# THE SECOND OLDEST PROFESSION

Phillip Knightley who worked for many years as special correspondent on the *Sunday Times* is also author of a number of distinguished books, among them *The First Casualty*, *The Philby Conspiracy*, *The Death of Venice* and *The Vestey Affair*.

An Australian by birth, Phillip Knightley lives in London with his wife and three children.

*For my family*

# Phillip Knightley

# *THE SECOND OLDEST PROFESSION*

## The Spy as Bureaucrat, Patriot, Fantasist and Whore

**Pan Books**
London and Sydney

First published in Great Britain 1986 by André Deutsch Ltd
in association with Burnett Books Ltd
This edition published 1987 by Pan Books Ltd
9 8 7 6 5 4 3 2 1
© Phillip Knightley 1986
All Rights Reserved
ISBN 0 330 29963 8
Printed and bound in Great Britain by
Richard Clay Ltd, Bungay, Suffolk

# Contents

# List of Plates

William Le Queux (Topham)
Captain Mansfield Smith-Cumming (Mrs Pippa Temple
and 'Secret Service' by Christopher Andrew)
Colonel Vernon Kell
Colonel Alfred Redl (BBC Hulton)
Mata Hari

Paul Dukes
Sidney Reilly
Robert Bruce Lockhart (BBC Hulton)
Somerset Maugham (Sir Gerald Kelly – Tate Gallery)
Feliks Dzerzhinsky (Topham)

Claude Dansey
Major R. H. Stevens and Captain S. Payne Best
Richard Sorge
General Filip Ivanovich Golikov

Vincent Astor (Associated Press)
Allen Dulles (Associated Press)
Klaus Fuchs (Camera Press)
G. N. Flyorov (Tass)

Ruth Kuczynski
Juergen Kuczynski
Sir Stewart Menzies (BBC Hulton)
Hans Oster

Charles Ellis
William Donovan (Library of Congress)
Kim Philby and George Blake (London *Daily Mail*)
Kim Philby (John Philby)

Oleg Penkovsky
Sir Roger Hollis (Press Association)
James Angleton (Associated Press)
William J. Casey (Associated Press)
John A. McCone (Associated Press)
William Colby
Marshal V. Chebrikov (Tass)


John Stockwell (Associated Press)
Jeremy Wolfenden (*Daily Telegraph*)
Frank Snepp (Associated Press)
Guy Burgess (London Express Service)
Donald Maclean
Anthony Blunt (The *Observer*)

# Acknowledgements

I would like to thank the following people and organizations:

Caroline Gathorne-Hardy, a multilingual researcher of infinite initiative, for her work in Britain, Germany, and France; David Leitch and Cherry Hughes, for interviews in the United States; Antony Terry for interviews in Germany; Lin Stowe for her typing skills; Murray Sayle for help in Japan and sound advice; James Rusbridger for some interesting documents; Dieter Pevsner for encouragement at a crucial stage; Carole Fries for her painstaking editing; and André Deutsch, Piers Burnett, and Edwin Barber for their almost limitless patience and faith.

Mrs Christa Wichmann of the Wiener Library took a great deal of trouble with my many inquiries; as did Michael Gasson of the Liddell Hart Collection, King's College, London, Centre for Military Archives; and Dr Gert Hirschfeld of the German Historical Institute, London.

I am also grateful to the Imperial War Museum library; the Royal Institute for International Affairs library; the library of the Royal Military Academy, Sandhurst; the Bibliothek für Zeitgeschichte-Weltkriegsbücherei, Stuttgart; the Institut für Zeitgeschichte, Munich; the Cambridge University library; the library of the University of East Anglia, Norwich; the Wandsworth Public Library, special collection at West Hill; and, of course, the London Library, an author's dream.

The Freedom of Information Act worked wonders with the Federal Bureau of Investigation, Washington. It worked less well with the Central Intelligence Agency. Compensation for this was the willingness of many former CIA officers to speak freely about events in which they had been involved – even though they knew that they would probably not agree with my conclusions.

Former officers of the British services were inhibited by the Official Secrets Act but were as helpful as they could be within its restrictions.

Aliya Knightley helped with the picture research. Acknowledgement to picture sources is made elsewhere. If any source has been missed this will be rectified in later editions.

NEXIS, of Mead Data Central, a full text information retrieval service, saved me many hours' work in analysing news coverage of espionage in the United States.

Crown copyright material is published by permission of HM Stationery Office. Reference to this material in the source notes is indicated by PRO (Public Record Office), CAB (Cabinet Papers) and FO (Foreign Office).

The first edition of this book included references in chapter 14 to Mr. Anthony Simkins, a former Deputy Director General of MI5. I now know that what I wrote about Mr. Simkins was incorrect and I have accordingly amended chapter 14 to remove all references to him.

# Abbreviations

| | |
|---|---|
| BSC | British Security Coordination (New York) |
| CIA | Central Intelligence Agency (United States) |
| CIG | Central Intelligence Group (United States) |
| COI | The Coordinator of Information (United States) |
| DIA | Defence Intelligence Agency (United States) |
| FBI | Federal Bureau of Investigation (United States) |
| GC and CS | Government Code and Cypher School (Britain) |
| GCHQ | Government Communication Headquarters (Britain) |
| GRU | Soviet Military Intelligence |
| IIC | Industrial Intelligence Centre (Britain) |
| JIC | Joint Intelligence Committee (Britain) |
| KGB | The Soviet Intelligence and Security Service |
| MI5 | The Security Service (Britain) |
| MI6 | see SIS |
| ND | Nachrichtendienst (Germany) |
| NIA | National Intelligence Authority (United States) |
| NSA | National Security Agency (United States) |
| NSC | National Security Council (United States) |
| OPC | Office of Policy Co-ordination (United States) |
| OSS | Office of Strategic Services (United States) |
| RSHA | Reich Security Agency (Germany) |
| RSS | Radio Security Service (Britain) |
| SD | Nazi Security Service (Germany) |
| SIS | Secret Intelligence Service (MI6) (Britain) |
| SLO | Special Liaison Officer (Britain and United States) |
| SLU | Special Liaison Unit (Britain and United States) |
| SOE | Special Operations Executive (Britain) |

Espionage is the world's second oldest profession and just as honorable as the first.
– Michael J. Barrett, assistant general counsel of the CIA, *Journal of Defence and Diplomacy*, February 1984.

# Introduction

The spy is as old as history, but intelligence agencies are new. Delilah was a secret agent of the Philistines, but she did not have to sign the Official Secrets Act or swear not to publish her memoirs without the director's approval. The Old Testament names the twelve spies Moses sent on a mission to the land of the Canaan, but they were amateurs. Alfred the Great was always interested in the Danish threat, but when it came to assessing its strength he went into the enemy encampment himself disguised as a bard.

Kings, especially those with shaky thrones, have always used spies, but more for internal security than to gather information from abroad. Akbar, the great Mogul ruler of India, employed 4,000 agents who reported to him – via a kind of National Security Council – every evening. Sir Francis Walsingham ran a security service, an early FBI or MI5, to protect Queen Elizabeth's kingdom from the Jesuits. He even sent spies abroad to gather intelligence about the Spanish Armada, but this was a private venture financed by Walsingham himself.

Spies for collecting military intelligence have flourished in wartime, but usually wilted when peace arrived. So although they did well in the Revolutionary War – an American agent who was doubling for the British stole Benjamin Franklin's secrets from the American Embassy in France – Lincoln found himself without an intelligence service when the Civil War began. He had to engage Alan Pinkerton's detective agency to fill the gap.

Wilhelm Stieber, the self-styled Prussian spy master, was said at this time to employ 40,000 agents. But he was a braggart and, again, those spies he did use gathered military intelligence and information for internal security purposes.

So it was not until 1909, in Britain, that the first intelligence agency came into being, a government department, financed from government funds, its employees largely civilians, created to steal secrets from other countries and to protect its own, empowered to operate in peace as well as in war. Once invented, the intelligence agency turned out to be a bureaucrat's dream.

3

As soon as one country had an intelligence agency, everyone had to have one. Germany followed Britain's lead in 1913, Russia in 1917, France in 1935, and the United States only as recently as 1947. Today even the poorest Third World government does not feel it has attained nationhood until it has its own secret service. From its humble beginnings in 1909 – one room and a budget of £7,000 a year – the intelligence business has become one of the twentieth century's biggest growth industries, expanding so rapidly as to be virtually out of control. Today no one knows – not even the governments who finance them – exactly what intelligence agencies cost to run or precisely how many people they employ.

This is partly because intelligence agencies use accountancy methods that would, if employed by public companies, lead to criminal prosecution. And partly because they collaborate with other friendly agencies in employing each other's staffs, which makes an accurate tally of staffing levels impossible.

The Central Intelligence Agency (CIA) spends at least $1,500,000,000 a year, more than the entire budget of many a Third World country. But this is only the best-known of American intelligence agencies. The National Security Agency (NSA), the technological side of the American espionage business, probably spends $3,500,000,000 a year. Taking into account the military intelligence services and the services of other American government departments, total expenditure on the intelligence community in the United States must be more than $7,500,000,000 a year.

The KGB budget is a Soviet state secret, but it is estimated at $1,650,000,000.* Again, if we include the Soviet military intelligence services and the internal intelligence sections of the KGB, then the intelligence community in the USSR must cost Soviet citizens at least as much as the American community costs Americans.

Britain officially spends about £92,000,000 on its Secret Intelligence Service (SIS) and the Security Service (MI5). But unofficial estimates put the figure at £300,000,000. Add the cost of the Government Communications Headquarters (GCHQ) and the various committees to which the agencies report, and the bill for Britain's intelligence community must come to at least £600,000,000 a year.

How many people work for all these agencies? It is difficult to say. Do we include only the 20,000 direct employees of the NSA or also

---

* The Russian Intelligence Service has had many names – the Cheka, the GPU, the OGPU, the NKVD, etc. Here it is referred to as the Cheka (during the Bolshevik Revolution) and thereafter, for simplicity's sake, as the KGB.

the 100,000 US servicemen around the world who do work for the agency? Do only those KGB staff engaged on foreign intelligence gathering qualify, or also those concerned with internal security? And what about satellite agencies under KGB control? If we include *all* those engaged on intelligence and security duties then the strength of the American establishment is at least 150,000, that of the Soviet Union close to a million, and Britain's about 25,000.

This means that the worldwide intelligence community consists of at least 1,250,000 people, costing, in the mid-1980s, at least £17,500,000,000 a year. These figures are hard for anyone to comprehend, but 1·25 million is Munich's entire population and £17,500 million is the budget for Britain's health service.

Any global group of this size must be very powerful and, like all specialist communities, intensely concerned with its own survival. Since it thrives best in time of international tension, it feels threatened by détente. Its member agencies, normally deadly rivals, then realize that they probably have more in common with each other than with the governments who supposedly control them. The CIA need the KGB to justify its own existence; and how would the KGB fare without the threat of a CIA?

So the intelligence community has produced a new sort of spy, one who spies on *everyone*, friend as well as foe. He uses high technology to sweep the entire electro-magnetic spectrum like a giant vacuum-cleaner, sucking up every imaginable piece of information that might be of use to someone somewhere: a telephone conversation in Moscow, a teleprinter message in Washington, a photograph of a missile silo or a ship at sea, the minutes of an OPEC meeting in Vienna, a bank crisis in Latin America.

Edward J. Epstein met some of the new spies at a conference in the United States in 1984. They were American; but since one of the curious features of intelligence agencies is that they gradually grow to resemble one another, they could equally have been Russians. Epstein was struck by their attitudes: 'They are not interested in espionage as a craft. They are not interested in the Soviet Union [USA]. They are not interested in communism [capitalism]. They are not Cold War warriors. They are systems analysts. They are technocrats. They are bureaucrats. They are good at putting together and working for a bureaucratically-efficient organisation.' How did a one-room outfit in 1909 grow into this monster without our having noticed?

There is some case to be made for intelligence organizations in wartime, although, in spite of the legends, their record even here is patchy. But once established, intelligence agencies have proved very difficult to get rid of – the American government failed in 1945 to wind up the Office of Strategic Services (OSS), the forerunner of the CIA; the British tried several times without success to run down the peacetime SIS or get rid of it entirely.

The agencies justify their peacetime existence by promising to provide timely warning of a threat to national security. It does not matter to them whether that threat is real or imaginary, and agencies have shown themselves quite capable of inventing a threat when none existed. It does not matter whether the agency is successful in giving timely warning or not. Over the years intelligence agencies have brainwashed successive governments into accepting three propositions that ensure their survival and expansion. The first is that in the secret world it may be impossible to distinguish success from failure. A timely warning of attack allows the intended victim to prepare. This causes the aggressor to change his mind; the warning then appears to have been wrong.

The second proposition is that failure can be due to incorrect analysis of the agency's accurate information – the warning was there but the government failed to heed it. (This was the British intelligence community's explanation for the Falklands' débâcle.)

The third proposition is that the agency could have offered timely warning had it not been starved of funds. In combination, these three propositions can be used to thwart any rational analysis of an intelligence agency's performance, and allow any failure to be turned into a justification for further funding and expansion.

Intelligence agencies have insulated themselves from the commonsense reaction which this sort of bureaucratic double-think might produce among the public by surrounding themselves with a thick wall of secrecy. This has enabled them to rebut critics by the simple and unanswerable expedient of saying, 'You are wrong because you don't know what really happened and we can never tell you because it's secret.' The chances of a dissenter from within the agency's own ranks revealing all is minimized by the rigorous use of the Official Secrets Act of 1911 (Britain), the Espionage Act of 1917 or the CIA's contract of employment (USA), and imprisonment (the Soviet Union).

Occasionally, when threatened by unsympathetic governments, or a change in the international atmosphere, the agencies emerge from behind the veil of secrecy to manipulate the media and mould public opinion. The head of OSS, William J. Donovan, helped by Allen Dulles, who was later to become head of the CIA, showed how effective this manipulation could be when they reversed a presidential decision not to have a peacetime intelligence agency in the United States.

There is, in fact, a discernible correlation between an easing of international tension and the willingness of intelligence agencies of all hues to 'go public'. The intelligence community has a direct interest in the continuation of the Cold War. Careers, promotion, pensions, travel, expenses, and a largely agreeable and stimulating way of life depend on it. So when all this is threatened by détente, the intelligence agencies open their doors to show the public that the menace still exists, that the need for timely warning has not ended, and that the efficient, reliable and patriotic intelligence agency is there to serve the nation.

But since agencies control the news they release, and ensure its uncritical dissemination through their own people in the media world, all spy stories should be treated with extreme scepticism. Even the 'now it can be told' variety, in which spies who have kept silent for forty years finally reveal the great triumphs of their agencies, turn out on closer examination to be, at best, exaggerations and, at worst, myths and legends.

But there is hope. The intelligence community may have finally overextended itself. As well as being out of government control, it may have also expanded beyond its *own* control. It now produces so much information, such an all-sources glut of words, images and electronic data that the number of intelligence officers who can understand it all, who see the overall picture, is rapidly declining. Soon they, too, may drown in their own intelligence. Nor can the computer take over. The NSA has already experienced difficulty in getting the material its customers want out of its computers and delivering to them.

Twenty years ago, a percipient CIA officer saw it coming. Thomas W. Braden, who had worked for the agency when it was still small, wrote:

> The [intelligence] community has grown to a vast industry which spends about 2½ billion dollars a year, employs more than 60,000 people and produces an amount of paper which God himself would have difficulty digesting even if He did not already know what the Russians were up to . . . And how can we make sure that all these people and all this paper is secure? By hiring more people to watch paper and people.[1]

Braden was in no position to do anything about it. In fact, since 1909 *no one* has successfully called the intelligence agencies' bluff. Various American presidents have taken office sceptical of the value of the intelligence community only to be rapidly won over. Some Soviet leaders have tried to challenge the KGB but without success. When Harold Wilson was Prime Minister of Britain he confronted his service but lost – he went, it stayed.

The trouble is that intelligence agencies have become wellsprings of power in our society, secret clubs for the élite and privileged. And as well as being highly skilled in the use of that power, they have been able to rely on the fascination that intelligence has held for many world leaders, from Winston Churchill to John F. Kennedy, a fascination based in part on the many works of fiction that have made the spy one of the most potent images of our age.

This inability to distinguish between the fiction and the reality of the intelligence world is ironically appropriate, because that was how it all began – in fantasy.

# 1. Governments, Spies and Fairy Tales

> The number of agents of the German Secret Police at this moment working in our midst on behalf of the Intelligence Department in Berlin are believed to be over five thousand.
> – Introduction to William Le Queux, *Spies of the Kaiser* (1909).

> On August 14, 1914 British authorities arrested 21 Germans suspected of being spies. One was brought to trial.
> – David French, 'Spy Fever in Britain, 1909–1915' (1978).

On Tuesday, 30 March 1909 a sub-committee of the Committee of Imperial Defence met in secret session at 2 Whitehall Gardens, Westminster, to consider the question of foreign espionage in Great Britain.[1] The membership of the sub-committee was impressive, an indication of how seriously the government regarded the subject. The chairman was the Secretary of State for War, R. B. Haldane, and others present included the First Lord of the Admiralty, the Home Secretary, the Postmaster-General, the Commissioner of Police, the Director of Military Operations and the Director of Naval Intelligence.

The first witness was Colonel James Edmonds, introduced as 'the officer in charge of that section of the General Staff employed under the Director of Military Operations on secret service'. This description was rather misleading in that it made Edmonds appear more important than he really was. His actual title was head of MO5 – military operations counter-intelligence – and his job was to uncover foreign spies in Britain. In fact, Edmonds did nothing of the sort; not through lack of will, or even skill, but through lack of money and resources: he had a miniscule budget – £200 a year – and only two assistants.

This was an important moment for Edmonds. The sub-committee had been appointed on the instructions of the Cabinet, and the Prime Minister, H. H. Asquith, was personally interested in the outcome. The future of Edmonds's department and his own job could well depend on his ability to convince the influential members of the sub-committee of the danger he believed Britain faced from German spies.

Edmonds began by setting out his credentials: he had studied the German army for practically all his life and he knew personally a German officer he described only as 'Major von X', who was head of the German secret service. Drawing on his experience, what he had heard from Major von X and what he had read, Edmonds outlined the German espionage system in Britain: the Germans had divided Britain into districts, each under a secret service officer who, in turn, had under him a number of agents, some 'stationary', that is settled in Britain for business or studies, and some 'mobile' or itinerant. Their duties were to collect information with which to supplement maps, to compile military reports, to buy secret information, and to make a reconnaissance of those docks, bridges, telegraph lines, magazines and railways which could be sabotaged on the outbreak of war.

The Germans were good spies, Edmonds said, because the German army openly recognized espionage as an essential and honourable weapon of war. With his own meagre budget no doubt in mind, Edmonds told the sub-committee what had happened to France. Prior to 1870 it had no secret service because no money was available. Two days after war started with Germany, the French government allocated 1 million francs for an espionage system. But, said Edmonds, Colonel Rollin, the officer entrusted with this task, had pointed out that, 'It was too late. Such a service cannot be improvised. It must be built up in the leisure of peacetime.'

The Germans had done just this, Edmonds said. They had an extensive system for collecting intelligence in peacetime and their spies were hard to detect because the use of motor cars enabled agents to live at a distance from the scene of their operations, where their presence attracted no suspicion. Edmonds claimed to have obtained, from a French source, a copy of the Germans' instructions to their spies on peacetime reconnaissance, but was able to quote to the sub-committee only the first paragraph. This read: 'The agent should be on the ground before daybreak so as to be able to commence work as soon as it is light in summer. This will always secure several hours of uninterrupted work.'[2] Members were, no doubt, impressed by this evidence of German efficiency and the threat which it posed to late-rising Britons!

Despite his reliance upon highly unconvincing material such as this, Edmonds found the sub-committee sympathetic to his case. Germany had been building up her navy ever since the turn of the century and the fear that the Kaiser was hell bent on an invasion of Britain had become widespread. The Germans, for their part, were equally convinced that the Royal Navy, unable to tolerate a rival on the high seas, would launch a surprise attack and sink Germany's new ships while they were peacefully in harbour. Officially, each country told the other that its fears were unfounded; unofficially, each was determined to make proper preparations to meet the threat that it perceived. With each government saying one thing while, apparently, doing another, an atmosphere of mistrust blossomed, especially in Britain where even the level-headed civil servants on the sub-committee were willing to believe that Germany was infiltrating the country and preparing to take by stealth and underhand tactics what it could not gain in open combat. ('Colonel Edmonds', asked Lord Esher, who apparently considered that Edmonds had spies on the brain, 'do you feel any apprehension regarding the large number of German waiters in this country?')

But when it came to hard evidence, Edmonds's case looked decidedly weak. Much of it was no more than hearsay and rumour. For example, two years earlier, in 1907, J. M. Heath, one of those patriotic seers who appears from time to time to warn their country of impending doom, wrote to the *Morning Post* claiming that there were 90,000 German reservists in Britain, 209,000 rounds of Mauser ammunition, caches of arms and uniforms concealed in warehouses and bank vaults, and plans to sabotage railways and telegraph lines. One of Edmonds's fellow officers in military intelligence clipped the letter from the newspaper and passed it to his superior, Colonel A. E. W. Gleichen, with a note saying: 'There is much truth in some of this, as you know. I heard last night of a German who has been seen constantly about the country between Brentwood and the River Thames at Tilbury, sketching and photographing. No one knows who he is or where he lodges. I can perhaps get more details, but what's the use?'[3] Gleichen, in turn, forwarded the note to Edmonds, testily asking, 'Is there no law under which these objectionable aliens can be got rid of?'

Edmonds had tried to document further instances of suspicious Germans out on sketching or photographic expeditions; but as he now told the sub-committee, Britain had no system or organization to detect and report such cases. The police had reported nothing to him, the Post Office knew nothing and civilians were curiously apathetic in the matter. Edmonds complained that one boarding-house proprietress at Wells, in whose house Germans had been living, had refused information, saying, 'German money is just as good as any other'. There was no direct evidence that Germany intended to carry out sabotage demolitions in Britain, only the assumption.*

The Commissioner of Police, Sir E. R. Henry, agreed that his department had reported nothing to Colonel Edmonds, but this was because there was nothing to report. On the occasions when his department had investigated allegations of espionage the results had been inconclusive: a foreigner named Boyen had been discovered working in the Devonport dockyard, but no suspicion was attached to him; a foreign-looking man was seen with a camera in a position to photograph the near side of Nothe Fort at Weymouth, but he turned out to be a missionary from East Africa; at Harwich nothing was discovered; but at Chichester, Miss Gordon-Lennox received German officers as paying guests 'and is reported to be aware of the objects they have in view' – whatever they may have been! The nearest the police had come to a real case was when a man named Alleyne, who had been suspected of espionage, broke his leg and was sent to hospital, thus enabling the police to search his hotel room. Details of shells and explosives were found among his papers but when these were sent to a government expert he reported that they were of no value whatsoever to any foreign government.

Edmonds was no doubt aware that this accumulation of hearsay, rumour, gossip, assumptions and impressions did not add up to evidence. He tried to strengthen his case by emphasizing the precautions that the Germans took against espionage in their own country. In Germany all strangers were watched and were liable to immediate arrest if their actions were suspicious. The law that prohibited the collection of military information was wide in scope and drastic in its effects. Finally, Edmonds tried to explain his lack of hard evidence by saying he had received a hint from someone in Germany that the attention given in the British press to the subject of German espionage had made German agents decide to lie low for a few years so as to lull suspicion.

The sub-committee was anxious to be convinced, but obviously

---

* But Edmonds made the point that the risk of such sabotage had increased dramatically since the Franco-Prussian War. In the intervening forty years gun-cotton and dynamite had become readily available. In the old days a horse and cart were needed to carry sufficient gunpowder to demolish the vital girders of a bridge. Now enough guncotton could be carried by one man.

hoped to obtain something rather firmer by way of evidence. Adjourning the first meeting, Haldane said it was quite clear that a great deal of reconnaissance work was being done by Germans in Britain and that probably secret agents were collecting information for sabotage purposes, although it was difficult to obtain precise details. Perhaps the chief constables of the coastal counties could say whether they had come across anything suspicious?

This suggestion would not have pleased Edmonds because it put matters back into the hands of the police, whereas he wanted *his* department to be expanded to cope with a menace he believed to be real and immediate. If he was to persuade the sub-committee to act when it reconvened in three weeks' time, he now realized, he would need to present it with a list of cases, packed with convincing detail, of German spies at work in Britain. Edmonds, of course, had no such list. But help was at hand in the unlikely person of one William Tufnell Le Queux, amateur spy extraordinary, traveller, lecturer, war correspondent, criminologist, wireless enthusiast, antiquarian collector and highly successful novelist – his books provided Queen Alexandra with her favourite reading.

Today we tend to imagine that the vogue for novels about espionage that has made the spy one of the most potent figures in contemporary fiction dates from the 1960s. But more than seventy years ago, Le Queux was already pioneering the curious cross-fertilization between espionage and literature that has subsequently been exploited by some of the most widely read writers of our time: John Buchan, Somerset Maugham, Rudyard Kipling, T. E. Lawrence, Compton Mackenzie and Graham Greene are but a few of those authors who, at one time or another, worked as intelligence agents. As a writer, Le Queux simply led where these, more distinguished, figures followed. But he was to play such an important role in the founding and development of Britain's first formal civilian intelligence agency that an examination of his amazing background is essential.

He was born in London in 1864 of a French father and an English mother. His name is an old Norman one and means 'the king's head cook'. He was educated partly in Britain and partly on the Continent so he spoke English, French, Italian and Spanish equally well. After a brief spell as an art student in Paris he turned to journalism, became foreign editor of the *Globe* and a war correspondent for the *Daily Mail*. In the course of his travels over the years he grew fascinated by espionage and began to do a bit of small-scale, amateur spying himself. He became an expert revolver shot, qualified as a telegraphist and extended his already wide circle of contacts – he claimed to know everyone in Europe worth knowing, from Sarah Bernhardt to the Chief of the Italian Secret Police, from Cardinal Manning to Madame Zola.

The trouble was that he was convinced that every country in Europe, but particularly Germany, deeply envied the British way of life and lusted after the wealth of the British Empire. He despaired that Britain, being populated by gentlemen and their faithful retainers, could not bring herself to think the worst of her Continental neighbours and was thus woefully unprepared for 'The Day', soon to come, when her enemies would invade her. All that stood between Britain and this fate was a nucleus of amateur intelligence agents, 'the most remarkable men, possessing shrewdness, tact, cunning, daring and – next to His Majesty's Secretary of State for Foreign Affairs – the most powerful and important pillars of England's supremacy'.

Le Queux used this description in one of his novels, but there is no doubt that he numbered himself among these 'remarkable men'. But the Foreign Office and the War Office, which he bombarded with reports, complaints and suggestions, refused to take him seriously. Soon 'the German menace' came so to obsess him that he readily accepted the most improbable stories, even touching them up a little himself if he felt that they lacked authenticity.

It is clear that he rapidly ceased to distinguish fact from fantasy. In 1905, for example, he claimed that a friend in Berlin, 'the under-director of the Kaiser's Spy Bureau', had decided to reveal to him the existence of a huge German spy network in Britain. This claim aroused immediate scepticism. What were the man's motives? Le Queux said that these were twofold. Firstly, the man felt bitter about his director who had not 'played the game' with him and, secondly, he had married an Englishwoman. This German spy, whom Le Queux had to call Herr N—— because he had promised never to reveal his name even after his death, arranged to meet Le Queux at the Dolder Hotel in Zurich on two occasions in order to pass documents to him. The first of these was a transcript of a secret speech that the Kaiser had given to the chiefs of the army and navy at Potsdam a month earlier.

The Kaiser had apparently spoken for more than two hours and had illustrated his speech with maps and diagrams, and with models of new aircraft and long-range guns. There is no other record of this speech anywhere and Le Queux's copy was, he said, later stolen by German spies from his publisher's office. Its tone and content smack of Le Queux's own obsession and there is every reason to believe that Le Queux wrote it himself:

> Do you remember, my generals, what our never-to-be-forgotten Field Marshal Gebhard Leberecht von Blucher exclaimed when looking from the dome of St. Paul's Cathedral upon the vast metropolis at his feet. It was short and to the point – 'What a splendid city to sack!' You will desire to know how the outbreak of hostilities will be brought about. I can assure you on this point. My army of spies is already scattered over Great Britain and France as it is over North and South America . . .[4]

Le Queux sent a copy of the speech to the War Office and he showed it to any high-ranking army or naval officer who was prepared to read it. But, he complained, he was ignored – as usual. After the second meeting with Herr N—— this no longer surprised him. For the second document Herr N—— had handed him was a list of British traitors, members of a secret organization called the Hidden Hand, who were working for Germany. 'I was aghast at the sight of this list. I sat staggered. It was appalling that persons whom the nation considered highly-patriotic and upright . . . should have fallen into the insidious tentacles of the great German octopus.' The list, Le Queux said, included members of Parliament, two well-known writers, and officials of the Foreign Office, Home Office, India Office, Admiralty and War Office. One of the main tasks of the Hidden Hand, Le Queux believed, was to frustrate his efforts to alert Britain to the German spy menace, and the fact that the British government had ignored his reports was a measure of its success.

The truth was that Le Queux was not taken seriously in Britain. This was partly because of the naïve content of his reports, but also because, even after he achieved outstanding success as a novelist, he was never really socially accepted. He was half-foreign, for a start, had not been to a proper school, was not a member of a decent club, spoke too many foreign languages too well, was too ostentatious about his patriotism, was a bore about the Germans, and if you did not do something about his blessed reports he would write about you in his books and newspaper articles. But, early in 1906, Le Queux confounded everyone. He teamed up with a disgruntled soldier, Field Marshal Lord Roberts, who was similarly obsessed with the German menace. Together they produced a fictionalized account of a German invasion of Britain four years hence and persuaded Lord Northcliffe to serialize it in the *Daily Mail*.

It was a well-planned operation. Northcliffe provided the money and three experts – Colonel Cyril Field and Major Matson (both army) and H. W. Wilson (navy) – contributed the professional advice. They toured the whole of East Anglia seeking a likely invasion route, and Roberts then put himself in the boots of a German general and planned a march on London that would ensure its capture while encountering the least resistance. Le Queux spent a year writing the material up in exciting fictional form and then proudly presented it to Northcliffe.

It was not to his lordship's liking. The line of march, it transpired, took the invading army through areas where the circulation of the *Daily Mail* was minimal. Northcliffe personally realigned the German attack to ensure that the Hun sacked those towns where chances of securing a boost to the *Daily Mail*'s circulation were strongest. Then he promoted the story by publishing, in *The Times*, the *Daily Telegraph*, the *Morning Post*, the *Daily Chronicle* and the *Daily Mail* itself, a list of those districts the Hun would hit the next morning.

On 'The Day' itself, the *Daily Mail*'s sandwichmen paraded up and down London streets dressed in spiked helmets and Prussian-blue uniforms. The Prime Minister, Sir H. Campbell-Bannerman, added to the public furore by telling the House of Commons that Le Queux was 'a pernicious scaremonger' and that the story was 'calculated to inflame public opinion abroad and alarm the more ignorant public opinion at home'. But, from Northcliffe's point of view, the whole thing was a tremendous success. The *Daily Mail*'s circulation soared. In book form *The Invasion of 1910* sold more than one million copies in twenty-seven languages – including Icelandic and Urdu. There were other, more important, results. Le Queux realized that he was on to something. He had found a way in which he could alert Britain to the danger from Germany and, at the same time, make a lot of money. From this moment on, the two motives, patriotism and profit, became inextricably mixed in Le Queux's mind with consequences he could never have foreseen.

Together, Lord Roberts and Le Queux now formed a voluntary Secret Service Department. 'Half a dozen patriotic men in secret banded themselves together', Le Queux wrote later. 'Each paying his own expenses, they set to work gathering information in Germany and elsewhere that might be useful to our country in case of need. Italy and the Near East were the regions allotted to me, but my travels took me also to Russia, to Germany and to Austria.' All the money Le Queux earned from *The Invasion of 1910* he spent on this private espionage work:

I parted with my money freely, leading a gay life, with the one idea of gaining information of use to Great Britain. I was the only Englishman who ever entered the gun factory of Erhardt's in Dusseldorf, where they were then constructing big guns. My escapade cost me a large sum in bribery, which I paid a certain adventurer in Constantinople, but I got the knowledge that I wanted. In due course the result of my adventure was reported by me, docketed, and sent to those dusty pigeon-holes in the War Office.[5]

When he was not spying abroad, Le Queux spent his time on counter-espionage work in Britain, flooding the War Office with reports of 'German officers in mufti' taking photographs, of hotels on the East coast with German proprietors, of forty-two cases of Germans living next door, or next door but one, to a telegraph office, 'ready to make a dash and seize or destroy the instruments on "The Day".' But, said Le Queux, his reports were ignored. This indifference he attributed to apathy or, more likely, to the intervention of the German sympathizers in the Hidden Hand.

Spurned by the government, Le Queux went back to his public. With the financial backing of D. C. Thomson, the Scots newspaper and publishing magnate, he travelled about Scotland looking for German spies, and published an account of this trip in Thomson's the *Weekly News*, which he then expanded into a book. Le Queux later described the *Weekly News* series as 'articles'. But the book itself, *Spies of the Kaiser: Plotting the Downfall of England*, was described as a novel, 'based on serious facts within my own personal knowledge', the result of twelve months' travelling Britain, 'making a personal enquiry into the presence and work of the 5,000 German spies here'.

As 'John James Jacox', barrister and amateur detective, of New Stone Buildings, Lincoln's Inn, Le Queux thus became the hero of his own story. With 'Ray Raymond', another 'typical, athletic young Englishman, aged about 30, clean-shaven, clean-limbed, an all-round good fellow', and his fiancée 'Vera', the fair-haired daughter of Vice-Admiral Sir Charles Vallance, Jacox/Le Queux motored around the country foiling German spies with 'bold strokes', intelligent deduction, patience and, come the crunch, with a new ·32 Colt revolver.

Le Queux was not first in the spy fiction field. Erskine Childers had led the way in 1903 with *The Riddle of the Sands* – a novel which Churchill said was largely responsible for Britain's decision to establish naval bases at Invergordon, Firth of Forth and Scapa Flow. But Le Queux, whose writing was arguably to be even more influential, was the first to claim that his stories were based on his own exploits and research: 'As I write I have before me a file of amazing documents which plainly show the feverish activity with which this advance guard of our enemy is working to secure for their employers the most detailed information.'[6]

*Spies of the Kaiser* is childish, the characters wooden and unconvincing, the plots of the various episodes all equally ludicrous. Germans disguised as Englishmen try to steal the plans for Britain's new silent submarine and the magnificent Kershaw army aeroplane, or they motor around (Le Queux here anticipated James Bond's obsession with fast and expensive automobiles) sketching railway stations and telegraph lines. Jacox sometimes uses his own name, at others he disguises himself as a valet or a chauffeur. He is, of course, aware of the spies' activities, but they put him out of action with drugged brandy – 1815 vintage – or a crack on the head. He is rescued by Ray Raymond and/or Vera and, together, they confront the Germans, bolstering their resolution for the showdown by telling each other, 'We must not show the white feather now'. The Germans always attempt to brazen it out: 'By what right, pray, do you enter here?' But their bluff is called: 'By the right of an Englishman, Herr Stolberg.' They realize that the game is up and, pausing only to utter a fierce oath in German, run away shouting 'You'll never stop me – you English cur!'

After 300 pages of this even Le Queux's imagination failed him and he had to move his hero out of Britain for an away fixture as a spy in Russia, trying to counter the German *agent provocateur*, 'Herman Hartmann', whose grey eyes are full of craft and cunning and who, when not fomenting revolution in Ostrog, controls 'an army of spies spread over our smiling land of England'. These spies make maps of the water mains in Leeds, North Shields, Sheffield and East London 'in order that, in the case of invasion, some of the German colony could . . . deprive half the metropolis of drinking water'. Or they import arms in small quantities and store them in safe houses in Chalk Farm, Canning Town, Chiswick and in Cowley Road, Leytonstone, ready for arming 'the horde of Germans in London on the day when the Kaiser gives the signal for the dash upon our shores'.

All this could be dismissed as harmless nonsense, adventure fiction fit for 15-year-olds, were it not for the powerful influence it was to exert on the findings of Haldane and his subcommittee. These, in turn, would determine the future of secret intelligence in Britain and, since Britain's service became the model for the CIA, in the United States.

There is no doubt that both Colonel Edmonds and Le Queux

believed Britain to be in deadly peril from German ambition, and were convinced that a German spy network was already established and at work throughout the country. Neither, of course, had a scrap of real evidence of this. But, to the evidence that the two men shared a common goal, can be added the fact that they were friends and, although this was never admitted publicly, the near-certainty that they exchanged ideas.

With all this in mind, compare Le Queux's view on how German spies operated in Britain, given in the introduction to *Spies of the Kaiser*, with Edmond's evidence before the sub-committee on the same subject. Le Queux wrote, well before the sub-committee had been set up:

> The number of agents of the German Secret Police at this moment working in our midst on behalf of the Intelligence Department in Berlin are believed to be over five thousand. To each agent, known as a 'fixed post', is allotted the task of discovering some secret . . . This 'fixed agent', is, in turn, controlled by a 'travelling agent' who visits him regularly . . .

It seems clear enough that, when Edmonds told the sub-committee that German agents in Britain were divided into 'stationary agents' and 'mobile agents', he was simply quoting Le Queux – the similarity in terminology was surely too close to be accidental.

We have already seen how Colonel Edmonds and his colleagues felt that they were hampered in their efforts against German spies by the lack of any law under which they could be prosecuted. In Le Queux's book, Jacox shows the same concern. He complains to Raymond: 'England is the paradise of the spy, and will remain so until we can bring pressure to bear to compel the introduction of fresh legislation against them.'

This could have been Edmonds speaking, so clearly did Le Queux's fictional characters express what Edmonds and his colleagues believed. Who influenced whom is impossible to say at this distance, but the answer is not important because Le Queux now became the dominant figure and Edmonds merely his conduit. *Spies of the Kaiser*, published early in 1909, was an instant best seller and it soon became clear that its thousands of readers considered it – as they had every right to do in view of Le Queux's ambiguous presentation of the book as fact in fictional form – as being totally true.

A wave of spy fever now swept the country. If there *were* any German spies in Britain at this time – a possibility we shall consider later – there were certainly not enough to satisfy every amateur spy hunter who, following in Jacox's footsteps, now set out to bag one. So Le Queux's readers had to fall back on their imaginations, and soon Le Queux was inundated with letters telling him of suspicious German travellers, army officers, barbers and waiters. These cases were almost the mirror images of those he had already presented in his novel, but instead of making Le Queux sceptical, this only reinforced his own view: if thousands of patriotic Englishmen were now observing the very same suspicious behaviour he had seen, then the gigantic German spy ring must indeed be a reality.

Le Queux hastened to pass on this new 'evidence' to Colonel Edmonds. It reached him at just the right moment – when he was trying to convince the sub-committee of the truth and extent of the spy menace. Edmonds quickly prepared a catalogue of 'Cases of Alleged German Espionage', and it was presented to the second meeting of the sub-committee on 20 April 1909.[7]

The summary at the beginning of the catalogue showed how infectious the spy fever had become: for example, in 1907 military intelligence had heard of only two instances of Germans behaving suspiciously; in 1908 this had gone up to sixteen; and in the early months of 1909 cases were being reported at the rate of one a week. Le Queux's cases, filed under 'from a well-known author', and those inspired by Le Queux's book, are easily identifiable. In the book, the hero, Jacox, makes motoring trips down unfrequented country lanes in his open forty-eight Daimler and, on one occasion, catches a German spy on a motorcycle observing something with fieldglasses. In Edmonds's catalogue one case reads: 'Informant while motoring last summer in an unfrequented lane between Portsmouth and Chichester, nearly ran over a cyclist who was looking at a map and making notes.'

The villains in Le Queux's book regularly betray themselves by 'cursing in German', or 'uttering a fierce oath in German'. The cyclist in the case above 'swore in German to ease his conscience'. In Le Queux's book, the German spies are always trying to get honest Englishmen, usually from the lower classes, into their power. In Edmonds's catalogue two Germans from Portsmouth 'consort with sick bay stewards, officers' servants, and similar ratings and take much interest in Navy gossip'.

In Le Queux's book, there are several references to telegraph lines and telegraph messages, and there is a case of a French naval officer who is seduced into being a traitor and working for Germany. In Edmonds's catalogue, Max Piper, of 54 Park Road, West Dulwich is accused of 'being a representative of Wolff's Telegraph Bureau, and being in frequent communication with the German embassy'. And a man called Simmonds, a photographer of 39 High Street, Portsmouth, is accused of being 'a Polish Jew, in communication with the French Naval attaché'.

In Le Queux's book, one German spy is portrayed as a barber. In Edmonds's catalogue there appears this passage: 'The firm of Henri et Cie, barbers of Osborne Road, Southsea, is a German named Beck. He is a well-educated man, has been eleven years in England, but is not naturalized. He had until recently an assistant named Schweiger, another German, who was discovered by accident to wear a wig over his own thick head of hair.'

The other cases in Edmonds's catalogue were as ludicrous as those provided by Le Queux – a mixture of malicious gossip, fantasy, envy, anti-semitism and xenophobia. They were all obviously worthless. A Lincolnshire Justice of the Peace reported that a man who called himself 'Colonel Gibson', but who was obviously a foreigner, stayed at Sutton-on-Sea in the summer, took much interest in the coast and was known locally as 'the German spy'. A member of the staff of a provincial newspaper reported that a German called Cobletz lived at Wellesley Road, Clacton-on-Sea, did not work, received remittances from abroad and 'makes a point of being on friendly terms with everyone'. A captain in the Royal Navy noted that a German called Schneider kept a barber's shop at Portsmouth and had formed it into a kind of club 'which is much frequented by sub-lieutenants of submarines'. A 'retired military man' reported that the English postmistress at Old Charlton, Kent, had married a German called Kerweder 'who lives in the Post Office'.

At first, the chairman, Haldane, tried to inject a note of sanity into the proceedings. He had recently returned from a visit to Germany and told the sub-committee that it was certainly not his impression that the German government was collecting information in Britain with the intention of invading it. But soon Haldane, too, succumbed to spy mania. The turning-point appears to have been a document which, very fortuitously, came into the hands of the War Office in the interval between the second meeting of the sub-committee on 20 April (when Haldane reported on his visit to Germany) and the crucial third meeting on 12 July (when Haldane joined the spy mongers). The document, its contents and the manner in which it reached the War Office, have all the hallmarks of a Le Queux novel, but since there remains no account of the affair in the British government records, we can do no more than report Haldane's version and leave it to the reader to decide how feasible the story sounds.

During the past week [Haldane said] the War Office received a document from abroad which throws some light on what is going on. This document had been obtained from a French commercial traveller who was proceeding from Hamburg to Spa. He travelled in the same compartment as a German whose travelling bag was similar to his own. The German, on leaving the train, took the wrong bag, and on finding out this the commercial traveller opened the bag left behind and found that it contained detailed plans connected with a scheme for the invasion of England. He copied out as much of these plans as he was able during the short time that elapsed before he was asked to give up the bag, concerning the loss of which the real owner had telegraphed to the railway authorities where the train next halted.[8]

Haldane admitted that he had at first been inclined to regard the plans as fakes, possibly concocted by the French government in order to wake Britain up and draw attention to her military short-comings. But, said Haldane, the Director of Military Operations, General J. S. Ewart, and the director of Military Training, General A. J. Murray, both of whom were on the sub-committee, were confident that the plans were not the work of amateurs, but showed great knowledge of the vulnerable points in Britain, and revealed that there were certain places where German agents were stationed whose duty it would be to take certain action on the outbreak of war, or during a period of strained relations preceding a war.

The whole story reeks of Le Queux's fertile imagination. The coincidence of the similar travelling bags; the fact that the German's bag, although supposed to contain plans of highest importance, was unlocked; the fact that the Frenchman was able instantly to recognize 'detailed plans for the invasion of England'; the convenient lapse of time to enable him to copy important parts; the speed with which these parts then reached Britain. But with two high-ranking military officers on the sub-committee assuring him that the plans were 'not the work of amateurs', what could Haldane do?

He succumbed. There was now no doubt, he said, that a great deal of German espionage was being undertaken in Britain to make a detailed study of the resources and of the topography of the country. The sub-committee then went on to make four main recommen-dations to deal with this threat: the introduction of controls to limit the freedom of movement of aliens; a scheme to defend vital installations against sabotage; a tightening of the Official Secrets Act so as to give the police increased powers against spies; and – our main concern here – the establishment of a regular secret service bureau.[9]

The idea of a secret service bureau had first been suggested by

General Ewart. Edmonds had hoped for a substantial increase in his own department – MO5 – to counter the activities of real, or imagined, German spies in Britain. Ewart had something else in mind: he wanted to match the Germans spy for spy; to obtain some decent agents without the opprobrium of being linked with them in any way. One can detect, even in these early days of British intelligence, a sentiment that still lingers in British ruling circles today. Spying is viewed as a dirty business more suited to foreigners than to Englishmen; but since circumstances compel Britain to tackle the foreigner on equal terms, then at least let the spying be done in such a manner that, if the spies are detected, the British can swear that it has nothing whatsoever to do with them.

The Foreign Office was particularly anxious to dissociate itself from anything that smacked of espionage. (Only a year earlier the consul at Cherbourg had reported, with some satisfaction, that when a spy offered him plans of French submarines for 1,000 francs he had sent the man packing.)[10] But if the Foreign Office did not know, and if the spy would be 'deniable' if caught, then, reasoned the War Office, why not recruit a foreigner or two.

It is appropriate then – since most spies are heavy drinkers – that the first recruit to what was to grow into an enormous espionage bureaucracy should have been an employee of Courage & Company, the London brewers. The War Office discreetly approached Courage's managing director, G. N. Hardinge, and he persuaded his Hamburg representative that his chances of continued employment with Courage would be better if he agreed to do a spot of spying for Britain. The man, known only as Rué, reported nothing of note, but became so hooked on espionage that by 1914 he was working for both Britain *and* Germany.[11]

Ewart was eager to build on this rather fragile foundation. But, in order to convince his fellow committee members, he put the emphasis on the contribution which his agents could make towards preventing espionage in Britain. 'We require information regarding espionage in this country,' he said. 'We also want to be in touch with foreigners with a view to ascertaining if there are any stories of foreign arms or explosives in the country.' He stressed that such contacts would be carried out through an intermediary so that the General Staff could 'be protected against being detected in any dealings with spies'. Haldane later re-emphasized this need for an expendable intermediary.

We have considered the question of how a Secret Service bureau could be established to deal both with espionage in this country and with our own foreign agents abroad, *and to serve as a screen* between the Admiralty and the War Office on the one hand and those employed on secret service, or who have information they wish to sell to the British Government on the other. (Emphasis added)

By the time the sub-committee was ready to report, the idea of having an intelligence system that officially did not exist had become the main reason for creating a Secret Service Bureau. It recommended, therefore, that the Bureau should be completely separate from the Home Office, the War Office, or the Admiralty; and that the Bureau serve as an intermediary between these departments and 'the agents that we employ in foreign countries'. The future path of British intelligence was largely determined by the sub-committee's next paragraph: 'By means of this Secret Service Bureau our naval and military attachés and government officials would not only be freed from the necessity of dealing with spies, but direct evidence could not be obtained that we were having any dealings with them.'

Once the idea of protecting the government from the dirty business of spying by having a non-existent intelligence service had gained acceptance, the next step was almost automatic: the non-existent service and the way in which it was created had to become a deep secret, otherwise the whole point was lost. So the secrecy that was to run like a leitmotiv through the history of British Intelligence began immediately. The sub-committee's report, issued on 24 July 1909, contained this conclusion:

The detailed recommendations of the sub-committee regarding the establishing of the Secret Service Bureau are of so secret a nature that it is thought desirable that they should not be printed or circulated to the members. These recommendations have been considered by the sub-committee, and a single typed copy has therefore been made and handed over to the custody of the Director of Military Operations.

It is one thing to declare something to be a secret; it is another to ensure that the secret is not revealed. The sub-committee now set about recommending the tightening of the Official Secrets Act to a degree that continues to inhibit open government in Britain even now. The first Official Secrets Act had been passed in 1889 to stop the disclosure of sensitive information by government officials. There had been an attempt to pass a new Bill in 1908 so as to prevent publication in the press of sensitive naval and military information, but the outcry from newspapers was so loud that the government abandoned the idea. The sub-committee wanted a new Act that would not only ensure that secrets remained secret in Britain, but that would enable spies to be prosecuted for the offence of publishing (which includes 'passing on', for example, from one agent to another) information prejudicial to the safety of the state. By the time government lawyers had worked over the sub-committee's recommendations it was clear that some subterfuge would be necessary to get the Bill through Parliament, so Draconian were its terms. They encapsulated the armed services' belief that there could be the *moral certainty* that someone was a spy, even if there were little or no evidence to prove it. All the prosecution would have to do would be to show that the circumstances of the case, the accused's character, or his general conduct made it appear *likely* that he was a spy.

The sub-committee had suggested at the beginning that the new Bill would 'excite less opposition' if it were introduced by the Secretary of State for War, rather than the Home Office, on the plea that it was a 'measure of precaution of great importance to national defence'. The government went further. The Bill was drafted in June 1910 and hustled through the Commons so quickly that almost no one noticed what it was. It was introduced late on a Friday afternoon – the unofficial start of the sacred British weekend – when only 117 MPs were present to vote on it. The government gave bland assurances that it was not aimed at anyone in particular and that it would infringe no one's liberties. Only two Liberals showed the slightest misgivings about it, and one of them was swayed by the government's soothing words into concluding, 'although I do not like some of it, I understand that it is necessary'. How false the government's assurances were can be gauged if we look forward, briefly, to consider two cases brought under the new Act: one the following year and the second early in 1914.

In November 1911, Max Schultz, a journalist living on a houseboat near Exeter – where he made no secret of the fact that he was German, even to the extent of flying the German flag – was charged with having tried to obtain information about the readiness of the British fleet for war. Schultz believed he had a cast-iron defence: he showed that the information was so far from being secret that it could be read in local newspapers. The jury took only four minutes to find him guilty.[12]

In April 1914, Robert Blackburn, an 18-year-old youth from Liverpool wrote to the German embassy in London offering his services as a spy. To demonstrate his skill he enclosed samples of the sort of information he was able to obtain. It was worthless and harmless, and Blackburn later admitted that he had collected it from local newspapers and by writing to the Liverpool Chamber of

Commerce. He also admitted that the idea of volunteering to be a German spy occurred to him after reading books – like Le Queux's – about German spy rings in Britain. The police intercepted Blackburn's mail and charged him with espionage. He too was found guilty and sent to prison.[13]

Meanwhile, the Secret Service Bureau's spies were up to much the same sort of thing in Germany, accumulating masses of information much of which could have been obtained from published sources. Even when the occasional grain of wheat found its way into the chaff it was of no value because the consumers of the intelligence usually dismissed it as false. For example, a report that German naval gunnery accuracy at long ranges was startlingly good was dismissed by the Admiralty, which said such results were impossible and that the agent must have been deceived.[14] The Admiralty was to learn at Jutland just how good German gunnery was.

So agents quickly learned from the questions the Secret Service Bureau asked them, and the reception their replies received, what their employer wanted to hear. Any information suggesting that Germany was preparing to invade Britain and that it had, as a preliminary step, flooded the country with spies and saboteurs, was bound to win praise and requests for more. But did the German spy menace have any basis in reality?

Germany certainly had a military intelligence service, the Geheime Nachrichtendienst des Heeres (known as the ND, or later, within the army, as Section IIIb), as did Britain, France, Imperial Russia and most European powers. But it was geared to war. Starved for funds in peacetime, it had to rely largely on the overt intelligence agents – military attachés, diplomats, consuls and the occasional journalist – to provide most of its information. After the Russo-Japanese War in 1905, Germany tried to improve its flow of information about Russia, and Russia's ally, France. A Russian section under Major Walther Nicolai was established, but Nicolai found that the whole ND had a budget of only £15,000 a year and that the Russian Section was expected to function with only four agents. These agents regarded espionage first and foremost as a source of income; it was a matter of indifference to them whether they worked for Germany or Russia. Discouraged, Nicolai gave up the job, only to be recalled in April 1913 and appointed as head of the ND, a post he retained throughout the war.

Within a year Nicolai had created a reasonably efficient organization, but it was directed only against Russia and France. Britain was considered to be a naval threat; therefore the intelligence section of the German navy theoretically looked after espionage in Britain. But German naval intelligence was even more starved for funds than the ND and, anyway, spying went against navy tradition. So, by the eve of war, Nicolai was preparing to bring Britain within his area of responsibility. Writing in 1924, he said: 'That was indeed to have been the next step in the organization of our intelligence service but that was hindered by the war. There was no talk even, of a service to deal with America.'[15]

Strong corroboration for Nicolai's statement can be found in the records of the British Home Office. On 4 August 1914, the day Britain declared war on Germany, the Home Office claimed that the authorities had arrested 21 German spies, hardly a massive espionage network, and falling somewhat short of Le Queux's 5,000 agents. But only *one* of these was ever brought to trial, a remarkably poor performance if all twenty-one were really German spies. The Home Office offered two excuses for this failure. It said, in October 1914, that it could not bring the spies to trial because evidence in open court would reveal how British counter-intelligence worked. Later in the war it offered, on several occasions, the further argument that it did not want to alert the Germans to the fact that their spy ring had been broken.

Neither excuse stands up to scrutiny. The Home Office had already revealed how British counter-intelligence worked – by watching and intercepting foreign telegrams and letters – in a statement it issued soon after the arrests.[16] (In any case, if it really was worried that the trials would reveal important secrets, it could have ordered them to be held in camera.) If the twenty-one Germans *were* spies, then their spymaster was alerted to their capture within hours because *The Times* printed all their names the morning after they had been arrested. The only possible explanation as to why the other twenty spies were not prosecuted but instead interned without trial is that the British authorities did not have any evidence to support a charge of espionage. In short, the German spy scare which gripped Britain in the years before the war was entirely without foundation. Why was it believed?

The spy stories of Le Queux, Childers and Buchan all had shared a basic plot, which is almost as ancient as man himself – the overcoming of the monster. The story of how the hero alone recognizes the danger the monster poses to the tribe, how he prepares for the confrontation, how he divines the monster's secret and eventually kills it, has been told for centuries in all civilizations as a harmless allegory for man's struggle against evil.

But Le Queux, a disturbed personality, projected his version of this fantasy into the real world and created a real monster – Imperial Germany. The authorities, while rejecting Le Queux himself, soon realized what a powerful nationalistic force he had discovered and used it for their own ends. As the First Sea Lord, 'Jackie' Fisher, one of the few who kept his head over the German menace, put it, the swarm of spies (real and imaginary) released in 1909 'served the double purpose of supplying false information to subserve expansion of armaments, and of increasing the ill-feeling which had already been worked up between England and Germany'.[17]

The repercussions were momentous: the establishment of the first bureaucratic intelligence agency – from which all others were to flow – and the realization by those who were to run it that the climate in which it would thrive best was one of international tension and foreign threat.

# 2. The Legends Grow

> Mata Hari, who could easily lay claim to the title of the most famous spy of the century, has had six books, three films and a musical created around her.
> – Nigel West, *Unreliable Witness* (1984).

> Mata Hari did not achieve anything for the German intelligence service. Her case was enormously exploited.
> – General Gempp, *Kölner Zeitung*, 31 January 1929.

Her Majesty's Secret Service Bureau, the child of the Haldane sub-committee, was divided into two sections – Home and Foreign. The Home department was to concern itself with catching foreign spies in Britain, that is, with counter-espionage, and was the forerunner of today's MI5, or Security Service. The Foreign department was to collect intelligence from abroad and was eventually to become MI6, or the Secret Intelligence Service (SIS).\* Inherent in this division of duties was the friction between the two services which has never entirely disappeared. Spy catching is basically policemen's work and MI5 officers tended to have a policeman's regard for the law and contempt for the law breaker. Spies, even one's own, are, at best, patriotic brigands and destroyers of other people's law. As William Skardon, the famous MI5 officer once said of SIS, 'You have to be a bit of a villain for that sort of work.'[1]

Having created the new Secret Service Bureau, the government tried to run it on a shoestring. MI5 was given a single room in the War Office and a budget of only £7,000 a year. No record exists of SIS's allocation, but it was sufficient to send agents only to Germany. More than fifty years passed before the service was given a proper financial structure and, in the meantime, it became customary for the chiefs of both departments to dip into their own pockets when cash became scarce. Intelligence work, therefore, was not a field

---

\* For the sake of convenience we shall use MI5 and SIS to refer to the departments from this point on.

that attracted young, career-minded officers, especially at the top. The pattern was set by the men who first took charge of the two departments.

The head of MI5 was Captain Vernon Kell. His credentials were sketchy: a background of hunting and shooting, and some experience as an intelligence officer based in Shanghai during the Boxer Rebellion, when he also doubled as foreign correspondent for the *Daily Telegraph*. Kell did, however, have a talent for empire building and MI5 grew from this single room in 1909 to a staff of 14 by 1914 and to 700 by the end of the war in 1918.

The head of MI-1c, as SIS was called until the 1930s, was Captain Mansfield Smith-Cumming, a genuine eccentric, even by the standards of the Royal Navy. It is difficult to write seriously about Cumming, the first 'C', as the head of the service is called to this day. He wore a gold-rimmed monocle, wrote only in green ink, and, after he lost a leg in an accident, used to get around the corridors by putting his wooden one on a child's scooter and propelling himself vigorously with the other. Visitors were intimidated by his habit of stabbing this wooden leg with his paper knife in order to drive home the point of an argument. His journal, a battered naval log book, contains entries such as, 'To Clarkson's today to buy a new disguise'.

All organizations, especially secret ones, need legends and one quickly grew up about Cumming. It was said that he had lost his leg in 1914 in a car crash while driving with his son near Paris. The son, dying of his injuries, complained of being cold, whereupon Cumming, who was trapped in the wreckage, pulled out his penknife and hacked off his own leg to free himself. He then crawled to the boy, covered him with a coat and was found hours later unconscious alongside his son's body. The reality is different. Cumming broke both his legs in the accident and one was surgically amputated in hospital the following day.[2] But the story was told in the secret world for years 'to show what sort of chap old "C" is'.

All this is relevant to Cumming's attitude to intelligence work. He thought it was a game for adults, played for fun with points being awarded for style rather than results. In conversation with recruits he frequently used sporting analogies. He once described espionage as 'time spent largely in enjoyment, full of sporting value'. When he was trying to persuade the author, Compton Mackenzie, to stay on in the service he told him: 'Here, take this swordstick. I always took it with me on spying expeditions before the war. That's when this business was really amusing. After the war is over we'll do some amusing secret service work together. It's capital sport.' He appointed Paul Dukes, one of his best agents in Russia, not because

Dukes spoke Russian and knew the country well – he was about to reject him despite that – but because Dukes happened to admire Cumming's collection of revolvers.

Since the government wanted to be able to deny all knowledge of SIS, Cumming's offices could not be in the War Office. Instead SIS inhabited part of the Liberator Building in Whitehall and also had space in Watergate House, near the Strand. Cumming spent most of his time in a small room in the east turret of the Liberator Building. One of his agents, Major Stephen Alley, has described what it was like: 'To approach Cumming's office it was necessary for a visitor to climb a staircase and wait while the secretary pressed a secret bell, whereupon Cumming would operate a system of levers and pedals which moved a pile of bricks revealing more steps.' In the office itself a row of half a dozen telephones stood at the left of a big desk littered with papers. Another table had maps, drawings and models of ships and submarines. Alley recalled that, 'This atmosphere of strangeness and mystery was rather destroyed by the fact that Cumming's secretary kept coming up through a hole in the floor.'[3]

The first agents Cumming recruited were Englishmen living in Germany. His idea was that if these agents noticed unusually heavy concentrations of troops or of shipping this could provide an early warning of possible invasion. Then in May 1910, SIS sent two Royal Navy officers, Captain Brandon and Lieutenant Trench, to reconnoitre the German coast. They were arrested and sentenced to four years' imprisonment of which they served thirty months. This episode confirmed the value of having an intelligence service that officially did not exist. When Germany raised the case of Brandon and Trench with the First Lord of the Admiralty, Reginald McKenna, he simply denied all knowledge of the two men. When Brandon and Trench returned to Britain, expecting, if not a hero's welcome then at least a little sympathy, they learnt that the government's official attitude was that they had been in Germany on leave for a personal pleasure trip, and that what had happened to them had been their own fault, thus establishing the service tradition that if a spy is caught he is on his own.

Cumming's main problem – one which was also to be of concern to his successors – was that the sort of man likely to be attracted to espionage often did not have the character to resist the many temptations it offered. The first of these was the temptation for the agent to invent intelligence in order to justify his own existence. The second temptation was to misuse the large sums of money an agent could command. Since it was unlikely that people who would provide an agent with the information in exchange for money would sign a receipt, SIS had no choice but to trust an agent's honesty. This trust was sometimes misplaced. An agent in Hungary staged a suicide and went off to the United States with all the SIS cash he was able to lay his hands on. Another shot himself when asked to explain what he had done with £28,000 that had been sent to him. Like many other outsiders, Captain Sigismund Payne Best, an army intelligence officer, did not think highly of the infant SIS: 'C always employed scoundrels', he wrote, 'and his people were always ready to do the dirty on me.'[4] (It must be added that, in the light of subsequent events – see Chapter 7 – Best's comment looks like a classic case of the pot calling the kettle black.)

This mistrust was no doubt one of the reasons for the proliferation of British intelligence agencies that occurred before and after the outbreak of the First World War. Lord Fisher, First Sea Lord from 1904 to 1910, set up his own intelligence organization based in Switzerland, and seems to have done rather well: 'I was able to obtain all the cypher messages passing from the various foreign embassies, consulates, and legations . . . and I also obtained a key to their respective cyphers.'[5]

There had been a Royal Navy intelligence section before the Haldane recommendation to create a Secret Service Bureau, and its director, Admiral Sir Reginald Hall, known to his colleagues as 'Blinker', advised the government on the setting up of SIS.

The army created its own secret service as part of the British Expeditionary Force and, in addition, the War Office had a section called Special Intelligence, under General G. K. Cockerill. There was also an Indian Secret Intelligence Section, which had an office near Sloane Street and concerned itself with German attempts to suborn the Indian sub-continent.

But most of these groups produced 'nuts and bolts' intelligence, useful only for tactical purposes at best. It was not intelligence in its broadest sense. In order to plan for the long term, the British needed to know what German morale was like; whether the economic blockade was hurting; how long the ordinary German civilian thought that the war would last; whether he was still confident of winning it; if he was still fond of the Kaiser; whether there were any political groups urging an early peace; if it was true that people had been arrested for revolutionary activity; what raw materials were in short supply; how much contraband Germany was getting through neutral countries; and what relations were like between Germany, Austria and Turkey.

In order to discover the answer to this sort of question, Cumming set up a large organization in Holland, a country which was neutral.

It employed more than 300 people and was divided into four departments: one concentrated on information about the German army, the second about the navy, the third dealt with propaganda and disinformation, and the fourth provided technical back-up (false identification papers, codes and methods of communication).

This Dutch branch of SIS recruited agents and sent them into Germany, sought out neutral war correspondents passing through Holland and tried to recruit them or, failing that, to pump them for information, and worked with German deserters who had fled across the border into Holland. Finding people willing to spy for Britain turned out to be relatively easy. Among those recruited by SIS was Leonhard Kooyper, a war correspondent for the daily newspaper, *Nieuwe Rotterdamsche Courant*, who made four trips to Germany to collect information, reporting much of it direct to London. SIS also succeeded in infiltrating its men into the internment camps in which the Dutch authorities held German deserters. Here they mixed with the Germans and tried to draw military information from them. They also tried, with little success, to win over suitable Germans with the aim of sending them back into Germany to spy for Britain.

The French, too, expanded their intelligence service at the outbreak of the war by actively recruiting agents. In an effort to attract a better-quality spy, they paid what were recognized to be the highest wages in Europe – until the Americans arrived.*

The Russians had been so blatant about their espionage activities before the war that they were something of a joke. It was generally accepted that some part of a Russian army officer's career would be spent travelling abroad on spying missions. The Russians imagined that this was the case with all armies and were sometimes angry that the custom was not tolerated in Europe as it was in Russia. Russian officers in Germany in prewar spying missions would become indignant when they discovered that they were being observed by detectives and some went as far as to summon uniformed police to complain about being followed by strangers. But when war actually came, the Russians had such bad experience with agents working for both sides – so as to earn double wages – that they discontinued espionage altogether.

---

* The official history of the intelligence section of the British Expeditionary Force comments, 'Six competing services which had been turning over the ground for agents for the greater part of the war had been joined since September, 1917, by a newcomer – the American service – who were not only complete novices, but had been given an apparently free hand as regards funds as long as they produced information'.[6]

With the British, the French and, later, the American intelligence services working against them, how did the Germans fare? Before the war they had relied largely on the overt gathering of intelligence abroad, that is, on the observations made by their military attachés, diplomatic and consular representatives, and foreign correspondents of the German press. But after British SIS agents had been caught in Germany in 1910, a German 'Le Queux' made his appearance.

Early in 1912 General F. von Bernhardi published a book called *Germany and the Next War*. The general saw Germany in much the same way that Le Queux had seen Britain: as an honest but naïve nation beset by devious and powerful enemies – in Germany's case by Britain, France and Russia. One of the most alarming pieces of evidence for this, according to the general, was 'the English espionage lately vigorously practised on the German coasts'. The book had the desired effect. By the summer of 1914, when a British naval squadron paid a courtesy call at Kiel, German spy fever was such that a British officer was detained when he wandered into part of the dockyard not on the official schedule, and the so-called goodwill visit dissolved into mutual hostility.

The German public soon became almost as obsessed with spies as the British. The most unlikely rumours were spread – and were believed. The British were said to have flights of homing pigeons, each carrying fastened to its tail a tiny camera operated at set times by clockwork. Spies in German cities would release the pigeons and since one flightline followed the course of the Rhine, and the other the railway between Thorn and Amsterdam, British intelligence could piece together aerial photographs of German military activity. Motor cars were said to be crossing Germany laden with gold to pay these British agents. As a result of this rumour, German vigilantes held up every large car and those that refused to stop were fired on.

A lady's maid was strip-searched when leaving Germany. The woman police officer reported with great excitement that the maid had 'secret writing' on her bottom. The maid was arrested, the writing photographed, and the prints sent to German military intelligence for evaluation. It turned out that the maid had gone to the toilet on the train on the way to the border and, for hygienic reasons, had covered the toilet seat with newspaper before sitting down. The secret writing on her bottom was from that day's *Frankfurter Zeitung*.[7]

The German army, sceptical of the value of espionage work,

34

resisted the demands, fuelled by these spy scares, to expand its Section IIIb, the small department of the Great General Staff, which ran the army's intelligence and counter-intelligence programmes on a budget of the equivalent of about £15,000 a year. But as war drew nearer, the German army realized that it needed a more efficient system of gathering and assessing information about its potential enemies, particularly France and Russia. The ND took over responsibility for this and posted officers, usually lieutenants or captains, to corps headquarters in the border regions of the Reich. By 1914 six such officers, usually working out of their private residence, were on duty in the west – at Münster, Koblenz, Metz, Saarbrücken, Karlsruhe and Strasbourg – while five others supervised the gathering of intelligence about Russia from Königsberg, Allenstein, Danzig, Posen and Breslau.

Contrary to the British belief that their country was overrun with German spies, the only plan that the ND had for espionage against Germany's enemies on the eve of war was for the use of its so-called 'tension travellers' (*Spannungsreisende*). These were volunteers – reserve officers, businessmen, and holiday-makers – who were to set off, at the first signs of political tension, ostensibly going about their normal affairs within the borders of France and Russia, in order to find out what they could. Nothing was planned for Britain, both because of the time needed to make a round trip across the Channel and because Britain, by tradition, was considered the concern of the Imperial Navy.

When the war started the new head of the ND, Major Walther Nicolai, had unlimited funds placed at his disposal. But he has recorded that this did not make up for the government's prewar neglect of intelligence because he lacked both trained men and bases abroad from which to operate. The United States makes a good example.

In the United States, military intelligence underwent an enormous expansion after America entered the war in 1917. Under Ralph H. Van Deman, a career army officer, the army's intelligence section grew from three men and a budget of $11,000 in 1916 to 250 officers, about 1,000 civilians and a budget of $2·5 million at the end of the war – an early indication that it is difficult, if not impossible, to have a small intelligence service.[8] Van Deman introduced the terms 'positive intelligence' (the use of all available means to gather information needed by American forces) and 'negative intelligence' (actions designed to deny intelligence to the enemy).

In the first sphere, American intelligence had some notable successes. It predicted Ludendorff's 1918 offensive, and the use of

'Big Bertha', the famous German artillery piece that could hit Paris from up to nine miles away. But the French were in charge of intelligence co-ordination at that time, and when reports from its own service disagreed with the American information, the French took no notice of it.[9]

Unfortunately, when it came to 'negative intelligence', the Americans went over the top. On the eve of war the United States became infected with the same sort of epidemic of spy hysteria as had occurred in Britain earlier. 'The state of the nation bordered on panic', says military historian, William R. Corson. The American Protective League (APL), founded by Albert M. Briggs, a vice-president of Outdoor Advertising Incorporated, set out to make every patriotic American citizen a counter-espionage agent. The APL was organized on a quasi-military basis; there are no official figures for its membership, but estimates of its peak strength range from 80,000 to 200,000. In their over-enthusiastic search for German spies and saboteurs, APL vigilantes often carried illegal weapons, posed as secret service agents, bugged rooms, tapped telephones and made illegal arrests. When the Espionage Act became law in June 1917, civil liberties took a double blow. Its provisions on censorship were so general that merely to be overheard by an APL member criticizing the government was to risk arrest.[10] Yet, as far as German spies were concerned, it was all a waste of time.

During the run-up to the war the Germans had maintained a general interest in the American army and its development. The German military attaché in Washington reported as much as he was able and the technical and general press was culled for further information. But when it became a distinct possibility that the United States would enter the war on the Allied side, the ND felt that it had to make some attempt to get up-to-date intelligence about the strength of the American armed forces and how much of it was likely to be committed to the struggle in Europe.

The difficulties immediately became apparent. There was no way that the ND could get agents into the United States. The route was barred in the West by Britain, France and Italy, and in the East by Russia and Japan. The British navy controlled the seas of the world and its surveillance made it virtually impossible to send agents, even on neutral ships. Before the United States entered the war, a few pro-German Americans offered their services to the ND but these offers were never developed into a real intelligence service. The ND felt that since it could not properly vet these volunteers, it could not run the risk that they might have been planted by one of the Allied secret services to feed the ND with disinformation. Nicolai concluded after the war: 'Of all the belligerents, America was the least threatened on her own territory by German espionage.'

This may not appear compatible with the reports at the time and with books written later describing widespread sabotage in the United States by German agents.[11] These, again, were not ND agents but pro-German Americans, frequently acting on their own initiative. Nicolai says of them, 'Their self-sacrificing attempts were of comparatively little use to Germany, and they contained in themselves from the very start all the dangers of aimlessness and lack of plan.'[12]

So, although there were thousands of arrests and convictions in the United States under the Espionage and Sedition Acts, most were for dissent and there was not one for active spying.[13] In the event, deprived of one enemy, the APL simply switched its attention to another: its paranoia was unleashed on labour unions, the International Workers of the World and other opponents of APL's main sponsor – American business.*

In Europe, intelligence at the front eventually proved no problem for the Germans. They, too, gathered information from prisoners and deserters and recruited agents from pro-German members of the civilian population in occupied areas who had ways of communicating with relatives and friends behind the Allied lines. The Germans were also energetic in developing the gathering of intelligence from aerial reconnaissance. Although this was useful in some circumstances, it often posed problems of interpretation. It could show the position of the enemy, but in trench warfare this was usually known. It could show marching columns, moving trains, towns, villages and smoking chimneys, but what did this mean? In most cases, aerial reconnaissance revealed the intention of the enemy only when this intention had already been translated into deeds, and it was then usually too late for the Germans to do anything about it.

But, like their British counterparts, the ND also desperately wanted to know what was going on far behind the lines. How did British civilians feel about the war? What was happening with war production? Was there a peace party on the British political scene? In an effort to obtain this sort of information the ND recruited agents who were sent to Britain to observe and report what was going on.

Legends have grown around the activity of German spies in

* This was the origins of the Red Menace of 1919–20, when the young J. Edgar Hoover, in charge of the Justice Department's General Intelligence Division, stamped hard on radicals, aliens, foreign organizations, unions, protest marchers and communists.

Britain during the First World War. Most of these can be traced to two men: the incredible William Le Queux, whose spy mania knew no limits when the outbreak of the war seemed to confirm all his prewar predictions about the German menace, and Dr Armgaard Karl Graves, a self-styled ND agent, who turned his prewar conviction on espionage charges to good account by writing a best-selling confession.

When the war started, Le Queux, spurned by MI5 – 'all the notice taken of [my reports] has been a mere *printed acknowledgement*' (original emphasis) – set out to catch German spies himself. Posing as an Italian he made the rounds of 'certain German quarters in London, notably obscure foreign restaurants in the neighbourhood of Tottenham Court Road'; he toured Surrey with an officer of the Naval Armoured Car Squadron investigating 'an intense white light being shown from a window in a country mansion'; he discovered other lights in places as far distant as Herne Bay, Sidmouth and Ilfracombe, all flashing in morse code the letters 'SM'; he reported suspicious advertisements in the personal columns of *The Times* ('M-Darling. Meet as arranged. Letter perfect. Should I also write? To the Day and to Kismet. – Vilpar').

Le Queux soon began to suspect that German spies had infiltrated the highest positions in the British government, otherwise why were the authorities taking no notice of his warnings?\* He put all his fantasy into a book called *Britain's Deadly Peril: Are We Told the Truth?* which was published in the autumn of 1915. It was an immediate best seller, confirming in the readers' minds the fears aroused by the confessions of Dr Graves, *The Secrets of the German War Office*, which had been published a year earlier and had sold 50,000 copies.

Graves had been sentenced in Edinburgh to eighteen months' imprisonment on 22 July 1912. He was released in December and went to the United States where an astute writer, Edward Lyell Fox, ghosted his memoirs, delivering the manuscript to the publishers six weeks before the start of the war. It is an amazing book in which Graves describes how he was recruited as a spy by Major the Count Freiherr von Reitzenstein during the Boer War in South Africa, where he was serving as a doctor and Reitzenstein as an observer for Germany. During his career, Graves claimed, he was

---

\* Le Queux was supported by other, equally xenophobic writers. An editorial in the magazine, *Referee*, demanded that the government publish 'a list of all men of German stock or of Hebrew German stock who have received distinctions, honours, titles, appointments, contracts or sinecures, both inside or outside the House of Commons, Lords and Privy Council'.

wounded five times, hauled before a firing squad in the Balkans, saved when a reprieve arrived as the squad took aim, and had spied in Singapore, South Africa, Turkey, Holland, Britain and Morocco. He also asserted that he had met the Kaiser, trapped two women spies and was eventually sent to Britain 'to watch the movements of British warships off the Scottish coast and promptly cable the German Admiralty Intelligence Department concerning them'.

The truth is that Graves was an adventurer, an impostor and a fraud. He may have tried some freelance spying in Scotland, but he did it in such an inefficient manner that in Edinburgh and Glasgow he was considered something of a joke, an eccentric old windbag. One Scotsman, with whom Graves had struck up an acquaintance in a Glasgow hotel, introduced Graves to his colleagues as 'my friend, the German spy'. In his book, Graves claimed that the reason he had been released so early from prison was that the British wanted to 'turn' him, that is, to use him against Germany. The truth is more likely that he had been in custody for nearly six months before his trial and this, plus the time he served, made him about eligible for parole anyway. The comparative lightness of his sentence also suggests that, although the government was prepared to make an example of him, it did not take his activities too seriously. But Graves's book was a best seller. Its skilfully created air of mystery – 'There are only three persons alive who know who I am. One of the three is the greatest ruler in the world. None of the three . . . is likely to reveal my identity' – and the entirely fictional, yet convincing, details which he gave about German espionage operations, confirmed in the British public's mind the concept of a country virtually overrun with master spies.

Let us compare the myth with the reality. Thirty German spies were arrested in Britain between 1914 and 1918. Twelve were executed, one committed suicide and the others were imprisoned.[14] The best known of these thirty was Carl Hans Lody, a lieutenant in the German Naval Reserve. Lody had been a tourist guide for the Hamburg–Amerika line, so he spoke good English with an American accent. He turned up in Edinburgh in September 1914 bearing an American tourist's passport which the Germans had stolen from a Charles A. Inglis in Berlin. Lody established contact with his controller by sending a telegram addressed to Adolf Burchard, of Stockholm, but made the mistake of exulting over recent German military reverses. The censors thought it odd that one neutral should waste cable charges expressing such sentiments to another neutral, and decided to monitor all correspondence addressed to Burchard. MI5 began to shadow Lody.

By October there was sufficient evidence to justify arresting him, and on 30 October 1914 he was tried before a court martial in London. His letters and telegrams were produced (only one had been allowed to go out of Britain, and this was because it repeated a rumour that SIS was anxious to spread in Germany, namely, that Russian troops had passed through Scotland on their way to the Western Front), and the prosecution emphasized their 'accurate observation and clear expression'. There was no defence, except that Lody had been acting from patriotic motives. He was found guilty, sentenced to death and a firing squad shot him in the Tower of London on the morning of 6 November.

Lody's case is the best known, but it is not typical. Most German spies in Britain were not German nationals. The ND rapidly realized that sending a German, even one who spoke good English like Lody, had distinct drawbacks: there was the need to create a false identity for him, the restrictions of the Defence of the Realm Act,* the problem of communication and, after Lody's well-publicized execution, a distinct lack of volunteers. On the other hand, there was no lack of neutrals willing to work for the Germans for money and, better still, the occasional British subject – if of exotic background – who could be forced into service for the ND. The ND's recruits were in fact a strange and rather pathetic assortment of misfits: people like Kurt de Rysbach, a dancer and former regular in the British army in Singapore; Eva de Bournonville, a Swede who spoke six languages; Leopold Vieyra, a Dutchman who had worked before the war as a film agent travelling between Britain and Holland; Leon van der Goten, a Belgian who had worked for the Belgian secret service; Adolfo Guerrero, a Spaniard sent to Britain under cover as a newspaper correspondent; and Frank Lauritz Greite, an American seaman who was caught when he contacted a German agent in Rotterdam.

From the secret reports of the trials of these German spies, from their petitions for clemency and remission of sentences, and from MI5 comments on these petitions, we can draw several important conclusions about the spies themselves, their effectiveness, their attitude to their work, and the way the counter-espionage authorities felt about them.[15]

In general, no matter how dangerous any of these spies *might* have become, their value to Germany was virtually nil. Even Lody,

* This Act, drafted by General G. K. Cockerill, and based on his experience in the Boer War, gave the government enormous powers. One of these was the registration of all foreigners in Britain, which kept their movements from one place to another under the constant notice of the British police.

whose military dedication to an assignment for which he was scandalously ill-prepared aroused the admiration of all those British officers who dealt with him, got nothing back to Germany except one rumour which turned out to be false. The other German spies could be classified as social misfits, criminals, adventurers, vagabonds, or romantics who were attracted to espionage by the prospect of easy money, or because it seemed to offer them an opportunity of living out their fantasies.

The attitude of the British authorities towards the pathetic group of inadequates was largely dictated by the need to deter potential spies and to make recruiting them as difficult as possible for the German ND. 'A sure and certain knowledge on the part of potential spies that their detection here will invariably involve heavy punishment with no likelihood of remission of sentence undoubtedly acts as a strong deterrent to individuals contemplating espionage', wrote MI5. 'Indeed it is practically certain that the comparatively high price which the Germans eventually found it necessary to pay for espionage in the United Kingdom (more than three times the price paid for similar work in France), was due to the severe sentences which invariably followed convictions.'[16]

So the sentence that a spy received bore little relation to what he or she had actually done. Instead the punishments meted out by the authorities reflected both their belief in deterrence and a series of moral propositions that relate to the state's attitude to spying in general. Some of these propositions were arbitrary and hypocritical. Thus German spies caught during the war were considered to deserve the death penalty, but were admired as patriots. Neutral spies, or 'traitor' spies, were considered beneath contempt but usually escaped capital punishment. German spies serving long terms of imprisonment were all released by 1920. But most neutral spies were forced to serve their full terms. MI5 was, apparently, conscious of this anomaly: 'Quite the best of the spies we got was Carl Lody, a patriotic German and an honourable man, and we shot him and cannot reduce his sentence. Greite on the other hand came here with an American passport, is presumably an American citizen, was treated as a friend, and abused our friendship for the sordid purpose of earning money. I would therefore regret any mercy being shown to him.'[17] Greite, in one of his petitions for his release, drew attention to inconsistencies in Britain's attitude to spies: 'Espionage for England is a commendable deed but espionage for Germany is a crime; an English spy is a man of honour, a German spy is a felon.'[18]

Thus German espionage in Britain achieved little during the war.

One assessment by a former MI5 officer was that, 'None of the German spies in Britain ever picked up much that could not have been read in our newspapers, most of which went to Holland and so found their way into German hands.'[19] But Germany could console herself with the knowledge that British spies in Germany did no better. In fact, of spies caught in Germany, the majority were Germans, numbering 235. Next came the French with forty-six and the British came well down the list with three, barely ahead of the lone Peruvian. The Germans admitted that the number of spies caught and charged represented only a fraction of those at work, but it is hard to believe that SIS under Cumming ever succeeded in getting any worthwhile information out of Germany from British agents.

Brigadier General W. H. H. Waters, a British military attaché of wide and long experience wrote after the war: 'My view always was – and experience has only tended to confirm it – that the results of a secret service are usually negligible.'[20]

W ere there then, no espionage successes in the First World War? The ND did have some success with its 'tension travellers' on the eve of war, particularly from the reports of an American, Wilbert E. Stratton, who worked for the Pyrene Company, London, and was frequently in Europe on business. Stratton had volunteered to report to the ND after visits to Russia and since he was in Germany as tension rose in July 1914, the ND sent him to Petrograd to see what he could discover. Stratton sent several telegrams in code from railway stations *en route* to Petrograd reporting what he interpreted as signs of mobilization. Although some of the telegrams did not get back to Berlin fast enough to be of much value, others did, and contributed to the early discovery of Russian military preparations. The ND, greatly pleased with Stratton, sent him on a mission to Stockholm and then again into Russia. When his office recalled him to London early in 1915, the ND naturally tried to persuade him to work there, but Stratton firmly refused to do so.*[21]

The French secret service got hold of the details of the Schlieffen Plan – the German scheme for a war against France based upon an

---

* The Pyrene Company say that they cannot trace Stratton in their records. But, curiously, the chairman of Pyrene after the war was Wallace Banta Phillips, who also ran a commercial intelligence organization in London.

attack through Belgium – from an officer of the German General Staff who wrote from Liège signing himself 'Le Vengeur' and offering 'documents of the highest importance'. The German, his head swathed in bandages as if he had just had a surgical operation, met a French agent, a Captain Lambling, three times – in Paris, Brussels and Nice. He told Lambling, 'I am perfectly aware of my shame, but they have behaved in an even more shameful manner to me and I am avenging myself.' He then proceeded to hand over the whole Schlieffen Plan, including a detailed chart of the 'zones of concentration'.

On several occasions the French Secret Service got other information that tended to confirm the accuracy of 'Le Vengeur''s account, including details of extensive railway improvements in the Western Rhineland, and High Command 'notes' on the principles which would inspire the army in the event of war with France. The Schlieffen Plan was, in any case, almost an open secret after the January 1909 issue of the *Deutscher Revue* published an anonymous article, obviously written by Schlieffen himself in protest at High Command changes in his plan. For, in order to make his case, the author of the article had to go into the broad outline of the original plan.*

But the French General Staff refused to the last to believe that the Schlieffen Plan was genuine, preferring the view that 'Le Vengeur' was a plant, designed to draw them away from the real area of attack. They were wrong; the route that the Germans took in 1914 was exactly as 'Le Vengeur' set out. When Marshal Pétain tried to hold an inquiry after the war he found that all the documents delivered by 'Le Vengeur' had been burnt in August 1914.[23]

The German ND obtained the Allied plan of attack for the Battle of the Somme from a French prisoner, and information about one of the first tanks from a British prisoner. The Frenchman provided so many details, and with such conviction, that the ND decided that an officer of his rank could not possibly have access to such information and dismissed him as a charlatan. The British prisoner had escaped unhurt from a tank which had exploded and, severely shocked, he gave the ND officer details of his work in a tank factory, described the design and construction of tanks, and the rate at which these new war machines were being manufactured. His information was so

* A student at the British Army Staff College brought the article to the attention of the then commandant, Sir Henry Wilson, later to be Chief of the Imperial General Staff. Wilson, who should have realized from what he read that the British Expeditionary Force would be endangered returned the article marked 'very interesting'.[22]

complete that a technician could have constructed a model of a tank by following it, but the ND doubted the whole story until, when it was too late to be of use, it was confirmed.[24]

The Russian secret service got hold of the details of Germany's eastern fortresses, as well as maps of the whole of the military road and rail network in eastern Germany, but this turned out to be of little use. As Nicolai said after the war, it was not difficult for a good espionage service to discover the location of the enemy's forces, their composition, and route and methods by which they would move. The difficulty was to determine the enemy's *intent* and, in this area, no spy of any service had any success.

Instead, the credit for the few coups of the period must go to the bureaucrats in communications intelligence, an aspect of espionage that had been underrated before the war, in part because of the British and American ethic that gentlemen did not open and read other people's mail, or intercept and decode their telegrams. Two of the belligerents, France and Austro-Hungary, had set up code-breaking organizations before the war, but elsewhere such activities were felt to be unnecessary – many countries did not even bother to encode their military traffic. The consequences of such naïveté became apparent at the Battle of Tannenberg in the last week of August 1914, when the Germans intercepted Russian radio messages sent in the clear and used the information to inflict a crippling defeat on the Tzar's forces – one of the great communications intelligence coups of history.

The British, who had started opening letters immediately after the outbreak of war,\* now quickly moved into radio interception and codebreaking. The Royal Navy staked out a claim to this work, 'Blinker' Hall realizing that communications intelligence was an unexploited area. He recruited a staff largely made up of amateurs – dons, clerics, schoolmasters, publishers – whose lack of the proper navy background was greatly to inhibit their effectiveness in the eyes of their more traditionally minded colleagues. (One can find some sympathy with the traditionalists' point of view: Dilly Knox, a classics scholar did his codebreaking in the bath, and historian Frank Birch fancied himself as an actor and later appeared regularly in pantomime on the London stage.)

The codebreakers, working out of Room 40 in the Old Block at the Admiralty, had their first breakthrough within two months of the

---

\* By November 1918 the postal censorship department – as it was euphemistically called – employed 4,000 people, including linguists, chemists and codebreakers.

start of the war when they received from the Russians the key that unlocked the secrets of the German naval code. This was the famous Magdeburg signal book, which the Russian navy had recovered from the body of a German petty officer killed when two Russian cruisers fired on the German light cruiser *Magdeburg* on 26 August 1914.

With the Magdeburg book, the *Handelsverkehrsbuch* (captured on the outbreak of war on a German merchant ship in Australia), and the *Verkehrsbuch* (found in the luggage left behind by the German diplomat, Wilhelm Wassmuss, when he fled from a British arresting party in Persia early in 1915), Room 40 was soon able to read virtually any message that the German authorities sent to their navy, merchant marine, consuls, embassies, submarines and Zeppelins.* During the war Room 40's codebreakers cracked about 20,000 German messages, some of which were vitally important.

Unfortunately, Winston Churchill, then First Lord of the Admiralty, decided this operation was so valuable to Britain that it had to be surrounded with secrecy. This secrecy was excessive and prevented the codebreaking operation from functioning properly: some navy departments never got to hear of Room 40's services; those who did, and were prepared to use them, were denied access to them on security grounds. Then when the moment was ripe to use the intelligence for a great naval victory, bureaucratic blunders lost the opportunity forever. This is what happened at Jutland in May 1916. The intercepts of radio traffic from the German High Sea Fleet could have provided Britain's Grand Fleet under Admiral Jellicoe with a British triumph. But security rules about the passing of information from Room 40 to Jellicoe led to a series of misunderstandings that not only allowed the Germans to escape, but shattered Jellicoe's faith in intelligence.[25]

A part from the limited success enjoyed by the communications intelligence, the intelligence community does not appear to have done very well in the First World War, and the individual agent did worst of all. How to explain, then, the enduring legends of spies such as Mata Hari, the beautiful 'Javanese temple

---

* The postwar German version of how the British had cracked their codes was that an Austrian, Alexander Szek, working at a Germany army wireless reception station in Belgium, had been suborned by British agents to copy the code book and deliver it to them. To explain why no one had ever heard of Szek, the German version added that the British had murdered him in case he inadvertently revealed that the British knew the German codes.

dancer' recruited by the Germans as their top agent in France, who became the mistress of a French Cabinet minister and died before a French firing squad; or Colonel Alfred Redl, director of the Austro-Hungarian counter-intelligence department and, simultaneously, a spy for Imperial Russia. The answer is that these are indeed legends, romantic nonsense that thrives in the intellectual twilight of the intelligence world, folk-tales on which new recruits are nurtured and trained.

Over the years, Mata Hari has become the very epitome of the dedicated spy – the beautiful girl who, for money and thrills, wormed out of her lovers the most important secrets of state: 'The most fascinating, the most beautiful, the most astonishing and the most conscienceless woman spy ever', says a typical account. Her story seems to have all the elements traditionally associated with spying – deception, excitement, high living, power, money and, in the end, amazing bravery. Even those accounts of her career which acknowledge that, as well as being a talented dancer, she was 'a demi-mondaine', 'a courtesan' and 'a devastator of men's hearts and pockets', also point out that, while appearing to surrender all to her clients, she held back the most important thing – she had a secret life, she was a spy; they were not using her, she was using them. When called upon to pay the price, the legend goes, she went to her execution steadfast and composed. One version has her dancing in her cell for her jailers; another says she waved at the firing squad with her gloves; a third describes how she bared her breasts in the conviction that the French soldiers would be unable to aim properly; a fourth relates that she had been promised that the soldiers were using blank cartridges and that she would later be smuggled out of France. The real story is much more sordid.

Mata Hari's real name was Margareta Gertruda Zelle. She was born in 1876 in Leeuwarden, Holland. After a disastrous marriage to an officer in the Dutch colonial forces, during which she spent six years in Java, she launched herself in Paris in 1905 as Mata Hari, 'The Eye of the Morning', a performer of erotic Indian dances, some of which she did naked. She was an instant success and in the prewar years performed in Paris, Berlin, London and Rome.* She also was a high-class prostitute and, although far from beautiful and nearing 40, she charged the many high-ranking citizens of these capitals who came to her stage door enormous fees for her favours. She was in

---

* Her finest performances were at private gatherings. One of the sensations at the rue Jacob garden parties of the famous American lesbian, Natalie Barney, was Mata Hari riding around naked on a large white horse.

Berlin when the war broke out and, subsequently, as a neutral, moved freely between Germany, France, Italy, Britain and Spain. The German, the French and the British intelligence services all suspected her of being a spy but no one could discover any evidence, apart from the fact that she had slept with German officers, and French Cabinet ministers and that, exasperated after a lengthy interrogation by Sir Basil Thomson, the head of Scotland Yard, she had confessed that she *had* come to Britain as a spy – for the French! She was arrested in Paris in 1917 and tried by court martial on 24–25 July. The main evidence against her was a list of payments which Germans, some of whom were in the ND, had made to her in 1916 and 1917. The French authorities had discovered these payments set out in telegrams (from the German military attaché in Spain to Berlin) which they had intercepted. How could she explain this?

Mata Hari said that the payments from the military attaché himself were gifts – she was his mistress – and that if he had claimed them back from the German government's espionage fund then he was not the gentleman she had taken him to be. She agreed that she had collected two payments from the Comptoir d'Escomptes in Paris in November 1916 and January 1917. If the French authorities had traced the origin of these payments to Germany then she would not disagree, but she thought that they had come from Baron van der Capellen, her lover in Holland, who had nothing to do with the ND. It was true, Mata Hari said, that she had also collected 20,000 francs in May 1916 from the German consul in Amsterdam, and she readily admitted that the consul had told her that this was advance payment for supplying information to the Germans on her next visit to Paris. But she had no intention of supplying the Germans with anything, and she regarded the money as compensation for her furs which the Germans had confiscated from her when she was in Berlin in 1914.

It is significant that the court, in weighing Mata Hari's guilt, was not asked to consider the evidence of these payments at all. Instead, it was asked to pronounce on a series of propositions relating to the prisoner's intentions and her relationship with various Germans: Had she entered Paris to obtain documents or information in the interests of Germany? Had she maintained intelligence contacts with the military attaché in Madrid and the German consul in Holland?[26] This was the best the prosecution could do because there was not a shred of evidence that Mata Hari had ever given the Germans any information at all, a fact that the French finally admitted in 1932 when the head of the Conseil de Guerre, Colonel

Lacroix, read the file and announced that it contained 'no tangible, palpable, absolute, irrefutable evidence'.

Moreover, Mata Hari was a neutral. As she told the court in her impressive final statement, 'Please note that I am not French, and that I reserve the right to cultivate any relations that may please me. The war is not sufficient reason to stop me from being a cosmopolitan. I am a neutral, but my sympathies are for France. If that does not satisfy you, do as you will.' The court found her guilty and sentenced her to death. She was shot by a firing squad on 15 October 1917 at Vincennes, her hands bound behind her back and without a blindfold. An army surgeon gave her the *coup de grâce* by firing a revolver in her ear.

There was some disquiet about her fate after the war. In 1933 Paul Allard, a French historian, wrote, 'I have read everything that has been written about the famous dancer-spy, and I am no further advanced than before. I still do not know what Mata Hari has done. Ask the average Frenchman or even the more intelligent Frenchman, what Mata Hari's crime was, and you discover that he does not know.'[27] Why did not the Germans clear up the matter once and for all? In 1929 Major-General Gempp, who had been in the ND during the war, wrote articles for German newspapers on the Mata Hari case. In the *Kölner Zeitung*, 31 January 1929, Gempp said, 'Mata Hari did not achieve anything for the German intelligence service. Her case was enormously exploited.' But, in 1941, another ND officer, Major von Roepell, disagreed with Gempp. Mata Hari, he said, had been recruited by Baron von Mirbach, a Knight of St John, had trained in Frankfurt and 'definitely spied for Germany'.[28] It would appear that the German secret service was as confused as everyone else as to Mata Hari's true status.

Certainly, on the evidence at her court martial Mata Hari was guilty, at worst, of associating with enemies of France. In Britain she would have been charged with 'doing an act preparatory to collecting information which might be useful to any enemy' – a catch-all charge, used when there was nothing more incriminating – and she might have got ten years' imprisonment. But France, at that time, was rife with defeatism, staggering from the shock of mutinies at the Front and the executions necessary to suppress them. Mata Hari's case served to remind the citizens of France of the dangers of subversion from within, and her execution acted as a deterrent to any other spies who might seek to undermine the French war effort. There were also political undertones to the case. Her diaries referred to an affair with a French minister whom she called 'M'. This was taken to refer to the Minister of the Interior, M. Malvy, and in the aftermath of the case he was driven from office. In 1926 General Messimy, who had been Minister of War in 1914, confessed that he was probably 'M', but insisted that he had resisted Mata Hari's attempts to seduce him.[29]

The conclusion must be that Mata Hari was shot not because she was a dangerous spy, but because it was militarily and politically expedient to shoot her, and because of what she was.

There are many versions of the Redl story. No spy anthology is complete without an outline of his career as a double agent. 'He caught some of Europe's cleverest spies', says one version. 'He wormed out many of the greatest secrets of several European powers. He never seemed to fail. Yet for more than half the time he held his appointment, Redl was acting as a spy for Russia.' The generally accepted version begins in 1905 when Redl was promoted to the Austro-Hungarian General staff's planning section. His successor, anxious to maintain Redl's reputation as a spy catcher, established a secret postal interception station, the Black Bureau. On 2 March the bureau opened two letters addressed to 'Opera Ball 13, Poste Restante, Central Post Office, Vienna'. The letters contained money: one the sum of 6,000 Austrian Kronen, and the other 8,000 Austrian Kronen (then about £240 and £320 respectively). Neither envelope contained anything else. It was this, and the fact that the letters came from Eydtkuhnen on the German frontier with Russia, that made the Austrian counter-intelligence agents suspicious and they kept watch to see who would collect the letters.

The agents bungled the job, so the story goes, and arrived at the Post Office too late to catch the man who had called for the letters. But they were in time to see him get into a taxi. While they stood on the pavement discussing what to do, they had an amazing stroke of luck. The same taxi cruised past them. The agents hailed it and learnt that their quarry had been driven to a restaurant called the Kaiser, where he had taken another taxi to the Hotel Klomser. While they were in the taxi the agents searched it and found the suede cover of a pocket knife on the seat. They gave this cover to the hall porter at the Klomser where it was claimed by none other than Colonel Redl. When he left the hotel the agents followed him, but so clumsily that Redl spotted them. One version states: 'Redl could not make a dash for it so he drew from his pocket some papers. He did not look at them to see what they were; it did not really matter now.

He tore them into pieces and threw them down. The men would certainly stop to pick them up.' One did, but the other continued to follow Redl back to the hotel.

At counter-intelligence headquarters the torn scraps of paper were pieced together and turned out to be three receipts for registered letters sent to Brussels, Warsaw and Lausanne. The Brussels address was the joint office of the Russian and French secret service, and the address in Warsaw was the local branch of the Russian intelligence bureau. This, the same account claims, was the proof Austrian counter-intelligence needed. Its director immediately informed the Commander-in-Chief of the army, General Conrad von Hoetzendorf who, the story continues, said:

> 'The scoundrel must be caught.'. . . 'Then' – a minute's pause – 'he must die. Immediately.' Again the General was silent. 'No one must know the reason for his death. Am I understood?'
> 'Perfectly.'
> 'Redl! Of the Eighth Corps too. Just the point where treason may be so deadly. My God! If Plan Three has gone . . .'[30]

Four officers went to Redl's room at his hotel, and found him sitting at his table writing letters of farewell. He said he knew why they had come and asked for an opportunity to 'depart his life'. They brought him a Browning revolver, and at 5 a.m. one of the agents checked and found Redl with his brains blown out. On a half sheet of notepaper was written, 'Levity and passion have destroyed me. I pay with my life for my sins. – Alfred.' When Austrian intelligence officers checked Redl's affairs it was discovered that he was a homosexual with a taste for luxury. He had a house in Prague and another in Vienna, an estate in the country, four expensive cars, and a cellar that included 160 dozen of the finest champagnes. Documents revealed that he had been receiving about £2,400 a year from the Russians – ten times his pay as a colonel – and that his main task for his employers was to name the Austro-Hungarian agents working in Russia. And, the story goes, he had betrayed Plan Three, the complete scheme for military action against Serbia in the event of war.

This certainly appeared to be confirmed when war came and the Austro-Hungarian forces went into action. The Serbian army repulsed three attacks, inflicting heavy losses. It took a great superiority of troops and Serbia's shortage of supplies for the Austro-Hungarians to succeed at their fourth attempt. Their casualties were estimated at half a million men. The account concludes,

'Redl was directly or indirectly the author of between 20 and 30 per cent of these.'

The Redl story is such an integral part of spy history, the first double agent of importance, that one hesitates to challenge it. Yet much of it sounds highly improbable. Redl certainly existed and there is little doubt that he was a Russian spy. But the accepted account of his detection, arrest and death, and the extent of his betrayal, that is, his importance as a spy, read suspiciously as if they were created both to inflate the efficiency of Austrian counter-intelligence and to explain away the country's humiliating defeats early in the war.

Let us, therefore, look at the story more closely. Redl collects the poste restante letters from the Post Office and signs for them. (The various accounts make no mention of what name he signed.) At this stage there is no evidence against him: he could have collected them for a friend. Redl then vanishes into a taxi but, with amazing luck, the very same taxi cruises past the agents a few minutes later. They are doubly lucky because Redl has left his pocket knife cover in the taxi and all the accounts make much of how this positively identifies Redl and enables the agents to follow him when he leaves his hotel. But Redl is suspicious and to delay the agents he takes some papers from his pockets. *'He did not look at them . . . He tore them into pieces and threw them down'* (emphasis added). Not only is the reader asked to believe that a man of Redl's experience would throw away papers without looking at them, but that these papers turn out to be the very documents necessary to prove Redl's guilt: receipts for letters he had posted to his spy masters. Would a spy keep on his person receipts of such an incriminating nature? Would he keep such receipts at all?

Redl was known to suffer from bouts of deep depression and had been consulting a doctor for 'psychological disturbances'. A more likely scenario is that he committed suicide during one of these depressions (the suicide note is open to many interpretations), that the subsequent ordering of his affairs revealed his treachery – probably his unexplained wealth was the starting-point – and that Austrian intelligence then created the story of Redl's detection and suicide to put a better complexion on a disastrous affair, carefully leaking its version to Prague and Berlin newspapers. As for Redl's importance, the chief of Austrian military intelligence, General August Urbanski von Ostrymiecz, felt compelled to reveal that Austria's early failures in the war were due to military deficiencies rather than betrayal.

In fact, Redl seems to have been a liability rather than an asset to his Russian masters. According to Professor A. Swetschin, of the General Staff Academy, Moscow, a member of the Russian Army High Command in the First World War, the information that Redl passed to Russian intelligence was out of date when the war began. Swetschin concludes, 'The work of the intelligence service hindered the Russian leadership more than it helped it.'[31]

By the end of the First World War, with bureaucratized intelligence still in its infancy, all the elements of its failures were easily discernible. In Britain, the Secret Service Bureau had attracted to it men of little merit, including leaders who, to put it kindly, were eccentric and inefficient. Their work had been surrounded with such secrecy that it nearly killed at birth the one form of intelligence that had proved its worth – communications interception and codebreaking. This secrecy, and the glamorized accounts of the work of spies like the pathetic Mata Hari, deceived the public into believing that the master spy was the new romantic hero whose influence on the course of the war had been immeasurable. Within the intelligence community there were a few, however, who saw only too clearly how useless the individual spy had been.

# 3. Crush the Red Terror

> With the world in its present condition of extreme unrest and changing friendships and antagonisms, and with our greatly reduced and weak military forces, it is more than ever vital to us to have good and timely information.
> – Winston Churchill, letter to Lloyd George, 19 March 1920.

> The buying of information puts a premium on manufactured news. But even manufactured news is less dangerous than the honest reports of men who, however brave and however gifted as linguists, are frequently incapable of forming a reliable political judgment.
> – Robert Bruce Lockhart, *Memoirs of a British Agent* (1932).

The end of the First World War saw British intelligence in crisis. Despite the success of the codebreakers, the service chiefs were not very impressed with what SIS or their own agencies had given them and the government had yet to be convinced that the growing expense of maintaining a full-time intelligence organization was justified in peacetime.

SIS was confident of being able to handle the service chiefs: they needed to be convinced that the intelligence failures during the war were as much the fault of military commanders as of the intelligence-gathering agencies. There was much evidence to support this argument. General J. V. Charteris, Field Marshal Haig's aide, through whom all intelligence had to be passed, had, for example, deliberately suppressed any information which he felt might depress his chief. Captain Payne Best recalled that he had reported firm evidence of plans for a German counter-attack after a British success at Cambrai, the first real tank battle, in November 1917. Charteris never showed the report to Haig and the Allies lost 50,000 men. When Best later tackled Charteris about this, he claimed that

Charteris replied, 'I didn't want to worry the poor dear Field Marshal.'[1]

Moreover, the army's own two intelligence units turned out to have been in competition not only with each other during the war, but also with Cumming's SIS, so much so that in some cases all three were paying the same agent for the same, often false, information. Thus, too close an examination of what had gone wrong was in no one's interests, and SIS was confident that it could carry the service chiefs with it in its plans for the future. The government was another matter. In the postwar drive for economy, the intelligence service was a natural target. SIS and MI5 had both been under War Office control. SIS was now hived off to the Foreign Office, as were the codebreakers, who were deliberately misnamed the Government Code and Cypher School (GC and CS). The navy continued to pay for the codebreakers, but the Treasury slashed SIS's budget in 1919 from £240,000 a year to £125,000, and MI5's from £80,000 to £35,000.[2]

The financial cut was a blow to SIS which was just beginning to build up a core of full-time agents recruited largely from the armed forces and the Indian Civil Service. The recruitment was largely haphazard. One of the older agents would remember that the candidate's grandfather had been 'knocking around Calcutta in the eighties', and someone else would recall having been at school with his father, and on the basis of these interlocking connections of the British middle and upper classes of the day, a new spy would enter the secret world. In SIS, this policy produced an atmosphere which was described by the late Henry Kerby, an agent at that time, as 'one in which no one thought of security breaches, knew the meaning of betrayal, and certainly would never dream of writing a book'.[3]

But they would fight to keep their service alive, and in Winston Churchill they found an ally. Churchill had a great belief in, and a fascination for, secret service work. When, in 1920, the Treasury proposed to cut SIS's budget down to a mere £65,000, and it became clear that the Foreign Office was not inclined to defend its adopted department, Churchill took up the cudgels. He wrote a 'most secret' letter to the Prime Minister, Lloyd George: 'With the world in its present condition of extreme unrest and changing friendships and antagonisms, and with our greatly reduced and weak military forces, it is more than ever vital to us to have good and timely information.' He said that it would take five to ten years to build up SIS and, 'It would in my judgment be an act of the utmost imprudence to cripple our arrangements at the present most critical time.'[4] He enclosed a memorandum, written in part by Cumming, showing how SIS had been spending its money and what cuts it would have to make if its budget was reduced still further. It is an illuminating document because it shows where SIS had stationed spies, why they were there, and what they were paid.

As might be expected, Germany still ranked highly in SIS's priorities. Cumming had agents in Berlin and Hamburg (paid £2,000 a year each) and men on every frontier with Germany. A network of agents in Holland, engaged solely in reporting on Germany, cost £30,000 a year, and there were men in Vienna, Prague, Warsaw, Bucharest and Copenhagen. There were plans for expanding in the Far East 'which should have proved of great value in the case of Japan', but since these would have cost £15,000 a year, 'they will have to be abandoned with the immediate result that little information from this part of the world will be obtained'. Espionage work in Italy, Spain and Portugal, which had cost £2,500, would also have to be abandoned if the budget cuts went through. Surprisingly, SIS had been spending £9,000 a year on espionage in the United States, only a year or so earlier Britain's valued ally. There is a hint in the memorandum of what this was for: if the budget were to be cut 'it will be impossible to watch the development of preparations for chemical warfare in any countries other than Germany. The General Staff are particularly anxious to have information on this subject from America.'[5]

In his accompanying letter, Churchill pleaded for the budget to remain as it was for a year. During that period, he said, it might be possible to make economies by combining the three 'distinct and very secretive organisations which exist at present: Sir Basil Thomson's civil organisation (the police Special Branch), Colonel Sir Vernon Kell's counter-espionage service (MI5) and "C's" Secret Service (SIS).' He was ignored. The cuts went through and, by 1921, SIS was operating on £65,000 a year and MI5 on £25,000. Yet, by 1927, it was up to £180,000, the highest budget since the end of the war and a record for peacetime. What had happened?

Admiral 'Blinker' Hall had fought as an MP against the Treasury cuts – 'methods of economy which only result in ruin' – because, back in 1918, he had already seen the path that British intelligence should follow. In his farewell address to his colleagues in naval intelligence he had said: 'I want to give you a word of warning. Hard and bitter as the battle has been, we now have to face a far, far more ruthless foe. A foe that is hydra-headed and whose evil power will spread over the whole world. That foe is Soviet Russia.'[6] This was a quick recovery by perhaps the most astute of the British spy masters. For the Bolshevik Revolution had caught most of Britain's intelligence chiefs unprepared.

Although SIS had agents in Russia – we shall discuss them later – their main assignment had been to keep the tzarist armies fighting and to counter attempts by German agents to persuade the Russians to sue for a separate peace. When Lenin and his followers came to power, Robert Wilton, *The Times* correspondent in Petrograd who also reported to SIS, was in London on leave, having told both his editor and Cumming that the Bolsheviks should not be taken seriously. Everything that other agents in Russia told Cumming about the Bolsheviks confirmed this view.

But after the murder of the Tzar and his family, and the total collapse on the Eastern Front as millions of Russian troops laid down their arms and headed for home, Cumming had to reassess the situation. Reports now poured in from agents warning of the Bolshevik menace. In January 1919, Walter Long, the First Lord of the Admiralty, sent the Prime Minister, Lloyd George, a long report from a former SIS agent. The agent, who had served during the war and had obviously kept in touch with his colleagues, felt that not enough was being done to stop a Bolshevik Revolution spreading to Britain. The report, despite its hysterical tone, nevertheless seems to have represented the views of most SIS members at the time.

I now find myself convinced that in England, Bolschevism [sic] must be faced and grappled with, the efforts of the International Jews of Russia combatted, and their agents eliminated from the United Kingdom. Unless some serious consideration is given to the matter, I believe that there will be some sort of revolution in this country and that before twelve months are past . . . At the present time the Secret Service receives reports from Switzerland, Holland, Scandinavia and Russia on Bolschevik [sic] activities, of agents being sent to France or England, of agitators and their schemes . . . Having won the war against Germany, a new enemy has sprung up which cannot be defeated except by organisation. Of what use divisions to fight Bolschevism unless they are sound of heart and contented; of what use a police force which may be on the verge of another strike. If twelve months ago anyone had foretold such a complete revolutionary movement in Germany, the average mind would have ridiculed the idea, and yet today the words Bolschevism, Soviet and Soldiers, and Workmen's Councils are heard everywhere, and are seen in every paper. To that extent have Trotsky and Company already imposed their will on Europe . . .

Bolschevism in the Army is a military matter, in the Navy a naval one, in the Police Force a police matter, but Bolschevism which includes all these forces and many industrial centres is a state matter, not for one department, but for the nation. Many will scoff at these ideas, yet how many 'extreme' British Bolscheviks are there; say 5,000. A bigger percentage in proportion to the population than Russia started with. The Bolschevik creed is a dangerous one, but enticing to a mass which is sick of soldiering, bureaucrats and politicians, as tired of these things as the Russian nation was of a corrupt monarchy . . . All the elements for the new explosive are about – there are plenty of provocateurs trying to mix them and bring them together.

Why not have some one person to see that those who try to mix them shall be prevented, in addition to those who rightly try to remove the grievances of those who may be dangerous. Someone with the power and no belief in 'paper'; someone who is straight, fearless and even unafraid of a question in the House [of Commons]?[7]

This mixture of anti-semitism, fear-mongering and political extremism only reflected what most of the members of the British intelligence community felt, as reports on the rise of the Bolsheviks filtered through from agents in Russia. As details of Lenin's new order became known, alarm spread throughout the upper classes in Britain and France. It was bad enough that the Bolsheviks had overthrown their betters in Russia; it was terrifying that they now spoke of spreading this appalling political dogma throughout Europe and the rest of the world. Thus the agent's report was passed on to sympathetic ministers with the hope that they, in turn, would alert the Prime Minister to the Bolshevik menace. Several did so. The First Lord of the Admiralty added his own comment: 'I am confident the danger is real. I am convinced that one of your most experienced ministers should be immediately charged with the duty of superintending the S[ecret] S[ervice] and have the power to act and, of course, report to you.'

This suggestion would not have been to the liking of SIS: to have a politician as intelligence overlord would have endangered the secrecy which it considered essential to protect its wide freedom of action. And even though Lloyd George saw no need to act on the First Lord's suggestion – he felt that some of his ministers were in danger of getting 'Bolshevism on the brain' – SIS thought it wise to step up its Russian operation. This was only in part because it felt that Bolshevism was a menace; it was also intended to stave off any attempts to take over its anti-Bolshevik activities. Thus throughout the 1920s and early 1930s, until the rise of Hitler showed that the threat to Britain could come from the extreme right as well as the extreme left, the Bolsheviks and their plans for world domination became SIS's main preoccupation. It devoted the largest single part of its budget to Russia (in 1920 it spent £20,000 on agents in Helsinki to cover North Russia alone; this should be compared with the £2,000 it spent in Berlin). It sent its best agents – fluent Russian speakers with long experience of the country and its people – to Moscow and Petrograd with virtually a free hand to establish networks, finance counter-revolutionaries, and to do all in their power to crush the Bolshevik menace in its infancy. They failed, but their exploits became the stuff of legend, and they entered the records of SIS and – via their memoirs and biographies – the public imagination, as 'master spies' and 'aces of espionage'. They became known as men of the greatest courage and ingenuity who 'laughed in the face of death', lived on danger like a drug, and always eluded the clutches of Bolsheviks anxious for their blood. Do they merit this reputation?

SIS's main officers in Russia were Sidney Reilly, George Hill, Somerset Maugham, who also worked for the Americans, and Paul Dukes. For the purposes of this assessment we shall also include Robert Bruce Lockhart, the British 'agent' in Moscow, because there is evidence that although not an SIS officer, he was deeply involved in SIS plots.*

Sidney Reilly was, without doubt, the most flamboyant of the four. His own version of his background was that he was born in Russia in 1874, the son of an Irish merchant sea captain and a Russian Jewish mother. He went to Port Arthur in China as chief agent of the Compagnie Est-Asiatique, returned to Petrograd to work with a firm of Russian naval contractors, helped in the negotiations for the repatriation of Russian prisoners of war after the Russo-Japanese War in 1905, and made an enormous private fortune from the commission he received from a German company on contracts for the rebuilding of the Russian navy. As well as Russian, he wrote and spoke English, French and German, but all with a foreign accent. At some stage in his business career he was recruited by SIS (where he had the code name ST 1). He was in Russia when the Revolution occurred and succeeded in establishing

---

* An agent was a compromise between official recognition and no recognition at all, and enabled the British government to have the best of both worlds. If criticized for having no relations with the new Russian regime, British leaders could reply that this was not so; British interests were represented by an agent. If attacked for dealing with the new regime they could reply that this was not so; Britain did not have an ambassador in Petrograd, merely an agent in Moscow.

himself as a Soviet government official with access to Soviet documents from Trotsky's office in the Foreign Ministry.

He organized what became known as the Lettish plot – the uprising of the troops from the Baltic province of Latvia, the Letts, who acted as bodyguards for the Bolshevik leaders. The Letts were to seize Lenin and Trotsky, and then Reilly and his followers were to establish a provisional government of anti-Bolsheviks 'to suppress the anarchy which would almost inevitably follow from such a revolution'. There was a sub-plot which required a fanatical socialist, Dora Kaplan, to shoot Lenin, if the opportunity arose. It did; but Dora Kaplan shot too soon, and the whole plot fell apart. Reilly had to flee the country using one of his many aliases – Comrade Relinsky of the Russian police; Georg Bergmann, a merchant; or Monsieur Massimo, a Turkish businessman.

In Britain, Reilly tried to warn SIS and various British ministers of the terrible danger of Bolshevism. He then got involved in White Russian politics and the many plots being hatched in Europe in the early 1920s for the overthrow of the Soviet government and, to finance these, travelled between the United States, Britain and France, trying to raise money. Then, believing that the best chance of success lay with an underground movement in Russia called the Trust, he went back into Russia across the Finnish border, even though, after the Lettish plot, there was a death sentence awaiting him. One version claims that he was caught and shot. He went underground, says another version, and continued the fight against Bolshevism until his death from old age.

Like almost everything about Reilly, this is a mixture of fact and fantasy. He was born in Odessa and both his parents were Russian – the story about the Irish sea captain being, like the name Reilly, one of his many fabrications. He made a considerable amount of money as a commission agent on arms deals in the First World War. His wide range of contacts and his brilliance in languages had probably attracted the attention of SIS in the immediate prewar years; but there is another possibility – that he had been used as a source of information by the Foreign Office and that when the FO took control of SIS, Reilly emerged as an intelligence officer. He was certainly in Moscow during, or immediately after, the Revolution where, with a Colt revolver in his back pocket and a seemingly endless supply of money in his wallet, he proceeded to recruit a network of agents.

He had a fanatical hatred of the Bolsheviks: 'a far worse enemy than Germany . . . a hideous cancer striking at the very root of civilisation . . . the forces of anti-Christ . . . a filthy flood . . . scum

. . . a drunken rabble.' He was the original proponent of 'we are fighting the wrong war' school of thought:

> Gracious heavens, will the people in England never understand? The Germans are human beings; we can afford to be even beaten by them. Here in Moscow there is growing to maturity the arch enemy of the human race . . . Here the foulest and most monstrous and most obscene passions which have been suppressed and bridled by the common decency of people at large and by the strong hand of the most beneficent authority since civilisation first began, gibber and swagger in the seats of government . . . What is happening here is more important than any war that has ever been fought. At any price this foul obscenity which has been born in Russia must be crushed out of existence . . . Peace with Germany? Yes, peace with Germany, peace with anybody. There is only one enemy. Mankind must unite in a holy alliance against this midnight terror.[8]

His fanaticism should have disqualified Reilly from representing SIS in Russia. It clouded his vision, distorted his judgement and made him unduly optimistic about the chances of a counter-revolution. SIS sent him to Russia to gather information, to assess the strength of various anti-Bolshevik movements and to recommend which ones the Allies should support. But Reilly, whose hobby was collecting Napoleoniana, saw himself instead as a new Napoleon: 'A Corsican lieutenant of artillery trod out the embers of the French revolution. Surely a British espionage agent, with so many factors on his side, could make himself master of Moscow.' When it all went wrong, he railed at fate and, having listed all the 'ifs', concluded, 'I had been within an ace of becoming master of Russia.'[9]

Back in Britain he was soon up to his neck in White Russian intrigues, refusing to admit that there was a logical inconsistency in his stance. On the one hand, he claimed, the Bolsheviks were all-powerful monsters but, on the other, that a mere handful of dedicated men could overthrow them with a well-organized plot. In 1923 he married Pepita Bobadilla – a well-known actress, the widow of the dramatist Haddon Chambers – and, such was the fascination both of Reilly's personality and the half-world of espionage, this apparently level-headed girl was soon swept into the spy fantasies of her husband and his friends.

In her account of her brief marriage Mrs Reilly writes, 'I learnt how beneath the surface of every capital in Europe was simmering the conspiracy of the exiles of Russia against the present tyrants of their country.' Reilly had warned her that no one could be trusted – 'The difficulty of this game is that you never know who is with you and who is against you. Many agents are taking the pay of both sides' – and she soon came to share his paranoia. She tells how she noticed that one of Reilly's agents, recently arrived in London from Russia, had a left ear that had been disfigured, probably from frostbite. When she went to Paris to meet some exiles, she spotted the same man in a welcoming crowd: 'He had shaved off his beard . . . he was so changed as to be almost unrecognisable, but there over his collar loomed one tell-tale ear.' Later, the Reillys sailed to the United States and one of the stewards on the ship appeared to be watching them closely: 'He was a tall shaven man, whom I would not have recognised but for his ear.' Later still, after Reilly had vanished, Mrs Reilly waited for him in a hotel in Paris, and in the lounge a man stares at her 'with a sort of triumphant smile', a man with a disfigured left ear.[10]

By this time Mrs Reilly was carrying her own gun and thought nothing of sending and receiving telegrams in code or of using a code name herself – Reilly was 'Mutt' and she was 'Jeff'. But neither Reilly himself, nor her own experiences, prepared her for the speed and manner with which SIS and the British government washed their hands of Reilly when he vanished over the Russo-Finnish frontier.

Reilly still had an SIS case officer, a Commander 'E' who worked under consular cover in Finland. Commander 'E''s main task was to finance Russian émigré organizations, and he used Reilly to advise him on which ones were likely to achieve anything. When Reilly vanished, Mrs Reilly sent Commander 'E' a telegram expressing her worries. At first, Commander 'E' was concerned, but when it became clear that Reilly had gone into Russia without informing him, his manner changed. He wrote: 'My dear Jeff: I certainly think that it would be a very good idea to consult the Paris surgeon. It is a very sad thing about poor old Mutt. I do hope he pulls through all right.' Mrs Reilly went to Paris, as Commander 'E' had suggested, and no doubt pondered over the sombre tone of his letter.

In Paris she received another letter from Commander 'E' saying that the position was much worse than he had previously realized, and that he would be coming to Paris within a few days to see her. Then, five days later, another letter arrived saying he did not know when he would have any further news of Reilly, 'as I find urgent business now which takes me abroad again immediately and prevents me coming to Paris. Furthermore I shall have no permanent address for some time.'

As time passed and it became clearer that Reilly was either dead or a prisoner of the Bolsheviks, SIS's attitude galled Mrs Reilly. Was Britain going to do nothing either to rescue or to honour its master spy? She wrote a personal letter to Reilly's great admirer, Winston Churchill. His reply confirmed what she had expected: as far as SIS and the British government were concerned, Sidney Reilly had been on his own; if the secret service did not exist (as the Haldane sub-committee had recommended back in 1909) then how could officers of the secret service exist? Churchill's secretary, Eddie Marsh, wrote:

> Mr. Churchill desires me to acknowledge the receipt of your letter of 13th December and to say that it appears to have been written under a complete misapprehension. Your husband did not go into Russia at the request of any British official, but he went there on his own private affairs. Mr. Churchill very much regrets that he is unable to help you in regard to this matter, because according to the latest reports which have been made public, Mr. Reilly met his death in Moscow after his arrest there.[11]

The British practice of denying any link with a spy who got into trouble is certainly a sufficient explanation of the callous dismissal of Mrs Reilly's efforts to help her husband or, at least, to discover the manner of his death. But there could well have been another reason why the British government was not anxious to delve too deeply into the Reilly affair and why, to put it bluntly, his disappearance may well have been both timely and convenient. This reason has to do with the notorious Zinoviev letter, the greatest 'communist scare' in British political history.

The letter, purportedly written on 15 September 1924, by Zinoviev, president of the Communist International, to the British Communist Party, instructed British party members to prepare for the British revolution by intensifying their work in the armed forces and by using their sympathizers in the Labour Party. The letter was published in British newspapers four days before the general election of 29 October 1924, and was generally held to have swung the voters away from Britain's first Labour government and to have brought the Conservatives back to power. It also eclipsed any prospect of the proposed Anglo-Russian trade treaties being ratified by the British Parliament and soured relations between the two countries for more than twenty-five years.

Yet the letter was a forgery, concocted by a group of Russian émigrés in Berlin, planted in the European intelligence network, and almost certainly brought to the attention of SIS by Sidney Reilly. SIS reported the letter to the Foreign Office which decided that it was genuine. This decision was based more on the conclusion that there was nothing obviously false in the tone and contents of the letter than on any evidence as to how the letter was intercepted and how the copy reached Britain. Now several groups of conspirators, each with its own highly dubious motives, swung into action to get the letter published.

There is little doubt that Reilly had a hand in the affair. The important questions are: Did he know that the letter was a forgery, but still go ahead and convince SIS that it was genuine? Or did his blind hatred of the Bolsheviks and their system lead him to convince *himself* that the letter must be true? The only source for the first, more damaging, accusation is a Russian one which must be suspect. It is a semi-fictionalized account of the Russian secret service by Nikulin, published in 1966. In the book, Nikulin states that Reilly had told a Russian émigré organization in Finland how to raise money for their cause, little realizing that the organization had been penetrated by the Russian secret service and that his words were being noted down. 'Above all [SIS] wants information about the Comintern', Reilly is alleged to have said. 'If you can't get some real documents from the Comintern you'll have to invent some. A letter from the Comintern's chairman helped the Conservatives to win an election. *They maintain it's a fake, but it's the result that counts*' (emphasis added).[12]

But there is another more likely scenario. Both Reilly *and* SIS knew that the document was a forgery but, nevertheless, went ahead because, even if Reilly did not in fact say that 'it's the result that counts', he would certainly have believed such conduct to be justified. This would mean accepting that Britain's first Labour government was the victim of a prolonged conspiracy by its own secret service, and that this conspiracy involved circulating a forged document and authenticating that document with further forgeries – the incoming Conservative government had claimed that evidence that the letter was genuine had come from *four* different and independent sources. Dr Christopher Andrew, editor of the *Historical Journal*, says of the twin conspiracy theory, 'that hypothesis cannot be completely dismissed. The intelligence services were considerably alarmed by some of the members and some of the policies of the Labour Government. And they showed themselves capable on this and on other occasions of exceeding (though in far less spectacular ways) their ill-defined authority.'

We can go further than that. What had alarmed SIS was the fact that the Labour Party was considering the suspension of SIS and the opening of its files – a proposal which would, if implemented, take effect in 1925. So SIS had every motive to sabotage Labour's election chances in order to make certain that this did not happen.[13]

In this context, Reilly's disappearance less than a year later could have been seen as something of a blessing for SIS. True, it had lost an agent, but one whose usefulness was diminishing as it became increasingly obvious that the Bolsheviks were in power to stay and that the feuding and ineffective émigré organizations were incapable of doing anything about it. On the positive side, with Reilly's disappearance, the only man who could link SIS with the forgers of the Zinoviev letter was gone and any risk that, in later years, Reilly, disillusioned and perhaps broke, might be tempted to tell his story (he had already started on his memoirs) was eliminated.

George Hill was not quite in Reilly's class as an adventurer and master of intrigue but, as Reilly's lieutenant on many a mission, he picked up much of his mentor's style. As well as being an adviser to Trotsky on the setting up of a new air force, Hill mixed freely with all the Bolshevik leaders and in the early days of the Revolution rolled up his sleeves and did his best to help sort out the chaos. His mission was to keep Russia in the war and, if this meant co-operating with the Bolsheviks, then Hill was prepared to do so. But he never forgot that first and foremost he was a British intelligence officer. So when he helped the Bolshevik military headquarters to organize its first military intelligence system, recruiting agents in all the eastern areas occupied by the German army, he made certain that London also got a copy of everything they reported. And when he helped the Bolsheviks to set up a counter-intelligence service to handle German agents in Russia, to decipher intercepted German messages, and to open mail to and from the German mission (established in Russia to negotiate a peace settlement), Hill again made certain that London knew everything the Bolsheviks had learned.

In parallel with this operation, Hill created his own network of agents, working mainly against the Germans. But he did not share the information that he gathered with the Bolsheviks – as they, albeit unwittingly, shared with him. In fact, part of his own network consisted of a courier section to carry messages to London because he did not want to risk using the Bolshevik telegraph. Hill was also prepared to provide arms, money and false documentation to any Russian group prepared to conduct guerrilla operations behind the German lines, which meant meeting and assessing some of the more peculiar groups that were springing up all over Russia in the wake of the Revolution.

Somerset Maugham had already served as a British military intelligence officer in Italy, Switzerland and the United States when he was recruited by Sir William Wiseman, the British intelligence liaison officer in America, to go to Russia in mid-1917. Wiseman wanted Maugham to report both for SIS and the State Department. Maugham seemed an ideal choice because he spoke Russian, had intelligence experience and was recognized as an author – an ideal cover up for a spy, since he could amass information under the pretext of doing research for a book.

Maugham went by ship to Japan and then to Vladivostok to embark on the trans-Siberian railway. In Petrograd he took a room at the Hotel Europa and set to work, using his renown as a writer to gain access to Russian literary circles. He met the liberal leader, Alexander Kerensky, and several prominent Bolsheviks and filed voluminous reports to Wiseman who passed them on to the State Department.

The Bolsheviks came to suspect Maugham soon after his arrival, but did nothing to interfere with his work. One reason could have been that since his reports stressed the growing strength of the Bolshevik movement they were content to let him be. Maugham's views, on the whole, were more accurate than most other reports reaching the West – he gave early warning of Kerensky's declining power, for example – but, perhaps because he was a writer, he was overoptimistic about the power of propaganda. One of his suggestions to the State Department for countering the Bolsheviks and keeping the Russians fighting was that the Americans should make newsreels showing 'the life of the working classes in America, pictures of Washington and New York, and some pictures of German militarism and what it means'.

The November Revolution put paid to Maugham's spying. He felt that he was now a marked man and that his work had been for nothing. He was also ill with tuberculosis, depressed and shocked by the sudden change in events. He slipped out of Russia and returned to Britain.[14]

Of all the British agents, the most successful was probably Paul Dukes. He had left England before the war to study music in St Petersburg where he had felt 'at home from the moment of arrival'. When the Anglo-Russian Commission was set up in 1915 to organize British war supplies to Russia, he was first given the job of preparing a digest in English of the Russian press and then, in 1917, returned to London to be the commission's representative at the Foreign Office. When the Bolshevik Revolution occurred, the Foreign Office sent him back to Russia to report on what relief might be needed in the chaos following the collapse of the Russian armies. To some extent, this was a cover assignment because Dukes was also told to file reports on whatever he saw, wherever he went. After six months, when he had shown he could do this competently, he was recalled to London and invited to join SIS. After a preliminary interview with Cumming's deputy, during which Dukes was initiated into the mysterious ways of the secret world,* Cumming himself briefed him. SIS believed that Russia might soon close its frontiers to all foreigners and it needed someone there to keep it informed of developments. He gave Dukes a free hand as to how he would enter Russia, where he would go and how he would report; he took care, however, to make it clear that if Dukes got caught, then SIS would deny all knowledge of him and do nothing to help him.

A series of secret manœuvres then ensued. A letter invited Dukes to call at the Passport Office about his passport application; there he collected a slip of paper saying 'Kingston station, midnight Sunday'; at Kingston a man got out of a train full of soldiers and told Dukes to take his place and get out at Newcastle; at Newcastle an SIS messenger met him and gave him a special passport and a berth on a troop ship. Dukes survived this paperchase and, in November 1918, as Joseph Ilitch Afirenko, Ukrainian, office clerk in the Cheka (the forerunner of the KGB), he slipped across the Finnish border and took a train to Petrograd.

At first sight it seemed foolhardy for Dukes to have adopted as his cover the identity of an employee of the Cheka, but he reminded himself of an old Russian proverb, 'If you must live among the wolves, then howl too, as the wolves do'. In fact, Dukes became even bolder during his assignment in Russia and, at one time or another, had twenty different identities, including that of a soldier in the Red Army. Under one alias he not only became a member of the

---

* The deputy, who was a collector of fine books, left Dukes alone in his office for a few minutes. Dukes took down Thackeray's *Henry Esmond* only to discover that it was a dummy containing in its hollow interior just one sheet of paper headed 'Kriegsministerium Berlin'. Dukes hastily put it back on the shelf and said nothing. At the next interview, the deputy deliberately drew Dukes's attention to his book collection and added, 'That, by the way, is a fine edition of Thackeray. Would you care to look at it?' Dukes, heart thumping, took down – as he thought – the dummy *Henry Esmond*, only to find that it was a perfectly normal de luxe edition, profusely illustrated. He never found out what this farce was all about.[15]

Communist Party, but took his seat as a delegate at plenary meetings of the Petrograd Soviet. Much of his time – and much SIS money – was spent in trying to get various anti-Bolshevik leaders out of prison. In order to keep one step ahead of betrayal, he made it a rule to spend each night at a different address, and to be known at each address by a different name.

All the while, he gathered information – through gossip, talk on the streets, casual conversations at restaurants and, occasionally, an item delivered to him by some anti-Bolshevik source, either for money or for idealism. A former army general gave him a report on the latest measures to be taken by Trotsky against Admiral Kolchak, the White Russian leader in Siberia. An ex-journalist told him of serious disturbances at Kronstadt, among sailors of several ships in the Baltic Fleet. A landlady, and his own observations, provided him with a list of food prices.

Dukes had few scruples about using his sources. Walking in Nevsky Prospekt he saw a little girl sitting on the steps of a music shop crying. She told Dukes that she had not eaten for a long time. The child was ill and, although Dukes brought her food and did what he could for her, she died a few days later. He helped the parents give her a proper burial for which they were touchingly grateful. At some stage Dukes learnt that the father was a foreman at the Putilov iron works and a member of the Social Revolutionary Party. Dukes then pumped him for information about conditions in the works, the feelings of the workers and the party's plans. On one of his trips to Finland to get out an important report, Dukes got frostbitten on both feet. For some time he limped around with the aid of a walking stick. To local party members who inquired about his disability he told a story of revolutionary work in Britain, imprisonment in capitalist jails and deportation to Russia after the Revolution. They expressed sympathy, arranged special privileges for him, trusted him and confided in him.

In fairness to Dukes, his life as a spy was not easy. He seldom had enough to eat and no matter where he spent the night, sanitary conditions were primitive. In winter months he nearly froze. In summer, when it was risky to go to one of his regular overnight addresses, he slept rough in fields or in a broken tomb he discovered in a disused cemetery. The Cheka knew he was in Russia and were after him, so he had to change disguises, identity documents, names, friends and habits with upsetting frequency. He never knew for certain whom to trust. One of the first contacts he made in Petrograd, a man to whom he paid thousands of roubles to get a leading anti-Bolshevik out of prison, turned out to be a Cheka agent, either playing Dukes along in order to trap others, or so as to get as much money out of him as possible before turning him in.

When he had gathered as much information as he could remember, or when what he had obtained seemed so important that it should be sent to London as soon as possible, Dukes wrote it all out in miniature handwriting on flimsy tissue paper and then began the dangerous business of looking for someone to take it out of Russia for him. Often he found a White Russian, usually a former member of the Tzar's army, who was planning to flee to Finland and who, for some money, would conceal the wad of tissue in his boots. When no one suitable was around, Dukes would make the risky trip himself. London tried to set up a courier service, using a Royal Navy high-speed torpedo boat that made a dash up the Gulf of Finland, past the guns of the Kronstadt fort, to rendezvous with Dukes waiting in a skiff off Petrograd. But this only worked when there was no ice and before the guns and searchlights of Kronstadt became too proficient in picking up the boat.

What was his reward for all the fatigue, hunger, strain and knowledge of the deceit he practised on people who trusted him? SIS sent him plenty of cash (though on one occasion it turned out to be counterfeit) but, for Dukes, the job itself and the approval of his chief was sufficient recompense. 'On the whole I was content and not without cause. I had been allowed the remarkable experience of viewing the greatest social experiment in history from a unique angle. And my work, I had been assured, was much appreciated.'[16]

This was certainly true. One of the strengths of the reports which Dukes sent to SIS was that they were not tainted with the anti-Bolshevik fanaticism of Reilly. They were level-headed, factual, brief and source-noted. His report of 30 April 1919 was typical. It began by describing factory strikes in March and the influence of agitation by the Social Revolutionary Party. Then followed an account of disturbances in the Baltic Fleet, and the mobilization of Communist Party members to meet the threat of Kolchak's recent advances. An economic section listed the Easter market prices, salary levels, the shortage of cash and the movement of food supplies by railway. There was a section on disease and mortality, sanitation and the population level in Petrograd. Finally, there was a description of the mood of the people as they strolled up and down Nevsky Prospekt in the brilliant sunshine of Easter Sunday.

SIS would have liked to have kept Dukes in Petrograd for as long as possible but by September 1919, after more than a year on the run, Dukes felt it was time to leave. The Cheka were getting closer, and his current cover as a driver in the Red Army could not be used for much longer – his commander had warned him that his section was about to be moved to the Latvian front. So, with three White Russians for company, he made the last dangerous trip through the battle lines to Riga in Latvia and from there back to London. Cumming gave him a warm welcome and he had a long meeting with Churchill who had become one of his most powerful admirers. Churchill tried to get the Prime Minister to meet Dukes – 'He will interest you greatly', Churchill wrote – but Lloyd George was concerned about the propriety of being too closely associated with an SIS agent. If Dukes was disappointed by this, Cumming made up for it by arranging for him to have an audience with King George V. In the course of this meeting, the king told Dukes that he thought the spy was the greatest of soldiers and that if he were the most detested by the enemy it was only because he was the most feared.

The Bolsheviks would certainly have agreed with the second part of this sentiment. For with British soldiers at Archangel, with White armies closing in from Siberia, Poland, the Ukraine and Estonia, with Dukes, Reilly, Hill and several lesser British agents operating in the chaos and confusion of those early post-Revolution days, the Bolsheviks saw enemies all around them. Before we consider how they reacted, and the importance of this reaction to the development of the world of intelligence, we should look briefly at one other British agent whom the Bolsheviks accused of nearly crushing the Revolution: Robert Bruce Lockhart.

Lockhart was a Scot who went to Moscow in 1911 as vice-consul. There he played football for the famous Motozovsti team, learnt fluent Russian and, despite his youth (the Americans called him 'the boy ambassador'), became acting consul-general during the war. When the Revolution occurred and the British government broke off relations with Russia, Lockhart went back in the diplomatic capacity of British 'agent', a semi-official posting which both sides accepted as a means of communication when no ambassador was recognized (see page 58). This twilight world suited Lockhart because there is little doubt that he was doing some sort of work for SIS as well.

He knew Trotsky, shook hands with Stalin and, at first, felt some sympathy with the Bolsheviks and their aims: 'I could not help realising instinctively that behind its peace programme, and its fanatical economic programme there was an idealistic background to Bolshevism which lifted it far above the designation of a mob movement led by German agents', he wrote. 'For months I had lived cheek by jowl with men who worked 18 hours a day and who were obviously inspired by the same spirit of self-sacrifice and abnegation of worldly pleasure which animated the Puritans and the early Jesuits.'[17] But as a loyal servant of his country, Lockhart put his own views out of his mind and tried to advise his government on the best means of carrying out its policies. Thus when it was considering intervention, he advised against this, but stated that if, nevertheless, Britain went ahead then considerable force would have to be used.

His advice was not taken, however. 'To have intervened at all was a mistake', Lockhart wrote. 'To have intervened with hopelessly inadequate forces was an example of spineless half-measures which, in the circumstances, amounted to a crime.' He put some of the blame for this on British SIS officers in Russia, of whom he had a very poor opinion. 'The buying of information puts a premium on manufactured news. But even manufactured news is less dangerous than the honest reports of men who, however brave and however gifted as linguists, are frequently incapable of forming a reliable political judgment.' Lockhart's main complaint was that the SIS officers, particularly Sidney Reilly, had convinced London that all it needed to overthrow the Bolsheviks was some money and a handful of British soldiers and suggested that once these were provided, the citizens would rise against their rulers and the counter-revolution would succeed overnight. In his own reports Lockhart tried to suggest that such optimism was simplistic, but he succeeded only in making enemies for himself in high places in the Foreign Office, and his wife had to warn him from London that his career was in jeopardy.

He was certainly swept up into the world of conspiracies and counter-conspiracies which characterized the period. Forty years later, he wrote: 'Russia has been the dominant influence in my life. Even today she haunts me like an unfaithful mistress whom I cannot discard.'

This should be taken into account when assessing Lockhart's role in the Lettish plot or, as the Russians called it, the Lockhart conspiracy. Two Latvians, Berzin and Shmidkhen, officers of the Lettish regiments which, as we have seen, were bodyguards for the Soviet leaders, came to see Lockhart. Lockhart said later that all they wanted was to be allowed to send a messenger to General Poole, commander of the British intervention force in Archangel, to try to arrange for the surrender of their troops, and that he agreed to put them in touch with Sidney Reilly to help them to do this. Two days later, according to Lockhart, Reilly told him that he wanted to try something much more ambitious: with help from the Latvians, he wanted to stage a counter-revolution. Lockhart said that he told Reilly to have nothing to do with 'so dangerous and doubtful a move', that Reilly then went underground and that he never saw him again.

Reilly's version is that he was already working on a plan for a counter-revolution and had 60,000 White Russian officers in Moscow awaiting the signal to mobilize. When Lockhart introduced him to the two Latvians, he realized that this was the opportunity he had been waiting for. The Latvians were mercenary soldiers; he would offer them more money than the Bolsheviks and the last barrier protecting the new regime would fall. Reilly said that he soon had hundreds of thousands of roubles and began to make regular payments to the officers while he finalized his plans. These depended on both Lenin and Trotsky being in Moscow at the same time, and when that happened Reilly would give the signal and the Latvian bodyguards would arrest the two Bolshevik leaders and parade them through the streets 'so that everyone should be aware that the tyrants of Russia were prisoners'. At the same time, the 60,000 officers would mobilize under General Judenitch and a provisional government, consisting of Judenitch and two of Reilly's friends, would take charge of the country. A similar uprising would occur in Petrograd where the signal was to be the arrest of the head of the Cheka, Uritzsky.

Reilly claimed that Lockhart knew nothing of all this. But it is highly unlikely that Reilly would have embarked on a plot of such importance without authorization, if not from London, then at least from London's representative in Russia, Lockhart. Lockhart in later years confessed that he knew more of Reilly's plans than he had at first admitted.

In the event, it all went wrong. The counter-revolutionaries in Petrograd did not wait for their Moscow colleagues and on 30 August 1918, shot Uritzsky dead in his office. The next evening the young Social Revolutionary, Dora Kaplan, shot Lenin twice at point blank range as he was leaving a factory meeting in Moscow. One of Kaplan's bullets penetrated Lenin's lung and the second lodged in his neck near the main artery and though he was not killed outright, his chances of survival were at first considered slim. (He recovered but his health was impaired. He died in 1924.) The Bolsheviks immediately hit back. A party of Cheka agents burst into the British embassy in Petrograd. Captain Cromie, the naval attaché, resisted the intrusion, shot dead a commissar and was, in turn, shot dead himself. All the British officials were arrested, the Latvians failed to rise, the 60,000 officers did nothing and Reilly, a price on his head, had to flee the country.

Nearly fifty years later, the Russians claimed that they had known most of the plot all along. In 1966 *Izvestia* published an interview with one of the Latvians involved, Shmidkhen, who revealed that he had actually been a Cheka officer, assigned to infiltrate counter-revolutionary groups.[18] Shmidkhen said that he and Berzin had met Cromie in a Petrograd nightclub, where Cromie had introduced them to Reilly, and Reilly had, in turn, sent them to Moscow to see Lockhart – a small but important change in the order of events as related by Reilly and Lockhart. If Shmidkhen's version is true, then this would explain the rapid arrest of Lockhart (who was eventually exchanged for the Soviet agent in London, Maxim Litvinov), and the attempt to arrest Cromie.*

But clearly Shmidkhen did not learn everything about the plot, otherwise why was the Cheka chief in Petrograd not warned, and how did Lenin become such an easy target for Dora Kaplan? The answer may lie in the confusion caused by another plot underway at the same time. This was a Cheka one to use the contact with Lockhart to lure the British force at Archangel into an ambush under the guise of accepting the surrender of the Latvian troops.[19] This plot, too, was overtaken by the speed of events described earlier.

The Bolshevik revenge for the Lockhart plot was a terrible one. The government promulgated an order to crush all counter-revolutionary activity – the Red Terror – and the Cheka was authorized to execute or sentence suspects at will. Lockhart saw three ex-tzarist ministers dragged from their cells and shot, not for what they had done, or for what they had said, but because they were class enemies and their death would be seen as a reprisal and as a warning. No one knows how many people were killed. Lockhart claims several hundred, others say many thousands. The British intelligence officers in Russia escaped, but some only temporarily.

Reilly, as we have seen, probably fell victim to the long arm and the long memory of the Cheka. Lockhart suffered serious pangs of guilt. For a while he considered settling in Russia; his Cheka interrogator pointed out that he had been happy there, he had a Russian mistress, his career in Britain would be blighted by

* Shmidkhen was rewarded with an apartment in Moscow where he was still living in 1966.

what had happened, and that there was interesting work for him to do if he stayed. 'I gave the suggestion more consideration than the English reader may suppose', Lockhart wrote. He recalled that three Frenchmen had accepted a similar proposal. 'They were not wilful traitors. Like most of us they had been influenced by a cataclysm which they realised would shake the world to its foundations.' But Lockhart decided that he could not forgo his official obligations. He returned to London and continued to work for the Foreign Office until 1928 when he became a journalist with Lord Beaverbrook. In the Second World War he was director of the Political Warfare Executive and, until his death in 1970, he wrote many memoirs and biographies of famous people. His diaries, published after his death, revealed that for most of this time he had wrestled with alcoholism.[20]

Hill was dropped by SIS and got by in the 1920s and 1930s with such casual jobs as came along, including a spell with Royal Dutch Shell, and a year as general manager to C. B. Cochran, the producer. But for a long time he was a nervous wreck:

> I seldom slept more than three hours in any twenty-four. Oh, the agony of wakefulness. It is then that the mind marshals its fears and cares into battalions . . . from where was one to get the courage to stumble through yet another day . . . I was groping my way through life, dazed and bewildered. No casual onlooker would have credited it; one had returned from the war with life and limb whole; all was well.[21]

But Hill survived and again served in Russia during the Second World War.

Dukes was knighted for his work in 1920 and remained in SIS until his retirement, when he received permission to write a sanitized account of his experiences. He lectured frequently on Russia and contributed his views on international affairs to many newspapers and journals. He died in 1967.

What did SIS's considerable effort in Bolshevik Russia actually achieve? The one item on the credit side was that the Russian experience forced SIS to introduce a grading of intelligence reports according to reliability. This came about in a rather humiliating manner.

The GC and CS had been intercepting and decrypting wireless messages between the Soviet government and its representatives in London. But in 1920 the Russians changed their codes. SIS stepped into the breach with an agent, code named BP 11, in Reval (Tallinn) who claimed to have penetrated Litvinov's office and was thus able to provide London with 200 summaries of telegrams between Litvinov and Moscow. The most interesting of these purported to show that the Bolsheviks were helping to finance the Sinn Fein rebellion in Ireland.

SIS also got its hands on a whole series of documents which it claimed to have purloined from the offices of the Soviet representative in Berlin. These purported to show Bolshevik subversion on India's borders. Lord Curzon, the Foreign Secretary, was furious at what he took to be evidence of Soviet duplicity, and sent off a strong note to Moscow. But his indignation quickly turned to ignominy.

The material from BP 11 was discredited, largely by Sir Basil Thomson, of Scotland Yard, who could discover no evidence of any Russian money reaching Ireland, and who pointed out that all the evidence from Ireland was that Sinn Fein was in serious financial difficulties. When SIS asked BP 11 to obtain the originals of the telegrams to authenticate his summaries he became evasive and thereafter was discredited.

The Soviet reply to Curzon's note said bluntly that the Berlin documents were forgeries, and that the information contained in them came from *Ostinformation*, a news-sheet published by an anonymous group in Germany and distributed to counter-revolutionary organizations. When the Foreign Office checked, it found that this was indeed the case: 'the bulk of our information did come from, or is at any rate in suspicious identity with, tainted sources [the German paper].'

Curzon exploded, 'I am positively appalled . . . I regard the position with dismay'.[22] In the reply which he sent to Moscow, his waffle, bluster and evasion could not conceal his acute embarrassment. SIS was immediately ordered to look at its procedures. The result was that all reports were to be submitted to careful consideration, 'both as regards reliability and value'. They were to be given one of three gradings: A1, A2 and B. To receive an A1 grading, a report not only had to be of 'primary importance', but had to be based on original documents actually in SIS's possession or to which an agent had access, or to have come from an agent of exceptional reliability. A2 was to cover reports which could not be classified A1 but which, nevertheless, were of significance both in subject matter and reliability. B was to be applied to reports of less importance, but whose interest and reliability still justified their being issued.

On the debit side, there are the obvious conclusions to be drawn. Misled by agents like Reilly into believing that a counter-revolution was just around the corner,* SIS advised the government that exploring any form of relations with the Bolshevik government was a waste of time because it would soon be replaced. SIS itself became infected with a fear of Bolshevik subversion and communicated its hysteria to several government leaders.

Yet so-called evidence of Red subversion in Britain at the time seems, in retrospect, ridiculously flimsy. There was, for example, the alleged sale of tzarist diamonds to finance the Labour newspaper, the *Daily Herald*. Although the newspaper seems positively respectable by the standards we are accustomed to today, Dr Andrew writes that for the heads of the secret service, the chiefs of staff and most members of the Cabinet, 'men who would subsidize the *Daily Herald* would stop at nothing'. SIS chiefs even set up a dining club known as 'the Bolo liquidation club'.[24] Those who stood against the tide of paranoia quickly became suspect themselves. Thus, Lloyd George, who tried to keep a cool head in the heated anti-Bolshevik atmosphere around him, was, according to Sir Henry Wilson, Chief of the Imperial General Staff, 'a traitor'.

There were other results of SIS involvement in the Russian Revolution which were less obvious but, it can be argued, far more important. It is, for example, arguable that the activities of SIS helped to create the Red Terror, poisoned a possible Anglo-Soviet détente, and were instrumental in leading to the formation and determining the subsequent direction of the KGB. The Red Terror may have occurred in any event. But Lockhart relates that in the early days of the Revolution the Bolsheviks were surprisingly tolerant and did their best to keep the hot-heads in the party under control. Reilly's abortive conspiracy and the attempt on Lenin's life gave the extremists in the party the opportunity they needed to justify the terror. Lockhart writes that, 'The whole situation seemed hopeless until Lenin was able to take a hand in affairs. After he recovered consciousness, his first remark, it was said, was "Stop the Terror".'[25]

The Zinoviev letter – where again Reilly was involved – hardened attitudes and marked a definite turning-point in Russia's view of the West and the West's view of Russia. Until then Britain had been gradually reaching a diplomatic *rapprochement* with Russia as the Bolsheviks turned away from world revolution to building socialism in one country. The Zinoviev letter strengthened the die-hard anti-Bolsheviks in the British government and the whole process

---

* In August 1921, Reilly was still writing reports for SIS which said that there would be a general uprising against the Bolsheviks in September.[23]

went into reverse, forcing Russia to become more isolationist and more suspicious of Western intentions, an attitude not really ameliorated until the Second World War.

The Cheka, the forerunner of the KGB, was set up by the Council of the People's Commissars on 20 December 1917. The word was formed from the organization's Russian title, which also describes what it was intended to do: All-Russian Extraordinary Commission for Combating Counter-Revolution, Speculation and Sabotage. Its first chief was Felix Dzerzhinsky, a Pole, and its first headquarters were in Petrograd. Dzerzhinsky later moved to the building formerly occupied by the All-Russian Insurance Company in Loubianka, Moscow, where the organization has remained ever since. (Although in the 1980s it expanded into other buildings.) The original intention was that the Cheka should be only an investigative body, and that prosecutions would be launched and punishments decided by the people's courts, but that altered during the Red Terror.

The Cheka began to wonder if it could cope with the class enemies in their many guises. A lot of the early officers in the Cheka had been recruited from the Tzar's secret police, the Ochrana, simply because there were not enough experienced officers available elsewhere. The Ochrana's method of combating subversion was to penetrate any suspicious organization, and this tactic was carried over into the Cheka. But the fact that Reilly's scheme got as far as it did greatly alarmed the Cheka.

In assessing the role that Reilly – and to a lesser extent Dukes – played in Russia, the Cheka chief, Dzerzhinsky, and his officers must have been impressed that these spies had not only been able to lose themselves amongst the Russian population, but had both masqueraded at various times as Cheka agents. Foreigners, it seemed, had penetrated the very organization which was supposed to be the guardian of Bolshevik purity. How should the Cheka respond? What could it do, not only to learn of the West's plans against Russia but to identify and neutralize Western agents before they could become a danger to the Soviet Union?

The obvious answer was to penetrate the West's intelligence agencies, as Western spies had penetrated those of the Bolsheviks. But the Russians were under a serious handicap. Reilly had been able to operate in Russia because he was a Russian. Dukes and Hill had spent so much time in Russia and spoke Russian so well that they could pass as Russians, any shortcoming in their accent or mannerisms being easily overlooked in a country of such diverse nationalities and languages. But, for a Russian agent, Britain posed a very different challenge. Even if an officer who spoke English well enough to pass as an Englishman existed in the Cheka – a highly unlikely possibility – such an agent would never master English mannerisms or acquire the necessary English background. With effort and time he might be able to deceive those Englishmen he might meet in every-day life in Britain, but the Cheka was aiming much higher: what they were seeking was a Russian who could become such a perfect Englishman that he could be recruited into SIS.

It could not have taken Dzerzhinsky long to realize that no such Russian existed, and was unlikely to do so for a long time, but there was an alternative. Although Reilly was a Russian, he had committed himself ideologically to the West and had worked for SIS. Could the Russians find an Englishman who would commit himself ideologically to Bolshevism and work for the Cheka? The idea was certainly feasible: three Frenchmen had thrown in their lot with the Revolution and even Lockhart had considered staying on in Russia. (It is appropriate to wonder here what was the 'interesting work' which his Cheka interrogator had in mind for Lockhart if he had accepted the offer?) Was it at this moment, perhaps, that the long-range plan for the Soviet penetration of Western intelligence agencies began?

The plan had to be long-range because of the difficulty in finding the right man. Lockhart had been influenced by the drama of the Revolution and had realized that it was 'a cataclysm which would shake the world to its foundations'. But Lockhart was exceptional in having had personal experience of the Revolution. In 1918 there were no likely ideological recruits for the Cheka in Britain or the United States because few people there understood what the Revolution was all about or what the Bolsheviks stood for. But in five years' time, or ten, would there be a young man in the West so moved by social injustice, or Marxist theory, or both, that he would be prepared to take the enormous step of committing himself to the Cheka for life, and to working against the country of his birth? The Cheka, with the patience that has since distinguished the Soviet intelligence apparatus, believed that there would be such men – and they were right. In Britain we so far know of only one – Kim Philby.*
It is significant that Philby, talking to his children in Moscow after his defection in 1963, told them, 'I was recruited in 1933, given the job of penetrating British intelligence and told it did not matter how

---

* There were also Guy Burgess, Donald Maclean and Anthony Blunt. But Burgess was not recruited to penetrate SIS, Blunt worked for MI5, and only briefly, and Maclean was never in either service. Philby is the only known KGB officer who had specific orders to penetrate SIS.

long I took to do the job.' It is also significant to recall that when Philby showed signs of complacency early on in his career in the KGB, his Soviet control reminded him of his lifetime mission: 'I [was] told in pressing terms by my Soviet friends that my first priority must be the British secret service.'[26]

There may appear to be gaps in this scenario. Why, for example, did the Cheka concentrate only on penetrating SIS? Why not American intelligence as well? One answer would be that there was no central American intelligence agency in 1918, and those American officials operating in Russia during and immediately after the Revolution who could loosely be called intelligence agents did not impress the Cheka. (One such official, Edgar Sisson, a State Department propaganda expert, fell victim to a British plot. British agents had bought some documents purporting to show how the Germans were financing the Bolsheviks; when they realized that these were forgeries, they put them back on the market again and could not believe their luck when Sisson eagerly bought them.)

There is, of course, the chilling likelihood that the Cheka *did* include American intelligence in its long-range penetration plans. It would be naïve to think that Philby was the only ideological recruit that Soviet intelligence located in the West. We know of Philby because, largely by accident, he was ultimately exposed. But it would have been logical for the Cheka to include the United States in its plans in 1918 and to look for recruits there even if, for the time being, there was no use for them.

The Russian Revolution, and the West's reaction to it, produced a major impact on the intelligence world. It began the intelligence race that led to the creation of the gigantic organizations that exist today. The Russians replaced the Germans as the threat to Britain, and from 1917 until 1939 the greater part of SIS's resources were to be devoted to the penetration of the Soviet Union and the defence of Britain against Bolshevism. Even during the Second World War, with Germany re-established as the monster, there were SIS officers who believed that Britain was fighting against the wrong enemy.

As for the Soviet Union, within three years the Cheka's strength grew from 15,000 to 250,000. One reason for this expansion was, obviously, the need to suppress dissent at home. But another was that its experience of British secret service officers during the Revolution had given it a special fear of SIS conspiracies – a fear that lingers even today.

# 4. Peacetime Professionals and Crackers of Codes

> An enterprising fortune teller had managed to convince
> some quite highly-placed officials that his glass ball could
> . . . advise on current affairs. For a short time he had
> enjoyed a monopoly in the field of Western European
> intelligence and was even patronised by Service
> intelligence chiefs. It was argued that since no
> information was coming in, any sort was better than
> none, and consequently crystal gazing was worth a try.
> – John Whitwell, *British Agent* (1966).

The real threat from the Soviet Union would come, SIS believed, in India. In the last days of the Allied effort to crush the Bolsheviks, a scattering of British agents in various disguises had gone into the Soviet Union from India on special intelligence missions. They had been singularly ineffective. Carried away by the romance of their assignments, they tended to exceed their instructions, thus worrying the British government and providing the Bolsheviks with ready-made ammunition for their anti-Western propaganda.* To a man, these agents reported that the Bolsheviks posed an immediate menace to India, and that they planned to bring revolution to the sub-continent by exploiting nationalist and religious sentiment.

Britain controlled India by a feat of political legerdemain: a few thousand sahibs kept in check a country populated by several hundred million Indians. Such a situation could continue only if subversive elements were identified and neutralized quickly. This was the task of the Indian Intelligence Bureau (IB), at first under Sir

---

* When the White Russians executed twenty-six Baku commissars in 1918, the Bolsheviks accused the British of masterminding the affair. Stalin wrote in *Izvestia* (23 April 1919) that it 'shouted the lawlessness and savage debauchery with which the English agents settled accounts with the "natives" of Baku and Transcaspia, just as they had with the blacks of central Africa'.

Cecil Kaye, a former Indian army officer, and then under Sir David Petrie, formerly of the Indian police. The IB was a highly efficient organization. It had a network of spies and informers throughout India, it intercepted and opened the mail of hundreds of suspects, it kept voluminous files on everyone who came to its notice, and it had several Indian penetration agents inside most local political organizations.

Its principal targets were M. N. Roy, an Indian nationalist who had been educated at the Bolshevik school at Tashkent and who lived in exile in Berlin and Moscow; his American wife, Evelyn Trent, also known as Helen Ellen, and her fellow members of the Friends of Freedom of India; and the American journalist, Agnes Smedley, 'a clever and unscrupulous revolutionary', according to the IB files, whom we shall encounter later in China. But the IB also kept files on many minor figures who came to the Bureau's attention when they visited India from Britain and the United States, and whose activities certainly suggest that the obsession with communism that gripped British intelligence in those interwar years was not entirely unjustified.

There was, for example, Percy Glading, also known as Cochrane, who arrived in India in 1925 as a member of the Amalgamated Union of Engineers, but was in reality an emissary of the Communist Party of Great Britain. His mission was to encourage Bolshevism in India and, if possible, 'to form a Labour Party with certain well-known Indian agitators as office bearers'. (He may also have had other aims because thirteen years later, in 1938, Glading pleaded guilty at the Old Bailey to trying to steal details of weapon developments from the Woolwich Arsenal and he was sentenced to six years' imprisonment.) Charles Ashleigh, also known as John Ashworth, an American who had served four years in Leavenworth prison, Kansas, for offences under the Espionage Act, arrived in India in 1922 'as an agent of the Comintern'. His passport was not in order, so the Indian authorities were soon able to deport him, but during his short stay, according to IB files, he saw several subversives and passed on instructions from M. N. Roy.

The IB suspected the existence of two communist networks in India: one associated with M. N. Roy and controlled, through him, from Europe, and a second, run in India by one 'Comrade Gamper, or Hamper', to whom had been sent the large sum of 150,000 English pounds 'for the renewal of agitation work in India in accordance with former instructions'. This ring appeared to be controlled from the Far East, probably from Shanghai. There were also Russian agents active on the north-west Frontier:

Information was received in October, 1925, that Soviet agents posing as traders were to be distributed in the large towns of northern Afghanistan . . . Secret information was obtained in France that one Jankel Lock, alias Anton Kanovalov, a Jew born at Dvinsk, a qualified mining engineer, knowing English and French and a smattering of two Indian dialects, had been sent to Afghanistan on a special mission. It was also stated that the Bolsheviks were employing a mixed gang of secret service agents in Kabul, including Ismail Effendi of Kapurthala. [This man] deserted at Batum during the Great War. He was since then reported to be employed as a Russian intelligence agent.[1]

Whatever the real strength of such evidence may have been, there is no doubt that in the eyes of the officers of the Indian Intelligence Bureau the threat of Soviet subversion was everywhere, and that they passed this attitude on to their colleagues in Britain. For SIS and MI5 not only received reports from the IB, they were also happy to employ IB men when they returned to Britain, relatively early in life, still active and looking for work. SIS recruited so regularly from this source that there was an SIS office clique known as 'the Indians', and MI5, for its part, maintained an up-to-date list of IB officers looking for employment. (The highest-ranking recruit, something of a triumph for the Indians, was Sir David Petrie, head of the IB in India from 1924–31, who began a second career in intelligence by becoming director general of MI5 in 1940.)

The effect of the Indian faction on the British services was to reinforce the assumption that Reds were under every bed and to exacerbate the obsession with secrecy that had marked SIS since its founding. The IB men brought with them the habit of never discussing certain subjects in front of the natives, and although there were no natives around anymore to listen – if they had ever bothered to do so – old habits are not discarded easily, and in Britain they continued to distrust anyone they did not know personally.

The two British intelligence services had their own evidence for what they believed to be far-reaching Soviet influence. In 1927, MI5 had stumbled upon a Russian spy ring led by Wilfred Macartney, a former British army intelligence officer, then an employee of Lloyds. It had planted an RAF manual on him to see what he did with it, and when he had handed it to a Russian working for the USSR Trade Delegation, MI5 got permission from the government to raid the delegation's City premises, which it shared with the All-Russian Co-operative Society, known as ARCOS. The manual, however, was not found. (Later Mr Macartney was convicted on other charges under the Official Secrets Act, and received a ten-year prison sentence. On his release he joined the International Brigades in the Spanish Civil War and became the first commander of the British battalion.)

In 1937, a Soviet intelligence officer, Walter Krivitsky, defected in France. In one of his debriefing sessions he said that he had come across a Soviet spy working in the British Foreign Office, but he was able to describe him only as 'coming from a good family'. Although, much later, it was decided that this probably referred to Donald Maclean, it could have been virtually anyone in the Foreign Office. The discovery that a former British army intelligence officer had been spying for the Russians, and a defector warning that there was a Soviet spy in the Foreign Office, convinced British intelligence that the danger came from the Soviet Union, and it reacted accordingly. All its resources became concentrated on the communist threat.

These resources were still rather meagre. In 1917 the young Captain Compton Mackenzie had had £12,000 a month to spend on intelligence work in Athens alone. SIS's entire budget in 1927–8 amounted to only £180,000. Even by 1936–7, with Europe in turmoil, the figure was only £350,000 and it went over the £1 million mark only after the outbreak of war.[2] The new chief of SIS, Admiral Hugh Sinclair, (Cumming died in 1923) complained in 1935 that the whole SIS budget equalled only the annual cost of maintaining one destroyer in Home Waters. At one stage, when there was insufficient office space in SIS, Sinclair's secretary had to work in the greenhouse where she complained continually of the cold. One year, after the auditors had been in, they told Sinclair that he had overspent his budget by £2,000. Sinclair, a short stocky figure with a single good eye and the smile of a friendly uncle, said, 'All in a good cause' and wrote out his personal cheque to cover the deficit.[*] This lack of funds and SIS's concentration on the Soviet threat had an effect on the service in two important areas: its overall efficiency and its recruitment policy.

Although SIS had done its best to monitor what was going on in Germany – mainly looking for breaches of the Versailles Treaty – it was slow to react to the rise of Hitler and National Socialism. Throughout the 1930s, its complement of full-time officers never

---

[*] This tradition of the Chief contributing to the running of the service continued. Robert Cecil, a young officer under Sinclair's successor, General Sir Stewart Menzies, asked for a transfer overseas because he could not manage on his salary and had run up an overdraft of £500. Menzies refused the transfer but wrote out his own cheque on Drummonds Bank for £500, signing it with a big green "C".[3]

exceeded thirty, and never more than six in Europe at any one time. The latter worked in a very relaxed manner, under cover as businessmen or as passport control officers in British embassies. They discreetly recruited local agents, usually for cash, and paid them small sums for small pieces of information. This they sent back to London with little or no indication of its reliability. Political and military information was often jumbled together, although there was an effort to get the SIS officer himself to give his own political assessment of local affairs at regular intervals. Leslie Nicholson, serving in Prague, had to sit down once a year and produce a report headed 'A Communist Summary'.

Occasionally an officer would strike gold only for the assessment system in London to fail. In the early 1930s, a recently recruited former journalist bought in Finland the blueprints of a prototype midget submarine. They were examined by Sinclair, himself a submarine expert, who decided that they were false and refused to pass them on to the Admiralty.[4]

Sinclair probably suspected that the blueprints had been planted on the SIS agent, a not unlikely event, because agents who sold information to British Intelligence officers were not above selling the same information to the Germans – and the Russians. Attempts by an officer to use an agent to mislead the opposition could take the instigator into deep waters, as happened to Charles Howard ('Dick') Ellis, an Australian who had been on intelligence work in Central Asia during the Allied intervention and who had later joined SIS.

Ellis's recruitment from the army into SIS had been regarded as something of a coup. He spoke several European languages, perfect Russian, and Turkish, Urdu and Persian. Posted to Berlin, Vienna and Geneva, Ellis became engaged in a dangerous double game for which he was ill-equipped. He complained later – and SIS chiefs acknowledged it to be true – that he should have been given more training and advice to help him avoid the pits into which he fell.

Ellis had married a White Russian, Lilia Zelensky, and through the exiled Russian community, he met a White Russian general known as Andrei Turkhul. Turkhul told Ellis that he had contacts with German intelligence and could probably obtain information from them. But he would need to offer them something in return. He suggested that he should tell the Germans that he knew a British SIS officer who had secrets to sell and then see what reaction this produced. The scheme appealed to Ellis on two levels. On a professional level, he felt that he could appear to be disenchanted with SIS and prepared to betray it at a price. In this role, any contact with the Germans was bound to be rewarding. The questions that the Germans would ask would reveal, for example, their areas of interest and ignorance, all of use to London. On a private level, his wife was ill, he was underpaid, and he needed money. Since, in order to establish his credibility, he would have to take German payment anyway, why not keep it – a not unusual practice. Unfortunately, his plan went wrong for several reasons. It seems that Ellis went further than he intended and, as he later confessed, he gave the Germans the SIS 'order of battle', that is, the exact hierarchical structure of the organization and who occupied what post – knowledge that intelligence organizations prize because it helps them to identify their exact rivals but which, over the whole intelligence spectrum, is of only minor importance.[5]

But worse was to follow. Turkhul turned out to be a Russian intelligence officer, sent to penetrate the White Russian community so as to keep Moscow informed of plots against the Soviet Union. When war broke out he disappeared only to surface later in his true colours. Ellis went on to become number two in the British Security Co-ordination Office in New York, an instructor in the fledgling Office of Strategic Services, forerunner of the CIA, head of SIS station in Singapore in 1946, chief of production in Europe and, after he retired, a key figure in the founding of the Australian Secret Intelligence Organization. We shall return to him later, because his contact with Turkhul made him one of the targets of a 'Red mole hunt' that was to wrack Western intelligence agencies in the 1970s and 1980s.

B y 1929, the information SIS was supplying to its consumers was proving so unsatisfactory that the Prime Minister, Ramsay MacDonald, moved to improve matters. He asked Major Desmond Morton, then number three in SIS, to set up the Industrial Intelligence Centre (IIC) which would work with SIS but which would have a large amount of autonomy, and which would report direct to the Prime Minister. Its mission would be to monitor the industrial capacity and growth of potential enemies. It would use open sources – trade returns, import and export statistics, companies' notices – and SIS assessments. It was a sound idea: for example, if it could be established that a country was importing, say, nine times as much manganese as it needed for normal steel-making, then it was obvious that it was stockpiling manganese. The IIC would then ask SIS if its agents could confirm the assumption that the stockpiling was part of a war plan.

In practice, IIC did not function as efficiently as envisaged. For a start, Morton carried over to the new department the SIS obsession with secrecy. The IIC office was in a modern block opposite 55 Broadway, SW1, and was linked by a tunnel to SIS headquarters and 'C's residence in Queen Anne's Gate. The IIC office was called the 'Import Control Department', later changed to the standard SIS cover, Passport Control Office. All Morton's staff were majors or colonels; all had been either to Eton or Harrow; all dressed in black coats, striped trousers and bowler hats; all carried tightly-rolled umbrellas. One of the sights in Broadway occurred precisely at 9.30 every morning when Major Morton marched along Petty France with his umbrella held at the slope. As he approached the IIC building he came to attention, presented his umbrella to the door-bell, pressed, and was admitted.

The female office staff were sisters or daughters of soldiers or Foreign Office officials, educated at Roedean, St Godrics, or in Switzerland, and wore tweed skirts and fawn sweaters. Occasionally, IIC would take on as a junior office assistant someone recommended by the headmistress of a school run by the Sisters of Charity. These girls were trained for the initial interview by being taught to recognize army badges, ranks and names, and to know regimental histories by heart. Part of the interview was a test in which the young applicant had to pick out on the walls a regimental badge which had been wrongly labelled.

One of these girls, Gwynne Kean, warned to be security conscious, slammed the door of her office on the foot of a man who had announced himself as 'Mr Stanley Baldwin'. She recalled, 'I didn't know who he was, although his face was familiar. But I did know he was not Stanley Baldwin.' In fact, he was Winston Churchill and he later sent Gwynne Kean a crocodile-skin handbag with a card reading, 'To our little watchdog'.[6]

The fact that Churchill, then in Opposition, could gain access to a secret government department for an information-gathering trip was the result of a curious arrangement that arose because Churchill was a close friend of Morton's and they were neighbours in Kent. Morton found it impossible to listen to Churchill airing his views on the threat of war without wanting to correct his industrial statistics, but he was reluctant to do this because it involved secret information. So he went to the Prime Minister, Ramsay MacDonald, and explained the situation. MacDonald took the view that it was preferable that Churchill should base his opposition on sound facts than on his fanciful imagination. He gave Morton permission to pass on the main points of his intelligence reports.[7]

Subsequent prime ministers, Stanley Baldwin and Neville Chamberlain, took the same view. Thus, throughout the 1930s, Churchill had access to a flow of information about intelligence matters, including – since Morton interpreted his authorization in the widest terms – a lot of SIS material. This was to account for the lively interest Churchill showed in intelligence when he became Prime Minister himself and, since he shared SIS's preoccupation with the dangers of communism, also his distrust and suspicion of the Soviet Union. (Lloyd George had once said that Churchill had 'Bolshevism on the brain'.)

SIS's concentration on the communist menace also had the effect of warping its recruitment policy and, indirectly, perpetuating its inefficiency. In the 1930s, while the prevailing political sentiment of the nation became vaguely leftist, SIS recruited against the trend. It sought out men whose hearts were in the preservation of Empire, the maintenance of an ordered society, and the protection of privilege and inherited wealth. To these men, communism was not a political theory but an abhorrent creed and any move to the left was felt to be a betrayal of all that was best in Britain. At this time, the universities were full of men with radical ideas, so no one could be recruited there. This led to the curious situation in which Russian spy masters were recruiting in British universities several years before SIS got around to doing so.

The bias against intellectuals and radicals knew no bounds. A recruit who joined after the outbreak of war recalls that absurd measures were still being employed 'to keep out lefties'. He had learnt that Edwin Muir, the poet, was working in the Food Office at Dundee, Scotland, so he mentioned to a colleague that Muir might be a good man to recruit. The colleague replied, 'He's been thought of but he's been turned down on political grounds. He's a communist.' When the recruit protested that this could not be true, his colleague replied, 'Oh well, he may not exactly be a communist, but he's rather suspect, you know. He's the kind of person who's been kind to refugees, so he wouldn't be suitable here.'[8]

Thus recruits came from the upper reaches of British society, men who would not merely defend the way of life they enjoyed, but whose physical presence actually embodied it. As John le Carré wrote in 1968:

> Within its own walls, its clubs, and its country houses, in whispered luncheons with its secular contacts, it would enshrine the mystical

entity of a vanishing England. Here, at least, whatever went on in the big world outside, England's flower would be cherished. 'The Empire may be crumbling; but within our secret elite, the clean-limbed tradition of English power would survive. We believe in nothing but ourselves.'[9]

The quality of these men is captured neatly in the description of his recruitment given by Bickham Sweet-Escott in his book, *Baker Street Irregular*. Sweet-Escott was joining SOE, but his story fits SIS equally well. He was ushered into a bare room at the War Office where he confronted an officer in civilian clothes who 'closely resembled Sherlock Holmes'. The officer questioned him on his background and then said, 'I can't tell you what sort of job it would be. All I can say is that if you join us, you musn't be afraid of forgery and you musn't be afraid of murder.'

The historian, Lord Dacre (Hugh Trevor-Roper) who joined SIS during the war was appalled by the quality of the prewar recruits.

It seemed to me that the professionals were by and large pretty stupid and some of them very stupid. They formed two social classes: the London end which consisted of elegant young men from the upper classes who were recruited on the basis of trust, within a social class. It is said that they were recruited in Boodles and Whites. I believe this to be basically true . . . Then there were the Indian policemen . . . They were of quite extraordinary stupidity in my opinion. They were socially distinct from the club men. They didn't move in the Whites Club Boodles world. They were rather looked down on.[10]

Leslie Nicholson, the SIS officer in Prague, described to me what it was like working with such people as an officer in the field. He had been recruited in 1930 from the intelligence section of the British Army of Occupation in Wiesbaden and given a three-week course in communications, codes and cyphers, and SIS accounting practices. It was only when he was *en route* to Vienna, where he was to meet the SIS head of station – 'one of the most experienced operators in the business' – that he realized that no one had told him what he was expected to do. His colleague in Vienna turned out to be of no help. He regaled Nicholson with stories of his predecessors: one had been an alcoholic and had ended up in the police cells, along with his briefcase full of communications from SIS in London; another, a public school product and a rugger blue, had got into a fight over a girl and was also arrested. The SIS officer then showed Nicholson the files, but these seemed to consist of little more than a series of question and answer sessions with London. Finally, Nicholson said, 'Look here. Can you give me a few practical hints?' 'The most experienced operator' looked nonplussed and then replied, 'I don't think there are any, really. You'll just have to work it out for yourself.'[11]

Nicholson found that maintaining his cover as an export-import agent took up as much time as running a real business and, in some ways, involved more strain. This, together with the need to keep the elaborate monthly accounts required by SIS's pay officer, meant that he had little time to spare for espionage. But he did manage to establish a small network of people who knew he was willing to pay for information about troop movements, armaments production, or new military inventions. It is likely, however, that the people who sold him this information also sold it elsewhere, because the British had a reputation among spies for being mean: on one occasion, Nicholson offered £10 for a tip about troop movements which he learnt afterwards fetched £50 from his German opposite number.

When he was transferred to Riga in Latvia, Nicholson discovered that the agents there were more open about their business.

> They used to take morning coffee together at a café near the stock exchange. They'd discuss the business among themselves, very much like the brokers on the other side of the street. They traded tit-bits of information and would sell their services to the highest bidder and then later, with no compunction, pass the same information to the opposition, usually at a higher price. But all the intelligence officers used them, even if only to plant false information on each other for our own purposes.[12]

Given that its information came largely from sources such as these, London never knew the strength of what it was getting, and the inconsistent way it evaluated reports confused its officers in the field even further. Information which Nicholson suggested should be treated with great caution often brought a bonus, while information he had gone to considerable lengths to confirm was dismissed out of hand. On one occasion, in 1938, an agent reported that a factory in East Prussia which had previously made bicycles had switched to producing light automatic weapons. The agent had hitherto proved reliable and Nicholson considered the item to be important, suggesting as it did that Hitler's remilitarization was gaining momentum. He sent it to London drawing attention to its source and commenting on its significance.

London did not reply for two months and, when it did, ordered that the agent was to be dismissed at once. At considerable expense, SIS had sent a senior officer from London to check the information. He reported that there was no company of the name mentioned by

the agent. It did not exist. Nicholson tackled the agent who produced a telephone directory from the Prussian town in question.
There, underlined in red pencil, was the entry, 'Waffenfabrik Wolf
u. Ebermann GmbH'. Nicholson sent the page off to London with a
short covering note suggesting that perhaps the SIS officer had gone
to the wrong town. Instead of the expected explanation, all he
received was a letter saying that since the agent had been officially
dismissed, nothing could now be done and the matter was closed.[13]

$\quad$ While SIS's network was blundering along in this
manner, another section of Britain's espionage establishment, GC
and CS, was showing distinct promise. Its Russian section was
headed by E. Stetterlein, one of the leading cryptologists of tsarist
Russia who had fled to London. His section kept the government
informed of Soviet intentions with a continuous flow of Soviet
government external communications. But this success ended
abruptly in 1924.

Austen Chamberlain, Foreign Secretary in the Baldwin government which took office in that year, found this secret information
inconsistent with his plans for a lasting peace in Europe and for
three years ignored growing evidence of 'hostile activities' by
Soviet agencies against the British Empire. Then, in March 1927,
MI5 turned him around. It brought to the Attorney-General, Sir
Douglas Hogg, a dossier on its surveillance of Wilfred Macartney.
This showed, as we have seen, that he had passed an RAF manual to
a Russian. The Cabinet now decided that it wanted to break off
diplomatic relations with the Soviet Union, and publicly to accuse it
of setting up 'an elaborate spy organisation in Britain' would provide
the pretext. The trouble was that MI5 wanted to allow Macartney
to continue to operate in order to discover how wide his network
was. If the government were to make the MI5 report public this
would alert Macartney and his fellow agents. Where else could the
government get concrete evidence of Russian spying to justify its
accusation?

In the end, the government decided that if it could not produce
evidence of a Russian spy ring in Britain, it could at least show that
the Soviet government ran a spy service and that Russians made
political propaganda against Britain. On 24 May, the Prime Minister, Stanley Baldwin, read out four intercepted Russian telegrams.
He was followed on 27 May by the Home Secretary, Joynson-Hicks,
who said that he had in his possession 'not merely the names, but

the addresses' of Soviet spies in Britain. (Needless to say, he did not read them out, since, if the government had *evidence* that they were spies, it should have prosecuted them.) That same day, Chamberlain told the Soviet chargé d'affaires that Britain was breaking off diplomatic relations with the Soviet Union because of 'anti-British espionage and propaganda'. As evidence of this, Chamberlain quoted a telegram that the chargé had sent to Moscow the previous April, 'in which you request material to enable you to support a political campaign against His Majesty's government'.

The message certainly justified a charge of political interference, but hardly one of espionage. The White Paper on the affair published later included some of the intercepted telegrams and these, too, contained no real evidence of espionage. The suspicion must be that the government was stampeded into an over-reaction by MI5, and MI5's success in the Macartney case and, once committed to a break with the Soviet Union, was forced to use the GC and CS intercepts to lend authenticity to its charges of widespread espionage. The results were disastrous. The Soviet Union rapidly introduced new codes and cyphers which GC and CS was unable to break. This, and the fact that it had been publicly compromised, did not help morale at GC and CS and left it with a lasting distrust of politicians.[14] (When GC and CS had some success in the Spanish Civil War and was able to assess German and Italian strengths, it kept the information to itself.)

Throughout the interwar period, Britain had forced the cable companies to submit all their traffic to GC and CS on the bogus grounds that there was a general state of unrest and emergency in the world. GC and CS had cracked the codes, not only of potential enemies, such as Japan, but also of friends like the United States, and had used the information gained in this manner to improve Britain's position at international conferences. But it had failed with Germany and the Soviet Union. (GC and CS's boss, Alastair Denniston, was heard to say to a codebreaker, 'I don't think that the Germans meant you to read their stuff, and I don't suppose you ever will.') So throughout the 1930s, when the two powers whose policies most concerned the British government were Germany and the Soviet Union, no one at GC and CS could break their codes, and what could have been a major source of high-grade intelligence vanished completely. By 1938 the chief of SIS had so lost faith in GC and CS that he noted, in an internal memorandum, that the organization was 'useless for the purposes for which it was intended'.[15]

Not that SIS itself was doing any better where Germany was concerned. It had, it is true, begun to awaken to the Nazi menace; but it had little success in discovering Hitler's strength and intentions. This brought increasing criticism from British government departments. By 1938 the War Office was complaining that SIS could not provide information about Germany's military capabilities, equipment, preparation and movements. The Air Ministry was more outspoken. It wrote off SIS intelligence as 'normally 80 per cent inaccurate'. The Foreign Office, SIS's traditional ally, did its best to defuse this criticism: it was an agent's job to report rumour as well as fact; it was up to London to weigh up all the information and draw conclusions from it. 'In that we may fail, and if so, it is our fault, but I do not think it is fair to blame SIS.'[16]

Belatedly, SIS was indeed making an effort to respond to the new challenge. It had broadened its recruitment, seeking to obtain new men with the resources of worldly knowledge and vigour that its previous recruitment policies had failed to provide. One obvious source was Fleet Street. Journalists got around; they knew how to gather and assess information; and, presumably, they knew something about international affairs since they had to write about them. And – very important in SIS affairs – there were precedents. In the 1920s Morton had apparently used *The Times* correspondent, Colin Coote, who later became editor of the *Daily Telegraph*, as network controller in Rome.[17] Now SIS widened its net, and eventually had journalists from the *Manchester Guardian* (Frederick Voigt), the *Daily Express* (Geoffrey Cox), and the *Daily Mirror* (David Walker) working for it. Walker's experience was probably typical: 'I was asked to lunch at a West End restaurant by a naval commander I knew. He said I might be interested in a job of national importance that I could do while continuing to work for the *Mirror*. He explained what it was, and I accepted. When it came to payment he asked me what I was getting at the *Mirror* and offered me the same.'[18] (Walker's career as a spy was a brief one. The *Daily Mirror* sent him to Romania. He fled as the Germans arrived, was captured by the Italians, then exchanged for some Italian journalists. On his return to London in 1941 he was told that his area had been 'blown' and that there was no immediate post for him. He joined SOE and after the war went into public relations. He says he never told the *Daily Mirror* of his SIS connection.)

There was also a remarkable piece of SIS–MI5 co-operation. Dick White, assistant director of B division, the counter-espionage section of MI5, went on a tour of Germany just before the war to recruit agents who would both assist MI5 in identifying German intelligence officers in Britain (MI5 work), and provide information about what was happening in Germany (SIS work). White, who spoke excellent German, was very successful because of his idealistic approach to intelligence work. He was not interested in the professional collector of intelligence titbits, the mainstay of SIS information in the 1930s, but in the ideologically motivated agent, 'the only worthwhile one'. He sought out the opposition to Hitler and found willing recruits 'who looked to Britain as a moral force against Fascism'.

A number of German officers, worried that Hitler would lead them into a war that could not be won, reported regularly to London, either through channels set up by White or while on visits to Britain. There was also a network of well-placed German civilians who did their best to warn of Hitler's intentions. Through these sources SIS learnt of the German army's order of battle, mobilization plans and the development of new equipment for the army. But this was one bright light in an area of darkness, and in any assessment of SIS's performance in the 1930s the failures heavily outweigh the successes.

It failed to provide reliable intelligence about the Russo-German negotiations in the summer of 1939. Its information about warship construction at Kiel in 1934 – which could have been important confirmation that Germany was breaking the Versailles Treaty – turned out to be partly wrong. During the Munich crisis, its service was interrupted because its field officers were not equipped with wireless transmitting sets and, when the Germans closed the frontier with Denmark, had no means of communicating rapidly with London. SIS was unable to give advance warning of the German occupation of the Rhineland in 1936, or of the Austrian *Anschluss* in 1938.[19]

There were warnings that Germany planned to attack Poland, the first of which arrived on 28 March 1939, five months before Germany moved, but these did not come from SIS. They originated from the British Embassy in Berlin and with a British journalist who had contacts on the German General Staff. When SIS did finally receive a series of warnings of the impending German attack it did not pass them on to the War Office, and the Chief of the Imperial General Staff had specifically to request copies from the chief of SIS.[20]

But the most serious failures of British intelligence related to the growth and intentions of the Luftwaffe. Under Hitler, German air strength underwent a period of accelerated expansion, beginning in

1933. Since this was a direct contravention of the Versailles Treaty, every effort was made to keep it secret. But it was impossible to carry out a major industrial programme, involving the construction of several thousand aircraft, without a lot of people being in the know. IIC picked up the first authoritative indications from German import requirements, industrial publications and labour force statistics. Other British intelligence-gathering organizations were not far behind.

The trouble was not that there was no information, but that each department of government interpreted the information according to its own set of prejudices. The Air Ministry, for example, flatly refused to believe that a German air force could be built up rapidly enough to pose a threat to Britain by the end of the 1930s. The Foreign Office, for its part, was convinced that the German air force was being created as a political weapon to back Hitler's diplomacy and that it had no strategic role at all. SIS could have dominated this debate because it had no departmental axe to grind, but it lacked a network of specialist agents in Germany and was regarded with scepticism, mistrust and suspicion by most Whitehall ministries. It had to rely on reports passed to it by the French Deuxième Bureau, which had an agent inside the German Air Ministry. In 1938 it was forced to confess that it lacked up-to-date and reliable information not only on the size of the German air force, but also on its organization and armaments, and the range and bomb-carrying capacity of its aircraft.[21]

Yet such information was available. There *were* sources in Germany, as the experience of the Foreign Office showed. In 1933 Malcolm Christie, a retired group captain who had been air attaché in Berlin from 1927–30, began to send private intelligence reports to Sir Robert Vansittart, permanent under-secretary at the Foreign Office. Christie was living in Berlin as a successful businessman and knew Goering, his deputy, Erhard Milch, and many officials in the German Air Ministry, one of whom, Hans Ritter, became a very valuable source. Vansittart described Christie as the best judge that Britain would ever get of what was going on in Germany. But when Christie sent tables showing, among other things, German aircraft production and projected strengths, and Vansittart passed this on to the Air Ministry, it was dismissed.

Under pressure from the Secretary of State, Lord Swinton, the Air Ministry looked at the information again and then tried to discover Christie's source. All he would reveal was that it was a senior official in the German Air Ministry. But to help prove Ritter's reliability, Christie acted as a go-between for a series of questions which were passed from London to Berlin: Although Ritter not only convincingly defended his figures, but also threw in details of the Dornier 17 bomber, the British Air Ministry remained sceptical.[22]

With SIS useless as a source, and Vansittart unable to convince the Air Ministry of the value of Christie's information, Britain's defence planners had to assess the threat from the Luftwaffe on a 'worst case' assumption, and this came to dominate British thinking in the 1930s. The worst case assumption was that the Luftwaffe would be capable of delivering a knock-out blow, probably a rain of high explosives and poisonous gas that would destroy British cities in hours and sap the nation's will to fight. This was a myth which proper intelligence could have quickly destroyed. The Luftwaffe was never capable of mounting anything like a knock-out blow during the 1930s and was neither equipped nor trained for such a purpose, but the Germans were brilliant at conveying the impression that it could. In this they were helped by American military intelligence and a number of credulous diplomats and politicians.

In 1936 American military intelligence brought in the famous aviator, Colonel Charles A. Lindbergh, specifically to obtain better intelligence on the German air force. The Germans could not have been finer hosts when Lindbergh went there and, after a second visit in October 1937, he reported that Germany's air force was stronger than that of all other European countries combined: 10,000 aircraft, of which 5,000 were serviceable bombers. Moreover, he reported, Germany was producing more than 500 aircraft a month and could, if necessary, triple this figure.

The truth was very different. The German air force actually had only 3,315 aircraft of which only 1,246 were serviceable bombers. Production was under 300 aircraft a month. During the Munich crisis, the Germans were able to mobilize only 1,230 aircraft of which only 600 were bombers. But Lindbergh's report circulated on the eve of Munich and was widely accepted by people such as the French Air Minister, Guy la Chambre, the French Foreign Minister, Georges Bonnet, and the American ambassador to Britain, Joseph P. Kennedy.[23]

The consequences of this were serious. When the British Prime Minister, Neville Chamberlain, flew to Germany the week before Munich he had read a summary of Lindbergh's report and during the crisis Chamberlain admitted to his Cabinet colleagues that he had a vision of London being laid waste by German bombs. As a result of this unjustified fear of the 'knock-out blow', Britain was out-bluffed by Germany, and SIS must accept some of the blame for failing to provide the intelligence that might have prevented this.*

The fact is that throughout the 1930s, SIS was a peripheral organization which made little impact on the British consumers of its intelligence. Government departments became accustomed to acting without help from SIS, basing their decisions on facts freely available, and using common sense to assess likely strategic and political developments. While SIS was still concentrating on the communist menace, the Defence Requirements Sub-Committee of the Committee of Imperial Defence decided in March 1934 that Germany was the principal potential enemy against which long-term defence would have to be prepared. The Foreign Policy Committee, set up in 1936 to advise the government on foreign policy decisions, used SIS material in only two of its reports during the following two-and-a-half years.[24]

Three penetrating pieces of intelligence about German military matters came not from SIS, but from the military attaché's section of the British embassy in Berlin. The attaché, Major-General K. Strong, recorded that intelligence reports in 1937 indicated that the German army would use armoured *Blitzkrieg* methods – as indeed it did, when it swept through France. The assistant attaché reported in 1939 that the Germans had a single weapon, the MG-34, that could be used both as a heavy and light machine-gun, and that the Germans appeared to be using anti-aircraft guns against tanks – technical innovations of striking success. The War Office refused to accept either report.[25]

Thus SIS's interwar period was one of penny-pinching, muddling through, being ignored and bypassed. It grew in upon itself, its officers running it like a gentlemen's club, contemptuous of the outside world and convinced that not only did they represent all that was best in Britain, but that they alone knew who the real enemy was – the Soviet Union.

* Two weeks after Munich, the Germans presented Lindbergh with the Service Cross of the German Eagle.

# 5. Business Is Better than Spying

> In every armament factory, in every shipyard in America, we have a spy, several of them in key positions. The United States cannot plan a warship, design an airplane, develop a new device, that we do not know at once.
> – Erich Pheiffer, Abwehr officer in 1934, quoted in Ladislas Farago, *The Game of the Foxes* (1972).

> In April 1934, the American commercial attaché in Berlin reported that American representatives were selling all kinds of aviation equipment – motor parts, crankshafts, cylinder heads, automatic pilots, gyro compasses and other instruments, and fine control systems for anti-aircraft guns, and not just in sample quantities but in volume.
> – Thomas H. Etzold, 'The (F)utility Factor' (1975).

However apparent SIS's weaknesses may have been in Whitehall, they were not immediately appreciated by the Germans. Leading Nazis told Hitler that SIS was the best intelligence service in the world and that Germany should build one modelled on it. But Hitler's attempts to do so were frustrated by bitter rivalries among existing intelligence agencies. The Abwehr, the army's intelligence section, appeared to be the most powerful. Its growth kept pace with the rapid expansion of the German armed forces. Its budget was a secret, but its dynamic head, Admiral Wilhelm Canaris, who took office on 1 January 1935, told his officers that he had 'millions of marks' at his disposal.

The Abwehr's natural rival was the Sicherheitsdienst (SD), formed by Reinhard Heydrich in 1931 for the chief of the SS, Heinrich Himmler. At first, the Abwehr and the SD worked well together. Abwehr officers welcomed the drive and efficiency of the secret police. This was how they had always conceived of fighting enemy espionage: hard, wholeheartedly, and in secret. They ignored the political concomitants because all that mattered to an expert was the efficiency of the new apparatus', Canaris's biographer wrote.[1] By the time that the Abwehr recognized that the ambitions of the SD reflected something more than the Nazis' desire for security, that its sights were set on achieving control of all the intelligence-gathering agencies in Germany, it was becoming too late to fight back. In the Night of the Long Knives those murdered included a former Abwehr chief, Ferdinand von Bredow, and relations between Canaris and Heydrich steadily deteriorated as Heydrich's ambition to expand into foreign intelligence-gathering became apparent.

In this atmosphere of rivalry, other minor agencies flourished, each under the protection of a different member of the Nazi leadership. A quasi-ministry, the Forschungsamt (research department) of the Reich Air Ministry – it actually had nothing to do with that body – intercepted radio and telephone traffic and broke diplomatic codes. It reported direct to Hermann Goering. Informationsstelle III (Information Post III), a spy service based on German diplomatic missions abroad, reported to Foreign Minister Joachim von Ribbentrop. The official German press agency, Deutsche Nachrichtenbüro, combined overt news gathering with clandestine operations, and reported to Propaganda Minister Goebbels. Deputy Führer Rudolph Hess had his own intelligence agency which gathered information abroad and kept him informed of the plans of his political rivals within Germany.

Inevitably, this blossoming of intelligence agencies led to duplication of effort, inefficient evaluation of information, rivalry in the field and general confusion. The Abwehr, for example, complained that the SD would seize any foreign intelligence agent the moment it uncovered him, thus frustrating the Abwehr which already knew about him and was allowing him to run free in the hope of discovering other agents or the source of his information. The greater the rivalry between agencies, the more reluctant each became to reveal its sources or to classify its material. This meant that the government departments using the information never knew what reliance to place on it. Major Oscar Reile, who handled Abwehr counter-intelligence in France from 1935 until the end of the war, revealed later that out of the hundreds of reports passed to him by the SD, there was only one in which the SD provided a source for its information.[2]

So, far from being the super-efficient apparatus portrayed in print and on the screen, the German intelligence system had a fatal flaw –

it was hydra-headed and each head was reluctant to abdicate its power because, as with all intelligence agencies, possession of intelligence titbits gave access to the leader. We can see how this handicapped German intelligence worked by looking at its operations in Britain and the United States.

If the German spies actually caught in Britain in the 1930s were a representative sample, German espionage was a spasmodic, unprofessional operation and the threat posed to British security by Nazi spies was heavily exaggerated.*

A typical case was that of Dr Hermann Goertz, lawyer and former army intelligence officer, convicted at the Old Bailey in March 1936 on espionage charges and sentenced to four years' imprisonment. He had come to the attention of MI5 when his landlady at Broadstairs, Kent, reported him to the local police for leaving without paying his rent – hardly the action of a professional intelligence officer.

In a raid on Goertz's bungalow, MI5 seized much of the evidence used against him at his trial: an Ordinance Survey map of south-east England with all the RAF stations marked on it, a camera, air magazines, letters and notebooks, the 1935 RAF list, and a reference book called *The Air Pilot*. One of the letters was a six-page application to join the Luftwaffe, in which Goertz recounted his successes as an intelligence officer in the First World War – again, hardly the sort of information a professional officer would leave behind in his rented bungalow.

Goertz's defence was that he was researching a novel to be called *Bridge over Grey Waters*, and all this material had been gathered for the novel. His counsel pointed out that the documents seized were freely available to anyone willing to buy them, a submission that MI5 agreed was correct. Goertz was convicted largely because the sketch he had made of Manston airfield, copied from *The Air Pilot*, included hangars and fuel dumps not shown on the original, which, as the prosecution pointed out, was proof of something more than amateur curiosity. It seems fairly obvious that Goertz was trying to gather material that would lend weight to his application to the Luftwaffe for a job as an intelligence officer. His case did not, as MI5

---

* I have excluded political warfare specialists, such as Dr H. W. Thost, a leading Nazi journalist expelled from London in 1935, and Dr G. R. Rosel, of the Anglo-German Information Service, expelled in 1939, because they were not true intelligence agents.

made out, presage a German intelligence offensive against Britain and no such offensive materialized.

Other cases in the 1930s were no more impressive. Mrs Jessie Jordan, of Dundee, a 51-year-old hairdresser who had spent so many years in Germany that she could no longer speak English fluently, was sentenced to four years' imprisonment in 1938 for acting as a 'post box' for the Abwehr – receiving letters from German agents in the United States and then forwarding them on to Germany. Donald Adams, aged 55, a racing journalist, of Richmond, Surrey, was given a prison sentence of seven years in September 1939, for sending information by letter to the Abwehr. His correspondence, first intercepted because the address was known to MI5 as an Abwehr cover, was allowed to continue for eight months because, as MI5 admitted, Adams was sending the Germans nothing that could not be easily obtained from British newspapers. In May of the same year, an Irish bricklayer, Joseph Kelly, working at the Royal Ordnance factory at Euston, Lancashire, was sentenced to three years for larceny and ten years, under the Official Secrets Act, for stealing a site plan of the factory and selling it to the Abwehr for £30.[3]

While these 'spies' were receiving heavy prison sentences for activities of a largely insignificant nature, people from a very different stratum of society were passing important material to the Germans with impunity.

Baron William S. de Rop was a native Lithuanian who had become a naturalized citizen of the United Kingdom and had served in the Wiltshire Regiment and the Royal Flying Corps in the First World War. De Rop took it upon himself to try to arrange a *rapprochement* between Hitler's Germany and Britain; together with his English wife he took up residence in Berlin and succeeded in winning the confidence of Hitler and other leading Nazis who referred to him as 'our English agent'. De Rop had two aims: one political, the other to gather intelligence. The political one was to convince influential British leaders of the need for Germany and Britain to stand together against the Bolshevik danger. To this end, he brought to Germany, among others, 'two generals, an admiral, a number of journalists', and many of his friends. The intelligence aim was to obtain for the Luftwaffe classified information about the British aviation industry and the RAF. Here de Rop decided to approach his friend, Squadron Leader Frederick Winterbotham who, from 1929, had been chief of air intelligence in SIS.[4]

The de Rop–Winterbotham relationship was a strange one and, at this distance, it is difficult to decide whether de Rop deceived

Winterbotham into helping him, or whether Winterbotham deceived de Rop. In his biography, Winterbotham makes no secret of his view that Britain's real enemy was the Soviet Union and he openly admits that he was in favour of an Anglo-German understanding on a united front against Stalin. On the other hand, he claims that he used the privileged position in Germany that these views gave him to gain as much information as possible about the new Luftwaffe.

The truth is that there was a two-way traffic. The Nazis almost certainly knew of Winterbotham's position in SIS – as he himself admits – and decided to trade information with him. This could be done at almost an official level: the Air Ministry, under Lord Londonderry and Lord Swinton, was keen for an understanding with Germany. An official German Foreign Office report in 1935 stated: 'When there are anti-German activities in London, enquiries always come to us from the Air General Staff as to what reply could be made to favour the German standpoint.' There were talks between British aero-engine representatives and the Luftwaffe; the Germans were invited to have a 'thorough look' at British air power and equipment; a British air attaché in Berlin, who was reporting with some alarm the rapid growth of the Luftwaffe, was replaced with a more sympathetic officer.

Winterbotham's role in all this could be defended as that of a classic double agent. But, as with all double agents, the employer is entitled from time to time to strike a balance and decide who is getting the fat and who the lean. The Foreign Office was doubtful. In 1937 it ordered Winterbotham to discontinue all contacts with the Nazis.[5] (He served loyally throughout the war, but remained convinced to the end that Britain was fighting the wrong enemy.)

De Rop is another matter. The information he gave to the Nazis – the strength of the appeasers in Britain, the possibility of co-operation between the Luftwaffe and the RAF, the sympathies of high-ranking officers in the Air Ministry, the prospects of the Luftwaffe being able to buy aircraft parts from Britain – was much more valuable to Germany than the floor plan of the Royal Ordnance factory, a sketch of Manston airfield, or the paraphrasing of reports from British newspapers. Yet there was never any suggestion that MI5 should arrest de Rop on one of his periodic visits to Britain and charge him under the Official Secrets Act, and, even after the outbreak of war, he continued to pass information to the Germans from his new residence in neutral Switzerland. The lesson would appear to be that a spy's chances of surviving are better if he operates at the upper end of the political and social spectrum.

While German intelligence operations in Britain were running at a low ebb, principally because Hitler remained convinced that he could reach an accommodation with British leaders, the effort against the United States was in high gear. The Germans concentrated on America because the level of its industrial development, research and innovation offered a rich field for a country in the middle of a vast rearmament programme. Even before the government intelligence agencies stepped up their operations in the United States, the giant German cartels and arms manufacturers such as I. G. Farben and Krupp had briefed their American representatives to report to head office any information on military and industrial development.[6]

When Canaris took over the Abwehr, he found that his predecessors had already established a small but active network of agents in the United States. Ladislas Farago has claimed in *The Game of the Foxes* that during the early and mid-1930s agents, such as William Lonkowski, Werner George Gudenberg, Otto Hermann Voss, Ignatz Theodor Griebl, Erich Pheiffer, Karl Eitel, Ulrich Hausmann and Gustave Guellich, succeeded in penetrating the American aviation industry and 'other sensitive areas of the nation's military machine'. Farago's account of the activities of these men often reads like spy fiction: one of the operations, for example, was code named 'sex'. The spies' sources included a Swiss-born captain in the US army, a draftsman in a firm of naval architects, workers in aircraft factories and a designer of guns in Montreal. The couriers were crew members of the German shipping lines plying to the United States; on one occasion, they were nearly caught in a random customs check, but the security officer, telephoned by customs, ordered that the spy should be allowed to go on condition that he agreed to return the next morning to be questioned!

According to Farago, the Germans boasted: 'In every armament factory, in every shipyard in America, we have a spy, several of them in key positions. The United States cannot plan a warship, design an airplane, develop a new device, that we do not know at once.'[7]

In Farago's opinion this was no empty boast and he claims that the daring and skill of German espionage in the United States in the 1930s enabled the Nazis to have the Luftwaffe ready for combat by 1939. Without espionage, he concludes, 'the Germans could not have gone to war as soon as they did'.

Farago's claim is a remarkable one and, if correct, the events he describes must be considered one of the great triumphs of intelligence history. The fact is, however, that the claim does not stand up to examination. German intelligence operations in the United States, spectacular though they may have appeared, were futile. Indeed, if the fact that some German agents were fed disinformation by the FBI is taken into account, Germany would probably have been better off with no spies in the United States at all.

The main aim of the German intelligence-gathering operation was to obtain economic and technological information relevant to Germany's military programme. German files examined after the war show the remarkably wide range of material that the Abwehr agents succeeded in obtaining: blueprints or samples of equipment, such as aircraft landing gear, new bombsights, new fuels, more efficient instruments, new ships and developmental aircraft; details of production capacity and expansion programmes; and timetables for a switch from a peacetime footing to all-out war production. But, as various Congressional investigations discovered, most of this information was freely available anyway, and could have been acquired (as in some cases it was) quite easily by overt means. In fact, the vigour of American salesmanship actually *forced* upon the Germans much of the material that they had set out to acquire by espionage.

In April 1934, Douglas Miller, the commercial attaché at the American embassy in Berlin, reported that American salesmen in Germany were selling aviation equipment of all kinds – aero engines, automatic pilots, gyro compasses and instruments. They were also offering control systems for anti-aircraft guns. Miller was able to forecast with great accuracy that American deliveries of this equipment meant that the Germans would have an air force of 2,500 aeroplanes by the end of 1935.[8]

Cartel agreements between American and German companies provided for the free exchange of new inventions and licences to cover their manufacture. Thus Dupont was freely exchanging information about explosives with several German companies in the early 1930s. Sperry Gyroscope licensed the Askania Company to manufacture blind flying instruments and sound locators in Germany, and supplied the Germans with gyros and other aircraft instruments. Pratt & Whitney sold engines, propellers and spare parts to the Germans, and provided Bayerische Motoren Werke with details of all the research and development work it was doing in the United States.

Standard Oil and I. G. Farben had an agreement to exchange patents and research under which Standard Oil provided the Germans with the formula and process for making butyl rubber, a major strategic material. Standard also gave Farben a superior method for making explosives. As late as 1940 Bendix Aircraft gave Robert Bosch details for manufacturing aircraft engine starters, running the British blockade of Germany in order to do so. In June 1940 there were twenty major items on the American government's list of scarce and strategic materials vital to the nation's defence. Of these twenty, no fewer than fourteen were produced by companies which had contracts with German firms.[9]

Sometimes these contracts worked to the disadvantage of the United States. The army asked Standard Oil to develop 100 octane fuel for aircraft engines, but warned Standard not to pass on the process to Farben. Standard replied that this would be in breach of an agreement it had signed with Farben in 1929 and that, rather than commit this breach, it would prefer not to develop the 100 octane fuel. Instead, Standard did the necessary research work and then built the necessary refineries for 100 octane fuel – in Germany! This gave the Germans knowledge not only of the process, but of the refinery capacity as well.[10]

Even the acquisition of the Norden bombsight, usually considered the Abwehr's most important intelligence coup in the United States, turns out to have been a hollow triumph. Nikolaus Ritter, a German who had lived in the United States for ten years, headed the Abwehr spy ring that obtained the plans for the bombsight. They were passed to him by Hermann Lang, an assembly inspector at the Norden plant, who simply took them home when he had an opportunity and copied them. By 1938 German scientists had filled in those sections that Lang had been unable to steal, and Germany had what was referred to as 'America's most jealously-guarded air defence weapon'. It turned out to be of limited use. The Luftwaffe did not have it installed in German bombers in time for the Blitz on Britain and, thereafter, it carried out relatively little bombing, its planes being used mostly for fighter and support functions.[11]

In the political intelligence field, the Germans did no better. Here their failure was one of interpretation. A vast mass of political information flowed to Berlin from the various German intelligence agencies; although some of it was perceptive, much of it was ignorant and prejudiced and any usefulness it may have had was then ruined by poor assessment.

The Abwehr failed to understand the nature of the American political process and tried to buy influence and to spread Hitler's views with paid propaganda. It believed the rumour that President Roosevelt was secretly the Jew 'Rosenfeld', and its agents painted him as timid, inept and of poor political judgement. They misunderstood race relations in the United States, and reported that prejudice would grow to such an extent that it would alter the government's foreign policy on the German persecution of the Jews. Even though the Abwehr succeeded in bugging the American embassy in Berlin and knew details of almost everything that was said, received and sent by the staff, its intelligence officers found no reason to challenge Hitler's conclusion that American leadership was mongrelized, timid and incompetent.[12]

Yet a traditional German diplomat, Hans Dieckhoff, who was the ambassador to Washington throughout 1937–8, told Berlin quite clearly that his assessment was that the United States would back Britain in any war with Germany. German diplomats noticed, if the spy masters did not, a change in Roosevelt's view of world affairs, a retreat from isolationism and a willingness to accept responsibility as a major power. This, combined with an emotional support for Britain, could only mean an increasingly firm stand against Germany. This perceptive conclusion fell on deaf ears. It did not tally with earlier intelligence assessments and it was based on diplomatic skills exercised openly without recourse to secret information. Hitler dismissed it.[13]

In the Soviet Union, the 1920s and 1930s saw the state intelligence system under its many names (it was called, successively, the GPU, OGPU, GUGB and NKVD) concerned mainly with internal subversion. Stalin used it to help suppress the peasants, to purge the army and to gather evidence for the great show trials of the period. Its overseas interest was concentrated on émigré organizations, such as the Trust, which received help from Britain and the United States. Most of these were successfully penetrated by Soviet intelligence, which allowed them to continue to function as long as they proved useful. It then eliminated them by luring their most important officers onto Soviet soil and arresting them.

When Dzerzhinsky died in 1926, the KGB had had no success in penetrating the British intelligence establishment. Its target appeared impossible – young Englishmen who would be prepared to make a lifetime allegiance to the Soviet Union and who would agree to 'remain in place', to serve Soviet interests wherever their careers in Britain took them. The qualities needed were rare: a political commitment at odds with their upbringing, a willingness to betray their class and their country, and a natural talent for duplicity because they would need to deceive not only their colleagues but their family and friends.

Fortunately for the Soviet Union, it turned out that soon a veritable pool of such young men was waiting to be tapped. There grew a deep disillusionment with British politics caused by the disastrous defeat of Labour in the autumn of 1931 and by Ramsay MacDonald's decision to continue as Prime Minister at the head of a national government that had no policy and no conviction. It was the third year of the Depression, unemployment was high and the Japanese invasion of Manchuria cast the early shadow of world conflict. Capitalism suddenly appeared not only wicked but vulnerable, and in the universities of Britain the talk was not of how it would crumble but when. Communist 'anti-war' groups were founded at Cambridge University, at the London School of Economics and at the University College, London, all at about the same time. They met at Easter 1932, to work out how to co-ordinate communist activity throughout British universities. [14]

The KGB was well aware of what was happening among the cream of British intellectuals. Conditions for finding a young Englishman to serve the Soviet cause might never be so favourable. But if the Russians were to attempt to recruit an undergraduate who, no matter how strident his public commitment to communism, was to find the thought of betraying his country a repugnant one, then the Soviet game could well end before it had begun. The Soviet Union would find it hard to cope with the scandal of an attempted recruitment of a spy at a time when public sympathy for communism was higher than ever before. Yet, as we now know, the Russians were remarkably successful in their recruiting campaign – Kim Philby, Guy Burgess, Donald Maclean and Anthony Blunt all made their commitment at this time. But – and this has puzzled everyone who has studied this period – not a single British undergraduate has ever come forward, then or now, to say, 'They tried to recruit me but I turned them down.'

It has been suggested that there could be only one explanation for this. The Russians approached only those undergraduates who they *knew* with almost total certainty would accept their proposition, and they could know this only if they had a talent spotter in a position of power and trust. According to this theory there must have been at least one Cambridge don who told the Soviet recruiters who to approach, a don who sought out those undergraduates who, because of their character, beliefs and attitudes, would be open to an offer to become a Soviet spy. Those who support this explanation have spent much time speculating on this don's identity, and wondering who his presentday successor could be.

There is a simpler but less exciting explanation. The Soviet approach was, at first, so oblique that many a student did not realize that it *was* an effort to recruit him. Those who responded were then taken slowly and carefully through an apparently endless process designed to test their sincerity and commitment. The KGB is renowned for its patience. For all but one of its prospective recruits of this period it was prepared to wait. The exception was Kim Philby.

We know now that if positive vetting had existed at the time of Philby's wartime induction into SIS he would have been rejected. A reasonably efficient check on his undergraduate days at Cambridge would have revealed – at the very least – that he had strong communist leanings. A contemporary says, 'Kim was almost certainly in the party'. There is no dispute that Philby first encountered communism at Cambridge. In our book, *The Philby Conspiracy*, my co-authors and I concluded that his actual recruitment occurred in Austria. Our reason for believing this was that when Philby came down from university in the autumn of 1933, he left immediately for Vienna, where the right and left were on the verge of civil war. Swept into the passions of European politics, both by choice and by his love affair with his landlady's daughter, Litze Kohlman, Philby was soon helping communists to escape abroad as the left was crushed by Fascist strength and ruthlessness. The lessons would have been obvious to him: only the Communist Party offered any hope for a Europe growing steadily darker.

We decided that it was at this moment that the KGB made its move. Everything the Russians knew about Philby's background pointed to him as a possible recruit: his birth abroad, his father's lack of attachment to Britain and Philby's activities at Cambridge. We speculated that the actual recruiter was a Hungarian refugee, Gabor Peter, who had fled from Admiral Horthy's dictatorship, and was later to become head of the Hungarian secret police.

I now believe that Philby was first approached in Britain, that Soviet intelligence *sent* him to Vienna and that, although Peter may have played a role in Philby's relationship with the KGB, a senior Russian officer would have been brought in at an earlier stage because of the highly important nature of Philby's assignment. Our mistake in our book was to think of recruitment as a one-meeting, sign-on-the-dotted-line affair. In fact it is actually a patient, long-drawn-out process of mutual testing that can go on for years and which starts with an approach so subtle that its significance may be entirely missed.

Our original reconstruction of events also runs into a problem of time-scale. In Moscow, years after the event, Philby told members of his family, 'I was recruited in June, 1933, and given the job of penetrating British intelligence and told it did not matter how long it took to do the job.'[15] Earlier we thought that Philby's experiences in Vienna had made him ripe for recruitment, but those experiences occurred in 1934, not 1933. In his remarks to his family he may have been compressing two events: he was recruited (in 1933); he was given his assignment (in 1934). So a more likely account of Philby's recruitment would be as follows.

He would have received an approach, a very oblique one, while he was still at university. On the basis of case histories we can speculate that this would have been a simple writing assignment. 'We are interested in what the young people in Britain feel about current political events. Could you write a paper for us with your interpretations of what is going on in this country today. Not for publication, of course. Just for private dissemination. And, naturally, no one need know that it was written by you.' The paper would have been lavishly praised, then after a short interval, there would have been a follow-up: Philby's perception of events had been so acute, would he consider an international assignment? Important events were occurring in Austria. The Comintern was in need of an outside, impartial assessment of what was happening and the likely outcome. The trip would also be valuable experience for a young man so interested in politics, and he might find when he got there ways in which he could help those whose struggle he no doubt supported.

After his Vienna experience, Philby would have been ready, politically and emotionally, to make his lifetime commitment. Whether he received his specific assignment, to penetrate British intelligence, at that moment does not matter. Other case histories suggest that an assignment of such importance would have come only after a much longer period of testing and trial. If it did come then – perhaps because the KGB was under pressure at the time and thus prepared to take a chance – then it is not difficult to suggest the nature of the proposition. The recruiter would have painted for Philby a grim picture of the coming struggle between Fascism and the left, a struggle which he had already witnessed being rehearsed in the streets of Vienna. He would have dwelt on the growing might of Germany and of the danger this posed for the Soviet Union. He would have recalled the days of the Allied intervention when half the world had joined forces to crush the Communist Revolution at birth. He would have voiced the Soviet Union's major fear: an alliance between Germany and Britain to try, once again, to overthrow the Soviet state.

The recruiter would have said that the Soviet Union could protect itself against this danger only by having someone at the centre of the British decision-making process, someone who could warn Moscow of any conspiracy against the USSR and its peoples. The details, initially, would have been left vague. The aim would have been to arouse Philby's interest in a secret assignment of international importance, to appeal to his ego and his sense of adventure. Philby would have returned with the impression that he had been offered a chance not only to take part in momentous events, but to have a hand in shaping their course. This would have been heady stuff for a 22-year-old; as he said later, 'It is a matter of great pride to me that I was invited at so early an age to play my . . . part . . . One does not look twice at an offer of enrolment in an elite force.'[16]

Perhaps the specific nature of his assignment was only made clear to him later. But we can see in retrospect that by the mid-1930s Philby had already begun to construct the disguise that would bring him to the attention of SIS as a possible recruit, and which would also protect him for the next dangerous thirty years. He gave up all political interests, got himself a minor job in journalism, edited the journal of the Anglo-German Fellowship, and started to establish himself as a quiet admirer of the Third Reich. He tried to start a trade journal designed to foster good relations between Britain and Germany and made several visits to Berlin for talks about this with the German Propaganda Ministry and the German Foreign Office, no doubt reporting to his Soviet controller on his return. This was his testing time, an attempt to measure his resolve. Philby must have passed, because in February 1937 the KGB gave him his first real assignment. It sent him to the Spanish Civil War.

Philby's task was to get 'first-hand information on all aspects of the Fascist war effort'. What better cover for this than to be an accredited journalist with the Franco forces, representing the London General Press, a news and syndication agency? The KGB financed the trip and when Philby ran short of money, sent him some more via Burgess – a blunder they were later to regret. But the investment itself paid off. Philby was not able to tell his Soviet masters much that they did not already know, but he took one important step closer to getting into SIS: he got a job with *The Times*.

On 24 May 1937, after submitting a string of articles 'on spec', he succeeded James Holburn as *The Times* special correspondent with General Franco. *The Times* had long been a source of recruits for SIS and Philby half expected an approach during the war in Spain. It did not come, but he had been noticed. The KGB's plan for Philby had taken an important step forward.

# 6. The Fantasies of Richard Hannay and Sandy Arbuthnot

> Now set Europe ablaze.
> – Winston Churchill, giving Hugh Dalton the charter for SOE on 22 July 1940.

> The fires that kept blazing were those of Europe's steel mills. Apart from the fact that most people are averse to running any great personal risk, we should realise that the tremendous complexity of the highly-industrialised societies of Western Europe make it difficult, if not impossible to tear up the fabric of social life.
> – Louis de Jong, 'Britain and Dutch Resistance, 1940–1945'.

The part played by British intelligence in winning the Second World War has become a legend. The legend goes something like this: SIS was in total disarray in 1939, following a series of organizational and operational disasters and after a long period of government penny-pinching; but with the outbreak of war it recovered rapidly. Legions of brilliant and dedicated amateurs were recruited from the backwaters of university life, from the City and from the professions. These men and women resolutely applied themselves to the task, brilliantly overcame the German opposition – which refused to the end to believe that the British could be so efficient – and then modestly resumed their civilian existences.

The view that Britain's intelligence war was a triumph is widespread. Zara Steiner, an author and a senior academic at Cambridge, has written that just as the Soviet army and the United States' industrial output were the keys to victory, so 'intelligence was the British success story'.[1] Another historian, Dr Christopher Andrew, director of studies in history at Corpus Christi College, Cambridge, concurred: 'Faced with a sophisticated German intelligence machine, British intelligence won a decisive victory.'[2] So did a British Broadcasting Corporation radio documentary which concluded that, taking the war as a whole, British intelligence had been a clear winner. In the United States, Ladislas Farago, a former intelligence officer, wrote in *The Game of the Foxes*, 'When I started my researches, I thought that the Germans had probably won the espionage war. When I finished them, I knew it was the British.'[3] Furthermore, Britain's wartime intelligence organization is also credited with helping the rebirth of American intelligence. General William Donovan, the first head of the American Office of Strategic Services (OSS), said that SIS 'gave us an enormous headstart which we could not otherwise have had'.[4]

This assessment of British intelligence in the war has largely been allowed to pass unchallenged. In keeping with the traditional secrecy surrounding SIS and MI5, it was never intended that their official history should be published along with that of other wartime services. A record was prepared, but was originally destined only for the archives. Then, in 1966, the government allowed publication of M. R. D. Foot's *SOE in France*, which opened the way for other books on intelligence such as Masterman's *The Double Cross System*, and Winterbotham's *Secret and Personal*.

Finally, the government agreed to an official history, written by Professor F. H. Hinsley and others, the first volume of which was published in 1979, and the fourth in 1984. It is, perhaps, scarcely surprising that in general Hinsley praises British intelligence – after all, he was in it! Even so, his work has not been universally welcomed by his ex-colleagues. His concentration on the *organization* of wartime intelligence resulted in what Maurice Oldfield, a former head of SIS, described as 'a book written by a committee, about committees, for committees'.[5] Hinsley was no doubt hampered by the problems that Malcolm Muggeridge, a wartime SIS officer, points out: 'Diplomats and intelligence agents, in my experience, are even bigger liars than journalists, and the historians who try to reconstruct the past out of their records are, for the most part, dealing in fantasy.'[6] But, given that the other books are largely personal reminiscences, Hinsley's remains the only attempt to provide an overview of the entire British intelligence effort. It is, therefore, regrettable that he barely essays a critical examination of the claims that have been made for British intelligence during the war.

The indications are that such an examination would reveal a picture very different from that set out in the legendary version. When war broke out in September 1939, SIS was indeed in serious difficulties. As we have seen, its intelligence gathering in the 1930s consisted of a series of second-rate, poorly paid officers in overseas stations buying minor items of intelligence from unreliable agents. These items were then sent back to London where headquarters staff graded and analysed them before distributing them to the various 'consumers'. The main consumers, the three armed services, had been unhappy with SIS material for some time, complaining that the items which were true usually turned out to be irrelevant to their needs, while items which seemed relevant usually turned out to be untrue. All three departments wanted more details of industrial production in Russia, Japan and Italy, as well as in Germany, and they wanted some sort of proof of authenticity.[7]

An opportunity to shake up SIS occurred when, on 4 November 1939, Admiral Sinclair, its head for fourteen years, died. After some intense lobbying, Cabinet agreed to the appointment of Stewart Menzies, who had been Sinclair's deputy. Menzies, then 49, was a regular soldier who had served with distinction in the First World War, winning the DSO and the MC. There was a widespread belief in the services that Menzies was the illegitimate son of Edward VII. He was certainly closely connected with court circles through his mother, Lady Holford, who was lady-in-waiting to Queen Mary. He also had considerable influence in important government circles and, as 'ruthless intriguer', used it shamelessly. He had no great intellect – one of his political masters described him as 'not quite illiterate'. But he had charm, many friends and a great natural facility for surviving.

Menzies left the day-to-day running of SIS to his subordinates – 'don't expect me to read everything that's put on my desk' – and devoted his attention to maintaining SIS's position in Whitehall. This annoyed ministers who dealt with him. One said, 'Whenever I ask Stewart about something on the telephone, he invariably says he must check and ring me back. I've got ninety-nine business interests but I have the details of them all at my fingertips.'[8] In personal relationships he was always polite, but never warm – 'hard as granite under a smooth exterior' is the description of one SIS officer's wife. He was a clubman, loved horses and racing, and drank heavily.

The Cabinet's approval of Menzies's appointment contained a caveat: there would be a major investigation of SIS and MI5. This would be carried out by Maurice Hankey, then the Minister Without Portfolio, and for fifty years the *éminence grise* of British intelligence. Hankey would look, in particular, at the cost of maintaining SIS since Menzies was demanding that his budget be substantially increased from its current level of £700,000 a year. But

Hankey's work was cut short; he had had time to produce only an interim report when Churchill's government replaced that of Chamberlain.

Churchill, a fanatical believer in the value of intelligence, was aware of the need to breathe new life into SIS. He had sacked Menzies's opposite number at MI5, Major-General Sir Vernon Kell, on 10 June 1940, and vested the political authority for MI5 with the Security Executive headed by Lord Swinton, the former Air Minister. Swinton's first task was to investigate and reform MI5 in order to improve its efficiency. He then intended to give SIS much the same sort of shake-up. Unfortunately, circumstances prevented him from doing so. He wrote a letter to *The Times* advocating an expanded general staff, as in the First World War. Churchill must have seen this as an attempt to dilute his role in running the war and Swinton was quickly made resident minister in West Africa. Duff Cooper, who replaced him as head of the Security Executive, showed no interest in reforming SIS.

But SIS's reprieve was only temporary. This first year of the war was a story of almost unrelieved disaster. The German *Blitzkrieg* of May 1940 virtually closed down its European network. It had already lost Czechoslovakia, Austria and Poland; Norway, Denmark, Holland, Belgium and France now followed. This was regarded as a terrible blow at the time, but Hugh Trevor-Roper (Lord Dacre), who joined SIS soon afterwards, thinks it was all for the good. 'We would have [been] drawing information from a lot of rotten spies on the continent who would have then been controlled by the Germans . . . The leaders of SIS, being of remarkable stupidity, would have accepted it . . . and would have presented it as hard information and it would have got mixed into real information and I think it would have done nothing but harm.'[9]

So SIS was reduced to a few stations in neutral countries and the hope that it would be able to use what was left of the agent networks of Allied governments exiled to London. Its reputation was not improved by the fact that it had been responsible for a grossly inaccurate assessment of France's fighting strength. SIS had accepted a French Deuxième Bureau argument that the answer to *Blitzkrieg* tactics was a fortified line, and that the Maginot Line would present a major obstacle to the German motorized forces. This view was circulated to consumers in London as an SIS assessment, and when it proved to be badly wrong SIS had to accept the blame.[10]

Even more serious was the failure of SIS to foresee the collapse of French morale. Here the question is whether SIS did not know, or whether it knew but failed to tell its consumers. At least one SIS officer who moved in important government and military circles in France reported to Menzies that the French would make a quick peace with Germany should war occur. The officer, Kenneth de Courcey, had joined SIS 'as an unpaid amateur' in 1936 at Menzies's invitation. 'I dined with Laval in 1937 and reported to Menzies what I had learned', de Courcey says. 'In early January 1940, I dined with a French general in Paris and saw various members of the French war cabinet. It was perfectly obvious to me that France would make a separate peace, either before a major military clash or after it. I told Menzies this. I suspect that he did not tell Churchill because he knew it was not what Churchill wanted to hear and Menzies needed to keep Churchill's favour.'*[11]

SIS was now scorned not only by the services, who were busy expanding their own intelligence departments, but by the Joint Intelligence Committee (JIC). This body had been set up in 1936 to co-ordinate all intelligence-gathering operations, and to assess and distribute the results. At the outbreak of war its head was William Cavendish-Bentinck. The three services, the Foreign Office, the IIC, and SIS and MI5 had representatives on it, and SIS soon found itself under attack from the others over its poor performance. There was a suggestion in June 1940, that SIS should be split up among the three services and it required all Menzies's skill at Whitehall in-fighting to prevent this from happening. Even Churchill was growing disillusioned with SIS and in November of that year asked the Chiefs of Staff to report to him on the feasibility of shutting down SIS completely and replacing it with a new inter-services intelligence group that would come under the Chiefs of Staff themselves.[12] As we shall see, Menzies and his empire were saved by his astute use of the codebreakers, GC and CS (later GCHQ) who came under his control, and by Churchill's romanticized view of the intelligence world.

Not that the performance of the JIC provided much support for the idea that a combined intelligence group would be any better than SIS. JIC appreciations of German intentions were equally ill-informed. It had an exaggerated opinion of the strength of the French army, largely due to the views of the army representative, the director of military intelligence, Major-General Frederick ('Paddy') Beaumont-Nesbitt, who claimed that France had 'five

---

* De Courcey's enemies in Whitehall said that he was not listened to because his information was suspect: 'De Courcey had hardly any French. It is no good meeting French generals clandestinely in the Bois de Boulogne if you are going to limit your responses to "Oui, mon Général".'

generals as good as Foch'. As a result of Beaumont-Nesbitt's assessment, says Cavendish-Bentinck, 'we didn't see how rotten the French had become'.[13] The JIC quickly became skilled at hedging its bets. In a report to the War Cabinet in July 1940 on 'The Imminence of a German Invasion of Great Britain', it concluded that Germany was preparing for an invasion or raids in force and 'might move at any time suitable to her, but that it was unlikely that her full strength would be developed until July 15.' In another report, the JIC canvassed the options open to Germany and then concluded 'which of these courses Germany will select will depend less on logical deduction than upon the personal and unpredictable decision of the Führer'. Other reports were superficial, trivial, or irrelevant. It did not help the War Cabinet to know, for instance, that 'information from a most reliable source is to the effect that the Germans will hold a parade of their armed forces in Paris some time after July 10'.[14]

With the War Cabinet in danger of vanishing under the sheer volume of intelligence reports, Churchill expressed his discontent in a memorandum to the secretariat of the War Cabinet: 'Please look at this mass of stuff which reaches me in a single morning. . . . More and more people must be banking up behind these different papers, the bulk of which defeats their purpose.'[15] It was this dissatisfaction with the committee approach to intelligence and his romantic desire to see the raw sources that pushed Churchill back into the arms of Menzies and SIS and helped ensure their survival, unreformed, throughout the war.

The wealthy upper-class young men recruited between the wars, together with the former members of the Indian police – who were sneered at and looked down upon by their colleagues – rapidly found themselves out of their depth as they struggled to shore up a crumbling institution. Wartime recruits could hardly believe the workings of the service they had joined. One recalls:

> The whole organisation was riddled with nepotism . . . dim, dreary people of utter unmemorability; sub-men who were doubled up with other sub-men to create an illusion of strength and only doubled the weakness; others [made] memorable only by poisonous, corrupt malevolence or crass, mulish stupidity; the whole run by a chain of command remarkable for its feebleness. The entire service was decrepit and incompetent.[16]

Yet, so thoroughly did the cultivation of secrecy protect SIS from exposure, that when the Dutch, Belgian and Norwegian intelligence services regrouped in exile in London, all still believed the myth that SIS was the best intelligence service in the world and were convinced that it had numerous networks still functioning in Occupied Europe.

The truth was very different. SIS had been taken by surprise by the speed of the German advance. Heads of station, officers and support staff fled to London or neutral territory. There were no contingency plans to create stay-behind networks – there was not even a supply of radio sets to help existing agents to remain in touch. Nor, at first, was there any way of infiltrating officers back in order to rectify this situation. The disillusionment of the service chiefs with SIS's performance made them increasingly reluctant to provide the transport and equipment necessary to get anyone into German-occupied countries. SIS now faced the humiliating prospect of seeking help from the European intelligence services that had been exiled to London for, without their help, it was unable to learn anything of what was happening in Europe. The Poles provided intelligence from their stay-behind agents and other European rings. Their arms sometimes proved surprisingly long: from 1941 onwards, for example, they were able to report regularly on the departure of German submarines from Bordeaux, Brest and Le Havre. The Czechs were exceptionally well informed, and the Dutch and French also helped. But SIS had to compete with other services which were also anxious to exploit the exiled European intelligence organizations: by late 1940 no fewer than five separate British intelligence sections were trying to organize joint intelligence operations with the French.

SIS was, of course, still functioning in neutral countries. Lisbon, in particular, had become an espionage capital and Stockholm and Geneva were both productive sources. Geneva SIS even had a radio but it could only receive, so outward messages had to be sent through the Swiss postal system! Madrid was potentially another important station; but the British ambassador there, the former Home Secretary, Sir Samuel Hoare, had been a leading appeaser and he still had hopes for a negotiated peace. A possible intermediary in any such negotiations would be the Spanish leader, General Franco, and Hoare was determined that nothing should upset the delicate relationship that existed between the British and Spanish governments. The last thing Hoare wanted was SIS operations against the Germans in Spain or, worse, SIS plots to overthrow Franco. SIS protested in Whitehall, but Hoare was not without influence from his Home Secretary days and his view prevailed.

Thus when SIS tried to open an office to debrief British and Allied prisoners who had escaped to Spain from German prisoner-of-war camps, Hoare protested and SIS was forced to transfer the office to Lisbon. He also resolutely refused to give his permission for an operation to knock out an infra-red searchlight station in Spanish Morocco which the Germans had set up to spot Allied shipping in the Straits of Gibraltar. At one point, under pressure from London, he did give reluctant agreement, only to change his mind and withdraw it again at the last minute. (The bombers ignored the message, successfully blew up the station and then claimed that the order had arrived too late.) In this manner, Hoare reduced SIS Madrid to impotency and in the later stages of the war, if it had not been for the Americans who obligingly carried out the odd operation for it, the station would have ceased to operate.[17]

Hoare was but one of the many enemies with whom SIS had to contend within the government machine. These were so numerous that at some stage during the war a bitter joke circulated about the SIS officer who, after enormous difficulty and delay, finally succeeded in mounting an offensive intelligence operation and reported how refreshing it was to be reminded that the real enemy was Germany. The traditional enmity between MI5 and SIS had been sharpened by MI5's successes* after its reorganization under its new head, Sir David Petrie. Menzies, worried about the deepening split, succeeded in arranging for an SIS liaison officer to work with MI5; an attempt both to stop the deteriorating relationship and to have an ear in 'the enemy camp'. But it was the War Cabinet's creation of an entirely new service that caused most distress to both MI5 and SIS.

SIS had had a section devoted to sabotage and subversion since 1930. Known as Section D (for 'destruction') it was supposed to initiate operations to attack what were thought to be Germany's Achilles' heels. Among the flights of fantasy considered by Section D were projects to blow up the Iron Gates of the Danube so as to interrupt the Germans' supply of Romanian oil, and to launch balloons over Central Europe in the hope that the incendiary bombs attached to them would set the grain fields on fire and cripple German food production. We can imagine the bewilderment of the KGB officer running Kim Philby, who had joined Section D in July 1940, when Philby described his department. 'My first factual

---

* An American State Department report of 1 August 1940 on MI5 said that it maintained a central index with 4·5 million names of everyone 'ever suspected in any part of the world of anti-British activity'. The fact that many of the names were fictitious and the information accompanying them was trivial, does not lessen the fact that MI5's image at this time was highly polished compared with that of SIS.

reports on the Secret Service inclined him seriously to the view that I had got into the wrong organisation.'[18]

Section D was starved of funds, distrusted by other sections of SIS, and viewed with extreme suspicion in Whitehall. It soon fell victim to the newly created Special Operations Executive (SOE) which came into being on 22 July 1940. The creation of SOE was a response to pressure from Churchill for some immediate counter-offensive steps against Germany, and it was put under the control of Hugh Dalton, the Minister of Economic Warfare in Churchill's coalition government. Its task, in Churchill's laconic phrase, was to 'set Europe ablaze'. Given the exclusive responsibility for sabotage overseas, one of SOE's first moves was to take over Section D without consulting Menzies, thus sowing one of the seeds that grew into a long-lasting enmity between the two organizations.[19]

A continuing source of friction was the basic difference in the aims of the two services. SIS's aim was to gather intelligence from the enemy so secretly that he did not know it had happened; SOE's aim was to destroy the enemy's property and strike fear into his heart. As Donald McLachlan writes, 'intelligence, in the true sense of the word, is incompatible with violent, subversive conspiratorial activity'.[20] Or as an SIS officer, quoted by Nigel West, says, 'SIS's role . . . was to watch enemy troops crossing a bridge while SOE's brief was . . . to blow up the bridge to prevent [those] movements'. Yet, despite these opposing aims, both services were forced to collaborate because neither could function unless it could get its officers into enemy territory and maintain contact with them. So they had to share such limited transport facilities as the services were prepared to make available to them. SOE wanted to run its own codes and signals, but Menzies regained some lost ground by insisting that SIS should conduct all SOE's communications.

This competition for facilities had barely been recognized when another cause of conflict arose. In the course of their sabotage activities, SOE officers could hardly help but gather intelligence items of interest to SIS. But SOE tended to pass on such information direct to the defence service most immediately concerned. After much bickering, a compromise was reached: SIS would allow SOE to act for it in specified areas and, in return, SOE would pass its intelligence on to the consumers only through SIS. The whole issue, however, was a shaming one for SIS because it had to acknowledge SOE's success in gathering material from countries that SIS officers were no longer able to penetrate. Seen in this light, SIS antagonism to SOE is understandable. As David Stafford writes, '[SIS] never fully accepted the SOE–SIS divorce of 1940 and its subsequent behaviour only too often resembled that of an embittered ex-spouse'.[21]

$A$t this point, it will be convenient to examine the performance of SOE. Although it was not strictly an intelligence-gathering service, its affairs became inextricably entwined with the two established intelligence organizations. For its origins lay within the intelligence world; a number of officers served in both SOE and SIS; and the conflict between SOE and SIS became, as one former SIS officer, Henry Kerby, has put it, 'The biggest, bitterest internal battle in the history of our intelligence services'.[22] (This battle was to have a vital influence on American intelligence and can be held to be partly responsible for a flaw at the heart of today's CIA.)

SOE's basic problem was that it was founded on a series of false premises. The most important of these was that a combination of subversion, sabotage, blockade and strategic bombing would win the war without the need for that direct confrontation with the German army which had produced the trench slaughter of the First World War. The Royal Navy was to create the blockade; the RAF would handle the strategic bombing offensive; sabotage and subversion would be the task of SOE. Its officers would provide the plans, the wherewithal and the leadership; the peoples of German-occupied Europe would contribute the manpower. Churchill envisaged a 'gigantic guerilla' which would snap at the German heels, bite its flanks, blow up its railways, slip sand into its war machinery, harry its patrols, mine its roads and kill its sentries.

There were several things wrong with this plan. First, at the time SOE was launched, Britain simply did not have the military means to carry out such an operation. She was on the defensive: arms, ammunition and supplies were scarce; so were the planes to deliver them. The strategic bombing offensive was given priority and the service chiefs were unwilling to divert aircraft from bombing missions to operations planned by SOE – an organization that Sir Arthur Harris, chief of Bomber Command, no doubt had in mind when he described the Ministry of Economic Warfare, SOE's Whitehall cover, as 'amateurish, ignorant, irresponsible and mendacious'. Even at its peak, SOE only had at its disposal four squadrons of aircraft to make supply drops to its agents and resistance fighters.[23]

Next, not having lived under enemy occupation for nearly a thousand years, the British failed totally to understand the attitude of the average European citizen who found his country occupied by the Germans. Both Churchill and Dalton romantically believed that every man, woman and child in Occupied Europe was just waiting for the right moment to rise and strike against the Germans. They did not understand the historic resignation with which most Europeans viewed the German occupation, their determination to make the best of defeat, to carry on with their lives as best they could, and to collaborate where necessary to ensure their survival. The fact is that most people collaborated most of the time. Only a month after the Armistice, French businessmen had concluded an agreement with their German counterparts to supply bauxite at a knock-down price. Danish businessmen offered capital and labour to the Germans to exploit conquered Eastern Europe, and by late 1941 nearly a million Poles had gone to work *voluntarily* in Germany.[24]

Both Churchill and Dalton extended their optimistic expectations to Germany herself. Churchill received in May 1940, a British intelligence assessment written by Gladwyn Jebb, later chief executive officer of SOE, which said, 'All our informants agree that the population of Germany as a whole is quite unelated by recent victories and generally depressed'. This was an amazing piece of self-delusion. Dalton was equally blinkered, looking forward six months he foresaw 'Famine, starvation and revolt, most of all in the slave lands which Germany has over-run'.[25] Such wildly unrealistic assessments, coupled with a natural tendency to underestimate the effectiveness and efficiency of German control over Occupied Europe's 260 million people, were the shifting sands upon which the very foundations of SOE rested.

And yet there were people within the occupied lands who *were* prepared to sacrifice their lives, and the lives of their families, for liberation. Dalton came close to identifying them in a letter he wrote in July 1940: 'We must organise movements in every occupied territory comparable to the Sinn Fein movement in Ireland, to the Chinese guerrillas now operating in Japan, to the Spanish irregulars who played a notable part in Wellington's campaigns . . .' Dalton, in short, saw that what was needed were revolutionaries, and the theory of a 'European Revolution' was much discussed in British left-wing circles at that time.[26]

But it soon emerged that most of these revolutionaries were communists. Only the communists, it seemed, had the organization, the discipline and the willingness to fight against fascism.

They would fight, however, not to restore a prewar Europe, one of 'kings and capitalism', but to replace them with an entirely new order. The British establishment and the European governments in exile – which it was committed to support – quickly recognized the danger. If SOE were to help resistance against the Germans in Occupied Europe, they risked opening the way for a postwar Europe dominated by communism. This explains the eagerness with which SOE supported other sources of resistance in the infrequent cases where they appeared. In the early days at least, royalists and right-wing groups who could show the slightest evidence of action against the Germans were showered with Allied aid. In the later stages of the war some of the most bitter infighting in SOE was over which resistance movement SOE should support – for example, Tito's communists or Mihailovich's monarchist chetniks in Yugoslavia.[27]

This political dilemma had implications for SOE's recruitment policies. Initially, Dalton, with his European Revolution in mind, wanted to recruit British working-class officers who could understand the mentality of the European industrial class. In particular, he wanted SOE to establish close relations with the French trade union movement. But Dalton soon found that it was impossible to recruit working-class officers in Britain who could speak fluent French, and when he got the sack because Churchill did not intend SOE to be the catalyst for a social revolution in Europe, or anywhere else, SOE's entire recruitment pattern changed.[28]

The top ranks of SOE were quickly filled by public school–Oxbridge men and women, recruited, in the tradition of SIS's old Section D, from the City of London. The first executive head, Sir Frank Nelson, was a former India merchant; his successor, Sir Charles Hambro, was a banker. Stockbrokers, businessmen, Lloyds underwriters and merchant bankers made up the bulk of SOE's recruits. The mixture was leavened by the occasional Foreign Office official, MP and journalist.* All were conservative by birth and upbringing. It is therefore understandable that some of the resistance groups these men were sent to help regarded SOE as a secret army of imperialism and the average SOE officer as a would-be Lawrence of Arabia – 'the perfidious arrogant champion of an Empire'.[30]

---

* The use of journalists for black propaganda was one of SOE's stronger points. Before the United States entered the war SOE cultivated American journalists who were friendly to Britain, such as Dorothy Thompson, Walter Winchell and Edgar Mowrer, and spread propaganda through a series of British front operations, such as Thompson's Ring of Freedom.[29]

Not only were many of SOE's agents politically illiterate as far as knowledge of Europe was concerned, but they also had a dangerously romantic conception of what they were about. They had been brought up on the assumption that the British were a superior race, natural owners of an empire on which the sun never set. They took it for granted that one Englishman was worth five Germans, ten Italians and an incalculable number of lesser breeds. Almost without exception, they had been avid readers, both as boys and men, of John Buchan, a writer who had worked for British intelligence and whose hero, Richard Hannay, was modelled on himself and his colleagues. Recruitment to SOE offered these Buchan fans a chance to act out their fantasies in a worthwhile cause. One of them has written that practically every officer he met in SOE imagined himself to be Richard Hannay, or Hannay's friend, Sandy Arbuthnot.[31]

The crucial point is that, like Buchan's heroes, SOE officers were amateurs – and proud of it. They considered the rigid discipline of the services to be not only useless but boring. Although at its peak SOE had a total staff of some 10,000 men and 3,000 women, it scorned too rigid a hierarchy and regarded the importance that the services placed on ranks with amused contempt. It delighted in secrecy and deniability; it relished the sense of being beyond society, beyond the law. It sported a plethora of cover names: its headquarters in Baker Street went under the title of Inter-Services Research Bureau, it often used War Office notepaper, its naval section called itself NID(Q). It had 200 unlisted telephone numbers and a series of furnished flats in the West End – but no central registry or proper filing system. Openness was a rare quality in SOE, and government departments were expected to provide assistance without really knowing what it was for, or even for whom it was intended. Often some valuable item, properly requisitioned, would be collected, only for the department concerned to find that the receipt had been signed by someone from 'Universal Export', a name to be used later – as an in-house joke – by the former naval intelligence officer, Ian Fleming, in his James Bond novels.[32]

Its obsession with secrecy meant that it had a 'once in, never out' attitude to recruits. But what could it do with those who failed to make the grade? Some had decided not to go through with their mission when told what it was; others had come under suspicion of being traitors; others had turned out to be alcoholics or to have psychological problems. While their knowledge of their own operation would, in time, become obsolete; their knowledge of SOE techniques, codes, contacts in Occupied Europe and the identities of other agents would not. These failed agents had to be kept silent, so at a series of meetings in March 1941, the Home Defence (Security) Executive, which consisted of representatives of SIS, SOE, MI5 and the Home Office, decided that what was needed was a special detention centre for 'those whose information was such that they could not be released before the end of the war'.

These rejects were not to be allowed any visits whatsoever, and every effort was to be made to prevent even the Red Cross from knowing about them. Government ministers were advised to lie if necessary to protect SOE's secret. In reply to people or organizations inquiring about an agent interned in the centre, 'the Home Secretary should inform them that there was no trace of that name in the index of persons in internment'. Stafford prison and the Isle of Man were considered as sites for the centre, but it was eventually located in Scotland at Inverlair Lodge, in Inverness-shire.[33] Guarded by the Cameron Highlanders, the failed SOE men (plus some colleagues from SIS) passed their time in considerable comfort. When hints about the bizarre episode emerged in the 1970s it became the inspiration for a novel (*The Cooler*, by George Markstein) and a highly successful television series (*The Prisoner*, starring Patrick MacGoohan).

Although the charge most frequently levelled against SOE officers was that they were 'amateurs', there were critics who had less charitable opinions. Henry Kerby has described SOE officers as 'a collection of talented roughnecks, activists, saboteurs and murderers – the dregs', and Robert Bruce Lockhart, of Bolshevik Revolution fame, now director of the Political Warfare Executive, thought that SOE was 'a bogus, irresponsible, corrupt sham which ought to be disbanded'.[34]

The moral aspect of what SOE was doing has received scant attention. In its attempts to 'set Europe ablaze' it killed not only Germans but many innocent civilians, including fervent supporters of the Allied cause. When an SOE team blew up a train in France, it may have disrupted German supplies but it also frequently killed the French train crew. The leaders of SOE must also have known that the Germans would exact terrible reprisals on the local population to deter it from helping SOE agents.

The assassination of Reinhard Heydrich, the Protector of Czechoslovakia, in May 1942, is a case in point. The operation was organized by Colonel Frank Spooner, head of SOE's training school. Two Czechs attacked Heydrich's car with machine-guns and grenades. The Germans responded by shooting a hundred hostages each evening until Heydrich died,* a week after the attack; and then executed the entire population of Lidice (the village where the SOE agents had landed by parachute), and razed the village to the ground. This savagery so crippled Czech resistance that, by the end of that year, the Germans were able to employ 350,000 Czechs on war work with only 750 Germans to supervise them. After the war, Spooner confessed that he wished he had not organized the assassination and that SOE tended to pay too little regard to the possibility of reprisals being taken against civilians.[36]

Sometimes the civilian casualties were accidents – although that was little consolation to their relatives. In March 1945 SOE persuaded the RAF – against its wishes – to mount a raid by Mosquito bombers on a Gestapo prison in Copenhagen where forty Danish resistance leaders were being held. SOE's justification for such an action was that the Danish resistance was valuable to the war effort. But the end of the war was only six weeks away and it was already clear that Germany's surrender was only a matter of time. The raid was a disaster. A bomber from the first wave crashed into a neighbouring Catholic school and the second wave of bombers mistook the resulting fire as their marker and bombed it. Thirty Danish resistance leaders escaped, but ten Allied airmen, twenty-seven Danish schoolteachers and seven Danish schoolchildren died. One of the children who survived recalled the raid in 1976 when the first full account of it emerged in Britain: 'There was a terrible crash and everything went dark . . . I thought maybe I am dead . . . Then I heard children crying and praying and crying . . . It had been such a marvellous day, you know. The first day of Spring.'[37]

Yet SOE certainly had its successes. It did raise the morale of the people in Occupied Europe. 'To have the least toe-hold in resistance gave back to millions of people the self respect they had lost at the moment of national disaster', writes M. R. D. Foot, 'and SOE was one of the largest of several bodies which provided opportunities and arms for taking part in the resistance struggle.' SOE's demolition of the German heavy water plant at Vemork in Norway in 1943 was a major achievement, as it probably deterred the Germans from trying to make an atomic bomb. Its contribution to the strike of French railway and telephone workers in the first week of June 1944 was never properly acknowledged. Its wartime support for Tito

---

* At first, German doctors were confident Heydrich would recover because his actual wounds were not too serious. His sudden deterioration has since been attributed to poisoning by botulinal toxin which, the German story goes, SOE had acquired in the United States and had used to impregnate submachine-gun rounds for the attack.[35]

helped him to build a powerful party, whose first loyalty was to its country, and enabled it to stand up to Stalin after the war. In Burma, SOE was responsible for bringing the formerly pro-Japanese security police over to the Allied side early in 1945 – at a crucial stage of the war.[38]

But against such successes, SOE's failures continue to weigh heavily. The most devastating of these was in the Netherlands and it nearly ended SOE's existence. The story of what the Germans code named 'Operation Nordpol' is now notorious. In brief, using radio direction-finding apparatus the Germans were able to locate and arrest a Dutch SOE radio operator, and then persuaded him to transmit to London under their control. The operator – at considerable risk to his life – managed not only to omit from his messages the standard, prearranged security check, thus indicating that he was under German control, but also to insert in one message the word 'caught'. The receiving operator ignored the warning, so that the Dutchman, trained in the world of double and triple cross, assumed that SOE headquarters had noted his capture but were keeping in touch so as to play some deep game against the Germans. He continued, therefore, to transmit whatever the Germans told him.

From then on, SOE's Netherlands division was, in effect, run by the Germans. Agents were lured to dropping areas where they found the Gestapo waiting for them. They, too, were forced to transmit under German control. At the peak of the operation the Germans were running seventeen transmitters and SOE was dropping an enormous quantity of arms, ammunition, explosives, food, clothing and money straight into enemy hands. This penetration of SOE's Dutch network was bad enough, but the damage spread to its operations in France and Belgium – where the disaster was even worse. Even when two SOE agents escaped from a Gestapo prison, painfully made their way to London via Madrid, and revealed that the Germans were in control of the whole Dutch operation, SOE disbelieved them, decided that they must have been 'turned' by the Germans, and put them in Brixton prison charged with helping the enemy. It was not until further escapes confirmed their story that SOE was forced to consider the possibility that it was being controlled by the Germans. The Germans finally wound up Nordpol in March 1944 when it became obvious that an Allied invasion of Europe was imminent. In September they shot the last forty-seven of the SOE agents they had captured. In all, the operation cost the lives of at least a hundred men and women.[39]

Meanwhile, SOE's enemies in Britain had their suspicions that all was not well. On 1 December 1943, Bomber Command announced that it was suspending all SOE's flights in Europe.[40] It was worried about German penetration of SOE and it was not prepared to risk the lives of air crew on dubious operations. Bomber Command demanded an immediate inquiry by the JIC. SIS seized this chance to lobby for extending this inquiry into a general review of SOE's work in Europe, and into its command structure and organization. The report that resulted was damning: it was laced with ridicule throughout, and ended with a series of suggestions that were tantamount to winding up the organization. Churchill, who still had a soft spot for SOE, despite his concern about the cost of running it,* had to intervene to save the service, even though this meant over-ruling the combined weight of the JIC, SIS and the Chiefs of Staff.[41]

SOE's fights with other services and with government departments may not have all been its own fault – certainly, in the case of SIS, blame must clearly be apportioned to both sides. But this cannot excuse the internal bickering, conspiracy, betrayal and character assassination that so often came near to crippling its operations. SOE in Cairo was the worst. Bickham Sweet-Escott has written: 'Nobody who did not experience it can possibly imagine the atmosphere of jealousy, suspicion and intrigue which embittered the relations between the various secret and semi-secret departments in Cairo during that summer of 1941, or for that matter, the next two years.'[42]

Within SOE itself the most notorious split of all was over Yugoslavia, and concerned the relative merits of Tito and Mihailovich. Churchill had sent a Tory MP, Fitzroy Maclean, to Yugoslavia to assess which leader was more effective against the Germans. Maclean reported that Tito was, and would win, but he had to warn the Prime Minister that Tito's Yugoslavia would be communist. Churchill, always pragmatic, asked Maclean: 'Are you going to live there?' When Maclean answered 'no', Churchill went on: 'Neither am I, so hadn't we better leave the Yugoslavs themselves to work out what sort of system they are going to have.'[43]

Churchill, who had periods when he distrusted SOE, decided on this occasion to bypass it, and he empowered Maclean to go to Tito as his own personal representative and ensure that SOE gave Tito the support that he needed. But some SOE officers had other ideas.

They felt that the communist James Klugman, who was attached

* No figures are available, but Churchill is said to have remarked: 'The great thing about Menzies is that, unlike SOE, he runs his service on pennies.'

to SOE's Cairo staff, and his left-wing associates – one SOE liaison officer with Mihailovich claimed in 1983 that SOE headquarters in Cairo had been 'a heap of Soviet moles' –[44] had sabotaged Mihailovich by losing or delaying his wireless messages requesting arms. It was a game two could play. Someone who was against Maclean's appointment sent Churchill a signal in the name of General Sir Henry Maitland Wilson, Commander-in-Chief in the Middle East, saying that Maclean was totally unsuitable for the job. (Wilson was furious when he found out.) Another of Maclean's enemies in SOE asked a black propaganda department to spread a whisper all around Cairo that Maclean was an alcoholic, a coward and an active homosexual. (Fortunately, the head of propaganda checked with General Wilson before starting the rumour.)

Maclean was dropped into Yugoslavia, taking care, he said later, not to accept the first parachute that SOE offered him. There he used his own separate and secret radio link from Tito's headquarters direct to General Wilson and Churchill because he did not trust elements in SOE, Cairo, to pass his messages to his superiors. The Americans were later drawn into this feud; they, too, divided into Tito supporters and Mihailovich supporters and, again, the two sides have continued the feud to this day.

Another failure was not to foresee what might happen to the arms and explosives that SOE had dropped all over Europe, and to the training and expertise it had supplied. SOE arms were smuggled from Greece to Cyprus and used against the British there. Palestinian Jews were trained by SOE in sabotage and subversion in case the Germans should occupy the country, and thus provided expertise to the Haganah, which no doubt was invaluable to that organization when it carried out SOE-type operations against the British in Palestine in 1946–7.[45]

The main trouble with SOE, however, was that it outlived its usefulness almost as soon as it was formed. The great equivocation at the heart of its policy – encouraging European liberation movements, while at the same time believing in the need for the restoration of the *status quo ante bellum* – destroyed its credibility. And even if its aims had been realistic there would never have been sufficient aircraft to achieve them. Finally, the United States' entry into the war, with its enormous production potential and its huge armies, plus the drain on German resources which the Soviet Union's resistance was exacting on the Eastern Front, altered Allied strategy. There was no longer any need to beat Hitler from within by detonating an explosion in Occupied Europe: the Allies would take it by superiority in men and materials. From then on, SOE was neglected and ceased to play a major role in Allied plans against Germany.

It had a brief renaissance when Britain and the United States were forced to contemplate a war with their former ally, the Soviet Union, and SOE was ordered to be ready to create resistance movements in countries which might be occupied by the Russians in such a war. But nothing happened and, in 1946, SIS reasserted its right to be Britain's sole secret service. On 30 June of that year SOE was officially disbanded. Its usefulness was outweighed by its failures, its military value was negligible, and the Allies would probably have been better off without it.

If SOE is remembered, it is largely because of the two hundred or so books about it, many by SOE officers themselves. As historian Anthony Verrier says, the real SOE 'bore little resemblance to an organization which remains associated in popular imagination with the liberation of Western Europe from Nazi occupation'.[46] The romantic fantasies of Buchan fans die hard.

# 7. Cross and Double Cross

> Plan Jael was renamed Bodyguard, a *ruse de guerre* that
> would come to be compared with the Trojan Horse.
> – Anthony Cave Brown, *Bodyguard of Lies* (1977).

> Military historians have developed a strong resistance to
> the story that ascribes the success of D-Day, for
> example, to the machinations of men with musical
> comedy names now allegedly forced to hide from
> neo-Nazi vengeance in remoter parts of Latin America.
> – John Keegan, *Sunday Times*, 12 August 1984.

On 9 November 1939, two months after the outbreak of war, two SIS officers, Captain Sigismund Payne Best, who had served in military intelligence in the First World War, and Major Richard Stevens, the head of the SIS station at The Hague, were kidnapped at gunpoint in the village of Venlo on the Dutch frontier and whisked into Germany. The British records relating to this incident remain closed for one hundred years and the German ones are unrevealing, but the basic facts are not in dispute.

Briefly, Best and Stevens believed that through one of SIS's agents in Holland, Dr Franz Fischer, they had established contact with a German opposition group which was anxious to overthrow Hitler and end the war. Unknown to them, Fischer was a double agent employed by the Gestapo. After a series of meetings designed to establish everyone's bona fides, the British officers pressed to be allowed to see the German general who was alleged to be leading the conspiracy against Hitler. A meeting was set for a café in the town of Venlo, only a few yards from the German border. Best and Stevens, accompanied by a Dutch intelligence officer, Lieutenant Dirk Klop, travelled together to Venlo for the vital conference. Klop had taken the precaution of arranging for protection from the local police, but the Englishmen and the Dutchman were late and, worried that they might miss the German general, drove to the rendezvous without giving the local police time to take up their positions.

Best, Stevens and Klop had barely parked when a large German car came roaring through the customs barrier, carrying several men armed with sub-machine-guns on the running boards. Klop reacted quickly. He jumped from the car, drew his revolver and ran towards the main road, firing at the Germans as he did so. But he was shot down, mortally wounded, when he had gone only a few yards. Best and Stevens were then ordered out of their car at gunpoint, their revolvers were taken from them and they were frogmarched across the border. There the Germans bundled them and the dying Klop into cars and they were driven at high speed to Düsseldorf.

The affair was an embarrassment to everyone; for SIS it was a humiliating disaster. The fact that it had been duped so easily made it reluctant even to admit that Best and Stevens were in the secret service. The Dutch government covered up its collusion with the British during a time of tension with Germany by disclaiming all responsibility for Best and Stevens, and by explaining Klop's presence as an error of judgement on the part of its intelligence chief, who was promptly sacked. Even the Germans were anxious to forget the incident. It exacerbated the strained relations that existed between the Abwehr, which had known little of the operation until it was well underway, and the Gestapo, which gloated over its triumph. (The triumph was short-lived, however, because although Hitler was anxious to link Venlo and the British to the Munich bomb attempt on his life, the Gestapo was unable to come up with any evidence for such a conspiracy.)

Best and Stevens survived the war and were found in April 1945 in a small village in the German Tyrol. They had not been able to resist Gestapo interrogation and had been the Germans' main source of information for the SIS order of battle. (Ellis, as we have seen, was another.) This had helped the Germans to prepare a document entitled *Informationsheft Grossbritannien* which contained a list, including a large number of SIS staff and their agents, of people whom the Gestapo planned to arrest when Hitler invaded Britain. Another section of the document, headed *Der Britische Nachrichtendienst*, described in detail the organizational structure of SIS, the headquarters, its sections and their duties, and even reproduced passport photographs of some SIS officers. Best and Stevens admitted giving information to the Gestapo – it would have been difficult to deny it, as the Germans had published a full acount of the affair at the time, including the list of SIS officers named by Best and Stevens. SIS decided not to prosecute them, but neither was offered further employment.[1]

The drama of the Venlo incident has led a succession of writers to concentrate on what happened, rather than on the motives of those involved in the affair. But it is only when we examine what Best, Stevens and the Germans thought they were *really* up to, that an unexpected and important political dimension to this intelligence operation emerges. In order to appreciate this, and to place it in context, we need to go briefly back to that ominous European summer of 1939 when there still remained hope, however slender, that war could be averted.

The German people were not 100 per cent behind Hitler. There was political opposition – a loose coalition of all other parties from Social Democrats to Conservatives – and military anxiety about the prospect of Germany becoming involved in another world war. Hitler's critics and opponents looked to Britain for encouragement but had, at that time, to tread a narrow path. On the one hand, they wanted Britain to show sufficient determination to deter Hitler from further military adventures, but not to do anything that would provoke a warlike response. This was a message, they felt, best conveyed through secret channels. So, in July, Colonel Count Gerhardt von Schwerin of the German General Staff arrived in London with an introduction to David Astor (later to become editor of the *Observer*) from Adam von Trott, who acted as a spokesman for the German opposition.

Von Schwerin spelt out exactly what Britain could do to convince Hitler that his present course would lead to war. Astor was so impressed that he arranged an appointment with SIS, hoping that it would agree to meet von Schwerin. Instead, a senior officer told him, 'I know who this man is; and if you want to know what I think of his coming over here, at a time when our country's relations with his are as bad as they are today, I think it's a damned cheek.'[2]

But the contact, indirect and unsatisfactory though it may have been, had been made, and it was duly noted in SIS that anti-Hitler elements did exist and apparently wanted to make approaches to SIS. This was confirmed by moves initiated soon after the outbreak of war. In Rome, Vatican officials were approached by the Germans to see if Pope Pius XII would act as an intermediary in securing a fair and honourable peace.[3] In Britain and – after war had started – in the United States, John Wheeler-Bennett, a leading British authority on the German army, had long talks with von Trott about British co-operation with the German opposition.[4] The desire for a deal with Germany, with or without the overthrow of Hitler, was to grow rapidly in the winter of 1939–40 but, at this stage, we are concerned with SIS's reaction immediately after the outbreak of war on 3 September 1939.

It began to bombard the Foreign Secretary, Lord Halifax,

with reports of dissension within Germany. On 11 September, for example, Halifax told the War Cabinet that, according to a secret source, very valuable results might be secured if Britain made a direct appeal to the German army 'along certain lines'. On 23 October he told the Cabinet that there was a lot of internal conflict in Germany and, four days later, that there was acute disagreement between Hitler and the German army. There was a general feeling that circumstances might come about in which it could be possible to achieve a quick end to the war and, with SIS encouragement, it became official policy to encourage dissent in Germany 'and then see what happens'.[5]

This was more easily ordered than done. Instructions were passed down the line and eventually stopped with Best in The Hague. In Holland, since the end of the First World War, Best had become a larger-than-life figure. He had acquired a Dutch wife, an export-import firm dealing in pharmaceuticals and bicycles and, for the Dutch, an eccentric manner: he wore spats and a monocle, and spoke in a loud, domineering voice. There was some doubt as to what, exactly, his relationship with SIS was. Stevens, who was head of station, had believed Best to be what he appeared: a prosperous expatriate businessman. But on the first day of the war, Best walked into Stevens's office and revealed himself as the local representative of the 'Z' organization, a super-secret branch of SIS run by the amazing figure of Claude Dansey.

Dansey, a former soldier, country club proprietor, and then MI5 officer, had joined SIS only to fall out with his chief, Sinclair, allegedly over some financial mismanagement. Sinclair, unable to stand Dansey in the office, got rid of him by allowing him to create his 'Z' network of amateur spies, mostly businessmen and journalists. They worked for little or nothing, and were controlled by Dansey – 'a man who thinks nine ways at once' – from a small office in Bush House, Aldwych. If the 'Z' organization had any good officers, then Best was certainly not one of them. Of thirteen 'head agents' which Best claimed to be running, eight turned out to be fictitious, and the considerable expenses those fictitious agents incurred had mysteriously found their way into Best's pocket.[6]

But one of the 'genuine' agents was Fischer who, as we have seen, was also working for the Gestapo. It is easier to understand what followed if we see events through Fischer's eyes. One of his employers, the British, had told him that they wanted to make contact with opposition groups in Germany to discuss possible peace negotiations. Fischer now faced two choices. He could do as Best wanted and say nothing to his other employers, the Germans, or he could reveal all to them. Fischer did not hesitate. Much of his political espionage for the Germans since Munich had been concerned with peace sentiment in Europe, so by telling them of his orders from the British he would be endearing himself to both his masters.[7]

Not unexpectedly, the Germans were happy to use Fischer as a go-between. They could see that they had nothing to lose by pursuing the contact. At the very least, they would learn something about SIS operations in the Netherlands. If negotiations were spun out, they might also learn something of SIS headquarters in London. But there were much higher stakes on the table. The peace overtures might be genuine. They might even provide a basis for a settlement between Germany and Britain that would be of mutual advantage. Fischer was working for the Gestapo and its head, Himmler, regarded the war with Britain as unnecessary. He felt that Germany's true mission was in the East, in the conquest of the Soviet Union. The war with Britain was a squabble between relatives that could be settled by common sense on both sides. Other German leaders agreed with him. Goering had encouraged Prince Hohenlohe, a Sudeten aristocrat, to contact his British friends and discuss peace terms with them. At one such meeting in Switzerland a month after the outbreak of war, Hohenlohe and retired Group Captain Malcolm Christie discussed a compromise peace which would free Germany to cope with the threat of Bolshevism.[8]

It is significant that the officer the Germans selected to run the operation was Walther Schellenberg, head of the Gestapo's counter-espionage section, a young intellectual who was in favour of a compromise with Britain because 'only Stalin can benefit from a European War'. At a meeting with Best and Stevens in The Hague on 30 October, some sort of an agreement on peace terms emerged. Hitler was to remain head of the German government for the time being; Ribbentrop would go, but a role would be found for Goering. Austria, Czechoslovakia and Poland would be restored and there would be a united anti-Soviet front. According to Schellenberg, Stevens referred these terms to the Foreign Office, Halifax approved them, and there was talk of another meeting in London to finalize an agreement.[9] The intriguing question at this stage is: How much did the British War Cabinet know about all this?

Chamberlain certainly knew of the meetings, but it would appear that, in presenting their account to him, SIS had laid more emphasis on the uncovering of a military conspiracy against Hitler than on peace negotiations. (But Chamberlain must have had some knowledge of the German terms, for on 5 November, in a letter to his sister predicting an early end to the war, he wrote that the Germans 'might have instant relief and *perhaps not have to give up anything they really care about*' – emphasis added.) On 1 November the War Cabinet was told about these secret negotiations for the first time. It was not happy with the news and Churchill, for one, wanted all contact with the Germans broken off at once. But it was, none the less, decided to continue with the operation. There remains some doubt as to whether all the members of the British War Cabinet knew all the story. SIS appears to have fudged the issue of whether the terms so far discussed firmly provided for the removal of Hitler. One man at the centre of the negotiations, Best, was in no doubt. As far as he knew, he said later, 'Adolf Hitler was to remain in power'. [10]

Hitler certainly knew of the discussions and approved of them. He had himself offered a compromise peace to Britain on 6 October, and without his agreement it seems unlikely that Himmler would have felt confident in instructing Schellenberg to pursue the peace negotiations as he thought fit. But, by early November, Hitler began to have second thoughts. His plans for an offensive against Britain and France were well advanced and further talk of peace began to smack of defeatism. Himmler, aware of his leader's views, decided that the operation should be wound up but, hoping to maximize any benefit, gave orders for the kidnapping of Best and Stevens. As we have seen, the Gestapo executed these orders with great efficiency on 9 November.

Schellenberg remained in secret radio contact with SIS for another fortnight, perhaps hoping that the political figures behind Best and Stevens might still wish to continue negotiations. But on 29 November he radioed from Berlin breaking off the last link. He did his best to protect Best and Stevens from a political show trial and even suggested that they should be exchanged for German prisoners. [11] (Schellenberg was rewarded after the war. Tried at Nuremberg, he was sentenced to only six years' imprisonment, of which he served two.)

But why should SIS have believed that the British government might have gone along with a settlement with the Germans when it did not necessarily include the removal of Hitler? The answer is that within SIS and in certain sections of the British establishment – a small but potentially powerful minority – there was agreement with the German view that both countries were fighting the wrong war, that the 'right' war would involve Germany and Britain fighting together against the Soviet Union.

Thus it was probably unfair for the British government to heap all the blame for the Venlo fiasco on SIS, adding yet another black mark to the service's record. Another consequence was that British policy towards German opposition to Hitler changed. From actively seeking out dissenters and peace supporters in Germany, Britain now adopted a passive role and treated any approach with extreme scepticism lest it prove to be another Gestapo plot. Churchill, in a directive issued shortly after he became Prime Minister in May 1940, wrote: 'Foreign Secretary: I hope it will be made clear to the [Papal] Nuncio that we do not desire to make any enquiries as to the terms of a peace with Hitler and that all our agents are strictly forbidden to entertain any such suggestions.'[12]

In May 1941 Hitler's deputy, Rudolph Hess, made his dramatic flight to Britain, apparently under the impression that he would be well received. He came armed with a list of prominent people in Britain whom he believed would be interested in a peace pact and an alliance with Germany now that Hitler was about to attack the Soviet Union.\* His list was out of date, and many people on it had swung behind Churchill's war effort during the Battle of Britain. But Hess's arrival was still embarrassing. Churchill had a reasonably united country and the last thing he wanted was for people to start asking the obvious question: Why did Hess imagine that his peace mission would be well received? Was it possible, for example, that Hess had come not because he was mad – as Churchill put out – but because he had been *invited* by a pro-Hitler faction in Britain?† This was certainly the explanation that the Soviet leaders considered, and Stalin became very suspicious after Hess's flight that Britain and Germany were about to do a deal. The last thing that Churchill wanted was SIS to complicate an already delicate situation, so, significantly, no SIS officer was allowed near Hess to interrogate him. Churchill himself took all the decisions about Hess and the main interrogations were carried out by politicians and Foreign Office mandarins.[14] SIS's role at Venlo had not been forgotten.

\* Harold Balfour, Under-Secretary of State in the Air Ministry; Kenneth Lindsay, an MP; Lord Dunglass (the present Lord Home); the Duke of Hamilton; Jim Wedderburn, Under-Secretary of State for Scotland; R. A. Butler, Under-Secretary of State at the Foreign Office; the late Lord Lothian, former British ambassador in Washington; Owen O'Malley, former British Minister to Hungary; Lord Halifax, at the time British ambassador in Washington; Lord Eustace Percy, an influential member of the Conservative Party; Sir Samuel Hoare, British ambassador in Madrid; and the Hon. J. J. Astor, owner of *The Times*.[13]

† This would explain Britain's ambivalent attitude towards Hess's imprisonment after the war. Although she blamed the Soviet Union for refusing to consider his release on grounds of his advanced age and deteriorating health, she did not make an issue out of it. It is one thing to say that Hess came of his own volition on his peace mission, and then to argue that he was mistaken in imagining that he would be well received. If Hess, however, were able to prove that he had been *invited* by prominent Britons, this argument collapses.

Its confidence shattered by its failures, SIS staggered through the war years in a state of internal strife and preoccupied by its war with SOE. It became so suspicious that the Germans were constantly trying to set it up for another Venlo that genuine approaches were rebuffed out of hand and first-class information disbelieved and dismissed. The best example of the latter is undoubtedly the Oslo report, probably the most remarkable intelligence document of the war. It was of enormous help to Britain, especially in scientific fields, but this benefit occurred in spite of SIS, rather than because of it.[15]

The report arrived at the British embassy in Oslo as a small, hand-delivered packet on 3 November 1939. It was expected. A week earlier, in a letter addressed to the naval attaché, Captain Hector Boyes, an anonymous Abwehr officer offered to provide important technical data if Boyes would indicate that it would be welcome. (This was done by a minor alteration to the BBC's German news broadcast.)

The SIS station chief, Commander J. B. Newill, immediately read the document. In retrospect it can be seen how sensational the information was. There were details of new fuses for bombs and shells, guided torpedoes, aircraft range finders, radar, remote-controlled shells, and the new Junkers 88 long-range bomber programme. But the choicest item concerned a testing range at Peenemunde where, the report said, the Germans were developing small remote-controlled aircraft which would carry a large explosive charge – a clear indication of the birth of the V1 and V2 weapons. Newill sent the report to London where it landed on the desk of the head of the air section of SIS, Wing Commander Winterbotham.

Winterbotham read it with some scepticism, but realizing that he did not have the scientific background to assess it properly,* he passed it on to Dr R. V. Jones, a scientist working on research for the Air Ministry. Jones studied the document and reported that it was genuine and very important. Not a soul in SIS believed him: the report was seen as a plant, another Gestapo trick. No single German, it was argued, could be so well informed about so many different subjects, and if some of the information survived the test of scientific scrutiny, then this was simply because the cunning Germans were using the old trick of giving something genuine away in order to make the rest seem convincing. Time proved the SIS

* Neither did anyone else in SIS. In a war in which science was to play such a major part, SIS had no scientific section.

136

assessment to be false, and nearly every detail of the Oslo report turned out to be genuine. But, by then, the Abwehr officer who had written it had vanished, no doubt wondering why no attempt had been made to acknowledge his material or to exploit the window he had opened.[16]

The damage done by this overcautious reaction was compounded in 1942 when Lisbon SIS station debriefed a central European who had escaped from a German slave labour camp. He told SIS that he had been working at a German research establishment on the Baltic near Peenemunde, and that although the project was secret it appeared to have something to do with rockets. Lisbon forwarded the debriefing to London where it was read by the case officer, Basil Fenwick, a one-time Royal Dutch Shell executive who had been part of Dansey's 'Z' network. Because of the 'need to know' principle, Fenwick had not been told of the Oslo report and so the slave labourer's statement meant nothing to him. He might have attached more importance to it if Lisbon had not had a reputation for acrimonious disputes and poor accuracy. As it was, he told Lisbon to treat the labourer's information as a plant. By the time someone at SIS who did know about Peenemunde had made the connection, the labourer had vanished into Portugal's teeming refugee community and the SIS station's frantic efforts to find him came to nothing.[17]

Such failures were by no means exceptional. SIS received warnings well in advance that the Germans planned to invade Belgium and Holland, but discounted the information. The first news came from the SIS station chief in Brussels, Colonel Edward Calthrop, who had a contact in the Belgian police. The contact passed to Calthrop some maps taken from a German military aircraft which had made a forced landing in Belgian territory. The maps appeared to be part of a plan for the invasion of Holland and Belgium, and the information they provided seemed to be confirmed by a Colonel Hans Oster, the deputy chief of the Abwehr, who was strongly anti-Nazi. Oster was a friend of the Dutch assistant military attaché in Berlin and had earlier given him warning of the German invasion of Poland. Now, in early May 1940, Oster warned that Hitler was preparing to attack Holland and Belgium. But, still smarting from Venlo, neither the Netherlands intelligence service, nor SIS, to whom Oster's tip was passed, believed the news. SIS decided that the German maps were forgeries and that Oster was playing a game with them. Their error became obvious when, on 10 May, German troops poured into Holland, Belgium and Luxembourg.[18]

Other information that could have had an important influence on events seemed to reach SIS without trouble, but then vanish into the cigar smoke. An SIS agent network in Vichy, France, code named 'Alliance', which had produced excellent information in the past, began in January 1942 to send regular situation reports on the state of readiness of the two German battle cruisers, *Scharnhorst* and *Gneisenau*, then in Brest. Two weeks before the ships broke out of Brest, prepared to fight their way up the Channel to their home port in Germany, an Alliance agent got a message to SIS in London via Madrid warning that they would sail at any time. It is unclear whether SIS sat on the report or passed it on to the navy which, in any case, was relying more on intercepts of German radio traffic to learn of the ships' departure. In the event, both ships, in convoy with the cruiser *Prinz Eugen*, left Brest on 12 February, boldly sailed through the Straits of Dover and docked safely in Wilhelmshaven some twenty-four hours later. The RAF had lost the only real opportunity it would ever get to attack German capital ships at sea; and the two battle cruisers were to be a constant threat to the Allied convoys making their way round the North Cape and the Soviet Union for many months to come.[19]

Another SIS report which proved to be absolutely correct seems simply to have got lost in the corridors of Whitehall. In the summer of 1940 there was increasing evidence that the situation in Iraq was deteriorating, as a result of powerful nationalist propaganda, and that the pro-British regent might be overthrown by German-backed elements. In the first three months of 1941, the SIS station in Baghdad poured out a stream of reports warning of a possible coup, and on 31 March emphasized that it was imminent. Three days later the coup took place. The British forces were caught unprepared and the regent had to flee the capital. SIS was quick to complain – Menzies went straight to Churchill – that the Eastern department of the Foreign Office had sat on its reports and had failed to forward them to the armed services.[20]

In one instance, a valuable source who had been rejected by the British – on the suspicion, yet again, of a German plot – walked across the street to the Americans and was given an enthusiastic welcome. This embarrassing episode happened in Switzerland in 1943. On 23 August of that year a German Foreign Ministry official, Dr Fritz Kolbe, arrived at the British Legation to see the military attaché, Colonel Henry Cartwright. Cartwright also represented MI9, the organization which helped and debriefed escapers from Germany. Cartwright's cover role was, however, well known in neutral Switzerland and the Abwehr had tried on several occasions to plant an agent on him for its own devious purposes. This had made

Cartwright very suspicious of 'walk-ins', and when Kolbe virtually came in off the street and said he wanted to help the Allies, Cartwright was on his guard.

Kolbe said that he was highly placed in the German Foreign Ministry, but that he was very anti-Nazi. He had taken advantage of his position to steal copies of secret documents from his office in Berlin and to bring them to Berne. He produced a bundle of these documents and said that he had hidden hundreds more. Cartwright did not even bother to read them. He decided that Kolbe was an Abwehr plant and a thief to boot. He had the German thrown out of the legation. Kolbe, amazed at the British reaction, mentioned the incident to a friend, who suggested that he try the Americans. The next day Kolbe called on Allen Dulles, special legal assistant to the American Minister. Kolbe now produced 183 flimsy file copies of German Foreign Ministry telegrams, left them with Dulles, who expressed great interest, and promised to return with more when he had a chance.

On 7 October, Kolbe came back with more flimsies and during the next sixteen months made three further visits to deliver in total more than 1,500 secret German documents. They provided a useful insight into the intentions of the German Foreign Ministry. Even though the Allies had to be sparing in the use of Kolbe's information, lest it reveal to the Germans the presence of a traitor in the ministry, he was, according to one American intelligence officer, 'one of the best secret agents any intelligence service ever had'. Kolbe remained in place and above suspicion until April 1945 when, as Germany collapsed, he managed to slip over the border into Switzerland. (He later gave evidence for the prosecution at the Nuremberg trials.)[21]

Of course, Kolbe *could* have been an Abwehr plant. (One reason for such an operation would have been to break Allied codes. When Dulles or SIS sent the contents of the telegram flimsies to London and Washington by wireless in code then the Germans could intercept the message and, since they knew the contents of the flimsies, would have been in a good position to work out the code that the Allies were using.) Or he could have been a confidence trickster interested only in money. The intelligence world abounded with such types – and still does. Many examples can be cited, among them the following cases.

The Czech government in exile ran a bureau in Lisbon during the war and, through its networks in France, provided SIS with a lot of material. But the second in command of the Czech network was also working for the Abwehr. When SIS found out, it fired him, although the damage had already been done. Undeterred, the double agent promptly got himself engaged by the Americans.

There was a waiter on the Taurus express, which ran from Istanbul to Baghdad, who was, in his own way, a classic case. He was recruited by SIS, but his trustworthiness was put in doubt after it was discovered that he had also been recruited by the Germans, the Italians, the Hungarians and the Japanese! His real loyalty probably remained with the Turks, because he was also a major in the Turkish army.

But for a real insight into the sordid world of espionage with its easily bought loyalties, loose morals, mind-boggling complexities and, if it were not for its murderous consequences, comic inanity, it is hard to do better than look at the case of William John Hooper, an intelligence agent for Britain or Germany (Hooper himself was unsure) in the Netherlands on the eve of the outbreak of war.

Hooper, a Dutch native, was a naturalized Englishman. He worked for SIS in Rotterdam, reporting to the station chief in The Hague. Among the many lucrative rackets that Hooper was engaged in were false sub-agents, padded expenses and dodgy information sold more than once. This came to light only after the senior SIS man in the Netherlands, Major Hugh Dalton, had committed suicide.

Dalton, who worked under cover as chief passport officer, found cover work beginning to overwhelm his intelligence duties when Jewish refugees, desperate for visas to Palestine, besieged his office. As a result, he ceased to gather intelligence but, worse still, he was tempted by the large sums of money the Jews were prepared to pay for their travel documents and helped himself to some £3,000 in bribes. Hooper somehow got to hear of Dalton's embezzlement and began blackmailing him. Dalton paid up for a while and then, in September 1936, put a revolver to his head and shot himself.[22]

London sent a two-man team to investigate Dalton's suicide which uncovered not only Dalton's visa racket, but also Hooper's blackmailing activities. He was immediately fired. (Dansey wanted him executed!) Apparently undismayed by his exposure, Hooper went to work for the Abwehr, at first as a casual agent and, later, as a senior officer. He won the Abwehr's trust by giving it the name of an important SIS agent in Germany, a retired naval officer who was arrested in July 1939, and who later committed suicide in his cell. The Hague SIS did not, of course, know of this betrayal when, just before the outbreak of war, Hooper approached them, confessing that he had been working for the Germans but claiming that now he wanted to work for the British again. He was, therefore, promptly re-engaged and told to play the double – to continue to pretend to be loyal to the Abwehr.

The complexities of this game did not end here. The Germans had managed to infiltrate a Dutch agent into SIS in the Netherlands, who reported to them what Hooper had done – that he was again in SIS's employ. It is possible that the Germans confronted Hooper with this and 'turned' him yet again. This would have meant that the British thought Hooper, originally their agent, had gone over to the Germans who then thought that he was working for them, when in fact he had come back to the British who were now using him as a spy in the German camp. In reality, however, Hooper was yet again working for the Germans who were using him as a spy in the British camp. Alternatively, the Germans did not bother to further complicate the charade and simply used Hooper to feed false and misleading information to the British.

Either way, Hooper was useless to SIS, and after Venlo when he automatically became suspect, Dansey again argued that he should be 'eliminated'. Instead, when SIS evacuated the Netherlands, Hooper and his family were brought to Britain and billeted with a senior SIS officer near Bletchley. Amazingly, SIS briefly considered infiltrating Hooper back into the Netherlands to continue his career as a double agent, but finally dropped the idea. Heaven knows what the result of this crazy scheme would have been, or where Hooper's loyalties now lay – if anywhere. SIS officers, who learnt the full extent of Hooper's dealings only after the war, have since claimed that there is no record of what happened to Hooper after his return to Britain, of what he did during the rest of the war, or of how he spent the rest of his life – he was only 42 when the war ended. One is left with the suspicion that Dansey's view on what to do with Hooper might in the end have prevailed.*[23]

The war, however, was not one long list of failures for SIS. It also had its share of successes, mostly minor ones. One of its recruits, an Indian army officer, Gulzar Ahmed – working under cover as a censor at the British consulate in Istanbul – was also employed by the Abwehr, but remained loyal to SIS and became one of the best double agents of the war. His information enabled other Abwehr agents to be identified and some of these were successfully 'turned'. A network of agents run by a priest in Bordeaux, which included other priests and many nuns, provided first-class information,

* The fact that an SIS agent had worked for the Germans did not, in SIS eyes, disqualify him from further employment. F. A. Van Koutrik had been a paid agent of SIS and the Abwehr before the invasion of the Netherlands. In Britain he was employed, until August 1943, on checking the credentials of refugees.[24]

especially about German troop movements. The Stockholm SIS station had a successful war and Cairo ran some excellent deception operations.

But SIS's main successes all shared one ominous common factor – the Abwehr was involved. We have already seen how the most important scientific intelligence coup of the war – the Oslo report – was handed to SIS on a platter by an anonymous Abwehr officer, and how the deputy chief of the Abwehr, Colonel Oster, told the Allies of forthcoming German military actions. However, to understand why it was really the Abwehr that was behind other British intelligence successes, we need to examine briefly the state of German intelligence at that time.

I f British intelligence organizations were riddled with wartime factionism and rivalry, those in Germany were just as bad. The prospect of imminent war had, if anything, increased the fissiparous tendencies of German intelligence. The Abwehr found itself isolated and increasingly thwarted by the Reich Security Administration (RSHA); both were held in contempt by Ribbentrop's Foreign Ministry intelligence section; each carried on a running feud with the other; and rival groups flourished *within* each organization.[25]

No German service had officers with sufficient experience of the United States and Britain to enable them properly to evaluate the intelligence that their agents collected, and all the services faced a major problem with their leaders – any report implying an Allied success was discarded as being defeatist, and its authors treated as near traitors. Hitler himself, though he had Churchillian fantasies about the importance of intelligence, made very little use of it and was reluctant even to hear anything which did not accord with his own evaluations. As can be imagined, this was no incentive to accurate, frank assessment – assuming, of course, that the input from agents was worthwhile in the first place. Frequently it was not.

Immediately after the war, Allied intelligence teams scoured German intelligence files, where these survived, and interviewed intelligence officers who were still alive. A report by one of these teams appeared in an Allied intelligence summary in the summer of 1945. Part of it read:

> It is obvious that the best type of agent is one who works from an idealistic motive and not from fear or financial reward. But virtually the only people of this type in the Reich were the party elite, and in

the nature of things few if any of them had any knowledge whatsoever of the British or American peoples and would have been far too conspicuous to be of much value abroad. Except in rare cases, therefore, the GIS [German Intelligence Service] had to recruit its agents not from idealists, but from the fearful, the avaricious and the opportunists.[26]

Thus German intelligence, too, was forced to rely upon agents who were frauds and confidence tricksters. Men like Karl-Heinz Krämer, the Stockholm Abwehr officer who, it emerged, gathered most of his information from newspapers and from aircraft manuals freely available in Swedish bookshops, or the senior official of Spanish military intelligence who also worked for the Abwehr, recruited by it especially to provide access to the Spanish agent network in London. When SIS managed to get access to this man's safe it discovered that many of his 'agents' in London existed only in his imagination and that his reports to the Abwehr were complete fiction.[27]

Even the story of the famous 'Cicero', the valet to the British ambassador in Ankara, Sir Hughe Knatchbull-Hugessen, turns out not to be quite the unqualified German success that was portrayed in the movie about him. 'Cicero', whose real name was Elyesa Bazna, had keys to the ambassador's safe and dispatch box and when Sir Hughe was safely in bed Bazna would photograph the contents of the safe and box, and sell the film to the Gestapo. He disappeared – with £200,000 from the Germans, but in forged notes – when a British security check, initiated by intercepts of German direct cypher telegrams from Ankara to Berlin which quoted the stolen material, began to get too close to him. The German payment to Bazna was false but his information was genuine and valuable. However, the Gestapo felt that the whole operation was too good to be true and must be a British game, so unless Bazna's information was confirmed from other sources – which seldom happened – they took the precaution of ignoring it.[28]

It was much the same story with Hitler's spies in the United States. They were interested in any disputes between Churchill and Roosevelt, the extent of American aid, war production figures and technological developments. Although their efforts were the subject of several books, published both at the time and subsequently, these were highly exaggerated. The German spies gathered little intelligence of any use and what they did get was frequently ignored by their employers. Edmund Heine confessed at his trial that he had gathered his information from scientific and technical publications on open sale. German scientists were quick to notice this and came to rely on their own research rather than on espionage. By the end of 1942 German espionage in the United States had virtually ended. Historian Hans L. Trefousse says, 'Despite the time, money and effort expended on its activities, the German intelligence service in America neither contributed materially to Hitler's power nor seriously impaired the contribution made by the United States in bringing about his destruction.'[29]

If SIS was uncertain of how the Abwehr was organized and run, then the German intelligence services, despite their success at Venlo, were not entirely sure about SIS. They could not believe that the famed British secret service could be as inefficient as it appeared, and thought either that there must be some super-secret organization which lay behind the façade, or that British perfidy was at work again. Thus they felt that if they took SIS at face value they would be led into some terrible trap.

The exception was a small but influential group of anti-Nazis within the Abwehr. The precise role of this faction has remained unclear and still creates considerable controversy. It is not difficult to see why. If the core of German resistance to Hitler was in the Abwehr, if this core was working secretly to help the overthrow of the Führer, then British successes against the Abwehr have to be seen in a new light. The crucial question becomes: Was British intelligence pushing at an open door?

One of the much-lauded triumphs of the intelligence war is the so-called double-cross operation. It is claimed that the British identified and captured every single German spy in Britain and then successfully 'turned' most of them, so as to use them for deception and disinformation. (The story is told in great detail in *The Double Cross System in the War of 1939 to 1945*, by Sir John Masterman.) Many spy books present the operation not only as a tribute to British astuteness but also as a consequence of German gullibility.

> Crucial to the successes of British intelligence during the Second World War was the remarkable fact that the Germans never suspected . . . that their entire espionage network in Britain had been taken over to be used against them [said the presenter in a BBC radio programme in 1980]. As the Third Reich entered its death throes in May 1945, it was still pathetically appealing to the agents who had betrayed it to stay in touch.[30]

That the *entire* German network in Britain was uncovered *and* 'turned' seems a remarkable claim to accept lightly; to go on to suggest that *no one* in Germany ever suspected that this had happened smacks of a victor's arrogance. A more sceptical look at the available evidence suggests that not everyone spying for Germany was even uncovered, much less 'turned' and, more important, that those who were uncovered were *meant* to be, and that – in some sense at least – they were 'turned' before they arrived in Britain.

The evidence for the existence of at least one German spy who was not exposed lies in an exchange of letters between an MI5 officer, Guy Liddell, and his contact at the American embassy in London, Herschel Johnson, early in 1940. In the first letter, headed 'Secret, personal, and confidential', Liddell wrote that the German secret service had been receiving from the embassy 'reports, sometimes two a day which contained practically everything from ambassador [Joseph] Kennedy's despatches to President Roosevelt, including reports of his interviews with British statesmen and officials'. Liddell stated that his source for this alarming story was an agent who had proved to be both reliable and accurate.

Johnson immediately passed on the story to Washington and, in doing so, ruled out the possibility that the leak was in the Berlin embassy. 'None of the ambassador's confidential telegrams were ever repeated to Berlin', he wrote. 'Either someone in this embassy or in the State Department is involved.' He went back to MI5 for more information and learnt that the British agent with whom the information had originated was an officer in the Abwehr. (Colonel Oster seems the most likely candidate, especially as MI5 described their man as being 'in constant touch with Admiral Canaris'.)

The British source had an acquaintance in Hess's office and had been visiting him there just before the war. A stenographer who did translations from English to German asked if she could leave because there was nothing in from the United States, and the Abwehr officer heard his acquaintance reply, 'No, the doctor is not dictating this afternoon'. There were few other clues. The British, who seemed to Johnson to be withholding something, would say only that the Abwehr officer had included in his report on 'the doctor' a lot of other material, all of which had proved to be correct; and that 'the doctor's' material came in regularly.[31]

Two months later, Johnson was no closer to identifying the source of the leak. In retrospect, the logical suspect would at first appear to be Tyler Kent, a code clerk in the American embassy in London. Kent was arrested on 20 May 1940 and later imprisoned for seven years for stealing some 1,500 documents from the embassy's cypher room. But 'the doctor' could not have been Kent, for the simple reason that Kent did not arrive in Britain until 5 October 1939 and 'the doctor' had already been passing his information to the Germans at least as early as August of that year. Moreover, since Kent was arrested, interrogated and tried in Britain, it is reasonable to assume that if he had been 'the doctor' then MI5 would have got this out of him. Yet a former head of MI5 has said that 'as to the identity of "the doctor", my recollection is that we never did solve that problem'.

If we rule out Kent as 'the doctor' then who could he have been? The files relating to the case that have been declassified give no further clues to his identity. There is nothing in the British archives. One suspect is Dr Hans Thomsen, a German Foreign Office official who worked in the German embassy in Washington at the relevant time. Ladislas Farago says that he interviewed Thomsen in 1966. Thomsen told him that he had an agent who was friendly with an employee of the State Department's code room. This employee was an isolationist and he freely discussed what was in Ambassador Kennedy's cables with his friend, not realizing that he was a German agent. Thomsen said that the agent reported to him and that he passed the information to Berlin.[32] Thus Dr Thomsen could have been 'the doctor'.

On the other hand, some MI5 officers suspected at the time that the leaks originated from Ambassador Kennedy himself. He was an isolationist, anti-British; he thought Hitler would win the war and said so frequently. He had access, through Chamberlain and Churchill, to what he called 'the whole picture – figures on Britain's land, sea, and air forces, the disposition of British units everywhere, Britain's home inventory of war materials, her prospective war production, and the fundamentals of her strategic plans'.[33] Week by week he forwarded these to Roosevelt in coded telegrams. At this time, of course, the United States was neutral, and if Kennedy somehow made the information available to the Germans as well, then he was not breaking any American espionage laws. But in Britain, MI5 was certainly suspicious of him and had him under surveillance, and later passed dossiers on the Kennedy family to the American authorities.[34] Unless further files are released, which seems unlikely, then we shall now probably never know the truth.

The success of the double-cross system has to be gauged against the background of the Abwehr's attitude to Hitler and the war against Britain. The head of the Abwehr, Admiral Canaris, held strongly anti-Nazi views but he was loyal to Germany and it would have been out of character for him actively to have worked for the British. What he appears to have done, however, was to allow anti-Hitler elements to shelter within his organization and to protect them from the Gestapo. So certain sections of the Abwehr became centres of conspiracy against Hitler, allowed to function by Canaris as long as they concealed from him what they were doing. One such group was headed by Colonel Oster.[35]

Oster, as Chief of Staff, had control of the section which looked after the service's administration. It also held all the files which meant that it was in a position to suppress information, withhold adverse reports, and mislead senior officers – all vital functions in covering for officers who were, in effect, working for Britain. Probably the most important of these was A-54, Paul Thümmel, who had started giving information to the Allies before the war and who continued to do so, using Czech intermediaries in neutral countries, until he was arrested by the Gestapo in Prague in March 1942. (The Abwehr managed to arrange his release but a British-backed attempt to get him out of Czechoslovakia compromised him. The Gestapo arrested him again on a charge of treason and executed him in April 1945.) Thümmel passed information about Germany's order of battle, mobilization plans and equipment, and, later, details of Hitler's actions against Czechoslovakia, Poland, France, Romania, Greece and Yugoslavia.[36]

Those agents sent abroad on missions by the Abwehr and 'turned' by the British come into a different category. Their value lay not in the information they provided, but in their use as part of Allied deception plans. The accepted view is that, once caught, these agents were 'persuaded' to work against Germany, either by argument or the threat of execution – a captured spy's traditional fate. This may have been true of some Abwehr agents. Yet consider the following facts.

German agents were 'turned' in London and Cairo at about the same time in separate and distinct operations and without consultation between British intelligence in the two centres. Was this sheer coincidence? Or was it, as David Mure, an intelligence officer in the Middle East during the war, says, a case of the same hand turning both sets of German agents – 'from the Axis side, not ours'?

The Abwehr was remarkably effective when it wanted to be. Hitler might complain that the service told him little of what was going on with the Allies in the West, but on the Eastern Front this was not so. Reinhard Gehlen, who was to be postwar head of German intelligence, says that the Abwehr ran a 'highly efficient intelligence service in the East'. Yet in the case of the 'turned' agents in Britain and the Middle East the Abwehr behaved in such a cavalier manner that Mure, for one, became suspicious.

147

I had not been chairman of a deception committee controlling several agents for more than a couple of months before I began to suspect, from my own transmissions and from the study of previous traffic, that the complacency and inefficiency displayed by my opposite numbers might well be deliberate.[37]

Mure gives examples. An agent code named 'Lambert' was sent on his mission with £1,500. He gave himself up to the British and functioned for them as a double agent for three years before it was noticed that he had 'forgotten' to ask the Abwehr for more money to live on. Yet, if the Abwehr was to be believed, no officer there thought it odd that 'Lambert' had survived for so long on so little cash. Neither, apparently, did the Abwehr consider it strange that while Lambert got the *detail* of various operations right in his reports he was invariably wrong about the *larger picture* – as his deception committee intended. Mure writes, 'why did [the Abwehr] never question why our apparently accurate information always led them to make mistakes of interpretation?'[38]

Masterman tells of another incident which must, surely, be seen as clear evidence of Abwehr complicity in the double-cross system. A senior officer in the Abwehr got in touch with a British agent in Lisbon in 1941, and asked him to make contact with London on his behalf and to say that there was strong opposition to Hitler which could be exploited for the benefit of both sides. The British agent was ordered to ask the Abwehr officer what he wanted, and was given the reply that information was needed indicating great British power and bombing potential, as this would strengthen the hand of those opposing Hitler. This can only be seen as a case of a senior German officer pointedly asking the British to provide the Abwehr with misleading information.

But no case illustrates better that the Abwehr knew of the double-cross system, and went along with it, than that of Dusko Popov, code named 'Tricycle'. Popov was a young Yugoslav who, from prewar years, knew a German, Johann Jebsen, who had become an officer in the Abwehr. Jebsen subsequently recruited Popov to be a high-grade agent in Britain. Popov went to SIS and revealed everything and, in doing so, insisted that Jebsen had *instigated* the whole thing – that is, that Jebsen *knew* that Popov would go to the British and would, in fact, work for them. Since Jebsen himself was later recruited by the British, Popov's account certainly rings true. If we do believe it, we must also accept that, as early as 1940, the Abwehr had deliberately recruited an agent whom they knew would be 'turned', who would then supply them with misleading information, and through whom they could supply the British with truthful and useful information about Germany.

This convoluted approach to espionage proved too much for the head of the FBI, J. Edgar Hoover. In March 1941, the Abwehr suggested that Popov should get himself sent to the United States and start another high-grade spy ring there. Popov met Jebsen in Lisbon and Jebsen gave him two crucial pieces of information. First, he told him that the Japanese navy was urgently seeking full details of the British navy's torpedo bomber attack on the Italian fleet in Taranto in 1940, *because the Japanese were planning something similar*. And, secondly, Jebsen provided Popov with the Abwehr's latest technical development, the microdot communication system. He was to use this on his first assignment in the United States – to report on all installations and the means used to protect them, *at the American base at Pearl Harbor*.

Popov, perhaps with a touch of hindsight, says that he made the connection immediately: the Japanese were planning a surprise torpedo bomber attack on Pearl Harbor. Jebsen even provided the answer to the question of when this would happen. The Abwehr's assessment, he said, was that the American oil embargo on Japan would force the Japanese government to go to war before Japan's reserves fell below twelve months' supply. This put the likely date of an attack as early December, five months away.

Popov reported all this to his British spy masters who agreed with his conclusions. But, at this point, everything began to go wrong. Masterman's committee decided, quite correctly, that it was up to the Americans to make their own deductions from Popov's material. It was politically sensitive, in that Britain was anxious not to leave herself open to accusations from isolationist groups in the United States that she was trying her best to drag America into the war. But through what channels should Popov's information be passed? Here Popov's mission as a double agent and his information about Pearl Harbor became disastrously entwined.

Had Popov not been going to the United States to establish a notional German spy ring, then his Pearl Harbor information would almost certainly have been given to William Stephenson's organization in New York, the British Security Co-ordination (BSC), whose job it was to liaise between British and American intelligence services. It would then have been passed to the Office of the Co-ordinator of Information – the forerunner of the OSS and the CIA – which was in regular touch with BSC. Had it followed this route, Popov's warning would doubtlessly have eventually landed on the desk of President Roosevelt himself.

But Popov's mission was to keep his German employer's trust by establishing an espionage network in America. This, of course, would be bogus but unless the Americans were put in the picture, the FBI might spoil the whole plan by arresting Popov as a 'real' German spy. The FBI would have to be told and its co-operation sought. The diplomatic niceties now came into play. Guy Liddell of MI5 consulted with Menzies, the head of SIS, and it was agreed that it should be Liddell who would inform Hoover (the FBI and MI5 being, so to speak, sister services) and that it would be up to Hoover, after hearing Popov's information about Pearl Harbor, to pass it on to the appropriate American authorities.

Popov duly called at the FBI and told Hoover what he knew about the Japanese plans. Hoover ignored the warning. The MI5 officer who 'ran' Popov, T. A. ('Tar') Robertson, said later, 'No one ever dreamed that Hoover would be such a bloody fool'. The trouble was that Hoover hated Popov on sight. I asked Kim Philby, the KGB penetration officer who knew both men well, if he could explain why. He said, 'I've a theory that what really infuriated Hoover was Dusko's entanglement with Simone Simon [the French film star who was in the United States at that time]. Hoover hated Slavs, Jews, Catholics, homosexuals, liberals, blacks and the rest: they blinded him to his real job, luckily!'[39]

There was more to it than that. Hoover had a policeman's mentality. He saw his job as that of catching spies and destroying spy rings. He felt that it would be difficult to establish and maintain the thin borderline between a bogus, notional spy ring and a genuine one, and he believed that, despite their apparent sophistication in these matters, the British had not established that borderline either. In short, Popov, this flashy Slav playboy, was probably working for the Germans at least part of the time, and Hoover was not about to allow him to create even a notional Germany spy ring in Hoover's domain. In fact, Hoover wanted Popov in prison.

So the FBI adopted a hostile attitude to Popov. Hoover would not allow him to go to Pearl Harbor to report – either actually or notionally – on its installations. He seized Popov's microdot communication system (and later wrote an article boasting about this as one of his successes against spies). When the Germans sent Popov a wireless set, Hoover took over its use and refused to tell Popov what messages the FBI sent on it, or what the replies were. In short, he not only ruined Popov's value as a double agent but made it so obvious to the Germans that Popov was under Allied control that his life would be instantly at risk if the Abwehr was ever able to get its hands on him again. Yet it did, and nothing happened.

After Pearl Harbor had been bombed on 7 December 1941, as Popov had, in effect, predicted it would be, and after Hoover had shrugged off any blame, Popov returned to Lisbon and met Jebsen again. Jebsen asked him some relevant questions about his failures in the United States, but told him that the Abwehr believed that the trouble had probably been caused by Popov's worry over family difficulties. He then said he was sending Popov back to Britain.

An illuminating exchange followed. Popov raised some minor question about his assignment for the Germans and Jebsen said pointedly: 'Sort it out with British intelligence.' Popov, playing the role which he thought was expected of him replied, 'I don't know British intelligence', whereupon Jebsen buried his head in his hands and said 'God, oh God! You don't mean that you've really been working for the Nazis all these years! I must be going crazy.'[40]

Time was getting short for the Abwehr conspirators. The Gestapo was closing in. In February 1944 it was given the opportunity it had been waiting for when a senior Abwehr officer and his wife, Erich and Elisabeth Vermehren, defected in Istanbul. The Vermehrens, devout Catholics, felt that they could no longer go on working for the Nazi regime. After contacting the British Legation, they agreed to be spirited away to Britain where they went to work for a black propaganda team.* Mrs Vermehren was a cousin of Franz Von Papen, the veteran German diplomat and politician, and the British authorities, anxious to get as much benefit as possible from such an important defection, released a press statement about it in the United States. There was an enormous *brouhaha* in Germany, and the resulting loss of face made Hitler decide to merge the Abwehr into the RSHA and an immediate purge of old Abwehr officers began. Canaris was sacked and Himmler became head of a new unified German espionage service.†

It is claimed that the 'turned' German spies in Britain still had one last role to play for the Allies: to help create a 'bodyguard of lies' around the Allied invasion of Europe, to deceive the Germans over the date and place of the D-Day landings in France in June 1944 – an operation that has been described as 'the greatest piece of military deception in the history of warfare'. This is an absurd exaggeration.

The story is that the 'turned' German spies reported to Berlin a

---

* They had a difficult time making a living after the war, eventually settling in Switzerland under another name.

† Canaris was hanged on 9 April 1945 for alleged complicity in the bomb plot on Hitler's life. Oster, who had been sacked by Canaris in 1943, was hanged at the same time.

host of fictional details, including the existence of notional divisions, heavy train traffic into the Dover area, but normal conditions around Southampton and Portsmouth, whereas the opposite was true. This helped to convince the Germans that the Allies intended to invade through the Pas-de-Calais and not through Normandy. The Normandy invasion thus caught the Germans by surprise, another feather in the cap of Masterman's committee.

But consider this. Firstly, the Germans were well aware that their agents in Britain may have been 'turned'. After the war, the US Office of Naval Intelligence, using the Germans' own documents, made an assessment of the effectiveness of German intelligence. It decided that the Germans had found that 'the value of many espionage reports was greatly limited by the uncertainty as to whether a report contained genuine information or *material which had been channelled by Allied counter-intelligence to mislead the German Command*' (emphasis added).[41]

Next, in the winter of 1943/44, the German armies in the West held their major war games in Normandy, not in the Pas-de-Calais, an indication of German thinking about the likely invasion route. Their view was reinforced in the Spring of 1944 by three separate items of evidence. One: they had spies in the French section of SOE who told them that twenty-six French Resistance groups had received orders to prepare sabotage plans to support the invasion. The sabotage was to be concentrated on the area between the Normandy coast and Paris. Two: German intelligence had learnt that there were no sabotage preparations in the Belgian and Dutch resistance movements, which there would have been if the Pas-de-Calais had been the chosen route. Three: Britain's deception plans had been called into question by the RAF's systematic bombing of the area between the Normandy coast and Paris, with the aim of destroying the approach routes for the Panzergruppe West. This made it clear that Normandy was to be the invasion route.[42]

This last statement is a controversial one. Some British historians insist that the RAF protected the real invasion route by deception raids and increased reconnaissance flights over the Pas-de-Calais. But some German historians disagree. They say that a map of the bombing kept by C.-in-C. West showed that every conceivable approach to Normandy that could be used by Panzergruppe West and its operational reserves was being substantially destroyed by Allied bombing. 'It was not long before the so-called Geländekammer [literally, terrain chamber] was recognisable', wrote Gert Buchheit. 'It had to be here that the broad battlefield of the invasion was being prepared.'[43]

Buchheit's conclusion is supported by the German Naval Staff War Diary for 5 June 1944 – the day before the invasion. It includes an intelligence appreciation dated 30 May reporting heavy Allied air attacks on German supply lines between the Seine estuary and Normandy. It concludes: 'This factor may indicate intentions of enemy command *against Normandy*' (emphasis added).[44]

Thus it is hard to disagree with Major Oscar Reile, the German officer in charge of intelligence for Frontaufklärung III West, when he says, '[We] were surprised neither by the time of the invasion nor by the place or direction of the enemy advance'.[45] This makes it difficult to strike a balance sheet. The German High Command may have preferred to believe its 'turned' spies in Britain in preference to genuine and correct intelligence from the front. But even if this were the case – and we have seen the doubt – to whom should the credit go for the 'turned' spies? Britain's double-cross committee, or the anti-Hitler officers in the Abwehr, who either 'turned' the agents before they were sent, or sent them knowing full well that they would be 'turned'?

Either way, the Abwehr's help was substantial – but it was to get little credit. David Mure writes, 'What has always astonished me was that there never seemed to be any consciousness in MI5 that important elements in the Abwehr were working against Hitler and, indeed, providing us with the opportunity to turn and use their own agents against them.'[46] If there were to be an intelligence triumph, then it would have to be an all-British one.

B y 1944 SIS was almost in dissolution, its few successes overshadowed by its disasters. Section V, the counter-espionage department had lost its importance and cohesion. An interdepartmental 'war room' had been created, outside Menzies's control, to deal with counter-espionage in Europe. True, SIS had one of its officers as joint head of the 'war room', but he seldom attended meetings because he was usually drunk by 11 a.m. From the early days of the war, when the commanders of Allied operations in Norway made decisions on the basis of intelligence that was 'little better than that of the newspaper reader', through the threat of the German invasion of Britain*, to the D-Day landings in June 1944, by

---

* At this time, the intelligence authorities 'consulted Channel tunnel experts, listened to a water diviner who claimed to be able to forecast the enemy's movements, and, aware of Hitler's interest in astrology, paid some attention to his horoscope.'[47]

which time SIS had not managed to establish a single officer in Germany, the story is one of dismal failure.

The SIS chief, Menzies, must accept a large share of the blame. He had a First World War cavalry officer's mentality. He failed to define SIS's role. He failed to get rid of men like Dansey, considered a joke by the few efficient officers in the service. He lacked the broad view of the war held by, say, the head of BSC, Stephenson. And, as we shall see in later chapters, he allowed his service to be penetrated by the KGB. How, then, did SIS manage to survive the war?

Menzies had two cards that he played so cleverly that his enemies were left breathless. Firstly, Menzies's personality appealed to Churchill. The two men got on very well together, and Menzies made sure that all Whitehall knew it. Secondly, by keeping bureaucratic control of the Government Code and Cypher School at Bletchley Park he grabbed the right to use the intelligence material provided by the interception and decoding of German wireless messages. This material, a small jewel in an otherwise rather tarnished intelligence crown, was known as Ultra.

# 8. An Ear to the Enemy's Mind

> Increasingly it looks as if Bletchley Park is the greatest achievement of Britain during 1939–45, perhaps during this century as a whole.
> – George Steiner, *Sunday Times*, 23 October 1983.

> The GC and CS at Bletchley did not single-handedly win WWII. At certain critical moments (such as the battle of the Atlantic and the Battle of Britain) intelligence was irregular or unavailable or even unusable because of a lack of defensive resources. For at least half the war poor British codes and cyphers probably gave away as much as was gained.
> – Duncan Campbell, *New Statesman*, 2 February 1979.

In 1974 Wing Commander Winterbotham, the former head of the air section of SIS, the officer who had played such a curious intelligence role in prewar Germany, published a book called *The Ultra Secret*. It caused a sensation. Breaking a generation's silence, Winterbotham revealed the best-kept secret of the Second World War: the Allies had cracked the Germans' codes and, throughout the war, had eavesdropped, as it were, on their conversations about vital military, political and economic matters.

Such an invasion of the enemy's mind was unprecedented in the history of warfare and it took a while for its significance to be appreciated. Astonished military historians began to realize that if Winterbotham's revelations were correct – and since his book had been vetted by the British authorities, it would appear that they were – they might have to re-examine their work. If, for example, Allied generals who had been praised for their brilliant conduct of a campaign had known in advance what their German opposite numbers were planning, did this not somewhat dull their brilliance? Should not the history of that campaign be rewritten to take into account the edge that the Allied generals had possessed? Some

155

decided that it should. 'Most of the significant volumes in the United Kingdom series of Official Histories of the Second World War are [now] fundamentally misleading, inadequate and out of date', said British historian Ronald Lewin. 'It was as though Ultra, now the new authority, had told the authors of countless volumes to begin anew', wrote Roger J. Spiller, of the US Combat Studies Institute.[1] Other books on the Ultra operation quickly followed. Their authors – Patrick Beesly, R. V. Jones, Ewen Montague, Ralph Bennett and Peter Calvocoressi – had all, like Winterbotham, been in some way connected with Ultra.

Faced with this flood of reminiscences, the British authorities released some of the files relating to Ultra, enabling Lewin to write *Ultra Goes to War: The First Account of World War II's Greatest Secret, Based on Official Documents*. Now it could be told that General Eisenhower had felt that Ultra had made 'a decisive contribution to winning the war', that General MacArthur attached 'supreme importance' to Ultra, that Churchill thrived on it, that Ultra was 'how we won the war'. When someone inevitably asked why, in that case, hadn't it been won sooner, Harold Deutsch, of the US Army War College, replied that the Allies *had* won it sooner, and the period saved was variously estimated at from one to four years.[2] One historian claimed that, without Ultra, the Second Front would not have been opened until 1946 and the war in Europe would have dragged on until 1949. The Pacific theatre would have been deprived of supplies and the war against Japan would have been prolonged: in 1945, instead of being at Japan's door, the Americans would still have been battling in the Philippines.[3]

Ten years after Winterbotham's revelations, Ultra had become far more than an intelligence victory. Bletchley Park, the country house headquarters of the Government Code and Cypher School (GC and CS) where the German cyphers were cracked, had turned into a legend and the entire Ultra operation had come to symbolize the British way of life at its best. Professor George Steiner wrote:

> Increasingly it looks as if Bletchley Park is the greatest achievement of Britain during 1939/45, perhaps during this century as a whole. Its organisation concentrated what is finest and most inimitable in British society and civilisation; the libertarian brilliance of amateurism working closely with professionalism of the utmost rigour; recruitment through channels of personal trust; the turning to imperative use of habits of ironic play, of mutual criticism, and efficient informality which were ingrained in the common room or the Royal Society Committee.

Euphoric assessments like this, probably the result of the thirty years' enforced silence which had deprived those involved in Ultra of proper appreciation, have obscured important aspects of the operation. Was Ultra really as crucial to victory as has been claimed? Did the Germans mount a similar operation against the Allies? Did the Germans never realize that their codes were being intercepted and read? And – in view of Soviet suspicion of Allied motives throughout the war – did we share with Stalin this 'priceless secret' that was, apparently, present in every victory, absent in every defeat?

Just after the First World War, a Berlin engineer, Arthur Scherbius, invented a machine to encypher messages. Patented under the name 'Enigma', it had a typewriter keyboard and, above this, the alphabet with a light under each letter. When the operator touched a key he set off a series of electrical impulses that ended with one of the letters lighting up. But it was not always the same letter. The first time the operator touched the key for P, the letter K might light up. But if he touched P again, this time the illuminated letter might be Q. Thus, the machine turned a sentence into a sequence of letters which had, apparently, no logical relationship to each other. When the sentence was received, all the operator had to do was to set his machine to use the same electrical impulses as the sender had used, and then tap out the message. The machine would then reverse the process and the letters lighting up would spell out the original sentence. For an eavesdropper to intercept the message and decode it he would need two things: the Enigma machine itself, and the particular setting of it used on that occasion by the sender and the receiver.

The Enigma was patented and offered on the commercial market, but did not do very well. However, the German navy took it up in 1926 and the German army in 1928. Polish intelligence succeeded in breaking the German Enigma traffic from about 1932 onwards by buying a commercial machine and getting hold of some drawings which revealed how the Germans had adapted it. But in 1939, on the eve of war, they had lost this ability because of the increasing complexity that the Germans had built into the machine. So, the Poles passed on to the French and the British an Enigma machine apiece, and all that they had been able to learn about it. Stewart Menzies, of SIS, personally took delivery of the British Enigma and handed it over to Commander Alastair Denniston, head of GC and CS at Bletchley Park.

Bletchley Park, a medium-size house in extensive grounds some fifty miles from London, had been bought by SIS in case London had to be evacuated. Now it became the home of GC and CS, eventually to employ 10,000 people, and the main source of Ultra, the name given to the material decoded from the Enigma machines. Briefly, the process went as follows. Wireless operators would tune in to frequencies known to be used by various branches of the German services and take down all that they overheard. This raw material would be relayed to Bletchley Park where the cryptographers would do their best to decypher it. Intelligence officers would then take over and try to interpret the messages and then pass on the material, with their comments, to those 'consumers' who would be most interested in the final product.

The people working at Bletchley Park were usually young – 25 to 30 – and had been recruited from similar backgrounds, that is, well-educated and middle-class: 'The place glowed white hot with talent' as someone said. These recruits shared much the same attitudes to life, work, discipline and values which, as Peter Calvo-coressi who was one of them, has pointed out, '[goes] some way to explain the astonishing fact that the Ultra secret was kept not merely during the war, but for thirty years afterwards – a phenomenon that may well be unparalleled in history'.[4]

For it would have been useless to have cracked the Germans' codes and then, inadvertently, have let it slip out that this was happening. Accordingly, stringent precautions were taken to keep the work at Bletchley Park a secret and to pretend that the Ultra material had come from somewhere else. All recruits to Bletchley were warned on joining that 'once-in, never out', so that there was no risk of an ex-employee falling into enemy hands, or being forced or tempted to betray GC and CS's secret. Next, distribution of Ultra material was restricted to four clients: the chief of SIS, the directors of naval and army intelligence, and the assistant chief of air staff intelligence. No Ultra signals were sent direct to commands below the level of any army headquarters or the equivalent, and anything passed on to a corps or a division had to be disguised in the form of an operational order – a restriction which, as we shall see, could have disastrous results. Ultra material that revealed movements of German ships and tanks could not be acted upon on its own, in case, the theory went, the Germans were provoked into considering the security of their signalling and thus into guessing Bletchley Park's secret. Instead, there had first to be an aerial reconnaissance, carried out in such an obvious manner that the Germans could not help but notice it, before the tanks or ships could be bombed.[5]

The Americans faced similar problems in making the best of their ability to intercept Japanese signals and decode them – what they called the 'Magic' and 'Purple' material. Breaking the Japanese 'ro' code* enabled American naval intelligence to catch the Japanese fleet by surprise at Midway in June 1942. But, first, it had to weigh the risk of using the intercepts – and thus compromising the codebreaking operations – against the prospect of inflicting a crushing defeat on the Japanese navy at a crucial stage of the war. It chose to risk its codebreaking, and the tide of the war in the Pacific was turned in the Allies' favour.

But the Japanese became suspicious after Midway. The following year Admiral Yamamoto Isoruku, commander-in-chief of the Combined Fleet, paid a visit to front line bases. His schedule was radioed in code to local commanders. But when the Commander-in-Chief of the Japanese Eleventh Air Flotilla learnt of this, he told his staff officers, 'What a damned fool thing to do, to send such a long and detailed message about the activities of the C.-in-C. so near the Front. This kind of thing must stop.'†[6]

At Bletchley, confident that the Ultra secret could be protected, expansion continued apace until its codebreakers seemed able to reveal every detail of enemy activity. Its cryptographers fought their way into the German codes by a mixture of luck, ingenuity and German errors. A German agent who had been 'turned' by the British gave them an Abwehr codebook; a naval codebook was captured from the submarine U110 in mid-1941; the Russians handed over a Luftwaffe codebook and another was captured in North Africa. Cryptographers thrive on repetition and, although regulations forbade it, day after day German radio men transmitted identically worded messages, such as 'nothing to report', or padded out three-letter words (which they were required to do by operating procedures) with the same three letters (which was against orders). Calvocoressi gives the example of the German operator at Bari who invariably used the three initials of his girlfriend, and never knew the harm he did to his service.

Among the first to realize that Bletchley Park could be an intelligence goldmine was the wartime head of SIS, Stewart Menzies. As

* There is disagreement over how this was achieved. The Americans say that it was through the brilliance of their codebreakers. The Japanese say that US navy divers recovered Japanese codebooks from submarine I-124, sunk in action off Darwin on 20 January 1941.

† He was right. The Americans intercepted the message and shot down Yamamoto, the man who planned the attack on Pearl Harbor, over Bougainville Island on 18 April 1943, killing him instantly.

we have seen, SIS was in such disarray at the outbreak of war that if the Ultra material, especially the Abwehr intercepts, had not suddenly been available from 1940 onwards, then Menzies and his organization would not have survived. Menzies had sufficient foresight to realize this, and more than enough cunning to make the most of this opportunity. Winterbotham, SIS representative at GC and CS, was told to provide a continuous supply of the best Bletchley Park material and, each day, Menzies or his personal assistant, David Boyle, took a packet of intelligence material direct to Churchill. (At weekends, Winterbotham would read the important items to Churchill over the telephone.) The daily package usually consisted of a mixture of Luftwaffe intercepts, a summary of Abwehr traffic, some German police signals and a few naval decrypts. Menzies, who brought the report in a special case, and Boyle, who carried it in his bowler hat, would give it to Churchill with a short commentary on GC and CS's current progress in the manner of a leader reporting on his staff. Churchill loved it – 'he ran the war on it', says Winterbotham – and his confidence in Menzies and SIS soared.[7]

Of course, this did not endear SIS to GC and CS which considered its subordination to Menzies to be a purely administrative arrangement. They despised 'the miserable SIS which lived on our credit', a feeling which persisted long after the war. Harry Hinsley, recruited to Bletchley Park while still an undergraduate, later to become Vice-Chancellor of Cambridge University and official historian of British intelligence during the war, has said of SIS: 'The espionage men were sort of lounge lizard types, you know. You had to be to do that kind of stuff. Whereas the Bletchley types were dour, upright, very charming-but-professional Englishmen and women. They were in a different kind of world. There was this quality difference between what their work was, and the old-fashioned spy stuff.'[8]

Yet in the early days of Ultra, field commanders were expected to accept the fiction that this marvellous intelligence coming to them from SIS had originated not only from one of these 'lounge lizards' (code named 'Boniface'), but a super one who could be in several places at once. This was Menzies's idea, a way of protecting his 'most secret source' and it resulted in some recipients of Ultra dismissing it out of hand. To overcome this problem, special liaison units were formed under Winterbotham's direction and attached to army headquarters to educate commanders in the importance and reliability of Ultra. But, even then, Ultra never made the impact its recent trumpeting would have us believe. An intelligence officer in the US Seventh Army may have said, after receiving one particularly useful Ultra item, 'This just isn't cricket', but one estimate has it that after a certain point in the war only 5 to 10 per cent of Ultra intelligence received in the field was ever used.[9] No general seems to have set down an account of the way he used Ultra, perhaps for the very human reason that to have done so might have detracted from his reputation.

There is, indeed, some evidence that at least one commander, General MacArthur, kept his Ultra material so close to his chest that the prosecution of the war was actually hindered rather than helped. If what is known about MacArthur's personality is taken into account, then his reasons for this action are easily discernible. As Australian historian, D. M. Horner, puts it: 'One is left with the tantalising question of whether MacArthur's confidence that the Japanese were not going to attack Australia directly was a result of these interceptions. If it was, then it was unfair of him to claim personal credit for reversing Allied strategy.'[10]

Other generals failed to understand the reluctance of junior officers to pursue a course of action that they were assured would succeed, but for which assurance they were offered no evidence. General John Lucas, an American corps commander at the Anzio landing in January 1944 was not authorized to receive Ultra, but his superiors, Generals Sir Harold Alexander and Mark Clark, were. They knew from Ultra that the Germans were in no position to resist Lucas if he decided to break out from his beach-head, but they were not allowed to tell Lucas this. They urged him to attack, but their optimism sounded more like false confidence in the face of Lucas's own assessment of his position and so he decided to be prudent and stay where he was. The Germans recovered and contained the Allied landings on the beach. Lucas, relieved of his command for lack of aggressive action, noted in his diary, 'apparently everyone was in on the secret of German intentions except me' – a fair summary of the facts.[11] On the other hand, there was a risk that the dissemination of too much Ultra material could be counter-productive. One special liaison officer wrote that Ultra could make commanders lazy, for it could become a substitute for analysis and the evaluation of other intelligence: 'Ultra must be looked upon as one of a number of sources; it must not be taken as a neatly-packaged replacement for tedious work with other evidence.'[12]

In short, Ultra could not turn a mediocre commander into a military genius. He still had to plan his campaign, motivate his officers, inspire his men and adapt to changing conditions once battle was joined. Ultra could actually inhibit a commander, because he knew that his political bosses had received the same secrets and would, rightly or wrongly, consider themselves in a position not only to advise him but to remove him if he failed to act as *they* would have. Churchill sacked two fine generals, Wavell and Auchinleck, early in the North African campaign because he felt that he knew from Ultra as much about the Germans and Italians as his generals did, and he disapproved of their performance in that light. Yet, in this case, Ultra was wrong.

Ultra has been described as 'over-hearing what the enemy himself is reporting to himself about himself'. But military commanders are subject to most of the human frailties: they lie, exaggerate, conceal, boast, delude themselves and alter their minds. Ultra dealt in absolutes. It could make no provision for changes of heart. It now emerges that German commanders sometimes deliberately exaggerated their *matériel* shortages in their reports to Berlin, and faked their estimates of Allied strength so as to make the German High Command take the enemy threat seriously. 'When Rommel wrote reports [from the desert] he developed a tactic of exaggerating in order to make sure of receiving at least part of the material he needed', wrote the German historian, Jürgen Rohwer. 'This meant that Churchill, who was fascinated by Ultra reports, forced the British commanders to mount attacks they did not intend, and which then failed. This led to the removal of Wavell and Auchinleck.'[13]

Rommel was also likely to disobey orders and tell Berlin one thing and then do another. He was an intuitive commander and, if opportunity beckoned, he would change his plans, often without bothering to say so. One of the reasons for the disaster at the Battle of Kasserine Pass in February 1943 was that Ultra indicated an attack in one direction, but Rommel disobeyed the order coming from Italy and attacked in another. The Americans, who had relied on Ultra, lost almost half an armoured division.[14] 'Reading a man's correspondence is not the same thing as reading his mind', wrote Peter Calvocoressi. 'Rommel's first campaign in Africa was a case in point. Rommel was ordered to attack in May. We knew this from Ultra and we knew that he did not dissent. But privately he determined to attack not in May but in March. At some stage he changed his mind without saying so, and since he did not say so we did not know of the change.'[15]

Allied estimates of the German forces that they would face when they invaded Europe appear to be much more accurate than German estimates of Allied strength. Allied intelligence had located almost every one of the fifty German divisions in France. The Germans, on the other hand, credited Eisenhower with seventy-five divisions – when, in fact, he had fifty – and with far more landing craft than were actually available. This was important because the thought that they were facing forces greater than really existed inhibited the German defence, and the knowledge of this inhibition, in turn, was of great help to the Allies. This double benefit has been hailed as an intelligence triumph, 'a central factor in the Allied victory', handed to Eisenhower by Britain's 'superb intelligence community, capped by the now famous Bletchley Park/Ultra system'. But was it?

After the war, in 1946, British army intelligence officers interrogated a German officer identified only as Colonel 'M'. He had been in German intelligence, the Foreign Armies West section, from May 1942 until May 1944 when he was appointed chief intelligence officer to Field Marshal Model of Army Group B. Colonel 'M', who could at that time have had no idea of the Ultra material, told his interrogators:

> Towards the end of 1943 my chief and I were summoned at least once a month to conferences at the Wehrmachtführungstab. We were always surprised at the completely illogical under estimation of the needs of the German defence forces in France, Norway, and the Balkans. Formations were continually being transferred to other theatres. Consequently my chief and I agreed to exaggerate our estimates of the number of Allied divisions in order to counter this tendency to over-optimism in the Wehrmachtführungstab. *Thus our estimate was too high by some 20 divisions*.[16] (Emphasis added)

So what has been hailed as an example of an intelligence triumph is really an example of how Ultra could be misleading. Fortunately, in this case, it was not so midleading as to affect the outcome.

In fact, there are large areas of the Second World War where it is clear that Ultra had no effect on events, others where its utility is in dispute, and only a few where it is clear that Ultra was crucial. To begin with, Bletchley Park was not a shadow German High Command, as Winterbotham more than once calls it. The first step in the long chain of events that produced Ultra material at a commander's headquarters could begin only when the Germans used wireless to send their messages. Without a wireless message, there was nothing for the Allies to intercept. In many ways, the German army clung to tradition. At the beginning of the war the bulk of its signals went by postal telegraph circuit which could not be intercepted in Britain. It even occasionally still used carrier pigeons and messenger dogs to transmit orders. Written orders were frequently carried by car, motorcycle, cycle and even horseback.[17] There was no Ultra from these sources. Even when the war was well advanced, the Germans displayed a natural preference for landline teleprinters and telephone, and used wireless only when the former were not immediately available.

According to Jürgen Rohwer, only about a quarter to a third of all German forces communications went by radio. 'The bulk of this would not have been at a high strategic level, but more on a middle operational or lower tactical level.' He gives a more precise figure for German navy traffic. 'In the year 1943 only 29 percent of all the German navy's messages were sent by wireless traffic encyphered on the Enigma machine. The other messages went by cable, either on the teleprinters or by telephone.'[18] (The exception to this was the Abwehr. With a secret organization's fascination for secret tools, it often used the Enigma machine even for communications within Germany in preference to secure landlines.) True, as orders came to be disseminated nearer the front, the likelihood that wireless would be used increased greatly. But often this meant that Bletchley would be confronted with an answer sent by wireless to a question that had been asked by landline, and the one was usually incomprehensible without the other.

By no means all messages that were intercepted could be broken. Bletchley Park's success with the Luftwaffe code was not repeated with the army and throughout the war the British cryptographers struggled with nightmarishly complicated naval codes for capital ships and submarines. Often the supply of decoded signals would falter at a critical moment. The Triton code, which the Kriegsmarine introduced in 1942, closed down this source of Ultra for ten months. A chart correlating Allied shipping losses and the flow of Ultra, recently declassified, shows how disastrous this loss turned out to be.[19]

Even when Bletchley made a break-through in December 1942, and once again could read the German U-boat traffic, the Admiralty could not cope with the sudden flow of information. The head of the enemy submarine tracking room, Rodger Winn, who earlier had to struggle along with insufficient staff – he even had to do the filing himself – collapsed from total mental and physical exhaustion. When decrypts were averaging 3,000 a day, his department could handle only what it considered to be of immediate operational importance. The rest of the decrypts were ignored.[20]

Some high-grade German cyphers were never read at all and, as the war progressed, even lower-level cyphers became harder to exploit because of the sheer number in use. At one point the German navy alone was using forty different settings of the Enigma machine at a time. Given the number of operations to be performed

– decoding, translating, intelligence serving, encoding the Ultra material for retransmission to the consumer – Bletchley Park was hard pressed to keep its service up to date. At its best, the interval between Enigma and Ultra times of origin could be as short as two hours. At worst, it could run to days.

Even a delay of hours could often be too late for the commander in the field to make any use of Ultra. The Coventry controversy is a good example. Several later books on Ultra have claimed that the British knew from intercepts that Coventry was to be the target for a heavy bombing raid on the night of 14/15 November 1940, but that Churchill decided not to evacuate the population or increase the city's defences for fear that this might reveal to the Germans that Britain was reading Enigma. The truth is that it was not until 2 p.m. on the day of the raid that Ultra material enabled the British to know that the attack was definitely on, and not until 3 p.m. that they were able, from other intelligence sources, to identify Coventry as the target – too late for any effective evacuation and too late to improve the city's defences.[21]

Apart from the sheer bulk of messages, Bletchley Park had to cope with the abbreviations, map and grid references, and service jargon. Sometimes the cryptographers would labour for hours over a message, only to discover it was of mind-numbing banality, as in the following case. The Abwehr sent a message to its head of station in Algeciras, Spain, an officer code named 'Cesar'. The decoded message said: 'Be careful of Axel. He bites.' Was this a code within a code? It turned out to refer to the arrival of a guard dog for the station compound, a theory confirmed a few days later with the decrypting of an Enigma reply which read: 'Cesar is in hospital. Axel bit him.'[22]

Operational codewords posed great difficulty. During the Battle of Britain, Luftwaffe decrypts made several references to 'Adlertag', which was to occur during the period 9–13 August 1940, but no one could work out what 'Adlertag' stood for. Then on 15 August, the day which is generally accepted as the turning-point in the Battle of Britain, the RAF managed to thwart a German plan involving diversionary attacks, without any advance warning from Ultra material.[23]

The same could be said for much of the Blitz. 'Ultra showed that a big air effort was coming against England and gave clues as to its scale', writes Calvocoressi, 'but it could not help with dates.' And, when the attack began, Ultra could not prevent the Germans from doing enormous damage to British cities. It is no help knowing where you are going to be attacked if your defences are not sufficiently strong to prevent it. Ultra gave nearly a month's warning of the gathering of German troops, transport aircraft, gliders, fighters and bombers on the Greek mainland, estimates of their strength, probable landing spots, and even the date of their attack on Crete. This was of no use to the commander defending the island, General Freyberg, because he simply did not have the forces to beat off the German attack. Arguments that it did, however, enable him to inflict on the Germans greater casualties than he would otherwise have been able to do, remain academic.[24]

Other commanders would ignore Ultra if it did not fit neatly into their preconceptions and plans. The Dutch Resistance got word to the Allies on 11 September 1944 that there were two German panzer divisions in Arnhem. Ultra reports tended to confirm this. Yet Field Marshal Montgomery went ahead with Operation Market Garden, of which the leading element was the parachute drop into Arnhem of the British 1st Airborne Division. It was cut to pieces. Ralph Bennett writes:

> Market Garden was not an operation planned entirely in relation to . . . intelligence about the enemy . . . There are slightly sinister undertones of excessive haste, Anglo-American rivalry and even desperation about it; the possibility that there were tanks at Arnhem was the one awkward fact that would not fit the desired pattern, so the best thing was to sweep it under the carpet.[25]

Ultra showed that the Allied strategic bombing of Germany had failed to crack German morale, and had made not a dent in German aircraft production. It showed, too, that American daylight raids in 1943 and British night raids on Berlin in 1944 were Allied defeats, because losses suffered were incommensurate with the damage inflicted.[26] All this was passed on to the proper authorities, yet the raids went on: the truth of Ultra did not suit the champions of heavy bombing.

For other failures there has been no explanation. On 8 September 1944, the day after the Allies had captured the Antwerp docks, Ultra provided the information that Hitler was about to strike back. He intended to deny them the use of the port, vital to supplying the Allies if they planned a quick advance to the Ruhr, by holding on to both banks of the River Scheldt. Two days later, a further Ultra intercept, of a message from Hitler to German forces in the Netherlands, confirmed the German plans. Yet, for ten days, the Allies did nothing to secure the banks of the river between Antwerp and the North Sea and by then they had left it too late. Bennett writes that even if ordinary logistical prudence had deserted them in all the excitement of their success, Ultra was there to bring them up short: 'Why its warning went unheeded is incomprehensible.'[27]

Other commanders, however, relied on Ultra to such an extent that they tended to believe that if there was no Ultra material, then nothing was happening.[28] That this was a dangerous assumption was made clear by the Ardennes offensive in December 1944 when the Germans made a desperate attempt to reverse the tide of the Allied advance. They achieved almost a complete surprise attack because Ultra had not been able to give a specific warning of their action: Hitler had imposed deliberate wireless silence and a special oath of secrecy on those who were given the job of planning the action.

The difficulty of assessing the contribution that Ultra intelligence made to the Allied war effort can best be summed up by an intriguing confrontation in Stuttgart in November 1978. At a conference organized to study the historical impact of Ultra, German historians repeatedly pressed the British participants, all of whom had been intimately involved with Bletchley Park during the war, to say whether Ultra had played a decisive role in this battle or that, and requested a summarized assessment of its overall wartime importance. The British were unable to give it to them.[29]

One reason for this reticence must be the nagging thought that the Germans knew that the British had broken the Enigma codes. Let us consider the evidence for this possibility. To begin with, the Germans were well aware that it was theoretically possible to break Enigma. One of their cryptanalysts, Dr Georg Schroeder, demonstrated a solution in the 1930s using alphabet slides and announced that 'The whole Enigma is garbage'. The lesson was not lost on German cryptographers who constantly suggested improvements because they knew that the machine was not absolutely secure and could be broken into, especially if the Allies had possession of one. The Germans must have assumed that they did, because the Enigma was originally sold to the public and, although it had been much modified, the basic layout remained the same.

Next, on 11 September 1942, the Germans captured the British gunboat MGB 335 and found, on board, documents giving current details of German convoy movements and mine-free channels. This information could only have come from cryptanalysis of Enigma signals. Moreover, in August 1943, Berlin had learnt via the Swiss secret service that a Swiss American working in the Navy Department in Washington, who had frequently visited Britain, had reported that the British were regularly reading German naval Enigma messages.[30]

Finally, the Germans' preference for landlines whenever possible suggests that they were alerted to the danger of the Allies intercepting and decoding wireless messages, as does the use of subterfuges of language in those wireless messages they did send. In the Coventry raid, for example, the operation was called Moonlight Sonata, and the actual targets were designated only by numbers. Hitler ordered radio silence prior to the Ardennes offensive because he suspected that the Allies had the capability to read the Enigma codes. Why would the Germans have tried to mislead the Allies about the location of certain units by sending wireless messages (implying that they were still in one place when in fact they were in another) unless they knew that the Allies could read the messages? The deception would have been useless otherwise. Why would the Germans have held a special conference on cypher security in the summer of 1944, at which Enigma's imperfections were recognized and steps taken to rectify them? The Germans were not fools. They knew that every transposition cypher is vulnerable, given the time to go through all its possible permutations, and that they would have to adopt a 'worst case' assumption – the Allies would find a way into Enigma, just as the Germans had found a way into Allied codes. For not only the spoils of war go to the victor, but the ballyhoo as well. To read the triumphs of Ultra one would believe that the Germans had no similar triumphs of their own. This was not the case.

Germany had many codebreaking agencies. The navy had its Beobachtungsdienst, or B-Dienst for short; as did the army and the air force. The armed forces High Command had its Chiffrierabteilung, the Foreign Office its Pers z. Goering had his own Forschungsamt; and for a while the SS's intelligence section, the Sicherheitsdienst also had its own codebreakers. Although there was an inherent weakness in their numbers and in the way they competed with each other – as compared with the concentration of Bletchley Park's effort – these agencies nevertheless achieved some amazing successes.

Unknown to the Allies, the Germans were reading French army cyphers which revealed the strengths and intentions of British and French units during those desperate days in 1940. If Allied successes later in the war are to be reassessed in the light of Ultra, then should not Guderian's *Blitzkrieg* also be reassessed in the light of German codebreaking? The British were greatly aided by Ultra in North Africa but Rommel, too, was not without help from the German codebreakers. The British army was guilty of appalling lack of radio security, including the abuse of low-grade codes like CODEX. A captured German radio intelligence lieutenant told his interrogators: 'We don't have to bother much about cyphers. All we need are linguists, the sort who were waiters at the Dorchester before the war.'[31]

In 1941–2 an American military attaché in Cairo, Colonel Bonner Fellers, confided to the Pentagon, using an American military code, all that was going on in North Africa, frequently revealing British plans and strengths. The Germans intercepted Fellers's messages and, as David Kahn relates, they were then 'rapidly broken down, evaluated, translated, encoded in a German system and radioed to General Erwin Rommel . . . In January 1942 [he] used them as he chased the British back 300 miles across the desert and approached the gates of Alexandria.' The success of German codebreaking won the sort of praise from the German High Command that Allied commanders were later to heap on Ultra, a head of Foreign Armies West, Colonel Ulrich Liss, calling it 'the darling of all intelligence chiefs'.[32]

The Germans even managed to tap into the radio-telephone circuit between London and Washington, and although important conversations on this line went through a 'scrambler' they succeeded in unscrambling them. Thus they were occasionally able to eavesdrop on conversations between Churchill and Roosevelt, but found what they heard disappointing. Both leaders were too guarded in what they said for the Germans to be able to make much use of it.

But their greater success was undoubtedly with British convoy codes. At the start of the war, one British naval code after another was broken or captured until by 1942–3, the B-Dienst was intercepting some 2,000 convoy messages a month, decoding them, and passing the information to the German U-boat fleet in time for it to inflict the slaughter that was known as the Battle of the Atlantic. 'All the time, while minds and technology were being pushed to the limit at Bletchley in the attack on German signals, the most elementary blunders were being made in defence of their own', writes Andrew Hodges, the biographer of the Bletchley genius, Alan Turing.[33]

The trouble was that GC and CS's responsibility for British cypher security had been neglected in favour of the more glamorous business of cracking enemy cyphers. Yet the very cracking of these cyphers should have set alarm bells ringing. GC and CS knew from German naval intercepts early in the war that the German naval attaché in Washington was remarkably well informed about British convoys leaving the United States. For example, one intercept read: 'Naval attaché Washington reports convoy rendezvous February 25, 200 sea miles east of Sable island; 13 cargo boats, 4 tankers, 100,000 tons cargo aeroplane parts, machine parts, motor lorries, munitions, chemicals; probably the number of the convoy is HX114.'[34]

But it was not until two-thirds of the way through the war that Britain realized that the German codebreakers were producing from their intercepts of British convoy communications information as detailed as, for example, that convoy SC2 would be at latitude 50°00' north and longitude 19°50' west at noon on 6 September 1940.[35] There was a crash programme to introduce new cypher systems. The Royal Navy received its new system on 10 June 1943, but the Merchant Navy's cypher system continued to be read by the Germans until the end of that year. By that time, it was nearly too late: the majority of the 50,000 Allied seamen who died in the war were already at the bottom of the sea.

The director of British naval intelligence, Admiral J. H. Godfrey, was made the scapegoat for the failure, the only naval officer of his seniority and rank to receive no recognition at the end of the war.[36] But the blame was not the Admiralty's alone. Cypher security was part of Bletchley's responsibility and it neglected it.

There were other German successes in penetrating British communications, including two notable ones achieved by old-fashioned methods. One of these ranks with much of Ultra in its strategic significance; both were British blunders so disastrous that today it is difficult to prise from the British authorities an admission that they even occurred.

The first took place on the morning of 11 November 1940 when the Blue Funnel Line steamer, the *Automedon*, was intercepted by the German raider *Atlantis* off the Nicobar Islands in the Indian Ocean. The ship's captain was carrying a bag of highly secret mail and codebooks to Singapore. So important was the material in this bag that it was kept on the bridge, sealed and weighted, ready to be thrown overboard should there be any danger of it falling into German hands. But the *Atlantis* hit the *Automedon*'s superstructure with twenty-eight rounds killing the captain and all the officers and crew on or near the bridge. The Germans found the bag intact and opened it. It proved to be a treasure trove of intelligence material.

There were copies of the Merchant Navy code, valid from 1 January 1941, and several issues of the Admiralty's weekly intelligence reports. But what delighted the Germans most were copies of British War Cabinet minutes and an appreciation by the Chiefs of Staff, discussed by the War Cabinet, of Britain's plans for the Far

East in the event of war with Japan. Basically, this said that Britain was too hard-pressed to be able properly to defend her interests and that she would have to 'retire to base from which it will be possible to restore our position later on'. Hong Kong, Malaya and Singapore were indefensible, there was no hope of sending a fleet to the Far East, and very little air power would be available to protect shipping in the Indian Ocean. Concentration of strong land forces in Malaya was a top priority and the Commonwealth would have to send one division there.

The documents were rushed to Kobe, in Japan, and taken from there to the German embassy in Tokyo where the naval attaché, Admiral Paul Wenneker, sorted and assessed them. Wenneker realized that the Chiefs of Staff report was 'of the very greatest significance for the Japanese', so he wirelessed a synopsis of it to Berlin and asked permission to hand over copies to the Japanese. In the meantime, the Japanese naval attaché in Berlin had received Wenneker's synopsis from the German High Command and he radioed this back to Tokyo on 12 December. (Thus, rather ironically, there were two opportunities for the British to intercept and de-cypher wireless messages which would have confirmed the capture of their secret documents. But Wenneker used a key for his Enigma machine which was never broken by Bletchley Park, and the Japanese naval attaché used the JN25 code which was not broken by the Americans until 1945.)

As soon as Japanese Naval General Staff saw the British documents it sent for Wenneker and told him repeatedly how valuable they were. There is a further indication of the importance the Japanese attached to the capture of the bag on the *Automedon*. When Singapore fell, Emperor Hirohito presented the captain of the *Atlantis* with a samurai sword, one of only three given to Germans throughout the war. (The other two recipients were Rommel and Goering.) But it appears that Churchill was never told about this loss, which leads to the conclusion that the documents must have been sent without War Cabinet approval, that their capture was hushed up and this cover-up has continued until today.[37]

The other British blunder concerns the capture by the German raider *Thor* of the Australian liner *Nankin* on 10 May 1942 while it was *en route* from Sydney to Colombo. The *Nankin*'s captain managed to throw overboard the ship's codebooks and confidential papers, but the *Nankin* was also carrying 120 bags of mail which contained reports from the Allied Combined Operations Intelligence Committee (COIC) in Wellington, New Zealand. Again, it was Wenneker who analysed the contents of the mailbags and wirelessed summaries to the German High Command. Apart from providing an indication of morale and attitudes to the war in Australia and Britain, the COIC reports made it clear that the Allies had penetrated Japanese cyphers. This information prompted a series of meetings between Japanese naval intelligence officers and a team of German naval signal specialists to find ways of improving Japan's signals security.

It is difficult to know what further use the Japanese made of the COIC reports because many of the documents concerning the *Nankin* incident are either still embargoed or are missing from both the British and German archives. The most likely explanation for this is British embarrassment that COIC papers were included in the *Nankin's* general mail – an elementary breach of security.

It is possible that the emphasis on the glamour of Ultra, on the secret, intellectual operation that 'won the war sooner', has concealed its main political importance: Did Ultra contribute to the Cold War? Two-thirds of the German war effort was expended on the Eastern Front, yet the role of Ultra in relation to this has remained a mystery. Did the Allies share with their Soviet allies their 'priceless' intelligence jewel? If not, did the Russians realize it? Is it possible that the Russians themselves had broken the Enigma code? (They certainly had cracked a variety of British cyphers.) Since the first Ultra revelations, such questions have done little more than create new Ultra myths. The best of these is that the Russians were so mistrustful of their Western allies that Churchill realized it would be no use passing the Ultra material to Stalin in a normal manner. For, if he did, Stalin would, as a matter of course, suspect Churchill of planting it on him for some ulterior motive. So, the myth goes, SIS fed disguised Ultra material into the famous Soviet spy network in Switzerland, the Lucy ring, and only when Stalin received it from his own trusted spies did he believe it was true. This theory, as we shall see, does not stand up to scrutiny.

There are other, more credible, versions of how Ultra material passed to the Soviet Union. Calvocoressi says that there was a justifiable reluctance to give Stalin *any* Ultra material, but when it became clear that the Soviet Union was going to put up a powerful resistance to Hitler, then both loyalty and expediency required that Britain should give the Russians everything that might help them to defeat the Germans. He says that there was no question of telling them the source of Ultra because Russian signals security was very bad and the secret of Bletchley Park might leak out. So Ultra material of use to Stalin was chosen and suitably disguised. It was sent to a British liaison officer, Major Edward Crankshaw, who was in Moscow representing Bletchley Park, SIS, military intelligence and the Admiralty. He informed the ambassador who, in turn, passed the disguised Ultra material directly to Stalin. Crankshaw, now a noted author on the Soviet Union, declined to discuss his role: 'I can neither confirm nor deny what Calvocoressi says about me', he said. Calvocoressi himself has doubts that Stalin ever used the Ultra material: 'In the case of the great tank battles of 1942 when we warned the Russians that they were pouring men and materials into a huge German trap, it is difficult to suppose that they gave full credence to warnings which, if heeded, would have saved them terrible losses . . .'[38]

Nigel West, however, says that SIS had one officer in Moscow, Cecil Barclay, whose job it was to provide his Soviet counterpart, General F. F. Kuznetsov, with selected Ultra material 'without compromising the source'. At one of their first meetings Kuznetsov produced the Luftwaffe codebook mentioned earlier, and asked Barclay to ensure that it got into 'the right hands'. At other meetings, Kuznetsov gave broad hints that he was well aware of Bletchley Park's function. There are several ways he could have known this.

Barclay had an opposite number in London – a Soviet intelligence officer whose job it was to liaise with SIS and SOE. This was Colonel I. Chickayev, and although his main work was with SOE he may well have learnt about Bletchley Park and its purpose and repeated this to Moscow. Or the information could have come from the Soviet penetration agents, Kim Philby, Anthony Blunt and John Cairncross.

At that time, Philby was in Section 5 of SIS and was certainly privy to Ultra material dealing with the Abwehr – in other words, he knew the source and authenticity of the intelligence he was handling. Whether he knew that Bletchley Park had broken the Enigma codes of the other German services is another matter, but it is reasonable to assume that he did. He told his fellow SIS officer, Leslie Nicholson, some time before the first V2 rockets that, 'The Germans have got a new weapon to hit London. I'm going to move my family to the country' – an important piece of information that came from intercepts of messages from the Japanese ambassador in Berlin to his superiors in Tokyo. And a secretary who worked in Philby's office recalls, 'There was a special room where material was available on application to sections which needed it for their work. It was common knowledge among the staff that the material was largely derived from Enigma intercepts.'[39]

Anthony Blunt, later Surveyor of the Queen's Pictures, her third cousin once removed, confessed in 1964 – in exchange for immunity from prosecution – that he had worked for Soviet intelligence during the war while a serving officer in MI5. Publicly disgraced in 1979 when the Prime Minister, Mrs Thatcher, revealed the earlier confession, Blunt gave a press conference at which he answered questions about his wartime work for the Soviet Union. He said that his Soviet controller was mainly interested in German intelligence and that, at his request, Blunt had passed to him information derived 'largely from intercepts, mainly intercepts', and from 'German codes'. So Blunt, too, knew about Ultra.

John Cairncross certainly knew about Ultra because he was employed at Bletchley Park until 1944 when he left to join Section 5. In 1964, then living in Rome, he admitted to MI5 that he had been recruited at Cambridge and had had regular meetings with his Soviet case officers *while at GC and CS*. It is inconceivable that three such highly motivated Soviet spies as Philby, Blunt and Cairncross could know about Ultra and not tell their Soviet controllers about it.

We must also consider the likelihood that the Russians had themselves cracked at least some of the Enigma codes. They had had long experience of codebreaking, had captured several Enigma machines and had at least one codebook. Although the Germans discounted this possibility during the war, they later had second thoughts. In a report in 1958, an intelligence officer wrote: 'It is absolutely certain that the Russians succeeded in deciphering Enigma messages in certain instances. The reason for this, besides the usual mistakes in cyphers, was the sending of too many messages with the same basic key.'[40]

Thus the evidence indicates that the Soviet Union knew about Enigma, knew that the Allies had broken at least some of the German codes, and knew that the Allies had kept this from them, officially at least. They may even have made efforts to force the Allies to reveal the Ultra secret. The present Duke of Portland, then, as Cavendish-Bentinck, chairman of the JIC recalls trying to convince the Soviet ambassador in London, M. Maisky, that Germany was going to attack the Soviet Union on 22 or 29 June 1941. Portland knew this from Ultra material, but he did not tell Maisky his source. Portland was irritated that Maisky flatly refused to believe him, saying, 'Oh no, we've got a treaty. These reports are put out to try to make mischief between the Germans and ourselves.'[41] But Maisky's response can be interpreted differently if we assume that he knew of Ultra; it can be seen as an attempt to induce Portland to be frank about his source.

We know that Stalin was sceptical of the depth of the Allies' commitment to defeat Germany. Their failure to reveal the Ultra secret to him now served to intensify his paranoia to the extent that he may have ignored what disguised Ultra material he *did* get, in the belief that the Allies were playing some deep and dangerous game with him. (This would be the explanation for the disastrous tank battles in 1942.) Seen in this light, the Allies' failure to share the secret of Ultra with an ally who was bearing the brunt of the war against Germany deepened Russian distrust of the West, and so contributed to the Cold War.

Thus Ultra made a significant contribution to the war effort in a few fields only, and little or none in others. It did not win the war and it is doubtful if it even shortened it. It made a negative contribution to Western–Soviet relations, and the failure to share it fully with the Russians so outraged several British officers working secretly for Soviet intelligence that they became absolutely convinced that their commitment was justified. The combination of a long-held wartime secret and the ability of articulate people to tell the story behind that secret once they were free to do so, has given Ultra an importance in intelligence history that it does not deserve.

# 9. KGB: Dzerzhinsky's Pride, Stalin's Prejudice

> Almost at the same time [5 June 1941], Richard Sorge sent Moscow in an astonishing compilation of data about 'Barbarossa', the objectives, the 'strategic concepts', the strength of the German troops to be committed and the opening date for the attack on the Soviet Union.
> – John Erickson, *The Road to Stalingrad* (1975).

> Stalin read all the reports flowing into Moscow warning of the forthcoming German attack, only to scrawl 'provocation' on them, and send them back to his intelligence administrator, F. I. Golikov, to be buried in the archives.
> – see p. 196 below.

If Feliks Dzerzhinsky, the founder of the modern Russian intelligence service, had been alive when Europe went to war in 1939 he would no doubt have been greatly pleased at how his organization had progressed. Long-term plans formulated soon after the Revolution had either achieved their goals or were about to do so. The Soviet approach to intelligence gathering – a huge, centralized effort in which it was impossible to see where traditional diplomacy ended and espionage began – had proved very effective. Intelligence, in the broadest sense of the word, was gathered by the NKVD (KGB) under the notorious Beria; the GRU, the military intelligence organization; the Soviet diplomatic corps; TASS, the main Soviet news agency; Amtorg, a trading company operating in the United States; and military, commercial and cultural missions.

The intelligence thus obtained was then forwarded to Moscow for collation and evaluation at one of the Soviet Union's largest government offices, the massive Central Information Department. A refined version was then passed to Stalin's own secretariat which, in turn, decided what to present to the Soviet leader himself. But just as Churchill had found himself overwhelmed by intelligence material and had taken steps to stem the flow, so Stalin, too, began to receive more than he could usefully absorb, and in 1940 there was a significant change in the system. F. I. Golikov was appointed chief of the General Staff Intelligence Administration, a Russian version of the Joint Intelligence Committee, and made responsible directly to Stalin. Golikov's staff undertook the responsibility for evaluating all incoming intelligence, matching it with earlier data, measuring it against the opinions of its own experts, and then passing it, via Golikov himself, to Stalin.[1] Thus, unlike its British and German counterparts, the Soviet system was highly centralized. But it, too, proved to have fatal flaws, human factors which led to disaster.

Firstly, Golikov was, understandably in the light of Stalin's record, anxious to please his master. It did not take him long to learn Stalin's views on a whole range of international issues. Any item, no matter what its source, which coincided with Stalin's opinions, Golikov classified as 'reliable'. He did not destroy those other items of intelligence which tended to contradict Stalin's preconceptions – he was too clever a bureaucrat for that – but he simply classified them as coming from 'doubtful' sources. Stalin returned these marked 'on file', so they were not circulated. As a result, no member of the Defence Commissariat or of the General Staff had any idea of the quantity or strength of the incoming intelligence material that conflicted with the views that they heard from Stalin.[2] The failures of the KGB, then, were just as serious as those of SIS, but attributable to different causes. SIS failed to provide a series of hungry consumers with sufficient raw material; the KGB, as we shall see, had, in general, excellent raw material, but Stalin, the one crucial consumer, often ignored it.

The KGB's priorities changed suddenly and dramatically after the German invasion of the Soviet Union in June 1941. In the earlier period it was the negotiations leading to the Soviet–German Pact of 23 August 1939 that were of prime interest to the KGB because Moscow had before it offers from the Western powers to sign an *anti*-German alliance. How sincere were these offers? What were the true objectives of Berlin, London and Paris? Once Stalin had signed the pact with Hitler, the Western powers, quietly at first and then with increasing urgency, began to warn him that Germany had no intention of keeping it; that the Nazis were only waiting for the right moment to strike eastwards and overrun the Soviet Union as they had overrun France and the Netherlands. Were these warnings genuine, or provocations designed to rupture the alliance? What *was* Germany's attitude to the Soviet Union after her stunning military success in the West?[3]

Once the German invasion of the Soviet Union began, the KGB's overriding priority became the British (and, later, American) attitude to German peace-feelers. Fear of a repeat of the Allied intervention of 1917–19, a switching of the war to a united German–British–American drive into the Russian heartland to end communism forever, gripped Moscow. This engendered a deep suspicion of Allied behaviour that was never entirely allayed throughout the war. What were the British up to? Who, exactly, in Germany was talking to them? America's entry into the war after Pearl Harbor in December 1941 provoked the same questions about the United States, plus the worry that Japan might attack the Soviet Union from the East.

There were, of course, nuts and bolts intelligence matters as well. The disposition, strength and morale of the attacking German forces, the battle plans of the German generals, the technicalities of German equipment, production figures, methods of communication, supply lines and troop movements, all interested the KGB. But these were not top priorities. Stalin saw the war with a broad political eye and, as a measure of this, it is significant that the KGB, even while the Soviet Union was still fighting for her life, maintained long-term interests. What sort of postwar Europe did the Western powers envisage?

Let us examine what dispositions the KGB had made so that we can answer these questions. The Red Orchestra led by the Pole, Leopold Trepper, operated in Belgium and later France and was the KGB's principal source of information from Occupied Europe. Richard Sorge, the half-German, half-Russian journalist and his Japanese colleague, Ozaki Hotsumi, ran from Tokyo what was probably the most influential Soviet spy network in the war. In Switzerland, the Lucy ring, or the Ring of Three – which included the Englishman, Alexander Foote – provided detailed operational information from German military sources. A Soviet intelligence officer in Rome had a source in the British embassy who was useful for political intelligence at a crucial stage. A network run by Ruth Kuczynski from her wartime home in Oxford, successfully penetrated the British War Cabinet, the RAF and the Supreme HQ Allied Expeditionary Force (SHAEF).

Finally, of course, there were the British sympathizers, those individuals from all sections of society, none part of any real network, some operating overtly, some covertly, some professional KGB officers, some not, who kept Moscow informed on a wide range of matters – Kim Philby, Guy Burgess, Donald Maclean, Anthony Blunt, John Cairncross, Ormond Uren, John King, Douglas

Springhall, and others yet unnamed.* It is the activities of this group that have fascinated readers in recent years, as book after book has tried to explain, firstly, why these men worked so willingly against what appeared to be Britain's best interests and, secondly, how they managed to do it. The latter question is the easier to answer.

Britain has a long tradition of civil liberties. It remains one of the few countries in Europe where citizens carry no official means of identification, where a letter from someone nominated by the applicant himself is usually considered to be a sufficient character reference for a job, where too close an inquiry into anyone's personal affairs – even for business purposes – is resented. It is understandable, therefore, that prewar government departments had seen no need for security checks within their ranks, 'which were thought to be safeguarded by the tradition of public service in the class from which it was recruited'.[5]

The Foreign Office, in particular, was like a club: 'entry to it automatically meant that you were assumed to be totally loyal and the most important virtue was keeping the club together'. Robert Cecil, who was in the Foreign Office at that time, has written that the principal private secretary, who, up to 1945, fulfilled the function of head of personnel, was reputed to have a file for staff labelled 'D' (for Drink) and 'A' (for Adultery) – worse offences were not contemplated. 'The service had the compactness of a family', Cecil wrote, 'and, as in all well-ordered families, there were areas into which one did not pry.'[6]

This state of affairs could not go on after John Herbert King, a 55-year-old cypher clerk in the Foreign Office was tried secretly on 18 October 1939 and convicted of passing information to the Soviet government. King had been recruited in Geneva in 1935, apparently accepting the explanation that all that was required of him was to pass information that would be of commercial use. The British

---

* Although, strictly speaking, the name Red Orchestra only applies to the Soviet network organized by Leopold Trepper in Belgium and France, MI5 discovered in German papers captured after the invasion of France, references to a Soviet network organized in Britain in 1939 by a German Jewish refugee, a friend of the singer, Richard Tauber. An MI5 officer found and interviewed the man. He frankly admitted that he had been recruited at a meeting at the Albert Hall and that he had organized a network to report to the Red Orchestra. The officer who interviewed the man, William Skardon, said, 'He named several people in the network. Some of them were quite prominent, others not. We decided to take no action against them.'[4]

security service had been alerted as a result of the American debriefing of the prewar Soviet defector, Walter Krivitsky, who had revealed that the KGB had 'a code clerk in the British Cabinet called King'. King, it turned out, had not been an active KGB agent for two years before his arrest, so had passed nothing of recent value to the Russians. Nevertheless, he was sentenced to ten years' imprisonment and steps were taken to institute some sort of security system in the Foreign Office – the most likely target for KGB penetration.[7]

In February 1940, the Foreign Office's first-ever security officer was appointed. William Codrington, a retired Foreign Office official, became unpaid adviser on security matters with direct access to the Foreign Secretary. He was given no staff until 1944 and it was not until 1946 that a security department, as such, came into being.[8] In the meantime, Codrington's attempts to introduce even a minimum standard of security and vetting were met with derision.

The British embassy in Ankara, a city with a considerable population of wartime spies, agents and informers, instituted a pass system for entry to the embassy building. Everyone, staff included, had to fill in a form stating their basic particulars before they could receive a pass. The head of chancery, Douglas Busk, stated on his application form that he was a Japanese midget, four feet high. The joke was not detected for weeks. Then the embassy visitors' book, containing the names of people of all nationalities to whom passes had been issued, vanished overnight. The staff were convinced that it had been stolen by someone working for the German embassy, just down the road. London also tried to vet the embassy staff in Moscow, worried that King might not be the only official who had been recruited by the KGB. The ambassador, Sir Archibald Clark-Kerr, received a parcel of forms with instructions to fill them in, commenting on his colleagues' background and attitudes. Clark-Kerr passed the forms on to his staff and told them to comment on themselves.[9]

The problem was a total failure to recognize the nature of the threat. Whitehall was ripe with professional distrust of the Soviet Union. The British security service maintained a file headed 'List of Foreign Communists Considered Dangerous by MI5', which contained twenty-one names, but its official attitude was that 'except for a few intransigent Communist doctrinaires and professional members of the Comintern, the rank and file have behaved themselves and have not entered into political controversies'.[10] The idea that the threat might come from *within* never occurred to anyone until the King case. And the King case was considered so out of the ordinary that it produced no change in this attitude. King was a desolate, poorly paid figure who had yielded to financial temptation. The concept of an ideologically inspired British recruit to the KGB was simply never considered.

Yet one such officer, Donald Maclean, was already in place in the Foreign Office; he was soon to be joined by Guy Burgess, a Comintern political agent; Anthony Blunt, another ideological convert, was shortly to join MI5; and Kim Philby, waiting in the wings as *The Times* war correspondent in France, would within months enter SIS itself, there to become the KGB's most valued British agent. Much has been written about the motives that led these men to betray their country and their class. When the *Sunday Times* first exposed Philby's full role as a KGB agent in a series of articles in 1967 we even consulted an eminent Harley Street psychiatrist in the hope that he could explain what had driven men like Philby to take such a different path. His reply was disappointing. He said that an ideology – Roman Catholicism, communism, or what you will – could give a person a sense of identity and masculine purpose. Secrecy was important psychologically: 'It may be a prolongation of the adolescent or pre-adolescent phase of the secret society which many schoolboys form when they are struggling to get away from parents, and gang up together in all-male groups. People who are not sure of their actual capability for achievement like to have a fantasy life in which they do great things, and to be a secret member of the party is obviously attractive to such people.'[11] Countless efforts since then to discover an answer have been equally unsatisfactory.

The error has been to imagine that the explanation must be a profound one and to ignore the obvious. As my colleague Bruce Page has written: 'The curiosity is that [so many people] should still be riveted, transfixed, astounded by the fact that the upper middle classes of the United Kingdom are capable of betraying the interests of the community they purport to serve. How odd a slant on matters: will a cat chase mice?'[12] The fact is that, despite their governing-class backgrounds, none of the four main Englishmen who served the KGB saw their action as a betrayal of anything.* As Philby said, 'To betray you must first belong'.[13] They had been shaken loose from their roots by the events of the 1930s: the Wall Street Crash; unemployment and hunger marches in Britain; the policies of the Baldwin–Chamberlain era which Philby called 'more than the

---

* Blunt's father was vicar of St John's Church, Paddington, and sent his son to Marlborough; Burgess's father was in the Royal Navy and Burgess went to Eton; Maclean's father was a lawyer and a leading Liberal MP and sent Donald to Gresham's. Philby's father was in the Indian Civil Service and sent Kim to Westminster.

politics of folly, the politics of evil'; and the apparent inability of any political system – except Marxism – to make a stand against the rise of fascism and the barbarity it foreshadowed (Germany had just revived beheading for political offences).

These young men rejected the liberal and Christian inheritance of their class and sought to purge themselves from the decadence and corruption of the period. But because it was not possible to cut themselves off completely from their backgrounds, their disgust was intensely personal and this sustained them through the doubts that brought many others of their generation, who had originally shared their views, back into the comfort of the fold. Thus the surprise is not that there were so many communist converts in the 1930s who made lifelong commitments to the Soviet Union, but that there were so few.

Contrary to other reports, their commitment to Marxism was initially quite open. Philby was well known among his contemporaries at Trinity, Cambridge, as a fellow-traveller. Donald Maclean was a most public communist and told everyone that, as soon as he had finished with Cambridge, he would be off to Russia to help the Revolution, probably as a teacher. He wrote an article in *Cambridge Left* on the capitalist society and spoke confidently in it of 'the rising tide of opinion which is going to sweep away the whole crack-brained, criminal mess'.[14] Guy Burgess was deeply involved in Marxist politics at Cambridge and during one vacation visited the Soviet Union. By 1937 he was telling people that he was a Comintern agent. Anthony Blunt's Marxist past was so open that he was rejected in 1939 for a commission in military intelligence because the War Office considered him to be politically unreliable.

Except for Blunt, who said that he began to have doubts in the late 1940s and, by 1951, had become hostile to the Soviet Union, none of them ever wavered in his commitment. Philby has written that even during Stalin's worst excesses he decided to stick it out 'in the confident faith that the principles of the Revolution would outlive the aberrations of individuals, however enormous'.[15] Burgess wrote from Moscow: 'I am loyal to the USSR, though that loyalty is, of course, based on . . . confidence in its wisdom, self-control and far-sighted statesmanship. There is so little room for our own old Foreign Office to display similar qualities.'[16] Maclean wrote a book, *British Policy since Suez 1956–1968*, which gave a Marxist analysis of British attitudes and actions, raised his children as Russians, lived an unobtrusive life in a flat in Moscow studiously avoiding other Westerners, and never expressed the slightest doubt about his actions.

After the German attack on the Soviet Union, the four could even argue that there was no conflict between their work for the KGB and their work for the British war effort. The Russians were our allies. Churchill, then Prime Minister, had publicly pledged that he would give the Soviet government 'any technical or economic assistance which is in our power', and the defeat of the Axis was the prime aim of all concerned. Philby has said of what he did for the KGB: 'I considered, and still consider now, that by this work I also served my own English people.'[17]

The one factor common to the recruitment of all four was an appeal by the recruiter, whoever he was, that they should not waste their talents by dying on some foreign battlefield but should continue with their education and career until the moment arrived when they could be of most service to the Soviet Union. This is typical of KGB practice. As Philby says, 'We have a tradition of foresight and patience laid down by that brilliant man, Feliks Dzerzhinsky'.[18]

The first of the four to find an opportunity to serve was Donald Maclean. In 1936, having finished eleven months' probation at the Foreign Office, he was posted to the British embassy in Paris as third secretary. At about the same time, Burgess had succeeded in establishing himself in London's political, financial and social circles. He advised Mrs Charles Rothschild, mother of his university friend Victor (now Lord) Rothschild, on her investments and any influence that current political developments might have on them – a perfect cover for asking his political friends what might otherwise have seemed too many pertinent questions. He was personal assistant to the Conservative MP for Chelmsford, Captain 'Jack' Macnamara, who was an important member of the Anglo-German Fellowship, a pro-German body which strongly supported appeasement. Burgess had a network of influential rightwing political contacts in Britain, and via his homosexual links, an important source in France, Edouard Pfeiffer, Cabinet chief to the French Prime Minister, Daladier. Philby was in Spain, under cover as *The Times* correspondent with the Franco forces, but working for the KGB with an assignment 'to get first-hand information on all aspects of the Fascist war effort'. Only Blunt, who had stayed on at Cambridge, and who had then gone to the Warburg Institute in 1937, was not in a position during those darkening years to be of service to the KGB other than as a 'talent spotter'.

The principal concern of the Soviet government in this early period was to decide with which country it should conclude an alliance. Until the Russians release their documentation on negotiations leading to the Soviet–German Pact of 23 August 1939, it is impossible to produce a definitive version of the process by which Moscow decided to sign with Hitler rather than the Western powers, who were offering an anti-Nazi alliance. But we can say what sort of intelligence would have had a powerful influence on that decision and how Maclean, Burgess, Philby, and others were well placed to supply it. The KGB would have been asking questions, such as: What is the real strength of the British and French desire for an alliance with Moscow? If we sign, and war comes, will Britain and France really fight Germany? Alternatively, how likely is an alliance between Britain, France, Germany and Italy against us? What are Japan's intentions? Would she join such an alliance? How powerful is the German war machine?

Maclean saw, as part of his duties in Paris, copies of virtually all the embassy's correspondence. The ambassador, Sir Eric Phipps, had previously been ambassador in Berlin, where he had been strongly anti-Nazi. In Paris, however, he came to believe (correctly, in contrast to SIS) that the French would not fight. Concerned about Britain's ability to stand alone, he turned to appeasement as the answer.[19] Phipps's assessment of the French will to fight, and the fact that such an important British diplomat favoured appeasing Hitler, would have greatly interested the KGB, especially as Burgess's reports from London no doubt confirmed the attitude of the French and painted a depressing picture of the extent and influence of pro-German feeling in Britain.

From Rome, the KGB would have had reports from the Soviet embassy, which had engaged an agent in the British embassy who regularly photographed the contents of the embassy safe and gave one copy to the Italian intelligence service and one to the Russians. Thus, a telegram sent by the Foreign Secretary, Lord Halifax, to the ambassador in Berlin, Neville Henderson, and forwarded by Henderson to Rome, found its way to Moscow. The KGB was no doubt intrigued to learn from it that while London was negotiating an alliance with the Soviet Union, the British would actually have preferred an agreement with Germany. As historian Dr M. Toscano comments: 'Given a question as difficult as that of choosing among offers presented simultaneously by London, Berlin and Paris, exact knowledge of the true objectives of Nazi policy and the lack of British enthusiasm for an entente with Moscow could not be but a factor of singular importance.'[20]

Journalist colleagues of Philby's in Spain recall that he was never content with knowing the general details of troop movements, but insisted on numbers, divisions, regiments, weapons – information which was far more detailed than *The Times* readers would have required and which, moreover, did not appear in his dispatches. Philby transmitted this sort of information, and his own assessment of the Fascist war effort, to Soviet contacts he met when he joined parties of journalists on visits across the border into France. He continued this sort of work for the KGB when he become *The Times* war correspondent in France. 'Luckily, apart from my censored dispatches to *The Times*', he has written, 'I was able to transmit news to another quarter which was not the least interested in the optimistic lucubrations of GHQ, only in the hard facts of military life: unit strength and locations, gun calibres, tank performances, etc. But for that, my time at Arras [British headquarters] would have been completely wasted.'[21] Maclean, too, until forced to flee from Paris when the Germans were at its gates, had access to information of strong interest to the Russians, such as the Anglo-French military plans to support Finland in her winter war against the Soviet Union, and to attack the Soviet oil wells at Baku in order to cut supplies to the German forces.[22]

But it was probably Richard Sorge and his Tokyo network who were rendering the USSR the most important service at this time. Sorge, a German national, was born in Russia in 1895, was educated in Berlin, and grew up to be an idealistic, hard-drinking, womanizing journalist who turned to communism while a soldier during the First World War as a way of preventing 'further imperialist wars' (a comparison with Philby is irresistible!) Tall, handsome, with a slight limp, he would normally have been considered too unreliable a personality to be a senior KGB officer. Once, speeding through Tokyo on his motorbike, drunk, he crashed into a wall, and one of his agents had to rush to the hospital ahead of the police to remove incriminating documents from Sorge's pockets. But the KGB was desperate for high-quality political intelligence from China and Japan and he was recruited by the Comintern intelligence section in 1925. After missions in Britain and Scandinavia in 1928–9, he was transferred to Red Army intelligence and was sent to Shanghai because Moscow was fascinated by the possible consequences of a Chinese revolution for the world communist movement.

By 1933 Sorge was back in Moscow being briefed for his new mission which was probably formulated by Stalin himself. The

Manchurian Incident in 1931* had made Moscow deeply concerned about Japanese expansionism and its attitude to the Soviet Union. Sorge, because of his success in China, seemed an ideal officer to post to Tokyo. Working with the patient thoroughness that was to characterize his ring, Sorge spent two years in preparation. Branko de Voukelitch, a Comintern intelligence officer, was sent to Tokyo under cover as a journalist working for the French magazine *Vue* and the Belgrade newspaper *Politika*. He was to be Sorge's aide. Miyagi Yotoku, a Japanese artist who had been educated in the United States and was a member of the American Communist Party, was ordered to return to Japan for a special mission. His job was to be the ring's translator of Japanese material into a language that could be encoded for radio transmission. The radio operator, known only as 'Bernhardt', a German communist, had been trained in Moscow and was already living in Tokyo. (He was later replaced by another German, Max Clausen.)

Sorge himself went off to Germany to create his own cover. He joined the Nazi Party; he got himself appointed Tokyo correspondent of the *Frankfurter Zeitung*, Germany's most respected newspaper, of the *Tägliche Rundschau* and of the *Berliner Börsenzeitung*. He armed himself with letters of introduction to the German embassy in Tokyo and to influential Germans in Japan. Then he travelled to Japan via the United States and set about recruiting the Japanese national who was to be the ring's most valued agent, and whose contribution to the KGB's efforts was equalled only by that of Sorge himself.

This was Ozaki Hotsumi, the brilliant son of a journalist, descendant of a long line of rural samurai. Ozaki was raised and educated in Taiwan where his father worked on a Taiwan newspaper, *nichi-nichi shimpō*. As a member of the ruling élite he attended special schools, learnt English, and returned to Tokyo to enter the Imperial University. The appalling treatment of Koreans, communists and labour leaders in the aftermath of the Kanto earthquake of 1923 (many were murdered by the police and mobs who claimed that they feared a rebellion in the chaos), had a profound effect on Ozaki who turned to Marxism to try to learn more about minorities, social problems and politics. He joined the *Asahi Shimbun* newspaper and, in 1927, was assigned to cover the Chinese revolution. At a Comintern bookshop in Shanghai in late 1930, he was introduced to Sorge by Agnes Smedley, the leftwing American writer and contributor to the

* The Japanese Kwantung army sabotaged the South Manchurian railway, accused the Chinese of doing it, and used this as a pretext for driving the Chinese armies from Manchuria.

American magazine *New Masses*. They became friends, had long discussions on politics and philosophy and when, back in Tokyo in 1934, Sorge put it to Ozaki that he could help the fight against fascism and militarism by gathering intelligence for the Comintern, Ozaki readily agreed to do so.

It was not until late 1936 that the ring was ready to operate. The intervening period was spent in establishing everyone's cover, in acquainting the foreign members with the nature of Japanese society, and in mastering the subject matter of the mission. By the time that Sorge decided that the ring was ready to begin its work it was a formidable organization, perhaps, indeed, the most formidable in espionage history. Sorge had so established himself in the German embassy that his position was second only to that of the ambassador himself. He was unofficial embassy adviser, with an office in the embassy building and full and free access to all the files. He knew all the local Nazis, all the German newspapermen and many others, including the Associated Press representative, Relman Morin, and the Reuters man, James Cox (killed by Japanese police in 1940). He had devoted himself to a rigorous study of Japanese politics, history, economics and art. He travelled extensively and had half-finished a book on Japan which would certainly have achieved considerable academic success. No other Westerner in Japan at that time had such a thorough knowledge of all aspects of Japanese life and affairs.[23]

Meanwhile Ozaki had risen in the world. As a writer of numerous books and articles on Sino-Japanese relations and, later, on the war between the two countries, he had established himself as the leading Japanese expert in this field, a high-level political analyst. He was a consultant to the Japanese Cabinet, had free access to the Cabinet secretariat, occupied an office in the official residence of the Premier, Prince Konoye, and, probably most useful of all, he was a member of the Breakfast Society, a Kitchen Cabinet, which advised Prince Konoye on a wide range of internal and international issues. This not only gave him access to the decision-making processes of the Japanese government, but enabled him to verify his personal opinions by testing them on the actual decision-makers. Like Burgess, he never had to pry for important information: people freely gave it to him in order to obtain his opinion. By 1938 Sorge and Ozaki were no longer merely reporting developments to the KGB; they were helping to make the very decisions that their espionage was supposed to uncover.

Up to this stage, the ring had one mission of overriding importance: to warn the KGB of any plans for a Japanese attack on the

Soviet Union. The reason for this mission can be quickly understood. Miyagi, the ring's translator told his interrogators that, 'Sorge told us that if Japan's attack on Russia could be forecast two months ahead, it could be avoided by diplomatic manoeuvres; if one month in advance, the Soviet Union could have large forces on the border and its defences ready; if two weeks ahead, a first line of defence could be constructed, and if only a week ahead, losses could be reduced.'[24]

The reasons for Soviet fear of a Japanese first strike were as follows. The Anti-Comintern Pact between Germany and Japan, signed in 1936, raised for Moscow the worrying spectre of a war on two fronts, one it could scarcely expect to win. Subsequent events during 1938–9 seemed to suggest that Japan was spoiling for a fight with the Soviet Union. In the summer of 1938 the Kwantung army claimed extra territory along the Russo-Japanese border south-west of Vladivostok. The Russians rejected the claim and sent forces to hold the area. The Kwantung army tried to dislodge them and in the furious fighting that ensued the Japanese advanced three miles into Soviet territory.

The KGB bombarded the Sorge ring with requests for information. Was this going to be a pretext for a Japanese invasion of Siberia? Ozaki attended Cabinet discussions on the incident. Sorge estimated the strength of the Japanese forces from German embassy sources. Miyagi established that no large troop movements were under way. Clausen transmitted all this to the KGB, ending with Sorge's opinion that Japan had no intention of allowing the incident to develop into a war. Without Soviet documents on the incident we cannot positively establish cause and effect. What the record does show is that Moscow refused any compromise on the issue and insisted on a return to the border as established before the incident. The Japanese backed down and agreed.

The following year the Kwantung army struck again. During the winter and spring it made repeated raids into Outer Mongolia to see whether the Soviet Far East Army would fight back. It did. On the morning of 20 August 1939 the Russians counter-attacked in force and, by the end of the month, had driven the Japanese out of Soviet Mongolian territory. This was a major Soviet victory and Moscow fully expected Japan to declare war. But, virtually in the middle of the battle, the Soviet–German Pact was signed, and the Kwantung army, bewildered by a diplomatic development it did not understand, lost heart for the fight, thus contributing to the switching of Japanese territorial ambitions towards the south.

Sorge's ring performed as before, but here its influence on events is less clear. Ozaki reported that the Breakfast Society wanted Japan to avoid war with the Soviet Union at all costs. His military contacts told him that the army had been stunned by the ferocity of the Russian counter-attack. Voukelitch visited the battlefield as a journalist and noted the numbers and types of Japanese aircraft in use; Miyagi established the strength and location of reserves that might be used as reinforcements; Sorge learnt from the German military attachés that their Japanese colleagues did not consider the battle to be the first stage of an invasion.

But the KGB's conviction that the Japanese were determined to attack the Soviet Union was so deep-rooted that Sorge's analyses were, he said later, 'unacceptable' and he was ordered to continue to concentrate his efforts on finding out the timing of the Japanese invasion. The need for this vigilance appeared to lessen after the signing of the Russo-Japanese Neutrality Treaty in April 1941.* Sorge regarded this as a diplomatic victory for the Soviet Union, and his efforts were switched to keeping a watchful eye for any signs that Japan might not abide by the treaty in the event of a German attack on Russia.

The likelihood of such an attack now occupied most of Sorge's attention. Three separate sources at the German embassy gave him details of Barbarossa, Hitler's plans for invading the Soviet Union. The senior military attaché told him sometime in April 1941, two months before the attack, that Germany's preparations had been completed. In early May a military emissary from Berlin arrived in Tokyo to brief the ambassador. He carried a letter of introduction to Sorge and had a meeting with him to explain Hitler's strategic reasoning for the invasion. Soon afterwards another German officer, *en route* to a new posting in Bangkok, stopped off in Tokyo and told Sorge that the invasion would occur on 20 June (it, in fact, started on 22 June) and that the main thrust would be towards the Ukraine. Sorge radioed this to the KGB at the end of May but, as we shall see, his warning, which was only one among many, was ignored by Stalin.

Once Germany had launched its invasion of the Soviet Union, Sorge's ring once more concentrated its efforts on discovering

* Japan might never have signed such a treaty – and the course of the Second World War might have been very different – if Hitler had told the Japanese Foreign Minister, Matsuoka Yosuke, when he visited Berlin in March 1941, that Germany was soon going to invade the Soviet Union. Hitler said nothing. So Matsuoka went on to Moscow where he signed a neutrality pact with Stalin. If Hitler had spoken frankly about his plans, then Japan may not have signed the pact with the Soviet Union and Stalin might well have found himself in June of that year defending an invasion by Germany in the West and by Japan in the East.[25]

Japan's intentions. There appeared to be two main schools of thought. One school held that the Axis alliance had the emperor's backing, that it therefore took precedence over the Russo-Japanese Neutrality Treaty, and that Japan would have to go to the aid of Germany. The other felt that the Axis alliance excluded the Soviet Union and that the treaty meant, therefore, a new area of obligation which took precedence over the earlier one. The question may have been one of honour for the Japanese; for the Soviet Union it was one of survival. For, as Hitler's troops overwhelmed the Soviet defences and pushed onwards to Moscow, Stalin's main hope of hitting back lay with the Soviet forces facing Japan – the fresh, well-equipped and combat-experienced Far Eastern armies. He could commit them to the struggle against Germany only if he were absolutely certain that his neutrality treaty with Japan would be honoured.

Sorge's ring redoubled its efforts to determine whether or not this would be so. Ozaki was the key figure. As a member of the Breakfast Society he was not only well placed to learn the government's decision on when and where to attack, but to influence that decision. The society, strongly supported by Ozaki, recommended that Japan should strike south against the Americans and the British and pursue its well-laid plans for taking the Dutch East Indies and Singapore. It should ignore Hitler's demand for an attack on Siberia and honour the neutrality pact with the Soviet Union. The government agreed to this on 2 July 1941 and the decision was confirmed by the emperor. For obvious reasons this was kept highly secret, but Ozaki managed to confirm it to his own satisfaction. Lunching with a high-ranking War Ministry official, Ozaki said that *he* was convinced that Japan would not attack the Soviet Union. The official told Ozaki that he was correct. Sorge had reached the same conclusion from his contacts in the German embassy. The ambassador had been frantically trying to convince the Japanese government of the need to enter the war against the Soviet Union and had obviously been making no progress.

In the first week of October 1941, Sorge weighed all the evidence and radioed the KGB: 'There will be no attack until the Spring of next year at the earliest.' Within days, half the ground strength of the Soviet Far Eastern armies was on the move westwards. But it is a long way from the Far Eastern frontiers of the Soviet Union to Moscow and, although legend has it that Sorge's message enabled the Siberian troops to reach Moscow in time to save the capital, this is not true. Only two regiments were assembled in time for the deciding battle,[26] so their presence was more a psychological boost than a military one. Just when the German High Command was convinced that the Red Army could not possibly have any further reserves, 'there came reports that fresh Siberian troops equipped in superb winter clothing were attacking our lines'.[27] By the time that the main body of the Siberian army had arrived the German advance had already been halted. They now turned the demoralized Germans around. The retreat from Moscow had begun.

This was the Sorge ring's greatest service to the Soviet Union, but it was accomplished in that grey area that divides the exercise of political influence from espionage. It can be argued that Sorge's message was merely a report on what he and Ozaki had already *achieved* – they had tilted the Japanese decision against an attack on Russia. Sorge himself certainly believed that his ring's exercise of political influence was more important than its spying.

There is some doubt, indeed, as to whether the ring's work was espionage in the legal sense. To begin with, all the best correspondents in Japan at that time cultivated political and military contacts because they were the only source of hard news. In fact, according to Professor Chalmers Johnson, 'It would have been difficult to find a competent newsman in Japan on the eve of Pearl Harbor who had *not* been accused by the police of being a spy.'[28]

Moreover, Sorge openly published much of the material that his ring sent to Moscow. For example, he was charged with telling the Russians, among other things, about the backgrounds of the young Japanese officers involved in a revolt on 26 February 1936. Yet everything in Sorge's report to Moscow on this incident was published in a series of his articles in the German magazine *Zeitschrift für Geopolitik*.

Finally, no state of war existed between Japan and the Soviet Union when the ring was operating, and Sorge gathered most of his intelligence at the German embassy which was technically German soil. But the Japanese judicial system, at that time, was weighted heavily against the defendant and by bringing charges against Sorge and Ozaki under both the Peace Preservation Law (easier to prove) and the National Defence Security Law (which carried the death penalty) the authorities virtually ensured both men's execution.

The ring had been uncovered almost entirely by accident. The Japanese police had been aware for some years of illegal radio transmissions originating somewhere in Tokyo. The navy and one or two government departments had complained about secrets leaking to the press. At the same time, Berlin had become concerned about Sorge's political past and a Gestapo officer going to Tokyo was instructed to report on Sorge. Against orders, this officer told the

Japanese police of his mission and they mistakenly got the impression that Sorge was under German surveillance because of security leaks from the embassy. They made a list of his associates and began to investigate them, looking in particular for members of the Japanese section of the American Communist Party who might have returned to Japan – a priority target because of steadily deteriorating relations with the United States. This led them to Miyagi Yotoku. Under torture, he confessed and named the other members of the ring.

It is likely that they were all tortured. Voukelitch, who was only 41-years-old and in good health, died in prison of unknown causes. So did Miyagi and three of the ring's Japanese sources. The Japanese prosecutor at Sorge's trial said that Sorge had been in 'poor health' for a week following his arrest. Clausen, who gave the prosecution all the help he could, seems to have escaped torture, as did Ozaki, who admitted everything but defended his actions vigorously. Clausen got life imprisonment and his wife three years. Sorge (49) and Ozaki (43) were hanged on 7 November 1944.*

For twenty years the Soviet Union made no reference to Sorge's role in the war. Professor Johnson wrote in 1964: 'The USSR has never so much as acknowledged the existence of Richard Sorge; and we do not know how many of Sorge's reports got through, or what relative weight was given to them in comparison with reports from other Soviet spies.'[29] One reason was that Stalin never completely trusted Sorge's information because Sorge's first boss, General Ian Antonovich Berzin, was executed in 1937 for being a Trotskyist and this made all his agents suspect. Stalin might have been even more concerned had he known of Sorge's contacts with German intelligence. From the moment he had consolidated his position with the embassy in Tokyo until his arrest, Sorge was sending reports not only to Moscow but also to Berlin. He told German intelligence that the Axis Pact would be of little military value to Germany because Japan would not renounce her neutrality treaty with the Soviet Union. In short, the key piece of intelligence which Sorge reported to the Russians, namely, that Japan would not attack in Siberia, he also gave to the Germans.[30] And it was as a possible *Nazi* agent that Sorge first came to the attention of the Japanese police.

* Some say Sorge was not hanged. They argue that the Japanese would not have wanted to antagonize the Soviet Union at a time when they hoped it would help them negotiate a peace settlement with the Allies. Also the prison authorities ordered a new suit for Sorge, a strange thing to do for a man about to be hanged. They claim that Sorge was handed over to the Russians and died in the Soviet Union in the early 1960s. There is no evidence to support this theory.

This does not mean that Sorge was a double agent – although the KGB would have regarded such behaviour with extreme suspicion. A more feasible explanation is simply that Sorge did not win the trust and confidence of the German ambassador and, through him, sources in Germany and Japan, without giving something in return. Like all collectors of information – journalists, spies, authors – he knew that the traffic had to be a two-way one. But everything about his life and death – his last words were in praise of the Communist Party and the Red Army – point to his being a dedicated servant of the KGB; it got the fat, the Germans only the trimmings.

The KGB appears finally to have accepted this. In 1964, the twentieth anniversary of Sorge's death, a flood of articles appeared in Soviet publications. They had titles, such as 'The Story of a Soviet Spy's Heroism' (*Izvestia*, 4 September 1964) and 'The Feat of Richard Sorge' (*Pravda*, 6 November 1964). Then, in March 1975, Tass news agency announced 'a new patriotic opera entitled *Richard Sorge*, celebrating the exploits of the Soviet espionage officer who exposed the German invasion plans . . . The work focuses on Sorge's wartime career during 1940–44 when he served as a Soviet intelligence agent in Japan.'[31] Soon afterwards Sorge was honoured with a commemorative stamp bearing his photograph. Among ordinary people in the Soviet Union, Sorge was the best-known Soviet intelligence officer of the Second World War – at least until the publication in Russian in 1980 of Philby's book *My Silent War*.

Ozaki's role continues to intrigue the Japanese. A crypto-communist who apparently became 'a traitor for the most patriotic reasons' – he thought that the Comintern offered the best hope of overthrowing the imperialist and militaristic rulers of Japan – he was also a brilliant and perceptive political analyst. He foresaw that the growth of Chinese nationalism, provoked largely by the actions of the Japanese army, would lead to a Chinese revolution that would transform the Orient. His rigorous intellectual approach to these matters, the clarity of his writing, and his deep concern that Japan should fulfil its destiny in South East Asia, have appealed to Japanese of varying political views. His letters from prison became a bestseller in 1946 and has been republished many times. There have been two films, a play, and several novels based on his life and his trial. As far as the KGB was concerned, it found in Ozaki and Sorge what every intelligence organization dreams of having – dedicated, ideologically motivated agents, in positions where they can not only report secret decisions but also influence those decisions.

As has been mentioned, Sorge's message giving the date of the German invasion of Russia some three weeks before it occurred was not the only warning that Stalin received – and ignored. Sorge was only one source used by the KGB to try to discover Hitler's intentions at this time. After a meeting in the Kremlin in January 1939, when Stalin told his senior military commanders that a future war might well be on two fronts – in the West against Nazi Germany, in the East against Imperialist Japan –[32] the KGB had done its utmost to obtain forewarning of both countries' war plans. Since this was one of the larger intelligence tasks of the Second World War it is worth charting how the KGB fared.

The British were probably the first to receive indications that Germany planned to attack the Soviet Union. In August 1940, SIS learned from its Czech agent A-54 that the German High Command, Foreign Armies East had embarked on a large-scale expansion of its intelligence section, and that the Abwehr in Romania had been reinforced with specialists on the Crimea and the Caucasus. None of the KGB agents serving in Britain was in a position to learn of this report. Philby had only just joined SIS and was in Section D discussing with Burgess some hare-brained schemes for blocking the Danube. Blunt had just entered MI5 and was in an unimportant section, with access to very little information. Ruth Kuczynski did not begin operating in Britain until May 1941. SIS, moreover, kept the report within its own service and failed to tell the JIC, the Chiefs of Staff, or the Cabinet about it, basically because it preferred to believe that Hitler was concentrating his efforts on planning the invasion of Britain, not the Soviet Union. (SIS stuck to this conviction, despite a report from its man in Helsinki in November that Abwehr officers had told him that Germany would attack the Soviet Union in the Spring.)[33]

So the first reliable news that Stalin received of German invasion plans came not via the KGB and its agents but through diplomatic channels. The American commercial attaché in Berlin, Sam Woods, had a source within the German military establishment. A civilian who was anti-Nazi, he not only told Woods about the planning for the invasion, but also revealed Hitler's intention of looting the Soviet Union of its economic resources. Woods put all this into a report and sent it to Washington in January 1941, where it was initially greeted with disbelief on the ground that this was not the sort of intelligence that could possibly come the way of a lowly commercial attaché. But after a team from the FBI had evaluated the report and said that it believed it to be genuine, the State Department took it seriously. It consulted the American ambassador in Moscow, who said that the Russians would not believe the report and would denounce it as provocation by the United States. Eventually, the American Under Secretary, Sumner Wells, chose an opportune moment to tell the Soviet ambassador in Washington of the report and its origins at a meeting on 1 March.[34]

But, in the meantime, the British ambassador to Moscow, Sir Stafford Cripps, who must have heard about the Woods material from his American colleague, acted, on his own initiative, and gave an informal press conference on 28 February at which he said he was convinced that Germany would attack the Soviet Union before the end of June.[35] Since Cripps would not have expressed this view publicly before telling the Soviet Foreign Ministry, we can assume that he had already done so.

Other diplomatic reports of German intentions now came thick and fast. The Swedish government heard of the planned attack through its missions in Berlin, Bucharest and Helsinki. On 3 April Churchill wrote personally to Stalin. He had learnt from Ultra intercepts that the Germans had started to move five panzer divisions from Romania to southern Poland, but that they had reversed the order because of an anti-Nazi coup in Yugoslavia. He interpreted this as evidence of Hitler's intention to attack the Soviet Union in May, but suggested that Germany's need to secure Yugoslavia first would now delay the invasion until June. Churchill invited Stalin to draw the same conclusion. But Cripps, who was supposed to deliver the letter, had seen how his earlier warning had been treated and delayed handing it over until 19 April because he believed that the Russians would regard it as yet another provocation. There is good reason for believing this caution to have been justified. Stalin already had ample indications of Germany's intentions, had he only been willing to heed them. KGB agents in Germany had confirmed the concentration of German troops and an agent in Czechoslovakia had reported that the giant Skoda works had been ordered to stop deliveries of war material to the Soviet Union. Later, the Czech government, which from its exile in Britain continued to run a network of well-informed agents in Occupied Europe, received details of the various 'occupation regimes' that the Germans were organizing for Russian areas. The KGB had news of German submarines arriving on station outside the Soviet base at Libau, and had received reports that German naval units in the Baltic had increased their state of readiness. The Soviet military attaché in Berlin reported that a German attack was pending, possibly scheduled for 14

May, and later his deputy reported that the attack was now firmly set for 15 June. Another report to the KGB read: 'Military preparations . . . are proceeding quite openly and German officers and men speak with complete frankness about the coming war between Germany and the Soviet Union as something already decided upon.' All this should have made Stalin treat the warnings from other, non-Soviet, sources with some seriousness. Yet on 14 May the Soviet Foreign Minister, V. M. Molotov, dismissed invasion predictions as 'British and American propaganda' and said that relations between the Soviet Union and Germany were excellent. Stalin read all the reports flowing into Moscow warning of the forthcoming German attack, only to scrawl 'provocation' on them, and send them back to his intelligence administrator, F. I. Golikov, to be buried in the archives.[36]

Whatever else he was, Stalin was no fool and his conclusions, which in retrospect look so pathetic, were nevertheless logical ones. Militarily, he did not believe that Hitler would be so foolish as to embark on a war on two fronts. Why then was Germany massing troops on her Eastern border? Because, Stalin argued, Hitler was determined to squeeze every ounce of profit from the Soviet Union and his military build-up was intended to give him the clout that would allow him to make economic demands which would probably go beyond earlier agreements. The warnings from Britain and the United States that Hitler planned to loot the Soviet Union, take slave labour to Germany and crush the communist system, Stalin dismissed as a Western conspiracy to entice him into a pre-emptive attack on Germany. Britain would then quickly make peace with Hitler, the United States would join them, and the Soviet Union would face her second Allied invasion in twenty years.

Hess's flight to Britain on 15 May, coming at such a crucial time, bolstered Stalin's analysis: the British were up to something with the Germans; a dangerous anti-Soviet conspiracy was afoot. Thus warnings of a German invasion from foreign sources should be discounted and KGB agents should beware of provocations. Even when the Lucy ring in Switzerland sent not only the exact date of the German attack – 22 June – but the German order of battle and first objectives, Stalin pointed out that any Abwehr plot designed to lead the Soviet Union to disaster would naturally begin by offering information so detailed as to make it appear to be true.

No doubt there was another thought at the back of Stalin's mind. Even if all the information that the KGB was giving him turned out to be true, then there was no need to be panicked into an immediate response – the Soviet Union still had plenty of time to prepare for war. The Soviet leader calculated that the Yugoslav resistance would keep the Germans busy for about three months, which would give the Soviet Union another year for its military preparations, since it would then be too late for Germany to launch an attack before winter came. The sudden collapse of Yugoslav resistance removed this comforting thought.

But Stalin was not alone in believing that, in the end, Germany would negotiate rather than attack. In Britain, conviction that Germany would attack had come only very late in the day. Throughout May the JIC still believed that although Hitler would invade the Soviet Union if he had to, 'agreement is the more likely event'. Despite a stream of Ultra intercepts showing German military preparations, Whitehall intelligence branches clung to their view that Germany would present the Soviet Union with a series of demands and an ultimatum, and that Stalin would probably give way. As late as 16 June Sir Stafford Cripps, showing none of the certainty he had displayed at his informal press conference four months previously, suggested to the British Cabinet that the Germans and the Russians were already secretly negotiating, and hinted that it was probable that the Soviet Union would agree to the concessions which Germany was demanding.[37]

But on 22 June 1941, with no ultimatum and no declaration of war, two million German troops supported by thousands of tanks and planes pushed into the Soviet Union. Operation Barbarossa had begun, the most bloody campaign of the Second World War was opened and Stalin now knew that, despite the wealth of intelligence available to him, he had got it all wrong. At least, he might have consoled himself, he was not the only one.

With the Soviet Union fighting for her life, the priorities of the KGB changed. At an operational level, it needed a regular flow of nuts and bolts information about the German armed forces. On a political level, information about Japan's intentions was a priority, and was provided by the Sorge ring. It was also anxious to keep a careful eye on any peace-feelers between Germany and the Allies that might presage a switch from an anti-Fascist war to an anti-communist one. This last task was the responsibility of its British penetration agents, especially Philby. After the fall of France, Philby, through an introduction from Burgess, was recruited into SIS where he went to work for Section D (training agents in underground work). (One of the prospective agents, a

Frenchman, said later that of all the lecturers Philby was the only one who gave the real flavour of what it was like to be an espionage agent in the field – in retrospect, an intriguing clue to Philby's own role.) When Section D was incorporated into the newly formed SOE, Philby found himself working as an instructor in underground political propaganda at SOE's training school in Beaulieu, Hampshire. On the face of it, this was not the best place for a KGB penetration agent to find the sort of political information his superiors wanted at that time, but Philby soon showed the ingenuity that distinguished his spying career.

He argued that it was useless to teach SOE agents merely the methods of disseminating propaganda; the content of that propaganda was equally important. If the SOE field agent was to inspire those under the Nazi heel to risk their lives, then the propaganda he put out would have to offer a better future. So Philby got permission to seek political guidance on Britain's view of Europe after victory. He turned to Hugh Gaitskell, a future leader of the Labour Party, at that time principal private secretary to Hugh Dalton, the Minister for Economic Warfare. Philby had known Gaitskell slightly before the war and Gaitskell did his best to help, sometimes taking Philby back to his office to consult Dalton himself. In this way, Philby, ostensibly a humble SOE instructor, learnt that the British government's view of postwar Europe was a simple return to the pre-Hitler status quo, with a reinstatement of those governments which had shown themselves to be reliable in maintaining the cordon sanitaire against the Soviet Union. This was very important information for the KGB because it meant that, although Britain might be willing now to support communist resistance movements in Europe if they were more effective than others in fighting the Germans, it would turn against them if they looked like becoming the postwar rulers. This knowledge coloured relations between the communist resistance movements and London throughout the war.

In September 1941, Philby was given an opportunity to move back into SIS. Friends in MI5 recommended him for a job in Section V, the counter-espionage section, where there were plans to expand the desk dealing with Spain and Portugal. Although this was, as Philby says, 'out on the flank of my real interest', he accepted and joined Section V's offices at St Albans. It proved a rewarding step for the Russians. The Central Registry housing the SIS archives was situated next door to Section V and Philby soon found a plausible reason for getting access to these files: he wanted to look at the records of SIS agents operating in his area – Spain and Portugal. He then worked steadily through the records of *all* SIS agents working abroad, paying particular attention, naturally, to those in the Soviet Union. So by the end of 1941, the KGB knew the identity and background of all those British intelligence agents working inside Russia.*[38]

Philby also discovered that he could volunteer for night duty once or twice a month at SIS headquarters in Broadway Buildings, London. The night duty officer received and, if necessary acted upon, reports that came in from SIS stations all over the world. Several government departments used the SIS communications network for their top-secret traffic – in the mistaken belief that it was more secure – and the night duty officer thus had access to an amazing amount of government business. One department that used SIS radio channels was the War Office and its messages to and from the British Military Mission in Moscow were on file for Philby to read when his spells of duty at Broadway came around. This meant that the British position on matters such as military aid to the Soviet Union, the arrangements for exchange of intelligence, and a British decision in June 1942 to reduce the flow of Ultra material to Moscow, was already well known to the Soviet authorities before their regular meetings with the British Military Mission in Moscow.

There were other sources of information available to Philby, their value impossible to assess. One of the difficulties of being in secret work is that the pleasure of talking about your job is so restricted. This tends to confine people in the intelligence world to the company of their peers where they can chat more freely. How much Philby gathered in this milieu only he can say. But one clue is that, in the latter part of the war, there was a fairly regular little drinking group that met at the house of Tomas Harris, in Logan Place, Chelsea. Harris was in MI5 and the group consisted of a mixture of MI5 and SIS officers, the most regular *habitués* being Harris, Blunt and Dick White of MI5, and Philby and Dick Brooman White of SIS. An occasional visitor was artist and publisher, Nick Bentley, then in the Ministry of Information. Asked what this gathering of intelligence and security officers talked about on these occasions, Bentley replied, 'Everything, just about everything'.[39]

* This coup of Philby's nearly proved his undoing. The details of SIS agents in the Soviet Union occupied two volumes. When Philby returned them, the filing clerk, to save space, amalgamated them into one without telling the officer in charge. So according to the records, Philby had signed two volumes out and had returned only one. Office regulations stipulated that the loss of a file should be reported immediately to the Chief of SIS himself. Philby, worried as to how he would explain his interest in files that had nothing to do with his duties, persuaded the officer to delay a few days. Fortunately for Philby, the filing clerk remembered in time what she had done.

By the end of 1943, Philby had become so well established in SIS that he acted as deputy to the head of Section V, Felix Cowgill, when Cowgill was away. His desk had been expanded to include North Africa and Italy. But it was from Spain and Portugal that matters of most interest to Philby, in his role as Soviet intelligence officer, originated. Since these countries remained neutral, it was where the Abwehr and SIS came face to face, and where peace-feelers – an attempt to discover an accommodation for Germany short of unconditional surrender – might be taken seriously rather than as a ruse. Stuart Hampshire, a temporary SIS analyst specializing on Germany, and historian Hugh Trevor-Roper's department produced a paper explaining the background which would make such approaches perfectly rational if they should come – as they did.

Since this was Philby's area – the approaches would be made in Spain or Portugal – the paper needed his imprimatur before it could go into general circulation in SIS and, perhaps, be shown to the Americans. Philby resolutely blocked the paper. It was, he said, 'speculative'. Later, in Moscow, he justified this action by saying: 'It would have been dangerous for the Russians to think that we were dickering with Germans; the air was opaque with mutual suspicions of separate peace feelers.'[40] Thus when Otto John, a Lufthansa lawyer, made contact with an SIS agent in Lisbon in March 1943, and said Canaris would like a high-level meeting, the agent's report naturally went to Philby. The reply was chilly. According to John, the agent told him that there would be no further contact and that the war would be decided by force of arms. When John persisted and later revealed that a conspiracy was being hatched against Hitler, this report, too, came to Philby who suppressed it as being 'unreliable'. In this instance at least, Philby was not only keeping Moscow informed but, like Sorge, was using his position to influence events in favour of the Soviet Union.

During this period there was one other major task that Philby was able to perform for Moscow, one which shows the range of information that becomes available once an agent has penetrated the opposition service. The Americans had given to SIS copies of the documents which Allen Dulles had obtained from the German Foreign Office official, Dr Fritz Kolbe. Because SIS suspected these documents of being a 'plant' – an operation by a hostile service – they came to counter-espionage, Section V, and eventually to its brightest, hardest-working officer, Kim Philby. Philby was only too happy to check their authenticity, which he did by asking Bletchley Park to compare the contents of the documents with the Ultra decrypts of German Foreign Office messages for the same period to see if any matched. This not only showed that the documents were genuine, but improved Philby's standing with GC and CS as it was able to use the documents to help break the German diplomatic code. But among the German material, now known to be authentic, was a series of telegrams between the German military attaché in Tokyo and his headquarters in Berlin. These included the Japanese order of battle and an assessment of Japanese military and political intentions. If Philby passed these on to Moscow, and we must assume that he did, they would have provided valuable confirmation of Sorge's reports.

What were the other KGB penetration agents doing at this time? Burgess was in the BBC producing a radio programme called 'Westminster at Work', which brought him into contact with many MPs, some of whom were to be of use to him later. He continued to mix with people in the intelligence and security worlds and no doubt picked up odd items from his wide circle of friends, especially at the parties he gave in his flat near Harley Street. But it is hard to credit the claim by the Soviet defector, Vladimir Petrov, in his statement in Australia in 1955, that 'the volume of material Burgess supplied was so colossal that the cypher clerks of the Soviet Embassy were at times almost fully employed in encyphering it so that it could be radioed to Moscow'.[41] Maclean was even less well placed to do anything useful for the KGB. Until he was posted to the embassy in Washington in 1944, he served in a backwater of the Foreign Office, the General Department, which dealt with the Allied blockade of Germany and other aspects of economic warfare.

Blunt was another matter. Recruited into MI5 by Guy Liddell, the director of the service's counter-espionage section, Blunt was given the job of keeping the neutral missions in London under surveillance. This included opening their diplomatic bags and photographing the contents. Thus he was in a position to pass on to the KGB what he learnt about the attitudes of neutrals to the war, their assessment of the British war effort, and any intelligence that the neutrals themselves had picked up from their own sources. As he rose in the ranks of MI5, Blunt's access to other secrets improved. He sometimes stood in as Liddell's representative on the JIC, and thus had access to SIS reports as well as those of MI5. And in 1944 he was seconded to SHAEF to work on deception plans in anticipation of the D-Day landings. But Blunt's greatest value to the KGB had come earlier when he was placed on the distribution list for certain Ultra material, mainly the intercepts of Abwehr radio traffic. It was this information that interested the KGB, according to Blunt, 'above everything else'. It is easy to see why. The KGB had no window on the Abwehr and no likelihood of getting one. That it should be given access to the Germans' top-secret intelligence traffic through a British officer was an unexpected bonus, especially as it provided the Russians with the means to cross-check the material which they were receiving from another source, the Lucy ring in Switzerland.

The Lucy ring, so called because of the code name of its main informant, remains one of the KGB's most intriguing operations. It consisted of Alexander Rado, a Hungarian who was the nominal chief; Rudolph Roessler, a German exile; and Alexander Foote, an Englishman who had fought with the International Brigades in Spain and who had been recruited as a radio operator by the KGB. Most of the ring's sixty-odd sources of information were within Switzerland, but it did have others outside, including one in the Vatican. The most vital source was 'Lucy', that is, Karel Sedlacek, a Czech military intelligence officer who worked as a journalist in Switzerland under the cover name of Thomas Selzinger.

Sedlacek gave Roessler, his controller, an amazing amount of detailed military information about the German army on the Russian front. Foote, who later abandoned communism and returned to the West, wrote in a book ghosted for him by MI5 that until the Swiss broke up the ring in 1943, 'Lucy provided Moscow with an up-to-date and day-to-day order of battle of the German forces in the East. This information could only come from the Oberkommando der Wehrmacht itself. In no other offices in the whole of Germany was there available the information that Lucy provided daily.'[42] Foote claims that Stalin fought the war on the Eastern Front largely on Lucy's material and, in another book on the Lucy ring, two French authors, Pierre Accoce and Pierre Quet, state that Lucy virtually won the war. These are impressive claims, but there is more to come. No member of the ring ever learnt from where Sedlacek got his information – although he hinted that it came from dissident officers in the German High Command known to him from the days when he worked in the Czech General Staff. But this explanation has proved too simple for writers on espionage and a more romantic version has been concocted.[43]

The British, the story goes, wanted Stalin to have the benefit of that Ultra material which related to the Russian front; and Dansey, the assistant chief of SIS, took it upon himself to make certain that they got it. But he had to do it in a way that protected the source, Ultra – the greatest secret of the war – and yet, at the same time, impressed upon Stalin the importance and reliability of the information. The suggestion is that Dansey did this by feeding the Ultra material into the Lucy ring via Sedlacek. In this way, the source of the material was disguised and Stalin believed and acted on it because it came from his *own* agents. Thus British intelligence has been credited with a major part in the espionage coup that virtually won the war on the Russian front. There is, of course, no truth in this nonsense.

To begin with, Dansey had no access to Ultra material about the Russian front. It went only to his chief, Menzies, and then only later in the war – when GC and CS first began to get Russian front Ultra in 1941, the existence of this source was not even known to SIS.[44] There can be no absolute certainty that, contrary to all the rules about Ultra, Dansey did not get to see this material sometimes; but he certainly did not see it on such a regular basis that he could conceivably have been Sedlacek's source. The main proof that the Lucy ring did not receive Ultra material is, however, very straightforward: it could not possibly have reached the ring in time. Eastern Front Ultra was always something of a problem at Bletchley Park. The Germans used a lot of teleprinter landlines in the East so not everything was transmitted by wireless. Where wireless *was* used, the distance and other factors frequently made for very poor reception in Britain. This meant garbled messages with missing words and a corrupt text: the first cause of delay. The next delay was in breaking that day's Enigma key. If the message was a German air force one, then this was not difficult. But the German army Enigma from the Russian front was broken only intermittently between June and September 1941, fairly regularly between October and December, and then was lost entirely throughout 1942.[45]

There was further delay because Russian front Enigma did not have a very high priority. GC and CS naturally preferred to work on material that was of immediate operational value to Whitehall and the British commands. So, at best, GC and CS's interception of Russian front Enigma was able to furnish little more than a guide to the scale, objectives and progress of the German offensive; and that only after a delay of two to three days, sometimes longer. If the proponents of the idea that SIS was Lucy's source are to be believed, this two-day-old material then made its way from Bletchley Park to London, from where Dansey found ways of sending it to Switzerland. Sedlacek in Lucerne then passed it to his controller, Roessler, in Geneva, who assessed it and then gave it to Rado. Rado then edited it and sent it to Foote in Lausanne, who encyphered it and, when he could get through, radioed it to Moscow.

Yet everyone agrees that the value of the Lucy material was its topicality: 'He fed Stalin every detail of Hitler's orders to his generals *as soon as the commands were issued.*' And 'plans and orders of the German High Command right down to brigade level were transmitted to Moscow *daily*'. Or, 'What increased the value was the speed with which the information reached us . . . On most occasions it was received *within 24 hours* of it being known at the appropriate headquarters in Berlin' (emphasis added).[46] It is clear, therefore, that Lucy's source could not possibly have been Ultra. The official historian of British intelligence in the Second World War, F. H. Hinsley, who worked at Bletchley Park himself, agrees with this conclusion. He writes: 'There is no truth in the much publicised claim that the British authorities made use of the Lucy ring . . . to forward intelligence to Moscow.'[47]

So who *were* Lucy's sources? There are two possibilities. One is the Swiss secret service. This allowed spies from all sides to operate in Switzerland throughout the war – providing they paid their dues by giving the Swiss a copy of anything interesting that they learnt. For their own purposes, the Swiss sometimes fed material that they had gathered in this manner to one side or another. But it is more likely that Sedlacek's own answer, 'officers in the High Command', was true. Sedlacek was a Czech and the Czechs ran the best espionage service of all the governments in exile. He had earlier made contact with Czech members of the German High Command, some of whom may well have been communist sympathizers. Sedlacek, who died in London in 1967, never named them, which provided an opportunity for the growth of yet another intelligence myth.

A KGB agent instrumental in recruiting Foote to the Lucy ring had been Ruth Kuczynski, code name 'Sonya', who left Switzerland in 1940 and set up a ring of her own based in Oxford. Kuczynski, a German by birth, had been spotted by Richard Sorge in Shanghai when she was living there in the 1930s with her husband, an architect. Sorge arranged for her to go to Moscow for training and she then returned to work for the KGB in China and later in Poland. It was Moscow's aim, however, to get Kuczynski into Britain, and after the Spanish Civil War it sent her to Switzerland to meet British veterans with instructions to recruit one and marry him. She was successful with a young English communist, Len

Brewer, and left for London with the two children of her previous marriage on 18 December 1940.

The KGB contacted her eighteen months later. She recalled the meeting thus: 'Sergei [her control] told me that Britain was at war against the Nazis, but that influential reactionary circles were continuously urging an understanding with Hitler and a move against the Soviets. Moscow wanted information. What contacts could I find. Military? Political? I was to try to build up a network.' This proved to be surprisingly easy. Her father, René, well known as a leading academic economist in prewar Berlin, had fled to Britain in 1935 with the other members of his family. He had become friendly with many Labour politicians and leftwing economists. (Ernest Bevin, then Minister of Labour intervened personally to get Professor Kuczynski's son, Juergen, also an economist, released from internment in June 1940.)

Ruth spoke to her father first, and then to her brother. Both agreed to help. Other members of her ring came from all walks of life. Juergen introduced her to Hans Khale, the *Time* and *Fortune* correspondent in London. Through a friendship with a housewife in Oxford she met 'James', an officer in a technical section of the RAF. She herself found 'Tom', a locksmith in a car factory, and she trained him as an alternative radio operator. Her husband, Brewer, recruited a specialist in amphibious landings. The material that Kuczynski's ring gathered divides neatly into technical and political information. Examples of the former came from 'James', who gave her details of new weapons and aircraft under development, including, on one occasion, an actual part for copying, and Brewer's specialist, who brought her an instrument that was part of a new radar system for submarines.

But it was almost certainly far more significant to the KGB that René and Juergen Kuczynski and Hans Khale were able to provide regular and detailed assessments of Britain's wartime politics, economy and military strength. It was probably the Kuczynski ring which first told Moscow in 1941 that Britain would be reluctant to provide military aid to the Soviet Union because the War Cabinet expected the Germans to triumph in a matter of weeks. Ruth Kuczynski says that her father got this information direct from the British ambassador to Moscow, Sir Stafford Cripps. Juergen's reports on wartime economic planning would have been important in helping Moscow decide whether the Allies really intended to open a Second Front. Two or three times a month, Ruth risked radioing her reports to Moscow, using a morse transmitter. She devised a pretext in order to persuade her landlord, the distinguished Judge Neville Lasky, to allow her to erect an aerial on the roof of his house. When not in use, the components of her transmitter were concealed in the stuffing of her children's teddy bears. She handed the aircraft and radar parts to her control at meetings in London during the blackouts. To all outward appearances she was a refugee housewife with two small children and another on the way, struggling to get by in wartime Britain. No one would have believed that she ran a spy ring and was in radio contact with Moscow.

Apart from her father and her brother, none of the other members of the ring knew exactly what Ruth Kuczynski did with the material they gave her. Some may have guessed, but it is unlikely that even if she had told them it would have made any difference. 'None of my agents wanted money', she says. 'The British people sympathised with the Soviet Union and the delay in opening the Second Front angered many of them. None of my British agents felt he was a spy; just that he was helping the Allied country that was fighting hardest and making the greatest sacrifices.'[48]

Early in 1944, when the Soviet Union became certain that the war would end in victory over the Nazis, the thrust of KGB operations began to change. The emphasis now switched from gathering information relevant to the fighting of the war, to discovering Allied intentions for postwar Europe and making preparations to counter any moves which Stalin considered to be against Soviet interests. Philby was at the centre of this operation. His work on the Iberian desk of SIS's counter-intelligence section, Section V, had drawn his superiors' praise. In a service filled with mediocrities he sparkled. But by 1944 Section V was no longer directly concerned with the war and now dealt with counter-espionage only in unimportant areas, such as South America or Arabia.

The decline of Philby's section coincided with the first indications of how SIS's priorities would be re-ordered after the war. Early in 1944 Churchill ordered a remorseless weeding out of every single known communist from all of Britain's secret services. He said he had decided to do this 'after having to sentence two quite high-grade people to long terms of penal servitude for this betrayal of important military secrets to the Soviet Union'.[49] This was probably a reference to the cases of Douglas Frank Springhall and Captain Ormond Leyton Uren. Springhall, national organizer of the British Communist Party, was sentenced to seven years' penal servitude in July 1943 – after a secret trial – for having obtained details of the jet engine from an Air Ministry clerk. Uren, a captain in SOE, received seven years' imprisonment in November 1943 for giving Springhall a description of SOE headquarters.

SIS took note of the way the wind was blowing and its senior officers began to think of reviving an earlier scheme to have a separate section (Section IX) devoted to anti-communist operations. Felix Cowgill, the former Indian Police officer, had been recruited in 1939 to run just such a section, but wartime work against Germany had kept him busy elsewhere. Now a modest stop-gap project was launched. Jack Curry, an MI5 officer, was brought in to head Section IX until Cowgill was free. The fact that the section was created so soon after Churchill's decision to weed out communists from secret organizations and that Curry came from MI5 suggest strongly that the first role of Section IX was a *counter*-espionage one, that is, its task was to seek out communist *penetration* agents. This makes what happened next all the more ironic. In October 1944, Philby, whose mastery of office politics allowed him to out-manoeuvre Cowgill, was appointed head of Section IX. Thus a KGB penetration officer became the head of a section set up to catch just such enemies within the SIS camp.

The irony grows stronger. Section IX expanded rapidly to become an offensive espionage operation, that is, it sought to collect intelligence from communist countries. Philby was thus in a position both to protect KGB penetration agents (including, as we shall see, himself) and to reveal to Moscow all espionage operations mounted against the Soviet Union. Cowgill's resignation from SIS made Philby's triumph complete. As one of Philby's colleagues writes, 'Philby at one stroke had got rid of a staunch anti-Communist and ensured that the whole post-war effort to counter Communist espionage would become known in the Kremlin. The history of espionage records few, if any, comparable masterstrokes.'[50]

The Kuczynski ring was also well placed to keep the KGB informed as the war against Germany drew to a close, and the Allies began to consider their future relations with the Soviet Union. In October 1944, Juergen Kuczynski joined the United States Air Force in Britain as a lieutenant-colonel. His job was to help produce the US Strategic Bombing Survey report on the damage being inflicted on the German economy. This top-secret SHAEF document was produced every fortnight and had a distribution list of only about fifteen, beginning with Roosevelt, Churchill and Eisenhower. Later, on the ground in Germany, Juergen Kuczynski worked with Kenneth Galbraith and George Ball in checking the accuracy of the survey assessments and reporting on the state of Germany's industrial base. In 1980 Kuczynski, then living in East Berlin, said: 'I passed to my sister to send to Moscow everything I learnt during this period. It was all of great interest to the Russians.'[51]

Juergen Kuczynski and the KGB had a further windfall. In the last stages of the war the Americans were dropping agents into Germany for sabotage and intelligence work. They recruited these agents from among German refugees in Britain. To help select the best recruits from the many who volunteered, the American authorities asked the German-born lieutenant-colonel in the USAF, Juergen Kuczynski, to vet their backgrounds. Kuczynski not only told the KGB of the operation, he also arranged for it to approve the list of recruits which the Americans submitted to him. This ensured that only agents sympathetic to the Soviet Union were dropped into Germany. 'The Americans never realised that their operation was in a sense masterminded by the Russians', Kuczynski said in 1980.[52]

Overall, the balance sheet for Soviet espionage in the Second World War is difficult to read. On the credit side, the penetration agents produced the political information expected of them. As Sir Maurice Oldfield, former head of SIS, says: 'Philby's single greatest achievement during the war, one that made his whole career worthwhile, was to keep the Russians informed of any British or American moves for a separate peace with Germany. This is why Burgess was so valuable to him; Philby knew the service attitude. Burgess could assess the political attitude.'[53] In the course of achieving this aim, Philby – and, to a lesser extent, Blunt – exercised an influence on the British view of German opposition to Hitler, hardly a straight espionage achievement, but of considerable importance.

Sorge's ring in Japan not only provided strategic military information, but influenced Japanese political decisions in favour of the Soviet Union. Ruth Kuczynski's ring in Britain gave the KGB political and economic information which complemented that obtained from the British penetration agents. The Lucy ring in Switzerland proved an unrivalled source of military information for fighting the war on the Eastern Front. However, much of the information that the KGB obtained was also available from non-secret sources. Soviet diplomats often told Stalin much the same as the KGB did. And if the KGB had cared to do so, it could have read about German plans to invade the Soviet Union – Operation Barbarossa – in the *Neue Zürcher Zeitung* and the *Chicago Daily*

*News* some six months before the invasion actually happened.[54] Sorge and Ozaki also published openly a lot of the material they included in their secret reports to Moscow.

On the debit side, the largest single item was Stalin himself. The Soviet leader provides a textbook example of two diseases which afflict virtually all those who put their faith in espionage. He came to believe that information obtained secretly was always more valuable than information obtained openly and when secret information appeared to contradict his own assessment, he dismissed it out of hand as being wrong, a provocation, or a plant. These attitudes, coupled with Stalin's suspicion that some KGB agents were Trotsky-ists (Sorge) or had been 'doubled' by the Germans (the Lucy ring), ensured that he never made the best use of the information that the KGB provided.

Still, the outlook for the KGB in 1945 was promising. The Sorge ring and the Lucy ring had been wound up, but Ruth Kuczynski was still operational, as were all the British penetration agents. Some, like Philby, were in key positions: Maclean was at the British embassy in Washington where Anglo-American plans for the post-war world were taking shape; Burgess was in the news department of the Foreign Office; Blunt was in SHAEF.

There was only one shadow on this otherwise bright scene – another Western intelligence agency had entered the field. Before the war, the United States had lacked a regular foreign intelligence-gathering organization. After seeing SIS and SOE in action, the Americans decided that they, too, needed a secret intelligence service. It was called the Office of Strategic Services, or OSS for short, and was to become the KGB's most deadly rival.

# 10. OSS: The Springtime Years

> After the birth of OSS, Donovan was launching
> operations every hour on the hour throughout the world,
> and while his defeats were spectacular and Byzantine,
> many of the operations were successful, and some of
> them would rank with the greatest exploits of human
> daring and bravery in the history of the United States
> and of World War II.
> – Anthony Cave Brown, *The Last Hero* (1982).

> The Americans had no intelligence service to speak of.
> OSS was an exact parallel to SOE, drawing on the ethnic
> dregs of America for skill in languages and knowledge of
> foreign countries. Their security was non-existent, but
> they were in constant liaison with SIS and SOE. Thus
> *our* security was bitched at one remove.
> – Captain Henry Kerby, MP, wartime SIS officer, in
> interview, 1968.

Like Churchill, President Roosevelt was fascinated by the world of espionage. He had done a little intelligence work himself as Assistant Secretary of the Navy in the First World War and, as President, he revived this interest. In the light of what happened, this can be seen to have almost certainly been a mistake. For, in spite of later hand-wringing about the woeful lack of proper intelligence on the eve of the Second World War, the United States was, in fact, not too badly served. The Office of Naval Intelligence had been operating since 1882, the Military Intelligence Department since 1885, and the FBI had been in existence – initially as the Bureau of Investigation – since 1910. There had even been, until 1927, a centralized collection and evaluation department, the Office of the Counsellor to the Department of State.[1] There was little wrong with this intelligence system that the injection of large sums of money could not have put right.

Yet Roosevelt chose to set the United States on a course that would eventually make intelligence a major part of the bureaucracy of American government. He began well before the outbreak of war by setting up in secret what can only be described as his own personal intelligence service. There were two distinct arms to this service, both performing professional intelligence missions, including intercepting cables and tampering with the US mail, both illegal acts. One arm was financed by Roosevelt from special unvouchered funds; the other appears to have financed itself.

This latter group had grown out of a secret society called the Room, founded in 1917 and run by a group of wealthy Anglophile New Yorkers, many of whom had service intelligence backgrounds, or for whom intelligence work held a romantic interest. They included Vincent Astor, a member of the American branch of the famous British family; Kermit Roosevelt who had fought in the British army in the First World War; Andrew Mellon's son-in-law, David Bruce; publisher Nelson Doubleday; banker Winthrop W. Aldrich; Wall Street lawyer Henry G. Gray; Judge Frederick Kernochan; and a distinguished selection of stockbrokers, philanthropists and academics. The Room met monthly at 34 East 62nd Street, New York City, in an apartment with an unlisted telephone number and no apparent occupant. The Room had links with the British SIS through the author Somerset Maugham and, later, through Sir James Paget and Walter Bell, SIS officers stationed in New York.[2]

Under the cover of mounting a scientific expedition, the Room surveyed Japanese naval establishments in the South Pacific and reported on political and economic conditions in the Panama Canal Zone, the Caribbean and Peru. After the outbreak of the war in Europe in 1939, the Room switched to a counter-espionage role. Using contacts furnished by its banker members, it checked bank accounts which might be used to finance foreign espionage and sabotage, looking in particular at the account of the Amtorg Corporation, the cover for the KGB in the United States. Astor used his power as a director of the Western Union Cable Company to monitor cables that might reveal useful intelligence; and the Room's good relations with the British also gave it access to information that they acquired by opening diplomatic pouches in Trinidad and Bermuda. On Roosevelt's instructions, the Room prepared plans to guard war industry factories against sabotage and to tighten controls on the border with Mexico to prevent foreign agents from slipping across.[3]

By 1941 the Room's efforts were being supplemented by those of another secret organization run by John Franklin Carter, a journalist friend of Roosevelt. Carter started work early that year, supplied by the President with $10,000 and a brief to report to him on American security. He hired researchers and agents and began to study everything from the stability of European governments to the loyalty of Japanese Americans and the threat of a Nazi fifth column. By the end of the year, with his budget now up to $94,000, Carter was in New York looking at Astor's operation, and complaining to Roosevelt about Astor's irritable reaction to the discovery that he was no longer the President's only intelligence source. [4]

Unknown to Astor and Carter (and, perhaps, unknown to Roosevelt himself), yet another intelligence agency was in operation during these prewar years. Although this organization was later to be funded by the Office of Naval Intelligence, it originated as an entirely private venture. Its founder was Wallace Banta Phillips, the chairman of the London-based company, Pyrene, at least one of whose employees was no stranger to espionage work (see Chapter 2). The claims made for Phillips's organization tend to be extravagant (it was said that he had 'no less than seven ex-Prime Ministers' on his payroll) and uncheckable. It was apparently designed primarily as a commercial intelligence service and, according to Phillips, had agents in the Soviet Union, France, Romania, Bulgaria, Turkey, Syria, Egypt, Afghanistan, Iran and Mexico. But reports from these agents were fragmentary and infrequent. Although some of them did have previous intelligence experience, most were businessmen, academics, or journalists, prepared to do a little espionage work for fun or for cash. [5]

This, then, was the extent of American civilian intelligence on the eve of war. Eisenhower recalled that when he went to Washington in 1941 to work on the War Department General Staff he found 'a shocking deficiency' in intelligence. Ray S. Cline, deputy director of the CIA in the 1960s, has written of mid-1941: 'It is still frightening to think how devoid of adequate intelligence assets we were when the war came to us.' [6] But any inadequacy lay more in the area of evaluation and collation than in collection, a situation that could have been easily remedied by setting up some centralized system for receiving, sifting and assessing information.

But Roosevelt was reluctant to create any such organization. America's traditions made it wary of anything that resembled a centralized police service, especially a secret one. Many of its citizens had experienced in Europe the workings of the secret forces of the state and were determined that the United States should remain free of such decadence. 'The creation of any super-espionage

William Le Queux (centre), the British author whose fantasies about German spies were a direct factor in the formation of the first bureaucratic intelligence service. Below (left), Captain Mansfield Smith-Cumming, who became head of the intelligence-gathering section, the Secret Intelligence Service, and (right) Colonel Vernon Kell, who ran the spy-catching section, MI5.

Colonel Alfred Redl, director of the Austro-Hungarian counter-intelligence department, was a homosexual *bon viveur*. To pay for his high life, the legend goes, he became Imperial Russia's most valuable spy. But the facts are different.

Mata Hari, the Dutch erotic dancer who was executed by the French in 1917, after being convicted of spying for Germany. Her name has come to be associated with the glamorous world of espionage, but there is little evidence that she did any serious spying.

Paul Dukes as

Joseph Afirenko

Sergei Ilitch

Alexander Markovitch

himself

Alexander Bankau

Paul Dukes, a British spy in Russia at the time of the Bolshevik Revolution, was a master of disguises. He had amazing success in adopting the identities of a variety of ordinary Russians.

Sidney Reilly (left), the British intelligence officer who nearly succeeded in staging a counter revolution in Russia in 1918, and Robert Bruce Lockhart, a British diplomat, who was involved in Reilly's plot. The author Somerset Maugham (below right) was there as an amateur spy but had little success. All three were up against the Pole who founded the modern Soviet intelligence service, Feliks Dzerzhinsky (below left).

Claude Dansey (below), who ran his own spy network. Sigismund
Payne Best (above right), one of Dansey's spies and another British
officer, Major Richard Stevens (centre); are shown here in a German
newspaper after the disastrous 'Venlo incident' in 1939. The Germans
tried to link them with Georg Elser (left) accused of a bomb attempt
on Hitler's life.

General Filip Golikov (above), Stalin's intelligence chief in the Second World War. Brilliant Soviet spies like Richard Sorge (left) sent Moscow much valuable intelligence but if it did not agree with Stalin's pre-conceived ideas, he simply ordered Golikov to bury it in the archives.

Allen Dulles (above), an
American spy in neutral
Switzerland during the Second
World War, and a future head of
the Central Intelligence Agency.
Dulles was carried away by the
glamour of intelligence work, as
was Vincent Astor (left) who ran a
private spy ring for President
Roosevelt before the war.

G. N. Flyorov (above), who as a young Soviet nuclear scientist, warned Stalin in 1942 that the United States was working on an atomic bomb. Klaus Fuchs (left), the British scientist who told the Russians all he knew about British and American atomic bomb programmes. But did it make any difference?

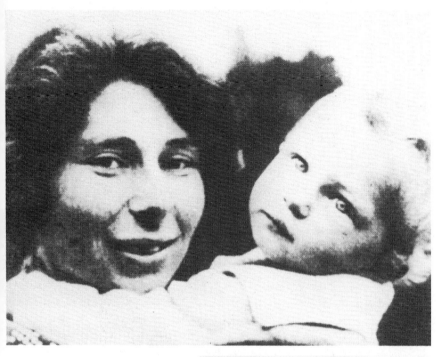

Ruth Kuczynski, a Soviet
intelligence officer who
worked in Britain during the
Second World War. She said
later that her young son,
Micha, and a washing line full
of diapers was a perfect cover
for espionage. Her brother,
Juergen (right) was one of her
agents. He became a
lieutenant-colonel in the
United States Air Force in
Britain and was never caught.

Hans Oster (above), a
German intelligence officer,
who was of great help to the
Allies during the war. Hitler
had him executed. The
wartime chief of the British
Secret Intelligence Service,
Stewart Menzies (left), whose
head was saved by his codebreakers.

British Chamber of Commerce (Inc.)
Vienna.

Telephone: 79-3-93          I. Kärntnerstraße 41

### 1927/8.May.

## Member's Ticket Nr.1083

This is to certify that

Mr. C. Howard E l l i s
is a Member of the British Chamber
of Commerce (Incorporated) Vienna,
subject to the Memorandum and Articles
of Association

Witness to Seal

Director

Director

Secretary

The long-serving British spy, Charles Ellis, under one of his many 'covers'. Ellis, who helped set up the American Office of Strategic Services (OSS), later came under suspicion for working for the Germans before the war and the Russians afterwards. He admitted the first charge, but vehemently denied the second. The head of the OSS was Colonel 'Wild Bill' Donovan (left), a tough New York lawyer.

A spies' picnic outside Moscow. Kim Philby, the KGB penetration agent who was SIS liaison officer with the CIA before he fled to the USSR, looks at his Russian wife, Nina. At the right of the table are George Blake, the KGB officer who escaped from a London prison where he was serving 42 years for espionage, with his Russian wife, Ida, and their son, Mischa.

Left: Philby as a young man. He was already committed to Moscow. Below: a game of spot-the-spy.

Three of the most controversial spies in the history of the profession: James Jesus Angleton (above left), the CIA officer sacked for insisting that the agency had been penetrated by the Russians; Oleg Penkovsky (above right), the Soviet intelligence officer who defected to the West – or did he? And Roger Hollis (below), the chief of the British Security Service, who was accused of being a long-term 'mole'.

The spy chiefs: John A. McCone (above left), head of the CIA from 1961–5; William J. Casey (above right) 1981–7 (dead); Marshal V. Chebrikov (below left), the chief of the KGB, and William Colby, CIA director from 1973–6.

The men in the field: Frank Snepp (above left), former CIA analyst in Saigon, who was punished for revealing CIA blunders; Jeremy Wolfenden (above right), a British correspondent in Moscow who was exploited by both sides; and John Stockwell, a former CIA officer in Angola who left the agency because he could not stand what he was doing.

Three of Moscow's men: Anthony Blunt, art historian and Surveyor of the Queen's Pictures, who worked for Moscow during and after the war; Donald Maclean, British diplomat and serving KGB officer; and Guy Burgess, friend of them both, one-time diplomat, but long-time drunkard, homosexual, and Soviet spy. All are now dead.

military agency is both unnecessary and undesirable', an editorial in the *New York Times* declaimed. 'It is alien to American tradition, and no glorified "OGPU" secret police is needed or wanted here.'[7] Whether Roosevelt would have eventually risked the political consequences of creating a centralized intelligence service we shall never know.

For, from June 1940, another possibility began to open up – collaboration with the British. Those who believed that America's intelligence resources were totally inadequate generally subscribed to the myth that British intelligence, in contrast, was superb. Thus, when an approach came from Britain suggesting co-operation in the intelligence field, Washington was more than ready to make a deal. It does not seem to have occurred to the Americans that Britain's motives were purely pragmatic or that 'co-operation' on British terms might be a euphemism for 'domination'.

Intelligence links between Britain and the United States before the war had been weak, infrequent and confined mainly to the two navies. Early in 1940 Menzies, the chief of SIS, had made informal contact with the director of the FBI, J. Edgar Hoover, to seek his co-operation in identifying German agents in the United States. In May, SIS attempted to expand and formalize this relationship by appointing Colonel William Stephenson as chief of SIS in the United States and liaison officer with the FBI. Stephenson arrived in New York on 21 June to set up what became known as British Security Co-ordination (BSC). The title is misleading, for Stephenson saw himself as something much more than a mere 'co-ordinator'. A Canadian who had fought with the Royal Flying Corps in the First World War, he had become friendly with Churchill during the 1930s when he regularly reported the evidence of Germany's growing military might which he had noted on his business trips to that country. Stephenson had become thoroughly imbued with Churchill's fervour for an Anglo-American alliance against fascism and in his plans 'co-ordinating' British security took second place to the task of bringing the United States into the war.

One of Stephenson's friends in New York was a 57-year-old Wall Street lawyer called William J. Donovan who had been a great hero in the First World War and it was on Donovan that Stephenson first began to exercise his persuasive gifts. There is no easy explanation for Stephenson's choice. Donovan was of Irish descent with strong Fenian leanings and no love for the British. He had, at that stage, no special relationship with the administration or with Roosevelt (although they did know each other fairly well and shared a close mutual friend, John Lord O'Brien, a lawyer who had advised Roosevelt on internal security matters), and therefore no real influence on American policy.

The most likely explanation is that Stephenson was steered in Donovan's direction by Sir William Wiseman, SIS representative in the United States in the First World War, then a New York banker, who knew Donovan and, what is more relevant here, knew one of his weaknesses – a fascination for intelligence and undercover operations. This interest had begun in 1916 when Donovan, in Europe on famine relief work, was recruited into an SIS ring as a courier, and had been revived in 1936 when he volunteered to report to the British Foreign Office on a visit he made to the Italian army during its invasion of Ethiopia.[8] Now Stephenson made Donovan an interesting proposition. The American ambassador to London, Joseph Kennedy, had been reporting to Washington that Britain was finished, and that it was only a matter of time before the Germans triumphed. Would Donovan like to come to London and see for himself how wrong this was? He could meet the king and the military chiefs and assess the national mood. Perhaps a meeting could even be arranged for him to see the head of His Majesty's Secret Intelligence Service.

Stephenson's offer coincided with a suggestion, originating with the Office of Naval Intelligence, that the Secretary of the Navy, Frank Knox, might himself go to Britain on a similar intelligence mission. Knox had rejected the idea on the ground that such a trip would alarm the isolationists, and it is possible that Stephenson had heard of this and was sounding out Donovan as a substitute. In the event, Knox and Donovan met for dinner on 11 July and it was agreed that Donovan should go, if Roosevelt agreed. He did, with the proviso that the American government should pay for the trip.[9]

Donovan arrived in London on 17 July – to Ambassador Kennedy's fury – and over the next three weeks fell victim to what can only be called a public relations campaign, one of the rare British intelligence triumphs of the war! Largely the idea of SIS chief Menzies, the whole exercise was designed to convince Donovan that Britain possessed both the will and the means to continue the war. At Buckingham Palace, King George VI said, quite truthfully, that the British government was determined to fight on, and wherever Donovan was taken he saw alert, well-equipped troops, and airfields in an advanced state of readiness to meet an invasion.

The reality was somewhat different. Not everyone shared

Churchill's determination to resist to the last, or his confidence that resistance would be successful. The gold reserves of the Bank of England had already been shipped to Ottawa. During June, July and August 1940, while Donovan was in Britain, over 6,000 children whose parents were rich enough to afford the fare went off to safety in the United States or the British Commonwealth. Churchill's own great-niece, Sally Churchill, was about to be evacuated to the United States before Churchill personally intervened, and the Minister of Information, Alfred Duff Cooper, had sent his son, John Julius, to Canada. The Swedish minister in London told his government that some MPs were in favour of an early peace with Hitler, and the British ambassador in Washington, Lord Lothian, the very man who had helped finalize arrangements for Donovan's visit, argued that nothing should be said that might close the door to peace negotiations. Dunkirk was just over; British ground forces of 3 or 4 modern divisions faced 150 German ones. The Battle of Britain was about to begin and the Battle of the Atlantic was already being rapidly lost.[10]

Had Donovan been more sceptical he might have got a more balanced picture of the real state of affairs. But he wanted to see only the bright side, and the British were eager to oblige. He was introduced to all the top personalities in the British intelligence community and they did their best to make him feel at home in their covert world. Menzies explained SIS's overseas operations – an unprecedented privilege for a foreigner. The director of military intelligence, 'Paddy' Beaumont-Nesbitt, gave Donovan a conducted tour of the War Office and revealed to him the German order of battle. He visited the Industrial Intelligence Centre, the Admiralty's intelligence division, and met Churchill himself in the Cabinet War Room deep under Whitehall.[11]

The plot worked. Donovan arrived back in New York on 5 August and lost no time in telling, first, Knox, then Roosevelt, and then anyone else he could buttonhole, that Britain had the will and the means to fight on, but that she could do with a little help from her friends. Donovan himself set an example of how this help might be provided by finding the loophole in American law that enabled Roosevelt to transfer destroyers to Britain in exchange for bases on eight British islands in the Atlantic. Seen from a business point of view, the British got a bad deal – none of the destroyers was battleworthy, some scarcely seaworthy – but that was not the point. The point was that SIS and its great admirer, Donovan, had moved the United States a step closer to joining the war. As Stephenson, anxious to consolidate his gain, told the Foreign Office when

Donovan was due to visit Britain for the second time, 'if the Prime Minister were to be completely frank with Colonel Donovan, the latter would contribute very largely to our obtaining all that we want of the United States'.[12]

Churchill played his part. Over the next few months, Donovan met him twice and early in 1941 he carried out a mission for the British Prime Minister – travelling to the Middle East, Greece, Bulgaria and Yugoslavia in order to put over the message that the United States was firmly behind Britain and that those countries which did not resist Axis pressure would lose America's sympathy and support.

In the course of his meetings with Churchill and other ministers and service chiefs, Donovan was made privy to virtually all British thinking about the future course of the war. As we have already seen, this was based upon the perception that Britain could not survive another war of attrition on the battle plains of Europe. Instead, Germany would be softened up by an economic blockade, strategic bombing, propaganda and subversive warfare. Then, at the right moment, the resistance forces in the Occupied countries, supplied and trained by Britain, would rise and attack the Germans as a prelude to an invasion, probably from the south, the soft underbelly of Europe.

We have seen that this strategy was almost totally illusory. It grossly overestimated the potential of SOE and its covert operations and vastly underestimated both the extent of German control in Occupied Europe and the willingness of defeated peoples to collaborate. But Donovan was seized by enthusiasm for the prospects which were laid before him. Already addicted to secret missions and international intrigue, he now became enamoured of the concept of shadow warfare, propaganda and covert intelligence gathering. On 10 June 1941, he wrote to Roosevelt saying that although the nation was in peril it lacked an 'effective service for analysing, comprehending, and appraising such information as we might obtain . . . relative to the intention of potential enemies . . . [Therefore] it is essential that we set up a central enemy intelligence organisation.'[13] From this small seed the enormous tree of the CIA was to grow.

Initially, Donovan and his supporters had to overcome opposition from the War Department, but on 11 July an order was promulgated establishing the Office of the Co-ordinator of Information (COI), with Donovan as its head. COI had the authority to collect and analyse information and data relating to national security and could, when requested by the President, carry out 'such supplementary activities as may facilitate the securing of information important for national security not now available to the government'. In other words, COI was empowered to carry out on behalf of the American government the sort of covert operations at which the British, Donovan believed, were so expert. Donovan was to have $450,000 in unvouchered funds but no salary, although his expenses would be reimbursed.[14]

Two questions immediately arise. What role had the British played in Donovan's success? And what change had there been in American public opinion that made Roosevelt feel that he could go so completely against tradition by establishing a centralized intelligence agency?

The early months of 1941 had not been a good time for Britain. By the end of April, Greece and Yugoslavia had fallen; by June, Rommel was on the border of Egypt and Crete had been evacuated. German submarines were sinking enormous tonnages of shipping in the Atlantic, and SOE had signally failed to start any major fires in Europe. A sympathetic voice which could press Britain's case to the President would clearly be of great help at this desperate time and, in Donovan, the British considered that they had found their man. No effort was spared to assist Donovan's candidacy for any sort of intelligence job that would bring him into close contact with Roosevelt. For the British envisaged, mistakenly as it turned out, that the head of an American central intelligence department would enjoy the same sort of relationship with the President as British SIS chiefs did with the Prime Minister.

Donovan was helped to prepare his submissions to Roosevelt by Stephenson and the SIS officers attached to his staff. Two senior British intelligence officers, Admiral John Godfrey and his personal assistant, Lieutenant-Commander Ian Fleming (later, of James Bond fame), crossed the Atlantic to work on the campaign. Godfrey got to speak to Roosevelt at a White House dinner party and Stephenson supplied Donovan with secret information calculated to impress the President.

There is no doubt about what the British were hoping to achieve, as the reports that Stephenson sent to Menzies make clear. He wrote that, at first, Donovan was not at all certain that he wanted the job of directing 'the new agency that *we* envisage' (emphasis added). When Donovan's appointment was announced, Stephenson wrote that Donovan was accusing him of having 'intrigued and driven' him into the job. Stephenson then expressed his relief that 'our' man was in a position of such importance to 'our' efforts. Major Desmond Morton of the Industrial Intelligence Centre was even blunter: '. . . to all intents and purposes US security is being run for them at the President's request by the British . . . It is of course essential that this fact should not be known in view of the furious uproar it would cause if known to the isolationists.'[15]

Only in a very extraordinary atmosphere would it have been possible for the British to mastermind the creation of a central secret intelligence service in the United States. This atmosphere was, in fact, the consequence of a spy scare remarkably similar to those which had nurtured the birth of SIS in Britain thirty years earlier and had so greatly aided the 'father of American military intelligence', Ralph H. Van Deman in 1917–18 (see Chapter 2).

On his first visit to Britain, Donovan had been accompanied by Edgar Mowrer, a senior journalist on the *Chicago Daily News*. Knox, who owned the newspaper, asked Donovan and Mowrer to look into 'the fifth column activities which had so helped the Germans in Norway, Holland, Belgium and France'. Knox's interest in the fifth column as a possible explanation for the stunning German victories in 1940, was shared by Roosevelt who had told Americans in his fireside radio chat on 26 May: 'We know of new methods of attack. The Trojan Horse, the fifth column that betrays a nation unprepared for treachery. Spies, saboteurs, and traitors are the actors in this new tragedy.'[16]

Donovan and Mowrer (who had covered the German *Blitzkrieg* and had written many stories about the German fifth column) did their job well. They produced a series of syndicated articles which appeared in the American press in the autumn of 1940. These were later published as a pamphlet, *Fifth Column Lessons for America*, with an introduction by Knox. Relying largely upon material provided by SIS, the authors stated that it was not German military genius which had inflicted such devastating defeats upon the Allies in 1940 but a fifth column, organized by the Gestapo and financed to the extent of $200 million a year. This, they suggested, was but a foretaste of what was yet to come. Hitler was determined to seize control of the whole world and the United States, 'crippled by all sorts of civilised inhibitions', would be unable to resist. She housed a 'German colony of several million strong'. There were 'thousands of German waiters' who were happy to serve as snoopers, and other German Americans could probably be blackmailed by the Gestapo. The conclusion, according to the authors, was obvious. In the event of war with Germany the members of this Nazi fifth column would seize the opportunity 'to destroy their own country, to sabotage its defences, weaken its war effort, sink its ships [and] kill its soldiers and sailors for the benefit of a foreign dictator and his alien political philosophy'.[17]

The similarity between the arguments set out in the Donovan–Mowrer pamphlet and those which fuelled the German spy hysteria in Britain during 1909 is striking. Even the same group of German workers – waiters – is singled out as being particularly untrust-worthy. The results were also similar. The FBI was flooded with reports of alleged spying and sabotage and, although the fear of a German fifth column never reached the fever pitch that it did in Britain (where thousands of innocent German refugees from Hitler were packed off to internment camps at home and in the Common-wealth), it served to break down isolationist sentiment, prepared the way for Roosevelt to bring the United States into the war and, our main concern here, created an atmosphere in which few questioned the need for the creation of America's first central intelligence agency.*

Yet the fifth-column threat was all a myth. It was created, in part, by British spy masters anxious to explain their own intelligence failures, and then it was allowed to flourish by governments who thought it no bad thing that Britain and the United States should be aroused by the threat of enemy subversion.

The myth had begun early in 1940, after the Norway débâcle when a British plan to invade and occupy the country was pre-empted by the Germans and the British force was ignominiously driven out. The British and American press had attributed the rapid German conquest of Norway to a gigantic conspiracy – the country had been 'honeycombed' with German agents before the invasion. This explanation soon received official backing. A phrase used by the American journalist, Leland Stowe, in his dispatches from Norway, Germany's 'Trojan Horse', was, as we have seen, repeated by Roosevelt in his fireside chat a month later. And when the British JIC met on 2 May to consider why British intelligence had apparent-ly been unable to provide even the slightest warning of German intentions in Norway, it also plumped for the fifth-column myth. In fact, the JIC had before it evidence from military and naval intelli-gence and from RAF Coastal Command which suggested that ample forewarning of the invasion had been available, if only it had been properly interpreted – the very job that the JIC was supposed to do. But the committee preferred to overlook its own shortcomings and to put the blame fairly and squarely on the presence of a German fifth column. It claimed that a special section of German intelligence

---

* When war started between the United States and Japan, however, the 'enemy within' scare led to the internment of thousands of American citizens of Japanese origin.

had been assigned the job of 'spreading false reports regarding German intentions, and misleading statements as to the objectives for contemplated operations'. In short, British intelligence believed it had not misread the signs that so clearly pointed to a German invasion of Norway – it had been deliberately duped. The JIC concluded: 'We cannot rule out the possibility that Fifth Column activities in this country, at present dormant, might well play a very active and highly dangerous part at the appropriate moment selected by the enemy.'[18]

Soon, as France and the Netherlands were overrun, in their turn, there were further defeats to be accounted for. Again, the fifth column provided a convenient explanation. Within a fortnight of the JIC completing its report on Norway, the former British Minister to The Hague, Sir Nevile Bland, was explaining the collapse of the Netherlands in very similar terms and taking the opportunity to warn his colleagues of 'the enemy in our midst'. Bland said that 'the paltriest kitchen maid not only can be, but generally is, a menace to the safety of the country'. Evidence of a fifth column could be, and was, detected almost everywhere. Admiral Godfrey, of naval intelligence, one of Donovan's sources, thought it necessary, for example, to tell a subsequent meeting of the JIC that an unknown Austrian had landed in Ireland and that Galway Golf Club had admitted several new Austrian members![19]

All this can now be seen to be the purest fantasy. The fifth column did not exist. British historian, A. J. P. Taylor, examined the evidence after the war and concluded: 'The fifth column of supposed traitors was the product of panic-stricken imaginations. It did not exist in reality.' Dutch historian, Dr Louis de Jong, accepted a brief from UNESCO in 1950 to write an account of the activities of the German fifth column as part of a permanent record of Nazi war crimes. He concluded that in Western Europe the fifth column was almost entirely mythical and that the fall of Norway and Denmark, in particular, were entirely explicable in straightforward military terms.[20]

But what about the United States? Were Donovan and Mowrer justified in importing British fears of a fifth column to America? Logically, it might be thought, if the Germans had not created an enormous fifth column in Western Europe, they could hardly have created one in the United States. In fact, Hitler specifically ordered Canaris and the Abwehr *not* to carry out sabotage in the United States because he did not want to give Roosevelt a pretext for entering the war.[21] So there were no such actions prior to Pearl Harbor and only a few minor ones afterwards. German intelligence operations in the United States throughout the war were poorly organized and of little value. The Germans remained ignorant right up to the end of the war, for example, of the fact that the United States was developing an atomic bomb.[22] There was also little German effort directed towards sabotaging British property in the United States. On the contrary, since one of the aims of Stephenson's BSC was to disrupt supplies bound from the United States to the Axis powers and carried in neutral shipping, it is probable that the British committed more acts of sabotage in the United States in 1940 and 1941 than any German fifth column.

Since America's first central intelligence agency was founded on fantasy, it is appropriate that fantasy should have been the predominant feature of its early operations. Donovan set the tone. Among his first proposals to Roosevelt were plans for half the Pacific Fleet and a force of 15,000 American 'commandos' to make a surprise strike on Japan or, failing that, an American attack from Alaska; and a suggestion that Errol Flynn, the Australian actor, should be sent to Ireland to persuade the Irish government to grant bases to the United States. Even more imaginatively, he proposed American sponsorship for the pretender to the Austrian imperial throne, Otto of Hapsburg, and outlined a plan to undermine the Italian economy by flooding the country with counterfeit currency.[23]

Roosevelt himself was briefly touched by this madness. When a citizen wrote to him saying that the Japanese were in mortal terror of bats, the President got Donovan to look at the possibility of bombing Japan with planeloads of American bats. The Army Air Corps and COI–OSS then actually spent several years carrying out experiments on ways of transporting bats in high-altitude aircraft and then dropping them so that they did not freeze to death before they landed.

Some of Donovan's actions were scarcely less outlandish than his words. He sent Armand Dennis, the ape expert, to Accra, under cover of a gorilla-capturing expedition, 'to observe German espionage and military activity', and to report on the attitude of native chiefs in the Belgian Congo and French Equatorial Africa. The mission was a disaster. Dennis complained to Donovan that most of the questions he had been briefed to ask could have been answered in the United States with a few telephone calls. He said that he was reluctant to ask the questions, anyway, because they would have made it apparent that he was a spy and he feared that he would be sent to jail; and that he could not travel around without a permit which was hard to get. (Eventually Dennis did obtain one, but he also caught a gorilla's disease, and he had to return to the United States.)[24]

Donovan bombarded Roosevelt with intelligence reports, many of which were either wrong, or irrelevant, or both. The Japanese were going to send convoys to Chile; the Germans were going to invade Spain; hordes of saboteurs were about to be landed in the United States where they would be received by 'the widespread German SA and SS *Standarten*'; there was to be a full Vichy Franco-German alliance. Few reports included any evaluation of sources and many contradicted each other.

Some of Donovan's black propaganda ideas were equally ill-considered. The month after Pearl Harbor, for example, he proposed announcing that Japan intended to attack Singapore, arguing that, when the attack failed to materialize, as he was confident would be the case, it would be possible to proclaim that this failure marked the turning-point of the war. His reaction when Japan *did* attack Singapore a month later is not recorded.[25]

One possible excuse for this wild flailing around on Donovan's part is that he was up to his ears in a civil war in Washington. The Joint Chiefs of Staff, who at first wanted nothing more than to do away with Donovan and his civilians, had belatedly recognized Donovan's influence at the White House and had decided instead to take him on board. The major elements of the COI, those concerned with intelligence and special operations, had been brought under the control of the Joint Chiefs of Staff and rechristened the Office of Strategic Services (OSS) – a move which Roosevelt approved in a Presidential Order on 11 July 1942. With Donovan at its head, the new organization now seemed secure. But a brief examination of these bureaucratic struggles, which preoccupied Washington at a time when there were more important battles to fight, shows that Donovan had only won a bloody round or two, certainly not the contest.

The first opponent into the ring was Hoover, who had keenly resented Donovan and his organization from the moment it was conceived. He saw it as a threat to his control of security in the United States and his intelligence gathering in South America. He was also suspicious of the close links between Donovan and the British. Covertly, Hoover started an FBI dossier on Donovan, infiltrated spies into his organization, and tried to sabotage his operations; at the same time, he attacked overtly by taking his jurisdictional dispute to Roosevelt. It was only when Donovan promised not to contest Hoover's monopoly on South American operations that Hoover calmed down – for the moment.[26]

The State Department, too, had seen Donovan's organization as a threat pre-empting the diplomat's role as collector of foreign intelligence: Kennedy had continued to protest bitterly at Donovan's visits to Britain, and Under Secretary of State, Sumner Wells, told Roosevelt bluntly that the State Department wanted the Donovan organization dissolved. The department also complained that Donovan recognized no demarcations of departmental responsibility and used information gathering as a pretext for meddling in everyone else's business. But Roosevelt, who had realized that Donovan would ruffle the State Department's calm, thought this no bad thing, and so did nothing about Wells's demand.

But the most powerful challenge to Donovan was mounted from military intelligence, in the person of General George Strong, one-time Indian fighter, who hated the idea of a civilian organization at the centre of military operations in wartime. He especially detested an agency that was secretly funded, reported directly to the President, had close links with the British and was, he believed, amateurish, insecure and open to communist penetration. Strong, known in Washington as 'King George' because of his power and aristocratic manner, set out to crush Donovan. Donovan had not been as cunning as Menzies; Strong controlled access to Ultra and Magic (the American decrypts of Japanese wireless signals) and he used this material to deride Donovan's intelligence operations. He kept a detailed dossier on Donovan's activities and never missed an opportunity to denigrate Donovan's organization and its work. [27]

It is easy to dismiss Strong's objections to Donovan as motivated by personal ambition. He undoubtedly saw Donovan as his main rival for a job he thought would grow out of the wartime chaos: director of the postwar intelligence service. But German documents recovered after the war revealed that, on one point at least, Strong was right – Donovan's organization was insecure.

In May 1942 Major Hermann Baun, chief of the Eastern desk of the Abwehr's espionage division, sent a report to the commander of the first echelon of the German army fighting the Soviet Union. It was a remarkable document in that it set out in some detail the American government's views on major strategic issues for the remainder of 1942. The main points were: the Soviet Union would hold out until American arms production built up to the point at which aid could be provided; once the Russians had dragged Germany into a second winter campaign, the Allies would be secure; the Russian strength was approaching 360 divisions, while the Germans were short of the 100 divisions needed to conclude the campaign before winter; the Allies would not open a second front in Europe in 1942, but would try to deceive the Germans into believing that they did plan an invasion; one element of this deception would be raids on the French coast.*

Baun said that his information came from several sources. One was merely said to be 'reliable'. The others were said to have reported what a foreign diplomat had learnt in Washington from 'the American Colonel Donovan'. Although there is nothing in German archives to indicate that the Germans realized the value of this important strategic information – perhaps because Germany had already concluded that there would be no second front in 1942 – a major intelligence leak could be traced back directly to Donovan.[28]

Strong did not, of course, know this at that time, and when he did attack Donovan for poor security, his ammunition turned out to be dud. He accused Donovan of endangering Magic by allowing his men to steal a cypher book from the Japanese military attaché in Lisbon. Strong claimed that this had been done in such a clumsy manner that the Japanese must have been alerted and, as a result, 'it is an even money bet that the codes employed by the Japanese are in imminent danger of being changed'. Magic had emerged as a major intelligence source after its contribution to American success at the Battle of Midway, so Strong's warning went all the way up to the President.

However, an investigation revealed a picture very different to that painted by Strong. The material taken from the Japanese military attaché's office consisted of duplicates of his messages recovered from wastepaper baskets. It had been sent in a simple cypher used for unimportant communications. The agents who took the material had been employed with Strong's knowledge and had carried out this particular operation with Strong's tacit consent, that is, he knew about it and had not objected. Finally, a check with the department that handled Magic showed that the theft in Lisbon had not been followed by any reduction in the traffic using the cypher which Strong was convinced had been compromised.[29]

This unproductive dispute, which took up much time and effort on both sides at a time when there was a war to be fought, would hardly be worth mentioning were it not for its repercussions. The Joint Chiefs of Staff, impatient with this internal warfare, determined to lay down a clear division of responsibilities. The result was a charter for the OSS, promulgated on 23 December 1942, and entitled

* One such raid did take place – Dieppe, on 9 August 1942. It was a disaster.

'Functions of the Office of Strategic Services'.* Its chief significance lay in the fact that it raised OSS to equal status with the Military Intelligence Department and the Office of Naval Intelligence and charged it with 'the planning, development, co-ordination, and execution of the military programme for psychological warfare', and with compiling 'such political, psychological, sociological, and economic information as may be required by military operations'.

But although this appeared to secure OSS a place in the major league, Strong still held one weapon which he used to virtually cripple Donovan – he was obliged to pass on to OSS only that Ultra and Magic material which was pertinent to national security. Strong gave Donovan as little as possible and used the rest to boost his own service. This ploy had the crucial effect of turning OSS away from intelligence gathering towards subversive operations – a change of direction that, in his heart of hearts, Donovan almost certainly welcomed.[30]

For Donovan saw himself, above all, as a man of action. Like General Patton, he had always longed to lead large bodies of men into mortal combat. Since that was not to be, he devoted his energies to OSS, a miniature army of inspired amateurs. He offered them a chance to live out their teenage adventure fantasies, to display their courage, to win the acceptance and approval of their fellows. They had to be action people – Donovan loved sports stars – and had to put their devotion to OSS above all other loyalties. The more hell they raised, the better Donovan liked them. He was the proud, grey-haired father of a bunch of barely controllable teenage sons. One OSS man recalls a meeting in France between Donovan, a huge ·45 handgun in a holster on his hip, eyes sparkling with delight, and a 27-year-old OSS captain returning from behind enemy lines. There were no snappy military salutes. Donovan shook the young man warmly by the hand and said: 'Well, what mischief have you been up to, boy?'[31]

Most OSS officers shared a similar background – East Coast, WASP, a good family. The majority had 'a good war'. The operations they took part in, no matter how fleetingly, gave them the sensation of being involved in great historical events. Freed from the disciplines and responsibilities of regular military service, an OSS officer

* The Joint Chiefs of Staff were impressed by OSS's intelligence before the Allied landings in Algeria and Morocco in November 1942. But a lot of this had come from a Polish spy network in North Africa which gave its reports to OSS, unsealed, to be sent in the US diplomatic pouch. OSS simply 'borrowed' the Polish material and took credit for it. (See John Herman's introduction to the English version of *In The Secret Service* by General M. Z. Rygor Slowikowski.)

was able to live out his dreams of adventure and, at the same time, feel that he was serving his country. For many of them the wartime years still represent a youthful springtime, to be looked back to with nostalgia.

There was, however, another OSS – one that is seldom mentioned. The Donovan adventurers had not been long in London – where the main hazard was probably being hit by a car in the blackout while trying to find their way between the Connaught Hotel and the American embassy – when they realized that they were not going to be able to set Occupied Europe ablaze. The reason was simple: none of them spoke a European language sufficiently fluently or had the 'cover' required for work as an agent. Recruitment policies – especially the one that did not favour Jews – had to change. Almost by definition, the largest single pool of recruits were refugees who had fled to the United States in order to escape from Hitler; many of them were, of course, Jewish.

They were highly motivated, and they desperately wanted American citizenship. One of them, John Weitz, recalls how he was plucked from the American army – a platoon sergeant at 21 – because he was German, and offered work with the OSS: 'I accepted because I wanted to remain in the United States and all I had at the time was a German passport with a big "J" for Jew stamped in it. If I got to be an officer I would automatically receive American citizenship.'[32] For Weitz, and others like him, the war was not glamorous but highly dangerous and deeply confusing.

Their lot might have been easier if they had been better trained. But Donovan had no time for organizational refinements, such as a proper training programme, and scorned those who were not prepared for instant adventure. 'In this kind of game', he said, 'if you're afraid of the wolves, you have to stay out of the forest.'

To be fair, no one received adequate training. As one of the early recruits, Lyman B. Kirkpatrick, recalls:

> We were all fresh to the business. I was sent to our so-called training area in Maryland. It seemed to be largely left to us to study what we thought would be useful. A couple of recruits were reading spy novels. Some others were working through a self-defence manual written by a British officer in the Hong Kong police. Others were doing the most amateurish codes. That was the basis of our training. We had to learn from the British who at least had a better idea of what could and could not be done, and who were much more politically sophisticated.[33]

Action, not training, appealed to Donovan and he took unacceptable risks himself. He insisted on going to Normandy soon after the invasion even though, as an officer aware of Ultra, his capture could have endangered the whole Allied interception and cypher-breaking operation. To an admiral who refused to take him to the invasion beaches, Donovan argued, 'What better end for us than to die in Normandy with enemy bullets in our bellies'. When he did get there by other means, he soon found himself lying in a ditch while German machine gun bullets clipped through a nearby hedge. According to David Bruce, later American ambassador to Britain, who was with him, Donovan said that they dare not be captured – they knew too much – and that if things got desperate they should take their lethal pills. Neither could find the pills, so Donovan reassuringly told Bruce not to worry, 'if we're about to be captured, I'll shoot you first. After all, I'm your commanding officer.'[34]

He had that appealing, if naïve, American belief that anything is possible, and that the inspired amateur can often do it better than the professional. This did not go down too well with traditional military thinking. One story, probably untrue but indicative of how some OSS men regarded their leader, claims that Donovan stood on the command ship during the Allied landing at Anzio, turned to Major-General Mark Clark, his superior and the architect of the operation, clapped him approvingly on the shoulder, and said, 'Well son, what're we going to do next?' He genuinely believed that any one of his 'boys' was worth at least ten conventional soldiers. It is said that he once assured Lord Louis Mountbatten, Allied Commander in South East Asia, that any time Mountbatten could not spare two or three thousand men for an operation, he should call on OSS and it would 'send in twenty or thirty men to do the job'.[35]

Yet this was the man and the organization whose activities in the Second World War established the precedent and prepared public opinion for American intervention in the revolutionary struggles of the postwar years. As a former OSS officer, Edmond Taylor, has written, 'However indirectly, many of our latter day Cold War successes, disasters and entrapments can ultimately be traced back to him [Donovan]'.[36]

Donovan's problem was that he believed his own propaganda. His report on the activities of the German fifth column had helped establish the atmosphere that made the founding of OSS possible. It is hard to believe that Donovan took his own overblown rhetoric about Nazi subversive prowess at face value. Yet his actions suggest that he did. Mistakenly, he thought that the Germans were particularly adept at secret warfare and concluded that an organization like OSS was the only way to counter this menace. He then compounded this error by imagining that the British held the key that could unlock all the secrets of the great game for his boys. Convinced that

SOE *was* setting Europe ablaze and that the war might well end before OSS had a chance to get a crack at the Germans, he turned to his friends in Britain for the expertise and sophistication that his organization needed to become truly operational.

The British welcomed the opportunity. They wanted American manpower, money and supplies. From the beginning they had worked to turn, first the COI, and then the OSS, into some sort of super SOE/SIS over which they would exercise complete, if indirect, control. It was no accident that London became the first overseas post for OSS, or that Donovan chose the cream of his recruits to serve there. They arrived in October 1942 and, after a suitable social reception, were sent for training at St Albans. The Americans recall the British as heavy drinkers fond of three-hour lunches. Lyman Kirkpatrick summed it up: 'Lunches would last from 1 p.m. through a good part of the afternoon. Our European friends were formidable consumers of alcoholic beverages, with apparently little effect. I always wondered whether they also put in the same long office hours that we did.'[37]

The British remember the rather charming unsophistication of their American 'cousins'. 'How well I remember them arriving like *jeunes filles en fleur* straight from a finishing school, all fresh and innocent, to start work in our frowsty old intelligence brothel', wrote Malcolm Muggeridge, who was in SIS at that time, 'All too soon they were ravished and corrupted, becoming indistinguishable from seasoned pros who had been in the game for a quarter century or more.'[38]

The initially happy relationship was not to last. Some British intelligence officers saw from the beginning that co-operation with the Americans would, in the long run, doom the British to junior status, that American power and resources would eventually outweigh British expertise, that the Americans, itching for action, would not be content forever to be under British control. They were soon proved right. All sorts of operational difficulties arose. OSS wanted to establish its own relationship with European governments in exile; the British argued that contact should be made only through them. The Americans wanted to be able to put agents into the field independently. The British insisted that they should be informed and that the theatre commander should approve. SIS tried to impose its codes and communications system on OSS. OSS refused, complaining that this would have enabled SIS to know all about OSS operations while keeping its own activities secret.[39] Early in 1943 the two organizations clashed again over missions which OSS in Algiers was sending into Occupied France, the British using their monopoly of aircraft available for covert operations to control OSS plans, much to Donovan's disgust.

An agreement to divide the world into spheres of influence was devised in the hope of damping down the developing antagonisms. OSS took primary responsibility for subversion in North Africa, China, Korea, the South Pacific and Finland, while SOE took India, West Africa, the Balkans and the Middle East. Western Europe was to be shared.[40] But there was considerable poaching by each organization. The Americans got a foothold in Yugoslavia – with British permission – and then when London swung its support from the royalists under Mihailovich to the communists under Tito, OSS did its best to continue to back Mihailovich. The Americans disapproved of the British political attitude towards Greece and OSS appears to have leaked stories to the press so as to show the British in the worst possible light.

The British resented the Americans' easy-going, open manner which won them many friends in areas where OSS operated. The very naïveté that the more experienced empire-builders in SOE laughed at proved an asset in the field. Edmond Taylor, then the OSS representative to South East Asia Command, has told of a young OSS officer just out of a Thai language-training course, who tried to deliver a short, but rousing speech to a conference of Thai guerrilla leaders. Fumbling for the right syntax, what he said came out as 'American officers hate Japanese, love Thai people. Otherwise [Americans] no good. All the time drink whisky, shoot crap, fornicate, masturbate.' Reports of this speech, Taylor says, spread throughout the entire Thai kingdom in a remarkably short space of time and 'enormously enhanced American prestige'.[41] One cannot help wondering if the Thais compared this incident with what befell a senior Thai officer who went to Ceylon bearing a gift of gold cufflinks from the King of Thailand for Lord Louis Mountbatten. He was met by an SOE officer who told him that Mountbatten could not accept the gift since it came from an 'enemy' nation.[42]

OSS recruited a former war correspondent, Therese Bonney, who had become close friends with Finnish leaders during the Russo-Finnish War. The idea was to send her to Helsinki under cover as a journalist working for *Colliers* magazine to try to persuade the Finns to abandon the Nazis. When SIS learnt of this it was appalled and did its best to sabotage the mission. OSS had to lodge a protest with the British ambassador in Washington before Bonney was allowed to go ahead. When OSS decided to send a thirty-man team to Norway to sabotage German rail movements, the British said that they were against the operation on political grounds and refused to provide

RAF planes for a parachute drop, so OSS had to use American aircraft with inexperienced crews. As a result, two planes crashed and ten OSS men were killed. It is no wonder that Lyman Kirkpatrick has described the later wartime relationship between OSS and SIS/SOE as 'a constant battle for power' in which, according to another OSS officer, 'the British are just as much the enemy as the Germans'.[43]

Nowhere was this battle more evident than in Britain's empire. OSS representatives were shocked by British behaviour in India. Edmond Taylor wrote home: 'Working with our Cousins has made me cynical about ideals – if we really believed our own propaganda, we would have to declare war on the British, for they have set themselves up as the master race in India. British rule in India is fascism; there is no dodging that.'[44] The British sensed how OSS felt. They were rightly worried that American anti-colonialism could boost Indian nationalist movements. Viewed from Delhi, the Americans posed as serious a threat to imperial postwar rule as did the Japanese. So everything possible was done to impose British control on all OSS operations in the area. London demanded the right to approve OSS plans and to vet all reports produced by OSS in India before they were sent to Washington. The American theatre commander, General Joseph Stilwell, in his pithy way, put an end to that idea, telling the US Joint Chiefs that he would rather lose OSS in India altogether than allow the British – especially SOE of which he had a low opinion – to control it.

Mountbatten and Donovan both became embroiled in the quarrel. Mountbatten told London that OSS activities in India were a mystery to him, but when Donovan called on him, Donovan came away with the impression that Mountbatten had agreed to create a large special operations force with a substantial OSS presence. Donovan seized the opportunity to develop several large, but vague operational plans for OSS, which only succeeded in further alarming the British. An accord was worked out, but both sides cheated. The British would discover an OSS team at work in an area where no such operation had been authorized. In reply to the British complaint, the Americans would then produce as a counter some grievance that they had been harbouring, such as a British broadcast to Thailand and Indo-China which announced that the Normandy invasion had begun and that France was being liberated by British and colonial troops 'with some Allied assistance'.[45]

The two agencies began to spy on each other. OSS staff in Delhi were warned that the British were experts at intrigue and had planted spies in all the American agencies. Carter, the journalist who had done some intelligence work for Roosevelt, told Donovan that the British had penetrated OSS and were 'thoroughly familiar with its methods, plans and personnel'. Donovan retorted that 'our allies . . . know less about our inner workings than we do about theirs'. Relations grew more sour by the month. One OSS report concluded 'Ditto for our foreign enemies – especially the British'. On the other hand, Captain Henry Kerby, an SIS officer, later described his OSS 'cousins' as 'the ethnic dregs of America' who 'bitched up our security at one remove'.[46]

There was more to this deep breach between OSS and the British services than the friction natural between an apprentice who has mastered his craft and now seeks his independence and his old mentor. There was a political factor at work. Most Americans in OSS were basically anti-imperialists. Roosevelt believed that European imperialism was one of the main causes of the war, and he saw America's participation in the Second World War as an opportunity to break up the old empires of Holland, France and Britain. The OSS was but one of the instruments he used to further this end.

SIS and SOE, on the other hand, were in business to restore Britain's empire to all its prewar glory and they were not about to allow an American organization, to which they had been midwife and which had only got going when the war was half over, to propagate its anti-colonial ideas in areas they regarded as essentially British. Colonel Sir Ronald Wingate, who was on Churchill's staff, summed up the British attitude: 'We had been at war with Germany longer than any other power, we had suffered more, we had sacrificed more, and in the end we would lose more than any other power. Yet here were these God-awful American academics rushing about, talking about the four freedoms and the Atlantic Charter . . .'[47]

Does this mean that OSS was essentially a radical organization, that despite being staffed by bankers, lawyers and big businessmen, it tended to the left, whereas SOE and SIS tended to the right? Certainly many OSS officers realized that men cannot be motivated to risk their lives in revolt against an occupying power without the carrot of a better future. William Phillips, one-time London chief of OSS, reported to Roosevelt that colonial peoples deserved 'something better to look forward to than simply a return to their old masters'. And Robert Solborg, Donovan's special operations chief, told his boss that 'oppressed peoples' could not be persuaded to resist by OSS acts of sabotage alone. 'It must be accompanied by efforts to promote revolution.'[48]

But no matter how radical the OSS officer in the field may have been, his masters in Washington were more interested in postwar American hegemony than in liberation for the colonial oppressed. Kim Philby, watching OSS in his dual role as SIS officer and KGB penetration agent, gave me a Marxist view of OSS's politics: 'It was radical, realist, and anti-colonialist only in the narrowest sense that it wanted the Open Door extended to the British, French and Dutch empires, for the same reason that successive US administrations pressed for it in China – economic domination. Realistic perhaps, but not radical.'[49]

There is some support for Philby's view. General MacArthur frankly defined the United States' wartime objectives as 'the development of markets and the extension of the principles of American democracy'. The French claimed to have evidence that OSS had suggested to the Vietnamese guerrilla leader, Ho Chi Minh, that business friends of Donovan's would be willing to reconstruct railways, roads and airfields in Vietnam after the war in return for commercial privileges there.[50]

There was also Project Bingo, an operation which OSS planned in India in April 1945. What OSS wanted was nothing less than a secret, continuing overview of the Indian economy 'for the protection of the United States' interests and security in Asia'. It sought an analysis of Anglo-Indian management trusts, cartels and capital structures, profiles of leading business and political personalities, sources of finance for industrial development, opportunities for foreign investment, postwar reconstruction plans, and political developments likely to influence economic policy. OSS realized that the British might take 'a dim view' of all this, and that it would be necessary to operate in secret and under cover. Nevertheless, OSS proposed that 'intelligence stations' should be located for this work in Delhi, Bombay, Calcutta, Madras, Karachi, Simla, Colombo, Rangoon and Kabul. How far Project Bingo proceeded is unclear. Although OSS files set out the scheme and its objectives in some detail, there is no operational order to show that it was ever implemented. But since CIA officers were later collecting just the sort of information demanded by Project Bingo, it seems likely that at least some OSS economic intelligence gathering, not entirely for security reasons, started in India in 1945.[51]

As the end of the war came into sight, OSS began to assess its relationship with its Soviet ally. Collaboration had been reasonably close. Despite his basic anti-communism, Donovan had realized that sheer self-interest dictated that there should be some co-operation with Stalin and, in December 1943, he had flown to Moscow and had hammered out an arrangement with the Russians for an exchange of intelligence material through the American Military Mission.

As a result, OSS and the KGB had shared information about agent equipment used in Nazi-occupied Europe. The KGB had provided intelligence data on strategic bombing targets in Germany and reports on conditions in German-controlled areas. In return, OSS gave the Russians miniature cameras, microdot manufacturing equipment and cryptographic materials. Donovan even tried to arrange for a KGB mission to go to Washington. But despite support from the Army Chief of Staff, George Marshall, and the American ambassador to Moscow, Averell Harriman, his scheme was never approved, probably because of opposition from Hoover who tended to see the war as an inconvenient, but only temporary, interruption in his never-ending hunt for communists.[52]

But OSS became increasingly alarmed at the growing power and confidence of the Soviet Union. Unlike the British and the Germans who were, in their different ways, both at their last gasp by 1945, the Russians were just hitting their stride. Their enormous armies, well equipped with modern weapons and brilliantly led by the triumvirate of Stalin, Zukhov and Vasilevsky, were storming into Europe. This was a new Russia, brimming with self-confidence, determined to establish her frontiers as far west as possible and to dominate the territory she had conquered so painfully by the most effective means, no matter how repressive. What was to be OSS's attitude to this?

One officer had already considered the problem. This was Allen Dulles, a successful businessman who had served as an American diplomatic representative in Switzerland in the First World War. Donovan had recruited Dulles in the COI days and sent him to Switzerland in November 1942 with a bank draft for $1 million and an assignment to penetrate Germany in order to discover the extent of German opposition to Hitler.

Dulles was deeply conservative and dedicated to the restoration of a prewar Europe. Within a month of his arrival in Switzerland, he was already raising with Donovan the spectre of communism taking over Europe as fascism collapsed. Dulles saw the Allies' policy of unconditional surrender as a mistake. He wanted to be able to negotiate with groups in Germany who could build up barriers against communism. There were obvious risks involved in such an undertaking: if the Soviets learnt of it all their fears of a German alliance with the United States and Britain to contain communism by military force would be reawakened . In the event, this is exactly what happened.

In the spring of 1945 Dulles was deeply involved in Operation Sunrise, the arrangement with SS General Wolff for the surrender of German forces in northern Italy. When the Russians were not allowed to participate in these surrender negotiations, they jumped to the conclusion that Operation Sunrise was a last-minute attempt at a separate peace with Germany, and that the Allies were conspiring, as they had always feared they would, with some of the worst elements of the Third Reich to switch the war to one against the Soviet Union.

Given Stalin's paranoia on this issue, it is nevertheless possible to appreciate the Soviet view. There *were* a rash of approaches from high-ranking Germans in the last months of the war suggesting that there should be an attack on the Soviet Union by Germany, Britain and the United States in order to prevent communist encroachment in Western Europe. The approaches to the British came from a German intelligence officer who 'defected' across the lines in France, and an Italian industrialist who called at the British legation in Switzerland. But the Germans concentrated on Dulles whom they considered to be 'an implacable enemy of Bolshevism', and in rapid succession an Italian cleric, an Austrian businessman and the German air attaché in Berne all offered the Allies, through OSS, a holy alliance against communism.[53]

Washington rejected them all; Roosevelt suggesting that the sole purpose of such approaches was to create suspicion and distrust between the Allies. If this was the Germans' intention – although the evidence suggests otherwise – then they certainly succeeded. The KGB knew that the Germans had been making overtures to OSS since 1943 and the Allies' refusal to allow Soviet representatives to join the surrender talks with Wolff seemed to confirm Stalin's worst nightmares. The Soviet Union openly accused the United States of double dealing, and Stalin and Roosevelt exchanged bitter telegrams. The wartime alliance was breaking up. Sensing the new atmosphere, OSS quickly moved to exploit it.*

It did so because, firstly, some of the German offers had included very tempting bait. One, for example, was a proposal that the Gestapo would hand over its valuable intelligence files on Japan if the Allies would agree to a ceasefire on the Western Front to allow

* The British were ahead of them. SIS had set up an anti-Soviet section in October 1944.

Germany to hold off the Russians. Although attractive, this proposal proved resistible. But when General Reinhardt Gehlen, commander of a German army intelligence section on the Eastern Front, took his men and his files and surrendered to the Americans, he made an offer they felt could not be refused. He claimed that he had an espionage network in Soviet territory and that it could begin work immediately for OSS. After approval from Washington, the Gehlen organization was given quarters in Frankfurt, and while the Soviet Union was still, officially, an ally of the United States, Gehlen's men pursued their operations against the communists, as they had under Hitler – except that now OSS was their master.*

But OSS also embraced the anti-communist cause so eagerly because to do so was very much in its own interests. Donovan had always at the back of his mind an ambition to see OSS develop into a peacetime intelligence service. As early as 1943 he was discussing with various generals the need for a long-term programme to establish 'an independent American secret service which should be maintained in time of peace as well as war'. By 1944 his thinking had reached the stage at which he could contemplate the possibility of 'a central intelligence service' which would concentrate on long-term strategic information and which would co-ordinate the functions of *all* intelligence agencies of the government. Since such ideas threatened the position of just about every powerful department in Washington, they ran into heavy opposition and OSS urgently needed convincing arguments to show why the United States needed such an agency. The Nazi menace had been useful in 1940 but now the Nazis were on the brink of defeat. Donovan turned to the Soviet Union.

Within OSS the change in the service's attitudes and priorities filtered rapidly down. One officer, serving with the advance guard of OSS in Berlin, recorded how, while sharing a bottle of vodka with a Russian major, he had realized sadly 'that our enemies had changed'. Others noticed it more in the attitude to the Germans. As yesterday's enemies became collaborators and yesterday's allies the new enemy, it was inevitable that many Americans should behave benevolently towards the Germans. John Weitz, the German refugee who had been recruited to OSS from the American army, remembers German officer POWs being allowed parole from a camp

---

* Many of the OSS officers made responsible for dealing with the Gehlen organization went on to become senior CIA officers: Frank Wisner, Harry Rositzke, Richard Helms and Dulles himself. Gehlen became head of West German intelligence until he retired in 1968.

near Munich to attend American parties. 'One German officer surrendered to me driving his own black BMW limousine. He asked me to make certain that his car was taken good care of, because he'd be needing it again soon.'

In this atmosphere American recruitment of German Gestapo and intelligence officers becomes easier to understand. Weitz recalls:

> The chances were that an OSS agent in Europe at that time was a German–Jewish refugee, about 20 to 25 years old. For him, the Germans were horrific people. There was no way any such agent was going to recruit Nazi types. Their recruitment was due to the opportunism of senior non German-speaking officers. They'd say, 'Look he speaks German and he knows the situation. Let's use him for the moment. We can always get rid of him later.' And, I suppose, some of them were useful characters in their day.[54]

This is the view from the field. There is another view. This is that some high-ranking Americans considered that the past deeds of Nazis – no matter how horrible – were of secondary importance when compared with their value as recruits to the anti-communist cause.

One example, at least, supports this theory. In 1945 Leon G. Turron was operations chief of CROWCASS (Central Repository of War Criminals and Security Suspects). Turron, a Pole, had fought with the Russian Imperial Army in the First World War and, after migrating to the United States, had been recruited by the FBI in 1929 because of his knowledge of communist affairs. As operations chief of CROWCASS, his overt task was to locate war criminals and catalogue their crimes. But this fanatical anti-communist also had a covert mission – he was given the freedom to hire, with no questions asked, former Nazis, especially SS members, to serve as American intelligence agents and sources about the Soviet Union. He carried out his covert job with such vigour that he has been called 'one of the Cold War's first spokesmen'.[55]

Once the new enemy had begun to replace the old, OSS wasted no time in mounting an intelligence operation against the Soviet Union. It was not the first. As far back as September 1943, OSS had taken the opportunity to recruit a part-time agent among the employees of a large American engineering company, E. G. Badger & Sons, which was supervising the erection of six oil-refineries being given to the Soviet Union under lend-lease. He was to collect industrial, agricultural, cultural and political intelligence over a two-year period. There is no indication in OSS files as to how this agent fared.

Operation Casey Jones was something else. Conceived by Donovan in 1944 and implemented in the spring of 1945, it was described as 'a project undertaken jointly with the British to use the post-war confusion to get photo coverage of all Central and Western Europe, Scandinavia and North Africa'. Some 2 million square miles, including all Soviet-occupied Germany, Yugoslavia and Bulgaria were photomapped from the air by sixteen squadrons of American and British bombers, some of the British planes flying unmarked. The Russians could hardly have failed to notice such a large operation and its purpose was probably betrayed to them by Juergen Kuczynski, the Soviet agent (see Chapter 9) who was then employed as a lieutenant-colonel in the USAF, working in the strategic bombing command near Frankfurt. Since Kuczynski's work – assessing the damage to Germany's industry – involved the use of aerial reconnaissance photographs, it seems reasonable to assume that Kuczynski knew of Casey Jones and passed the information to the KGB.

That the Russians did know of Casey Jones there is no doubt, for the records show that a series of secret air battles between American and British planes and the Soviet air force took place in the last months of the war and the early days of peace. On one day alone, 2 April 1945, six engagements occurred during which one American Mustang fighter was shot down. The Russians grounded all Allied aircraft in the Soviet Union and, to show that they were serious, shot down two RAF Ansons near Klagenfurt, Austria, in July 1945. The following month they filed more than 300 complaints about Allied violations of their airspace.[56]

D onovan's opening salvo in the battle to ensure that OSS remained intact when the war ended was fired in October and November 1944. In a long memorandum to Roosevelt he made out a case for a permanent central intelligence service which would co-ordinate all government intelligence activities touching on national policy. This proposal was so wide-sweeping and threatened intrusion into so many Washington bailiwicks that it was promptly attacked from all sides. Roosevelt himself was far from convinced and when Donovan's enemies leaked his proposal to the press early in 1945, the President made no effort to protect him from the uproar which followed. Although much of the criticism was on the lines of super Gestapo agency, there was some thoughtful, and prescient, comment. Admiral Ernest King, for example, saw an element of danger in a central intelligence service because 'over a long period of time such an agency might acquire power beyond anything which had been intended for it'.

Donovan became increasingly isolated. Even his British friends who had found him so useful in the early stages of the war now abandoned him.[57] Thus, when Roosevelt died on 12 April 1945, in the middle of the intelligence battle, Donovan's plans to carry OSS into the postwar era died too.

The new President, Harry Truman, had none of Roosevelt's fascination for intelligence. He did not welcome unsolicited reports or informal callers at the White House. He was suspicious of secret organizations, did not trust security services (including the FBI), and was anxious to abolish all those wartime agencies involved in undercover operations. So he simply passed to the Bureau of the Budget all suggestions about a central intelligence agency and left it to the bureau to decide – within the need to reduce government spending to peacetime levels – what, if anything, it was prepared to fund.

Donovan fought back by trying to win public sympathy. OSS officers were authorized to reveal details of their wartime adventures and soon newspapers, magazines and even comic books were full of exaggerated, glamorized accounts of OSS operations, which goes some way towards explaining the romantic image that OSS retains with many older Americans to this day. But it was to no avail. Truman signed the order dissolving the OSS on 20 September 1945 and the United States' first central intelligence agency was formally dead. Or was it?

The great game was too deep into the hearts of too many Americans for a mere presidential order to kill it. Donovan and his colleagues quietly created an organization of former OSS men, the Veterans of Strategic Service (VSS), which had 1,300 members within three years. Its aim was to keep alive, by any means, 'the idea and functioning of central intelligence'.[58] Amongst its members were those OSS officers of the research and analysis section who had been reassigned to the State Department and who were still there, ready and willing, when the Central Intelligence Agency (CIA) came into being in 1947. Other VSS members came from the one thousand or so academics who had joined OSS to become men of action as well as men of intellect and who, seduced by the secret world, had gone back to academia to inspire and help recruit a new generation of American intelligence officers. Still more VSS members were to be found in the newspaper world, in publishing, in law firms, on Wall Street, and in positions of power in Washington – a unique network of men of influence devoted to the ideals of Donovan and OSS.

Admirable in many ways though this may have been, one cannot help but feel that it involved an element of self-deception. Some OSS exploits involved acts of enterprise, valour and self-sacrifice of the highest order. Yet the contribution which OSS made to victory was minimal. It did not really get going until late in 1943 when the war was already half over. A history of the early days of OSS is a story of blunders, sabotage by its enemies in Washington, and battles for its independence from the other American services, SIS and SOE. In 1947 an American naval intelligence officer said that wartime relations between OSS and the service intelligence sections were so bad that 'You would have thought that one was the enemy rather than the Germans and the Japanese'.[59]

OSS was excluded from a major part of the war, the Pacific theatre, by General MacArthur; it spent a lot of its time in South East Asia fighting with, and spying on, the British; and, by failing to support its field officers who wanted to back Ho Chi Minh and his nationalist movement, probably missed a crucial opportunity to change the tragic history of Vietnam over the next quarter of a century. Its efforts in China were handicapped by a lack of cultural sensitivity and language fluency, and in Europe it was no more than a minor cog in the enormous industrial military machine which really won the war and, without which, OSS would not have been able to function.

It failed, as did SOE, to appreciate fully the realities of life in German-occupied Europe, the pragmatism of populations which, over the centuries, had seen occupying forces come and go. OSS officers were bewildered, for instance, when French industrialists wanted guarantees of postwar compensation from the United States before they would allow French resistance teams to sabotage their plants producing supplies for the Germans. And the resistance movement itself was rightly suspicious of OSS exhortations to revolt. Thousands of members of the maquis were sacrificed in June 1944 by Allied calls for a general rising so as to conceal the main thrust of the invasion of France. Bureaucratic muddling by the OSS in London, and changed military priorities, cost the lives of countless French and Italian resistance fighters when OSS support failed to reach them and the Germans exacted a bloody revenge. It is enlightening that OSS casualty figures – 143 killed and 300 wounded out of a peak establishment of 16,000 – specifically exclude sub-agents and make no mention, even in passing, of those resistance fighters and those ordinary European civilians killed by the

Germans in reprisal for OSS/SOE activities.[60] As historian Jean Overton Fuller has pointed out, when people speak of the massive rising of the Resistance to support the Allied armies, it was mainly not the old *Résistants*, because most of them were dead.*

As far as intelligence gathering is concerned, OSS never really got behind Hitler's borders until the very last months of the war. But in the research and analysis (R and A) area, it undoubtedly did better. The output of R and A was prodigious and its quality generally high. But there were two main drawbacks. The first was that OSS introduced academics to the seductive world of intelligence, causing them to look back on their service with OSS as 'the best years of their intellectual lives', and beginning that link between academia and American intelligence that goes on to this day. The second was that occasionally an R and A report was seriously flawed, with significant consequences. One such report, for example, put the Soviet Union's war dead at 3·4 million – an underestimation by a factor of six or seven. (This might not appear important, but it helped form the State Department's view that the Russians would be able to recover quickly from the war and that, therefore, East–West relations would not be harmed if the United States went back on its promise of a recovery loan – an assessment that turned out to be wrong.)[61]

A lot of adventurous young Americans were attracted into OSS and they found within its ranks an opportunity to develop those qualities that, unfortunately, seem to be best stimulated by war: initiative, enterprise, daring and self-reliance. But it also attracted psychopathic characters because it offered fantasy, sensation, intrigue, the lure of being a mysterious man on a mysterious mission. To such people intelligence work rapidly becomes an end in itself, rather than one of the many paths to victory.

If there is any one story that captures the essence of OSS – an attractive flamboyance, too-often concealing a basic futility – it would be how David Bruce and his OSS staff joined forces with war correspondent Ernest Hemingway during the Allied drive to Paris in August 1944.

Bruce made Hemingway an honorary OSS officer and, although their official assignment was to collect intelligence that might be useful to the Allied advance, they joined the advance units entering the capital in the hope of being the first Americans into Paris. While Generals de Gaulle and Leclerc, whose troops had decided the issue, formally received the German surrender, and while the

* The figures are: 24,000 executed; 115,000 sent to concentration camps, of which 75,000 died in captivity.

communist resistance, which had begun the uprising and had borne the brunt of the casualties, buried its dead, the OSS officers took their men down the Champs-Elysées to the Ritz Hotel. The manager looked at them askance and asked if there was anything they wanted: 'How about seventy-three dry martinis', Hemingway replied.[62]

The historic importance of OSS was that it introduced American leaders to the attractions of the secret world, and in such a manner that intelligence gathering and covert action, or shadow warfare, became inextricably linked. The British better understood the importance of keeping the two functions separate and, when the war ended, they were able to dissolve their covert action force, SOE, and leave their traditional intelligence service, SIS, intact. But, because of the way Donovan had structured the OSS, Truman's September order virtually wiped out both operations. The campaign between 1945 and 1947 for a peacetime intelligence agency used OSS as a model, thus making it inevitable that intelligence also involved covert action, and covert action now meant American intervention in the affairs of countries with which the United States was not at war. For the CIA, this confusion of purposes was to prove a dangerous inheritance.

# 11. CIA: Bigger than State by Forty-eight

> I do not believe in a big agency. If this thing gets to be a great big octopus, it should not function well. Abroad you will need a certain number of people, but it ought not to be a great number. It ought to be scores rather than hundreds.
> – Allen W. Dulles, giving evidence on the National Security Act of 1947, 27 June 1947.

> For some time I have been disturbed by the way the CIA has been diverted from its original assignment. It has become an operational and at times a policy-making arm of government.
> – Harry S. Truman, *Washington Post*, 22 December 1963.

Only four months after President Truman had signed the order dissolving OSS he had a change of heart. Donovan's enemies had buried his organization, but there remained a nagging suspicion in Washington that his idea of a central agency to co-ordinate intelligence collected by the army, the navy and the State Department was a sound one. Peter Vischer, the secretary of the intelligence committee of the Joint Chiefs of Staff, later expressed this view as follows:

> Everybody said intelligence is a mess, we have to have a Central Intelligence Agency to correlate and co-ordinate all these activities. It was held, and rightfully so, that collection was not too bad. After all, the information on Pearl Harbor was all over Washington. It was that it was not pulled together and given to the right person at the right time. Everybody agreed, all right, we will have a Central Intelligence Agency charged with the correlation, evaluation, and dissemination of the stuff that is already flying all over the place.[1]

Truman was won over. This would be nothing like the swashbucklers of OSS. As Vischer described it, the central agency was to be a small Washington office co-ordinating material already collected by the existing intelligence services – it would not be a collector in its own right, but a clearing house. On 22 January 1946 the President signed a directive, drafted mainly by Vischer, creating the Central Intelligence Group (CIG). This was to consist of personnel assigned from the army and navy operating under a director appointed by the President, and would report to a National Intelligence Authority (NIA) composed of the secretaries of state, war and navy, with the President's personal chief of staff.

Did Truman, a man by nature suspicious of secret intelligence activities, harbour doubts after his about-face? At a private lunch at the White House two days after signing the directive, he produced wooden daggers, black hats, cloaks and false moustaches and presented them to his chief of staff, Admiral William Leahy, and the CIG's first director, Admiral Sidney Souers. He told the two officers that they should 'accept the vestiments and appurtenances of their respective positions, namely as Personal Snooper and Director of Centralized Snooping'.[2]

If Truman did have reservations then they turned out to be absolutely justified. Setting the pattern for the Central Intelligence Agency (CIA) which was soon to succeed it, the CIG showed that there can be no such thing as a *small* intelligence agency. Within eighteen months the CIG had extended its role from mere collation and distribution to include the *collection* of intelligence. Seizing the opportunity created by a weak State Department the CIG confronted and defeated the FBI, abolished the FBI's foreign intelligence networks, and seized control of the intelligence organizations of the very three departments it was meant to report to: state, war and navy. It discovered the existence of a secret intelligence service which had been founded within the War Department in October 1942, and was known throughout the war only to the State Department and Roosevelt himself, and wiped it out. In one year the CIG expanded six times over, absorbing in the process all the bits and pieces of OSS that had managed to survive in the State and War Departments. It also succeeded in winning Truman over so completely that from 1948 – by which time the CIG had become the CIA – his first caller of the day was invariably the director of central intelligence.[3]

CIG's 'bending' of the original presidential directive so that it could expand into collecting intelligence set the precedent for the old boys of OSS to expand still further into covert action until the growth of the CIA became unstoppable. It became a huge bureaucracy in its own right with its own revenue, its own banks, its own airline, its own policies. The British historian, Christopher Andrew, has said that modern intelligence systems emerged not so much by the conscious will of the central government as by a process of creeping bureaucratic growth. With the CIA the growth was explosive. Its secret slogan in 1947 was 'bigger than State by forty-eight' – and it was. With its expansion the CIA became increasingly difficult to control – 'if not a rogue elephant, at least a major instrument of foreign policy operating in semi-independence'.[4] Its conception of its own role changed. It was not merely in the business of collecting information about what was happening in the world; it saw its duty as making things happen. The CIA became virtually a government within the government of the United States.

One small clause in the presidential directive of January 1946, a clause that was not in the original draft, opened the way for the CIG's initial expansion. It is impossible to state with certainty who, between the drafting and the President's signature, inserted the clause, but what evidence there is points to Admiral Souers. In the first draft, the clause defining the director's duties said they were to 'accomplish the collection, correlation and evaluation of intelligence'. The word 'collection' was removed, most likely by the Joint Chiefs of Staff who correctly saw the threat that this posed to their own intelligence collecting services. But the final directive, while still omitting 'collection', added a new clause charging the director to 'perform such services of common concern as the National Intelligence authority determines can be more efficiently accomplished centrally'.[5]

Souers used this catch-all clause as a mandate to expand the CIG. A first-class organizer – he had been a Missouri businessman before joining the navy – he employed his talents, in what was his last job before retiring, to create a new bureaucracy. Colonel John Grombach, the last head of the War Department's intelligence service before the CIG liquidated it, asked to explain the growth of the CIG, said: 'I just think the people who had these co-ordinating agencies started to build an empire.' Certainly, the next head of the CIG, General Hoyt S. Vandenberg, who took over from Souers in June 1946, had no intention of limiting himself to co-ordinating intelligence collected by other services. Asked by a CIG staff member how he saw his job, he replied: 'I will tell you this; I do not believe in any damn co-ordinating sewing circle.' The same staff member said later that half the CIG wanted to keep strictly to its co-ordinating role, but the other half, who were ambitious, said, in effect, 'Gentlemen, which is this going to be, a super-dooper agency? This is going to have all the powers that OSS had and more.'[6]

The ambitious men won. Within six months of the presidential directive, the CIG had gone to the NIA and had persuaded it to redefine the director's functions. NIA Directive No. 5, marked 'Top Secret', was issued on 8 July 1946. It ordered the director of the CIG to conduct 'all Federal espionage and counter-espionage outside of the United States for the collection of foreign intelligence information required for national security'.[7]

This was an extraordinary surrender of the NIA's power. The first 'oversight' body whose duty it was to control the fledgling CIG handed over that control without a murmur, setting the precedent that would later enable the CIA to proceed to its worst excesses unchecked. In retrospect, the reasons for the NIA's surrender are not difficult to pinpoint. Its members – the secretaries of state, war and navy, and the President's personal chief of staff – were men heavily occupied with their own duties and would hardly have time to concern themselves with intelligence matters unless the CIG came up with something as urgent as another Pearl Harbor. In any case, these members of the NIA had to rely on the director of the CIG to initiate meetings. Thus, although the NIA appeared on paper to control the CIG, in reality power rested with the CIG's director.

Another reason for the unchecked rise of the CIG was that the climate was right. At the end of the war, there was an outpouring of books and articles about American intelligence agencies and their activities. (These, as we have seen, were encouraged by Donovan as part of his propaganda campaign to keep the OSS alive.) With few exceptions these publications gave a glamorous view of intelligence, presenting it as an essential activity which it was desirable for a government to sponsor.

The CIG could not help but feel frustrated in this climate. There was little glamour in sitting at a desk in Washington co-ordinating and evaluating intelligence collected by other people. An army intelligence officer, quoted by Peter Vischer, summed up the attitude of many a CIG staff member: 'Evaluation has no sex appeal; this . . . stuff [clandestine collection] carries a kick. Everybody wants to do it; they just love to do it. Once you get started in it, you lose all interest in your normal operation. You forget everything else you are supposed to do because you get excited.'[8]

How quickly Vandenberg translated his mandate to collect intelligence information outside the United States into a charter for covert action can be seen from the fact that in July 1946 the CIG was arguing to the NIA the case for funding 'covert activities'. Seven months later Vandenburg reported to Truman: 'The clandestine operations of the CIG are being carefully established in the most critical areas outside the United States and are proceeding satisfactorily.'[9] Given the time that it would take to plan and then establish these clandestine operations, this means that the United States had embarked on covert action overseas well before the CIA came into being, and that it did so not only without any public discussion, but without debate – secret or otherwise – in Congress.

For when congressional hearings began on the National Security Act of 1947, the Act that created the CIA, the intelligence community gave not even a hint that covert actions had already started. In fact Vandenberg and other intelligence officers who testified in secret session before the Committee on Expenditures in the Executive Departments in June 1947 gave the impression that they were merely seeking approval to *collect* intelligence abroad – a revival of the co-ordination versus collection debate over the role of the CIG that had already been settled. The vision of the CIA's future set out in the 1947 testimony bears so little resemblance to today's reality as to be virtually unrecognizable.

Allen Dulles, a future director of the CIA, after greatly inflating his wartime role in OSS – he said that he had about 10 per cent of Germany's Abwehr working for him – went on to describe how he envisaged the Central Intelligence Agency which the new Bill would create. The CIA would be quite small, Dulles said, because 'if this thing gets to be a great big octopus it should not function well'. Pressed on just how many officers the CIA would need, Dulles said:

> On the evaluation side, there you require a certain number of people. On the side of collecting business information, I should think that a couple of dozen people throughout the United States could do it, two in New York, one in Chicago, and one in San Francisco . . . Abroad, you will need a certain number of people, but it ought not to be a great number. It ought to be scores rather than hundreds.[10] [The CIA now has about 16,000 employees.]

Dulles had ideas about where these people might be found:

> American businessmen and American professors, and Americans of all types who travel around the world are the greatest repositories of intelligence that we have . . . I should think that in the collecting field, in what we might call the clandestine collecting field, Americans who have no official connection with the government would furnish quite a high percentage of the valuable intelligence.

And he stressed how essential the CIA would be: '. . . in my opinion the British have saved themselves several times by their intelligence service . . . This is vital, you know. It is terribly important for our national security.'[11]

Dulles's evidence, like that of the other witnesses, was given under the cloak of anonymity – he was designated as 'Mr B'. Only an original was prepared of the transcript, both the stenographer and the typist being sworn on oath to secrecy. The original was kept by the chairman of the committee, who introduced the Bill, but the CIA later borrowed it and made a copy. This turned out to be fortunate because the chairman destroyed the original in 1950.[12]

The secrecy of hearings, plus the fact that the main purpose of the Bill was the unification of the armed forces (the CIA is not even mentioned in the Bill's full title), enabled the new agency to come into being without wide public discussion and with its exact function left rather vague. Congress believed that the CIA would have no domestic role, that it would have limited operational functions, and that it would act primarily as an information co-ordinator (although its right to collect information itself remained vague). It was certainly not going to carry out covert operations overseas. Yet, as we have seen, the CIA's predecessor, the CIG, had already been *collecting* intelligence and already carrying out covert operations. The new agency was certainly not about to surrender those functions.

Although the established collectors of intelligence, such as the State Department, poured scorn on the CIA, they were outgunned within the bureaucracy. The CIA had two crucial advantages: it reported directly to the President and was accountable only to the National Security Council, which the President headed. Thus if the President could be convinced of the benefits of timely intelligence, nothing would stand in the way of the CIA's march to a bigger and better future.

That is what happened. In 1948 the communists took power in Czechoslovakia and made alarming gains in the polls in Italy and France. The Commander-in-Chief of US European Command warned President Truman of the danger of imminent war with the Soviet Union. Truman responded by issuing a series of directives expanding the CIA's powers and duties. National Security Council Paper 10/2 widened the scope of CIA missions against the USSR to include covert paramilitary operations. National Security Council

Paper 68 assigned the CIA a major role in the Cold War against the Soviet Union, including psychological operations and covert action. Amendments to the National Security Act in 1949 granted the CIA exceptional secrecy, empowering its director to withhold, even from Congress, details of the agency's size, budget, methods, operations and sources.

Licensed to conduct what was, in essence, a secret Third World War, the CIA underwent explosive growth. In one year – from mid-1946 to mid-1947 – the CIG had expanded six-fold. Now its successor, the CIA, expanded six-fold again between 1947 and 1953. Most of this expansion took place in its covert operations section. In 1948 it had a staff of 302, 7 overseas stations, and a budget of $4·7 million. By 1952 it had a staff of 2,812, 47 overseas stations and a budget of $82 million, soon to be increased to $200 million. By this time almost two-thirds of the agency's staff could be described as clandestine operators, and running them accounted for three-quarters of the agency's budget.[13] The agency came to be dominated by these covert action officers, many of whom were ex-OSS men. (Donovan lived long enough to see this, but it is unlikely he appreciated his triumph. He suffered from brain atrophy and was given to reveries and visions – including one in which he saw Russian battalions marching over Washington's Fifty-ninth Street Bridge! He died in 1959.)[14]

The accepted view is that this rapid growth of the CIA was justified and necessary; that the United States had to react to a realistic appraisal of the postwar Soviet threat; that the expansion of the CIA's covert operations was essential to counter this threat; and that the threat receded because of the effectiveness of these operations. My view is that the Soviet threat was deliberately exaggerated by an agency intent on becoming an empire; that there was a conspiracy to further the growth and influence of the CIA; that President Truman, Congress and the American people were manipulated into authorizing and funding this expansion; that clandestine operations were often ineffective and counterproductive; and that, when the CIA was in danger of being found out, it was saved by the resurrection of that oldest of intelligence service weapons – the domestic spy scare.

An intelligence service thrives on threat. Its continued existence and its funding depend upon its ability to convince its political masters that the nation is in danger and that intelligence is both a sword and a shield. In the closing days of the Second World War, with the Nazi threat about to be eliminated, OSS had transferred its attentions to the Soviet Union, hoping that the dangers of communism would ensure the need for a postwar intelligence service. As we have seen, it at first looked as if these hopes were not to be realized. But then Truman became increasingly concerned about the Soviet Union and began to demand that the CIG provide him with more analysis about Soviet intentions. Vandenberg began to send top-secret memoranda direct to the President.*

Truman's interest in Soviet intentions came as a godsend to the CIG. It ended any debate on whether the United States needed a large, centralized peacetime intelligence agency. The CIG quickly made it clear that its ignorance of the Soviet Union was enormous – due to present and past neglect – and could be remedied only by vast injections of money and men. This, of course, was simply not true. OSS had recruited the Gehlen spy network in Eastern Europe. SIS, whose officers the Americans still erroneously believed to be the supermen of espionage, had been hard at work since 1944 establishing an anti-Soviet intelligence operation and, in the early postwar years, had re-engaged many of its old agents in Eastern Europe and had recruited freely from Nazi intelligence groups which had run anti-communist operations. There was a solid core of American and British experts on the Soviet Union, many of whom had served in Moscow during the war. The fact is that it suited the CIG, and then the CIA, to exaggerate their lack of knowledge of the Soviet Union and the shortcomings of American intelligence, and to magnify the operations of the all-powerful KGB so as to justify their own existence and expansion.

Once this expansion had started there was no point in reporting that, perhaps, the Soviet threat was not as serious as had been first believed. Instead, generalized anti-communist sentiments were given free rein, while to the CIA's own deep distrust of the USSR was added SIS's traditional anti-Bolshevism. The alarm that such 'intelligence' created in the United States must have played an important part in the development of the Cold War.

Even some CIA officers thought that the agency's assumptions about the Soviet Union were off the mark and they tried to redress the balance. A small group of officers got together in 1949 and wrote a top secret review of the Soviet Union's intentions. The paper, called 'Project Jigsaw', reviewed world communism and concluded that, even if Moscow manipulated communist parties in Western

* At least one was alarmist and, as it turned out, based on false information from Britain's SIS. This stated that Russian rockets were being fired on Sweden and Norway. SIS claimed that there had been many sightings of rocket trails, but no debris had been recovered because the rockets had been fitted with 'self-destruct' devices. The 'rockets' turned out to be meteors.

nations such as France and Italy, there was no Soviet masterplan for world domination. But this was such an heretical view that the paper was suppressed, even for internal circulation.[15] Instead, the expansionist view of the Soviet Union prevailed. The CIA claimed that Russia intended to take over Finland and Austria. Tito and the Greek guerrillas were under the Kremlin's thumb. France could go communist any day – unless it decided instead for the authoritarian leadership of General de Gaulle! The Italian Communist Party might decide on armed insurrection, and unrest in Europe could seriously undermine stability in Britain.

This alarmist view suited the administration. Truman was committed to the Marshall Plan – basically American aid for the recovery of those European nations which would exclude communists from power – but Congress was delaying its approval. Truman needed something to shock the American public into immediate recognition of the need for the plan and a continuing menace to ensure the plan's implementation. The communist coup in Czechoslovakia provided the former, and the CIA's assessment of the Soviet threat the latter. Covert action became the natural ally of the Marshall Plan because it was seen as a way of countering communist opposition to it.

In December 1947 a CIA operation began in Italy to make certain that the communists did not win the forthcoming elections. About $10 million was used to pay bribes, support the Christian Democrat election campaigns, and to produce and distribute anti-communist propaganda. In the subsequent election the Christian Democrats gained a majority of forty seats. At the same time, the CIA was running a covert operation in France to encourage and finance a split in the communist-dominated trade union, the CGT – a scheme that was successful at the cost of about $1 million a year. In Greece, the CIA took over from SIS an operation supporting the nationalists against the Greek Communist Party.[16]

These operations were the forerunners of a programme of covert CIA operations in foreign states that still continues today. Their initial successes encouraged CIA covert action officers to press for the setting up of a permanent group to plan and carry out covert action. As a result, in August 1948 the Office of Policy Co-ordination (OPC) – a quaint and misleading title – was established under Frank G. Wisner, a tough, hard-drinking, hard-working, aggressive and ambitious officer with an abiding hatred of communism.\* This

---

\* Wisner killed himself in 1961. One story claims that he had committed himself to the Hungarian uprising and was emotionally shattered by the CIA's failure to help the Hungarians.

meant a radical departure from American foreign policy in peace-time. Indeed, no nation had ever before formally espoused covert action – later defined by a CIA legal officer as 'special activity conducted abroad in support of national foreign policy objectives and executed so that the role of the government is not apparent or acknowledged publicly'.[17] Yet it appeared to offer attractive solutions to problems which traditional methods could not solve.

In the complex postwar world, the United States had found itself time and time again faced by situations which would not yield to diplomacy alone. Covert action 'more forceful than diplomacy, less hideous than war' offered a way out. The Italian, French and Greek experiences suggested that such action could achieve results. Since it was secret the United States would not be seen to be an inter-national bully. It had the political advantage of allowing the American government to maintain its high moral tone. It got around the fact that, despite the Soviet threat, Congress was wary of vast increases in military expenditure; for as covert action came under the general CIA budget, it was safe from curious Congressmen. In short, covert action came to be seen as a miracle cure for all international ills, and with the OPC dominated by ex-OSS officers who had exaggerated ideas about the success of their wartime operations, it began to appear as if it could accomplish miracles.

Covert operations started in the Ukraine, Lithuania, Poland and Albania. They were stepped up in Italy, France and Greece. They spread to Iran and Guatemala – and later to Indonesia, Angola, Cuba and Chile. (There may be many more: those foreign governments which *asked* for CIA help will not have talked about it.) Indeed, if we include under covert action the secret funding of anti-communist publications, the planting of CIA officers on newspapers and all the major news agencies, and the bribing and suborning of trade union officials and politicians, then there was hardly a country in the world in the 1940s and 1950s – friendly to the United States or otherwise – which did not knowingly or unwittingly play host to a CIA covert action operation.

Money and cynicism were unlimited. When the Communist Party made a comeback in Italy in the 1953 elections, polling 37 per cent of the vote, only 3 per cent behind the Christian Democrats, the CIA went into action. William E. Colby, a future director, was rushed to Rome from Stockholm, given $25 million a year to spend, and ordered to liaise with the American ambassador, Clare Booth-Luce and the Roman Catholic Church, in a secret operation to pump money into the anti-communist parties. In France financial support for anti-communist unions was increased, a Cabinet minister was put on the CIA bribes list and a plan considered – but eventually rejected – which involved trying to sway the entire French Chamber of Deputies with $700,000.[18]

The Albanian operation – an attempt to stimulate the overthrow of the government of Enver Hoxha by training émigré Albanians and then infiltrating them back into their country – was an enormous operation mounted with SIS help. It involved recruiting anti-communist exiles, training them in camps set up in Malta and Cyprus, and then parachuting them into the Albanian mountains or slipping them ashore by boat on remote parts of the Albanian coastline opposite the Greek island of Corfu. The Ukrainian operation was equally ambitious. It involved supporting Ukrainian nationalists in their attempted resistance against Soviet control by financing and training émigré organizations and helping them get men back into their country to spread revolt.

Probably the most-celebrated example of covert action during this period was the CIA operation designed to restore the Shah to the throne of Iran in 1953. The Iranian Prime Minister, Mohammed Mossadegh, had overthrown the Shah with the help of the Iranian Communist Party and had nationalized the Anglo-Iranian Petroleum Company. SIS and the CIA moved to reverse this. The CIA gave one of its covert operations officers, Kim Roosevelt, a budget of $2 million to mount a campaign to restore the Shah to power. Mossadegh was duly ousted and Roosevelt was secretly awarded the National Security Medal.

But, looked at over the long term, how effective were these CIA operations? The short answer is that covert action, as a substitute for a coherent foreign policy, turned out to be little more than a gimmick, effective only when the internal forces were *already* moving in the direction that the CIA wished to push them.

Where this was not so, covert action either failed or was counter-productive. It failed in the Ukraine, Lithuania, Poland and Albania. Hundreds of agents and millions of dollars were lost in Lithuania and the Ukraine, where CIA intervention hindered rather than helped the resistance movements. These failures were to leave an awkward legacy which came to the surface only twenty years later. Many of the émigrés that the Americans had recruited for these operations were former Nazi collaborators who were subsequently smuggled into the United States. It was only in the 1970s that evidence began to emerge that numbers of Nazi war criminals had safely lived out their final years as American citizens with the connivance of the CIA.

In Poland the CIA became an unwitting tool of the communist authorities who used the old Bolshevik tactic, perfected after the Revolution, of setting up dummy resistance groups to milk the opposition of hard currency and then mounting a propaganda coup by revealing everything.

But Albania was, perhaps, the classic failure. Here hundreds of CIA émigré agents went to their deaths between 1949 and late 1953. Dropped by parachute or landed by boat, they never managed to get very far before the Albanian security police found them and either shot them on the spot or arranged state trials to show what happened to saboteurs and traitors. Since this was a joint CIA–SIS operation, under the joint command of James McCargar for the CIA and Kim Philby for SIS, the official explanation for the débâcle is that Philby, the long-serving KGB penetration officer, betrayed it. This does not stand up to close examination.

For the last two years of the operation Philby had nothing to do with it, having been recalled from Washington in June 1951 in the aftermath of the flight of Burgess and Maclean. Moreover, although Philby's role as 'commander' gave him overall knowledge of the operation, he would not have known in advance details like the time and date of landings which, since they depended on the weather, tides and other local factors, had to be left to the field officers.

Philby would have told the KGB about the *existence* of the operation – valuable-enough information. But it is unlikely that the KGB used him to obtain details. Why would the KGB risk their most valuable penetration officer, just when he had finally manœuvred himself into the heart of SIS *and* the CIA, by getting him to report on an operation that had no chance of success in a country with which Moscow did not enjoy the closest of relations? It is significant that Philby, not slow to take modest credit for his other betrayals, claims nothing for Albania. For what it is worth the then Albanian leader, Enver Hoxha, also said bluntly that it was the vigilance of the security police, their 'radio game' and the incompetence of the CIA–SIS controllers which caused the operation to fail 'and not the merits of a certain Kim Philby, as some have claimed'.[19]

The most likely explanation for the débâcle seems to be that the Albanian authorities had penetrated the émigré organizations from which the agents were recruited, and that one of these communist penetration agents managed to get himself chosen for infiltration into Albania. Once there, he handed over his team to the security authorities who then forced the radio man to work for them. From that moment, Albanian security would have controlled the whole operation and could have played a 'radio game' in order to lure the rest of the CIA–SIS teams to their doom.

Ironically, it only emerged in the early 1980s that the CIA was not as committed to the success of the operation as it made out. It knew it could not succeed. The Albanian exiles were dupes, sent to make a noise, to show that the CIA was active in the fight against communism. They were sacrificed for wider political interests. As it turned out, Albania soon formed a close friendship with China anyway and, by doing so, probably became a bigger headache for the Soviet Union than if the CIA had actually succeeded in installing a pro-Western government.

The Italian operation, according to Colby, was necessary because Moscow was pouring $50 million a year into the Italian Communist Party in the 1950s and Communist participation in the Italian government would have introduced 'a subversive fifth column' into NATO's military defences. But Colby is vague and unconvincing about Moscow finance for the Italian Communists. A fellow CIA officer, Robert Amory Jnr, at the time in the intelligence section of the CIA and therefore able to look at covert action with a sceptical eye, felt that an accidental combination of people especially sensitive to the Soviet menace – Booth-Luce, Gerald Miller (the OPC head of European operations), and the staff of the Italian desk at the State Department – had resulted in the communist threat in Italy being exaggerated. And what of the political cost? Kennedy Memorial Trust scholar, Trevor Barnes, concludes: 'The strident anti-communism of the Christian Democrats, stimulated and sustained by infusion of CIA money, may have become a surrogate for necessary reforms and as a result the communists' position was not undermined in the long-term.'[20]

It is difficult to measure the CIA's influence on French politics during this period. The money spent on bribes and subsidies to anti-communist trade unions, plus the secret funding of newspapers and magazines must have had some effect, but it is hard to pinpoint anything significant. Perhaps the main effect of the CIA's covert action was to burden French politics with a multitude of powerless parties, a situation which aided the communists rather than hampering them.

To claim that the CIA saved Western Europe from communism is clearly an exaggeration. The fact that no Western European nation went communist at that time was due more to open American aid – the Marshall Plan – inherent internal cohesion, and traditional political and economic conservatism than the secret machinations of the covert action clique in Washington.

Iran, again a joint CIA–SIS operation in 1953, has been hailed – largely by the CIA itself* – as an almost textbook example of the quiet efficiency of covert action. Key Iranians were successfully bribed (two agents were each getting $50,000 a month), a propaganda campaign was mounted to frighten the people with the prospect of a Soviet takeover, and anti-Mossadegh sections of the army were supplied with American equipment. Yet the evidence is that Mossadegh was a nationalist, not a communist: he had organized his National Front on the issue of who was to own Iranian oil and he had refused to legalize the Communist Party or to accept its co-operation.[21] And, although the CIA's objectives were achieved, it remains doubtful whether it was instrumental in replacing Mossadegh with the Shah. The Iranian army, police and political leaders seem to have played a more important part in the coup than the CIA is prepared to acknowledge.

In Guatemala, in 1954, the CIA toppled the elected government of the leftist Guzman Jacob Arbenz by using the 'big lie' technique – the bigger the lie, the more likely it is to be believed. The aim was to convince the Guatemalan middle class that the Arbenz government was a puppet of the Soviet Union. The lie, repeated frequently in radio broadcasts from 'The Voice of Liberation' (in reality, the CIA) on the eve of the coup, was that a shipment of Soviet arms destined for Guatemala had been sighted at sea. (This was so effective that the CIA, apparently convinced that the public had short memories, tried it again in Nicaragua in 1984 – this time unsuccessfully.) The result of the coup was the installation of the corrupt government of Carlos Castillo Armas – a development that even the CIA officer in charge of the operation, David Atlee Phillips regretted.[22]

In short, the CIA's covert intervention in the affairs of countries where it was concerned about communist influence was frequently counter-productive, worse, it threw away the United States' moral advantage over the Soviet Union. The United States had a reputation for respecting the sovereignty and the right to self-determination of other countries. The CIA's use of covert action led many to believe that there was little to choose between the United States and the Soviet Union. In those countries, notably the Third World ones, where most CIA covert actions took place, people no

* Although Prime Minister Churchill and the Foreign Secretary, Anthony Eden, were deeply involved in the plan to restore the Shah to his throne, the British government archives on the operation which were due for release in 1983 remain secret.

longer distinguished between the CIA and the KGB; both were symbols of imperialism. Unwittingly, the American covert action operators had acquired the faces of their Soviet opponents.

Yet these Americans *were* often honourable men – as the CIA has been at pains to emphasize – and, ironically, often of liberal political views. Intelligence tends to attract religious and altruistic people of high ability – David Atlee Phillips, the CIA officer in Guatemala mentioned above, has described William E. Colby, who was to become a director of the CIA from 1973 to 1976, as 'a soldier-priest'. These men believed that they had embarked on a crusade but, ironically, like Marxists, they came to the conclusion that the nobility of their aims justified any means that came to hand. Operating in semi-independence, they assumed the initiative in deciding what covert operations were needed to further American foreign policy and went ahead and implemented them under minimum control.

At first, the State Department was regarded by the CIA as a rival and often kept in ignorance of what the agency was doing. Sometimes situations arose in which CIA covert operations were in direct conflict with the policies being pursued by the State Department. But under the reign of the Dulles brothers an alliance was struck which was, if anything, even more dangerous than the rivalry that preceded it. Allen Dulles, the former OSS officer, rejoined American intelligence in 1951 as chief of covert operations and became director of the CIA in 1953. His brother, John Foster Dulles, was already installed as Secretary of State and establishing his reputation as the Cold War warrior *par excellence*, speaking of liberating Eastern Europe and 'rolling back communism'. Covert action by the CIA offered a sharp and apparently efficient tool for doing this, and the bond between the State Department and the CIA thus became so close that the CIA was easily able to ward off attempts to establish congressional committees to oversee the agency's activities. Allen Dulles was able to say, with considerable justification, that 'Intelligence has a more influential position in our government than Intelligence enjoys in any other government in the world'.[23]

Not everyone was happy with this situation. With hindsight, Lyman Kirkpatrick, who was the CIA's inspector-general during Allen Dulles's regime, says: 'We are talking about a period in which, the more I look back at it and try to be objective, the more horrified I am by those two Dulles bothers, conferring four to five times each day on the telephone, meeting every night, running bombing operations over Indonesia, neither of them having had military experience of this type.'[24]

And here, for what it is worth, is a KGB view of the CIA at that period:

> Allen Dulles, through John Foster Dulles, had far too much power, which President Eisenhower could not curb and John Foster Dulles would not. (Eisenhower probably knew very little about it.) Allen Dulles, for his part, was the genial chairman, who could never get his mouth around the essential 'no'. So, side by side with a lot of very sensible chaps, a lot of maniacs were allowed to go off every-which-way and do more or less as they liked. The dirty tricks multiplied of their own momentum. Naturally, if you think in terms of a global struggle, dirty tricks are inevitable; but without control and purpose they become incredibly wasteful and too often counter-productive. The Mad Mullah succeeds Mossadegh.[25]

Certainly, in an agency dominated by covert action men, intelligence collection and evaluation got relegated to second place. This fatal flaw had its origins in the days of OSS, when Donovan and others had seen how the British system of two independent organizations, SOE (covert action) and SIS (intelligence), had led to bitter rivalry. The chairman of the British JIC, William Cavendish-Bentinck, recalls a wartime trip to Washington.

> I remember saying to Bill Donovan 'Don't have two organisations; one for skullduggery, tripping people up, cutting throats, and any other nasty business like our SOE; another like our SIS for intelligence. Because they'd be quarrelling the whole time and trying to get the better of one another instead of getting the better of the enemy. Have one control organisation.' I didn't know that I was acting as a midwife for that monster, the CIA.[26]

The memory of what they had seen, and the problems it had caused for the British, made some senior OSS officers, who became the backbone of the CIA, determined to have covert action and intelligence under one umbrella. But the attractions of covert action – the freedom it gave people of ability to exercise power, money, secrecy, the appeal of patriotism, the frontline of the Cold War – are greater than those of intelligence evaluation. The older covert action men relived the halcyon days of the war, the younger recruits tasted real power, and both were reluctant to see things change. (When Admiral Stansfield Turner became director of the CIA in 1977 and gave orders to rein in covert operations he was simply ignored.) Policy-makers ceased to look to the CIA for information and analysis as the intelligence branch wilted. It took the shock of the Soviet atom bomb to reveal how badly the CIA had failed its true purpose.[27]

On 29 August 1949, as dawn broke over Kazakhstan, Central Asia, a huge mushroom-shaped cloud blossomed skywards. Four years after the United States had exploded the world's first atomic bomb, the Soviet Union had also entered the nuclear world. President Truman, who had assured Americans that the United States had an atomic monopoly which would last for ten to fifteen years, refused to believe first reports of the explosion, and it needed radioactive rainwater samples from contaminated clouds to convince him.[28] Even then, he could not accept that it necessarily followed that the Russians had an atomic bomb – in his announcement to the American people on 23 September, more than three weeks after the event, he implied his own view – that there had been a nuclear accident – by speaking only of an 'atomic explosion' in the Soviet Union. He avoided the word 'bomb'.

But five days later Moscow told the world. Americans were stunned and frightened. How could a country ravaged by war, without the industrial muscle of the United States, apparently without the properly qualified scientists, without the necessary raw materials and, above all, without the vital know-how, produce an atomic bomb in such a short space of time? How could the Soviet Union take one of the most important weapon decisions this century, implement that decision, and succeed in its aims without the CIA knowing about it? Worse, how could American intelligence be so faulty as to insist that a Russian atomic bomb was ten to twenty years away – the greatest miscalculation of the Cold War?

There was a chorus of protests. The director of the CIA, Admiral Roscoe Hillenkoetter, had sent Truman a memo only a year earlier in which he wrote that 'the earliest date by which it is remotely possible that the USSR may have completed its first atomic bomb is mid-1950, but the most probable date is believed to be mid-1953.'[29] Hillenkoetter took the blame and was eventually replaced by General Walter Bedell Smith. But it needed more than one head to appease the CIA's critics. Dr R. E. Lapp, a consultant to the US Atomic Energy Commission, stated that the Soviet Union's development of the atomic bomb represented a major deficiency in American intelligence. Bernard Baruch, the American representative to the UN Atomic Energy Commission, complained to the State Department of poor intelligence evaluation, and the president of the Reservists' Association demanded a strengthening of American intelligence so that 'we can more effectively pierce the Iron Curtain and be warned of hostile moves'.[30]

Criticism of an intelligence failure, no matter how fierce, can, if properly handled, be turned to the intelligence agency's advantage. The best ploy, tested over the years, is to suggest that the failure was due to the insidious skill of the enemy's intelligence organization whose spies had penetrated the castle and had stolen its secrets, and that the only way to counter the enormous efforts the enemy puts into these intelligence coups is to match him agent for agent and dollar for dollar. This was the tactic adopted by the CIA.

The CIA's failure to detect that the Soviet Union would build an atom bomb so quickly was explained away by suggesting that the estimates of ten to twenty years before Russia got the bomb were correct, but had been invalidated by Soviet espionage rings in the United States which had 'stolen the most important secrets ever known to mankind and delivered them to the Soviet Union'. There was no evidence, at that time, that any atom espionage rings existed, but this did not stop Congressman Richard Nixon from initiating the hunt for them by writing in the New York *Journal American* demanding that President Truman reveal 'the facts about the espionage ring which was responsible for turning over information on the atom bomb to agents of the Russian government'.[31] Hoover ordered the FBI to find the spies who had enabled the Russians to build an atomic bomb so quickly and the United States was soon swept up in a massive spy scare that was to lead in 1953 to the execution for treason of Julius and Ethel Rosenberg. In the United States and Britain a number of 'atomic spies' were caught, tried and imprisoned. Others, accused or about to be accused, fled to the Soviet Union. What did those spies give away? How did they help the Soviet Union to develop the atomic bomb? And what could the CIA have learnt about its development? To answer these questions we must first look briefly at the history of the atomic bomb.

Soviet scientists, along with their counterparts in other countries, certainly realized that an atomic bomb had become a theoretical possibility in 1939 after German physicists discovered the nuclear fission of uranium. Igor Kurchatov, later hailed as the father of the Soviet atomic bomb, and a group of young researchers, including Georgy Nikolayovich Flyorov (who was to play an amazing role in the Soviet bomb programme) were urging crash development of atomic research early in 1940 – a full year before the American programme began. In June of that year the Soviet authorities decided to set up a uranium authority to work out a plan of atomic research for 1941 and to determine what materials would be needed.

Early in 1941 the scientists put it to the Soviet government that it might be possible to create an atomic bomb far more powerful than any existing conventional bomb.

But before the government had responded, the German invasion brought a halt to all Soviet nuclear research. Soviet scientists have since claimed that, had it not been for the war with Germany, they might well have achieved a chain reaction before the Americans did in Chicago in December 1942. This is one of those 'ifs' with which history is littered, but David Holloway, of the University of Edinburgh and the Center for International Security and Arms Control, Stanford University, California, who has written definitively on Soviet atomic energy policy, says that 'The claim is not a wild one'. He believes that if the Soviet scientists' plan to attempt a chain reaction had been adopted, and if the Germans had not invaded then 'the first chain reaction might have taken place in the Soviet Union, for Soviet physicists did not lag behind their American, British or German counterparts in their thinking about nuclear fission'.[32]

Immediately after the German invasion, Kurchatov decided to abandon work on nuclear fission. The laboratory was closed down and most of his younger scientists joined the armed forces. G. N. Flyorov went into the Soviet air force from where this 28-year-old lieutenant bombarded Kurchatov, the State Defence Committee in Moscow and the members of the Academy of Science with letters urging that nuclear fission research be resumed. But, by now, the German army was on the outskirts of Moscow and the very survival of the Soviet Union was in doubt; so it is scarcely surprising that most of Flyorov's letters did not even receive a reply. But the young lieutenant did not give up his interest in atomic research, and when he was posted to an airbase at Voronezh in February 1942 he took the opportunity to visit the university's library where there was a comprehensive and up-to-date stock of Western scientific journals. What he found there dismayed and alarmed him.

Back in 1940, Flyorov and a colleague had published an account of the spontaneous fission of uranium and had been nominated for a Stalin Prize for their work. But the award had been withheld on the ground that Western scientists had shown no interest in the discovery, not even responding to Flyorov's paper in the July 1940 issue of *Physical Review*. Puzzled by this silence – for, before the war, physics was perhaps the most international of the sciences – Flyorov spent hours ploughing through all the scientific journals in the Voronezh university library. What the Stalin Prize referee had said was true: there was *nothing* about Flyorov's work. But then

Flyorov realized *that there was nothing about nuclear fission at all.* All the great names in the field – Fermi, Szilard, Teller, Andersen, Wheiler, Wigner – had completely vanished from the journals. Flyorov drew the only possible conclusion: nuclear research in the United States had been made a state secret because its scientists were working on an atomic bomb. *

Flyorov, a junior officer, decided to go direct to Stalin, his Commander-in-Chief. He wrote to the First Secretary, setting out the evidence and his conclusions, and said it was vital to the Soviet Union that no time should be lost in reopening nuclear research and building an atomic bomb. Now things happened quickly. Although the war was at a crucial stage, the State Defence Committee approved, in principle, the renewal of atomic research and Flyorov was called to Moscow for consultations. Some senior scientists had an uncomfortable interview with Stalin who wanted to know how it was that a junior lieutenant at the front had seen the danger to the Soviet Union, while his scientific advisers had not.† The scientists had to admit to Stalin – who might well have had them shot had he not needed them so badly – that work on an atomic bomb was probably going on not only in the United States and Britain, but in Germany as well.[33]

Kurchatov was put in charge of the Soviet bomb project and, as the war swung in the Soviet Union's favour and the Red Army moved into Germany, he made extensive efforts to recruit German nuclear scientists for his work. An indication of the international attitude of nuclear physicists can be seen in the decision of Nobel Prizewinner, Gustav Hertz, who was an expert on the gaseous diffusion process for separating the isotopes of uranium. He decided not to move Westwards as Germany collapsed but to offer his services to the Soviet Union, giving as his reason that there were so many brilliant scientists in the United States that his abilities would be better appreciated by the Russians.[34]

Yet, even now, the Soviet Union did not press ahead with its bomb programme with any high degree of urgency. This came only after the dropping of the bombs on Hiroshima and Nagasaki on 6 and 9 August 1945. The American test explosion of the atomic bomb had taken place on 16 July. The Potsdam Conference was in progress and

---

* Flyorov was not quite right. American scientists *themselves* had decided in April 1940 not to publish papers on nuclear fission, fearing that they might help Germany to develop an atomic bomb.

† Flyorov became an outstanding Soviet physicist, a Lenin Prize winner, and member of the USSR Academy of Sciences. For the past twenty-eight years he has headed the Laboratory of Nuclear Reactions in Dubna.

after the session on 24 July Truman approached Stalin and told him about a new weapon 'of unusual destructive force'. Accounts differ as to what Truman actually said, and what Stalin *understood* him to mean. The Western version is that Stalin failed to understand that Truman was referring to the atomic bomb. The Soviet version is that Stalin knew only too well, and actually said later that day that he would have to talk to Kurchatov about speeding up work on the Soviet bomb. The truth – hinted at in some Soviet versions – is most likely that Stalin knew that Truman was referring to the atomic bomb, but did not appreciate the full significance of the American achievement.

This was brought home to him only when the United States used the bomb against Japan. Now Stalin got the message: America had a powerful weapon; it alone possessed it; it was prepared to use it to achieve its political objectives. There is a Soviet account of Stalin's reaction (discovered by David Holloway). Stalin summoned the People's Commissar of Munitions, his deputies and Kurchatov to the Kremlin. 'A single demand of you, comrades', said Stalin. 'Provide us with atomic weapons in the shortest possible time. You know that Hiroshima has shaken the whole world. The equilibrium has been destroyed (*ravnovesie narushilos*). Provide the bomb – it will remove a great danger to us.'[35]

The race for a Soviet bomb was now on. We have seen how the atomic spies played no part in the early development of the Soviet bomb – the vital knowledge that the West was developing a bomb came from Flyorov and he was tipped off, inadvertently, by American nuclear physicists themselves, when they ceased publishing papers on nuclear fission. Did the atomic spies now play a major role in helping speed up the Soviet bomb? Firstly, it must be appreciated that the chances of keeping secret the most important single piece of scientific information about the bomb – that it worked – were absolutely nil after Hiroshima. The American government itself thus gave the Soviet Union more than all the atomic spies put together. It then followed up this unavoidable gift with a gratuitous one. It released the Smythe Report on Atomic Energy for Military Purposes in August 1945. The Soviet Union, anxious to get Soviet industry behind the bomb project, rushed through a translation of the report and published and distributed 30,000 copies within six months.[36]

As for the atomic spies we can eliminate the Rosenbergs immediately. They were convenient scapegoats but, as David Holloway puts it, 'I've never seen anything to suggest that the Rosenbergs told the Russians anything of value about the atomic bomb'.[37]

Donald Maclean, the Soviet spy who, in 1947–8, was Britain's representative on the Combined Policy Committee (which made recommendations to Britain, the United States and Canada on the division of programmes in the atomic energy field) can also be discounted. In 1968 I wrote (in *The Philby Conspiracy*) that Maclean had a non-escort pass to the Atomic Energy Commission's headquarters and that he used this pass after office hours, several times a week and over a period of months. I concluded from this that Maclean was an atomic spy of major importance. Since 1968 further information leads me to believe that I overrated Maclean's usefulness to the Russians and that he was able to tell them little of value about nuclear weapons, as such.

A British geologist, Professor C. F. Davidson, who had an office in the AEC, told me: 'By regulation strictly adhered to, all files were housed at night in security safes with combination locks. Maclean did not know the combinations of my safes, and I find it difficult to accept that the Americans made him their confidant.'[38] Caroll L. Wilson, general manager of the AEC at the time, said that Maclean's non-escort pass would not have given him access to anything he should not have had. Others who worked in the AEC at the time have also confirmed that security was very tight – guards at the end of each corridor at night; people recalled to the building if their papers had not been locked away. In short, although Maclean may have been able to tell the Russians about political differences between Britain and the United States on atomic energy matters, and to provide them with organizational details about both countries' atomic programmes, he was not in a position to tell them anything that would help them to speed up the production of their own atomic weapon.

That leaves us with the spy who is generally considered to have been most important to the Soviets and most damaging to the West, Klaus Fuchs. Fuchs, a refugee from Hitler, who had arrived in Britain in 1933, had been shipped to a Canadian internment camp in 1940. In 1942 he was brought back to Britain to work on the British atomic bomb programme and two years later was seconded to the American project where he worked in Chicago, New York and Los Alamos. He returned to Britain in 1946. In 1949 CIA cryptographers, working routinely through a mass of coded material stolen in 1944 from the New York offices of the Soviet Government Purchasing Commission, a known front for industrial espionage, came across Fuchs's name on a report about progress at Los Alamos. It was passed to MI5, Fuchs was interrogated and on 10 February 1950 confessed – on the promise, later broken, of a light sentence – to passing classified information to Soviet agents in Britain and the United States.*

Fuchs's spying breaks down into four periods. In the first period, from early 1942 to December 1943, he was working with Professor Rudolph Peierl's team at Birmingham University. Fuchs told the Soviet Union that Britain considered an atomic bomb to be a definite possibility, that similar work was being done in the United States, and that there was collaboration between the two countries. He gave his Soviet contact carbon copies of his own calculations on the theory of the gaseous diffusion process for separating the isotopes of uranium, and his conclusion that uranium 235 produced in this way might be used in an atomic bomb.

It is unlikely then, given the state of nuclear knowledge in the Soviet Union in 1940–1, that Fuchs's information would have been either new or important to Russian scientists, except in so far as it confirmed what Flyorov had deduced from the absence of papers on nuclear fission in scientific journals: Western scientists were working on an atomic bomb. Fuchs himself noted that his Soviet contact was in no way surprised to hear that Britain and the United States were working on an atomic bomb. In fact, the Soviet contact surprised Fuchs by asking him what he knew about electromagnetic techniques for separating uranium 235. Fuchs knew nothing of any work on this method and had never considered it.[39] The conclusion must be that, at this stage, the Soviet Union was already studying the technical problems of producing an atomic bomb.

During the second period, from December 1943 to August 1944, Fuchs was a member of the British Diffusion Mission. In this capacity, he learned a good deal more about the American programme, in particular its general scale and effort. In the third period, from August 1944 to the summer of 1946, Fuchs was at Los Alamos. There he realized for the first time the full nature and magnitude of the American atomic energy programme. He wrote a report for his Soviet contact summarizing the whole problem of making an atomic bomb as he then saw it. He later gave the contact a sketch of the American test bomb and its components and all the important dimensions. But there was other, equally crucial, information such as details of production, of pile design, construction and operation, that he did not know and could not have passed on to his Soviet contact.

---

* Fuchs, whose confession put the FBI on the trail of the Rosenbergs, was sentenced to fourteen years' imprisonment, served nine, and then on his release went to live in East Germany.

In the fourth period, while working at Harwell atomic energy research establishment, Berkshire, Britain, from the summer of 1946 to the spring of 1949, Fuchs filled in the picture of the plutonium bomb that he had already given the Russians from Los Alamos and provided mathematical details, such as the blast calculations of the Hiroshima and Nagasaki bombs. He also described the ideas in Los Alamos on the design and method of operation of a super bomb which were current at the time he left.

The Soviet Union has never acknowledged that it received *any* information from Fuchs, a surprising omission considering the propaganda mileage it could have gained from using him as an example of the 'international attitude which should inspire all nuclear scientists'. This lack of recognition means, however, that there is little indication in Soviet sources of what actually happened to Fuchs's reports. David Holloway says that his extensive researches leave the issue unclear except for the following item. 'In one of his confessions Fuchs noted that questions had come back to him from the Soviet Union about the derivation of the Bethe-Feynman formula for estimating bomb efficiency. Fuchs had passed on the formula, which was basically a heuristic device, and evidently it had reached the appropriate Soviet physicists.'[40]

As to Fuchs's value to the Russians, Holloway cannot reach a positive conclusion. He says Fuchs did provide potentially useful information. Some of this the Soviet scientists already knew, or else they would have discovered it: 'But I think it is hard to dismiss it as worthless, especially as it gave the Soviet authorities some indication of what the Americans were up to. The estimates I have (from scientists who worked with Fuchs) suggest that he might have saved the Russians as much as a year or eighteen months in building the atomic bomb.'[41]

We do, however, have Fuchs's own assessment of what help he had been to the Soviet Union. This should, of course, be treated with caution, but the Harwell scientist who took down Fuchs's confession felt obliged to note that he seemed to be 'trying his best to help me evaluate the present position of atomic energy works in Russia in the light of information that he had, and had not, passed to them'. Fuchs claimed that he had been extremely surprised that the Russian explosion had taken place so soon as he had been convinced that *the information he had given could not have been applied so quickly* (my emphasis), and that the Russians would not have had the engineering design and construction facilities that would be needed to build large production plants in such a short time.[42]

To sum up: the atomic spies, unforgivable though their treachery may have been, did not give the atomic bomb to the Soviet Union. The spies may have advanced the date of the first Soviet bomb, but even this remains somewhat doubtful and it would appear to be a matter of months rather than years. Ultimately, their actions merely hastened the end of a process as futile as trying to keep secret the discovery of the wheel.*

Moreover, the American scientific and intelligence community was well aware of this. Twelve days after the explosion of the atomic bomb on Hiroshima, Gregory Bateson, an officer in the research and analysis section of OSS wrote a paper, 'The Influence of the Atomic Bomb on Indirect Methods of Warfare', in which the following sentence appears: 'The general principle on which these bombs operate are already known to a large number of physicists' and therefore 'no high degree of security in regard to the A-bomb can be expected' because 'all the major powers are likely to have this sort [of weapon] within the next ten years.'[43]

So it was not the fact that the Soviet Union had *developed* the atomic bomb that caused panic in American intelligence, it was the CIA's own failure to predict when this would occur. The CIA owed its very existence to its promise to prevent surprises of this nature – Allen Dulles had specifically assured the 1947 Congressional Committee that the CIA would know if 'some people across the seas' had managed to develop an atomic bomb and were prepared to use it.[44]

There was no excuse for this major intelligence failure. A study of the files of *Izvestia*, for example, would have turned up an article on 21 December 1940 naming numerous Soviet scientists, including Kurchatov, who were engaged in nuclear research. Proper debriefing of Nazi nuclear scientists after the war would have revealed that Kurchatov had tried to buy a kilo of refined uranium from the Nazis in 1940. The Americans knew that the Russians had tried in 1944 to persuade the brilliant Danish nuclear scientist, Niels Bohr, to leave Britain, where he had taken refuge, and settle in the Soviet Union. Bohr himself had told President Roosevelt on 26 August 1944 that the Russians knew that the United States was making great efforts to develop an atomic bomb, that the Russians were themselves studying the matter, would be free to increase their efforts when Germany was defeated, and that they would probably obtain the German secrets.[45] Given all the available information, any competent nuclear scientist would have realized that intelligence

---

* By 1954 Churchill had recognized this. According to a Cabinet paper yet to be released, he said that the tragedy was that the West did not tell the Soviet Union everything it knew about the atomic bomb when the United States still had the monopoly.

predictions of no Soviet bomb for ten to twenty years were ludicrous. As with Pearl Harbor, all the relevant facts were floating around the United States waiting for someone to collate and evaluate them – the CIA's real job.

But the device of shifting the blame for this intelligence failure to betrayal from within, allowed the CIA not only to survive, but actually to expand. When General Walter Bedell Smith took over as director in October 1950 he prepared a memorandum entitled 'Intelligence Requirements and Mobilization' in which he requested a supplement to the agency's budget for the 1951 financial year. The increase, which was granted, was in addition to another 'very substantial increase' given to the agency to enable it to implement National Security Council Paper 68 which was aimed at stepping up intelligence operations against the Soviet Union.[46] But the shock of the Soviet bomb, followed by the North Korean invasion of the South in June 1950, yet another intelligence surprise, meant that virtually anything the CIA asked for was granted. And this despite the fact that, in the case of Korea, American intelligence had even less excuse for its failure.

The CIA had been carrying out covert operations in Korea for at least two years prior to the invasion. At the peak, these operations involved about two thousand armed agents who had been infiltrated into the communist-held area of the country. The North Koreans had become increasingly hostile to these American-controlled operations and any responsible evaluation of the prospects of war between North and South Korea should have taken this hostility into account.

But there was no such evaluation. The covert action officers so dominated the CIA's thinking that it saw in the enemy a mirror image of itself. If it was obsessed with subversion, then the communists must be too. Therefore, since war was unlikely in Asia (in the early 1950s it was generally believed that any war would involve an all-out confrontation with the Soviet Union), the main danger to American interests in the Far East was communist subversion, and the communists would always draw back from direct military action. Thus, while ample evidence existed to show that North Korea was preparing an attack on the South – and, later, that China would enter the war – it was ignored in Washington because it conflicted with the CIA's prevailing view on the East–West confrontation. As Secretary of State Dean Acheson observed later, the United States had sufficient intelligence warning of the North Korean attack, but nowhere was it correctly evaluated. In June 1950 the CIA, the State Department, and the army all agreed that North Korea might invade, but that 'this attack did not appear imminent'.[47]

The surprise that the invasion had taken place at all, quickly changed to alarm at the speed of the communist advance. This, too, caught the CIA unawares because the army's 'Report on Korea', written in 1947 by General Albert C. Wedemeyer, which showed that the North Koreans were strong enough to over-run South Korea very quickly, never reached the director of the CIA.[48]

It then became necessary correctly to assess Communist China's reactions to the intervention of the United Nations forces. Here the picture is less clear because, after the invasion, General Mac-Arthur's headquarters had become solely responsible for intelligence on Korea. But the CIA had a China section with many China experts and, according to MacArthur, it offered its views on the likelihood of Chinese intervention if United Nations troops were to invade North Korea. Chinese intentions were hardly secret. In September, Peking officially informed the Indian ambassador, Sardar Pannikar, that China would respond, and authorized him to pass this on to Washington, which Pannikar did. It was shrugged off. On 3 October, the Chinese Foreign Minister made the warning more specific. He told Pannikar that if United States troops, or United Nations troops other than South Koreans, crossed into North Korea, China would send troops to defend the frontier. Radio Peking repeated this statement a few days later.

We know what MacArthur's views were. One of his senior intelligence officers told war correspondents that China had not recovered from the Revolution; large sections of the country were opposed to communist rule; the army was badly equipped; much of it was pinned down by Chiang Kai-shek's Kuomintang forces on Taiwan which were poised to return to the mainland; the Chinese army had only a few thousand troops on the frontier and could not bring up reinforcements without detection.[49]

Unfortunately, we only have MacArthur's version of what the CIA was telling him – or not telling him:

> In November, our Central Intelligence Agency here had said that they felt that there was little chance of any major intervention on the part of the Chinese forces . . . Now you must understand that intelligence that a nation is going to launch a war is not an intelligence that is available to a commander limited to a small area of combat. That intelligence should have been given [to] me.[50]

All this smacks of buck-passing. The military débâcle and the tens of thousands of lives lost when China did exactly what it had announced it would do (that is, responded to the United Nations counter-invasion of the North in massive strength), led to all sorts of inquiries, culminating in congressional committee hearings into the war and in MacArthur's dismissal by President Truman. But the important point is not whether MacArthur was attempting to blame the CIA for his own intelligence shortcomings, but that Korea was another example of the very intelligence failures the CIA had supposedly been created to prevent. The CIA was supposed to co-ordinate the intelligence activities of government departments, collect its own intelligence, evaluate intelligence from all sources and provide the results to all agencies, including the armed forces. The main reason for the Korean failure was not a lack of raw information, but the CIA's obsession with covert action and subversion which led the agency to ignore or misinterpret the information available to it.

In the months following the Korean invasion, the CIA did its best to recover its position by concentrating on communist military preparations. Its reports made gloomy reading. The summary for 10 August 1950 said: 'Throughout the Soviet orbit the trend towards . . . preparedness for war has continued. There is, moreover, evidence that certain phases of the programme are being accelerated with some urgency.'[51] Czechoslovakian factories were switching from consumer to military production, Soviet MIG 15 fighters had been seen in Hungary, the Eastern Bloc countries were crushing internal opposition. The CIA believed the Soviet Union would be ready for all-out war by 1952; SIS thought 1955 a more likely date.

Not everyone within the CIA agreed. A section of covert action officers argued that the Soviet leaders were essentially conservative and cautious. They were happy to seize opportunities to extend the Soviet Union's sphere of influence, but they shrank from using all-out war as a means for achieving this, preferring to rely upon subversion as their principal weapon.[52] This view of the Soviet Union suited the CIA officers' convictions about their own roles: to meet Soviet subversion with CIA covert action. Ray Cline, one of the CIA officers who in 1950 saw the main Soviet threat as subversion has, thirty-five years later, not changed his conclusion or his views on how the United States should react. 'The United States is faced with a situation in which the major world power opposing our system of government is trying to expand its power by using covert methods of warfare. Must the United States respond like a man in a bar room brawl who will fight only according to Marquis of Queensbury rules?'[53]

When a war with the Soviet Union failed to materialize, the hand of the covert action officers was strengthened. The accepted view became that the Soviet Union was now intent on worldwide subversion, and that the United States had to reply in kind. 'There are no rules in such a game. Hitherto accepted norms of human conduct do not apply', a special committee of the Hoover Commission reported in 1955. 'We must learn to subvert, sabotage, and destroy our enemies by more clever and more sophisticated, and more effective, methods than those used against us.'[54] Aping the adversary became CIA policy. Communism was to be contained by reacting in kind to the real or imagined covert activities of the Soviet Union. But how many of these activities were real, and how many imagined?

As Professor R. W. Johnson, of Magdalen College, Oxford, has pointed out, the curious thing about American intelligence histories is that they have failed to produce any hard evidence of KGB covert action. 'Not a single major KGB covert action – comparable, say, to the Bay of Pigs, or the Chile de-stabilisation – has been uncovered. No intelligence service is that good or that lucky for 40 years on the trot, so one is forced to the conclusion that the KGB employs covert action sparingly, if at all.' When confronted by a rebellious client state – of the sort the United States faced in Chile or Nicaragua – the Soviet Union has either intervened militarily and openly, as in Czechoslovakia and Hungary, or allowed the rebellion to run its course, as in Yugoslavia and Albania. Johnson accepts that an exception could be Poland, with the Jaruzelski coup planned and managed like a classic CIA operation.[55] But this might only mean that the Russians have been learning from the Americans.

It would appear, then, that the Soviet bogeyman, if not created by the CIA, was given giant status largely to justify the existence of the agency's covert action section. This was done, in the main, by honourable men with good intentions – although some self-interest, such as a rewarding career and the building of an empire, was also a factor. Perhaps the creation and rapid rise of the CIA was an inevitable part of the de-colonizing process of the postwar world and the assumption of great power status by the United States. For what had looked like imperialism by the OSS when practised by Britain, became justifiable counter-insurgency when practised by the CIA.

# 12. SIS: Treachery and Decline

> To betray, you must first belong. I never belonged. I
> have followed exactly the same line the whole of my
> adult life. The fight against fascism and the fight against
> imperialism were, fundamentally, the same fight.
> – Kim Philby, in interview with Murray Sayle, *Sunday
> Times*, 17 December 1967.

> A kind of institutional and national conceit was a more
> telling indication of decline than the treachery which ate
> into SIS and MI-5, and of which perceptive and
> antagonistic intelligence officers in Washington became
> unhappily aware.
> – Anthony Verrier, *Through the Looking Glass* (1983).

Britain, of course, did not willingly accept the declining role in world affairs that history in 1945 assigned her. Politicians from both parties assumed that the aim of British foreign policy was to continue to exercise the functions and responsibilities of a great power; but the reality was that the country had neither the will nor the resources to do so. In such circumstances the secret world appeared to offer a solution. SIS would maintain Britain's position on the cheap. Intelligence would enable her to protect vital interests. The empire might be disintegrating, the United States and the Soviet Union might be emerging as new world powers, but Britain could remain great by bluff and sleight of hand.

The new role that the first postwar government, a Labour one, envisaged for SIS came as something of a shock to its wartime chief, Stewart Menzies. He had emerged in 1945 with the reputation of his service high, largely because of his control of GC and CS and its Ultra material. But Menzies looked forward to the day when SIS could return to what he saw as its real business: the straightforward collection of raw intelligence by stalwart men in the field. He wanted to re-establish his European networks, wiped out by the

Germans in 1939–40, and get back to frustrating the expansionist ambitions of the Soviet Union.

The Foreign Office, which under Anthony Eden had made a determined bid for firmer control of SIS in 1944, had a wider view of what the service should be doing in the postwar world. It wanted to use SIS to fend off American encroachment in the Middle East, and to ensure that, as the British empire contracted, new regimes would remain friendly to Britain and would be willing to protect British commercial interests. But convincing Menzies was no easy task. Depressed that the government did not seem to share his views on how best to tackle the Soviet menace, Menzies dug his heels in and used all his Whitehall skills to resist any attempt to redirect SIS. Thus no major reorganization took place in the service, no internal examination of how it functioned or what its aims were was even considered. Menzies got rid of most of the amateurs who had disturbed SIS's calm in the war years, retaining only those he considered to be the best and brightest, like Kim Philby, and concentrated on consolidating his service's position in Whitehall.

The same cunning which had enabled Menzies to recognize and exploit the value of Ultra, enabled him to foresee the continuing role that signals intelligence would play, and he moved to consolidate his control of this activity. Although the Americans lagged in the field in 1945 it was clear that their superior technology would soon put them ahead. Menzies pressed for an agreement under which SIS would provide intelligence from its anti-Soviet section, functioning under Philby since late 1944, in return for access to signals intelligence from American sources. This was made part of a wider agreement on Anglo-American intelligence co-operation concluded between Prime Minister Attlee and President Truman in 1946–7. [1]

But this co-operation was put at risk almost immediately when Igor Gouzenko's revelations made apparent the success that the KGB had enjoyed in recruiting agents in Britain. Gouzenko, a cypher clerk at the Soviet Embassy in Ottawa, had sought asylum from the Canadian authorities on 5 September 1945, and the information which he poured out to Canadian, British and American security officers led to several major Soviet rings being smashed. The most obvious impact in Britain was the arrest and conviction in 1946 of Dr Alan Nunn May, the British scientist who had spied for Russia while working at Chalk River, Ontario, on the Allied atomic bomb project during the war. But, behind the scenes, there was a major move of communists and sympathizers from sensitive government posts. A special Cabinet committee under the chairmanship of the Prime Minister, and advised by a senior MI5 official, Graham

Mitchell, laid down a procedure to examine the loyalties of suspect civil servants. Largely due to Mitchell's moderation, the methods adopted were very different from those used during the McCarthy purges in the United States (where some 9,500 civil servants were sacked and 15,000 resigned), and concentrated on quietly shifting suspects to non-sensitive work. (In the thirty-five years that the British system has been in operation only twenty-five officials have been dismissed for security reasons; none was named.)*[2]

No such review of loyalties took place in SIS, still basking in the myth that it had had a brilliant war, and still regarded by most American intelligence officers as a model for their own fledgling service. In reality, SIS's performance in this early postwar period was patchy, ranging from the sort of rank incompetence that had marked the prewar service, to some professional, if morally dubious operations. Alistair Horne, the author, then a young lieutenant in the intelligence corps in the Middle East in late 1945, remembers how the Jerusalem SIS changed its cover from Interservices Liaison Department (ISLD) to Combined Research and Planning Office (CRPO). Immediately all mail from headquarters in Cairo ceased. Sacks of confidential documents were eventually located at the Jerusalem base of the real CRPO – the Command Regimental Pay Office![4]

But in London more serious issues were at stake. The anti-Soviet section of SIS (Section IX) had expanded rapidly under Philby, the KGB penetration agent whose enthusiasm for his new job would have calmed any suspicions about him. In the event, there were none; if anything his critics felt he was *too* anti-communist! Since the size and scope of Section IX involved financial implications and questions of cover for its officers in British embassies, the Foreign Office had to be consulted on Philby's plans. In February 1945 Philby submitted his ideas to Menzies's personal assistant (PA/CSS), since 1942 a Foreign Office appointee, at that time Robert Cecil. Cecil remembers:

> I was shocked, both at the size of the operation and its aims. It included a substantial number of overseas stations to be held by SIS

* The minutes of the special committee remain secret, despite the thirty-year rule for releasing government documents. But its very British approach can be judged by an incident at a meeting in 1948 at the height of the Berlin airlift. Senior civil servant Sir John Winnifrith was taking the minutes when his wife telephoned from their farm. A cow had just started a difficult labour; could he hurry home to help. Sir John asked the Prime Minister if he would mind if a deputy took the minutes instead. Not at all, said Attlee, with a civilized sense of priorities, off you go.[3]

officers under diplomatic cover and who would be directly responsible to [Philby]. I sent it back to Philby with a note suggesting he might scale down his demands and adding, 'I don't think that this is the Foreign Office view of post-war Europe or our part in it'. Within hours Philby had descended on me upholding his requirements and insisting that these be transmitted to the F.O. With hindsight it is easy to see why Philby pitched his demands as high and why he aimed to create his own empire within SIS. Quite apart from his covert aims, it is also clear that he foresaw more plainly than I the onset of the Cold War, bringing with it more menacing surveillance and making necessary more permanent use of diplomatic cover.[5]

Within eighteen months Philby had transformed a one-man, one-room section into a major department occupying a whole floor and employing a staff of more than thirty. It began by building up files on anti-communist movements in Eastern Europe, but the section's long-term aims can be judged by Philby's drunken outburst to Malcolm Muggeridge whom he went to visit in Paris. Philby insisted on going off to inspect the Soviet embassy where he marched up and down shaking his fist at the silent building and shouting: 'How are we going to penetrate them? How are we going to penetrate them?'[6]

SIS began to recruit agents in newly liberated Europe, seeking to re-establish and expand its prewar anti-communist network. The spy business being what it is, SIS was not surprised to discover that some of its agents, arrested by the Abwehr in the general round-up of 1939–40, had been recruited to work in Eastern Europe against the Soviet Union. With a typical display of pragmatism, some of these agents were now rehired by SIS, which argued that their anti-Soviet experience would be invaluable. Other former German intelligence and security officers were recruited because they were considered to have intact organizations behind the Iron Curtain or, like Klaus Barbie, the 'Butcher of Lyons', because he could be of help in identifying other officers in hiding, and recruiting them.

In the end, of course, it was all counter-productive. Philby, the Soviet penetration officer, ensured that most of the postwar effort against the Soviet Union was known in the Kremlin and, as was inevitable, some of the agents SIS had recruited then went on to work for the Russians as well, either for money or for ideological reasons. Heinz Felfe is a good example. Felfe had joined the SD, the counter-espionage section of the SS, in the Occupied Netherlands in December 1944. Arrested by the British in May 1945, he was held until autumn 1946 and then employed by SIS in the British occupation zone of Germany. In 1950 he was recruited for Soviet intelligence by a former SD colleague, Hans Clemens, and soon afterwards signed up with the Gehlen organization (the German intelligence agency at that time being run by the CIA), where he was in charge of a key department – counter-espionage, Soviet section.

For the next ten years Felfe and Clemens supplied the Russians with some 15,000 photographs of secret documents, including weekly and monthly progress reports of the German Federal Intelligence Service, the successor of the Gehlen organization. The Russians paid the men a regular salary of the equivalent of about £500 a month and, in 1961, gave them a certificate attesting to their 'ten years' faithful service', sent with a personal letter of appreciation from the head of Soviet intelligence. At their trial (Felfe got fourteen years, Clemens ten) the two men said that they were Nazis at heart and they gave 'hatred of the Americans' as their motive for spying for the Russians.

The postwar errors of SIS were not to become apparent for years. In the meantime, Menzies compounded his mistakes by starting to groom Philby as his successor. Menzies ran a crown prince system and had, at first, chosen Jack Easton as his heir apparent. Then, for some reason, he decided that Philby would make a better chief.* Philby was sent off to get some field experience and served from 1947 to 1949 in Turkey where, he has said, his patience was tried by requests from SIS for information about Turkish harbours which had actually been built by British concerns. Then in 1949 came the last stage of his preparation. The relationship between SIS and the CIA was so important to the British that experience in Washington was considered to be essential for a future 'C'. Philby was, therefore, posted to Washington to be liaison officer with the CIA and the FBI.

He was very welcome. His wartime reputation preceded him and some of the many friends he had made among OSS officers who had served in London were now in the CIA. They hoped that Philby's experience in creating SIS's anti-Soviet section would be useful for the agency and they opened their doors to him. As liaison officer, he had access through every level, including the director, General Walter Bedell Smith, whom he saw frequently. Lyman Kirkpatrick says: 'Philby's job was to smooth the exchange of information between the two American services, the CIA and the FBI, and the two British ones, SIS and MI5. No other relationship in the intelligence world was so close. And because intelligence officers talk

* The reason could well be set out in Menzies's memoirs, but they are unlikely ever to be published. The few SIS officers who have seen them say that they are self-serving and, what would be even more damaging to the service, reveal Menzies to have been a fantasist.

trade among themselves all the time, Philby was privy to a hell of a lot beyond what he should have known.'[7]

This does not mean, however, that every officer in the CIA told Philby everything – or even that Philby was able to use everything that he *was* told. In the secret world of intelligence even close friends are never entirely trusted. The CIA turned down an offer from Philby to allow it to use SIS's worldwide communications system – at that stage faster and more efficient than that of the Americans – because it did not want SIS reading its messages. And – an example given by a former CIA officer – if a CIA committee was working on analysing strategic sections of the Soviet economy it would make a point of keeping its findings from the British because, 'We wouldn't want that damned nation of shopkeepers using our information to do some strategic selling'.[8] There was other information which Philby did receive, but could not use because so few people knew about it that, if the Soviet Union had acted on it, the CIA would be bound to have been suspicious of him.

This is not intended to minimize the damage which Philby caused to the CIA and SIS. But the damage was not so much in operations areas as in the lasting suspicion he sowed both within the CIA and FBI and between the American and British services. After Philby, the special relationship was never to be the same again, and his treachery so poisoned the minds of some CIA officers that, as we shall see, they were never again able totally to trust even their closest colleagues.

In the end, Philby was exposed not – as the accepted account would have it – because of his loyalty and friendship for Burgess, another Soviet officer, but because the KGB was, and is, fallible and made a stupid mistake. If it had not bungled the rescue of its man in the Foreign Office, Donald Maclean, then Philby might, just might, have become 'C' and have gone down in the history of espionage as the most accomplished spy ever.* Maclean had gone to Cairo from

* Before Philby left for Washington, Menzies and his deputy, Sir John Sinclair, let the Foreign Office know that they favoured Philby as successor to Menzies when he retired. SIS was obliged to do this because the Foreign Office had, in the changed postwar atmosphere, demanded a say in the selection of 'C'. The Foreign Office sent a senior officer along to SIS to see Philby and report on Menzies's recommendation. The officer had known Philby during the war and had been impressed by him. Now, he decided, Philby had deteriorated. He appeared worried and tense, even shifty. He was drinking heavily. The Foreign Office report was that Philby was unsuitable for such an important post and that when the time came it would resist Philby's nomination vigorously. Menzies did not abandon his intention that Philby should succeed him, but it was clear that he would have had to reckon on Foreign Office opposition. In the event, it never came to a departmental conflict because Philby was exposed in time.[9]

Washington in the autumn of 1948. In Cairo he no doubt learnt that his career as a Soviet spy was drawing to a close. The FBI had been working for three years to crack the code the Russians had used in radio transmissions from the Soviet Consulate in New York to Moscow in 1944–5. In the spring of 1948 they began to get results. One of the first pieces of information to emerge was that in the early summer of 1945 the British embassy had housed a spy, code named 'Homer', who was sufficiently well placed to have access to telegraphic messages between Churchill and Truman. [10]

Working in tandem, the FBI and MI5 had started to concentrate on those people who had been serving in Washington at that time and who would have had access to this material. Philby had been briefed on this investigation before he went to Washington and was able to follow its progress there because of his liaison duties with the FBI. [11] Naturally, he was keeping his KGB controller in Washington informed and it seems reasonable to assume that the KGB warned Maclean in Cairo that he might well have to make a dash for safety. This would explain Maclean's degeneration – his drinking, his violence – and his convoluted confession to a colleague that he was harbouring guilty secrets.

The generally accepted version of what occurred next is that Maclean returned to London in May 1950 suffering from a mild nervous breakdown – 'overwork', said the department's psychiatrist – had a few months' sick leave, and was then posted to the American desk at the Foreign Office. He seemed to realize that exposure was not far away. When drunk he would accost patrons at bars with, 'Buy me a drink. I'm the English Hiss', and at a Chelsea party he tried to provoke a friend by saying he should report him because 'I'm working for Uncle Joe'.

Meanwhile in Washington, Philby and his KGB controller had decided that it would be safest to get Maclean away by the middle of 1951 at the latest. Philby claims that, with the permission of his controller, he told Burgess, who had been posted to Washington in August 1950 and who was staying in Philby's house, all about the Maclean case. Philby says that an idea emerged – 'I do not know whose' – that Burgess could help in the Maclean rescue. 'If Burgess returned to London from the British Embassy in Washington, it seemed natural that he should call on the head of American Department. He would be well-placed to set the ball rolling for the rescue operation', Philby writes. He states that Burgess could not simply resign and return, however, because that would look suspicious: 'Matters had to be so arranged that he was sent back, willy-nilly.' [12]

The story continues with Burgess deliberately getting booked for speeding three times in one day, the Governor of Virginia protesting to the State Department at this abuse of diplomatic privilege, the State Department complaining to the ambassador, and Burgess being ordered back to London. There, he contacted Maclean at the Foreign Office and they later met for lunch at the Royal Automobile Club. Meanwhile, at a meeting on Thursday, 24 May 1951 of officers of SIS, MI5 and the Foreign Office, it was decided to apply to the Foreign Secretary, Herbert Morrison, for permission to interrogate Maclean the following Monday. Morrison signed this permission on the Friday.

The accepted account now enters the 'tip-off' stage. Someone – Philby is the most popular choice – learnt of this decision and tipped off Burgess that Maclean was to be questioned on Monday. About 10 a.m. on the Friday, Burgess had a telephone call or a visit that drastically changed his plans. He had booked a two-berth cabin on the cross-channel steamer *Falaise* due to sail from Southampton at midnight, planning to go with an American friend, Bernard Miller. At 10.30 a.m. Burgess met Miller and told him, Miller remembers clearly, that 'A young friend of mine in the Foreign Office is in serious trouble. I am the only one who can help him.'

Burgess ordered a hire car, packed a suitcase, said a brief goodbye to his live-in friend, Jack Hewit, then drove to Maclean's house in the country. He dined with Maclean and his wife, Melinda, then drove Maclean to Southampton, arriving at 11.45 p.m. They rushed on board, leaving the car unlocked. When a sailor noticed the car and shouted after them, one of them called, 'Back on Monday', and they were gone.

When the news reached Washington, Philby tells us that the fact that Burgess had also gone caused him great concern – with good reason, because the CIA, the FBI, MI5, and perhaps even his own service would consider him guilty by association. (How could Philby, a trained counter-intelligence officer, share his house with Burgess and not become suspicious of Burgess's behaviour?) This is exactly what happened. Philby was recalled, questioned by MI5 and, after Menzies had received a letter from Bedell Smith saying that the CIA would never work with Philby again, asked to resign.

This account suffers from one major flaw: the whole involvement of Burgess in Maclean's rescue does not make sense. Burgess's escape with Maclean proved a disaster for the KGB because it blew Philby, the Soviet's white hope, the penetration agent who might have become the next 'C' and who, even as it was, had proved a most valuable officer in a most rewarding post. So the crucial question which, in turn, exposes Philby's and other accounts as wrong, is: Why did Burgess go?

Philby claims that he drew Burgess into the secret of the search for 'Homer', after consulting his Soviet contact, because 'Guy's special knowledge of the problem might be helpful'. What special knowledge? Philby, via his Washington control, had the whole Russian intelligence network to warn Maclean and the skill of its service to spirit Maclean to safety. What knowledge or skill did Burgess possess to contribute to the rescue, which the KGB did not already have in London? The whole tip-off theory rings untrue, and Philby's account in his own book reads like disinformation. The reason for such an exercise is not hard to find. Anyone examining the tip-off theory must quickly conclude that the final warning that is said to have galvanized Burgess on the Friday morning could *not* have come from Philby – although he did indeed know that Maclean was to be interrogated on the following Monday. It could not have come from Philby because there was insufficient time.

Former CIA officer George Carver points out that MI5 was obliged to give Hoover time to comment on the decision to question Maclean and that MI5 would have waited until Morrison signed his approval.

> It would have been terribly embarrassing to have told the Americans that he was going to sign it if for any reason he baulked at doing so. So it is unlikely that there would have been a notification until after the fact, and there just isn't time for a cable to go to Washington and action to be taken in the fortyfive odd minutes that seem to have elapsed between Morrison signing his name and Burgess getting the alert that changed his course of pattern.

And Carver then goes on to draw exactly the conclusion that Philby no doubt hoped would be drawn:

> Since the witting circle of those who knew that Morrison had signed was terribly small, to me a much more logical explanation is that someone in that witting circle passed the information along. Now you can't really chalk it off to Blunt because Blunt had left MI-5 several years before . . . My thought has always been that the sequence of events on that day alone certainly raised the possibility that there was yet another person in the net who presumably has not been discovered to this day, who occupied a very senior position, possibly in Six, but more likely in Five.[13]

Thus Philby's account of the tip-off sows the suspicion that even after he, Burgess, Maclean and Blunt had been uncovered there remained yet another KGB penetration agent in place. This doubt, as we shall see, was to poison Anglo-American intelligence relations, and to divert energy in both services from more rewarding tasks.

There is a much more logical explanation of events that led to the flight of Burgess and Maclean, and some evidence to support such an explanation. Maclean's escape was planned well in advance. Philby says that his own tour of duty in Washington was scheduled to end in the autumn of 1951 and he might have been posted to Cairo or Singapore, well out of touch with the Maclean case, so 'it seemed safest to get Maclean away by the middle of 1951 at the latest'. Philby did not take Burgess into his confidence. He had no need to. All Philby's duty required of him was that he kept his Washington controller informed of the progress of the search for 'Homer'. The KGB would decide when and how Maclean would be lifted to safety. The less Philby knew about such plans, the better.

Philby's story about Burgess and his method of provoking his recall to London is disinformation for the reasons set out above. Against Philby's version there is the evidence of the head of Burgess's department at the embassy in Washington, Denis Greenhill, that Burgess, far from being delighted that his plan had worked, was 'boiling with rage' on leaving the ambassador's room after being told that he was being sent back to Britain.[14] Next, the timescale for Philby's account does not support his version. Burgess's speeding offences were on 28 February. The State Department lodged a complaint on 14 March. Burgess was sacked a few days later, but he hung on in the United States for a further *six weeks*. When he finally arrived in London on 7 May, he spent his early days looking for a job and did not bother to contact Maclean until at least a week later. Then they lunched openly together at the Royal Automobile Club, a club frequented by Foreign Office officials. Yet Philby has written, 'despite all *precautions* Burgess might be seen with Maclean and enquiry into his activity might lead to doubts about me' (emphasis added).

So Philby's version of telling Burgess about Maclean's difficulties, of engineering Burgess's precipitate departure from Washington and, after properly warning him to be discreet, of using Burgess as a courier to put Maclean in the picture, is full of flaws. What Philby is trying to conceal is that 'the élite service', to which he secretly owed allegiance, botched things – with a little help from its quartet of spies. This is understandable. Philby, Burgess, Maclean and Blunt were originally a group of interconnected amateurs which the KGB had inherited from the Comintern. They followed none of the golden rules of the KGB – Philby and Burgess living in the same house in Washington must have driven Moscow mad. Faced with a situation of the highest potential value, but in which it was able to exert none of its usual discipline, the KGB lost control.

Burgess learnt of Maclean's problems when Maclean told him, 'I'm in frightful trouble. I'm being followed by the dicks', and pointed out two men. This was true; Maclean was under MI5 surveillance and these watchers would certainly have noted Burgess's presence. He would have become a suspect for the role of Maclean's contact. It is even possible that Burgess, too, was then watched. This would have added to the concern that he had been experiencing since a chance meeting in Washington, just before he left, with Michael Straight, the American recruited for the KGB by Blunt at Cambridge. Straight had had second thoughts – he eventually unmasked Blunt – and, according to his account of the meeting, he threatened to turn Burgess over to the security authorities: 'If you aren't out of the government within a month from now, I swear to you I'll turn you in.'[15] So we have Burgess, a man whose overt and covert careers are both at an end, worried whether Straight has reported him to the FBI, and knowing he has come to the attention of MI5: what more natural than that he should turn to the only man who could advise him – his Soviet controller in London, 'Peter'.

Since Burgess was worried that he was being watched he did not contact 'Peter' directly, but asked Blunt, who was also controlled by 'Peter', to act as an intermediary, and we have Blunt's confirmation that he did so. What advice did 'Peter' give? We know something of 'Peter''s rule for a KGB officer who feels the policeman's hand reaching for his collar: play it safe. (Blunt has said that when he told 'Peter' about his interrogation, 'Peter' advised him to make a quick escape.)[16] It seems probable that he would have given the same advice to Burgess, who was clearly in no state to bluff his way out of trouble. And since the KGB had arranged for Maclean's escape, what better solution than that Burgess should go with him?

So Burgess's haste on the Friday had nothing to do with a tip-off that Maclean was about to be interrogated. It was much more likely to have been the result of a message from 'Peter' approving his escape, and instructing him that he was to leave Britain with Maclean. Burgess got this approval on Thursday night – we have Hewit's account that when he returned to Burgess's flat after dining out on Thursday, Burgess and a foreigner were deep in conversation in Burgess's room. But, in giving this approval, 'Peter' blundered. He did not know how closely Philby and Burgess had been connected during the Washington period because he had no liaison with his KGB colleague controlling Philby in Washington. It would not have occurred to him to ask his superiors about this because he would never have imagined that two KGB officers would have broken so elementary a rule. So 'Peter' had no comprehension that by allowing Burgess to escape he was effectively 'blowing' Philby. Philby's Washington controller could have warned 'Peter' about this, but the Washington officer, for his part, was not to know that Burgess wanted to escape from Britain.

The KGB quickly realized its error. Burgess was not welcomed with open arms when he arrived in the Soviet Union. He was packed off to a KGB centre in Kubishev in Siberia, where he was subjected to hostile interrogation to establish whether he was a British intelligence plant. He was never honoured for his work, as Philby was, or allowed to write a book about his political views, as Maclean was. Even when Philby came home to Moscow shortly before Burgess died in 1963, the two do not seem to have met. When Western journalists besieged Burgess for news of Philby after he had vanished from Beirut, Burgess passionately denied that Philby could be in Moscow because 'I am the first person he would contact if he were here'.[17] It was not until Burgess, with his detailed knowledge of the 1930s and appeasement, told the KGB that Macmillan and not Butler would become Prime Minister after Eden's fall in 1956, that the Russians forgave him for his part in destroying Philby's career.

If this version of the Philby–Burgess–Maclean affair is correct then Philby's own account can be seen for what it is: an attempt to cover up a Russian intelligence mess and – by sowing suspicion in the Western services that a further Soviet penetration agent remained in place – to salvage something from the disaster that Burgess's departure caused. For, as Philby admits, the sharper brains in the CIA were no longer taken in by Philby's smooth charm once Burgess's escape became known. 'I had no fear of the bumbling Dulles . . . But Bedell Smith was a different matter. He had a cold, fishy eye and a precision-tool brain . . . Bedell Smith, I had an uneasy feeling, would be apt to think that two and two make four rather than five.'[18]

But the mistakes were not solely on the Soviet side. Philby was put out to pasture in Britain, a man under such suspicion from MI5 that, despite continuing to receive the confidence of his colleagues in SIS who thought him a victim of McCarthyism, the chances of him being of any further use to his Russian masters were very bleak. But then a Hoover–MI5 conspiracy went sour and put Philby back in business for another seven years.

Hoover was appalled that the British government's 1955 White

Paper on the Burgess–Maclean defection made no mention of any suspicion attaching to Philby, and in September of that year he decided to do something about it. Motivated partly by his anti-communist zeal and partly by a sense of personal betrayal – he had been a dinner guest in Philby's Washington home – Hoover set out to plant a story in British and American newspapers naming Philby as the third man in the case. He had a meeting with an International News Service reporter and gave him all he needed for 'a hot story'. Philby, Hoover said, had been employed by British intelligence in Washington; he was a heavy drinker; he had access to highly confidential information; he had been recalled after the Burgess–Maclean disappearances and (here Hoover was wrong) a representative of British intelligence had come to Washington to accompany him back to London.

'But I cautioned him that in the White Paper . . . there was no mention of Philby's name, apparently because of lack of direct proof against Philby and the fact that Philby was in contact with lawyers and threatening heavy libel suits if any paper prints his name in connection with this matter', Hoover wrote in his FBI memorandum of the meeting.[19] He then went on to suggest to the International News Service reporter that the place to apply the pressure was in London with the British.

The seed matured quickly. By the first week in October, the editor of the *Empire News*, Jack Fishman, who had a very close working relationship with MI5, had confirmed that Hoover strongly suspected Philby. Fishman, presumably with MI5 approval, tried to get Philby's name into the open by persuading a Labour MP, Norman Dodds, to ask a parliamentary question in which Philby's name would be mentioned. (Since parliamentary speeches, and reports of them, are privileged in law, this would have avoided the libel problem.) But Dodds was dissuaded from this course by a senior Labour MP, George Wigg, who said it was better to ask for a Foreign Office inquiry because it was wiser 'never to frighten the rabbits when there may be much bigger game around'.

Assured that there was not much bigger game than Philby, Fishman switched his attack. He says:

A colleague and friend, Henry Maule, then headed the New York Daily News London Bureau. I deliberately gave Maule the story to break it in America knowing it would be cabled back here and quoted in the Commons. I also spoke to both Norman Dodds and Marcus Lipton [another Labour MP] about the background to my enquiries to prepare them for possible supplementary questions and debate.[20]

The *Sunday News* of 23 October named Philby as the third man and, on the following Tuesday, Lipton asked in the Commons: 'Has the Prime Minister made up his mind to cover up at all costs the dubious third man activities of Mr Harold Philby who was First Secretary at the Washington embassy a little while ago . . . ?' With this, nearly a month after Hoover had played the first note of a carefully orchestrated campaign to expose Philby, Philby's name was well and truly out in the open. The government committed itself to make a statement and to allow a debate in the Commons.

Hoover was delighted, and moved quickly to consolidate his advantage. On 2 November he cabled the head of the FBI in London explaining what he was doing:

> Public identification of Philby as individual who may have tipped off Burgess Maclean and requests of Bureau from other government agencies for information on Philby's role in case make it necessary that Bureau furnish information on Philby to certain high US government officials stop Bureau plans to advise certain high-level government officials of Philby's role – Hoover.[21]

It is not difficult to see what Hoover was doing. Other FBI files make it clear that American intelligence officers suspected that Philby was being protected by his brother officers in SIS and by high-ranking Foreign Office officials. If the FBI gave its dossier on Philby to every high-ranking American government official up to, and probably including, the President, it would be difficult for the British government to resist American demands for a full-scale investigation of Philby.

But Hoover had reckoned without several peculiarly British factors which, together, wrecked his scheme. He did not allow for the anti-McCarthy feeling in Britain which regarded the pursuit of Philby as persecution. He did not allow for the rivalry between MI5 and SIS which prevented either service taking an overview of Philby's case. For example, Menzies, in his final years as 'C' and drinking very heavily indeed, regarded the Burgess–Maclean disappearance as nothing to do with SIS. When a friend of Burgess's, Rosamond Lehmann, telephoned Menzies immediately after the two men had fled to offer him information, Menzies said that he was sorry, he would love to talk to her, but he had to take his little girl to Ascot that week.[22]

And, most important of all, Hoover had no way of knowing the distaste that the Foreign Secretary, Harold Macmillan, and his advisers had for the whole secret world, and their reluctance to have anything to do with it. Macmillan's secretary, Lord Egremont, considered all intelligence agencies a waste of time and money: 'Much better if the Russians saw the Cabinet minutes twice a week. Prevent all that fucking dangerous guesswork.'[23] Macmillan himself made the right noises about SIS in public, but in private had a low opinion of the intelligence it produced and thought that the Philby affair was a squabble between SIS and MI5 which they should have settled themselves. He thus became involved with great reluctance, but quickly arranged a compromise.

Philby had not been fired, SIS told him, because, despite what the Americans said, there was no evidence against him; he had simply been too friendly with Burgess. Macmillan said the problem would always remain while Philby did – he would have to go. When SIS muttered about innocent-until-guilty, Macmillan replied, 'We're not jailing the bugger, just firing him'.[24] Macmillan then agreed to issue a statement virtually clearing Philby in return for a reorganization of SIS and 'a general clean-up'. So on 7 November Macmillan made the following short statement to the Commons, the contents of which were true, but unwittingly wrong:

> No evidence has been found that Philby was responsible for warning Burgess or Maclean. [True, no evidence had been found.] While in government he carried out his duties ably and conscientiously. [True.] I have no reason to conclude that Mr. Philby has at any time betrayed the interests of this country, or to identify him with the so-called 'third man', if, indeed, there was one. [True, Macmillan had no reason to conclude this.]

Philby was cleared. He held a relaxed press conference which he handled so brilliantly that at least one of his old SIS colleagues rang up to congratulate him. Confirmed in his role of injured hero, a martyr to security, he was kept on the SIS books as a field officer and in 1956 went off to Beirut, under cover as a newspaper correspondent for the *Observer* and *The Economist*.

The CIA and the FBI were appalled. Hoover was forced to call off his men and officially the FBI, too, cleared Philby. On 29 December 1955 it closed its file on him: 'Subject – Donald Stuart Maclean et al. During a recent review of all references in *BUFILES* on Harold A. R. Philby abstracts were made and placed on 3 × 5 cards. Philby is suspected of tipping off subject that he was under investigation. From this review there does not appear any basis or justification for an investigation of Philby.'[25]

The Philby case was placed in the FBI archives and remained there until 23 January 1963. On that day, Philby, his career for the KGB having been unexpectedly extended by a further seven years, vanished from Beirut, after an SIS colleague had failed to get a confession from him in return for immunity from prosecution. He surfaced in Moscow six months later, his true role revealed at last. Hoover was vindicated, but his quarry had eluded him. In fact, it was probably the attitude of the Americans that weighed heavily in Philby's decision not to confess and to flee to Moscow: he could trust the British to keep their bargain and not prosecute him, but he could not be certain that Hoover or the CIA would not try to snatch him from Beirut for an unpleasant debriefing in the United States, or, perhaps, try to terminate his career for good.

Hoover – and, to a lesser extent, Bedell Smith – felt that he had been betrayed by the British old boy network. Hoover remained distrustful of SIS and of the British in general until his death in 1972. Bedell Smith made it clear that the CIA's special relationship with SIS could not continue until the British put their house in order. SIS now set about doing this.

After the clean-out of the amateurs in 1945, SIS had continued to be immune from interference until the Foreign Office acted in 1952 to improve relations between the two departments. The post of Foreign Office adviser to 'C' was upgraded and George Clutton, later British ambassador to Warsaw, was appointed in a higher rank than any of his predecessors.[26] He had a difficult task: the last few months of Menzies's reign were followed by the installation of Sinclair, a 6 ft. 7 in. Old Wykehamist, whose three years as head of SIS were beset by such disaster that SIS officers referred to the period as 'the horrors'. When not planning some amazing operation, Sinclair spent a lot of his time trying to reassure an increasingly worried CIA that British intelligence was basically sound.

He was not very successful. Early in 1956 CIA officers in London remember listening in dismay as an SIS representative outlined a plan to engineer a coup in Syria, as an encore to follow the success of the operation which had restored the Shah in Persia. Iraq was to stir up the Syrian desert tribes, Lebanese Christians were to raid across the border, and Turkey was to promote frontier incidents. It sounded more like a plan for a general Middle Eastern war than a coup. Fortunately, it never got off the ground. Another CIA officer, Wilbur Eveland, recalls a meeting in Beirut where the SIS representative, much the worse for drink, revealed that the British service had plans to assassinate Nasser, the Egyptian leader. He then rambled on about the Middle East being turned over to the communists until 'his voice trailing off, he finally sank in his chair and passed out'.[27]

Following yet another meeting, this time in London, the CIA officers reported to Washington:

> After sitting around a table in a desultory fashion for an hour or two, one Englishman finally said, 'I say, why don't we get old Henry up here? He knows about this'. A day or two later old Henry finally showed up from down in Sussex and agreed to undertake the task, although as he said, 'This will wreak havoc with the garden, you know. Just getting it into trim.'[28]

The climax came with the SIS operation in April 1956 to examine the hull of the Russian cruiser *Ordzhonikidze* in Portsmouth Harbour. A similar operation in October 1955, on a sister ship, the *Sverdlov*, had been successful and SIS was tempted to try again in the hope of learning more about the ship's anti-submarine and mine-detection equipment. But the *Ordzhonikidze* was carrying the Soviet leaders, Bulganin and Khrushchev, to Britain and the frogman hired by SIS, Lionel 'Buster' Crabb, was too old and too frail. He vanished forever, the Russians lodged a complaint, and Prime Minister Eden had to apologize in the Commons on 4 May.

An internal Foreign Office–SIS inquiry placed the organizational blame on the Foreign Office adviser. His sanction was required for any SIS operation which might have political repercussions. SIS had asked his permission for Crabb's mission very late one evening and he had signed it without properly considering it. (He was moved to a very obscure corner of the Foreign Office and his successor, Geoffrey McDermott, made it a rule never to consider such SIS requests after 6 p.m.!)[29] But the real blame clearly lay with Sinclair. Behind the scenes in SIS, the Foreign Office and the Cabinet Office, the feeling grew that Sinclair's imminent retirement would be an opportunity to change the whole tradition of SIS's leadership.

Two senior civil servants took the initiative. They were Sir Norman Brook, Secretary to the Cabinet, and Sir Burke Trend, Deputy Secretary to the Cabinet. Their argument for a radical change in the tradition of having a military or a naval man as chief of SIS found a sympathetic hearing with Macmillan. The man they chose was Dick White, who had been recommended by Patrick Dean, Assistant Under-Secretary of State at the Foreign Office and a one-time private secretary to Menzies in SIS.[30] At that time, White was head of MI5, where he had spent virtually his entire adult life. Educated at Bishop's Stortford College and Christ Church, Oxford, with a spell at the universities of Michigan and Southern California, White was an elegant, cultivated intellectual. He was a complete contrast to the Menzieses and Sinclairs of the secret world, and his appointment was greeted by the Americans with undisguised delight. Robert Amory recalls the meeting at which the news reached Washington.

> It was sometime in July 1956. We were at a routine meeting – Dulles, Helms, Bissell, me, and a few others. We'd finished the morning session and were clearing away for lunch. I said, 'By the way, I've just heard from a contact in the British embassy who the new "C" is.' Helms and Bissell almost fell off their chairs. It turned out that this information had been made the number one priority for their man in London. When I told them it was White they were utterly astonished. They had lined up two or three names as candidates and White's name was not even on the list. But they were delighted. They'd formed a very favourable opinion of White – smooth, professional and decent. As someone said 'White's persona very grata with us.'[31]

White's appointment turned out to be a landmark in Western intelligence because it changed the emphasis from the thrills and spills of the great game, to the harder but more rewarding field of intelligence analysis. The CIA under Dulles – 'the great white case officer', as one of his staff dubbed him – did not appreciate the change, but Richard Helms, who became director in 1966, did. From his first day as 'C', White made it clear that SIS was not a peacetime continuation of SOE, that sabotage and assassination were not part of its duties. (For example, SIS ignored an order from Eden to examine ways of murdering Nasser.)[32] If the government imagined that SIS would provide a cheap way of maintaining power in a post-imperial world, then White was going to disappoint them. SIS would operate in keeping with the moral climate of the times.

One of the changes, noted especially by the Treasury, was that SIS began to pay more attention to economic and industrial intelligence. In 1958, for example, a Belgian agent tipped off SIS that a refrigeration plant, being exhibited by the Soviet Union on its stand at the Brussels Expo, contained a vital part in its mechanism which British refrigeration engineers had been trying to perfect for several years. SIS wanted to raid the stand at night, remove and examine the part and replace it before the Russians missed it. Since this was an operation which could have political repercussions, the Foreign Office adviser, at that time Geoffrey McDermott, had to be consulted. McDermott had grave misgivings and gave his approval only reluctantly. Fortunately, the operation went off without a hitch.[33]

Under White, SIS's recruiting policy changed. The 1930s practice of recruiting by personal recommendation had led to such inbreeding that many senior SIS officers were related to each other: Anthony Blunt, Stewart Menzies, Claude Dansey and Guy Liddell, for example, were all related, however distantly. Those who were not related tended to hold the views of their recruiter, with the result that SIS in the 1930s was heavily penetrated by officers who had been talent spotted and signed up by spy author John Buchan, of *The Thirty-Nine Steps* fame.

Members of Parliament and journalists became preferred recruits in the early postwar period. Captain Henry Kerby, a Conservative MP, made little secret of the fact that he was a long-serving, full-time SIS officer. Others turned down recruitment offers. Tony Benn, a Labour MP, has said that SIS approached him twice: when he was 22 and President of the Oxford Union, and after he became an MP in 1950.[34]

White stepped up recruitment from universities and broadened SIS policy to include women. One recalls:

> I had got a moderate degree from Bristol and was wondering what to do. My tutor said, 'Well, there's this interesting job in Foreign Office co-ordination. If you like I'll arrange an interview for you.' At the first interview it was unclear what the job was. At subsequent meetings it gradually became clear what 'Foreign Office co-ordination' really was. I gave it a go and spent a month in SIS registry. I didn't really like it and I left.[35]

But the main source of SIS recruits became, and remains, university graduates who failed, or fail, the Foreign Office or Civil Service examination.*

SIS did not lack for agents. White once told a French colleague that SIS was constantly inundated with offers from British businessmen going abroad who wanted to do a little espionage work on the side. His French colleague replied that this highlighted the difference between the British and the French character. 'When a French businessman goes abroad', he said, 'it's not a bit of spying he wants on the side.'

---

* The main difficulty in aiming at a higher standard of recruit is not that the SIS cannot offer a proper career structure – under White it succeeded in doing this – but that, on retirement, often early, SIS officers find it difficult to get another job because they cannot explain what they have been doing all those previous years. And SIS, so clever at creating other legends, has flatly refused to create fictitious CVs for its retiring officers. Things are very different in the United States, where retiring CIA officers go on to lucrative careers in industry, commerce and academia.

One of the first shocks awaiting White when he took over as 'C' was to discover that Philby was still on SIS books and was about to be sent to Beirut. Arrangements had gone too far to be stopped – the Foreign Office was keen that Philby should do the job. White was persuaded to agree on the ground that if Philby *were* a Soviet agent, his work in Beirut would provide opportunities to expose him and that, in the period of his appointment, more evidence might arise to make his guilt clear. If he were innocent, then at least SIS would have treated him decently.

In the meantime, White still had to cope with one of the most successful KGB agents left over from 'the horrors' period. This was George Blake who, like Philby, was a British intelligence officer who turned out to be working for Moscow. Blake's damage to Western intelligence was so great – he confessed to having passed to the KGB every important official document which had come into his hands – that his trial was held in camera and the British government did its best to persuade the British media to conceal the fact that Blake had ever been in intelligence work. Even today, the accepted story of Blake and his treachery is riddled with disinformation, part-British, part-Soviet.

Blake was born in the Netherlands; his father was an Egyptian Jew, his mother a Dutch Lutheran. Blake's father held a British passport, was overly patriotic – he christened Blake 'George' after King George V – and seems to have done some intelligence work for SIS in the First World War. On his father's death in 1936, a delayed result of German phosgene gas, George Blake was sent to live with an uncle in Egypt. He was on a visit to his mother in the Netherlands when the Second World War broke out and he was trapped by the German advance. Interned by the Nazis, he escaped, joined the Dutch Resistance, and eventually made his way to Britain where he served in the Royal Navy. After the war, he was posted to Hamburg in naval intelligence. He later studied languages, including Russian, at Downing College, Cambridge, then joined the Foreign Office and was appointed vice-consul in Seoul, Korea. At some stage most likely before he even went to Hamburg, Blake was recruited by an SIS officer, Kenneth Cohen. He was seen as an ideal candidate: wartime experience, foreign languages, and clearly a man who could take care of himself in difficult circumstances.

Blake arrived in Seoul just before the Korean War, and during the fighting he was captured by the North Koreans and held for three years. On his release, SIS gave him leave to recuperate and in April 1955 posted him to the SIS station in the Olympic Stadium in West

Berlin as deputy director of technical operations. His special assignment was concerned with studying the Red Army in East Germany and looking for potential defectors amongst its officers. His main act of betrayal in this posting was to tell the KGB about the Berlin Tunnel, which had been bored by SIS–CIA so that Western intelligence could tap into the landlines linking East Berlin with Moscow. Blake's tip-off to the KGB made what was later presented as an SIS–CIA coup (they could intercept secret Soviet traffic) into a fiasco, because the KGB was able to use the Berlin Tunnel operation to plant deception material on the Western intelligence agencies. Then, when it suited them, the Russians moved into the eastern end of the tunnel and turned the operation into a propaganda victory. But the SIS damage report credits Blake with political betrayal as well – by revealing to the Russians each new plan and move of the West in the delicate East–West Geneva negotiations of 1959 on the Berlin question.[36]

In London in 1961, SIS finally got the results of a lead given by Howard Roman, a CIA case officer who had been handling a communist intelligence officer still in place and known then only as 'Heckenschütze'. (He later defected and revealed himself as Michael Goloniewski, vice-chairman of Polish military intelligence.) The lead revealed that the KGB had a list of twenty-six Polish officials which had been compiled by SIS men in Warsaw as potential targets for recruitment. Investigations showed that the list could only have come from George Blake's safe.[37]

When SIS realized this, Blake was in the Lebanon, studying Arabic at a language school favoured by Western intelligence services. He was recalled by a low-key message, and allowed to move freely in Britain for twenty-four hours in the hope that he might try to contact Soviet officers. But when he was on his way to SIS headquarters on the second day, he was arrested and charged under the Official Secrets Act. He confessed, was tried at the Old Bailey and sentenced to forty-two years' imprisonment, the longest term ever imposed under English law. He had served barely five and a half years when he made a dramatic escape from Wormwood Scrubs prison, West London, and vanished, only to surface in Moscow a year later.

Blake, one story in the West claimed, had been a loyal and efficient SIS agent until captured by the communists in Korea. They had brainwashed him and tricked him into working for Moscow. At first it was thought that the KGB must have organized his escape, but then an Irish criminal came forward and described how he and Blake had arranged the escape themselves. Some laborious psychoanalysing of Blake's motives followed. Labour MP, Leo Abse, wrote:

> His whole early life was punctuated by events calculated to make him at least unconsciously, yearn for revenge on Britain. With a father who had betrayed George by his choice of nationality, by his unnecessary death, by condemning his son to exile and finally to arrest in Holland and alienation in Britain, it would indeed be astonishing if the son's deep resentment was not to be worked out against his father's first love. Only our Secret Service could have been so accommodating as to provide full facilities for George Blake to commit posthumous parricide.[38]

The facts are more prosaic. Blake was attracted to communism as a youth. He has said that early in his life he had thought of becoming a Roman Catholic priest, but chose instead the alternative faith of the communist world. His cousin in Cairo, Henri Curiel, with whom he lived, was a founder member of the Egyptian Communist Party.[39] Blake has said that his experiences with the communist resistance in the Netherlands, Churchill's 'Iron Curtain' speech and the American bombing of Korea reinforced his commitment to the Soviet cause. Thus the idea that Blake, a patriotic British Foreign Office official, was brainwashed and recruited in Korea while a prisoner of war, does not stand up to examination. Instead, it serves only to conceal the fact that even a superficial check on Blake's life before he joined SIS would have turned up his communist connections. Or was it the case, as I shall speculate, that SIS knew about Blake's communist links and hoped to exploit them?

For there are indications that one of the reasons why the British authorities are so sensitive to this day about the Blake case is that Blake played a brilliant triple game in which SIS came off second best to the Russians. At Blake's trial, it was obvious that he could not have been convicted without his confession. The ordinary evidence used so effectively in other spy trials – contact with known KGB officers and the passing of information – would not have worked in the Blake case 'because of the nature of Blake's work', as his former colleagues have said. This can mean only one thing: Blake was *authorized* to have contact with Russians. One of the reasons given for Blake's rapid rise in SIS was 'a remarkable string of successful recruitments of Communist officers in Germany'. And Blake himself told how, after his escape, when he put himself in the hands of the East German authorities, they sent for the KGB officer 'I had been in contact with years before when I was with the Secret Service in Berlin'.[40]

It is my belief that Blake actually reported to SIS that the Russians had recruited him and himself suggested that this could be put to good advantage for Britain. His SIS chiefs agreed with him. They saw a rare opportunity to beat the KGB at the game at which it excels. Firm in their belief that Blake was really loyal to SIS – he was married to a fellow SIS officer, and he had, after all, reported his Soviet contacts – Blake's chiefs authorized him to pass to the KGB carefully selected material, some of which would have to be genuine, in the hope of convincing the KGB that Blake was a loyal communist. Blake's KGB superiors would have done the same, in the hope of convincing SIS that Blake was loyal to Britain. In this dangerous game – surrendering some information with the expectation of eventually gaining far more – the winner is the one who gets the fat. It would, therefore, have come as a considerable shock to SIS to learn that Blake's final loyalties were to the Soviet Union and that while SIS *thought* it was getting the fat, it was actually getting the lean. A triple agent can do immense damage and is very difficult to uncover because he can explain away treacherous behaviour by saying, 'Ah, but that is what it is *meant* to look like'.

The triple agent scenario explains the severity of Blake's sentence – 'one year for each of the 42 agents whose lives he cost', was one comment at the time of his trial. And it explains the high esteem that the Russians had for Blake's loyalty to the KGB. He was awarded the Order of Lenin when he arrived in the Soviet Union, the same award which was given to Philby. But why would a spy of Blake's calibre confess? The answer must be that SIS offered him a substantial inducement to do so: the promise of a light sentence and exile on release. But even SIS cannot guarantee that a British judge will not follow his own instincts in passing sentence, and Blake suddenly faced the prospect of spending at least twenty-eight years in prison.

Normal KGB procedure in a case such as this is to arrange a prisoner exchange, so as to get their own man out. But this can take a long time and there is always opposition to such deals from Western security services, who resent that the effort they put into trapping Soviet spies counts for little when a spy is promptly exchanged by their colleagues in the intelligence services. Moreover, the West seldom benefits from such deals. As Philby has said: 'We will just have to face the fact that the Western side always comes out worst in this type of exchange for the simple reason that we have more and better agents than you have. We get Colonel Abel, a first-class man, for Gary Powers, who was only a pilot, for the simple reason that you have no one as good over here for us to catch.'[41] The KGB considered that it might have to wait a long time to arrest a

Western spy as good as Blake for exchange, so it sprang Blake from prison.

The main account of Blake's escape is given by the Irish criminal who organized it, Sean Bourke, in his book *The Springing of George Blake*. According to Bourke, he met Blake in Wormwood Scrubs prison, liked and sympathized with him (Bourke wrote an article for the prison newspaper called 'In Defence of Spies'), and readily accepted a suggestion from Blake that he should organize his escape.

Bourke claims that he did not do this for money, and had to borrow £700 to buy the car and other items needed for the escape operation. Blake's mother was asked for this sum, but refused, as did Blake's sister. Bourke then went to three friends: a married couple and 'Pat', all Anglo-Irish, but neither IRA members nor communists. None of them was well off, according to Bourke, but they all managed to raise loans to help Blake, whom they had never met. Bourke's own motivation was, he explained, 'an opportunity to strike a blow against authority', but he offers no reason as to why Blake should have chosen him in the first place.

Blake's escape, says Bourke, involved breaking an iron-framed window, sliding down a roof, dropping to the ground, climbing over an 18-foot wall on a rope ladder made by Bourke, and dropping the final few feet. Blake, an unathletic man, accomplished this in a matter of minutes. After hiding Blake in various flats in London, Bourke states that the Anglo-Irish couple then smuggled him to East Berlin, hidden in a secret compartment in a camping van. Bourke later joined him in Moscow travelling, he says, on a false passport. He then fell out with Blake, began to feel that his life was in danger and appealed, of all places, to the British embassy for help. Two years after the escape, he finally got back to Ireland where he showed great and, as it turned out, justifiable confidence in the refusal of the Irish government to extradite him to Britain.

None of this is plausible. It has the ring of a story concocted after the event for political reasons. The idea of Bourke, a drunkard and a petty criminal, agreeing to spring Blake just for the thrill of a blow against authority is ludicrous, as is the involvement of Bourke's friends. A more accurate figure for the cost of the operation would be £10,000 – not the kind of money that Bourke and his friends could easily raise.[42] Why would Bourke go to Moscow at all? He says he wanted a refuge until the furore over the escape died down, but he could have gone to Ireland with greater ease.

The only story which fits the facts is that the escape was organized by the Russians who contracted out some of the work to the IRA. Bourke was a minion, hired because he knew Blake and was about to be released under the hostel system, which allowed him free access between the outside world where he spent the days, and the prison where he slept at night. The Russians moved Bourke to Moscow with Blake because they could not trust Bourke not to blab about the whole story once Blake was gone. Bourke claims that he wrote his book during his time in Moscow, but the Russians seized the manuscript when he tried to smuggle it out, and only returned it to him, with excisions and amendments, in the spring of 1969.

This, too, sounds false. The Russians would have known that there was nothing to stop Bourke from reinstating the censored material and ignoring the amendments – as he says, this is exactly what he did.[43] What probably happened was that Bourke wrote most of the story in Ireland, inflating his own role to make the account a more saleable book. The KGB sprang Blake because he was one of the best officers it had ever had, and it wanted to show that it looked after its men. It hushed up its role because the period was one of relative détente and because it did not want to publicize its use of the IRA.

Blake thrives in Moscow. He married a Russian girl, Ida, and they have a son, Mischa. They are friendly with the Philbys and spend summer weekends in the country together. Bourke died young (47) and mysteriously in Ireland. He lived in a borrowed caravan in Kilkee, County Clare, claiming poverty but boasting of having an almost unlimited supply of whiskey. On 26 January 1982, he was found dead in his bed, apparently from alcohol poisoning.[44]

No one denies that the Philby and Blake cases did harm to the Anglo-American intelligence relationship; the only differences of opinion are on the extent of that harm. Some CIA officers say that liaison on *intelligence* matters went on much the same as before; only *counter*-intelligence relations were damaged, because the CIA counter-intelligence men became convinced that the British were not secure. But Robert Amory, for one, believes that the damage went deeper than that because of the close relationship that Philby had built up with Bedell Smith and other senior CIA officers. 'The Philby Affair poisoned Bedell Smith against SIS and he remained so for the rest of his life', Amory says.[45]

The point is that the damage occurred at a crucial point in the changing relationship between the CIA and SIS. The British were relinquishing their leadership of the Western intelligence world – a position they had retained thus far largely by invoking legend and by sheer bluff – and were adapting to a new role as the Americans' subordinates. Lack of resources, as we have seen, was the main reason for this. Miles Copeland, a former CIA officer, states: 'It is in most parts of the world a primary duty of the British station chief to use his superior prestige and cunning to persuade his CIA colleague to join with him in joint Anglo-American operations for which he supplies the brains and the CIA colleague supplies the funds.'[46]

It was crucial to this collaboration between the CIA and SIS, especially in its early days, that SIS enjoy the full trust of its American cousins. Philby and Blake endangered this trust, not simply because of their own betrayals but by leaving behind them the continuing suspicion that there could well be other Soviet officers within SIS and MI5 ranks.

If this suspicion had been confined to SIS, then it would have been destructive enough. As it turned out, it also infected the CIA where some counter-intelligence officers argued simply: Why should the Russians have limited their penetration efforts to Britain? One CIA officer, in particular, pursued this line of thought: James Jesus Angleton. Angleton had been closer to Philby than most. Philby had been one of his instructors when Angleton, then in OSS, first arrived in Britain, and Philby had become the American's 'prime tutor in counter-intelligence'. In Washington the two men had lunched together and, when Philby was recalled to London, he had made a point of saying goodbye to Angleton. The two men liked and respected each other, Angleton looking upon Philby as an elder-brother figure.

The shock that Angleton felt at Philby's betrayal can, therefore, be easily imagined. This one act alone would probably have tipped Angleton into a state of permanent suspicion, but it was reinforced by the arrival in the United States of one of the most amazing defectors ever to leave the Soviet Union.

# 13. The Defection Game

> Of all the Soviet citizens who provided the west with
> intelligence information, the best-informed,
> highest-placed, most courageous, and, indeed, the
> noblest of them all, was Colonel Oleg Penkovsky.
> – Christopher Dobson and Ronald Payne, *Dictionary of
> Espionage* (1984).

> Skulking in the shallows and shadows of the American
> intelligence community may be found a few old-timers
> who remain convinced that Penkovsky is the prime
> example of the KGB at its fiendish best.
> – Anthony Verrier, *Through the Looking Glass* (1983).

Defectors are the lifeblood of Western intelligence agencies. They rank only just behind a penetration agent in value. A penetration agent can tell you the opposition's strengths and weaknesses. He can learn its intentions – through the information his agency is asked to provide. He is in a position to neutralize these intentions – by providing misleading or incorrect information. He can be used to confuse your enemy, or to manipulate him to your advantage. And he can ensure that your own service remains free from penetration by giving timely warning of any such attempt. The KGB, with infinite Russian patience (it took ten years from his KGB recruitment for Philby to manoeuvre himself into the right place in British intelligence), prefers to play the penetration card. Western agencies, always under pressure to get quick results, prefer the defector.

The defection of an important officer from the other side's intelligence agency is a major event. He brings information to up-date your knowledge of the opposition agency, the nuts and bolts of his organization, his order of battle, training methods, strategy and tactics, and the relationship between his agency and the opposition government. If he is well placed in his service, or if he has prepared for his defection, then he brings clues to the identity of opposition agents and moles in your country – almost every major counter-

297

intelligence coup since the war in the United States, France, Britain, Germany, Scandinavia and Australia has been sparked off by a defection. The pursuit and capture of these moles will help enhance your service's image with your government – a factor vital to your survival and growth. He can bring an assessment of what the opposition service knows and thinks about you – a matter of importance to professionals trying to improve their performance.

Defectors, both genuine ones and those who 'change their minds' soon after coming over, can be used as messengers via whom agencies can exchange information – or disinformation. At the very least, a defector provides an agency with the opportunity to 'go public' with all the information that the agency has gathered over the years from poor sources, such as gossip, stolen papers and unreliable newspaper reports. Since this would not normally be believed, the agency has been forced to sit on it. Then a defector arrives. The agency can now attribute to him all this poorly sourced information. Many a defector must have been greatly surprised to learn how much secret information he knew, how important he was before he came over and, above all, what a high rank he had achieved in his old job. Finally, there is always the exciting prospect that a potential defector can be persuaded to stay in place, thus enabling you to penetrate the opposition the easy way.

It is small wonder then, that Western intelligence agencies spend so much time, money and energy trying to identify a possible defector from among the ranks of KGB officers serving abroad, and then in attempting to persuade or blackmail him into coming over. Is he the fun-loving, heavy-drinking type who seems to enjoy the high-life outside the Soviet Union? Does he appear happy in his job? Has he any observable weaknesses that could be exploited – drink, drugs, sex, money? CIA whistle-blower, Philip Agee, has described how a large part of his working life as a CIA officer in three different Latin American countries was spent observing, making contact with, and trying to recruit, local KGB officers, and the agency's China desk seems to have devoted nearly forty years to an effort to recruit its first Chinese official.[1]

But defectors, rewarding though they may be, are also both dangerous and difficult. They are dangerous because of the need to decide whether they are genuine or acting under orders as part of a plan to plant a mole, however briefly, in your service, or to confuse and confound you with disinformation. A defector who arrives unexpectedly, who 'walks in', is therefore regarded with great suspicion. Western intelligence services prefer a defector they have targeted themselves, worked on for a long while, and who comes reluctantly, preferably kicking and screaming. Even then, suspicion lingers. It is an exaggeration, but not a great one, to say that defectors are *never* trusted, and few ever achieve total acceptance from all sections of the service. The rationale is simple and cynical: if he can be 'turned' once, he can be 'turned' again.

Defectors are difficult men because of the heavy emotional pressures they are under. These begin from the moment the decision to defect is taken. Few betray lightly and the thought of permanent exile is not a happy one. The defector is likely to develop a close attachment to the officer who has persuaded him to defect, both needing him and blaming him for what has happened. He is worried about retribution (although the days when the KGB pursued and murdered defectors is generally acknowledged by Western agencies to have ended). He wants reassurance and admiration.

The Western intelligence agencies' needs are different. They want the defector to tell them everything he knows as quickly as possible. 'They are interested in everything', Czech intelligence officer Josef Frolik, who defected in 1968, has written. 'It can all be exploited one way or another. They want to know the names of the officers, how you worked, how much you were paid, the operations, where you were recruited, even what the office looked like. I was talking, talking, for about three years, five days a week, hours on end. When you have been working for 17 years you have a lot of information.'[2]

This pressure to empty the defector of all he knows does not imply that an agency is uncaring. The CIA guarantees a defector a lifelong pension. His physical needs are taken care of – housing, medical attention, a welfare officer, financial advice and, if he wants it, training for a new job. (Few are ever employed by the CIA, and, if so, usually only in a consultancy capacity.) But no matter how favourably this future may be presented to him, the ex-KGB officer soon sees it for what it is – the defectors' scrap heap. He has little to look forward to except seeing out his days, probably in the suburbs of Washington, surrounded by fellow defectors, with, if he is lucky, an occasional visit from his CIA officer, who will have moved on to other cases and developed other interests.

The smarter defector realizes this in his early days in the West and tries to do something about it. He exaggerates his former role in the KGB, making himself out to be of higher rank and of greater importance than he really was: he had access to files not normally available because he was alone at weekends; he knew a gossipy registry clerk; he had been selected for special training; he once met Stalin; and so on. He hints that he was privy to great secrets. He rations information, pleading a poor memory. He is sparing with clues; asks for access to certain Western files to help complete the crossword; complains he is not being taken seriously enough and that his information is not being acted upon. All of this is to put off the dreadful day when he will be finished, pumped dry, his life's work over, an alien in a free but strange land.

In the history of postwar espionage two Soviet defectors stand out: Anatoliy Golitsyn and Oleg Penkovsky. Both were 'walk-ins', Penkovsky volunteering his services in such a blatant, demanding manner that the CIA refused to touch him and he had to turn to the British. Both changed the course of Western intelligence. Penkovsky influenced history; Golitsyn may yet do so. Their stories illustrate all the problems and rewards mentioned above – with an added dimension. They were certainly difficult and dangerous. But they also posed vital questions about their role and motives that, twenty years on, have remained unanswered.

On 22 December 1961, the CIA station chief in Helsinki, Frank Friberg, answered his doorbell to find a stranger outside. The man was short, heavily built and spoke in English with a heavy Russian accent. He came quickly to the point. His name, he said, was Anatoliy Klimov; he was a major in the KGB. It was imperative that he be flown to Washington immediately because he had information of the utmost importance for the leaders of the Western alliance. Friberg was quickly on his guard. CIA officers are warned about a 'walk-in' or 'a dangle', as unheralded defectors are called in the business.

But it took only hours to establish a prima facie case for believing Klimov to be genuine. To begin with, he had previously been targeted by the CIA as a possible defector. Seven years before, he had been spotted in Vienna, where he was serving as a junior counter-intelligence officer. CIA officers noted that he was deeply unpopular with his colleagues, and so marked his file as worth a cautious approach to see if he would be interested in a new life in the West. But before the CIA could move, Klimov had been transferred back to Moscow. When he turned up in the West again, in Helsinki, the CIA did not realize that Klimov was the same Vienna officer because he had used a different name there – a Russian tactic to make the West's job of tracking Soviet officers all the more difficult.

Klimov was quickly flown to an American army base near Frankfurt, where a team hastily assembled by Richard Helms, then the

CIA chief of operations, began an exhaustive interrogation. His real name, he said, was Anatoliy Golitsyn. He had been born in the Ukraine of a Ukrainian mother and a Russian father. The family had moved to Moscow in the 1930s and the father became a fireman. Golitsyn related how, when a boy, he wanted to be either a sailor, a pilot, or a spy. But, at the end of the war, he enrolled at a school for artillery officers at Odessa. He was an enthusiastic Komsomol leader and attracted the attention of the KGB recruiter who sent him to Moscow for training.

There he studied at the University of Marxism–Leninism, at the High Diplomatic School and at the KGB's own institute, where he took a law degree. Between his posting to Vienna and that to Helsinki, he worked as a deskman in the first chief directorate of the KGB, which conducted aggressive intelligence operations against the Western world. For two years he served in the NATO section of the information department. This meant that he saw all the intelligence that the KGB was receiving on NATO but, in accordance with the 'need to know' principle, he was told no more than was strictly necessary about the sources who were supplying it. The CIA tested Golitsyn by giving him a batch of NATO documents in which genuine and fake papers had been mixed. Golitsyn quickly identified the genuine ones.[3]

Golitsyn's first message to the CIA was that it had grossly underestimated the scale of the Soviet intelligence attack on the West. He was in a position to assess this because of the volume and importance of Western secret documents that had passed through his hands. He had prepared for his defection by memorizing information and gathering clues to agents' identities that would help expose important Soviet spies in the West.

The CIA officers were jubilant. If Golitsyn was able to deliver even a part of what he promised, then the agency had its hands on one of the most important defectors in espionage history. But when Golitsyn was finally flown to the United States after several weeks in Frankfurt, his CIA handlers had a foretaste of what was soon to become a major problem: the man was unbelievably difficult to handle.

The problems were twofold. The first difficulty was that Golitsyn claimed that the KGB not only had an army of agents in high positions in the West, but that it had also succeeded in penetrating most of the Western intelligence services. There were Soviet moles, he said, at the heart of the French service, SIS – and the CIA. As a result, he was very choosey about whom he dealt with in the CIA. If he had the slightest doubts about an officer, if he felt that he was not being taken seriously, or if he thought that the case officer was not bright enough or senior enough he would clam up and refuse to co-operate. An official CIA report refers to Golitsyn as 'a very difficult individual to accommodate'. In the heat of the moment, one officer put it more bluntly, 'The man's a total son-of-a-bitch'.[4]

And yet, in those early days, Golitsyn consistently delivered exactly what he had promised. He revealed that the KGB's access to the French section of NATO was so free that it used the NATO filing reference to select the documents it wanted, which usually reached Moscow within days of the request being made. Golitsyn's revelations led to the resignations of two French intelligence chiefs, the defection to the United States of another senior officer (worried that his service had fallen under KGB control), the departure of President de Gaulle's intelligence adviser,[5] and, eventually in 1983, the sentencing of Professor Hugh Hambleton, a Canadian and former NATO official, to ten years' imprisonment in Britain for passing NATO documents to the KGB.

The second problem with Golitsyn was that he insisted that his information on Soviet agents was only a minor part of the message which he had brought to the West. The other part was political, and so important that it was for the ears of the President of the United States alone. Golitsyn was so insistent that the CIA duly wrote to President Kennedy requesting a meeting and was subsequently able to show Golitsyn a reply on White House notepaper, signed by a White House official, General Maxwell Taylor, politely rejecting the request and expressing confidence in the CIA's ability to make the most of Golitsyn's message. (Golitsyn did, however, have three meetings with the Attorney General, Robert Kennedy.)

The thrust of Golitsyn's message was that the whole basis on which the West had been dealing with the communist world for the past thirty years was fundamentally unsound because of the success of a deliberate and systematic campaign of disinformation orchestrated by the world's communist parties and their intelligence agencies. At its simplest, Golitsyn's hypothesis was that a fresh long-term strategy for world communism had been worked out in Moscow between 1957 and 1960. The KGB had been given a new and influential political role in implementing policies that were based on long-term strategic deception. The main aim of this deception was to convince the West that the communist bloc was torn by dissension and then to pursue Soviet political objectives by taking advantage of the complacency which this induced in the West.

Thus, once you accept Golitsyn's theory, the Soviet–Yugoslav split of 1958 becomes phoney, as does the Soviet–Albanian split. The emergence of Solidarity ceases to be a spontaneous occurrence and becomes a carefully controlled Soviet-bloc plan to revitalize communism in Poland. The dissident movement in Russia is revealed as a KGB-controlled front, and dissidents, such as Andrey Sakharov, as loyal servants of the Soviet Union. Most important of all, the Soviet Union's break with China becomes a mere ruse, a façade of rhetoric behind which the two nations remain as firmly united in communism as ever before. The Soviet military build-up on the Sino-Soviet border and the armed clashes are elaborate tricks planned to give substance to the deception. Clearly, acceptance of Golitsyn's thesis involved a complete reappraisal of everything and anything that happened in the communist world.[6]

Even for the most fervent anti-communist, such a scenario was hard to swallow and the manner in which Golitsyn expounded it did not help. Harry Rositzke, a senior officer in the CIA's Soviet bloc division, recalls:

> I was in India when Golitsyn defected but I met him later. He was a man full of enormous nervous tension, so convinced of his message that there was no room for what one might call political conversation or analysis, or even to consider that there might be other factors involved. He was a man on horseback, a man with a mission. The main reason that he had come out was to let the West know what was really going on and because he felt that only *he* knew what was going on, his attitude was, 'you'd damn well better listen to me.' He saw himself as a missionary, a prophet even. He had to warn us poor, unenlightened westerners – unanalytic, uncomprehending, uncomplicated people – that we could not comprehend the KGB's devilish conspiracies. It was a paranoid approach to history.[7]

But Stephen de Mowbray, former head of Soviet counterintelligence in SIS, disagrees. De Mowbray and Arthur Martin, a Soviet expert from MI5, got to know Golitsyn well, spent many hours in his company and gradually became convinced by his thesis. De Mowbray says:

> The subject of how Golitsyn was handled by the CIA and ourselves is a thorny one. His relations with the CIA in 1962 were stormy. I don't think anyone in the CIA would deny that they had never handled a case like this and that mistakes were made on both sides. Having kicked over the traces in the Soviet system, Golitsyn did not fit easily into a bourgeois bureaucratic system.
>
> It should be kept in mind . . . that the sensitivity of his counter-

espionage leads has dictated that contact with him has always been limited to a small number of individuals whose primary interest has normally been in the identification of spies rather than in political questions . . . Descriptions of Golitsyn as a paranoiac and a self-styled prophet are grotesque and contemptible. He is an exceptionally dedicated and tenacious individual. What is striking is the way in which he has maintained his balance and consistence in the face of endless frustration.[8]

In March 1963 Golitsyn moved to Britain. The CIA was far from pleased. It had provided him with a new identity, a pension and a house in Washington where it could keep an eye on him and guarantee his security. (The Soviet courts had sentenced him to death *in absentia*.) But Golitsyn spent only four months away from the United States. He had barely settled into his English rural retreat when the *Daily Telegraph* inadvertently blew his cover with a news story saying that a high-ranking Soviet defector was hiding out in Britain. It is impossible to prove that the CIA indirectly planted the story on an unsuspecting *Daily Telegraph*, but it certainly achieved what the CIA wanted: Golitsyn packed his bags and went back to Washington.[9]

There he presented his political thesis to a panel of Sino-Soviet experts. He did it badly: he became angry and overbearing when the experts challenged him, and made the mistake of trying to shift the burden of proof on to them: 'How do you *know* that the split is genuine?' He demanded to see every classified document, with its true source identified, that reported on the split, insisting that he could prove that the reports were part of a KGB deception operation. The CIA naturally refused. ('How the hell could anyone in his right mind give a KGB officer enough information [from CIA files] to make a valid analysis', one division head said.)[10]

Rositzke, who was on the panel, remembers the approach that so angered Golitsyn:

We asked him who were the people in the KGB responsible for all these deception actions, because, theoretically, they would need continuity? What was the role of the local party authorities? Were they directed by the Politburo? Were they controlled by the Politburo or were they acting on their own? How was it all arranged? Who acted for the other side? Who acted for the Yugoslavs, the Albanians, and the Chinese? To make the deception work would have involved the participation of hundreds of people, Soviet and non-Soviet, KGB and non-KGB. How is it that nobody has ever come out of the Soviet Union and described any of this? Golitsyn could not satisfactorily answer any of these questions and the panel agreed unanimously that his thesis had no basis in fact; that if one started from a common-sense point of view then the whole thing was ridiculous.*[11]

Golitsyn realized that piecemeal revelations of his thesis was counter-productive, and he retreated until he could produce it in writing, as a complete argument and with research to back his conclusions. In 1968 he made a brief sortie into the American academic and publicity worlds through a few introductions to reliable people. But he claimed that he soon found himself in touch with others who were unacceptable to him on security grounds and he was obliged to retreat again. But he did allow a few intelligence officers to read his manuscript as it then stood. Stephen de Mowbray and Arthur Martin went to the United States and, under carefully controlled conditions imposed by Golitsyn – they were not allowed to make a single note, for example – they read the book, the only British officers to do so. De Mowbray recalls: 'Being by then familiar with his argument, I was able both to understand the manuscript and see that he had gathered a good deal of evidence to support it. If, however, I had approached it cold, I would very probably have written it off as a mishmash of ungrammatical, repetitive gobbledegook.'[12]

It was not surprising, therefore, that when Golitsyn showed the draft manuscript to the CIA, hoping that the agency would publish it, a number of CIA officers read it and rejected it. Then, a few months later, the Soviets intervened in Czechoslovakia, something that Golitsyn had not predicted and which could not be reconciled with his thesis as it then stood. Once more Golitsyn retreated to his drawing board to rework his theories. This took him most of the 1970s, and by 1978 he was again ready to publish. Realizing, by now, that there was no hope of achieving this through the CIA he decided to do so through normal commercial publishing channels. But the manuscript was too long – at least a million words – to interest a commercial publisher. So four Golitsyn supporters – de Mowbray and Martin from Britain, Scotty Miler, former chief of operations of CIA counter-intelligence, and Vasia Gmirkin, a Sino-Soviet expert, all intelligence or security officers of distinction – volunteered to cut and edit it.[13]

* Some officers apparently later changed their minds. When President Nixon's opening towards China occurred, the China desk of the CIA felt very threatened. Its existence was tied into keeping China as one of the primary enemies of the United States. The Golitsyn thesis suddenly became very acceptable to officers on this desk. Former CIA officer Ralph McGehee relates how a member of the CIA's East Asia division 'tried to convince me that the Chinese and the Soviets had secretly agreed to split in order to lull and conquer the rest of the world'.

This was a difficult and time-consuming job and finding a publisher, even for the new version, was not easy. But, finally, in 1984, the book, *New Lies for Old*, was published in both the United States and Britain. It failed to create the debate which Golitsyn and his editors hoped it would. Reviewers felt that it strained credulity, the style was too assertive, the thesis too all-embracing and of interest only to students of conspiracy theories. The Oxford historian, Professor R. W. Johnson, wrote, 'It is possible that the ultimate source for this nonsense lies in bureaucratic conflicts within the CIA'.[14] This appeared to be the end, for the time being, of the political side of Golitsyn's message for the West, although de Mowbray continued to work at the archives testing Golitsyn's thesis against the historical account of Soviet–Western relations before the Tehran and Yalta conferences in 1943 and 1944.

Golitsyn had another message for the West – you have been penetrated by Soviet moles – and here he exercised an influence which continues to this day, both in the CIA and SIS. He offered a different interpretation of KGB operations to justify his claims about KGB penetration. It went something like this. What is the use of the KGB merely catching Western spies? The West will simply send more and the process will become endless. What the KGB aims to do, in the short term, is to plant agents in Western services so they can warn of spies in the Soviet Union, and so that if these Western spies do succeed in getting genuine information about us, our moles can discredit that information and destroy its value.

In the long term, Golitsyn argued, the KGB aimed to achieve nothing less than a complete takeover of Western intelligence services so that it could not only discredit genuine information, but sow disinformation as and when required. If the KGB was successful, the West would be at Russia's mercy, unable to distinguish genuine Soviet policy from the false explanations that the KGB supplied.

Golitsyn's message was that the KGB had already achieved its short-term aim and was well on the way to achieving its long-term goal of exploiting its penetration for political purposes. The first task for the CIA and other Western agencies was to discover the extent of Soviet penetration.

Golitsyn's message was music to many ears in the CIA. Some officers thought that the agency had become complacent about possible Soviet penetration. Others reasoned, more cynically, that promotion, foreign travel and assignments abroad all depended on maintaining the KGB threat. Both groups argued that every Western intelligence agency had discovered Soviet penetration –

except the CIA. Why should it have had special immunity from KGB moles? Lyman Kirkpatrick relates that at top levels in the CIA much thought had been given to this question:

> The idea that the Russians would try to penetrate us had been on our minds ever since the Agency had been created. No skilled intelligence operator would fail to consider the possibility that the opposition was working in his service. So nights when I couldn't get to sleep I'd thrash around and think who it would be, how they would approach, and how they would get by us, and so on. The odds are strong that sooner or later there will be one, if there isn't one now. [15]

In 1980, at a series of conferences, 'Intelligence Requirements for the Eighties', sponsored by the Consortium for the Study of Intelligence, Dr William Harris, a consultant to the Senate Select Committee on Intelligence, said that the CIA had to operate on the assumption that it was 'a partially penetrated' service. He asserted later, in private, that he had no doubt that the KGB had succeeded in placing moles inside the CIA. Even if the CIA had the best conceivable 'quality control' procedures to screen its officers – which might be, say, 99·8 per cent successful in detecting potentially disloyal individuals – 0·2 per cent would slip through. This would be the equivalent of several hundred potentially disloyal recruits in the previous ten years. Moreover, the cases of Soviet moles in other government departments had shown that polygraph (lie detector) tests on which the CIA relied, were not an effective means of detecting disloyalty. In these cases, the Soviet moles had undergone periodic lie detector tests without arousing any suspicion. [16]

Golitsyn's warning was therefore welcomed by many in the CIA, but by none as warmly as James Angleton, the brilliant chief of the agency's counter-intelligence division. Angleton, poet, orchid-grower, ex-OSS officer, 'a super spook who wouldn't even come to monthly staff meetings because he didn't want his cover blown', [17] had, as we have seen, been a friend and admirer of Kim Philby.

Angleton's reaction to Philby's treachery differed from that of many of his colleagues. In the years after Philby's betrayal it became customary to blame him for virtually everything that had gone wrong with Western operations against the Soviet Union. The Albanian débâcle, which we have already examined, was just one case among many that were cited. Philby was, for example, accused of being the source of leaks during the Second World War from the British embassy in Washington, 'where Philby had then served'. [18] Such claims may have been convenient; they were hardly sustainable. Philby did not serve in the British embassy in the war years, but from 1949 to 1951. Angleton, therefore, resisted the idea that it was possible to heap all the blame on Philby. Instead, he asked, in effect: If it was possible for Philby to be a traitor, then who else? If the KGB were able to seduce Philby, why not others? Position, past performance, appearance might mean nothing. It was Angleton who originally coined the phrase, 'a wilderness of mirrors', to describe 'the strategies, deceptions, artifices and other devices of disinformation which the Soviet bloc and its co-ordinated intelligence services use to confuse and split the West'.[19]

Angleton now became Golitsyn's champion. It was Angleton, according to espionage author, David C. Martin, who arranged for Golitsyn to meet Robert Kennedy. (Kennedy was rather taken aback, Martin says, by Golitsyn's request for $30 million to finance special intelligence operations against the Soviet Union.) Under Angleton, the leads which Golitsyn had provided since his defection were followed up with vigour, and security officers from Britain, France, West Germany, Canada and Australia, queued up in Washington for a chance to question Golitsyn and obtain clues to the identities of KGB moles operating in their services. But nowhere was the hunt as intensive as in the United States.

Within the CIA the ten-year-long search for a KGB mole at the heart of operations was shatteringly divisive. Angleton believed that he had narrowed the search for KGB penetrators down to the Soviet bloc division of the CIA and, in 1963, he began steps to get rid of four possible suspects in this department. When this did not appear to work, he cut off the Soviet bloc division from information about highly sensitive cases, leading, according to Angleton's critics, to the near-paralysis of the department.

The hunt went on. Loyal officers with years of service were investigated in secret; although nothing was ever proved against them, several careers were ruined. Nobody was above suspicion. Even a distinguished ambassador, Averell Harriman, was briefly suspected of being a KGB agent on the basis of clues provided by Golitsyn. The difficulty was that much of what Golitsyn had learnt in the KGB (from files that passed through his hands, from KGB 'training cases' in which the real identities had been altered but often insufficiently, and from office chat) was tantalizingly incomplete.

Yet when there was sufficient information to begin an investigation, Golitsyn's tips were seldom wrong. In Britain his information helped finally to pin down Philby, put MI5 on the trail that led to Anthony Blunt and aroused suspicions about a spy in the Admiralty (William John Vassall). Why then did his information about moles in the CIA not also produce results?

Golitsyn's main piece of intelligence for the CIA was that in 1957 the head of the KGB's second chief directorate (the American embassy section), M. V. Kovshuk, paid a visit to the United States. Golitsyn said that the only reason that such a senior KGB officer would undertake such a trip would be to meet with a high-level mole in a sensitive position within the CIA. Having revealed this, Golitsyn then said that, from his knowledge of the KGB technique for neutralizing genuine information which it considered dangerous, he would make a specific prediction: the KGB would send to the United States false defectors to discredit his account of Kovshuk's trip.

Events certainly appeared to support Golitsyn's predictions. Within a few months, two important Soviet officials volunteered to work for the United States. One, code named 'Fedora', appears to have been Victor Lessiovski, a long-time Soviet employee at the United Nations.* 'Fedora' became a prized agent for the FBI, highly rated by J. Edgar Hoover himself. The other Russian was Yuri Nosenko, a KGB officer with a Soviet group in Geneva who had first contacted the CIA in June 1962; two years later, he suddenly insisted on defecting. Everything that both these sources said cast doubt on what the CIA had heard from Golitsyn, especially where Kovshuk's trip to the United States was concerned.

Nosenko stated that Kovshuk had not come to the United States to see a high-level mole in the CIA, but to see a lowly agent code named 'Andrey', an American serviceman who had been recruited while serving in Moscow. Golitsyn had spoken of American agents 'blown' by the mole in the CIA. No, said Nosenko, there was no mole; the KGB had got on to the agents by routine surveillance. But how reliable was Nosenko? The CIA asked the FBI to check Nosenko's credentials with its man-in-place, 'Fedora'. 'Fedora' not only confirmed Nosenko's KGB background but said that the Russians were so upset over Nosenko's defection that they had shut down all KGB operations in New York.

There were other indications that Nosenko must be genuine. He gave the lead that pointed *directly* to Vassall – 'A homosexual who had served in the British naval attaché's office in Moscow'. He revealed the existence and location of all the KGB bugs in the American embassy. But Angleton and other Golitsyn supporters were far from convinced. The KGB, they said, regarded Vassall and

---

* David J. Garrow identifies 'Fedora' as Lessiovski in a book *The FBI and Martin Luther King Jnr*. Garrow says he got the name from fellow author Ladislas Farago who got it from former top FBI official William C. Sullivan. Both men are now dead.

the American embassy bugs as having been blown by Golitsyn anyway, and it would be willing to sacrifice them to convince the CIA that Nosenko was genuine.

So a CIA faction set out to show that Golitsyn was a genuine defector by trying to force Nosenko to confess. He was confined for three and a half years, sometimes in conditions as bad as those in any Soviet *gulag*. Deprived of sufficient food, natural lighting, blankets, toothbrush and toothpaste, bathing facilities (except an occasional shower), reading material and exercise, Nosenko was subjected to hostile interrogation, some of the questions being supplied by Golitsyn. But he did not confess and, at the end of the day, the CIA was no closer to knowing the truth.[20]

Within the agency, three schools of thought emerged: the anti-Nosenko, the pro-Nosenko, and the official. The anti-Nosenko school, continued to maintain that he was a KGB plant. These officers maintained that Nosenko had lied on at least twenty occasions, particularly about his background, and that there were many examples of his ignorance about matters within his claimed area of responsibility in the KGB. He could not even describe the KGB cafeteria. This school did not believe that there could be any innocent explanation for this.

The pro-Nosenko school held that a defector's bona fides should be judged by the quality of the information he gave, and that the information from Nosenko had been at least as valuable as that from Golitsyn, and possibly more so. According to an internal CIA report, after Nosenko had weathered his hostile interrogation, a further but friendly debriefing had enabled him to provide the FBI with nine new cases of Soviet espionage.

The official school of thought was represented by Rufus Taylor, a deputy director of the CIA. He studied the internal report and decided that there had been no significant conflicts between Nosenko's information and Golitsyn's. Taylor's advice to his director was that Nosenko should be accepted as a bona fide defector. Nosenko's supporters in the CIA increased and in 1975 he was hired by the agency as a counter-intelligence consultant – a job he still holds at the time of writing – a position attained by few defectors.[21]

Yet suspicion about Nosenko has never entirely died. In 1978 the House Select Committee on Assassinations was looking into the background of Lee Harvey Oswald. It called for Nosenko's file because one of Nosenko's statements to the CIA after he had defected was that the KGB had never shown the slightest interest in Oswald when Oswald was in the Soviet Union. After hearing Nosenko's evidence and cross-examining him, the committee's conclusion was devastating. It found significant inconsistencies between statements which he had given to the FBI, the CIA and the committee: 'For example, Nosenko told the committee that the KGB had Oswald under extensive surveillance, including mail interception, wire tap and physical observation. Yet in 1964 he told the CIA and the FBI that there had been no such surveillance of Oswald.' The official report states further:

> Nosenko indicated that there had been no psychiatric examination of Oswald subsequent to his suicide attempt, while in 1978 he detailed for the committee the reports he had read about psychiatric examinations of Oswald. In the end the committee was unable to resolve the Nosenko matter. The fashion in which Nosenko was treated by the Agency – his interrogation and confinement – virtually ruined him as a valid source for information on [Kennedy's] assassination. Nevertheless the committee was certain Nosenko lied about Oswald. The reasons range from the possibility that he merely wanted to exaggerate his own importance to the disinformation hypothesis with its sinister implications.*[22]

We have already seen how Nosenko and 'Fedora', the long-time Soviet employee at the United Nations, were linked; it was 'Fedora's' evidence which confirmed Nosenko as a genuine defector. Thus Nosenko's detractors felt that their case was boosted when the FBI began to have doubts about 'Fedora'. By 1980 the bureau was 90 per cent convinced that 'Fedora' was, in reality, a Soviet agent and that he had been under Moscow's control during his years as an FBI informant, including the period when he was supporting Nosenko's story. (The 10 per cent doubt vanished in 1981 when 'Fedora' returned to Moscow after his tour of duty with the United Nations ended.) Logically, if 'Fedora' falls, so does Nosenko, and Golitsyn is vindicated.

But in the secret world, life is not that simple. One CIA counter-intelligence officer, Clare Edward Petty, decided to apply the 'who benefits' method of analysis to the events since Golitsyn's defection. Petty accepted the Angleton assumption that the CIA had been penetrated with the aim of damaging America's intelligence efforts. He then made out a case that Golitsyn, Nosenko and 'Fedora' were all part of a KGB plot to protect the *real* mole, the man who had

---

* There is, of course, another possibility. Nosenko, as a CIA employee, would have discussed his evidence with the agency before he appeared before the committee. He would not have made statements to the committee directly contradicting his original story to the CIA without the agency's knowledge and approval. Thus a third possibility is that in 1978 the CIA, for reasons known only to itself, wanted the committee to believe that the KGB had been greatly interested in Oswald.

greatly damaged CIA operations with unfounded suspicions, who had turned officer against officer, who had caused alarm in friendly intelligence services and delight to the KGB – James Angleton! (At least one chief of SIS had had similar thoughts. Discussing what he called 'the Angleton sickness' he told me: 'If one considers the dissension Golitsyn sowed in the CIA then one could theoretically conclude that *he* was the most effective agent the KGB ever had.') It is not clear from Petty's report, or his statements, whether he sincerely believed that Angleton was a Soviet mole, or whether he embarked on his exercise in order to demonstrate the futility of the path into which Angleton had led the agency. He says simply that the case against Angleton was 'a great compilation of circumstantial material . . . a long and unpleasant solitary effort'.[23] (He resigned immediately after submitting the report.)

The director who received it, William Colby, had had enough. He thought it the ultimate example of the conspiratorial mentality at work, but he accepted that it was no more than a response to Angleton's equally conspiratorial approach to intelligence work. Colby had spent hours listening to Angeleton expound Golitsyn's theories about Soviet strategy, moles, false defectors and devilish KGB plots, and admits that he could not swallow them; either because he did not have Angleton's labyrinthian mind, or because the evidence did not justify Angleton's conclusions. Colby drew up a balance sheet: Angleton's pursuit of Golitsyn's leads was more harmful than beneficial. He sacked him. As Colby explains:

> This was a professional disagreement between Mr. Angleton and myself. I thought we spent an inordinate amount of time worried about possible false defectors and false agents. I'm perfectly willing to accept that if you try to go out and get ten agents, you may get one or two that will be bad. You should be able to cross-check your information well enough so that you're not led very far down the garden path by that kind of problem. And at least you'll have eight good ones. Whereas if you spend all the time protecting yourself against the possibility of having a bad one, you may end up with no good ones.[24]

Supporters of Golitsyn and Angleton argue that the CIA simply decided that an admission that Nosenko is wrong and Golitsyn right would be too embarrassing, and that it has, in effect, reconciled itself to the idea that a KGB mole (or more than one) remains at the heart of the Agency.

The detractors of Golitsyn and Angleton argue that the CIA got rid of Angleton just in time; that if allowed to stay he would have brought its operations to a complete standstill. As for Golitsyn, they say that, valuable though his early leads may have been, he then became a past-master at the game of maintaining his importance and avoiding the defectors' scrap heap. 'What Golitsyn has done is to say that only *he* can interpret the reality of Soviet actions; only *he* understands the Soviet conspiracy; only *he* can identify which defectors are genuine', says Harry Rositzke.[25] There are officers in this latter group who offer an intriguing explanation for Golitsyn's apparent ability to provide a never-ending supply of leads about Soviet penetration. They say that no single KGB officer could ever have had access to so many KGB cases. They therefore conclude that Golitsyn *did* get to see CIA files, that Angleton showed them to him, and that Golitsyn then used this information to develop clues and patterns about Soviet penetration of the CIA and about mole suspects. In short, the CIA found itself following up leads to moles that originated in its own files.

Whatever the truth of the matter, the upshot was that for a period in the 1960s and early 1970s the CIA was wracked by a mole hunt of unprecedented fury and vigour. The hunt ruined the careers and reputations of several fine officers, disrupted relations with other Western services, and nearly brought the agency's offensive intelligence operations against the Soviet Union to a standstill. Yet no mole was ever found. Although it is too easy to blame Golitsyn for these wasted years – as many have – the fact is that he could only have had the influence he did, if the CIA had been in a mood to hear him. And here the blame must genuinely be Philby's. His unmasking as a long-serving Soviet penetration agent at the very heart of Western intelligence – a coup unprecedented in espionage history – left behind an atmosphere of distrust, suspicion and paranoia that prepared the way for Golitsyn's conspiratorial theories. This was Philby's real legacy to the CIA.

The Penkovsky case offers a further insight into Angleton's 'wilderness of mirrors' where nothing may be what it at first seems. There are many versions of, and variations upon, what has been described as the most important defection in the history of postwar Western intelligence. The most generally accepted version goes as follows.

In Ankara, in 1955, Western military officers noticed the assistant military attaché at the Soviet embassy, Colonel Oleg Vladimirovich Penkovsky, sitting forlornly in dreary cafés with a faraway look in his eyes. On this slim evidence, the British marked Penkovsky as a possible future defector. In London, at about the same time,

Greville Maynard Wynne, a British businessman who had served in MI5 during the war, was approached by a former colleague 'James', now transferred to SIS, with the suggestion that Wynne might combine business in Eastern Europe and the Soviet Union with some part-time spying. Wynne readily agreed.

In November 1960, in Moscow, Wynne made contact, at SIS's suggestion, with the Foreign Department of the Soviet State Committee for Science and Technology which was involved in arranging visits to the Soviet Union by foreign technologists and engineers, and which controlled visits overseas by their Soviet counterparts. The chairman of the Foreign Department was Dzherman Mikhailovich Gvishiani, who was the son of a KGB general and was married to Ludmila, daughter of the Soviet leader, Kosygin. Gvishiani's deputy was Yevgeny Illich Levin, a colonel in the KGB and the KGB representative in the department.

Among the officials that Wynne met in the course of his discussions with the committee was Penkovsky, who was the Red Army's intelligence directorate (GRU) representative in the department. When Wynne told 'James' about Penkovsky, 'James' showed particular interest and encouraged Wynne to maintain and encourage the relationship. On his next visit to Moscow, Wynne did so and soon he and Penkovsky were on first-name terms calling each other Grev and Alex, which Penkovsky preferred to Oleg. 'James' was pleased when Wynne reported this and he told Wynne that Penkovsky had already tried to make contact with the West. He urged Wynne to gain Penkovsky's confidence and then wait to see what happened.

Sure enough, in April 1961, on Wynne's last evening in Moscow, when Penkovsky and Wynne were walking across Red Square, Penkovsky suddenly said that he was in possession of certain facts which he must, at all costs, pass on to the appropriate authorities in the West. In Wynne's hotel, the National, Penkovsky gave him a double-wrapped, double-sealed envelope which turned out to contain a full account of his career and enough secret information to convince SIS of his bona fides.[26]

Two weeks later, Penkovsky arrived in London as part of a Soviet trade delegation. Each night, after his official duties were over, Penkovsky would slip away from the Mount Royal Hotel, Marble Arch, where he was staying, to a safe house where he met with SIS and CIA officers who questioned him until the early hours.[27] In order to encourage Penkovsky to 'stay in place' and gather more secret material, he was introduced at one of the meetings to twenty high-ranking Soviet defectors brought to London from all over the United States and Britain: 'We brought them along, Colonel Penkovsky, so that you may know that you are among friends, that you are welcome.' Penkovsky went back to Moscow laden with the tricks of the spy trade – camera, radio, film, secret writing paper, arrangements for dead letter drops – and a small army of SIS officers to service his needs.

During two subsequent meetings, in London and Paris, SIS and the CIA continued to milk Penkovsky of all the information he had gathered during his career, in particular the nine months he had spent at the Dzerzhinski Military Artillery Engineering Academy where he had passed out first on a missiles course. In addition Penkovsky passed to SIS, over a period of sixteen months, some 5,000 Soviet documents dealing with missiles, Soviet politics, KGB operations and military strategy. He also provided his assessment of Soviet leaders, and the gossip and scandal of Moscow's ruling circles.

Then on 22 October 1962 Penkovsky was arrested and charged with treason and on 2 November Wynne was seized in a Budapest street and taken to Moscow to be tried with Penkovsky. On 11 May 1963 a military tribunal of the Soviet Supreme Court found both men guilty of spying. Penkovsky was sentenced to be shot; Wynne to eight years' imprisonment. The Soviet authorities later announced that Penkovsky had been executed five days after the sentence. Wynne served one year and then was exchanged on 22 April 1964 for the Soviet intelligence agent, Conon Molody, who, as Gordon Lonsdale, had been arrested in Britain in January 1961.

Attention in the West focused on Wynne's trial, and Penkovsky's role emerged only slowly over the next two years. Perceptions changed with the publication of *The Penkovsky Papers*. These purported to be a collection of diary-type jottings, written by Penkovsky during his spying period and hidden by him in a desk drawer in his Moscow flat. There they were discovered by CIA agents and smuggled out.[28] Penkovsky was now hailed as the most highly placed Western agent ever to penetrate the Soviet Union, the most important spy in the Cold War, a main factor in President Kennedy's triumph over Krushchev during the Cuban missile crisis, 'a dream spy of the type who hardly ever exists in reality', a brave and honourable man whose vision had played an important role in preventing a nuclear war.

The difficulty with this account is that it depends largely on evidence produced at the Moscow trial, which must be suspect; on *The Penkovsky Papers* itself; and on the recollections and statements of Wynne, principally contained in his book, *The Man from Moscow.* But *The Penkovsky Papers* turned out to have been written at the behest of the CIA by Frank Gibney, a former *Life* writer, and Peter Deriabin, a Soviet defector. Their source material was the recordings which SIS made of Penkovsky's interrogations and debriefings and, since publication of the book was intended to benefit the CIA, it also must be suspect.[29]

As for Wynne, his book provoked a rare comment from the British Foreign Office: 'Certain passages dealing with alleged activities by British authorities, and with Mr Wynne's relations with those authorities, would almost certainly have been objectionable on security grounds had they been true.'*[30]

New material, only recently available, in particular the recollections of SIS and CIA officers concerned with the Penkovsky Affair, make it possible to construct a version radically different in many essentials from the received account and to examine three startling conclusions about Penkovsky's real role currently being canvassed in intelligence circles.

These are as follows. One: that the Russians needed a Western intelligence officer to exchange for Conon Molody (Gordon Lonsdale) and the Penkovsky affair was an elaborate provocation to make SIS or CIA provide one. When CIA proved too cautious, SIS obligingly put Wynne's head into the trap. Second: that Penkovsky was a straight disinformation agent, sent into the arms of Western intelligence to feed it misleading and seductive stories as part of a long-term disinformation process designed to lead the West into a state of false security. Since this was an important strategic programme, the Russians were prepared to sacrifice some tactical intelligence pearls in order to give Penkovsky the vital credibility which he needed to succeed in his mission – which he did. Third: that Penkovsky was a pawn in a bizarre Kremlin power struggle played out on the international intelligence stage. He was used, probably unwittingly, to pass vital information to Western leaders about this power struggle and so avert a nuclear confrontation based on misconceptions. This channel of communication was chosen by Soviet leaders because they knew that their Western counterparts had so fallen under the spell of their intelligence agencies that they would give greater credence to information obtained by an

* SIS objected to Wynne's disclosures and he eventually left Britain to live in Majorca. There he made news when arrested for allegedly hurling a beer crate and a flower pot from his tenth floor apartment onto a seafront boulevard. Wynne complained that this was actually the work of communist agents who wanted him away from his flat so that they could ransack it.

espionage coup than they would to that obtained openly or through traditional diplomatic methods.

Let us now re-examine the Penkovsky affair in the light of the fresh evidence and, most important, in the context of the international events occurring at the time, in particular, the American difficulties with Cuba that culminated in the Cuban missile crisis.

Each new President of the United States had, in the early days of office, faced a major problem: Is he running the CIA or is the CIA running him? Under Eisenhower, Allen Dulles and his CIA covert action warriors did virtually what they liked. When the first U-2 flew in 1955 and flights over Soviet territory became routine – at least fifty in four years – Dulles initially did not bother fully to inform the President and refused to reveal numbers to a senate committee.[31] State Department curbs on the CIA had ceased to work because its section for clearing covert operations was different from the one that cleared intelligence operations, and there was no co-ordination between the two.[32] The whole intelligence area was ripe for reform and many of the bright young men who came to power with John F. Kennedy in January 1961 were confident that he would be the President to initiate it.

They were disappointed. They had underestimated Dulles, and they had ignored the potent emotional attractions of the secret world. As historian Arthur Schlesinger Jnr has noted, there is present in every President 'a James Bond signalling to be let out'. Kennedy was no exception. When *Life* magazine published in 1961 a list of the President's ten favourite books it included the James Bond adventure *From Russia with Love*. Dulles, moreover, knew exactly how to handle the President. CIA files contained a psychological profile of Kennedy which went back to his days in London during the war, when his father Joseph Kennedy was the American ambassador. As we have seen, MI5 was sufficiently suspicious of Joseph Kennedy's pro-German sympathies to keep him under surveillance and to open files on him and his son. These had been passed to the OSS in 1942 and became, in turn, part of the CIA archives and source material for the profile on John F. Kennedy and an assessment of how best the CIA should 'stroke' him.[33]

It seemed easy. Kennedy was not interested in detail, only in the broad overview. The CIA used this as an excuse to tell Kennedy as little as possible, while continuing to run the agency according to Dulles's own perceptions. Dulles and his friends also worked on the

President's brother, Robert Kennedy, the Attorney General, to convince him that the CIA had provided a haven for radical and liberal refugees from the excesses of McCarthyism. As one CIA historian has described it, the CIA leaders 'stroked' John F. Kennedy so effectively that he readily fell in with their belief that the way to show the communists that the new President had the will to resist them was through low-risk covert operations. The invasion of Cuba, at the Bay of Pigs, was to be one of them.[34]

At a presidential briefing on 25 January 1961, the CIA took Kennedy through the forthcoming operation. He was told nothing about reservations expressed both outside the agency – principally by the military – and within the agency itself, where the plans had been kept from several senior officers. Lyman Kirkpatrick recalls:

> James Angleton, Richard Helms, Robert Amory and I were not cut into the operation. But you can't be in such senior positions and not know something about what is going on. I felt that the plan could never work, that it was based on false intelligence from Cuban refugees, namely that an invading force would get help, that there'd be an uprising. But I had heard what had happened to a team dropped into the Cuban mountains, ten men or so. There were two thousand Cuban militia after these guys and they couldn't even get food from the locals. I finally wrote to Dulles and asked permission to put two inspectors into the Bay of Pigs operation as a regular, routine measure. Dulles replied in twenty-four hours, 'Permission denied'.[35]

The operation was a disaster and Dulles paid the price for it. The President said that he wanted to 'splinter the CIA into a thousand pieces and scatter it to the winds'.[36] He considered appointing Robert Kennedy to replace Dulles as director, but decided instead on John McCone who turned out to be just as tough. In the meantime, it was undeniable that the United States had lost a round to the Soviet Union. Kennedy and Khrushchev met in Vienna and Kennedy said, 'The Bay of Pigs was a mistake'. Khrushchev replied, 'Yes. Castro isn't a communist but you're going to make him one.' And the Soviet leader went on to say that Moscow would now extend to Cuba 'all the necessary aid for the repulse of armed attacks'. Paul Nitze has described the Vienna meeting as 'hours and hours of abuse from Khrushchev, emphasising that he, the steel worker, knew how to run a super-power, and Kennedy, the nice kid, was not fit to run anything at all'.[37]

Small wonder that Kennedy came away from Vienna obsessed with Khrushchev. What did he want? What would he do next? The answers were not encouraging. In the following months the Soviet Union resumed nuclear tests in the atmosphere, dashing Kennedy's hopes of an agreement to end such experiments; the Berlin Wall went up; and Russian defence chiefs began to boast about the accuracy of their intercontinental missiles.

It became essential for the United States to know whether Khrushchev was acting from a position of real strength. Kennedy had fought his election on the promise to 'end the missile gap' – to provide resources to enable the United States to catch up with the Soviet Union. After his election, the CIA told him that their assessment was that the gap did not in fact exist. But the Bay of Pigs fiasco made Kennedy suspicious of anything the CIA said, so he ordered Dulles's successor, McCone, and the Defence Secretary, Robert MacNamara, to find out the truth.

Immediate difficulties arose. How do you *measure* a gap? The CIA had tried counting missile sites. But did every site actually contain a missile? It tried counting missiles. The U-2 photographs provided evidence but there were arguments about interpretation. 'To the Air Force every flyspeck on a film was a missile. At various times ammunition storage sheds in the Urals, a Crimean War monument, and a medieval tower were identified as the first Soviet missiles.'[38] And even if you could accurately measure the Soviet Union's *capacity* to wage a nuclear missile war, were not her *intentions* more important? What were Khrushchev's intentions and did he really represent the feelings of the rest of the Soviet leadership? The British Prime Minister, Harold Macmillan, was convinced that Khrushchev was a show-off and a bully rather than a real threat, and that his antics were a source of concern to the more conservative Soviet leaders who were afraid that he might provoke a dangerous response from the West. The CIA was unable to help: its concentration on covert operations had left it without the means of obtaining reliable political intelligence about Khrushchev, his relationship with other Soviet leaders, and Moscow's real thinking on its relationship with the West.

At this very moment, most fortuitously, there appeared on the scene the 'dream spy', the man in a position to provide everything Kennedy had demanded to know – Colonel Oleg Penkovsky. The British had been running Penkovsky since April 1961, the CIA having earlier turned him down. For, contrary to the received version, it was not Penkovsky's lonely evenings in Ankara cafés that had brought him to the notice of Western intelligence agencies, but his persistent opportuning. He haunted diplomatic functions, cornered CIA, SIS, and military officers, and breathlessly offered them his knowledge of Soviet plans for the Middle East. The Western officers concerned duly reported these offers, and were duly told to keep well away from Penkovsky. His background, his war record, his marriage to a general's daughter and his steady progress up the Soviet promotion ladder did not fit a defector's profile. Angleton warned strongly that Penkovsky's approaches had all the marks of a KGB conspiracy. CIA bosses accepted his judgement and all NATO embassies in Ankara were warned to rebuff the persistent colonel.

Five years passed. Khrushchev came to power in the Soviet Union. Now back in Moscow, Penkovsky began to repeat his Turkish performance, haunting receptions and telling alarmed Western diplomats that he wanted to reveal important Soviet secrets – 'Here is a package for your authorities.' Finally, he was successful in making contact with someone willing to listen. It was not initially Wynne, but a Canadian diplomat. Penkovsky thrust a bundle of papers into his hands at a party and walked out. The diplomat gave them to his intelligence officer who passed them to the SIS station head. He sent them to London for assessment. [39]

There, the Ministry of Defence experts in SIS read Penkovsky's material, decided that it was genuine, and asked for more. Dick White then took the decision that the CIA had been wrong about Penkovsky and gave the station chief in Moscow the go-ahead to contact Penkovsky and to accept his conditions for more material. Wynne now came into the picture as a go-between because he was already 'in place', acceptable to the Russians as a businessman, brave and reliable. A summary of Penkovsky's first offerings were sent to the CIA, and arrangements made for the CIA to participate in Penkovsky's debriefing sessions on his visits to the West. (Eventually the CIA had three bi-lingual case officers and eighteen back-stop officers working full time on the Penkovsky operation.) [40]

At first, neither SIS nor the CIA could believe their luck. Penkovsky's knowledge appeared too wide-ranging, his access to documents too easy, his memory too prodigious to be true. But apart from the access to gossip and shop talk which his marriage and professional contacts gave him, he was required, as a GRU officer, to do a regular stint as duty officer at the GRU central registry. By playing the good fellow and volunteering for weekend duty, Penkovsky told his case officers, he was able to spend a lot of time in the heart of the GRU files, frequently alone. Many of the doubts – but not all – about his bona fides faded in the light of one intelligence maxim. If Penkovsky *was* a Soviet conspiracy, either to disinform or to plant a mole in Western intelligence, then the Russians had gone overboard on information to establish Penkovsky's credibility – he had too much genuine and valuable material to be a plant.

In Washington the CIA was in a quandary. It could not afford to be wrong about Penkovsky. Another fiasco and Kennedy might really scatter the agency to the winds. The chief of Soviet operations, John Maury, gave the Penkovsky raw material to a Russian-speaking officer to read. It consisted almost exclusively of technical data relating to the Soviet missile programme, particularly guidance systems on intercontinental missiles. (The significance of this will be discussed later.) It took the officer until the end of 1961 to read the material and write his report. This concluded that the intelligence was genuine, that it indicated that the Soviet Union was behind in its missile development programme, and thus that, if there was a gap, it was not in Russia's favour but America's.[41]

This startling news did not reach the President immediately. For one thing, some senior CIA officers remained unconvinced: Angleton still insisted that Penkovsky had not proved himself genuine. Others worried about the effect that such news could have on the hawks in the Pentagon: the temptation to strike first at a weak Soviet Union might be overwhelming. Maury moved cautiously, discussing with McCone how best to present the Penkovsky material and, more important, to whom. There appeared no need to hurry. Penkovsky was still in place and might well come up with more information that would convince even the doubters.

Then, in July, Khrushchev decided to put missiles into Cuba to deter an American invasion of the island, preparations for which were well under way. Khrushchev had to overcome strong opposition from other Soviet leaders. Some saw his decision as dangerous adventurism; others were worried that the move could seriously weaken the Soviet Union's own defensive system. The opposition was such that Khrushchev had to sack two generals before he got his way.

The United States' reaction to the idea of Soviet rockets virtually in its own backyard is now history. Kennedy and Khrushchev took the world to the brink of a nuclear war in the twelve days between 16 and 27 October. (War was so close that the White House discussed the list of who would be allowed in the Administration's nuclear shelter.)

It is accepted that Penkovsky played a major part in preventing that war. Firstly, his information about the Soviet Union's methods of building and arming a missile site enabled the CIA to calculate that it would take sixteen to eighteen months before the Cuban missiles would pose an actual threat. (In the event, the sites were never finished and no missiles ever arrived in Cuba.)[42] Secondly, the copies of Soviet missile manuals which Penkovsky supplied enabled the Americans to identify the type of missile for which sites were being prepared. Finally, most important of all, Penkovsky's evidence, by revealing that the missile gap was in America's favour, helped Kennedy to decide that Khrushchev must be bluffing and that his bluff could be called.

On this last count, Penkovsky's most valuable service would appear to have been to get himself arrested. Not only did this happen at a vital moment, 22 October, but it occurred in a manner that enabled SIS to know about it within hours. This not only ensured that the CIA (and the President) now fully accepted that Penkovsky was genuine, but that Kennedy's hand was doubly strengthened. For not only did Kennedy know for certain that the missile gap was in the United States' favour, but Khrushchev *knew that Kennedy knew*. No one can continue to bluff if he realizes that his opponent has seen his cards, and within twenty-four hours of learning of Penkovsky's relations with SIS and the CIA, Khrushchev had written his famous letter: 'Only lunatics or suicides who themselves want to perish would seek to destroy your country.'[43] Kennedy offered a deal: dismantle your rocket sites and we shall leave Cuba alone. Khrushchev agreed, and the crisis was over.

Penkovsky subsequently entered into intelligence history. Dick White, speaking to SIS officers later that year, conveyed the CIA's gratitude for the Penkovsky material which SIS had passed to its 'cousins'. 'I am given to understand that this intelligence was largely instrumental in deciding that the United States should not make a pre-emptive nuclear strike against the Soviet Union, as a substantial body of important opinion in the States has been in favour of doing', White told them. 'I would stress to all of you that, if proof were needed, this operation has demonstrated beyond all doubt the prime importance of the human intelligence source, handled with professional skill and expertise.'[44]

Up to this point, the differences in the received account and the new and up-dated one seem minimal. Wynne's role is different; there is more detail about Penkovsky's revelations and the influence it had on United States policy and actions. But there are some peculiarities in both accounts that need explaining.

No one has ever managed to establish Penkovsky's motives. All explanations sound trivial, or simply untrue. It is said that he had an abiding hatred of Khrushchev, but his wife says that he actually admired the Soviet leader.[45] It is also suggested that when he learnt that his father had died as a White Army officer fighting the communists, he wanted to avenge his father's death. But his father was probably a White conscript, not a volunteer, and he died when Penkovsky was only four months old. He hated the communist system, it is claimed. But he was a member of the Soviet élite who had benefited from communism, not suffered under it. The frequent references in *The Penkovsky Papers* to religious motivations and Penkovsky's (rather late) discovery that communism was a fraud, smack of CIA propaganda. Vanity, a delight in treachery, anger at slow promotion, the compulsions of a manic depressive, moral corruption, have all been suggested as explanations, but they all fail to carry conviction. We are left with the important but unanswered question: Why did Penkovsky do it?

Next, we are told that Penkovsky's value was not only in the documents which he could copy or remove from the GRU central registry where, with suspicious convenience, he did weekend duty for colleagues (did no one ever wonder why Comrade Colonel Penkovsky was so willing to work weekends?), but in his assessment of Soviet leaders and policy and his brilliant technical brain. But Western scientific officers at his debriefings describe Penkovsky's knowledge of missile technology as rudimentary, 'a gunner who had taken his courses and passed them, just'. The material which the CIA so thoroughly analysed had nothing to do with the character or intentions of Soviet leaders but dealt exclusively with Soviet missile capability. On Russian leaders, especially Khrushchev, Penkovsky was considered to be unreliable and not to be trusted.[46]

The intelligence tradecraft, as described in the received version of the Penkovsky affair, is frequently ludicrous: meetings in hotel rooms in Moscow with taps running to beat the bugs (rather than a walk in a quiet street or park); the use of 'Alex' as Penkovsky's SIS code name (when Alex is well known as Penkovsky's nickname); and the gathering of twenty Soviet defectors to meet Penkovsky before he returns to Moscow as a Western agent-in-place (a vital breach of the 'need to know' principle, as John le Carré pointed out – '"Boys", I expect [Penkovsky] said, "keep it under your hats".')[47]

What we need to help us reach an informed conclusion on Penkovsky is an outside view, one that comes neither from Western intelligence agencies, which have obvious interests to push, nor from the Soviet Union, which produced a caricature of the degenerate traitor at Penkovsky's trial, again for obvious reasons. Fortunately such a view is available. A British career diplomat with long experience of Soviet affairs, a Russian-speaker with some good contacts in Soviet official circles, was in Moscow throughout the relevant period. This diplomat had established a rewarding relationship with members of the foreign department of the State Committee for Science and Technology, especially the head of the department, Gvishiani, and several others, including Penkovsky. He also knew Wynne.

Wynne at this time was making himself something of a nuisance at the embassy, demanding all sorts of services, not normally expected by British businessmen. Some of the staff who, of course, were not aware of Wynne's SIS role, could not understand why the Russians took him so seriously. Finally, one of them made this point informally to a senior member of the committee's foreign department who said that he found this most interesting.

But the result was surprising. Instead of showing *less* interest in Wynne, from then on the Russians chased him even more enthusiastically and the person chosen to do this was the low-ranking protocol officer, Penkovsky. There are several points to make about this. The first is that the State Committee for Science and Technology's foreign department was clearly more than it appeared to be. It no doubt had a covert function, probably to keep up-to-date on Western developments in the electronics field. *This would explain the presence of so many members who had KGB or GRU backgrounds.

These intelligence officers showed unwarranted interest in Greville Wynne from the moment he arrived in Moscow, probably suspecting his real role as an SIS agent. When British officials, in the dark over Wynne's SIS work, suggested to the Russians that there were many other business visitors who seemed likely to be able to make a more useful contribution than Wynne to Anglo-Soviet trade, Soviet interest in Wynne actually *increased*. Why?

The diplomat, although not at the time aware of the intelligence activities of either Penkovsky or Wynne, has, over the years, considered the Penkovsky affair in the light of what he saw and heard in Moscow during the period and what he has learnt since. Although necessarily tentative, his conclusions are clear.

> All the incidents and the vivid impressions which I recall are very hard indeed to reconcile with the received version of this affair, but relatively easy to reconcile with the idea of a KGB plant from the start. My conclusion is either that Penkovsky had been shunted off to the low-level post he had with the state committee with few real high-level secrets to offer, so that he could be safely kept under observation

---

* During this period, 1960–3, the British government was taking trade promotion with the Soviet Union seriously, and British electronics experts were frequent visitors to Moscow. One, employed by a firm on the fringe of the defence industry, arrived at the British embassy one day in a very shaken state and implored the staff to use its influence to get him on the first plane to London. He said that he had been brusquely ordered into a car that morning, driven to an address he could not identify and introduced to an official who told him that his services in the Soviet Union for the next two years would be of great value. He had been offered a princely salary and pressed very hard to accept. He said he had got away only by promising to think about it. He left for London within hours.

without being able to do much harm; or that he had a real job with the committee, as an intelligence officer and missiles expert, keeping tabs on Western developments in this field, but with the additional role of trapping Wynne by offering 'secrets' which looked only-too convincing.

If the first interpretation is correct (which I think is less likely), then, as a disappointed, fun-loving officer who had failed to make the grade, he might well have been in the mood for treachery. In this case he would have had some military-technical material to offer, especially on missiles. But if he had had genuine high-level political or strategic information, the KGB would surely have stopped him in his tracks at an earlier stage.[48]

But there is a third possibility, quite consistent with the diplomat's impressions – Penkovsky was used by a faction in the Kremlin to pass a vital message to the West. The period during which Penkovsky operated saw an alarming deterioration in East–West relations: the U-2 incident; Eisenhower's insistence that the United States had the right to send planes over Soviet territory, which genuinely infuriated Khrushchev; the collapse of the summit conference in Paris; the Berlin Wall; the crisis over East Germany; American and Soviet tanks facing each other in Berlin; the Soviet resumption of nuclear tests in the atmosphere; and the hawks, on both sides, arguing for a pre-emptive first strike.

The doves in Moscow were deeply worried by Khrushchev's increasingly hard line with the United States, by what they called his 'adventurism', his strident tone with the newly elected Kennedy, his insistence on imposing his own personal defence policy on the military and, in particular, by his decision to raise the nuclear stakes by putting missiles in Cuba. A nuclear war in defence of the Soviet Union was one thing, but a nuclear war caused by Khrushchev's bluffing was an intolerable, but increasingly likely, possibility. The structure of Soviet authority being what it is, there was no way that the anti-Khrushchev faction, which included senior military officers, could let the West know that the Kremlin was not united behind Khrushchev's policies. What the faction needed, clearly, was a channel through which they could let the West know that whatever Khrushchev might *threaten*, he did not have the *capability* to carry out that threat. I believe that Penkovsky was that channel.*

* Penkovsky was not the only channel. At the same time, Yevgeny M. Ivanov, significantly also a GRU officer, under cover as assistant naval attaché for the Soviet embassy in London, was trying to pass peace messages to the British government via MI5, Members of Parliament and influential citizens. It is significant, also, that Penkovsky and Ivanov knew each other, and that Ivanov was well connected with Moscow's ruling circles.

It could be that Penkovsky's early attempts to make contact with Western intelligence were a Soviet intelligence plot, and this was reactivated when the 1960–2 crises began (in which case, Penkovsky is alive and well and living in Moscow). Alternatively, Penkovsky was genuine from the start, but was spotted by the KGB – not a difficult task! – and then allowed to run until the moment came to use him (in which case his execution was genuine).

But by far the most convincing explanation for what followed is the one I have outlined. It accounts for Penkovsky's timely arrival on the scene with exactly the sort of information that the CIA desperately needed; for the persistence with which Penkovsky's superiors courted Wynne (a man they had every reason to believe was a British intelligence agent); for their persistence in thrusting Penkovsky and Wynne together; and, above all, for the amazing timing of Penkovsky's arrest. Why arrest Penkovsky at that particular moment? Why not allow him to run further to see who else he might incriminate? Why not feed him disinformation to confuse Western intelligence? Best of all, why not try to 'turn' him, then 'allow' him to defect and become a mole in SIS or the CIA? All this is standard KGB procedure but it was not applied in this case.

Instead, Penkovsky was publicly arrested just as the Cuba missile crisis moved to its climax – because only by arresting Penkovsky could the Russians provide the final proof that the information he had been giving the West was genuine. After Penkovsky's arrest the CIA was convinced, the President was convinced and – a double bonus – Khrushchev quickly learned that his hand had been exposed to his opponent. The dangerous guesswork on each side was over. The Soviet Union did not have the ability to attack the United States with intercontinental missiles; the Kremlin did not speak as one voice; the Russian doves had made themselves heard and, in doing so, had strengthened the hand of Americans who did not want war. The downfall of Khrushchev had begun, the leaders of both countries had been educated into the realities of the nuclear age, and from this was to grow the improved East–West relationship that marked the next ten to fifteen years.

At the time, the CIA and SIS must have considered the possibility that, although Penkovsky's information was genuine, he could well be operating with the connivance of some faction within the Soviet intelligence community – the GRU, the KGB, or others. And they must have decided that the value of Penkovsky's message overrode the implications of this collaboration. For in an unguarded moment in 1971, the director of the CIA, Richard Helms, let slip something which tends to confirm the above analysis. In his first public speech since taking office in 1966, Helms said that 'a *number* of well-placed and courageous Russians had helped the United States during the Cuba missiles crisis' (emphasis added).[49] Pressed by reporters, he agreed that Penkovsky had been one, but he declined to name others. His reticence – and that of the Russians – is easily explained. The Cuban missile crisis was a major turning-point in East–West relations. Statesmanship, the world believes, triumphed. But if the two intelligence services, Soviet and Western, collaborated to allow vital information to reach Kennedy and Khrushchev so as to save them from the consequences of their misconceptions, then it is understandable that everyone concerned would prefer that this should be kept secret.

There remains one unanswered question: Would the Soviets have been prepared to give away valuable military details in a plot which might not have worked? There is a curious postscript to the Penkovsky affair. Although, at the time, every little morsel that Penkovsky dropped was avidly seized by Western intelligence experts, in retrospect, they now find it difficult to identify any single piece of military information that Penkovsky brought which proved to be of major value.[50] Penkovsky wrote his message in broad brush strokes. It dealt with capabilities and intentions. Kennedy read it and understood.

CIA operations against the Soviet Union may have been disrupted during the Golitsyn period, but its worldwide efforts to contain communism went ahead. President Johnson, briefed by the agency on the nature of the threat, became almost obsessed with three countries which, he believed, threatened American security. These were Cuba, Vietnam and, curiously, Zanzibar.

Kennedy had promised the Soviet Union to leave Cuba alone, but Johnson and the CIA interpreted this promise in its narrowest sense – there would be no more attempts at a military-style invasion. But the ludicrous plans to assassinate Castro, now well known, went ahead. Less well known were CIA efforts to destabilize the Cuban economy by manipulating the international commodities market.

In 1963 James Rusbridger, the managing director of a City of London commodity brokerage house, J. A. Goldschmidt Limited, had a telephone call from 'Bob', a friend who ran a small commodity house on Wall Street. 'Bob' said that he had a client who wanted to do some heavy trading on the London sugar futures market, and perhaps Goldschmidt would be interested in placing the business. Rusbridger flew to New York and met the prospective clients: 'I recognised them instantly as CIA, typical of the agency during that period: sharp, bright and full of weird ideas about bringing down Castro. They also knew a great deal about me personally and of some work I had done for SIS in Eastern Europe.'[51]

The plan the CIA outlined to Rusbridger was bold and simple. The United States had stopped importing sugar from Cuba after the rupture of diplomatic relations. This should have hurt Castro, for sugar was his country's main export, but he had found other markets. The Soviet Union was helping by taking a quota from Cuba, paid for in roubles. Cuba's most important new market, however, was Japan. Japan was paying on the basis of the LDP (London Daily Price), a price for world raw sugar issued every morning by the London Sugar Market. Cuba was doing quite well on this deal because a cyclone in the Caribbean had damaged crops and forced up the LDP. The CIA scheme was to force down the LDP by manipulating the market. Then the price for Cuban sugar sold to Japan would drop, Cuba's foreign currency earnings would fall, and the Cuban economy might be sufficiently damaged to topple Castro.

Rusbridger listened to the scheme with scepticism. He warned that commodity prices could only be pushed out of line for a very short period before the law of supply and demand reasserted itself. The CIA men were undeterred. They wanted to sell sugar short on the London sugar futures market – they would offer for sale sugar which they did not have, at a price lower than the prevailing one – but for delivery in, say, three months' time. The normal reason for doing this is the hope, sometimes backed by intelligent anticipation, that when the three months have passed and the time has come to deliver the sugar, it will be possible to buy the necessary amount at a current price that will be less than the price agreed three months' earlier. Commodity dealers trade in this way to make a profit. Since the CIA wanted it done to force the price of sugar down (who would buy sugar currently at the full price when Rusbridger's firm was offering it for future delivery at a lower price?) it would be a risky business, so Rusbridger demanded a deposit of $500,000 before he would agree to start trading. He thought that this would frighten off the CIA but when he got back to London two days later, the money had already arrived.

Goldschmidt began selling sugar short, using its various European offices and different floor traders in order to give the impression that there was a general downward trend in sugar prices and not just one company at work. Soon Rusbridger asked the

CIA for a second $500,000 which arrived by return. A million dollars spent selling sugar futures short had to have some effect, but Rusbridger says that it probably did no more than hasten a return to normality as the effect of the cyclone damage subsided. 'The CIA could have saved its money but it felt it had succeeded and the two officers I dealt with were very pleased. My friend in New York and I were also happy – we had done well from our commissions.'

There is a postscript to this story. Whether the KGB got to hear of the operation, or whether the Soviet Union learnt of Rusbridger from other sources, is not known. But that same year the Soviet trading agency asked Goldschmidt to sell the sugar which the Russians had bought from Cuba with roubles. They stipulated that it must be sold for hard currency – without Cuba getting to know about it! Rusbridger says he managed to do this by 'a complex laundering deal' and that the Russians were as pleased as the CIA had been.

The Zanzibar Revolution in January 1964 greatly alarmed the CIA. The Afro-Shirazi Party had quickly accepted offers of aid from communist countries and there had been an inflow of technical and diplomatic personnel from the Soviet Union, China and East Germany. During an anti-imperialist demonstration outside the United States embassy, one embassy official reported that he had distinctly heard someone shout *Venceremos*, and this was interpreted in Washington as evidence of possible Cuban involvement. The State Department shared the CIA's worry. 'With relatively slight effort, the East can implant symbols of economic progress and make this relatively tiny area a credible display case for communism, somewhat as the US has used Puerto Rico to dramatise the benefits of free enterprise', one State Department intelligence report said.

The CIA considered three options to prevent this: quarantine the island, heighten the American presence and outdo the communists with aid programmes, or 'uninvited military intervention'. One and three were ruled out as being counter-productive and likely to lead to 'far-reaching anti-Western sentiment throughout much of Africa'. Option two, a heightened American presence with increased aid, money and expressions of goodwill was adopted. There were two sides to this operation. There was an overt one – American ambassadors in all countries allied to the United States were told to urge their governments to establish missions in Zanzibar to raise the Western presence and to offer aid. And there was a covert side: the

CIA set out to 'buy off' Zanzibar's left-wing leaders.[52] The prime target was Abdul Raman Mohamed Babu, a leading revolutionary and the island's newly appointed Foreign Minister.

The month after the revolution, Babu travelled to Geneva for a meeting of the United Nations Conference on Trade and Development. One evening, after a committee session, Babu was approached in the Intercontinental Hotel by a CIA officer using as a cover a large American shipping company. The CIA man said that his company wanted to help Zanzibar become economically independent. He understood that there were prospects of a trade agreement between Zanzibar and Indonesia for the export of cloves, but since Zanzibar had no shipping line then transport would be a problem. His company would be prepared to enter into an agreement to provide charter ships at a very reasonable price. Babu said that he would report this to his government and it would certainly consider the offer.

The CIA man then removed one layer of his cover. 'Now, as to your own position,' he said, 'we would like to help you personally. We realise that you feel indebted to certain countries, China for example, for help they have given you. We would like to assist you achieve true independence because only by being truly independent can you achieve your full political potential.' 'Yes?' said Babu, intrigued. 'Well,' said the CIA officer, 'we would like to open an account for you here in Switzerland with, say, an initial deposit of three million dollars. Would that be satisfactory?'

Babu was suitably non-committal. The CIA man pressed on. 'Think it over', he said. 'We'll get in touch with you in Zanzibar to get your answer. In the meantime, here is a little gift from us – a gold Rolex watch. Keep it as a memento of our meeting. Now listen carefully. Here is the guarantee for the watch. It has on it the number of the watch. Our man will approach you in Zanzibar and say "That's a nice watch you've got there" and you'll say "Yes, I got it in Geneva". He will then produce this guarantee and the number on the guarantee will match the number on your watch. If our man has to telephone you first, he will introduce himself as Marcellino from Milano. When you are certain he is our man you can tell him your decision about the three million dollars and you can pass on to him any little pieces of information you think might interest us. Is that understood?' Babu replied that it was. The CIA officer then rounded off this le Carré-style meeting by reaching in his pocket and pulling out a thick wad of $100 bills. 'I forgot about your expenses', he said. 'Here's $20,000 so that you won't be out of pocket on our behalf.'

Babu took the money and the watch and on his return to Zanzibar went directly to President Karume, reported what had happened and handed over the $20,000 and the Rolex. When he was in Nairobi some weeks later, he had a telephone call from 'Marcellino from Milano' who said that he was in Dar es Salaam. They arranged to meet in Zanzibar the next day but when Babu reached Zanzibar, Marcellino had been and gone.[53] Either he had come to an arrangement with a more 'flexible' minister, or the CIA had been warned off by the State Department which was moving quickly to solve the Zanzibar issue by its own political means.

These aimed at persuading Kenya, Tanganyika and Uganda that an independent socialist state off the East African coast was a danger to the stability of their governments, and that these three countries, in turn, should convince Karume that Marxists in his government would topple him unless he allied himself with a mainland state. This is what happened. With American urging, the Tanganyika–Zanzibar union was settled. Tanzania came into being, and the Marxists in Zanzibar were relegated to unimportant posts. Some were later imprisoned.* President Johnson could rest easy where Zanzibar was concerned. Vietnam was another matter.

Allen Dulles believed implicitly in the domino theory – that if one country in South East Asia fell to the communists, the others would fall like dominoes – and through the late 1950s this was the CIA's official position. So its covert action officers were active in Indo-China even before the French had departed, organizing tribes into paramilitary groups to fight the Viet Cong and manipulating Vietnamese politics to put the anti-communist Ngo Dinh Diem into power. But these were comparatively small operations and, by their nature, slow to produce results. In Washington, as pressure grew for more effective action, two views of the nature of the struggle emerged.

One view was that the Viet Cong were inspired and backed by Moscow and Peking and could thus be defeated only by American military force. The other upheld that the Viet Cong was an anti-colonialist, nationalist movement whose leaders happened to be communists by an historical accident. The only way to defeat them was through widespread reform. If American troops were sent, the

---

* Babu served six years' imprisonment without trial, charged with having taken part in the abortive attempt in 1972 to overthrow Karume's regime in which Karume himself was killed. Babu was released in 1978 after pressure from Amnesty International. He now lives in the United States and Britain.

population would be driven into the communists' arms.[54] Any assessment of the CIA's part in the Vietnam War must take this sharp division among the policy-makers into account, for a CIA report that was seen as accurate, relevant and prescient by one of these schools in Washington would be rated as disgraceful and defeatist by the other. And, as in other CIA activities, we need to separate the agency's covert operations in Vietnam from its intelligence-gathering and analysis role.

The CIA's covert actions and paramilitary operations were a failure. The propping up of Diem; the organizing, training and supplying of anti-communist forces; the black propaganda and dirty tricks; and programmes like Operation Phoenix (the 'neutralizing', often by execution, of some 20,000 to 30,000 communists and communist 'suspects') may have enjoyed short-term success. Phoenix, for instance, helped to cripple the communist political structure in the South. But, in the long term, they all turned out to be counter-productive. Phoenix forced the North Vietnamese to take over the fight from the Viet Cong and when Phoenix's excesses became known in the United States, they added to the backlash against the war in general, and the CIA in particular.[55] The CIA was blamed for America's entrapment in Vietnam, the secrecy, desirability and effectiveness of covert operations became a major issue, and the agency lost its immunity from public scrutiny.

But in the strategic intelligence field, the CIA did well in the Vietnam War, especially during its early stages. Unfortunately, the agency's achievements in this area were overshadowed by its covert action disasters, and no one in Washington was listening anyway. The problem was overload, and a reluctance to hear bad news. As often occurs with modern intelligence, the supply of finished analyses, reports, communications intercepts, bulletins and battlefield statistics flowing upwards through government departments, each of which felt the need to add their own interpretations to justify their existence, exceeded the capacity of the men at the top to read and absorb them. During the Vietnam War the CIA sent presidents current intelligence daily reports, weekly reports, daily intelligence information cables, occasional special reports, and specific memoranda and special analyses. The presidents had time to read little of it, and were reluctant to take notice of what they did read. 'No power had yet been found', said former CIA director, Richard Helms, 'to force presidents of the United States to pay attention on a continuing basis to people and papers when confidence has been lost in the originator.'[56]

Yet, as early as 1954 the CIA warned that, even with American support, it was unlikely that the French or the Vietnamese would be able to establish a strong government and that the situation would continue to deteriorate. Ten years later the CIA even challenged the sacred domino theory. It reported to President Johnson that, with the possible exception of Cambodia, no nation in South East Asia would quickly fall to communism as the result of a communist victory in Vietnam. Furthermore, the CIA report claimed, a continuation of the spread of communism in the area would not be irreparable and that China could probably be deterred from overt military aggression against South East Asia in general.[57]

The CIA confronted the air force and Washington policy-makers on the effectiveness of the bombing of North Vietnam. In 1964 it reported that it did not believe that the bombing would create unmanageable problems for the North Vietnamese government and that the regime there would be willing to absorb bomb damage to test its will against that of the United States. When this proved correct and the US Joint Chiefs of Staff raised the stakes by deciding to bomb North Vietnam's petrol storage facilities, the CIA put forward the view that this would not surprise Hanoi and that it had probably already planned against such attacks. When the raids took place in June 1966, it soon became clear that North Vietnam had indeed dispersed its oil reserves around the countryside.[58]

While the American air force, realizing that the only part of the Vietnam War in which it could play the leading role was in the bombing of the North, faked and exaggerated its successes there, the CIA tried to tell the truth. In 1967 a CIA study concluded that twenty-seven months of bombing had had remarkably little effect on Hanoi's overall strategy for the prosecution of the war and its long-term confidence in victory.[59] When the United States mined the ports of Hanoi and Haiphong in 1972, the CIA warned that this would have little practical effect because the North Vietnamese would activate overland routes of supply through China. (True, the CIA did not foresee that the Soviet Union's failure to react to the mining would shatter Hanoi's confidence in its ally, but that would have required a crystal ball.)[60]

Two CIA reports on the overall situation in Vietnam had a profound influence, both on American policy and on the agency itself. John McCone, since acknowledged to have been one of the best directors the CIA has ever had, frequently tried new ways of gathering intelligence in Vietnam, often to the annoyance of his staff. In 1962 he sent a group of 'old Vietnam hands', gathered from CIA stations all around the world, back to Saigon. From there they spread out around the country, by-passing the established CIA stations, to make an independent survey of the situation. This was then used to pinpoint weaknesses in the system. In 1964 McCone sent Kirkpatrick, his executive director, on a similar mission. Kirkpatrick's report was dynamite. He said that the North Vietnamese Regular Army was the best jungle army in the world. At that time, it had committed only a token force in South Vietnam and its main body had been virtually untouched. The bombing of North Vietnam could not significantly affect the situation. Kirkpatrick concluded that the United States could not win the war in Vietnam, short of using tactical atomic weapons.[61]

McCone, on the basis of this report and other information, strongly advised Johnson against increasing the American commitment. Johnson and McCone did not get on well together – 'they were not really on the same wavelength', according to McCone's colleagues – and McCone's recommendations infuriated the President. 'Policy making is like milking a fat cow', Johnson told a group of CIA officers. 'You see the milk coming out, you press more and the milk bubbles and flows, and just as the bucket is full, the cow with its tail whips the bucket and all is spilled. That's what CIA does to policy making.'[62] So Johnson seized on those parts of CIA analysis that were sufficiently ambiguous to support his own predispositions and buttressed them with the more optimistic conclusions that came through command channels on pacification, interdiction, enemy casualties and defections. McCone was not willing to be a party to this. He was allowed to resign.

The Tet offensive of 1968 changed matters. The Pentagon estimates of communist forces in the field were about half that of the CIA's figure and the real figure was higher again – an under-calculation due mainly to the United States' total lack of understanding of the Vietnamese Communist Party and how it operated.[63] The fact that the communists were able to mount an operation as large as Tet – even though they were defeated – showed that the CIA was closer to the truth than the Pentagon. Armed with this knowledge, the conclusion that the bombing of the North had not weakened Hanoi's will, and that pacification was not working, CIA analyst George Carver wrote a report saying, in effect, that there was only darkness at the end of the tunnel. He persuaded Johnson that this was a more accurate picture than anything the President was hearing elsewhere.[64] Soon afterwards, Johnson stopped the bombing and decided not to stand for a second term.

But the agency's whole relationship with the Johnson administration had taught it an important bureaucratic lesson – it was better to be wrong and in the team, than right and on the sidelines. The

CIA now began to tell Washington what it wanted to hear. John Stockwell, a CIA case officer in Vietnam from 1973 to 1975, was warned by his station chief not to file any more reports on corruption in the South Vietnamese Army. 'If we sent them in, he said, he would send them back to us. If we persisted, he would put notes in our personnel files. He was saying, in effect, that Washington had decreed that Vietnamisation was working and that it would be disloyal to report that it was not.'[65]

Vietnamization – the process of withdrawing American forces and handing over the war to the South Vietnamese – meant a reduction in the CIA presence which it tried to compensate for by stepping up its recruitment of local agents. This eventually proved a costly failure. Hundreds of agents on the CIA payroll turned out to be fraudsters whose main source of information was newspapers and gossip which they inflated into 'valuable' secrets. In one reassessment alone, 300 agents were dropped for fabrication or lack of contact. The truth is that, during its entire time in Vietnam, the CIA was unable to recruit a single high-ranking Viet Cong agent.[66] The agency came more and more to rely on the South Vietnamese government for its information and, naturally, the government exaggerated its successes because congressional funding depended on showing that its chances of long-term survival were good.

Occasionally the truth slipped through. In late 1974 two reports cabled directly from Vietnam arrived on the desk of Ralph McGehee, a CIA headquarters officer. One claimed that 30 per cent of the military and government officials of a particular province had deserted the South Vietnamese government to join the Viet Cong. The other stated that, in another province, apart from the capital city, the communists 'owned' the rest. When the station chief in Saigon heard about the cables he warned against disseminating them, claiming that they were poorly sourced, inaccurate and gave a false impression of the war. McGehee, who had served in Vietnam himself, recalls: 'In fact, these were the only two reports I saw that were accurate at all. Based on these two reports I wrote an end-of-the-year report saying that the place was coming apart, just deteriorating before our eyes. I knew nobody would do anything about it – and nobody did. A few months later the Thieu government collapsed.'[67]

The CIA's determination to 'get on the team' led it onto dangerous ground within the United States. Students of the historiography of the CIA note a distinct change in the attitude of writers at the time of Vietnam. Prior to the mid-1960s, intelligence literature, in general, glamorized the CIA; even scholarly works were friendly in tone and criticism was notable for its absence. During the Vietnam War this changed dramatically: publications by outsiders, with few exceptions, showed considerable hostility to the CIA. This trend grew throughout the late 1960s and reached a peak in the mid-1970s before more balanced works began to appear.[68]

The attitude of elected representatives underwent a similar change. In 1960 a US Senate document said: 'The golden word of intelligence is silence. More can be lost by saying too much too soon than by saying too little, too slowly.' In 1976, the same US Senate committee felt that 'The shortcomings of the intelligence system, *the adverse effects of secrecy* were major subjects of the Committee's enquiry. The Committee is of the view that many of the unlawful actions taken by officials of the intelligence agencies were rationalized as their public duty' (emphasis added).[69]

A combination of factors led the CIA into the actions that brought about this change in American attitude: it wanted to influence public opinion to ensure continuing support for the war; it wanted to identify and neutralize dissent; and it wanted to defend itself against its critics. Getting over the agency point of view on Vietnam, once it had decided to go along with the Administration, was a routine operation. It would be naïve to imagine that any intelligence agency does not use journalists, and the CIA was no exception. Since its founding it has employed up to a hundred working American newspapermen and some twelve to fifteen CIA officers have used full-time journalistic cover on foreign assignments. As many as eight hundred foreign journalists have been used as 'propaganda assets' by the CIA.[70]

This network was used to help shape home and foreign opinion in support of American policy. In addition, sympathetic editors and senior editorial staff were given special briefings on the agency's view and urged to write articles supporting the war, stressing that the communists were hard-pressed and that the Saigon government could survive if given sufficient aid.

To complement this operation, the CIA and the FBI waged a secret offensive against publications which were avowedly anti-war. When *Ramparts* magazine began preparing, in early 1967, to publish an exposé of the CIA's funding of the US National Students Association, the CIA decided that this was 'an attack on the CIA in particular and the Administration in general', and put the magazine's editors under surveillance to see if they were in contact with hostile intelligence services. This project was later expanded into Operation Chaos, an examination and analysis of the whole anti-war movement; the exercise was, of course, in violation of the CIA's charter which prohibited it from performing any 'internal security function'.[71]

When Operation Chaos came to an end after six years, the computerized list of Americans whose name had surfaced during the investigation totalled 300,000. Of these, as Seymour Hersch revealed in his famous report in the *New York Times* on 22 December 1974, some 10,000 – among them Congressmen and government officials – had been singled out for surveillance, phone tapping, mail interception and investigation.

Although no evidence has ever been revealed to show that American war dissidents were being financed or controlled by foreign powers, the CIA and the FBI put several dissident publications out of business by persuading big advertisers, usually record companies, to withdraw their support. The publications' bank records were scrutinized – to try to identify any overseas' funding, but also to locate domestic financial support – their tax returns checked for irregularities, and their editorial staffs infiltrated by agents to sow disinformation and suspicion.

From the plethora of committees which were set up to investigate Hersch's allegations and other allegations of misconduct, primarily by the CIA, but also by departmental intelligence agencies, thousands of pages of evidence, opinion and accusation emerged. Some of the wider allegations against the CIA did not stand up, but what remained was bad enough. The agency had indeed spied on law-abiding American citizens; it had developed a horrific repertoire of dirty tricks; it had interfered in the politics not only of hostile regimes but in those of friendly countries as well; and it had organized unsuccessful assassination plots against heads of state. The time had come to get into the open what the CIA had been doing in the service of the United States. The Church Report of 1976 concluded: 'There is a clear necessity, after 30 years of substantial secret activities, for public debate and legislative decisions about the future course of our intelligence system.'[72]

The CIA was appalled by what appeared to be a concerted effort by Congress and the press to destroy it, and did its best to restore its public standing. But nothing could be done to prevent the damage which, it claimed, the hearings had caused to the agency's operations. Lyman Kirkpatrick told a high-ranking Congressman, 'If I had been head of Soviet intelligence in 1975 I would have given a million dollars for what you published in those hearings. And if any committee gets complete intelligence oversight then the KGB can forget about penetrating the CIA or any other agency – just penetrate the committee.'[73]

But the Senate revelations did encourage some conscience-stricken officers to reveal what they felt was wrong with their agency. Some had general complaints; others criticized specific operations, especially in Vietnam, where the CIA strength had reached some 700 officers. One of these men, Frank Snepp, who had been chief strategy analyst in Saigon, felt that the CIA should face up to its part in the panic-stricken evacuation that occurred when the war ended in 1975 with the North Vietnamese occupation of the South. Snepp suggested to his superiors that there should be an official report on the evacuation and the events leading up to it. No one was interested.

After several abortive attempts to get a post-mortem started, and after learning that the agency was leaking a highly selective and largely favourable account of its role to sympathetic journalists, Snepp resigned in 1976 to write a book, *Decent Interval*. It charged the Secretary of State, Henry Kissinger, the last American ambassador in Saigon, Graham Martin, and CIA station chief Tom Polgar, with refusing to accept intelligence reports that the North Vietnamese were intent on a military victory over the South.* Thus, Snepp claimed, preparations for an evacuation were subordinated to Kissinger's peace negotiations.

When Saigon fell, the Americans had to leave in such a hurry that they left behind thousands of Vietnamese who had worked for them, together with most of their files and dossiers, thus making it an easy matter for the communists to identify them. 'It is not too much to say', Snepp wrote, 'that in terms of squandered lives, blown secrets, and betrayals of agents, friends and collaborators, our handling of the evacuation was an institutional disgrace.'[74]

The CIA's reaction was to sue Snepp for breaching his contract by publishing his book without first clearing it with the agency. The courts ruled that Snepp had not only breached his contract, but had also breached a position of trust – even though classified material was not held to be at stake. Snepp was permanently prohibited from circulating any of his writing arising from his years in the CIA, unless it was first cleared by the agency, and was ordered to hand over all present and future profits from *Decent Interval* to the government – an unprecedented punishment that left Snepp impoverished and angry, and the publishing and legal worlds greatly alarmed. Constitutional lawyer Professor Thomas Emerson, of Yale, wrote, 'For a

---

* Kissinger never took much notice of the CIA alone. He preferred to be his own intelligence officer. He liked to get reports from the CIA, the Defence Intelligence Agency and elsewhere. But they were then processed and analysed by his own staff.

government to impose that kind of blanket inhibition on its employees is a kind of action that is simply not governed by normal contract rules. It raises First Amendment rules about the right of the public to obtain information and the right of the press to publish it.'[75]

But Snepp's experience reflected the CIA's burning desire to put Vietnam and the disasters of 1975 behind it, not only in its public stance but within the agency itself. Lyman Kirkpatrick says:

> We were disgraceful in Vietnam. We were overconfident that these little Orientals could not really compete with us. My God, the Vietnamese were all over us. Our house in Saigon had two Vietnamese guards who spent most of their time fifty feet from the gate talking to pretty girls. We had two explosions. The second one was a booby trap on a field where GIs played baseball. Every night when the GIs played, there were lots of Vietnamese urchins there, picking up Coke bottles and Coke cans. On the night the bomb went off there wasn't a single urchin there. Why weren't they there that night?
>
> Then Tet really shook us. It was a clear indication that the communists were everywhere. They had penetrated the whole bloody system, right up and down. And we never really understood that, and when the CIA said that they had, then the CIA got reprimanded by the government. There was basic disagreement between intelligence and policy makers, and when you can't convince the policy makers that you're true, then you're almost negated. Vietnam was a classic intelligence failure.[76]

But when Kirkpatrick suggested that there should be a major appraisal of the involvement of the CIA (and the armed services) in Vietnam, his idea was rejected.

> I wanted the spring electives at the Naval War College to take a different form. I said that instead of each of us giving an elective we should collaborate and give one elective dealing with Vietnam – do a scholarly, dispassionate, objective analysis of how we got in, what we did when we were there, and what the results have been. I got shot down very fast. Emotions were too high and too intense. Still are. We'll have to wait a few years until this generation moves on and you can sit down with younger people – ones who didn't see their comrades killed – before you'll get a real analysis of our failures in Vietnam.[77]

# 14. Myths, Moles and Conspiracies

> Over the last three weeks the defence and espionage expert, Chapman Pincher, has revealed the evidence which has persuaded him and many other security insiders to believe that the late Sir Roger Hollis was a Soviet mole even while he was director general of MI-5.
> – *Sunday Times*, 11 November 1984.

> Secret Services provide, apparently, natural ambiences for romantics and myth-makers, and the greatest of their artefacts is the Myth of the Mole.
> – Bruce Page, *New Statesman*, 21 September 1979.

The wave of reform that swept over the CIA in the 1970s washed away much of the agency's secrecy. Never before had a secret intelligence organization received such public scrutiny. 'It is indeed a unique event', *Time* magazine wrote, 'that a modern nation is exhaustively examining one of its chief weapons of defence for all the world to see – including its adversaries.'[1] Covert action was drastically curbed. The Hughes–Ryan amendment to the Foreign Assistance Act of 1974 required the director of the CIA to report to four congressional committees and four Senate committees on anything it did in the covert action field. The CIA was appalled. 'That effectively kills covert action', commented CIA director, Richard Helms. 'One simply cannot assume that literally scores of Congressmen and Senators and their staffs are all going to keep the secrets.'[2]

Jimmy Carter made promises of further reforms of the CIA part of his platform in his presidential campaign of 1975–6, with the full support of his vice-presidential nominee, Senator Walter Mondale, who had sat on the Church Committee which had examined CIA excesses. After his election, Carter put all American intelligence agencies under the direct budgetary and administrative control of Admiral Stansfield Turner, Carter's own nominee as director of the CIA. (Previously, directors had not changed with an incoming President because they had no fixed term of office.) Turner slashed jobs in the agency's covert operations section – 212 positions were eliminated – and phased out a further 600 elsewhere in the agency, provoking an outburst of protest. 'What do you want?' Turner responded, 'Happy spies or effective and well-controlled spies?'[3]

Turner, who basically did not like the agency and the kind of people who worked for it, also set about changing its attitudes. He felt that there had been too much emphasis on covert action and on the threat from the Soviet Union. 'The Soviet military is the number one intelligence issue and must remain so', Turner said. 'But without neglecting the cardinal line of defence, we've got to be able to tackle a much wider range of subjects. Today we've got to look at most of the 150-odd countries of the world.'[4] On 24 January 1978 President Carter issued his intelligence executive order, implementing most of the recommendations of the Church Committee pending a new charter for the CIA. It began to look as if the agency was finally back on the path it was originally meant to take – the collection and evaluation of information.

But there was a basic problem with the CIA – and, for that matter, all intelligence agencies – that no legislation, no director's hand, could eliminate. The mole hunts that tore the CIA apart in the 1960s were a symptom of it, and were recognized as such by some more perceptive officers. It has many names: conspiratorial neurosis, clandestine mentality, dream-world spookology, and the crude but explicit 'sick-think'. The point is that those who practise secret intelligence work are always likely to fall prey to destructive fantasies and a conspiratorial view of the world.

The very nature of intelligence work makes for an élitist attitude, one of easy superiority, in which membership of the élite is felt to be a privilege. The new member is taught to trust no outsider and soon finds that he can relax only with his own kind. Intelligence officers tend to eat together, drink together and socialize exclusively with one another. Soon, the club – whether CIA, SIS, or KGB – becomes a small, self-sufficient society. The outside world becomes more and more remote and its realities less and less important. Lyman Kirkpatrick comments: 'After 23 years in intelligence, when I left the agency and went to Brown University, I was surprised at the different attitudes in the outside world.'[5]

At the same time, the intelligence officer's personality is under stress. Since he can tell no outsider what he is really doing, he is forced to invent cover stories. He may need different cover for different people or different situations. 'When you wake up in the morning, your mind goes *click*, okay, who am I today?' says Philip Agee. 'All day long there is the same problem. Somebody asks you a simple question, "What did you do over the weekend?" *Click.* Who does he think I am? What would the guy he *thinks* I am do over the weekend? You get so used to lying that after a while it is hard to know when you're telling the truth' (original emphasis).[6]

Along with the divorce from everyday reality goes what intelligence officers call 'obligatory paranoia'. The CIA believes that this is healthy on the job and will help an officer to survive in a hostile environment. But once established, it is difficult to eliminate and separates the officer still further from the outside world. He begins to grow suspicious of it: Is it plotting against him, as he has plotted against it? At this stage, symptoms of his 'sick-think' most often take the form of alcoholism and divorce. (The CIA had an alarmingly high divorce rate in the 1950s for the simple reason that officers were not supposed to tell even their wives what they were doing. The rate dropped when the policy was altered to allow limited disclosure, but marital difficulties remain a major problem.) As the clandestine neurosis progresses it generates other symptoms: a free-floating suspicion, the belief that outsiders are intent on penetrating the happy secret family to destroy it from within. The last stage is the full conspiracy conviction: the officer is certain that he is the victim of a fiendish plot in which even his fellow officers may be involved. No one can be trusted; the enemy is everywhere.

When Turner took over the CIA in 1977 he had long discussions with senior serving and retired officers about this problem and how it might be tackled. They were not optimistic. They told him that during the Golitsyn–Nosenko–'Fedora'–Angleton upheavals various schemes had been tried to prevent the spread of the clandestine mentality. One scheme was regularly to rotate officers from covert operations to other sections of the agency. But the operations officers fought this, arguing that it would 'contaminate' them by revealing their identities to officers outside operations, thus disqualifying them for use on truly secret missions. Those officers who did agree to be rotated, then found that their colleagues in operations would not accept them back.

Another scheme involved assignments to do specific tasks in other government departments for limited periods. But that did not work either, because if the officer was any good the other government department insisted on keeping him.*

---

* The State Department is a good example. Many CIA officers who were sent there on assignment did not return. At one stage, four assistant secretaries were former CIA men. On another occasion the State Department asked the CIA to provide it with a director of communications and a director of security because it did not have any people of its own with the necessary qualifications.

A third scheme was to give officers sabbaticals on the understanding that, during their year away from the agency, they would go into industry, commerce or academia, and that they would avoid the intelligence fraternity as far as possible, living in and mixing with an outside community. But all these schemes turned out to be either ineffective or impracticable. Indeed, no other intelligence service appears to have solved the problem either.[7]

In Britain SIS was as interested in a solution as the CIA. For the 'sick-think' had crossed the Atlantic in the 1960s, a fact seldom admitted and even less often discussed, and which infected both SIS and MI5 alike. Although it was never as virulent as in the United States, it persisted much longer in a peculiarly British mutation. The CIA's obsession with secrecy had its beginnings with SIS which, as we have seen, was in many ways the model from which the CIA was moulded. But the Americans never went to the lengths that Britain did to preserve the anonymity of its secret services.

Although, officially, there were no such departments as SIS and MI5, most people were vaguely aware of their existence, largely because of books lauding their wartime exploits. But ignorance of their functions, their place in the administrative bureaucracy, and their accountability to the government extended to high-ranking politicians, even to the government itself. For example, it was only when Lord Denning issued his report on the Profumo Affair* in 1963 that the public learnt that SIS was responsible to the Foreign Secretary and MI5 to the Home Secretary.

According to Harold Wilson, then leader of the Labour Opposition, this came as a complete surprise, both to his party and to most of the government. 'It is quite clear to me that no one knew of the existence of this brief except the security services themselves. The Home Office don't seem to have known about it, the Home Secretary doesn't seem very clear about it, and I'm sure that the Prime Minister didn't know very much about it.'[8] This was all in keeping with the original aim of distancing the government from SIS, so that if any intelligence operation went badly wrong the government could convincingly deny all knowledge of any such service and any such operation. But it also gave the services great autonomy and a degree of power that could easily get out of hand, especially when a faction within the services developed conspiratorial neurosis. This is exactly what happened. It began when the KGB, apparently in a

* The Secretary of State for War, John Profumo, resigned in 1963 following a sex scandal involving himself, a call girl named Christine Keeler, and the Soviet naval attaché, Eugene Ivanov.

moment of aberration, gave two spies the same code name – 'Elli'.


In September 1945 Igor Gouzenko, a 25-year-old cypher clerk who had been based at the Soviet embassy in Ottawa between 1943 and 1945, defected in dramatic circumstances. (The Canadians were at first reluctant to accept him and his embassy colleagues almost caught him.) The Royal Canadian Mounted Police (RCMP) hid Gouzenko at a wartime special training school on the north shore of Lake Ontario. Gouzenko was questioned, at first by RCMP officers, later by an SIS officer, Peter Dwyer, and then by Roger Hollis, at that time head of MI5's section dealing with political parties, in general, and the British Communist Party, in particular.[9] Gouzenko's value was that he had brought with him clues to the identity of KGB spies working in the West. Some of these clues he had gathered while he was posted in Ottawa, and some while doing routine duty in Moscow.

From these clues, the Canadians amassed evidence which led to a Royal Commission on espionage and the prosecution of eighteen people, of whom nine were convicted. One of those convicted was Kathleen Willsher, who worked in the British High Commission's registry. She was arrested on 15 February 1946, pleaded guilty to passing secrets to the Russians and, since they were minor secrets, given only three years' imprisonment. The clues that led to Willsher included Gouzenko's information that she worked in 'administration' and that her code name was 'Elli'.

But later, Gouzenko claimed that he knew of yet another spy for the KGB, also code named 'Elli'. Gouzenko said that he had learnt of this second 'Elli' when he was doing night duty in Moscow and a colleague had passed him a telegram from a Soviet intelligence source in Britain. Again, Gouzenko furnished a number of clues as to this person's identity: he was a man, despite the female code name; he was in British counter-intelligence; he was so important that he could only be contacted through messages left at prearranged hiding places; and, finally, he had 'something Russian in his background'. This could mean, Gouzenko explained, no more than that he had visited the Soviet Union, had a wife with a Russian relative, or had a job to do with Russia.

If Gouzenko was right, then the Russians had a spy at the heart of Western intelligence (the CIA had not yet been formed), and a hunt began to identify this second 'Elli'. No progress was made until

1948. In that year the FBI began to get results from the code-breakers working on radio messages sent from the Soviet Consulate in New York in 1944–5. One of these, as we have seen, put the authorities onto Donald Maclean. But another message – to the Soviet embassy in London – provided a new clue to the identity of the second 'Elli'. This message advised that Gouzenko had defected and asked that 'Stanley' be warned of this fact 'as soon as he returned to London'.[10]

MI5 interpreted this as meaning that a highly placed KGB officer working in London was in danger of being exposed by Gouzenko and could not be warned at that moment because he was abroad and out of contact. The new clue was filed away in the hope that eventually other developments would solve the mystery. Over the years the possibilities were whittled down. When Maclean was exposed in 1951, it was realized that he could neither be 'Elli' nor 'Stanley'. He was in Washington at the relevant time and in regular contact with his Soviet case officer. It could not be Burgess because he was in London.

In fact, 'Stanley' was almost certainly Kim Philby. He was abroad at the right time, undertaking a desperate mission to save himself from the revelations of Konstantin Volkov, a Soviet intelligence officer in Turkey, who had approached the British embassy, offering to defect and claiming to have clues to the identity of a Soviet agent in Britain who was 'head of a counter-intelligence organisation in London'. Philby, who was dispatched to assess Volkov for SIS, naturally tipped off his Soviet case officer about Volkov and, by the time he reached Istanbul, Volkov had already been bundled aboard a Soviet airliner never to be seen again.

But was Philby also 'Elli', if the second 'Elli' did indeed exist? The identification of the second 'Elli' became a major priority for MI5 after Philby's defection in 1963, followed by Blunt's confession in 1964, had made MI5 aware of the extent of Soviet penetration of the British intelligence community. Events now took a bizarre turn, fully worthy of the convoluted spy world and the complex thinking of its inhabitants. The then head of MI5, Roger Hollis, launched an investigation to establish whether there might be other Soviet moles who had escaped detection. No one, up to and including himself, was to be exempted from this inquiry. This was the beginning of events unique in MI5's history, a trauma which split it for two decades, and the repercussions of which continue to influence its behaviour even today.[11]

A joint MI5 – SIS body, known as the Fluency Committee, was set up to conduct the investigation. It was staffed largely by what came to be known as Young Turks – young officers whose political views were coloured by the Cold War, who did not regard, as many of their superiors did, the Soviet Union as a fact of life, like the weather, that had to be lived with, but rather as a grisly monster, capable of the most devilish conspiracies. They felt passionately that anyone who had at any stage so much as flirted with this monster should be hunted down and destroyed. The Young Turks were thus all for exposing and prosecuting any suspected 'guilty men', no matter how long ago the offence had occurred and what the suspect's current position might be.

But the service chiefs, particularly Dick White, argued that in the ever murky world of intelligence, the truth is never simple. Many factors must be considered. It is very easy, in secret work, to draw two vastly different conclusions from the same set of facts: one innocent, the other sinister. It is virtually impossible in espionage cases to prove guilt without a confession. Even if you have a confession, taking the man to court will expose your weakness to the enemy and shake public confidence in your service. Such risks are not worth taking, especially if the offence is a minor one. Exposure of a suspect also deprives you of the opportunity of making better use of him – by persuading him to play the double game, for example. This was the practice during the war when, at White's suggestion, spies were not automatically considered for execution, as in 1914–18, but given an opportunity to be of use to their captors.

The Young Turks were not swayed by these arguments and saw them not as a realistic approach to espionage work but as something much more sinister. They were exactly the sort of arguments, the Young Turks claimed, that a KGB mole would put forward to prevent his being uncovered. Was there, then, a KGB mole among the service leaders? They submitted a proposal that there should be an investigation to find out. Basically this involved compiling a list of all MI5 operations that had gone wrong since the 1950s and examining each one on the assumption that it had gone wrong because it had been betrayed. Hollis rejected the suggestion. He responded that operations could go wrong for a number of reasons – human failure being one of them. An internal investigation, working on the premise that failure was indicative of guilt, would destroy the service's morale. No officer could continue to function efficiently if he felt that his every move was being watched because his role in a past failure had cast suspicion on his loyalty. 'I'm not having any Gestapo around here', he is reported as saying.[12]

Hollis was so vehemently opposed to the Young Turks that their dislike of him – he was a rather cold, aloof man with no taste for office socializing – turned quickly into suspicion. Could Hollis himself be the KGB mole who they were looking for? Could Hollis be the second 'Elli'? They began to compile a secret dossier on him, a task which became almost an obsession as Golitsyn's views about Soviet penetration of the West crossed the Atlantic. Golitsyn placed great emphasis on a British 'ring of five' highly placed Soviet penetration agents.* Philby, Burgess, Maclean and Blunt made four. Who was the fifth? They devoted their energies to finding him.

At this stage, it must be asked how a group of intelligence and security officers could pursue an investigation which their superiors did not like, which followed lines their superiors had expressly forbidden, and which eventually turned into an investigation of the director general of MI5 by junior members of that service? One possible answer is that the Young Turks' bosses weakly acquiesced to the growth of the investigation because they did not want to lose the talent and dedication which the Young Turks had brought to the services, and they thought that the investigation could be controlled. But there is a tendency in the intelligence world for operations to gather a dynamism of their own and to cease to respond to higher control. This is what happened in what has become known as the Hollis case, an example of conspiratorial neurosis which, although not as dramatic as the Angleton–Golitsyn upheavals in the CIA, has lasted longer, and continues bitterly to divide serving and retired intelligence officers into pro-Hollis and anti-Hollis factions to this day – even though Hollis died in 1973. For if the director general of MI5 had indeed been a long-time Soviet agent, then the damage he would have caused would be beyond calculation. It would be as if J. Edgar Hoover were to be revealed as a long-serving colonel in the KGB.

The Young Turks dismissed the fact that while Hollis was in the service it had caught at least eight major Soviet spies, and set about collecting information to support their conviction that he was guilty. This consisted of a mass of circumstantial evidence, some of it so trivial as not to be worth considering. But the thrust of their case (with my possible explanations in parenthesis) is as follows:

During a nine-year stay in China in the late 1920s and 1930s, Hollis got to know Agnes Smedley, the American communist. He probably also knew Ruth Kuczynski, an important Soviet intelligence officer, in China and, later, in Caux, Switzerland. (Everyone

* The expression 'ring of five' originates from the Comintern practice of creating self-contained cells of five communists. Since Maclean, Burgess, and probably Philby and Blunt, originally worked for the Comintern, it has been assumed that there must have been one other member of their cell.

in the European community in Shanghai at that time knew Agnes Smedley. If Hollis did indeed know Ruth Kuczynski, did he necessarily know that she was a Soviet agent?)

Hollis could offer no reason why he had been so doggedly determined to join MI5 in 1938. (Hollis needed the job. There were 3 million unemployed at the time. The service needed Hollis because it was about to expand its Far Eastern operations and his experience there would be useful.) When Hollis was head of MI5 he often remained late in the office; he walked home instead of using the office car, thus giving himself a chance to meet his Soviet contact; he knew the writers Claude Cockburn and Maurice Richardson, both one-time communists, and Tom Driberg, a left-wing influence at Oxford and later a Labour MP. (One, Hollis was a hard-worker who thrived on long hours. Two, he walked because he felt he needed the exercise. Three, many other people, including some who remain in sensitive positions and whose loyalty has never been doubted, knew these people.)

The KGB did not press Blunt to remain in MI5 after the war. This could only mean that they already had someone in place there, namely Hollis. (Blunt had a brilliant and lucrative career awaiting him in the postwar art world. If, on the insistence of his Soviet controller he had asked to stay on in MI5, with its pitiful pay, it would have looked very suspicious.)

Hollis asked Gouzenko very few questions, reported a minimum of information about Gouzenko's interrogation to his office and tried to deride Gouzenko's reliability. (The Canadian government provided Britain with a transcript of Gouzenko's full, formal debriefing. Hollis knew that this would be forthcoming and may well have felt it a waste of time to go over the same ground with Gouzenko. Hollis's job included making an assessment of Gouzenko's reliability, but an adverse conclusion could be an error of judgement rather than anything more sinister.)

No record exists of inducements and immunities offered to spies prior to 1964 to ensure that they confessed, and the tapes of some 200 hours of interrogation of Blunt between 1964 and 1972 are missing, so Hollis must have destroyed the records and tapes, on instructions from his controller, before his retirement in 1965. (There is a simple and innocent explanation for the absence of records of this nature before 1964. This is that the director general of MI5 and law officers from the Director of Public Prosecutions had, before 1964, met for informal discussions on each spy case. At these meetings, the chances of successfully prosecuting a suspect were weighed against the possibilities of getting information from him if he were to be offered inducements or an immunity. Since these meetings were very informal, no records were kept of them. But the Blunt case in 1964, because of Blunt's position in society, was thought to be too important to be discussed without a record being kept. As for the tapes of Blunt's interrogation, these are not missing at all and have been carefully preserved.)[13]

The difficulty with rebutting allegations like this is that Hollis's detractors never once give him the benefit of the doubt, never once do they admit the possibility of an innocent explanation, never once do they take into account the possibility of human error. By piling coincidence, generalizations and probabilities one on top of the other, such a strong case is built up that the uninformed reader begins to think, 'Well, there must be *something* to it'.

For example:

Hollis was with MI-5 in Woodstock, near Oxford, during the war. Sonia [Ruth Kuczynski] lived in Woodstock too. Sonia sent radio messages to Moscow. Hollis's *department* was responsible for locating such a radio. It did not do so. Hollis's *department* was responsible for preparing a list of dangerous communists. Sonia's brother was a Soviet agent, yet he was not on the list. When Sonia's cover was 'blown' after the war, MI-5's interrogation was farcical; she was not put under surveillance, and no attempt was made to interfere with her continuing espionage activities. Hollis was *involved* in the decision.

MI-5 made mistakes in giving Fuchs, the atom spy, security clearance. Hollis's *department* was responsible for *most* of them . . . When Hollis was sent to Australia following code-breaks of KGB traffic to and from that country, the KGB changed the codes . . . The leak that the British diplomat, Donald Maclean, was to be interrogated on the morning of May 28, 1951, *almost certainly* originated from MI-5 and it gave Maclean a chance to defect, along with Guy Burgess. Hollis was *one of the few* who knew of the forthcoming interrogation. While Hollis was director-general cases fell apart with suspicious regularity. Philby was *almost certainly* forewarned that he was to be approached and interrogated in Beirut in January, 1963. Hollis was *one of the few* who knew of this decision. (Emphasis added.)[14]

And so on. In short, the Young Turks concluded that their own director general was a long-serving Soviet officer; that he was the second 'Elli' named by Gouzenko; that his agent-runner during the war had been Sonia, the self-confessed Soviet intelligence radio operator who had moved to be close to him in the Oxford area; and that Hollis had been systematically undermining the services' anti-Soviet activities for nearly thirty years. By this time Hollis had retired, but it remained important as a matter of principle to the Young Turks to prove their case against him. They took their case to the new director general, Martin Furnival Jones, and asked for permission to recall Hollis from retirement to face hostile interrogation.

Furnival Jones was in a quandary. The Young Turks included some of the brightest officers both services had had in years – Stephen de Mowbray of SIS, and Peter Wright, Arthur Martin and Anthony Motion of MI5 – and no one wanted to lose them. On the other hand, to allow them their freedom to pursue a former director general who had had a distinguished career, who came from an establishment family and whose whole background, upbringing and character were in keeping with service to his class and country, was not something to be decided lightly. Furnival Jones consulted Dick White and other former high-ranking intelligence officers. Dick White read the Young Turks' case against Hollis and, in a response remarkable for its cold intellectual analysis, tore it to pieces as circumstantial, inconclusive and bearing all the marks of having been compiled with 'a conspiracy theory basis, instead of by analysis of facts'.

Nevertheless, White and his fellow officers agreed with Furnival Jones that the only way to satisfy the Young Turks and, perhaps, restore some calm to the service was to allow them to interrogate Hollis and to conduct a full investigation of the accusations against him. Hollis, with some embarrassment, presented himself for interrogation, answered the Young Turks' questions, and returned to retirement. The result of all this was that nothing emerged to identify Hollis as 'Elli', or, as the official report said, 'pointed specifically or solely in his direction'. The official conclusion therefore was that Roger Hollis had not worked for the Russians. The investigating team was disbanded.

This did not satisfy the Young Turks. They believed, at best, that the service was covering up because it did not want a scandal and, at worst, that other Soviet moles in the service were sabotaging their investigation. They now pressed for an independent review, Stephen de Mowbray taking the extreme step of approaching Number 10 Downing Street to seek an interview with the incoming Prime Minister, Harold Wilson.[15] The Young Turks were successful. In July 1974, even though Hollis had died the previous year, Lord Trend, former Secretary of the Cabinet, looked at the files again and met at least two Young Turks to hear their accusations. Trend found that the original investigation by the joint SIS–MI5 committee had been carried out exhaustively and objectively, that there had been no cover-up, and that there was no evidence that Hollis had been a Soviet agent.

This sort of inquiry could not be conducted in a total vacuum. Although they never became public at the time, the allegations did have political repercussions of an amazing nature. The Prime Minister, Harold Wilson, was stunned when he learnt of the case against Hollis. His political secretary, Lady Falkender, remembers: 'Harold told me "I've heard everything now. I've just been told the head of MI-5 may have defected to the Russians."'[16] When Trend reported, Wilson began to wonder whether Hollis might have been the victim of a right-wing faction within MI5 and when damaging rumours about Wilson's government – especially that he and Lady Falkender had communist links and that there was a 'communist cell' at Number 10 – began to spread in Whitehall, he briefly became convinced that the Young Turks were out to get him as well.

There was some truth in this. Golitsyn certainly believed that Wilson was, if not a Soviet agent, then certainly a Soviet asset (and that the KGB had poisoned the previous head of the Labour Party, Hugh Gaitskell, so that Wilson would get his job!) Golitsyn's views had crossed the Atlantic, along with his warnings of Soviet penetration at high levels. Whether the Young Turks did no more than repeat Golitsyn's views and this then became Whitehall gossip, or whether they took active steps to gather evidence against Wilson, is impossible to prove. But Wilson certainly came to believe that he was under surveillance, and his Lord Chancellor, Lord Gardiner, the highest legal officer in Britain, considered that his office telephones were being tapped. 'I thought it more likely than not that MI-5 was bugging the telephones in my office', Lord Gardiner said later. 'When I really had to speak to [the Attorney-General] in confidence, I took him out on one or more occasions in the car because I knew the driver, and I knew that she would never have allowed the car to be bugged without my knowledge.'[17]

In August 1975 Wilson called in the director of SIS, then Maurice Oldfield, and the head of MI5, then Michael Hanley. From them, Wilson said later, he learnt that there were indeed officers in both services who were strongly anti-Labour. (Given the nature of their work, this is not surprising.) But both officers assured him that the services would remain under ministerial control, irrespective of which political party was in power. Wilson did not entirely believe them. On 10 February 1976 he asked his publisher, Lord Weidenfeld, to visit him at the House of Commons. There he made a surprising request.

The Prime Minister of Britain had decided to go over the heads of

**351**

his own two services and appeal secretly to the CIA. He asked Weidenfeld to carry to Washington a letter to a mutual friend, Senator Hubert Humphrey. The letter contained the names of a number of SIS and MI5 officers of whom Wilson was suspicious. Wilson wanted Senator Humphrey to ask the director of the CIA, George Bush, whether the CIA knew anything about these officers. Was it possible, for example, that they were actually working for the agency and that, perhaps unknown to Bush, it was a faction in the CIA which had the British Prime Minister under surveillance? (Remember, this was at a time when the CIA was reeling as each new day brought fresh revelations of its excesses.) Bush took Wilson's letter so seriously that he flew to London to see the Prime Minister, and assured him that if he had been under surveillance it was not the CIA which had been responsible.[18]

Wilson had resigned before Bush saw him, and now Wilson quickly began to seek ways of getting a Royal Commission set up to investigate the activities of MI5 and its role during Labour's period in government. He put out feelers to the editors of various newspapers to see what support they would offer; but he was unwilling to give them his grounds for seeking a Royal Commission until they committed themselves, and they were reluctant to do so without some evidence to justify such a serious move. Wilson then turned to the BBC and began an extraordinary series of interviews with two BBC reporters, Barrie Penrose and Roger Courtiour. Later Lady Falkender expanded the detail of Wilson's broader charges. These interviews, all tape recorded, went on over a period of months.[19]

The allegations ranged from what Wilson had heard of the Young Turks' case against Hollis, to stories of people compromised by the KGB, to plans for a military coup to overthrow the Labour government which had been discussed in 1968 by Lord Mountbatten and others. The reporters found it difficult to decide what was the main thrust of Wilson's charges. On the one hand, he seemed to accept some of the allegations made by the Young Turks – that there were more instances of Soviet penetration of British public life than had been admitted. (Blunt's confession in 1964 was not made public until 1979.) But Wilson believed that MI5 had known about the plans to oust his government and had failed to warn him. (MI5 did tell the then Home Secretary, James Callaghan, but Callaghan apparently decided against informing either Wilson or the Cabinet.)[20] All this was fascinating material, but Wilson blurred and confused the issue by bringing South Africa into the story. He charged that officers of BOSS, the South African intelligence service, were somehow involved in spreading disinformation about his government.

Wilson's allegations – and the detail provided by Lady Falkender – were impossible to use on the BBC for legal and journalistic reasons. Penrose and Courtiour wrote a book based on the interviews, *The Pencourt File*, but they, too, were restrained by the risk of libel and lack of admissible evidence. Then, in 1979, Lady Falkender teamed up with a well-known Fleet Street defence correspondent, Chapman Pincher, to write a book, *The Infiltrators*, about the penetration of the Labour movement, which was to be published by Sidgwick & Jackson. In 1980 Pincher told the publishers that he would prefer to write a different book, one which would expose Hollis as a KGB agent. The head of Sidgwick & Jackson, Lord Longford, checked the synopsis with his own Whitehall sources and agreed to publish the book, *Their Trade Is Treachery*, which appeared in 1981 to quite a furore: 'MI5 Chief was Russian Spy Suspect' was the front-page headline in the *Daily Mail*.[21]

But in the House of Commons, the Prime Minister, Mrs Thatcher, made a dismissive statement: 'Lord Trend, with whom I have discussed the matter, agreed with those who, although it was impossible to prove the negative, concluded that Sir Roger Hollis had not been an agent of the Russian Intelligence Service.' The Prime Minister did, however, promise an inquiry into security procedures and an investigation into the sources for Pincher's book. These were probably Lady Falkender, repeating what she had learnt from Wilson who, in turn, was relying on the Young Turks' case. Pincher says simply that his sources were 'his [Hollis's] own colleagues inside MI5 and from the Secret Service'.

What the Young Turks (by now many were not so young, and some had retired or resigned) had discovered was the power of publicity. They had exhausted the official channels open to them and had failed. Trained in secrecy, taught to be suspicious of the media – unless they are manipulating it – intelligence officers have an inbuilt reluctance to air grievances in public. But this was different. Peter Wright, the senior MI5 officer who was the most possessed by the conspiracy demon, had retired to Australia and, out of the jurisdiction of the British courts, was beyond the threat of an Official Secrets Act prosecution.

In loose liaison with his former colleagues, Wright began to leak information about the Hollis investigation, about other MI5 cases on Soviet penetration, and the Soviet use of agents of influence, that had never become public because the Director of Public Prosecutions had decided not to prosecute. Throughout the early 1980s there was a spate of revelations and confessions: a civil servant who had given information to Guy Burgess; a former British ambassador to Moscow who had been to bed with the Russian maid who turned out to be (surprise) a KGB officer; a military intelligence officer in postwar Germany who had spied for the Russians; an apparently endless list of often old and insignificant men who had performed services for the Soviet Union decades before.*

The British press was a willing party to this manipulation because, correctly, it judged the British public to be fascinated with espionage and betrayal – more so, perhaps, than readers in any other country. (The reason for this would make a book of its own but, briefly, it has to do with post-empire decline and the bluff with which Britain tried to sustain its grandeur. As Meredith put it: 'We are betrayed by what is false within.') So, as 'spy confesses' headlines followed each other in regular succession, the Young Turks rejoiced. Every time a new suspect was named, especially when he publicly confessed, the Young Turks believed that they had taken a step closer to vindicating their stance.

Getting the Blunt story into the open was particularly rewarding. The Young Turks were appalled that Blunt appeared to have escaped the consequences of his treachery by his confession in 1964. Blunt's work for the Russians before, during and, occasionally, after the war, had been exposed by an American friend, Michael Straight, one of Blunt's recruiting failures. Blunt had then done a deal with the British authorities. He would not be prosecuted and both his treachery and the deal would remain secret forever. In return, he would do all he could to help the authorities by answering their questions frankly and honestly.

This appeared to the Young Turks to be a disgraceful surrender to Blunt's social and professional position. But there were good reasons for striking such a deal. The lawyer in the office of the Director of Public Prosecution who agreed to it, Maurice Crump, says that even with Straight's testimony it would have been impossible to prosecute Blunt because there was no evidence against him. On the other hand, he had valuable information to give. He was prepared to give this in return for 'a valueless undertaking not to do the impossible' – not to prosecute him.

Moreover, says Crump, the information which Blunt gave was not

* One newspaper published its list under the headings 'confessed', 'partially confessed' and 'unresolved'. They were not always accurate. An apology read: 'Our list of MI-5 spy suspects included Cedric Belfrage whom MI-5 officers said had made a partial confession and we said was dead. We are glad to make it clear he is alive, never made any confession and maintains he should not have been on the MI-5 list at all.'

a confession because, under British legal rules of evidence, it could never be used against him. 'It is understandable that [Blunt] wanted the undertaking such as he was given, because he was not to know that we had no evidence', says Crump. 'If I had denied this country information it needed in order to avoid saying that I would not do what I could not do, my conduct would indeed have been questionable.'[22]

It is clear, then, that the authorities got the best of their bargain with Blunt, and that if he had kept his mouth shut he might well have escaped unharmed. But the Young Turks saw no reason why Blunt should continue to enjoy his career, his honours, and his professional and social esteem – he was Surveyor of the Queen's Pictures. They wanted him exposed and, from within and without the service, they worked to achieve this. Blunt's name as a possible 'fourth man' in the Philby, Burgess and Maclean so-called 'ring of five' was a rumour in Fleet Street for years. My co-authors and I heard it in 1968 when we were writing *The Philby Conspiracy* and tried to interview Blunt about it. He wisely refused to see us and we did not persist; we were interested in a bigger mole, Kim Philby.

Then, in 1977, *The Times* claimed that the fourth man may well have been Donald Beves, a wealthy and highly respected Cambridge don who had died in 1961. The story had been planted on *The Times* and, after an outcry from Beves's colleagues and former students, and a flood of outraged letters to the editor, Sir William Rees-Mogg, the paper apologized and said that its suspicions about Beves were wrong and that it regretted having reported them. (Privately Rees-Mogg remained convinced that Beves played a role in the secret world, perhaps as a recruiter for SIS, and that the Russians, having got Philby, Burgess and Maclean, then steered them in Beves's direction hoping that he would recruit them for SIS.)[23]

But the effect of the Beves story was that interest was reawakened in the identity of the fourth man, and two authors were soon deep into books which pointed a finger at Blunt. The first was by a veteran espionage writer and wartime intelligence officer, Donald McCormick, and was withdrawn for libel reasons unconnected with Blunt. The other, *The Climate of Treason* by biographer Andrew Boyle, published in 1979, used a cunning stratagem to avoid actually naming Blunt but, at the same time, making it crystal clear to the reader that Blunt was the fourth man. Boyle gave the fourth man the code name 'Maurice', presumably from the homosexual hero of E. M. Forster's last published novel. Then Boyle gratuitously mentioned Blunt's name in the text as many times as possible, often in the most forced manner, and as physically close as possible in the text to any mention of Maurice. At the same time, someone 'leaked' stories to the gossip magazine *Private Eye* alleging that Blunt was threatening to sue Boyle when his book was published. When the book came out and Blunt did not sue, Boyle announced that he was able, if need be, to name the fourth man. Ten days later, on 15 November, in a written Commons answer to a question tabled by Ted Leadbitter MP, the Prime Minister revealed the 1964 deal with Blunt. In the furore which followed, Blunt was stripped of his knighthood and resigned most of his public offices. He died in 1983, aged 75.

Even with Blunt's treachery out in the open, the Young Turks still appeared no closer to proving that Hollis was the 'King mole'. However, there were still a number of minor spies whose confessions could be adduced as evidence of the extent of Soviet penetration. In bringing the names of these to light, the Young Turks were unwittingly helped by a new arrival on the espionage writing scene, Rupert Allason, and by a second split in the secret world, this time due to piqued egos.

Allason, who writes under the name of Nigel West, is the son of a former Conservative MP, Lieutenant-Colonel James Allason. He was educated at university, has been a special constable in the Metropolitan Police (he once arrested two men on a beach in the Bahamas on suspicion of smuggling cannabis) and, at the time of writing, is a Conservative Party candidate. He became interested in the intelligence world when he was employed as a researcher for Ronald Seth, the author of an encyclopaedia of espionage and a former intelligence officer with a rather unusual wartime career. With Donald McCormick, Allason researched and helped to write the book of a BBC documentary series, 'Spy', in 1980. Allason produced a number of major works on espionage and intelligence.[24]

The remarkable thing about these books is their attention to detail. The first book – about MI5, 1909–45 – for example, contains eight organizational charts, listing not only all the major posts within MI5 but the names of the officers who held them. The book on MI6 is equally well documented. Both books are packed with the names of service officers, and their exploits are described in great detail. At least ten double agents – Abwehr officers who were 'turned' and worked for the British – granted Allason interviews, even though they had led anonymous lives since the end of the war through fear of reprisals. Four former MI5 officers checked Allason's manuscript for accuracy and Rear-Admiral W. N. Ash of the Ministry of Defence's 'D' Notice Committee (a government body that 'advises' the media on sensitive issues) is thanked by Allason for his 'guidance'. The deputy Treasury solicitor said of Allason's work: 'It's pretty clear that some of these things have not come from the imagination of the author. To use the vernacular – it looks like an inside job.'[25]

So what help did Allason get and why? Allason himself says, 'In the course of the BBC series I met in 1978 an ex MI5 officer and he passed me to other officers and eventually to ex-senior officers of MI5. They were interested in getting the history right.'[26] But there is more to the story than that, and to understand it we need to look at earlier publications about the secret world. In 1960 the then Prime Minister, Harold Macmillan, gave his approval for the publication of an official history, *SOE in France. An Account of the Work of the British Special Operations Executive in France 1940–1944* by M. R. D. Foot. The first author to take advantage of this precedent was Sir John Masterman, the Oxford don who had been chairman of MI5's 'double-cross' committee. After the war, Masterman had been invited to write the history of the committee to be kept for the historical record. Masterman now saw no reason why this should not be published, especially since, he argued, it would improve the image of British intelligence after the disgraces of the 1950s. When MI5 tried to stop him, he simply arranged publication in the United States, beyond British jurisdiction. After the book, *The Double Cross System in the War of 1939 to 1945* came out in 1972, long and bitter negotiations followed before the Heath government finally agreed to allow a British edition.

Its publication caused considerable resentment. Many MI5 officers felt that Masterman had taken all the glory for himself, and that their own roles, particularly those of the case officers who 'ran' the German double agents, had been overlooked. The government, aware of this resentment and anxious to prevent a repetition of the wrangling with Masterman, decided that the solution would be to allow publication of an official history of the entire British intelligence effort during the war. A team of Cambridge historians under Professor F. H. Hinsley, a wartime intelligence officer himself, undertook the work, and the first volume, *British Intelligence in the Second World War*, was published in 1979.

Instead of alleviating resentment in the services, Hinsley's book exacerbated it. Security officers were appalled to find only ten references to their service in the book's 601 pages, and these references were largely to do with liaison matters. SIS officers were equally upset. Although the book dealt with intelligence activities, few SIS officers were mentioned by name. Under the index for 'D', for example, there were fifty-one entries. Only five of these referred to people, and none of these was an SIS officer. Yet there were twenty-five references to committees, including the Defence Committee (with eleven sub-references), the Defence Policy and Requirements Committee, and the Defence Requirements Sub-committee.

Maurice Oldfield, a wartime intelligence officer and head of SIS from 1973 to 1979, told me: 'You get the impression that the intelligence war was won by committees in Whitehall, rather than by people. I'm thinking about doing a review of the book and the first sentence will be "This is a book written by committees, for committees, about committees".'[27] But while SIS only simmered, MI5 officers decided to do something about it.

Towards the end of the war both SIS and MI5 had been concerned that their funds would be drastically cut when peace returned, as had happened after 1918. (The rapid abolition of SOE seemed to confirm the likelihood of this, as did the austerity measures of a Labour government.) So both services, independently, prepared a substantial documentary history of their wartime achievements. These were 'house histories', never intended for publication, but meant to be used as reference works in the Whitehall exchanges which would precede any attempt to reduce service budgets. They were compiled by asking each departmental head to produce a comprehensive account of his section's achievements, and these were then welded into one document.

When publication of Professor Hinsley's official history proved so disappointing to many MI5 officers there were moves to press for a separate history of the service. The problem was that Mrs Thatcher took intelligence matters very seriously and considered that the secret service should remain secret. She would have preferred that even Hinsley's official history had not been published. It had been commissioned under the Heath government in the early 1970s at the same time as an official history on strategic deception in the Second World War, to be written by Professor Michael Howard, Regius Professor of Modern History at Oxford.[28]

Hinsley's first volume was cleared for publication in 1978 during the final year of Mr Callaghan's premiership. Mrs Thatcher was less than happy with the project but felt unable to halt the work in midstream. But when Professor Howard finished his book in 1980 and submitted it to the Cabinet Office, Mrs Thatcher personally decided against publishing it. 'When I was called to the Bar, the first and best piece of advice that I received was never to admit to more than you have to,' she is reported to have said in support of her decision.[29]

Then Allason, who was keen to write on intelligence, came on the scene. Allason insists that he was 'never given access to *files* in MI5's famous registry' (emphasis added). Allason believes that the initial impetus to give him this help came from officers who felt that their work, especially during the war, had never been properly appreciated. But he adds that there were other factors, such as the desire of some former officers to air the accusations against Hollis. Allason insists that he remained impartial. 'I didn't question the motives of these people,' he says. 'You don't look a gift horse in the mouth.'

With the right introductions, Allason then went on to interview many wartime MI5 officers and to build up a history of the service's early days. The result delighted most MI5 officers. Nearly every wartime officer got a mention, no matter how brief ('Miss Dicker . . . ran the female personnel section') and Whitehall committees were virtually ignored. Under the index letter 'D', the same letter we used in the earlier example from Hinsley's official history, there were 109 entries in Allason's book, of which 77 were for named people and only 1 for a committee. The more astute reviewers noticed this. The *Yorkshire Post* wrote that the book was 'numbingly thorough' in its detail, and a former wartime intelligence officer, Peter Calvocoressi commented in the *Sunday Times* that 'Unlike Professor Hinsley and his colleagues, Mr West seems to have set out to mention as many of MI5's operators as he can find. The result is a clutter of names, barely distinguishable by the reader.'[30]

A second book, *A Matter of Trust. MI5 1945–1972*, quickly followed, appearing the next year. This was less of a house history than the first volume and dealt largely with what appeared to be the service's decline in the postwar period, culminating in the damaging divisions over the Hollis affair.

With two books on MI5 published in two years, both with wide sales and much publicity, SIS was now very much in the shade. But not for long. A year later Allason's third book *MI6. British Secret Intelligence Service Operations 1909–1945* appeared. Like the first MI5 book, this was the house history of SIS. For example, four of the wartime chapters are divided into geographical areas representing SIS's own operational divisions. But because some operations overlapped, Allason's account of these operations is repeated in more than one chapter, sometimes with slight variations, sometimes with contradictions.

Where there was friction within a department, or where it was geographically remote from SIS headquarters and Section V (the counter-espionage section and, it would appear, the prime mover in getting the official history written and in helping Allason with his book) then there was no section history for anyone to draw on. The corresponding sections of Allason's book are weak, and sometimes wrong. For example, GC and CS could not have contributed, because Allason inverts ISOS and ISK, using the term ISK for hand cyphers and ISOS for Enigma, when exactly the reverse was the case. No one at GC and CS or Radio Security Service (RSS) would make such a mistake; a member of SIS headquarters at Broadway or Section V, who saw only the intercepts in final, translated form, might easily do so. Allason rounded off his literary quartet with a book on the Police Special Branch, published to coincide with its centenary. He has said he hopes that his books will be used as reference works, as indeed they are. But in the course of his relations with former MI5 and SIS officers, particularly the Young Turks, Allason learnt secrets he did not include in his books. He was willing to leak, to selected newspapers, clues to the identity of people MI5 had investigated for their pro-Soviet activities, who had worked directly for Soviet intelligence, who had helped Soviet agents, or who had been indiscreet in their relationships with Russians. These newspapers followed Allason's clues, located the people and, in many cases, persuaded them to confess. If they were dead and unable to sue, they could be named anyway. In this manner, the Young Turks' case was further advanced. Suspects they had been unable to prosecute were exposed and thus punished and the extent of Soviet penetration of British life could be revealed.

Encouraged by this, the leading Young Turk, Peter Wright, from his remote residence in Tasmania, Australia, now began to leak parts of the document which has become the bible of the Young Turks movement: 'The Security of the United Kingdom against the Assault of the Russian Intelligence Service', 160 pages devoted largely to the case that there was a senior Soviet penetration officer highly placed in MI5 in the postwar years, and that the evidence pointed to Sir Roger Hollis.[31] Wright's disclosures attracted the attention of two members of Granada Television's 'World in Action' team, which made a documentary about Wright. But the writer most intrigued by Wright's allegations was Chapman Pincher, who had been pursuing the Hollis case since his book *Their Trade Is Treachery* had appeared. Pincher now rushed into print with *Too Secret Too Long*, basically the

Young Turks' case against Hollis coupled with Pincher's own theories and investigations.

$T$he whole affair had clearly got totally out of hand. The case against Dick Ellis, the Australian officer in SIS who had given the Germans his service's order of battle before the war, was resurrected to show the extent of Soviet penetration of Britain. The Young Turks alleged that Ellis, who died in 1975, a lifelong anti-communist, had been blackmailed into working for the KGB because it knew of his prewar relations with the Germans. The argument went like this: If Ellis, an instructor in OSS, number two in Stephenson's British Security Co-ordination Office in New York and effectively number three in postwar SIS, could be a Soviet mole, is it too much to accept that Hollis could also be one? And how many more? No one was above suspicion. Sir Dick White and other retired heads of MI5 and SIS supported Hollis and argued that the Young Turks' allegations were ludicrous. Was it possible, then, that White and the others were, if not Soviet agents, then at least Soviet assets? Allason says he was sent to see Graham Mitchell, a former deputy director who had retired in 1963 to get a deathbed confession from him that *he* had been the Soviet mole, not Hollis.[32] Mitchell did not oblige, and when he died in January 1985, Dick White wrote his obituary in *The Times*. White said that Mitchell had been under 'unjustified suspicion' and that he bore the publicity that the Young Turks had thrust upon him 'with dignity and indeed magnanimity'.[33]

There will be no end to the Hollis affair until all the accusers are dead and a new generation of officers shreds the files. For it is ironical that, in the secret world, to defend someone against accusations like those made against Hollis does him a kind of disservice. Support becomes equivocal. There is no evidence that Hollis was a Soviet spy; therefore he must have been the most cunning of all spies not to have left a trace of his treachery. Yet the most obvious answer is most likely the correct one. The Soviet mole in British counter-intelligence was Philby. All the main clues fit him as well as they do Hollis. Gouzenko simply mistook the agency in which the mole was at work. He confused MI5, the Security Service, with Section V of SIS, Philby's section. The chief suspicion against Hollis arose through an error, and the rest of the case against him would be laughed out of any British courtroom.

It could be argued that it does not really matter. Hollis is dead and the slurs cannot hurt him – although they distress his family. It all happened a long time ago and the suspects who have eventually confessed in public have got it off their consciences. Everyone enjoys a good spy story, and the publication of them keeps us alert to the Soviet menace. But disgruntled security officers who feel that they have been thwarted in the pursuit of their quarry can be dangerous. Wright's group demanded that the government should radically alter the way Britain approaches security. It wanted the formation of a super security service (to be called 'The Guardians') which would watch for Soviet penetration of SIS and MI5 – another example of the ability of intelligence departments to expand in an almost limitless manner – and it wanted, against all British legal tradition, to have the burden of proof in espionage cases reversed; the onus, they suggested, should be on the accused to prove his innocence.

The Soviet Union is, of course, well aware of the damage that mole hunts can inflict on the Western intelligence world and does its best to encourage them. One of the jobs of KGB officers in London is to take advantage of the British obsession with treachery by planting doubt about the loyalty of civil servants and politicians. Richard Cox, a former Foreign Office official who later became a senior Fleet Street defence correspondent, has told how a KGB officer, Prokopy Gamov, would take him to lunch and then never talk to him about defence. Instead, he would ask intriguing questions about the Prime Minister's Office and the Cabinet Office and the making of policy. Cox said:

> They [the KGB] must have presumed that the questions they were asking me would get back to the British authorities and that if they asked the right questions which suggested that there was a spy in the Cabinet Office, then that could cause a lot of alarm and despondency. [Government offices] are very frightened of Russian agents and if it conceivably tied up with any other suspicions that they had, then they would have to begin a witch hunt in the Cabinet Office, not knowing who they were looking for, and nothing demoralises anybody's office more than to think that you've got a spy in it.[34]

So the seeds of suspicion that were sown in the United States found fertile ground in Britain, where the secret world had grown accustomed to the idea that virtually everything that happens is part of a KGB conspiracy. The services were divided and damaged and found it difficult to recover. Whereas the CIA ultimately shook off Philby's legacy of distrust, suspicion and paranoia, something in the British character, an almost religious fervour for seeking out treachery, made it less easy to do so. Cyril Connolly foresaw it. When Burgess and Maclean defected in 1951, and the hunt was on for Philby, the third man, Connolly wrote: 'After the third man the fourth man, after the fourth man the fifth man; who is the fifth man always beside you?'

# 15. Overcoming the Monster

Free societies as well as closed ones need to have secret
services, otherwise the closed ones will take them over.
– *The Economist*, 15 March 1980.

Secrecy corrupts individuals and institutions; it invites
the concealment of negligence and malpractice; it nearly
always spreads unnecessarily; it damages international
relations; and it can become pathological.
– Galen Strawson, reviewing *Secrets* by Sissela Bok, in
*Sunday Times*, 29 April 1984.

The 1980s were boom years for intelligence agencies, especially
the CIA. Although Jimmy Carter made intelligence reform part of
his platform, although a bi-partisan Bill for an all-embracing charter
for the CIA was introduced in the Senate in 1978, the American
mood had changed entirely by the end of the 1970s.

Carter, the man who had promised to put the CIA on a short
leash, sensed the swing. In January 1980, in his state of the union
address, he was still saying there should be guarantees that there
would be no further abuses of CIA power, but he also delighted the
intelligence community by stressing that 'an effective intelligence
capability is vital to our nation's security' and promising to remove
'unwarranted restraints on our ability to collect intelligence'.[1] The
bi-partisan Bill died, a less comprehensive one failed. Instead,
legislation was passed cutting the number of committees to which
the CIA reported from eight to two, and giving the agency the right
to carry out covert operations without notifying the committees in
advance, if there were special circumstances.* What had brought
about such a volte-face?

The main cause was a changed perception of the Soviet threat,
heightened by the Soviet invasion of Afghanistan. But even before

---

* The chairman of the Senate Select Committee on Intelligence, Barry Gold-
water, complained in 1984 that he had not been told about the CIA's role in mining
Nicaraguan waters.

that, the CIA had take steps to present the American public with a scenario of communism on the move against an increasingly ill-informed and defenceless United States. In Angola, for example, a team of CIA propaganda experts was employed to plant stories in the Western press highlighting Russian and Cuban aggression. Sometimes a propaganda officer got carried away. One planted a story that Unità forces had captured forty-two Russian advisers. When journalists from all over the world came flocking into Angola to see what would happen to the Russians, the Unità leader, Jonas Zavimbi told them: 'What Russians? They're aren't any Russians in this country.'[2] But mostly they were successful. A story that Cuban soldiers who had raped some Angolan girls had subsequently been captured, tried and executed by their victims appeared widely in the Western press, complete with a photograph of the 'firing squad'. In 1985 John Stockwell, one of the CIA officers in charge of the propaganda exercise, admitted that the story was fiction and the photograph a fake.[3]

Even the débâcle in Iran – the Shah was overthrown early in 1979 just five months after a CIA report had said that there was no sign of any revolution – was turned to the agency's advantage. In the last years of the 1970s there had been a 40 per cent reduction in the funding for the intelligence community and a 50 per cent cut in the work force.[4] If you emasculate us, the CIA argued, then you cannot blame us if you are caught unprepared. If we got it wrong in Iran, then this was because we did not have the money or the men to do a proper job. The way to correct this is obvious: fund us properly; let us off the leash. This was exactly the line that Ronald Reagan made a major issue in the 1980 election: 'We will revitalise the nation's intelligence system.'

Reagan was as good as his word. As his administration moved from détente to confrontation with the Soviet Union, the intelligence community's role was broadened and strengthened. Its budget was increased: by 15 per cent in 1982, and a huge 25 per cent in 1983, not allowing for inflation, more generous even than the increases granted the Defence Department. By 1985 the CIA was spending at least $1,500 million a year, more than the entire budget of many a Third World country. It was also the fastest-growing major agency in the Federal government.[5]

The man who presided over this expansion was William J. Casey, former millionaire, tax lawyer, businessman and, more significantly, a former OSS officer who had worked with Donovan on covert operations behind German lines in the closing days of the Second World War. It is, therefore, no surprise to find that the major growth in the agency took place in the operations division. Donovan's boys were back; the lean years were over; the morale of the covert action warriors, badly dented by Vietnam, was quickly restored. Under Casey, the first CIA director to have Cabinet rank, there was a five-fold expansion of the CIA's worldwide covert operations in three years. At one stage there were twenty different secret operations underway in Africa alone as the agency got back into business on a scale and with an enthusiasm unmatched since the heyday of the 1960s.[6]

Industrial psychologists have long theorized that a company does not have to change a much-criticized commercial practice if it can alter public perception of that practice. Sometimes a simple change of terminology is sufficient. It is interesting to note, then, that as the covert action warriors dusted off their cloaks and daggers, the CIA changed the term 'covert action' to 'special activities'. It rehired, on short-term contracts, some of the 800 'special activity' veterans who had been let go between 1977 and 1980 and began a recruitment and training programme to bring this section up to staff levels that could cope with Casey's expansion programme. In one year, 1982, more than a quarter of a million young Americans, many attracted by the agency's glamorous recruiting advertisements, contacted the CIA about jobs; 10,000 submitted applications and 1,500 were hired, bringing the CIA's workforce to well over 16,000.[7]

These new recruits spent a large part of their training learning how to navigate through the maze of interlinking organizations that formed the greatly expanded intelligence community: the CIA, the National Security Agency, the National Reconnaissance Office, the Defence Mapping Agency, the air force, navy, army and marine intelligence organizations, the State Department's Intelligence and Research Bureau, the FBI, the intelligence divisions of the Department of Commerce, Agriculture and the Treasury, the Drug Enforcement Administration, and the Federal Research Division of the Library of Congress.

Expansion of secret intelligence services always seems to be accompanied by a reduction in civil liberties and this new growth in the CIA and other organs proved no exception. What had been seen as unacceptable abuses in 1975–6 were quickly made legal under the Reagan administration. The CIA was authorized to investigate foreign-sponsored activities in the United States, a role never envisaged for it back in 1947, and one which must have made J. Edgar Hoover turn in his grave. It was given the right to carry out covert actions, or rather 'special activities', within the United States, to open mail in the United States, to co-operate with local law enforcement agencies, and to put American citizens abroad under surveillance.[8] (Richard Helms, a former CIA director, once highlighted the major difference between the CIA and the KGB: the KGB acted abroad as an intelligence agency, and within the Soviet Union as a security agency; the CIA did not. But now the CIA's new internal role has begun to erode this distinction.)

To prevent a recurrence of the trouble caused when Philip Agee revealed the name of every serving CIA officer he could remember, and when Richard Welch, the CIA station chief in Athens was murdered after being named in a journal called *Counterspy*, the CIA got an Act through Congress making it a crime to print the names of CIA agents.[*] American civil liberties groups complained that the law was harsh (it applied even if the names had been gathered from public sources and printed before); that the penalties were excessive (ten years' imprisonment and a $50,000 fine for former intelligence officers, and three years' imprisonment and a $15,000 fine for others); and that the law, in effect, imposed censorship in peacetime.[9]

The new mood of super-secrecy extended to everyone. The CIA was no longer anxious only about officers like Frank Snepp, who had published his experiences with the CIA without the agency's prior approval, it was also keen to end the practice by which former directors published their memoirs. Admiral Stansfield Turner, head of the agency under President Carter, spent years making his book innocuous enough to satisfy the new CIA. The agency insisted on deleting general references to covert actions against Nicaragua – while the operations were being described in detail on the front pages of American newspapers – and refused to allow Turner to quote from his own public speeches.[10] The aim was, clearly, to establish secrecy for secrecy's sake.

The KGB, on the other hand, sought to improve its image with Soviet citizens by becoming less secretive as the 1980s progressed. The process began under Yuri Andropov, head of the KGB for fifteen years before he became Communist Party chief in 1982. Anxious to get rid of the almost universal KGB stereotype – a

---

* It is not entirely clear whether the left-wing group which claimed responsibility for the murder identified Welch from reading *Counterspy*, or because his house was well known to have belonged to a succession of CIA station chiefs over the years. The CIA had actually suggested that Welch should occupy another house.

thug in an ill-fitting suit – Andropov changed the service's recruiting and training procedures and then began a public relations campaign worthy of any Western advertising agency.

A new breed of intelligence officers began to be recruited from Soviet universities. Recruiters looked for the élite of the graduates, preferably with at least one foreign language, and lured them with a mixture of patriotic appeal and visions of good pay, large apartments and foreign travel. Those posted to the 10,000-strong First Chief Directorate, which covers foreign affairs and is housed in a new building on the outskirts of Moscow, away from the poor image presented by the old headquarters at 2 Dzerzhinsky Square, were turned into sharply dressed, highly sophisticated and exceptionally bright officers. A former African politician complained that he found it increasingly difficult to tell the difference between the local CIA officer and the local KGB officer: 'They look alike, they speak alike, they want the same information, and they use the same inducement to get it – money.'

In 1979 Andropov devoted some of his greatly expanded budget – usually about 10 per cent more than the CIA – to making an hour-long documentary film on the KGB. No expense was spared. Officers he specially favoured were brought back to Moscow from overseas postings to help prepare it. At about the same time, books, films and television dramas began to present idealized KGB officers as principal characters. One television serial, 'Seventeen Moments in Spring', had as its hero a KGB officer called Maxim Isayev, code name 'Stirlitz', who penetrates Nazi headquarters during the war. The gap left by the Soviet boycott of the Los Angeles Olympics was filled by the spy thriller called 'Tass Is Authorized to State', depicting a battle of wits between the KGB and the CIA in an imaginary African country, Nagonia, which had asked for Soviet help after suffering destabilization by a CIA covert action. The series was based on a novel by Julian Semyonov which had been a best seller in 1979. Finally, the KGB announced its own literary prize for the best work showing KGB officers as scrupulous and honourable men trying to defend the Soviet Union against its internal and external enemies.[11]

As in the United States, the intelligence service's influence with the nation's political leaders increased. Just as Casey became the first director of the CIA to have Cabinet rank, so the KGB achieved two political 'firsts' in two years. Andropov became first secretary of the Communist Party in 1982 – previously, it had been thought that no KGB chief could ever become party leader. And then, in 1984, under the new KGB boss, Marshal Victor Chebrikov, it was announced that the Supreme Soviet had introduced a new

KGB rank, that of 'Generalissimo' – a rank previously confined to the army and only ever held by Stalin.[12]

There was, however, no evidence that the KGB had streamlined the rigid, vertical chain of command that, its Soviet critics say, led to promotion of favourites, patronage, cronyism and bureaucratic blunders. (A KGB defector, Stanislav Levchenko, studied Japanese at Moscow University for six years, wrote his master's thesis on the Japanese peace movement, and was then told that his assignment in a state of war alert was to proceed to Scotland to report on the readiness of British nuclear strike forces!)[13]

Britain did not escape the bureaucratic explosion that the 1980s had brought to the international intelligence community. The British services may have been in a different financial league, but their organizational complexities were far richer than anything the Soviet Union or the United States could invent. The budget for SIS and MI5 was officially £92 million a year, but unofficial studies based on the space the services occupy – eight large office blocks in London alone – suggested that the real budget was more likely about £300 million. GCHQ also probably spends £300 million a year. It is, of course, entirely possible that because of the secrecy surrounding the intelligence services, *no one* knows what they cost. As Dr Christopher Andrew has pointed out: 'All governments, of course, conceal from their subjects the sums spent on their intelligence services by accounting methods which, if employed by public companies, would lead to prosecution.'[14]

Other aspects of the British intelligence community became slightly more visible, not because the government or the services wanted it that way, but because of the uncovering and subsequent trials of officers who had been working for the Russians, and because of a union dispute involving GCHQ.* Subsequent calls for the intelligence services to be made properly accountable led to revelations about the bewildering structure of the British intelligence community and the depth to which it had penetrated many areas of Whitehall.

One example, the reporting procedures of SIS, MI5, GCHQ and the Defence Intelligence Staff (DIS), gives an idea of how many bureaucrats have an interest in the survival and expansion of the

---

* In 1983 the British government banned unions at GCHQ and asked GCHQ staff to sign away their right to join a trade union in return for £1,000. Most did so.

intelligence world. At the time of writing, SIS reports to the Joint Intelligence Committee (JIC), the Overseas Economic Intelligence Committee (OEIC) and the Co-ordinator of Intelligence and Security (CIS) in the Cabinet Office. MI5 reports to OEIC, CIS and the Official Committee on Security (OCS). GCHQ reports to JIC, OEIC, CIS and the London Signal Intelligence Board (LSIB). DIS reports to JIC, OEIC and CIS. JIC, OEIC, CIS, LSIB and OCS report to the Permanent Under Secretaries Committee on Intelligence Services (PSIS). OEIC reports to PSIS and the Prime Minister (PM). CIS reports to PSIS and PM. LSIB reports to PSIS and PM, as does OCS.

This catalogue of acronyms by no means exhausts the list of Whitehall committees dealing with the gathering and protection of secrets. There are, among others, the Security Commission, the *ad hoc* Ministerial Group on Security, the Security and Policy Methods Committee, the Personnel Security Committee and the Electronic Security Committee. All these chiefs deal with the work of some 14,000 'Indians' in the intelligence and security services.[15] This all seems a far cry from the days when SIS had sufficient money to send spies only to Germany and MI5 worked out of one room at the War Office on a budget of £7,000 a year.

But the expansion of the traditional intelligence agencies, the ones that rely on people to gather their information – HUMINT (human intelligence) in the bureaucratic jargon – was almost insignificant when compared with that enjoyed by the new intelligence growth sector, SIGINT (signals intelligence), with all its associated high-technology equipment: satellites, listening posts and computers. The expansion here, led by America's National Security Agency (NSA), has been enormous. NSA, with its main partner, Britain's GCHQ, now monitors the entire globe, helped by similar but smaller agencies in Canada, Australia, New Zealand and some NATO countries.

NSA/GCHQ monitors military, diplomatic and commercial messages sent by radio, telex, teletype and microwave. It eavesdrops on satellite communications and private telephone calls. It has lists of individuals and organizations whose communications are automatically intercepted. These include certain oil companies, banks, newspapers, commodity dealers, civil rights leaders, radical political groups, politicians, embassies, trade missions, terrorists and their sympathizers. NSA's computers, which cover eleven acres at the agency's headquarters at Fort Meade, Maryland, can be programmed to home in on a telex or cable-message by picking up a 'key' word that the intelligence consumer considers significant. The computers look for the key words at the rate of 4 million characters a second, which means that they can read the average daily newspaper before you could pronounce its title.

NSA/GCHQ picks up and transcribes the radio telephone conversations of Soviet officials driving in Moscow in their limousines, and listens to Soviet ships talking to each other in the Atlantic. It can monitor Soviet satellites calling from space, or record the report of a construction boss at a Siberian missile site telephoning Moscow long distance. In a rare public reference to NSA/GCHQ's ability to read global communications traffic, an NSA official said in 1980: 'There are three satellites over the Atlantic, each capable of transmitting on about 20,000 circuits. There are eight transatlantic cables with about 5,000 circuits. We listen to them all.'[16]

The scale of the NSA/GCHQ operation has only recently emerged, yet the collaboration between the two agencies and its purpose go back to 1947, when a secret treaty known as UKUSA linked the then senior partner, GCHQ, with the embryonic NSA. NSA has since become the undisputed boss but, with occasional hiccups, the relationship has remained as warm as that described by a director of GCHQ, while addressing his opposite number in the United States: 'Between us we have ensured that the blankets and sheets are more tightly tucked around the bed in which our two sets of people lie, and like you, I like it that way.'

Until the 1980s, NSA/GCHQ concentrated mainly on listening to people communicating with each other, but rapid technological changes soon had the agency talking of 'sweeping the entire electromagnetic spectrum' – that is, listening to *all* noises *and* looking at all images. Thus, NSA/GCHQ now monitors not only COMINT (people to people) but ELINT (electronic emissions of all types) which includes FISINT (Foreign Instrumentation Signals Intelligence) which comprises machines talking to their masters, or vice versa. And in the imagery area, NSA takes satellite pictures by ordinary means; image intensification photographs; infra-red pictures which show the targets by the heat they emit; and radar pictures, although not very good ones. It also does a lot of its surveillance from spy aircraft, like the EC 121 which carries a crew of thirty to service six tons of electronic equipment.

The enormously expensive machinery required for all this naturally needs a whole army of technicians to work it, and a bureaucracy of managers to run the technicians, oversee the budgets, and to make certain that the operation runs efficiently. But, in the nebulous world devoted to gathering other people's secrets and protecting one's own, the search for efficiency always leads to further expansion.

Jeffrey Richelson, who makes a professional study of the American intelligence community, has given a recent example of this. The National Reconnaissance Office (NRO) which operates all American photo satellites, needed to know in advance when possible areas of interest in the Soviet Union were clear of cloud. So the First Space Wing of the Air Force Space Command beefed up its Defence Meteorological Satellite Programme in order to provide NRO with the weather information it needed. But if the United States was efficiently photographing the Soviet Union, then it must be assumed that the Soviet Union was doing the same to the United States. So the First Space Wing's Space Defence Operations Center (SPADOC) undertook to monitor what the Soviet satellites were doing and to issue Satellite Reconnaissance Advance Notices (SATRANS) to American defence installations. These gave warning that a Soviet satellite would soon be overhead and if the recipients did not want their secrets photographed then they had better put them under wraps.

The waterways of the world enjoyed the same attention during this intelligence explosion as did the skies. If the air force could pinpoint the movements of Soviet satellites, then the US navy was not about to be left out. Fleet Ocean Surveillance Information Centers (FOSICS) were set up to correlate information from underwater sensors, ships, satellites and aircraft, to produce Contact Area Summary Position Reports (CASPERS) on all classes of shipping all around the world. And since ships are usually on the move, not always in the direction they had originally planned, FOSICS produces a Daily Estimate Position Locator (DEPLOC) on ships in harbour and at sea.[17]

As can easily be imagined, none of this came cheaply. At its imposing headquarters at the edge of Fort Meade, ringed by a double-chain fence topped by barbed wire with strands of electrified wire between them, NSA employs at least 20,000 people (and lines of shredders to handle the 40 tons of unwanted paper it produces each day). But abroad the agency has control of some 100,000 servicemen and civilians who are employed by the army, navy and air force.[18] It thus became difficult to know what the end cost of NSA actually was, and if there was a government figure, not only was it inevitably secret, but in all probability it was only an estimate. David Kahn, the author who specializes in signals intelligence and its history, puts the annual cost of NSA in 1976 at $1,500 million. Allowing a 10 per cent per annum increase since then for inflation and expansion, this would put the cost of NSA in the mid-1980s at more than $3,500 million.[19]

Much of what applied to NSA also went for GCHQ. Not only was its budget secret, but until 1983, when one of its employees, Geoffrey Prime, was charged with spying for the Russians, the government had refused to reveal what GCHQ's true role was – no doubt because its operations in peacetime were without a legal basis. Its secrecy had been maintained by massive and deliberately intimidating security. Newspapers were discouraged from mentioning it; a book by a former GCHQ employee, Jock Kane, was seized by Special Branch police officers in 1984; and a still photograph of GCHQ headquarters at Cheltenham, Gloucestershire, was banned by the Independent Broadcasting Authority in 1973, leaving a blank screen in the middle of a 'World in Action' programme.[20]

As with NSA, the size of GCHQ's staff at Cheltenham, about 6,500, gives no real indication of its strength. It has major monitoring stations in Cyprus, West Germany, West Berlin, Australia and Hong Kong, and smaller ones elsewhere. Like NSA, much of its overseas work is done for it by service personnel. This adds at least another 4,000 employees to its strength. So GCHQ's total budget runs to some £300 million a year, a large part of which is funded by the United States in return for the right to run NSA stations in Britain, where it has at least four major independent establishments (Chicksands, Bedfordshire; Edzell, Scotland; Menwith Hill, Harrogate; and Brawdy, Wales), and on British territory around the world.[21]

The collaboration between the two agencies offers many advantages. Not only has it made it easier to monitor the globe by dividing responsibility – GCHQ, for example, took Africa and Europe east of the Ural mountains – but it has solved what could have been tricky legal problems. If GCHQ eavesdrops on telephone calls made by American citizens and NSA monitors calls made by British citizens, each government can plausibly deny that it is tapping its own citizens' calls – as, indeed, they have. Yet the NSA station at Menwith Hill in Yorkshire intercepts all international telephone calls made from Britain, and GCHQ has a list of American citizens whose telephone conversations are of interest to NSA.[22]

In spite of the secrecy surrounding NSA/GCHQ – or perhaps because of it – SIGINT received a wonderful press. Most of the claims made for its efficiency and effectiveness have been accepted uncritically. It is said that nothing escapes NSA/GCHQ, that they can even read the number plates on Soviet cars in the KGB car park. 'Nothing militarily significant in the world escapes their attention', warned the *Indian Express*. 'We read not only the minds of the Argentines,' said former Labour minister Ted Rowlands, 'we also read their telegrams.' One British newspaper described the rise of NSA/GCHQ as 'Exit Smiley, enter IBM'.

When Caspar Weinberger became America's Defence Secretary in early 1981, he was given a briefing on the Soviet menace by John Hughes, an intelligence community photoanalyst. Hughes's standard briefing on the Red menace, classified at a level above top secret, lasts up to four hours and comprises hundreds of satellite and spy plane photographs of military installations and weapons in the Soviet Union. Those who have heard Hughes say that his graphic presentation of the Soviet military machine left them almost rigid with fear. Weinberger, for one, was absolutely convinced; he was soon telling friends that he believed that the Soviets, like the Nazis, were bent on world domination. [23]

Now while it is true that NSA/GCHQ probably has the technological competence to do the things it claims it can do, it seems worth examining whether it has been able to do this consistently, whether the intelligence it gathers has any value, whether it can provide it when its customers need it, and whether it is then capable of being interpreted so as to be useful and, finally, whether, as is claimed, it is free from the suspicion that blights a spy's reports – that he might be a double agent. Or does NSA/GCHQ conduct operations for operations' sake and is its first imperative to ensure its own continued existence?

The first myth that needs attention is that NSA/GCHQ has been carrying on the Allies' wartime successes in codebreaking. NSA/GCHQ has not been able to drag the encoded messages sent by the Soviets or the Chinese, or any other major power, out of the ether, crack their cyphers, translate the results, and have this intelligence on the right desks in time for great diplomatic or intelligence victories. In fact, neither the United States nor Britain has broken a major Soviet code since the 1940s for the simple reason that modern computers can generate random cyphers that other computers cannot, in practice, break. True, during the Strategic Arms Limitations Talks in 1972, NSA reported on the precise Soviet negotiating position. But this was due to a Soviet encyphering error and no doubt the Russians will take care that this does not happen again. So, at best, NSA/GCHQ has been able to break the 25 per cent of Soviet coded communications which consists of low-level stuff the Russians did not consider worth spending time and money to protect. Geoffrey Prime, the GCHQ Russian expert jailed for spying for the Soviet Union, ended his career as a section head of a group concerned with the analysis of the few Soviet signals GCHQ could break. Most of GCHQ Soviet bloc division staff were employed to listen to Soviet telephone conversations. The importance of these can be gauged by the complaint of an NSA technician, trained in Russian, who worked in a listening post in West Germany. He said that the amount of Russian conversation he overheard was so little that he began to lose his fluency in the language.[24]

In fact, in the codebreaking area, NSA/GCHQ's usefulness has been declining in direct relationship to the rapid development of computers and their manufacture. In the 1950s and 1960s and early 1970s, although the Soviet Union and China may have been closed areas, NSA/GCHQ could milk the Third World for useful information. But as computers became better and cheaper this source, too, began to dry up. David Kahn says:

> For the same amount of money as it spent five years ago, a nation can buy a cipher machine today with double the coding capacity. But doubling the coding capacity squares the number of trials the cryptanalyst has to make. Very quickly this work rises beyond practical limits . . . So the number of countries whose systems are still being able to be broken is constantly declining. The window, as it were, through which NSA, GCHQ and other code breaking agencies can look is constantly closing.[25]

But, in the secret world, as one window closes another can be made to open. NSA/GCHQ did not tell its consumers that, owing to a reduction in its capacity for codebreaking, it would be reducing its establishment and its budget. It simply said that it would substitute analysis of routes of communication and volume of communication for codebreaking as a means of obtaining information. This meant that many more people had to be employed in these areas. As Kahn says, 'They [had] to build up their empires and increase their manpower to get the same amount of information that they were able to get before with fewer people.'[26]

But was the information as accurate? Even with codebreaking there is always a possibility for deception. If your opponent learns, or suspects, that you are reading his messages he may decide to deceive you as to his real intentions by transmitting false information. The potential for deception in intelligence that is based upon analysing routes and volume of the enemy's communications is much greater – he does not have to create plausible messages, but simply increase their number and vary the source – and too heavy a reliance on these methods can lead to nasty intelligence failures.

The enemy also knows that any system for monitoring and processing information that works on the basis of the volume and route of signals traffic can be easily overloaded to the point where it will fail to function. So a potential attacker could deliberately spew out large amounts of information to overload the opposing system and thus create confusion and delay in decision-making.

Sometimes there are no signals, and thus no volume or route from which to draw conclusions. The Iranians successfully countered the billion dollar technology of NSA/GCHQ by sending important military communications with a man on a motorbike, *à la* First World War. Lyman Kirkpatrick comments: 'If the Soviets ever decided to go for broke, they wouldn't put anything on electronic communications or do anything visible by satellite. All the orders would go by officer couriers, which was what Hitler did at the Battle of the Bulge and caught us totally unprepared. We were relying too heavily on communications intelligence.'[27]

The technocrats of NSA/GCHQ scoff at the idea that anyone anywhere could successfully conceal or fake their intentions today. 'We monitor the entire electro-magnetic spectrum', one technocrat said at the US Air Force Academy symposium at Colorado Springs in June 1984. 'No-one is going to fake his entire electro-magnetic spectrum.' But there are instances which show that it is possible to fake certain key areas of that electro-magnetic spectrum in a manner which makes the deception practised on human intelligence agencies look like a kindergarten game.

For years NSA has been intercepting Soviet missile testing data. This has enabled it to offer its customers information on the range and accuracy of the Russian missiles and, on the basis of this information, a number of crucial decisions were taken in the late 1960s and early 1970s about the number, location and defence of American missiles. Yet it later turned out that the raw intelligence, the information gained by the relentless electronic monitoring of Soviet missile tests, was seriously flawed.

It was not until new and better methods for analysing this missile data became available in the mid-1970s that the reason for the flaws emerged: the Russians had faked their tests. They had systematically duped the American satellites and antennas. Knowing that the Americans were monitoring the tests, the Russians developed a way of double-crossing the American machines to make them report that the missiles were less accurate than they really were. At the same time, Soviet agents in the United States made such blatant attempts to acquire the American technology that could correct this inaccuracy that they came to the attention of the FBI. When the FBI reported this it seemed to confirm what NSA was learning from satellites and antennas. The Soviet deception was complete.

But, as we have seen, defeat can always be used in the intelligence world to justify expansion. What was needed to prevent this happening again, some sections of the intelligence community argued, was an 'all source counter-intelligence unit' which would keep an eye on technical spies, as well as human spies, for signs that they might have come under Soviet control. The supporters of the scheme argued that a Soviet deception involving the use of 'turned' satellites, faked electronic signals, KGB officers and false defectors could be perceived only by a counter-intelligence unit with access to all these sources and able to look for a master plan.

The scheme's opponents were, firstly, NSA officers who doubted that their monitoring procedures had ever been deceived in the first place. There were also those who, while accepting that the deception had taken place, considered that an 'all sources unit' would be both destructive of morale in the intelligence services and a target for anti-intelligence jokes on the lines of 'next they'll be looking for a Soviet mole among our satellites'. There were deep and intense divisions in the intelligence community, one sudden resignation – that of the deputy director of the CIA, Admiral Bobby Inman, who opposed the scheme – and the National Security Council took it no further.

Edward J. Epstein, the writer on intelligence who first exposed the split over the plan, says: 'While Congress and the informed public have been under the impression that satellites and electronic wizardry can be relied on for foolproof intelligence, the story of the misestimates of Soviet missile accuracy demonstrates that these "national technical means" are at least as susceptible to Soviet deception as less exotic means of intelligence gathering.'[28]

NSA/GCHQ would argue that the wealth of intelligence it produces every day more than compensates for the risk of an occasional deception. But there are other limitations to non-human intelligence. Satellites, as we have seen, can be prevented from taking ordinary photographs by the weather. So when American satellite photographs of the Soviet port of Nicolayev showed that the dockside was stacked with crates of a type normally used to house MIG fighter planes, there was considerable intelligence interest in what would happen to those crates. Would they be loaded into a ship moored nearby? And where was the ship headed? Unfortunately, cloud cover prevented photography which might have provided the answers. The next set of photographs showed that both the crates and the ship had gone. Then when the ship was photographed off the coast of Nicaragua, someone made an enormous leap in logic – Soviet MIGs were on their way to the Sandanistas.[29] When this proved wrong, the weakness of satellite intelligence was revealed. It is true that American satellites can take infra-red photographs, but when cloud cover is thick, as it often is in the northern hemisphere, these do not work. Even radar pictures through cloud are often too blurred to be of any use.[30]

Since the Soviets know that the Americans are photographing them, and vice versa, it is accepted that both sides do their best to conceal their secrets or to disguise them. No doubt the art of photoanalysis is now so advanced that no one in NSA/GCHQ could be fooled by what occurred in Moscow in 1962, but the story is worth recounting as an illustration of the *type* of tactic either side might use to try to deceive the camera in the sky (or on the ground). A Russian-speaking British diplomat decided, by way of a change, to *walk* to a Red Square parade.

> We wanted to assess the atmosphere in the back streets where the crowds were assembling, rather than in Red Square itself. In one remote back alley, we found a unit of rocket artillery, lounging by their parked trucks bristling with those sinister, silvery missiles. At a range of two feet, no more, we noticed that they were all wooden mock-ups, freshly-painted with aluminium paint. To make absolutely sure, since the soldiery did not seem to be worried, we turned back to examine at six inches range, and tap; not a shadow of a doubt.

When, next day, the diplomat told the British military attaché, who had no doubt been busy at the parade snapping away with a sub-miniature camera, he was dragged into the attaché's office for interrogation, shown dozens of photographs of missiles and asked to identify the ones he had seen. Subsequently, the military attaché reported to his chiefs in London that his colleague 'claimed to believe that the missiles were only wooden mock-ups'.[31] So not only can photoanalysis be misleading, but the analysts can scarcely be persuaded, even by eye-witness evidence, to modify the conclusions to which they have become wedded.*

There is also the problem of overload. American satellites and spy planes produce more photographs than anyone could ever look at, much less analyse. Communications intercepts, especially in times of crisis, pour in at such a rate that the analysts sometimes get to read the few important ones only when the crisis has already past. And

---

* This is not the only communist use of dummies on record. In 1986 East Germany began to use dummy guards in watch towers along the fortified frontier with West Germany.

the technology has become so esoteric that the number of intelligence officers who understand the overall picture, already limited through the 'need to know' principle, grows smaller each year. Harry Rositzke says that the American intelligence analyst in the 1980s faced 'an all-source glut: millions of words daily from foreign radio broadcasts, thousands of embassy and attaché reports, a stream of communication intercepts, cartons of photographs, miles of recorded electronic transmissions – and a handful of agent reports'.[32]

Sometimes the analyst is so overwhelmed by this *embarras de richesse* that when a little gold glimmers in mud he imagines he has struck a mother lode. An analysis of developments in world oil prices produced in 1974, largely from NSA/GCHQ intelligence, and distributed with the required international designations 'Codeword material, Top Secret, Top Secret Umbra', turned out to contain little that had not already appeared in the *Wall Street Journal* or the *Financial Times* and its conclusions could have been reached by any competent reporter. For example: 'Some OPEC members are trying to increase their production levels, oil is being discovered elsewhere, and alternative energy sources are being developed. We cannot, however, specify what reduced level of imports will break the cartel, or if and when this will happen.'[33]

The intelligence on the Argentinian invasion of the Falklands (Malvinas) in 1982 was voluminous. NSA/GCHQ was reading Argentinian military and diplomatic traffic, two American reconnaissance satellites were passing over the Argentinian coast once a day (the ports were free of cloud so there were photographs of the build-up of the invasion fleet), the American navy had spy satellites reporting on Argentinian electronic emissions, and an American air force spy plane, an SR 71 was making flights in the area.[34] Yet, as James Schlesinger commented, you cannot photograph an intention, and the best source for Argentinian intentions turned out to be *La Prensa*, the country's leading newspaper. On 24 January 1982 its front page proclaimed that 'it is believed that if the next Argentinian attempt to resolve the negotiations with London fails, Buenos Aires will take over the islands by force this year'.*

So what went wrong? The Falklands was a failure of interpretation. The JIC believed what it wanted to believe – that Argentina

---

* This is not to say that NSA/GCHQ were of no use when fighting started. GCHQ, in particular, had made a policy switch in the late 1970s that led to greater concentration on *tactical* intelligence, rather than strategic, and this proved of great value in the Falklands campaign.

was bluffing. Despite SIS station reports on the mood of Argentinian leaders, despite all the communications intelligence, despite summaries from the British embassy of sentiments like that expressed in *La Prensa*, the JIC decided that an invasion was neither imminent nor likely, and when the Argentinian marines waded ashore to occupy the Falklands, the British Cabinet slept soundly in their beds.

The failure of communications intelligence to measure up to the claims made for it have led some of its customers to investigate ways of improving it. The practice had been for agencies within the intelligence community to tell the United States Intelligence Board what information they needed. After board approval, the director of the CIA would ask NSA or one of the services to carry out the assignment. But this sometimes led to overlaps because one agency would be reluctant to share with another information it had asked NSA to provide.

In an effort to prevent this, the directors of the various intelligence services agreed on an *ad hoc* basis to rationalize their requirements. From this arrangement there grew, in the early 1980s, the practice of 'putting together an IC (intelligence community) package' for the NSA to carry out. This can mean allotting to satellites and antennas assignments as diverse as photographing Soviet planes for the American air force, listening to the chatter of private planes for the Drug Enforcement Agency, and eavesdropping on Latin American banks for the Treasury to learn if they will repay their loans.

This, in turn, had led, by the mid-1980s to 'vacuuming the entire electromagnetic spectrum' on the basis that there would be a customer somewhere for virtually anything which NSA collected. The problem became how to feed the intelligence to this customer. Some service customers began to complain that they were getting less usable information than before. This was one of the topics discussed at the US Air Force Academy conference in 1984 at Colorado Springs. The air force case was, basically, that its own intelligence service was becoming inferior because it was not always getting the information it expected from NSA. One of the air force officers gave an example. There was supposed to be sixty Soviet divisions on the Chinese border. The air force had asked NSA to find these divisions by imagery, without success. It then asked for radio traffic volume and analysis. NSA could not find it, or could not segregate it. The only indication that the Russians were there was the daily radio intercepts which gave the Soviet order of battle. But, of course, these could be easily faked.

The NSA case was that the information had been collected; it was a matter of finding it and feeding it to the consumer. Important intelligence – for example, if the Soviets started to heat up their missiles – would be quickly known and conveyed, but low-grade intelligence that nevertheless might be important to someone was difficult to isolate and distribute, unless the consumers were prepared to build a system compatible with NSA's. Edward J. Epstein, who was chairman of one of the panels at the conference, was struck by the attitude of the intelligence officers: 'They are not interested in espionage. They are not interested in the Soviet Union. They are not interested in communism. They are not Cold War warriors. They are systems analysts. They are technocrats. They are bureaucrats. They are good at putting together and working for a bureaucratically efficient organisation.'[35]

In a way it is somewhat heartening to know that these 'bureautechs', coldly applying their skills to the technical problems of eavesdropping on the world, have failed to replace the spy who, with all his faults, is motivated by warmer emotions. Communications intelligence actually needs the most old-fashioned of the spy's skills: theft and subversion. The United States may spend on SIGINT seven times what it spends on HUMINT, but a spy who can break into a foreign embassy and photograph its codebooks without being detected is worth three computers, and a spy who can subvert and recruit an opposition cypher clerk is worth ten.

No, it is not all over for James Bond yet. Bond and his employers in Washington, London, Moscow, or wherever are thriving in the 1980s. It may be apparent to observers that the intelligence explosion is already out of hand, but intelligence agencies and their officers are looking for ways of intensifying it. The new thrust is on the economic front. In a polycentric but economically interdependent world, intelligence about trade, commodity prices, tariffs, financial pacts, currency levels, oil prices, producers' cartels and government attitudes to them, has become as important – more important in many peoples' view – as military information. CIA covert action in a Third World country now carries a new risk of being counter-productive: to destabilize a country may threaten the international economic system, especially the already perilous balance of international debt, and eventually rebound on the United States.[36]

The interest in economic intelligence means that the targets of intelligence agencies have broadened. The Soviet Union remains uppermost in all Western agencies' priorities but hardly a country in the world, however small, escapes the attention of the spy. And, of course, the Western allies all spy on each other. There are no longer any friendly intelligence services, only the intelligence services of friendly countries. France, for example, has spied on Germany because she is concerned that the German 'Green' political movement might spread to France and make French nuclear testing an issue in its environmental campaign. She has also spied on Britain and the United States to monitor Greenpeace's anti-nuclear activities. And when French intelligence officers blew up the Greenpeace ship, the *Rainbow Warrior*, in New Zealand in 1985, the carefully planned operation included an attempt to plant the blame on Britain's SIS.

Germany spies, and is spied upon, to such an extent that swapping East German agents caught in West Germany with West German agents caught in East Germany has become an almost routine procedure, and an East German lawyer, Wolfgang Vogel, makes a very successful living out of organizing the exchanges. The CIA has estimated that there are no fewer than 30,000 East German agents in West Germany at any one time.

Israel not only spies on Arab countries* but also spies on targets in the United States, in spite of her special relationship with the CIA. Lyman Kirkpatrick says, 'The Israeli intelligence service is very active in the United States, perhaps not in the direct penetration area, but certainly in lobbying.'[37]

Despite all this evidence of duplicity, many intelligence buffs still found it difficult to accept that the United States would spy on Britain. Yet, in 1984, the CIA announced that it had identified 300 companies in the West, including some in Britain, that were illegally exporting high technology to Soviet-bloc countries. According to a British MP, the information about the British companies had been obtained by CIA operations, an allegation the then CIA director, William Casey, did not deny.[38]

SIS and GCHQ have spied on Britain's partners in the EEC, especially France, in order to find out their negotiating position in talks about trade and financial matters relating to the organizing of the community. 'It gives you a tremendous advantage in negotia-

---

* In intelligence circles Israel is considered the classic case where HUMINT (human intelligence, or the old-fashioned spy) is more important than communications intelligence. Israel needs knowledge of her enemy's *intent* and, it is said, the best way of getting this is by penetrating the opposition's intelligence service.

tions if you know the opposition's limit', a British EEC official said. 'But you have to use your intelligence carefully so as not to reveal to the other side that you've read his hand.' There were other problems that limited the usefulness of this intelligence. According to one civil servant, the Treasury usually insisted that it knew it all anyway and, as the SIS officers who brought the intelligence to the Treasury were often second-rate, it made it easy for Treasury officials, who resented this intrusion into what they regard as their patch, to dismiss it.

The KGB has become equally interested in economic matters. One student of Soviet espionage, Roger Hilsman, of Columbia University, claimed that if the Kremlin was forced to choose between subverting the national security adviser to the President or a subscription to the *New York Times*, it would take the *Times* because the Russians prefer a wide range of information to narrow, if high-level, stuff.[39] Harry Rositzke describes the typical KGB officer of the 1980s as a sophisticated economics or science graduate hard at work in New York and in the great cities of Europe, 'developing friendly contacts with persons of influence across the spectrum of private and public elites: politicians of the Centre and Right as well as the Left, labour leaders of all political complexions, key editors and journalists of all hues, and prominent members of the business and banking communities'.[40] Rositzke claims that the KGB is interested in people who can sway decisions on truck assembly plants, loan terms, or Siberian investment projects.*

The point about economic information is that, in the West, most of it is available from open and semi-overt sources so that the KGB is able to obtain 75–90 per cent of what it needs in a perfectly legal manner. KGB agents plough through newspapers, magazines, trade, technical and commercial papers. They read government publications and congressional reports and sit as observers at open sessions of government committees. They match up published material with agents' reports and send this as a package back to Moscow where it is distributed, largely without analysis or

---

* This is how the misconception of 'agents of influence' arises. Although these people might technically be called agents, and may appear on any list that a Soviet defector might bring to the West, they are not spies, may not have done anything to advance the Soviet interest any more than, say, a farmer who sells wheat to the Soviet Union, and may be greatly surprised that they have been considered worth a place on any KGB list. Rositzke says that thousands of influential New Yorkers and Washingtonians are considered 'agents of influence' by the Russians but that this does not mean that they have been disloyal to the United States. Newspaper stories of Soviet defectors arriving in the West with lists of hundreds of agents should, therefore, be treated with great scepticism.

comment, to the intelligence consumer for him to make his own decision on its value.[41]

But the time-honoured work of the spy still goes on, despite this new emphasis on economics and trade. In many ways, little has changed in thirty years. George Young, a former deputy director general of SIS, recalled that in the 1950s it was 'a matter of the utmost importance' that the West should discover the thickness and strength of the armour on Soviet tanks. 'The only way of finding that out was to find somebody on the other side of the Iron Curtain.' And there, in the 1980s, was the CIA still trying to find out exactly the same information. The CIA station in New Delhi suborned four Indian service officers and plied them with questions about Soviet arms supplied to the Indian army. Among the questions was: 'Can you bore a hole in the armour of a Russian T-72 tank if we supply you with special instruments?' (The Indians replied that this was too risky.)[42]

And the traditional work of intelligence agencies also continues. For the most part, this is not, as the public which paid for them might naïvely believe, the gathering of timely information useful to decision-makers, but the gathering of information about other intelligence agencies. What the CIA and SIS would most like to know is what the KGB is up to, and vice versa. As we have seen, this is why defections are such exciting events in the intelligence world and why agencies attach such importance to them. Defectors bring knowledge of the rival agency which enables the CIA, or SIS, or whoever to update their voluminous files about the rival's order of battle, the personal details of his officers, their postings and promotions, and the quirks and preferences which might, one day, make one of them a target in the defection game.

In between defections, intelligence officers spend a lot of their time in the 1980s, no matter where in the world they are posted, keeping an eye on officers from the opposition agency. Thus, in Iran, before students seized the American embassy in 1979, the CIA station spared no effort to track down every Russian in the country, find out whether he was KGB, and decide what he was doing. No private detail in the Russian's life was too mundane to note, sometimes inaccurately. When the station located a Soviet journalist, Levon Vartanyan, probably KGB, who had arrived in Tehran from Kabul, it asked CIA headquarters in Langley for any trace it had on him.

The Tehran CIA station request read: 'It is said Vartanyan's wife is or was a Kosygin mistress. The Vartamians [sic] apparently enjoy perks accruing to this kind of intimacy, dacha, etc. Seems likely Vartamian's [sic] colourful background may serve to identify him. Is he known to HQs?' Langley confirmed that Vartanyan was known to it, corrected the Tehran station's misspelling of the name, and put it straight about Mrs Vartanyan: 'His wife was secretary (not mistress) of Kosygin.'[43]

It has puzzled some observers of the intelligence world that most defectors seem to come from intelligence agencies themselves and not from other government departments. 'It is a strange commentary that members of these supposedly high security organisations should be most susceptible to subversion', wrote Herbert Scoville Jnr in *Foreign Affairs*.[44] The answer, although few intelligence officers would admit it, is that intelligence officers have often more in common with officers from a rival agency than they have with their own employers.

The former CIA officer, John Stockwell, has described how a CIA case officer on a foreign posting is always under bureaucratic pressure to show that he is active: 'If you don't recruit agents, if you don't generate operations, your fitness reports are at best bland and you don't get promoted. If you do all this, then you get a reputation for being an operator, as they call it, and nice things begin to happen to you and you get the good posts.' Exactly the same pressure is on the KGB case officer, so rival officers tend to develop some sympathy with each other's professional problems and often reach unspoken agreement on certain rules of the game. Stockwell said: 'It is a lot like professional football. You knock heads on Sunday then on Monday you're getting drunk together. I played with KGB officers at a couple of my posts and went to lunch with them. It's like a five-year-old's game, but deranged five-year-olds.'[45]

By the mid-1980s none of the major agencies played the game so that the players themselves got hurt. The KGB no longer killed CIA officers, and vice versa. But there were other casualties. Stockwell recalled: 'I had an agent I had recruited picked up and shot. No trial, just bang and he was dead. He left behind a wife and six children. When I reviewed his file there wasn't one report, not one report in five years that we hadn't gotten from some overt source somewhere. There was nothing he had done that had saved the world from anything.'[46]

No agency was innocent of the charge that it used and manipulated people, no matter what the cost. The tragic story of Jeremy Wolfenden is a graphic illustration of this. Wolfenden, son of Sir

John Wolfenden, director and principal librarian of the British Museum and a distinguished educationalist noted for his public service, went to Moscow in 1962 as the *Daily Telegraph* correspondent. Jeremy Wolfenden had learnt Russian as a National Service member of naval intelligence and the KGB probably knew this. In the event, the Russians crudely compromised Wolfenden, who was a homosexual. As he was going to bed with the Ministry of Foreign Trade's barber, a man jumped out of the wardrobe in Wolfenden's room at the Ukraine Hotel and took photographs of the two men. The KGB then blackmailed Wolfenden. It wanted him to pass on information about the Western community in Moscow. Wolfenden resisted, but he was worried that the KGB would tell the *Daily Telegraph* and that he would lose his job. Uncertain of how long he could hold out, he warned his colleagues not to confide in him and then, with some courage, he reported the incident to the British embassy. The embassy must have passed this on to London, because on his next visit home he was called to see an SIS officer who asked him to 'co-operate with the Russians', but report back to SIS whenever he was in London.

Well and truly hooked by both services, Wolfenden, always a heavy drinker, now had frequent bouts of alcoholism. (The other correspondents nicknamed him 'Green' because of his pallor.) He did 'co-operate' with the KGB. In 1964 he wrote a story for the *Daily Telegraph* saying that British firms which had been associated with Greville Wynne – the British spy in the Penkovsky case – were to be blacklisted by the Soviet Ministry of Foreign Trade. He later told colleagues that he had sent the story, knowing it to be untrue, because the Russians had made him do so. But he also 'co-operated' with SIS. Martin Page, a correspondent for the *Daily Express* who had been in Moscow during Wolfenden's time, was questioned by SIS about a Soviet diplomat, Yuri Vinogradov, who had precipitately left a post in the United Nations to return to Moscow. Page refused to answer questions about Vinogradov on the ground that what he knew about him could serve no counter-espionage purpose. When he later told Wolfenden about this, Wolfenden confessed that he had given Page's name to SIS as someone who had had close contact with Vinogradov in Moscow.

By now Wolfenden was making desperate efforts to break away from both intelligence services. He had married an English girl, Martina Brown, whom he had first met when she was working in Moscow as a nanny for Roderick Chisholm, visa officer at the British embassy. (Chisholm was later named in the Wynne–Penkovsky trial as the SIS contact man for the two spies.) Wolfenden renewed the friendship with Martina when on a short posting to Washington, but after their marriage, when he was due to return to Moscow, his British controller advised him not to take his wife with him. (A possible explanation for this advice will become apparent.) Wolfenden eventually solved the problem by arranging a permanent transfer to the *Daily Telegraph*'s Washington bureau and told a friend that he hoped that now he could forget about his intelligence experiences. But, at the Queen's birthday party at the British embassy in Washington in 1965, Wolfenden's SIS controller came up to him, greeted him warmly, introduced himself under a new name and began a close association with Wolfenden again.

Wolfenden began to deteriorate. His marriage was not going well. His bouts of drunkenness became more frequent. He ate hardly at all. On 28 December 1965 his death was announced. He was 31. It was said that he had fainted in the bathroom, cracked his head against the washbasin and suffered a cerebral haemorrhage. His wife returned to London for a while and then decided to live in the United States. One of Wolfenden's friends met her for a farewell drink and asked what she planned to do there: 'I don't know', she said. 'I can't go back to my old job. I'm getting a bit old for looking through keyholes. Anyway, I've lost all my Russian contacts.'

Whether Wolfenden knew the extent to which SIS had gone to involve him must remain speculation. But some of his friends believe that, whatever the physical causes of his death, the KGB and SIS between them had driven him into a state of such desperation that he had lost the will to live. They also doubt what real use he could have been, except as part of the intelligence agencies' game between themselves, because the weakness they exploited led him to tell each side all he knew about the other.[47]

Wolfenden's story is exceptionally tragic but there are many other instances of lives, careers and marriages ruined in the intelligence world. Greville Wynne, a simple patriot who believed he was helping his country in the Cold War, now cannot bear to live in Britain and says his espionage activities changed his life: 'When I came back [from a Soviet prison] I was rejected by my wife, my family, and my business associates . . . My first wife knew me as a businessman and never forgave me for keeping the other side of my life a secret from her . . . My relationship with my son, Andrew, ended with my marriage. I don't even know if I have grandchildren . . . My life was totally changed by what I became involved in.'[48]

Nikolai Khokhlov, a KGB officer on an assassination mission in West Germany in 1953 (his target was the leader of NTS, a Russian

The Second Oldest Profession

exile movement) had pangs of conscience and warned his victim. He then planned to return to Moscow and report that his mission had been a failure. But his victim told American military intelligence and it was decided to force Khokhlov into defecting. He recalled later: 'Without my knowing what was going on the Americans called a press conference and announced that I had defected. They publicly demanded that the Russians allow my wife and child to join me in the West . . . My family disappeared immediately. I never heard another word from them.'[49]

It is an interesting reflection on human character that these tragedies, and many others, were created by high-minded people, often of deep religious faith, who wanted to do good. There is, of course, an element of self-deception at work. Normal people develop, alter their views in the light of new information, change to new circumstances. An intelligence officer must remain absolutely fixed in the attitudes that made him decide on his career in the first place. The tiniest crack in his ideological motivation and he risks collapse.

He has strong support. Within the CIA and SIS there is no lack of high-minded discussion on the role of intelligence services in saving the world from communist aggression; and in the KGB no lack of emphasis on the officer's role as the sword and the shield in the fight against capitalist encirclement. But the officer will also pay a price. 'You can't spend your life bribing people, seducing people into committing treason, betraying their own movements, sometimes betraying their own families – and that's the nice-guy stuff – and come away a healthy, whole person whatever your rationales are', John Stockwell has said. 'You can't go through your entire career with a plausible denial to your own conscience.'[50]

Some officers try to convince themselves that there is a moral justification for their work. Donald Maclean said that spying was as necessary and as disagreeable as cleaning out lavatories. Others argue that in an imperfect world it is the duty of a nation to survive and that any means justifies that end. Michael J. Barrett of the CIA has suggested that spies of *both* sides may be morally correct in what they do, and that in protecting the interests of their respective countries *both* can be acting honourably.[51] Dick White, the former chief of SIS, has warned that spies can work only within the moral climate of the day, and that society will not for long tolerate its intelligence agencies going outside the moral climate. The Americans have also considered the dangers of excesses in the spy war. 'Finally there remains the ultimate moral and ethical question', says Roger Hilsman, of Columbia University, 'whether the means we use will eventually corrupt our values so as to change the nature of our society just as fundamentally as if we were conquered.'[52]

All the argument about the morality of espionage is superfluous if, in fact, spies are unnecessary. There is some case to be made for their use in wartime, although even here their record, as we have seen, is patchy. As David Kahn has pointed out, in only one of Creasy's *Fifteen Decisive Battles of the World: From Marathon to Waterloo* does the author ascribe victory to an intelligence coup, and the very many decisive battles fought since Creasy's book came out in 1851 yield few additional examples. But is there justification for expensive, virtually uncontrollable, intelligence agencies in peacetime?

We have seen how intelligence agencies have ensured that there is seldom failure in the secret world. Indeed, the agencies discourage discussion of success and failure, as such, arguing that in many situations it is impossible to distinguish one from the other. If there is intelligence of a surprise attack and the intended victim mobilizes in time, the aggressor, realizing that surprise has been lost, may cancel the operation. The successful prediction then appears to have been wrong.

Other rationalizations are common. 'We have had great successes but we cannot reveal them; we do, after all, inhabit the secret world.' And, 'We could have offered the vital intelligence if only we had not been starved of funds. The failure was, therefore, not one of intelligence but of government lack of foresight.' Or, 'We may appear to have been wrong, but the failure was one of analysis, not of collection. See, here in our files is the correct information.' The CIA is usually well prepared to offer this last excuse: since the Iranian débâcle it is now careful to arrange for a dissenting analysis which it can produce from its archives when its main analysis proves incorrect. And SIS has widened its recruiting to try to inject a 'nonestablishment' view into the service. In 1985 it recruited its first CND (Campaign for Nuclear Disarmament) member.

By removing themselves from the scrutiny which other governmental organizations undergo to ensure their efficiency, intelligence agencies have been able to proliferate unchecked for much of this century. Governments no longer know the real cost of their intelligence agencies, or how many people they employ. The agencies defy government control. George Young, a former deputy director general of SIS, has said that during his time in office some politicians did not know their job properly so, 'I was quite certain of my judgement to carry out the operations, and to tell them afterwards that's that'.[53] The CIA showed in Nicaragua that it was prepared to act first and inform its oversight committees later.

The KGB, originally formed as a small defence group to counteract foreign sabotage and subversion in the chaos following the Bolshevik Revolution, grew to be a major force in Soviet government, producing from its ranks leaders of the nation, including one head of government.

So far, all efforts to check this growth, to rationalize the structure and purpose of intelligence agencies, seem to have resulted only in their further proliferation. The US Defence Intelligence Agency (DIA) was created in 1961 to unify all American military intelligence and to prevent the three service intelligence agencies from duplicating each other's activities. Logically, this should have led to a reduction in the size of the three agencies, and at first it did. But the agencies regenerated themselves and in less than ten years they were larger than they had been before the DIA had been created.[54] The really explosive growth was in small countries which felt that they had to follow the major powers' lead. In six years, 1978–84, the budget for the Australian intelligence community increased by 270 per cent.[55]

How did they get away with it? The history of intelligence agencies has shown us that they justify their existence by promising to provide timely warning of a menace. In the Western world we have become so accustomed to this menace being the Soviet Union – and its intelligence arm, the KGB – that one wonders what the agencies did before the Red threat existed. The answer is: they invented one. We have seen how, before the First World War, William Le Queux, Erskine Childers and John Buchan acted out their fantasies in spy novels which used that most ancient of plots, the overcoming of the monster. But these pre-1914–18 spy writers projected their fantasies into the real world. Le Queux bore some direct responsibility for the creation of Britain's Secret Intelligence Service, from which all others flowed; Buchan became a recruiter of SIS spies. Both decided that the monster menacing Britain was Imperial Germany, a proposition enthusiastically supported by the intelligence services, who quickly realized that without a threat they were out of business.

When the monster was beheaded in 1918, SIS's future looked bleak. There was no need for the intrepid spy-hero in peacetime. Fortunately, an even more convincing monster was to hand. Imperial Germany had suffered from one major drawback for the part of out-and-out villain: it was a Christian country that bore too close a likeness to the hero to be portrayed as irremediably evil. But

Bolshevik Russia was, on its own admission, Godless, a murderer of princesses, and bent on world domination. Buchan quickly saw the trend. His *Huntingtower*, published in 1922, was the first anti-Bolshevik thriller; ever since, fictional KGB agents have continued to meet their match at the hands of Her Majesty's Secret Service or the CIA – except, that is, in Soviet fiction where it is the other way round.

Bolshevism proved a godsend to the intelligence agencies. It was here, there, and everywhere. It was as much a threat in peace as in war, and it was capable of corrupting the hero's own kith and kin. Therefore, it was not only necessary to discover the monster's secrets but to protect your own from the monster's disciples who could be, like the fifth man, always beside you. So intelligence agencies were able to insinuate themselves into politics, suggesting or inventing uses for their skills, until they were rewarded with constitutional acceptance, and became an institutionalized part of the government in virtually every modern nation. They have become a focus of power in our society, secret clubs for the élite and privileged, which demand – and are too often granted – the right to define reality for their fellow citizens.

Like the spies who work for them, these clubs have much in common. Each owes its survival to the existence of its fellows. What would the CIA and SIS do without a KGB, and vice versa? Each has helped create the state of tension in which all thrive. All feel threatened by détente. All have a direct interest in the continuation of the Cold War. 'The Russians are coming' is as potent a stimulus to intelligence power in the West in the mid-1980s as 'the Germans are coming' was in 1909. 'The capitalists surround us' gives power to the KGB in the 1980s, as it did to its forerunner, the Cheka, more than sixty years earlier.

In this can be found a possible explanation for the spate of spy stories – defectors, double agents, espionage coups, mole scares – which appear in the media the moment that there is a likelihood of a thaw in the Cold War. It is the intelligence agencies 'going public' in a way they would not contemplate at other times. All these stories are, in effect, controlled by the agencies themselves: if they did not provide the information, no one outside the secret world would know about it.

What I have looked for, as some evidence of this theory, has been a correlation between the number of published spy stories and the state of East–West relations. There were 2,258 stories about espionage in the *Washington Post* between 1977 and 1985.[56] A month-by-month breakdown of these stories shows a distinct increase in their frequency when international events indicated an *improving* climate of relations with the Soviet Union.

For example, there was a dramatic rise in the number of espionage stories as the Soviet Union and the United States moved towards the Geneva summit in November 1985. Obviously, it would be a mistake to place too much emphasis on an unscientific study like this. But we have seen in this book how intelligence agencies are skilled at using the media to advance their cause when an outbreak of peace has threatened either their funding, or, in the case of OSS in 1945, their very existence. It is only reasonable to assume that in times of approaching détente the intelligence and security services of both sides feel the need to justify their bureaucratic existence by drawing attention to the monster.

So in the mid-1980s we are faced with an intelligence community which has grown to a size and power which is unprecedented. It is so big and so expensive that we can only guess at its size and cost. But there is no doubt about its power. In the Soviet Union national leaders come from its ranks. In the United States its influence on presidential decisions is such that it is sometimes difficult to decide whether the President is running the CIA, or the CIA is running the President.

The intelligence community hates the government of the day, of whichever party. It juggles all our destinies in the name of protecting them. And it is able to do all this because of the secrecy with which it surrounds itself, a secrecy which corrodes a democratic society; it is no accident that as intelligence agencies have expanded, our civil liberties have contracted.

There might, just might, be some justification for the intelligence community if it did what it claimed to do: provide timely warnings of threats to national existence. But, as we have seen, this claim is exaggerated even in wartime and, in peacetime, intelligence agencies seem to have spent more time trying to score off each other, protecting their budgets and their establishments, and inventing new justifications for their existence, than in gathering intelligence.

Perhaps this is because – when not deep in their fantasy world – the intelligence community knows that open, published information, and that obtained through traditional diplomatic and other overt contacts, have proved this century by far the most useful source of military, political and economic intelligence for both sides. 'What role does [the spy] play?', said Harry Rositzke, once one himself. 'It's way down there.'[57]

# Source Notes

## Introduction

1 Thomas W. Braden, 'Kim Philby of Her Majesty's Secret Intelligence Service', *Washington Post*, 12 May 1968.

## Chapter 1

1 PRO, CAB/16/8/ERE 9077.
2 ibid., p. 3.
3 PRO, WO/32/8873/ERE 9077.
4 William Le Queux, *Things I Know about Kings, Celebrities and Crooks* (London: Evelyn Nash & Grayson, 1923), p. 242.
5 ibid., p. 251.
6 William Le Queux, *Spies of the Kaiser: Plotting the Downfall of England* (London: Hurst & Blackett, 1909), p. xi.
7 PRO, CAB/16/8/ERE 9077, Appendix I.
8 PRO, CAB/16/8/ERE 9077, p. 10. Further quotations in this chapter come from this document, unless otherwise stated.
9 PRO, CAB/16/8/ERE 9077, Secret Report and Proceedings.
10 Slade Papers III, microfilm MRF 39/3, National Maritime Museum, Greenwich.
11 Recounted by Nicholas P. Hiley, 'The Failure of British Espionage against Germany, 1907–1914', *Historical Journal*, vol. 26, no. 4 (1976), pp. 867–89.
12 *The Times*, 4 November 1911.
13 *The Times*, 29 October 1914.
14 Hiley, 'Failure of British Espionage', p. 887.
15 Walther Nicolai, *The German Secret Service* (London: Stanley Paul, 1924), pp. 52–3.
16 The statement was printed in *The Times*, 9 October 1914.
17 Hiley, 'Failure of British Espionage', p. 888.

## Chapter 2

1 Skardon in interview with author, 1967.
2 Nigel West, *MI6. British Secret Intelligence Service Operations 1909–1945* (London: Weidenfeld & Nicolson, 1983), p. 7.
3 Alley in interview with Page, Leitch and Knightley, 1967.
4 'The Profession of Intelligence', part 1, BBC Radio 4, 5 March 1980.
5 Nicolai, *German Secret Service*, p. 18.

6 PRO, WO/106/45/ERE 9077, p. 15.
7 Herbert von Bose, 'Verdun, Galizien, Somme, Isonzo . . . Oder Wo?', in Hans Henning Freiherr Grote (ed.), *Vorsicht! Feind hört mit!* (Berlin, Neufeld und Henius, 1930), pp. 73–4.
8 R. J. Jeffreys-Jones, *American Espionage* (New York: The Free Press, 1977), p. 49.
9 Fletcher Pratt, 'How Not to Run a Spy System', *Harper's*, September 1947, p. 243.
10 William R. Corson, *The Armies of Ignorance* (New York: The Dial Press, 1977), pp. 591–2.
11 See, for example, Henry Landau, *The Enemy Within* (New York: Putnam's, 1937).
12 Nicolai, *German Secret Service*, p. 109.
13 Corson, *Armies of Ignorance*, p. 65.
14 S. T. Felstead, *German Spies at Bay* (London: Hutchinson, 1920), p. 20.
15 PRO, WO/32/4898/ERE 9077.
16 ibid., Minute sheet 12D, 8 November 1920.
17 ibid., Minute sheet 13, 12 November 1920.
18 ibid., Petition from Greite in Parkhurst Prison, 12 September 1921.
19 Felstead, *German Spies*, p. 135.
20 W. H. H. Waters, *Secret and Confidential* (London: John Murray, 1926), p. 36.
21 Ulrich Trumpener, 'War Premeditated?', *Central European History*, vol. 9, no. 1 (March 1976), p. 67.
22 *Army Quarterly*, vol. 18, no. 2 (July 1929), p. 287.
23 See Maurice Paléologue, 'Un prélude à l'invasion de Belgique', *Revue des deux mondes*, vol. 11 (October 1932).
24 Nicolai, *German Secret Service*, p. 186.
25 See Patrick Beesly, *Very Special Intelligence* (London: Sphere, 1978), pp. 21–6.
26 Sam Waagenaar, *The Murder of Mata Hari* (London: Barker, 1964), pp. 251–2.
27 ibid., p. 250.
28 Letter from Major von Roepell to Major General Gempp, 24 November 1941, in ND collection, Military Archives, Freiburg, West Germany.
29 *World's Pictorial News*, 25 April 1926, p. 3.
30 Nicolai, *German Secret Service*, pp. 287–8.
31 A. Swetschin, 'The Strategy', in Max Ronge (ed.), *Kriegs und Industrie Spionage* (Vienna: Amalthea, 1930), p. 86.

**Chapter 3**

1 'The Profession of Intelligence', part 1, BBC Radio 4, 5 March 1980.
2 House of Lords Record Office, Lloyd George MSS, F/9/2/16, 'Reduction of Estimates for Secret Services', 19 March 1920.
3 Kerby in interview with Page, Leitch and Knightley, 1967.
4 Lloyd George MSS, F/9/2/16, Churchill to Lloyd George, Bonar Law,

First Lord of the Admiralty, Lord Curzon, and Chancellor of the Exchequer, 19 March 1920.

5 Lloyd George MSS, F/9/2/16, 'Reduction of Estimates for Secret Services', p. 2 (vii).

6 'The Profession of Intelligence', part 2, BBC Radio 4, 12 March 1980.

7 Lloyd George MSS, F/33/2/3, Long to Lloyd George, 9 January 1919.

8 Sidney Reilly, *The Adventures of Sidney Reilly* (London: Elkin Mathews & Marrot, 1931), pp. 28, 44.

9 ibid., p. 43.

10 ibid. Mrs Reilly tells her story in the second half of Reilly's unfinished book.

11 ibid., p. 238.

12 Quoted by Lewis Chester, Stephen Fay and Hugo Young, *The Zinoviev Letter* (London: Heinemann, 1967), p. 194.

13 Christopher Andrew, 'The British Secret Service and Anglo-Soviet Relations in the 1920s', *Historical Journal*, vol. 20, no. 3 (1977), p. 705.

14 Maugham's spell in Russia is best told in R. J. Jeffrey-Jones, *American Espionage* (New York: The Free Press, 1977), ch. 7.

15 Paul Dukes, *The Story of ST-25* (London: Cassell, 1938), pp. 32–3.

16 ibid., p. 293.

17 R. H. Bruce Lockhart, *Memoirs of a British Agent* (New York: Putnam's, 1932), p. 288.

18 'Russian Agent Planted on Sir R. Bruce Lockhart', *The Times*, 14 March 1966.

19 The Cheka plot is explained in Richard K. Debo, 'Lockhart Plot or Dzerzhinski Plot?', *Journal of Modern History*, vol. 43, no. 3 (1971), pp. 413–39.

20 Kenneth Young, *The Diaries of Sir Robert Bruce Lockhart: Vol 1. 1915–1938* (London: Macmillan, 1973).

21 Respectively: Dukes in interview with Page, Leitch and Knightley, 1967; and George A. Hill, *The Dreaded Hour* (London: Cassell, 1936), p. 260.

22 Andrew, 'British Secret Service', pp. 690–1.

23 Lloyd George MSS, F/203/3/6, Folder 5, 'Memorandum on the Situation in Russia'.

24 Bruce Page, David Leitch and Phillip Knightley, *The Philby Conspiracy* (New York: Doubleday, 1968), p. 117.

25 Lockhart, *Memoirs*, p. 341.

26 Kim Philby, *My Silent War* (London: MacGibbon & Kee, 1968), p. xv.

## Chapter 4

1 Sir David Petrie, *Communism in India, 1924–1927* (Calcutta: Editions Indian, 1972), pp. 174–5.

2 Page, Leitch and Knightley, *Philby*, p. 118.

3 Cecil in interview with author, 1980.

4 Nicholson in interview with author, 1967.

5 There are many versions of the Ellis story. This one comes from an interview with one of Ellis's senior officers. The author will forward letters to him.

6 Gwynne Kean, letter to author, 4 March 1980.

7 Interview with Page, Leitch and Knightley, 1967.

8 'The Profession of Intelligence', part 2, BBC Radio 4, 12 March 1980.

9 Page, Leitch and Knightley, *Philby*, p. 10.

10 'The Profession of Intelligence', part 2.

11 Nicholson in interview with author, 1967.

12 ibid.

13 John Whitwell, *British Agent* (London: Kimber, 1966), pp. 70–1.

14 Christopher Andrew, 'How Baldwin's Secret Service Lost the Soviet Code', *Observer*, 13 August 1978.

15 Christopher Andrew, 'Governments and Secret Services: a Historical Perspective', *International Journal*, vol. 34, no. 2 (1979), p. 180.

16 F. H. Hinsley *et al.*, *British Intelligence in the Second World War* (London: HMSO, 1979), vol. 1, p. 56.

17 Morton in interview with Page, Leitch and Knightley, 1967. Morton said that his network controller was '*The Times* man in Rome'. *The Times* staff records list Coote as its correspondent there during the relevant period.

18 Walker in interview with Page, Leitch and Knightley, 1967.

19 Hinsley, *British Intelligence*, vol. 1, pp. 57–8.

20 ibid., p. 83.

21 Wesley K. Wark, 'British Intelligence on the German Air Force and Aircraft Industry, 1933–1939', *Historical Journal*, vol. 25, no. 3 (1982), p. 640.

22 Wark, 'British Intelligence', pp. 636–8. Christie's informant is identified as Ritter in C. Andrew and D. Dilks (eds), *The Missing Dimension* (London: Macmillan, 1984), p. 123.

23 Barton Whaley, 'Covert Rearmament in Germany 1919–1939: Deception and Misperception', *Journal of Strategic Studies*, part 5 (March 1982), pp. 3–39.

24 Hinsley, *British Intelligence*, vol. 1, pp. 49, 80.

25 ibid., pp. 46, 76–7.

## Chapter 5

1 Heinz Hohne, *Canaris* (London: Secker & Warburg, 1979), p. 161.

2 Gert Buchheit, *Der Deutsche Geheimdienst. Geschichte der militarischen Abwehr* (Munich: List, 1966), p. 175.

3 Nigel West, *MI5. British Security Service Operations 1909–1945* (London: The Bodley Head, 1981), pp. 92–104.

4 The de Rop–Winterbotham relationship is described by Winterbotham himself in *Secret and Personal* (London: Kimber, 1969).

5 Ladislas Farago, *The Game of the Foxes* (London: Hodder & Stoughton, 1972), p. 86.

6 David Kahn, *Hitler's Spies* (New York: Macmillan, 1978), p. 63.
7 Farago, *Foxes*, p. 36.
8 Thomas H. Etzold, 'The (F)utility Factor: German Information Gathering in the United States, 1933–1941', *Military Affairs*, vol. 39, no. 2 (1975), p. 78.
9 ibid., p. 79.
10 ibid.
11 ibid.
12 ibid., p. 80.
13 Manfred Jonas, 'Prophet without Honour: Hans Heinrich Dieckhoff's Reports from Washington', *Mid-America*, vol. 47 (July 1965), pp. 222–33.
14 Page, Leitch and Knightley, *Philby*, p. 46.
15 ibid., p. 61.
16 Philby, *My Silent War*, p. xix.

## Chapter 6

1 R. J. Jeffreys-Jones, 'History on Trial: a Critique of the CIA and its Critics', p. 6. Paper delivered at the 9th Annual Meeting of the Society for Historians of American Foreign Relations, Catholic University of America, Washington DC, 4–6 August 1983.
2 Andrew, 'Governments and Secret Services', p. 181.
3 Farago, *Foxes*, dustjacket.
4 Corey Ford, *Donovan of OSS* (Boston, Mass.: Little, Brown, 1970), p. 112.
5 Oldfield in interview with author, 13 July 1979.
6 Malcolm Muggeridge, *Chronicles of Wasted Time. II: The Infernal Grove* (London: Collins, 1973), p. 149.
7 Hinsley, *British Intelligence*, vol. 1, p. 91.
8 Page, Leitch and Knightley, *Philby*, p. 121.
9 'The Profession of Intelligence', part 2, BBC Radio 4, 12 March 1980.
10 West, *MI6*, p. 109.
11 De Courcey in letter to author, 16 May 1981.
12 West, *MI6*, p. 137.
13 Interview with Peter Gilman, 23 March 1978, unpublished.
14 PRO, CAB/66/9/WP(40)244, 4 July 1940, 'Imminence of a German Invasion of Great Britain'.
15 JIC(40)376, 12 November 1940, quoted in Hinsley, *British Intelligence*, vol. 1, p. 295.
16 Private letter to author, 7 September 1967.
17 West, *MI6*, p. 109.
18 Philby, *My Silent War*, p. 4.
19 Hinsley, *British Intelligence*, vol. 1, p. 278.
20 Michael Elliot-Bateman (ed.), *The Fourth Dimension of Warfare, Vol. 1. Intelligence/Subversion/Resistance* (Manchester: Manchester University Press, 1970), p. 53.

21  David Stafford, *Britain and European Resistance, 1940–1945* (London: Macmillan, 1980), p. 209.
22  Kerby in interview with Page, Leitch and Knightley, 1967.
23  M. R. D. Foot, 'Was SOE any Good?', in W. Laquer (ed.), *The Second World War* (London and Beverley Hills, Calif.: Sage 1982), p. 251.
24  See Werner Rings, *Life with the Enemy: Collaboration and Resistance in Hitler's Europe 1939–1945* (London: Weidenfeld & Nicolson, 1982) for examples.
25  David Stafford, 'The Detonator Concept: British Strategy, SOE and European Resistance after the Fall of France', *Journal of Contemporary History*, vol. 10 (1975), pp. 215 and 196 respectively.
26  See, for example, R. Crossman and K. Martin, *100,000,000 Allies If We Choose*, pamphlet, July 1940.
27  Foot, 'Was SOE any Good?', p. 247.
28  Anthony Verrier, *Through the Looking Glass* (London: Cape, 1983), p. 37.
29  Bradley F. Smith, *The Shadow Warriors: O.S.S. and the Origins of the C.I.A.* (London and New York: Deutsch and Basic Books, 1983), p. 85.
30  Milovan Djilas quoted in Stafford's book *Britain and European Resistance*, p. 210.
31  Richard Usborne, quoted in Mark Wheeler, 'The SOE Phenomenon', in Laquer, *Second World War*, p. 195.
32  Foot, 'Was SOE any Good?', p. 243.
33  PRO, 32/10611/MA/08233, Home Defence Security Executive, 20 March 1941.
34  Respectively: interview with Page, Leitch and Knightley, 1967; and quoted in Verrier, *Looking Glass*, p. 350.
35  The Stockholm International Peace Research Institute has investigated the German story without any conclusive result.
36  Jean Overton Fuller, *The German Penetration of SOE* (London: Kimber, 1975), pp. 175–6.
37  William Stevenson, *A Man Called Intrepid: the Secret War 1939–1945* (London: Macmillan, 1976), p. 457.
38  Foot, 'Was SOE any Good?', pp. 248–9.
39  Louis de Jong, 'The "Great Game" of Secret Agents', *Encounter*, January 1980, pp. 12–21; and West, *MI6*, p. 180.
40  Stafford, *Britain and European Resistance*, p. 137.
41  ibid., p. 142.
42  Bickham Sweet-Escott, *Baker Street Irregular* (London: Methuen, 1965), p. 75.
43  Basil Davidson, 'Scenes from the Anti-Nazi War', *New Statesman*, 4 July 1980, p. 11.
44  Private letter to Peter Calvocoressi.
45  Stafford, *Britain and European Resistance*, p. 180.
46  Verrier, *Looking Glass*, p. 24.

**Chapter 7**

1 There are many versions of these events. The best is to be found in Callum A. MacDonald, 'The Venlo Affair', *European Studies Review*, vol. 8, no. 4 (October 1978), pp. 443–64.

2 David Astor, 'Why the Revolt against Hitler was Ignored', *Encounter*, June 1969, p. 7.

3 Telegram from D. G. Osborne (The Vatican) to London, 1 December 1939, in 'Papst Pius XII, die britische Regierung und die deutsche Opposition in Winter 1939/40', *Vierteljahreshefte für Zeitgeschichte*, vol. 22, no. 3 (1974).

4 Astor, 'Revolt against Hitler', p. 8.

5 MacDonald, 'Venlo Affair', p. 445.

6 West, *MI6*, p. 71.

7 MacDonald, 'Venlo Affair', p. 448.

8 Christie Papers, CHRS 1/27–8, Churchill College, Cambridge.

9 W. Schellenberg, *The Schellenberg Memoirs* (London: Deutsch, 1956), p. 106.

10 S. Payne Best, *The Venlo Incident* (London: Hutchinson, 1950), p. 7.

11 MacDonald, 'Venlo Affair', p. 459.

12 PRO, FO/371/C/7324/89/15, Churchill directive, 28 June 1940.

13 C. Simpson and P. Knightley, 'The Secret List of Rudolph Hess', *Sunday Times*, 7 November 1982.

14 Churchill's secretary, Sir John Colville, in interview with Colin Simpson and author, November 1982.

15 Hinsley, *British Intelligence*, vol. 1, p. 100.

16 West, *MI6*, p. 112.

17 ibid., pp. 186–7.

18 ibid., p. 110.

19 ibid., pp. 152–3.

20 Hinsley, *British Intelligence*, vol. 1, p. 367.

21 West, *MI6*, pp. 84, 225.

22 ibid., p. 44.

23 ibid., pp. 50–2, 74.

24 Louis de Jong, 'Britain and Dutch Resistance, 1940–1945', p. 21. Notities voor het Geschied werk, no. 109 (undated), Netherlands State Institute for War Documentation.

25 See Hans L. Trefousse, 'The Failure of German Intelligence in the United States, 1939–1945', *Mississippi Valley Historical Review*, vol. 42, no. 1 (June 1955).

26 Joint Weekly Intelligence Summary, British Troops, Austria. Liddell Hart Collection, 9/24/229, University of London, King's College Centre for Military Archives.

27 West, *MI6*, pp. 173, 184.

28 ibid., pp. 200–1.

29 Trefousse, 'Failure of German Intelligence', p. 100.

30 'The Profession of Intelligence', part 2, BBC Radio 4, 12 March 1980.

31  The correspondence between Liddell and Johnson, and Johnson and the State Department is in the National Archives, Washington under: US Embassy, London, 1940–1941, RG 84, Box 4/820/02/C/1940.

32  Farago, *Foxes*, pp. 472–3.

33  *The Times*, 6 September 1944.

34  Corson, *Armies of Ignorance*, pp. 30–1.

35  David Mure, *Master of Deception: Tangled Webs in London and the Middle East* (London: Kimber, 1980), p. 190.

36  Hinsley, *British Intelligence*, vol. 1, p. 58.

37  Mure, *Master of Deception*, p. 165.

38  ibid., p. 37.

39  Letter from Philby to author, 27 March 1978.

40  Dusko Popov, *Spy/Counter Spy* (London: Panther, 1976), p. 223.

41  'German Naval Intelligence, Part B: Naval Intelligence and the Normandy Invasion', 15 October 1946, p. 44, US National Archives, Washington DC.

42  See Gert·Buchheit, *Spionage in zwei Weltkriegen* (Landshut: Politisches Archiv, 1975), p. 326; and O. Reile, 'Wer täuschte die deutsche militärische Führung über die Stärke der in England für die Invasion bereitgestellten Streitkräfte?' *Wehrwissenschaftliche Rundschau*, no. 3 (1979), p. 83.

43  Buchheit, *Spionage*, p. 326.

44  'German Naval Intelligence', cit. at n. 41, p. 68.

45  Reile, 'Wer täuschte', p. 83.

46  Mure, *Master of Deception*, p. 176.

47  Hinsley, *British Intelligence*, vol. 1, pp. 137, 187.

## Chapter 8

 1  Respectively: Ronald Lewin 'A Signal-Intelligence War', in Laquer, *Second World War*, p. 185; and Roger J. Spiller, 'Assessing Ultra', *Military Review*, vol. 59, no. 8 (August 1979), p. 14.

 2  Harold Deutsch, 'The Influence of Ultra on World War II', *Parameters: Journal of the U.S. Army War College*, vol. 8 (December 1978), p. 6.

 3  David Kahn, 'The International Conference on Ultra', *Military Affairs* vol. 43, no. 2 (April 1979), p. 98.

 4  Peter Calvocoressi, *Top Secret Ultra* (London: Hutchinson, 1979), p. 36.

 5  Ralph Bennett, *Ultra in the West* (London: Hutchinson, 1979), p. 36.

 6  Agawa Hiroyuki, *The Reluctant Admiral* (Tokyo: Kadansha International, 1979), p. 347.

 7  'The Profession of Intelligence', part 2, BBC Radio 4, 12 March 1980.

 8  'The Profession of Intelligence', part 3, BBC Radio 4, 27 January 1982.

 9  Spiller, 'Assessing Ultra', p. 19.

10  D. Horner, 'Special Intelligence in the South-West Pacific Area in World War II', *Australian Outlook*, vol. 32, no. 3 (1978), p. 316.

11  Spiller, 'Assessing Ultra', p. 22; and Ralph Bennett, 'Ultra and Some

Command Decisions', in Laquer, *Second World War*, pp. 223–4.

12 Stephen E. Ambrose, 'Eisenhower and the Intelligence Community in World War II', *Journal of Contemporary History*, vol. 16 (1981), p. 158.

13 'Der Einfkuss alliierten Funkaufklärung auf den Verlauf des Zweiten Weltkrieges', *Vierteljahreshefte für Zeitgeschichte*, vol. 27, no. 3 (1979), pp. 362–3.

14 Ambrose, 'Eisenhower', pp. 158–9.

15 Calvocoressi, *Top Secret Ultra*, p. 108.

16 'Interim', *British Army of the Rhine Intelligence Review*, no. 19 (4 March 1946), in the Liddell Hart Papers under German Intelligence in the West, 1944–1945, File on Col M. University of London, King's College Centre for Military Archives.

17 Gunther Blumentritt, 14 August 1942, Liddell Hart Papers, 9/24/229, Intelligence.

18 J. Rohwer, and E. Jäckel (eds), *Die Funkaufklärung und ihre Rolle im Zweiten Weltkrieg* (Stuttgart: Motorbuch, 1979), p. 111.

19 Spiller, 'Assessing Ultra', p. 18.

20 Andrew Hodges, *Alan Turing: the Enigma of Intelligence* (London: Unwin Paperbacks, 1985), p. 244.

21 Aileen Clayton, *The Enemy Is Listening* (London: Hutchinson, 1980), pp. 79–85.

22 Philby, *My Silent War*, p. 38.

23 Hinsley, *British Intelligence*, vol. 1, p. 178.

24 Calvocoressi, *Top Secret Ultra*, p. 58.

25 Bennett, 'Ultra and some Command Decisions', p. 232.

26 Peter Calvocoressi, 'Ne Plus Ultra World War', *The Times*, 3 May 1984.

27 Bennett, 'Ultra and some Command Decisions', p. 231.

28 Spiller, 'Assessing Ultra', p. 20.

29 Kahn 'International Conference on Ultra', p. 98.

30 James Rusbridger, 'Secrets of Enigma', *The Times*, 17 May 1985.

31 F. D. Shirreff, 'Some Experience with Special Signals', *Mercury. The Magazine of the Royal Signals Amateur Radio Society* (1981–2).

32 David Kahn, 'Codebreaking in World Wars I and II', *Historical Journal*, vol. 23, no. 3 (1980), p. 624.

33 Hodges, *Alan Turing*, p. 261.

34 Calvocoressi, *Top Secret Ultra*, p. 85.

35 Kahn, 'Codebreaking', p. 624.

36 His obituary in *The Times*, 31 August 1971.

37 See James Rusbridger, 'The Sinking of the *Automedon*, the Capture of the *Nankin*', *Encounter*, May 1985.

38 Calvocoressi, *Top Secret Ultra*, p. 94.

39 Respectively: Nicholson in interview with author, 1967; Thomas O'Toole, 'World War II – Some Additional Postscripts Come to Light', *International Herald Tribune* (Paris), 14 September 1978; and interview with Page, Leitch and Knightley, 1967.

40 Waldemar Werther, as reported in Rohwer and Jäckel, *Funkaufklärung*, p. 65.

41 'The Profession of Intelligence', part 3, BBC Radio 4, 27 January 1982.

## Chapter 9

1 John Erickson, *The Road to Stalingrad* (London: Weidenfeld & Nicolson, 1975), p. 89.

2 ibid.

3 See M. Toscano, *Designs in Diplomacy* (Baltimore, Md: Johns Hopkins Press, 1970), pp. 406–10.

4 Skardon in interview with Leitch, 1980.

5 Robert Cecil, 'The Cambridge Comintern', in C. Andrew and D. Dilks (eds), *The Missing Dimension* (London: Macmillan, 1984), p. 181.

6 Cecil, 'Cambridge Comintern', p. 181.

7 Gordon Brook-Shepherd, *The Storm Petrels* (London: Collins, 1977), pp. 172–5.

8 Cecil, 'Cambridge Comintern', pp. 181–2.

9 Geoffrey McDermott in interview with Page, Leitch and Knightley, 1967.

10 Letter from Liddell of MI5 to Johnson of American Embassy, 26 December 1940, US National Archives, Washington DC.

11 Private letter to Page, Leitch and Knightley, 3 August 1967.

12 Bruce Page, 'The Endless Quest for Supermole', *New Statesman*, 21 September 1979, p. 414.

13 M. Sayle, 'Conversations with Philby', *Sunday Times*, 17 December 1967.

14 Page, Leitch and Knightley, *Philby*, p. 51.

15 Philby, *My Silent War*, p. xviii.

16 Letter to Harold Nicholson, undated.

17 Nigel Wade, 'Soviet Press Praises Philby', *Sunday Telegraph*, 10 August 1980.

18 Sayle, 'Conversations with Philby', cit. at n.13.

19 Cecil, 'Cambridge Comintern', p. 19.

20 Toscano, *Designs in Diplomacy*, p. 409.

21 Letter from Philby to author, 18 February 1974.

22 Cecil, 'Cambridge Comintern', p. 175.

23 See Chalmers Johnson, *An Instance of Treason* (Tokyo: Charles E. Tuttle, 1977).

24 C. Johnson, *Treason*, p. 154.

25 ibid., p. 154.

26 Erickson, *Road to Stalingrad*, p. 239.

27 Heinrich Haape, quoted in Desmond Flower and James Reeves (eds), *The War 1939–1945*, vol. 1 (London: Panther, 1967), p. 339.

28 C. Johnson, *Treason*, p. 18.

29 ibid., p. 159.

30 ibid., p. 172.

31 Reported by the Associated Press in the *Japan Times*, 17 March 1975.
32 Erickson, *Road to Stalingrad*, p. 54.
33 Hinsley, *British Intelligence*, vol. 1, pp. 435–6.
34 Erickson, *Road to Stalingrad*, p. 58.
35 Hinsley, *British Intelligence*, vol. 1, pp. 443–4.
36 Erickson, *Road to Stalingrad*, p. 75.
37 Hinsley, *British Intelligence*, vol. 1, pp. 480–2.
38 Philby, *My Silent War*, pp. 44–5.
39 Bentley in interview with Page, Leitch and Knightley, 1967.
40 Philby, *My Silent War*, p. 61.
41 Evidence of Petrov to the Australian Royal Commission, 1955, quoted in Andrew Boyle, *The Climate of Treason* (London: Hutchinson, 1979), p. 216.
42 Alexander Foote, *Handbook for Spies* (London: Museum Press, 1949), p. 81.
43 See, for example: Anthony Read and David Fisher *Operation Lucy* (London: Hodder & Stoughton, 1980); Chapman Pincher, *Their Trade Is Treachery* (London: Sidgwick & Jackson, 1981); Richard Deacon, *A History of the British Secret Service* (New York: Taplinger, 1970); and Constantine Fitzgibbon, *Secret Intelligence in the 20th Century* (London: Granada, 1978).
44 Letter from Hinsley to author, 25 April 1984.
45 Hinsley, *British Intelligence*, vol. 2, pp. 69–70.
46 Respectively: Deacon, *British Secret Service*, p. 366; Read and Fisher, *Operation Lucy*, dustjacket; and Foote, *Handbook for Spies*, p. 82.
47 Hinsley, *British Intelligence*, vol. 2, p. 60.
48 See Ruth Werner (pseudonym for Kuczynski), *Sonjas Rapport* (East Berlin: Verlag Neues Leben, 1977); and A. Terry, 'The Housewife who Spied for Russia', *Sunday Times*, 27 January 1980.
49 Cable, Foreign Office to Ambassador, Algiers, 6 April 1944, Eden Papers, SOE/44/17/192, Birmingham University.
50 Cecil, 'Cambridge Comintern', p. 179.
51 Kuczynski in interview with Anthony Terry, for author, 17 January 1980.
52 ibid.
53 Oldfield in interview with author, 13 July 1979.
54 Hinsley, *British Intelligence*, vol. 1, p. 441.

## Chapter 10

1 R. J. Jeffreys-Jones, *Eagle against Empire. United States Opposition to European Imperialism 1898–1981* (Aix-en-Provence: European Association for American Studies, 1983), p. 61.
2 Jeffrey M. Dorwart, 'The Roosevelt–Astor Espionage Ring', *New York History* (July 1981), p. 309.
3 ibid., p. 317.
4 ibid.

5 B. Smith, *Shadow Warriors*, p. 63; and Dorwart 'Roosevelt–Astor Espionage', p. 321.

6 R. J. Jeffreys-Jones, 'History on Trial: a Critique of the CIA and its Critics', p. 3. Paper delivered at the 9th Annual Meeting of the Society for Historians of American Foreign Relations, Catholic University of America, Washington DC, 4–6 August 1983.

7 *New York Times*, 1 December 1938.

8 West, *MI6*, pp. 202–3.

9 Corson, *Armies of Ignorance*, p. 114; and Anthony Cave Brown, *The Last Hero: Wild Bill Donovan* (New York: Times Books, 1982), p. 153.

10 Phillip Knightley, *The First Casualty* (New York: Harcourt Brace Jovanovich, 1975), p. 237.

11 West, *MI6*, p. 204.

12 Cave Brown, *Last Hero*, p. 156.

13 ibid., p. 168.

14 ibid., p. 169; and B. Smith, *Shadow Warriors*, pp. 68–9.

15 Cave Brown, *Last Hero*, p. 170.

16 B. Smith, *Shadow Warriors*, p. 21.

17 ibid., pp. 38–9.

18 Peter and Leni Gillman, *Collar the Lot!* (London: Quartet, 1980), p. 85.

19 ibid., p. 108.

20 ibid., p. 77.

21 B. Smith, *Shadow Warriors*, p. 22.

22 Professor Margaret Gowing, British Atomic Energy Authority official historian, interview with author, 1984.

23 B. Smith, *Shadow Warriors*, pp. 100–5.

24 Cave Brown, *Last Hero*, p. 182.

25 B. Smith, *Shadow Warriors*, p. 104.

26 Cave Brown, *Last Hero*, pp. 226, 233–4; and B. Smith, *Shadow Warriors*, p. 117.

27 Cave Brown, *Last Hero*, pp. 306–7.

28 See Timothy P. Mulligan, 'According to Colonel Donovan: a Document from the Records of German Military Intelligence', *The Historian*, November 1983, pp. 78–86.

29 Cave Brown, *Last Hero*, pp. 306–8.

30 ibid., pp. 315–16.

31 Cave Brown, *Last Hero*, p. 593.

32 Weitz in interview with author, 14 September 1984.

33 Kirkpatrick in interview with David Leitch, on behalf of author, 1979.

34 R. Harris Smith, *OSS* (Los Angeles, Calif.: University of California Press, 1972), p. 185.

35 ibid. p. 9.

36 Edmond Taylor, *Awakening from History* (Boston, Mass.: Gambit, 1969), pp. 350–1.

37 Lyman Kirkpatrick, *The Real CIA* (New York: Macmillan, 1968), p. 24.

38 Malcolm Muggeridge, 'Book Review of a Very Limited Edition', *Esquire*, May 1966, p. 84.

39 Hinsley, *British Intelligence*, vol. 2, p. 53.

40 Stafford, *Britain and European Resistance*, p. 90.

41 Edmond Taylor, *Richer by Asia* (Boston, Mass.: Houghton Mifflin, 1947), pp. 225–7.

42 Sweet-Escott, *Baker Street Irregular*, p. 252.

43 Respectively: interview with Leitch, September 1979; and R. Smith, *OSS*, p. 34.

44 Taylor, *Richer by Asia*, p. 233.

45 R. Smith, *OSS*, pp. 289–90.

46 Respectively: R. Smith, *OSS*, p. 286; Cave Brown, *Last Hero*, p. 625; ibid., p. 644; and Kerby in interview with Page, Leitch and Knightley, 1967.

47 Cave Brown, *Last Hero*, p. 609.

48 R. Smith, *OSS*, p. 27.

49 Letter from Philby to author, 1978.

50 Respectively: Michael Howard, 'The Black Record of the Anglo-Saxons', *Sunday Times*, 26 January 1978; and R. Smith, *OSS*, p. 354.

51 Cave Brown, *Last Hero*, pp. 645–8.

52 B. Smith, *Shadow Warriors*, pp. 339–48; and Cave Brown, *Last Hero*, pp. 423–6.

53 Respectively: Whitwell, *British Agent*, pp. 202–7; and R. Smith, *OSS*, p. 229.

54 Weitz in interview with author, 14 September 1984.

55 Corson, *Armies of Ignorance*, pp. 87–8.

56 Cave Brown, *Last Hero*, pp. 641–2.

57 Cave Brown (ed.), *The Secret War Report of the OSS* (New York: Berkley Medallion, 1976), p. 7.

58 B. Smith, *Shadow Warriors*, p. 410.

59 Thomas Inglis, Chief of Naval Intelligence, testifying before Congress. National Security Act Hearing, 27 June 1947 (Washington DC: US Government Printing Office, 1982), p. 68.

60 Cave Brown, *Last Hero*, p. 757.

61 B. Smith, *Shadow Warriors*, pp. 381–2.

62 Larry Collins and Dominique Lapierre, *Is Paris Burning?* (New York: Simon & Schuster, 1965), p. 304.

## Chapter 11

1 National Security Act Hearing (Washington DC: US Government Printing Office, 1982), p. 41.

2 David C. Martin, *Wilderness of Mirrors* (New York: Ballantine, 1981), p. 39.

3 Respectively: National Security Act Hearing, pp. 38, 55; Pratt, 'How Not to Run a Spy System', p. 242; and Trevor Barnes, 'The Secret Cold War. The CIA and American Foreign Policy in Europe, 1946–1956, Part 1', *Historical Journal*, vol. 24, no. 2 (1981), pp. 400–4.

4  Harry Howe Ransom, 'Secret Intelligence in the United States, 1947–1982: the CIA's Search for Legitimacy', in Andrew and Dilks, *Missing Dimension*, p. 206.
5  National Security Act Hearing, p. 32.
6  ibid., p. 46.
7  ibid., p. 38.
8  ibid., p. 35.
9  Memo in the Leahy Papers, 25 February 1947, Box 20/132, US National Archives, Washington DC.
10  National Security Act Hearing, pp. 28–9.
11  ibid., pp. 22, 27, 29.
12  ibid., pp. vi, 1.
13  Respectively: Barnes, 'Secret Cold War. Part 2', p. 656; and Ransom, 'Secret Intelligence', p. 203.
14  Cave Brown, *Last Hero*, p. 785.
15  Barnes, 'Secret Cold War. Part 2', p. 651.
16  Barnes, 'Secret Cold War. Part 1', pp. 412–13.
17  Michael J. Barrett, 'Honorable Espionage', *Journal of Defence and Diplomacy* (February 1984), p. 14.
18  Barnes, 'Secret Cold War. Part 2', pp. 660, 663.
19  Enver Hoxha, *The Anglo-American Threat to Albania* (Tirana: 8 Nëntori, 1982), p. 430.
20  Barnes, 'Secret Cold War. Part 2', p. 664.
21  Harry Rositzke, *The CIA's Secret Operations* (New York: Reader's Digest Press, 1977), p. 188.
22  See David Atlee Phillips, *The Night Watch* (New York: Atheneum, 1977).
23  In a speech at Yale University, 3 February 1958, quoted in R. Hillsman, 'On Intelligence', *Armed Forces and Society*, vol. 8, no. 1 (Fall 1981), p. 136.
24  Kirkpatrick in interview with David Leitch, on behalf of author, 1979.
25  Letter from Philby to author, 27 March 1979.
26  'The Profession of Intelligence', part 3, BBC Radio 4, 27 January 1982.
27  R. W. Johnson, 'Making Things Happen', *London Review of Books*, 6–19 September 1984, p. 12.
28  Tad Szulc, 'When the Russians Rocked the World', *The Times*, 29 August 1984.
29  David Holloway, in letter to author, 2 August 1985.
30  *New York Times*, 7 May 1950.
31  Quoted in Robert Kimball, 'Criminals of the Century?', *Unsolved*, vol. 2, no. 21 (1984).
32  David Holloway, 'Entering the Nuclear Arms Race: the Soviet Decision to Build the Atomic Bomb, 1939–1945', *Social Studies of Science*, vol. 11 (1981), p. 169.
33  ibid., p. 175.
34  ibid., p. 179.

35  ibid., p. 183.
36  ibid., p. 186.
37  Holloway in letter to author, 2 August 1985.
38  Davidson in letter to author, 16 October 1967.
39  Fuchs's confession to Dr Michael W. Perrin, atomic scientist, British Ministry of Supply, quoted in letter from Hoover to Souers, 2 March 1950. Harry S. Truman Library, President's secretary's files.
40  Holloway, 'Entering the Nuclear Arms Race', p. 194.
41  Holloway in letter to author, 2 August 1985.
42  Fuchs's confession to Dr Perrin, cit. at n. 39.
43  B. Smith, *Shadow Warriors*, p. 389.
44  National Security Act Hearing, p. 29.
45  Margaret Gowing, 'Niels Bohr and Nuclear Weapons' (manuscript of chapter for Massachusetts Institute of Technology), p. 10.
46  Barnes, 'Secret Cold War. Part 2', p. 654.
47  H. A. DeWeerd, 'Strategic Surprise in the Korean War', *Orbis* (Fall 1962), pp. 439–40.
48  ibid., p. 438.
49  Louis Heren, 'Korea: the Blame that Rests on MacArthur', *The Times*, 3 January 1981.
50  DeWeerd, 'Strategic Surprise', p. 449.
51  Barnes, 'Secret Cold War. Part 2', p. 652.
52  ibid., p. 655.
53  'Should the U.S. Fight Secret Wars; a Forum', *Harper's*, September 1984, p. 44.
54  Ransom, 'Secret Intelligence', p. 209.
55  R. W. Johnson, 'Making Things Happen', p. 14.

## Chapter 12

1  Verrier, *Looking Glass*, p. 98.
2  P. Hennessy and G. Brownfeld, 'Britain's Cold War Security Purge: the Origins of Positive Vetting', *Historical Journal*, vol. 25, no. 4 (1982), pp. 971–2.
3  ibid., p. 973.
4  'The Profession of Intelligence', part 4, BBC Radio 4, 3 February 1982.
5  Cecil, 'Cambridge Comintern', p. 180; and Cecil in interview with author, 31 January 1984.
6  Page, Leitch and Knightley, *Philby*, p. 172.
7  Kirkpatrick in interview with author, 1967.
8  Robert Amory in interview with Page, Leitch and Knightley, 1967.
9  Retired SIS officer in interview with author, 26 June 1984.
10  Cecil, 'Cambridge Comintern', p. 186.
11  ibid., p. 188.
12  Philby, *My Silent War*, p. 129.
13  'The Profession of Intelligence', part 3, BBC Radio 4, 27 January 1982.
14  Cecil, 'Cambridge Comintern', p. 193.
15  Michael Straight, *After Long Silence* (London: Collins, 1983), p. 251.

16 Cecil, 'Cambridge Comintern', p. 195.

17 Page, Leitch and Knightley, *Philby*, p. 291.

18 Philby, *My Silent War*, p. 137.

19 29 September 1955, FBI Archives, Washington DC.

20 Letter from Fishman to *Sunday Times*, unpublished, 13 February 1977.

21 FBI Archives, Washington DC.

22 Rosamond Lehman in interview with Page, Leitch and Knightley, 1967.

23 Lord Egremont in interview with Page, Leitch and Knightley, 1967.

24 ibid.

25 FBI Archives, Washington DC.

26 Geoffrey McDermott, former Foreign Office adviser to the head of SIS, in interview with Page, Leitch and Knightley, 1967.

27 Respectively: 'The Profession of Intelligence', part 4, BBC Radio 4, 3 February 1982; and Wilbur Eveland, *Guardian*, 29 August 1980.

28 Unsigned article, *New Statesman*, 7 July 1978.

29 McDermott in interview with Page, Leitch and Knightley, 1967.

30 Lord Egremont in interview with Page, Leitch and Knightley, 1967.

31 Amory in interview with Page, Leitch and Knightley, 1967.

32 Verrier, *Looking Glass*, p. 158.

33 McDermott in interview with Page, Leitch and Knightley, 1967.

34 A. J. McIlroy 'Tried to Recruit Me to Be a Spy', *Daily Telegraph*, 9 December 1980.

35 The woman in interview with author, 4 December 1982.

36 Honoré Catudal, *Kennedy and the Berlin Wall Crisis* (Berlin: Berlin Verlag, 1980), p. 246.

37 Edward J. Epstein, 'The Spy War', *New York Times Magazine*, 28 September 1980.

38 Leo Abse, 'How to Recognise Tomorrow's Spy', *The Times*, 26 October 1981.

39 Respectively: John Vassall, *Vassall: the Autobiography of a Spy* (London: Sidgwick & Jackson, 1975), p. 158; and Christopher Dobson and Ronald Payne, *The Dictionary of Espionage* (London: Harrap, 1984), p. 16.

40 Respectively: Epstein, cit. at n. 37; and Sean Bourke, *The Springing of George Blake* (London: Cassell, 1970), p. 242.

41 Philby in interview with Sayle, 17 December 1967.

42 *Observer*, 30 October 1966.

43 Atticus, *Sunday Times*, 27 January 1982.

44 'Spy Blake's Jail-break Helper Dies', *Daily Mail*, 27 January 1982.

45 Amory in interview with Page, Leitch and Knightley, 1967.

46 Miles Copeland, *Real Spy World* (London: Sphere, 1978), p. 94.

## Chapter 13

1 Ralph W. McGehee, *Deadly Deceits* (New York: Sheridan Square, 1983), p. 119.

2 C. Sweeney, 'The Price of Freedom', *Sunday Times Magazine*, 1 December 1974.

3 'Has the KGB Fooled the West?', *Sunday Times*, 4 March 1984.

4 David C. Martin, *Wilderness of Mirrors* (New York: Ballantine, 1981), p. 109.

5 Edward J. Epstein, 'When the CIA Was almost Wrecked', *Parade Magazine*, 14 October 1984.

6 see Anatoliy Golitsyn, *New Lies for Old* (London: The Bodley Head, 1984).

7 Rositzke in interview with Cherry Hughes for author, 1984.

8 Stephen de Mowbray, former SIS officer in unpublished letter to *Sunday Times*; and Epstein, 'When the CIA Was almost Wrecked'.

9 Martin, *Wilderness of Mirrors*, pp. 148–9.

10 ibid., p. 192.

11 Rositzke in interview with Cherry Hughes, 1984.

12 De Mowbray in unpublished letter cit at n. 8 above.

13 Epstein, 'When the CIA Was almost Wrecked'.

14 R. W. Johnson, 'Making Things Happen', p. 14.

15 Kirkpatrick in interview with Leitch, 1979.

16 Epstein, 'When the CIA Was almost Wrecked'.

17 Kirkpatrick in interview with Leitch, 1979.

18 Joseph C. Goulden, *Korea: the Untold Story* (New York: Times Books, 1982), p. 245.

19 Angleton in undated statement first issued on publication of Martin's *Wilderness of Mirrors*.

20 Martin, *Wilderness of Mirrors*, pp. 155–77.

21 Henry J. Hurt, 'Is this American a Soviet Spy?', *Reader's Digest*, October 1981.

22 ibid.

23 Martin, *Wilderness of Mirrors*, p. 210.

24 'The Profession of Intelligence', part 5, BBC Radio 4, 10 February 1982.

25 Rositzke in interview with Cherry Hughes, 1984.

26 Fitzroy Maclean, *Take Nine Spies* (London: Weidenfeld & Nicolson, 1978), pp. 305–6.

27 ibid., p. 306.

28 Chapman Pincher, 'U.S. Intelligence Agents Find Shot Russian's Story Hidden in Drawer', *Daily Express*, 29 April 1965.

29 Catudal, *Berlin Wall*, pp. 242–3.

30 John le Carré, 'Wardrobe of Disguises', *Sunday Times*, 10 September 1967.

31 Verrier, *Looking Glass*, p. 197. See also Executive Sessions of the Senate Foreign Relations Committee (Historical Series), Vol. XII, testimony of Hugh L. Dryden of NSA, 1 June 1960.

32  Hillsman, 'On Intelligence', p. 142.
33  Corson, *Armies of Ignorance*, pp. 30–1.
34  ibid., pp. 26–9.
35  Kirkpatrick in interview with Leitch, 1979.
36  Corson, *Armies of Ignorance*, p. 30.
37  Verrier, *Looking Glass*, p. 206.
38  Lawrence Freedman, *U.S. Intelligence and the Soviet Strategic Threat* (London: Macmillan, 1979), p. 71.
39  Verrier, *Looking Glass*, pp. 210–11.
40  Kirkpatrick in interview with Leitch, September 1979.
41  Verrier, *Looking Glass*, pp. 217–18.
42  ibid., p. 229.
43  Robert Kennedy, *13 Days: the Cuban Missile Crisis* (London: Macmillan, 1968), p. 87.
44  Sir Dick White, then head of SIS, quoted in Verrier, *Looking Glass*, p. 193.
45  Robin Stafford, 'False, False, that Book about My Husband', *Daily Express*, 23 November 1965.
46  Edward Crankshaw, 'The Dispute about Penkovsky', *Observer*, 21 November 1965.
47  Le Carré, 'Wardrobe of Disguises', cit. at n. 30.
48  The diplomat in correspondence with the author. The diplomat, for professional and personal reasons, wishes to remain anonymous. But he has agreed that I may forward to him serious inquiries sent care of me.
49  'Russians Helped CIA during Cuba Crisis', *The Times*, 15 April 1971.
50  Herbert Scoville, 'Is Espionage Necessary for Our Security?', *Foreign Affairs*, vol. 54, no. 3 (April 1976), p. 488.
51  Letter from Rusbridger to author, 16 July 1985.
52  Teresa Stern, 'The Tanganyika–Zanzibar Union: a Look at U.S. Non-Interference', unpublished paper, in present author's possession.
53  Babu in interview with author, 4 September 1985.
54  Hillsman, 'On Intelligence', pp. 133–4.
55  Frank Snepp, 'The Intelligence of the Central Intelligence Agency in Vietnam', Part 1 in Harrison Salisbury (ed.), *Vietnam Reconsidered* (New York: Harper & Row, 1984), p. 57.
56  Richard K. Betts, 'Analysis, War, and Decision: Why Intelligence Failures are Inevitable', *World Politics*, vol. 31 (October 1978), p. 68.
57  Chester L. Cooper, 'The CIA and Decision Making', *Foreign Affairs*, vol. 50 (January 1972), pp. 229–30.
58  ibid.
59  ibid., p. 232.
60  Snepp, 'Central Intelligence Agency', p. 60.
61  Kirkpatrick in interview with author, 1967.
62  Henry Brandon, *The Retreat of American Power* (New York: Doubleday, 1973), p. 103.
63  Respectively: Snepp, 'Central Intelligence Agency', p. 56; and Kirkpatrick in interview with Leitch, September 1979.

64 Snepp, 'Central Intelligence Agency', p. 56.
65 John Stockwell, 'The Intelligence of the Central Intelligence Agency in Vietnam', Part 3 in Salisbury, *Vietnam Reconsidered*, p. 64.
66 McGehee, *Deadly Deceits*, p. 156.
67 Ralph W. McGehee, 'The Intelligence of the Central Intelligence Agency in Vietnam', Part 2 in Salisbury, *Vietnam Reconsidered*, p. 63.
68 David H. Hunter, 'The Evolution of Literature on United States Intelligence', *Armed Forces and Society*, vol. 5, no. 1 (November 1978), p. 32.
69 ibid., p. 32.
70 John M. Crewdson, 'CIA's Propaganda Efforts', *The Times of India* (Bombay), 7 January 1978.
71 Angus Mackenzie, 'Sabotaging the Dissident Press', *Columbia Journalism Review*, March/April 1981, pp. 57–63.
72 Church Committee, *Final Report*, Vol. 1 (Washington DC: US Government Printing Office, 1976), p. 14.
73 Kirkpatrick in interview with Leitch, 1979.
74 Frank Snepp, *Decent Interval* (Harmondsworth, Middx: Penguin, 1980), back cover.
75 Richard Eder, 'Why Decision in Snepp Case Disturbs Publishers', *New York Times*, 11 March 1980.
76 Kirkpatrick in interview with Leitch, 1979.
77 ibid.

## Chapter 14

1 'Shaping Tomorrow's CIA', *Time Magazine*, 6 February 1978, p. 24.
2 Kenneth Harris, 'Did the CIA Fail America?', *Observer*, 9 December 1979.
3 'Shaping Tomorrow's CIA', p. 29.
4 ibid., p. 31.
5 Kirkpatrick in interview with Leitch, 1979.
6 Philip Agee, *Playboy*, August 1975, pp. 60–2.
7 Kirkpatrick in interview with Leitch, 1979.
8 'The Profession of Intelligence', part 5, BBC Radio 4, 10 February 1982.
9 Nigel West, 'The Hollis Affair and that Spy Called Elli', *The Times*, 23 October 1981.
10 ibid.
11 Obituary of G. R. Mitchell, in *The Times*, 3 January 1985.
12 see 'The Hollis Affair', *Sunday Times*, 29 March 1981.
13 Former head of SIS in interview with author, 3 December 1981.
14 Phillip Knightley, 'Cock-up or Conspiracy?', *Sunday Times*, 11 November 1984.
15 Nigel West, *A Matter of Trust. MI5 1945–72* (London: Weidenfeld & Nicolson, 1982), p. 178.
16 'Hollis Affair', cit. at n. 12.

17 'The Profession of Intelligence', part 5, BBC Radio 4, 10 February 1982.
18 ibid.; and 'Hollis Affair', cit. at n. 12.
19 'Hollis Affair', cit. at n. 12.
20 S. Freeman, B. Penrose and C. Simpson, 'Military Coup Was Aimed at Wilson', *Sunday Times*, 29 March 1981.
21 'Hollis Affair', cit. at n. 12.
22 Maurice Crump, letter to *The Times*, 19 April 1984.
23 Rees-Mogg in interview with author, March 1979.
24 West, *MI5. British Security Service Operations 1909–1945; A Matter of Trust. MI5 1945–72; MI6. British Secret Intelligence Service Operations 1909–45; and The Branch – a History of the Metropolitan Police Special Branch, 1883–1983* (London: Secker & Warburg, 1983).
25 The Deputy Treasury Solicitor, *Sunday Times*, 17 October 1984.
26 Allason in interview with author, 1981.
27 Oldfield in interview with author, 13 July 1979.
28 Ian Black, 'Second Wartime Spying Book Stopped', *Guardian*, 8 December 1983.
29 ibid.
30 Peter Calvocoressi, 'Action that Day', *Sunday Times*, 18 October 1981.
31 'Sons of Stalin's Englishmen?', *The Times*, 2 August 1984.
32 Allason in interview with author, 1984.
33 Mitchell's obituary in *The Times*, 3 January 1985.
34 'Panorama', BBC 1 television, 19 October 1981.

## Chapter 15

1 M. R. D. Foot, 'Britain. Intelligence Services', *The Economist*, 15 March 1980.
2 John Stockwell, a former CIA officer in Angola, in interviews with Christopher Hird of Diverse Productions for Channel 4 television, London, September 1985.
3 ibid.
4 Philip Taubman, 'Bolstered by Budget Increases Casey's CIA Comes Back', *International Herald Tribune* (Paris), 26 January 1983.
5 John Stockwell, 'The Heart of the Matter', BBC 1 television, 22 September 1985; and Taubman, cit. at n. 4.
6 David M. Alpern, 'America's Secret Warriors', *Newsweek*, 10 October 1983; and *Guardian*, 12 June 1984.
7 Taubman, cit. at n. 4.
8 Ransom, 'Secret Intelligence', p. 224.
9 Jeff Stein, 'Spooking the Spook-namers', *Village Voice*, 12–18 November 1984; and Peter Hennessy, 'Intelligence Chiefs Draft Secrets Law', *The Times*, 9 April 1984.
10 Jeremy Campbell, 'A Silly Season for Secrecy', *Standard*, 4 July 1984.
11 Respectively: 'KGB Spy Thriller Fills TV Gap', *The Times*, 9 August 1984; and J. Kohan, 'The Eyes of the Kremlin', *Time*, 14 February 1983.

12  Richard Owen, 'Generalissimo Rank Confirms Political Rise of KGB', *The Times*, 28 May 1984.

13  Murray Sayle, 'The Spy Who Lost Me', *Spectator*, 11 June 1983.

14  See A. Bevins, 'A Record £11m Rise for Secret Services', *The Times*, 20 March 1986 for figures; and for quotation see Christopher Andrew, 'Whitehall, Washington and the Intelligence Services', *International Affairs*, July 1977, p. 391.

15  Peter Hennessy, 'Can this Web Catch Them All?' *The Times*, 16 April 1984.

16  Linda Melvern, 'Exit Smiley, Enter IBM', *Sunday Times*, 31 October 1982.

17  Andrew Cockburn, 'Tinker with Gadgets, Tailor the Facts', *Harper's*, April 1985, p. 66.

18  Duncan Campbell, 'Threat of Electronic Spies', *New Statesman*, 2 February 1979.

19  David Kahn, 'Big Ear or Big Brother?', *New York Times Magazine*, 16 May 1976.

20  Duncan Campbell, 'The Spies Who Spend What They Like', *New Statesman*, 16 May 1980.

21  Estimates of the cost of GCHQ range from £80 million a year (*The Times*, 10 April 1984) to £200 million (*New Statesman*, 2 February 1979), to £300 million (*The Times*, 20 March 1986). £300 million is probably conservative.

22  See David Leigh, 'US Agency "Bugged" Labour MPs', *Guardian*, 7 February 1981; John Peacock, 'Spy Centre on the Moors', *Daily Mirror*, 17 July 1980; Will Bennett, 'US Taking Control of British Spy Base', *Daily Mail*, 27 January 1985.

23  John Connell, 'Cap the Knife Faces the Flak', *Sunday Times*, 10 February 1985.

24  See David Martin, 'Unveiling the Secret NSA', *Newsweek*, 6 September 1982; and Kahn, cit. at n. 19, p. 64.

25  Kahn, cit. at n. 19, p. 67; and Kahn in 'The Profession of Intelligence', part 4, BBC Radio 4, 3 February 1982.

26  'The Profession of Intelligence', part 4.

27  Kirkpatrick in interview with Leitch, 1979.

28  Edward J. Epstein, 'Disinformation. Why the CIA Cannot Verify an Arms Control Agreement', *Commentary*, July 1982.

29  Cockburn, cit. at n. 17, p. 65.

30  ibid., p. 67.

31  The British diplomat. See Chapter 13, note 48.

32  H. Rositzke, 'America's Secret Operations: a Perspective', *Foreign Affairs*, vol. 53 (January 1975), p. 338.

33  Richard Hall, *The Secret State: Australia's Spy Industry* (Melbourne: Cassell Australia, 1978), p. 241.

34  Respectively: Robert Harris, 'The Falklands Inquest', *Listener*, 24 June 1982; and Jeremy Campbell, 'Spy Plane Denied', *Standard*, 7 April 1982.

35  Edward J. Epstein in interview with author, London, 29 June 1984.
36  R. J. Jeffreys-Jones, 'The Historiography of the CIA', *Historical Journal*, vol. 23, no. 2 (1980), p. 495.
37  Kirkpatrick in interview with Leitch, 1979.
38  Kevin Cahill, 'Sh . . . the Following May Be a US Secret', *The Times*, 17 April 1984.
39  Hillsman, 'On Intelligence'.
40  Rositzke, 'America's Secret Operations', p. 340.
41  Richard Helms, 'The Secrets of Russian Espionage', *Observer*, 16 December 1979.
42  Respectively: 'Heart of the Matter', cit. at n. 5; and 'Can You Bore a Hole in the T-72?', *Sunday Observer* (Bombay), 4 March 1984.
43  Shyam Bhatia, 'Revealed – How the CIA Kept Watch on the Russians', *Observer*, 14 July 1985.
44  Herbert Scoville, 'Is Espionage Necessary?', p. 494.
45  Stockwell in Hird interviews, and in 'Heart of the Matter', cit at n. 2 and 5.
46  Stockwell in Hird interviews.
47  Martin Page in interviews with author, 1967 and 1986.
48  Hilary Bonner, 'The Spy Who Stayed Out in the Cold', *Mail on Sunday*, 30 December 1984.
49  David Jones, 'The Price of Freedom', *Sunday Times Magazine*, 1 December 1974.
50  Stockwell in 'Heart of the Matter', and in Hird interviews cit. at n. 5 and 2.
51  Barrett, 'Honorable Espionage', p. 13.
52  Hillsman, 'On Intelligence'.
53  Young in 'Heart of the Matter', cit. at n. 5.
54  Betts, 'Analysis, War and Decision', p. 79.
55  Richard Hall, *National Security and the Agent of Influence Myth* (Sydney: Corradini Press, 1983), p. 19.
56  Information provided by NEXIS, a news retrieval service from Mead Data Central.
57  Henry Allen, 'The Spy Game,' *International Herald Tribune* (Paris), 23 September 1981.

# Select Bibliography

Adams, Ian. *Portrait of a Spy* (New York: Ticknor & Fields, 1982).

Agee, Philip. *Inside the Company: the C.I.A. Diary* (Harmondsworth, Middx: Penguin, 1975).

Ainsztein, Reuben. *Jewish Resistance in Nazi-occupied Eastern Europe* (London: Elek, 1974).

Akhmedov, Ismail. *In and out of Stalin's G.R.U.* (London: Arms & Armour Press, 1984).

Allen, W. E. D., and Muratoff, Paul. *The Russian Campaigns of 1944–45* (London: Penguin, 1946).

Ambrose, Stephen E. 'Eisenhower and the Intelligence Community in World War II'. *Journal of Contemporary History*, vol. 16 (1981).

Andrew, Christopher. 'The British Secret Service and Anglo-Soviet Relations in the 1920s'. *Historical Journal*, vol. 20, no. 3 (1977).

Andrew, Christopher. 'How Baldwin's Secret Service Lost the Soviet Code'. *Observer*, 13 August 1978.

Andrew, Christopher. 'Governments and Secret Services: a Historical Perspective'. *International Journal*, vol. 34, no. 2 (1979).

Andrew, C., and Dilks, D. (eds). *The Missing Dimension* (London: Macmillan, 1984).

Astor, David. 'Why the Revolt against Hitler Was Ignored'. *Encounter*, June 1969.

Bamford, James. *The Puzzle Palace: a report on N.S.A., America's Most Secret Agency* (Boston, Mass.: Houghton Mifflin, 1976).

Barnes, Trevor. 'The Secret Cold War. The C.I.A. and American Foreign Policy in Europe, 1946–1956, Part 1'. *Historical Journal*, vol. 24, no. 2 (1981); Part 2, ibid., vol. 25, no. 3 (1982).

Barrett, Michael J. 'Honorable Espionage'. *Journal of Defence and Diplomacy* (February 1984).

Barron, John. *K.G.B. Today: the Hidden Hand* (New York: Reader's Digest Press, 1983).

Beesly, Patrick. *Very Special Intelligence* (London: Sphere, 1978).

Bennett, Ralph. *Ultra in the West* (London: Hutchinson, 1979).

Bennett, Ralph, 'Ultra and Some Command Decisions'. In Walter Laqueur (ed.), *The Second World War* (London and Beverley Hills, Calif.: Sage, 1982).

Best, S. Payne. *The Venlo Incident* (London: Hutchinson, 1950).

Bethell, Nicholas. *The Great Betayal* (London: Hodder & Stoughton, 1984).

415

Betts, Richard K. 'Analysis, War and Decision: Why Intelligence Failures Are Inevitable'. *World Politics*, vol. 31 (October 1978).

Bickel, Lennard, *The Deadly Experiment* (London: Macmillan, 1980).

Bittman, Ladislav. *The Deception Game* (New York: Ballantine, 1981).

Bloch, Jonathan, and Fitzgerald, Patrick. *British Intelligence and Covert Action* (Dublin: Brandon Books, 1983).

Bose, Herbert von. *Verdun Galizien Somme, Isonzo . . . Oder Wo in Vorsicht!* (Berlin: Feind Hort Mitl, 1930).

Bourke, Sean. *The Springing of George Blake* (London: Cassell, 1970).

Boyle, Andrew. *The Climate of Treason* (London: Hutchinson, 1979).

Brandon, Henry. *The Retreat of American Power* (New York: Doubleday, 1973).

Brook-Shepherd, Gordon. *The Storm Petrels* (London: Collins, 1977).

Buchan, John. *Greenmantle* (London: Thomas Nelson, 1917).

Buchheit, Gert. *Der Deutsche Geheimdienst. Geschichte der militärischen Abwehr* (Munich: List, 1966).

Buchheit, Gert. *Spionage in zwei Weltkriegen* (Landshut: Politisches Archiv, 1975).

Burke, Michael. *Outrageous Good Fortune* (Boston, Mass.: Little, Brown, 1984).

Calvocoressi, Peter. *Top Secret Ultra* (London: Hutchinson, 1979).

Catudal, Honoré. *Kennedy and the Berlin Wall Crisis* (Berlin: Berlin Verlag, 1980).

Cave Brown, Anthony (ed.). *The Secret War Report of the OSS* (New York: Berkley Medallion, 1976).

Cave Brown, Anthony, *Bodyguard of Lies* (London: Star Books, 1977).

Cave Brown, Anthony. *The Last Hero: Wild Bill Donovan* (New York: Times Books, 1982).

Cecil, Robert. 'The Cambridge Comintern'. In C. Andrew and D. Dilks (eds), *The Missing Dimension* (London: Macmillan, 1984).

Chester, Lewis, Fay, Stephen, and Young, Hugo. *The Zinoviev Letter* (London: Heinemann, 1967).

Clayton, Aileen. *The Enemy Is Listening* (London: Hutchinson, 1980).

Cline, M. W., Christiansen, C. E., and Fontaine, J. M. (eds). *Scholar's Guide to Intelligence Literature* (Baltimore, Md.: University Publications of America, 1983).

Cline, Ray, and Alexander, Yonah. *Terrorism: the Soviet Connection* (New York: Crane Russak, 1984).

Colby, William. *Honorable Men: My Life in the C.I.A.* (New York: Simon & Schuster, 1978).

Collins, Larry, and Lapierre, Dominique. *Is Paris Burning?* (New York: Simon & Schuster, 1965).

Cooper, Chester L. 'The C.I.A. and Decision Making'. *Foreign Affairs*, vol. 50 (January 1972).

Copeland, Miles. *Real Spy World* (London: Sphere, 1978).

Corson, William R. *The Armies of Ignorance* (New York: The Dial Press, 1977).

Davidson, Basil. 'Scenes from the Anti-Nazi War'. *New Statesman*, 4 July 1980.

Deacon, Richard. *A History of the British Secret Service* (New York: Taplinger, 1970).

Deacon, Richard. *The Israeli Secret Service* (London: Hamish Hamilton, 1977).

Deacon, Richard. *The British Connection* (London: Hamish Hamilton, 1979).

Deacon, Richard, and West, Nigel. *Spy* (London: BBC Publications, 1980).

Deacon, Richard. *A Biography of Sir Maurice Oldfield* (London: Macdonald, 1985).

Debo, Richard K. 'Lockhart Plot or Dzerzhinski Plot?' *Journal of Modern History*, vol. 43, no. 3 (1971).

Deutsch, Harold. 'The Influence of Ultra on World War II'. *Parameters: Journal of the U.S. Army War College*, vol. 8 (December 1978).

DeWeerd, H. A. 'Strategic Surprise in the Korean War'. *Orbis* (Fall 1962).

Dobson, Christopher, and Payne, Ronald. *The Dictionary of Espionage* (London: Harrap, 1984).

Dorwart, Jeffrey M. 'The Roosevelt–Astor Espionage Ring'. *New York History* (July 1981).

Dukes, Paul. *The Story of ST-25* (London: Cassell, 1938).

Dulles, Allen. *Great True Spy Stories* (London: Robson Books, 1984).

Elliot-Bateman, Michael (ed.). *The Fourth Dimension of Warfare, Vol. 1. Intelligence/Subversion/Resistance* (Manchester: Manchester University Press, 1970).

Erickson, John. *The Road to Stalingrad* (London: Weidenfeld & Nicolson, 1975).

Etzold, Thomas H. 'The (F)utility Factor: German Information Gathering in the United States, 1933–1941', *Military Affairs*, vol. 39, no. 2 (1975).

Farago, Ladislas. *The Game of the Foxes* (London: Hodder & Stoughton, 1972).

Felstead, S. T. *German Spies at Bay* (London: Hutchinson, 1920).

Fitzgibbon, Constantine. *Secret Intelligence in the 20th Century* (London: Granada, 1978).

Foot, M. R. D. *SOE in France. An Account of the Work of the British Special Operations Executive in France 1940–1944* (London: HMSO, 1966).

Foot, M. R. D. 'Britain. Intelligence Services'. *The Economist*, 15 March 1980.

Foot, M. R. D. 'Was SOE any Good?' In W. Laqueur (ed.), *The Second World War* (London and Beverley Hills, Calif.: Sage, 1982).

Foote, Alexander. *Handbook for Spies* (London: Museum Press, 1949).

Ford, Corey. *Donovan of OSS* (Boston, Mass.: Little, Brown, 1970).

Freedman, Lawrence. *U.S. Intelligence and the Soviet Strategic Threat* (London: Macmillan, 1979).

French, David. 'Spy Fever in Britain, 1909–1915'. *Historical Journal*, vol. 21, no. 2 (1978).

Frolik, Josef. *The Frolik Defection* (London: Leo Cooper, 1975).

Fuller, Jean Overton. *The German Penetration of SOE* (London: Kimber, 1975).

Gillman, Peter and Leni. *Collar the Lot!* (London: Quartet, 1980).

Golitsyn, Anatoliy. *New Lies for Old* (London: The Bodley Head, 1984).

Goulden, Joseph C. *Korea: the Untold Story* (New York: Times Books, 1982).

Hall, Richard. *The Secret State: Australia's Spy Industry* (Melbourne: Cassell Australia, 1978).

Hall, Richard. *National Security and the Agent of Influence Myth* (Sydney: Corradini Press, 1983).

Hallin, Daniel C. *The Uncensored War* (New York: Oxford University Press, 1986).

Heaps, Leo. *Thirty Years with the K.G.B.* (London: Methuen, 1984).

Hennessy, P., and Brownfeld, G. 'Britain's Cold War Security Purge: the Origins of Positive Vetting'. *Historical Journal*, vol. 25, no. 4 (1982).

Hiley, Nicholas P. 'The Failure of British Espionage against Germany, 1907–1914'. *Historical Journal*, vol. 26, no. 4 (1976).

Hill, George A. *Go Spy the Land* (London: Cassell, 1932).

Hill, George A. *The Dreaded Hour* (London: Cassell, 1936).

Hilsman, R. 'On Intelligence'. *Armed Forces and Society*, vol. 8, no. 1 (Fall 1981).

Hinsley, F. H., Thomas, E. E., Ransom, C. F. G., and Knight, R. C. *British Intelligence in the Second World War* (London: HMSO, 1979–84).

Hiroyuki, Agawa. *The Reluctant Admiral* (Tokyo: Kadansha International, 1979).

Hodges, Andrew. *Alan Turing: the Enigma of Intelligence* (London: Unwin Paperbacks, 1985).

Hohne, Heinz. *Canaris* (London: Secker & Warburg, 1979).

Holloway, David. 'Entering the Nuclear Arms Race: the Soviet Decision to Build the Atomic Bomb, 1939–1945'. *Social Studies of Science*, vol. 11 (1981).

Hood, William. *Mole* (New York: Norton, 1982).

Hopkirk, Peter. *Setting the East Ablaze* (London: John Murray, 1984).

Horner, D. 'Special Intelligence in the South-West Pacific Area in World War II'. *Australian Outlook*, vol. 32, no. 3 (1978).

Hoxha, Enver. *The Anglo-American Threat to Albania*. (Tirana: 8 Nëntori, 1982).

Hunter, David H. 'The Evolution of Literature on United States Intelligence'. *Armed Forces and Society*, vol. 5, no. 1 (November 1978).

Hyde, H. Montgomery. *Room 3603* (New York: Ballantine, 1977).

Hyde, H. Montgomery. *The Atom Bomb Spies* (London: Sphere, 1982).

Jeffreys-Jones, R. J. *American Espionage* (New York: The Free Press, 1977).

Jeffreys-Jones, R. J. 'The Historiography of the CIA'. *Historical Journal*, vol. 23, no. 2 (1980).

Jeffreys-Jones, R. J. *Eagle against Empire. United States Opposition to European Imperialism 1898–1981* (Aix-en-Provence: European Association for American Studies, 1983).

Johns, Philip. *Within Two Cloaks* (London: William Kimber, 1979).

Johnson, Chalmers. *An Instance of Treason* (Tokyo: Charles E. Tuttle, 1977).

Johnson, R. W. 'Making Things Happen'. *London Review of Books*, 6–19 September 1984.

Jonas, Manfred. 'Prophet without Honour: Hans Heinrich Dieckhoff's Reports from Washington'. *Mid-America*, vol. 47 (July 1965).

Jong, Louis de. 'The "Great Game" of Secret Agents'. *Encounter*, January 1980.

Jong, Louis de. 'Britain and Dutch Resistance, 1940–1945'. Notities voor het Geschied werk, no. 109 (undated), Netherlands State Institute for War Documentation.

Kahn, David. *Hitler's Spies* (New York: Macmillan, 1978).

Kahn, David. 'The International Conference on Ultra'. *Military Affairs*, vol. 43, no. 2 (April 1979).

Kahn, David. 'Codebreaking in World Wars I and II'. *Historical Journal*, vol. 23, no. 3 (1980).

Kennedy, Robert. *13 Days: the Cuban Missile Crisis* (London: Macmillan, 1968).

Kettle, Michael. *The Allies and the Russian Collapse: March 1917–March 1918* (London: Deutsch, 1979).

Kirkpatrick, Lyman. *The Real C.I.A.* (New York: Macmillan, 1968).

Knightley, Phillip. *The First Casualty* (New York: Harcourt Brace Jovanovich, 1975).

Landau, Henry. *The Enemy Within* (New York: Putnam's, 1937).

Laqueur, Walter (ed.). *The Second World War* (London and Beverley Hills, Calif.: Sage, 1982).

Leigh, David. *The Frontiers of Secrecy* (London: Junction Books, 1980).

Le Queux, William. *Spies of the Kaiser: Plotting the Downfall of England* (London: Hurst & Blackett, 1909).

Le Queux, William. *Britain's Deadly Peril: Are We Told the Truth?* (London: Stanley Paul, 1915).

Le Queux, William. *Things I Know about Kings, Celebrities and Crooks* (London: Evelyn Nash & Grayson, 1923).

Lernoux, Penny. *In Banks We Trust* (New York: Doubleday, 1984).

Lettow-Vorbeck, P. E. von (ed.). *Die Weltkriegspionage* (Munich, 1931).

Lewin, Ronald. *Ultra Goes to War: the Secret Story* (London: Book Club Associates, 1978).

Lewin, Ronald. 'A Signal-Intelligence War'. In Walter Laquer (ed.), *The Second World War* (London and Beverley Hills, Calif.: Sage, 1982).

Lockhart, R. H. Bruce. *Memoirs of a British Agent* (New York: Putnam's, 1932).

Lotz, Wolfgang. *The Champagne Spy* (London: Valentine Mitchell, 1972).

MacDonald, Callum A. 'The Venlo Affair'. *European Studies Review*, vol. 8, no. 4 (October 1978).

McGehee, Ralph W. *Deadly Deceits* (New York: Sheridan Square, 1983).

Mackenzie, Compton. *Gallipoli Memories* (London: Cassell, 1929).

Mackenzie, Compton. *First Athenian Memories* (London: Cassell, 1931).

Mackenzie, Compton. *Aegean Memories* (London: Cassell, 1940).

Maclean, Fitzroy. *Take Nine Spies* (London: Weidenfeld & Nicolson, 1978).

Manchester, William. *American Caesar* (Boston, Mass.: Little, Brown, 1978).

Martin, David C. *Wilderness of Mirrors* (New York: Ballantine, 1981).

Masterman, J. C. *The Double Cross System in the War of 1939 to 1945* (New Haven, Conn.; London: Yale University Press, 1972; Sphere, 1973).

Mathams, R. H. *Sub-Rosa: Memoirs of an Australian Intelligence Analyst* (Sydney: Allen & Unwin, 1982).

Meissner, Hans-Otto. *The Man with Three Faces* (Tokyo: Charles E. Tuttle, 1976).

Mosley, Leonard. *Dulles* (London: Hodder & Stoughton, 1978).

Muggeridge, Malcolm. *Chronicles of Wasted Time II: The Infernal Grove* (London: Collins, 1973).

Mulligan, Timothy P. 'According to Colonel Donovan: a Document from the Records of German Military Intelligence'. *The Historian*, November 1983.

Mure, David. *Practice to Deceive* (London: Kimber, 1977).

Mure, David. *Master of Deception: Tangled Webs in London and the Middle East* (London: Kimber, 1980).

Nicolai, Walther. *The German Secret Service* (London: Stanley Paul, 1924).

Page, Bruce. 'The Endless Quest for Supermole'. *New Statesman*, 21 September 1979

Page, Bruce, Leitch, David, and Knightley, Phillip. *The Philby Conspiracy* (New York: Doubleday, 1968).

Paléologue, Maurice. 'Un prélude à l'invasion de Belgique'. *Revue des deux mondes*, vol. 11 (October 1932).

Petrie, Sir David. *Communism in India, 1924–1927* (Calcutta: Editions Indian, 1972).

Philby, Kim. *My Silent War* (London: MacGibbon & Kee, 1968).

Phillips, David Atlee. *The Night Watch* (New York: Atheneum, 1977).

Pincher, Chapman. *Their Trade Is Treachery* (London: Sidgwick & Jackson, 1981).

Popov, Dusko. *Spy/Counter-Spy* (London: Panther, 1976).

Pratt, Fletcher. 'How Not to Run a Spy System'. *Harper's*, September 1947.

Pringle, Peter, and Spiegelman, James. *The Nuclear Barons* (London: Michael Joseph, 1982).

Raina, Asoka. *Inside R.A.W. – The Story of India's Secret Service* (New Delhi: Vikas Publishing House, 1981).

Ransom, Harry Howe. 'Secret Intelligence in the United States, 1947–1982: the CIA's Search for Legitimacy'. In C. Andrew and D. Dilks (eds), *The Missing Dimension* (London: Macmillan, 1984).

Read, Anthony, and Fisher, David. *Operation Lucy* (London: Hodder & Stoughton, 1980).

Rees, Goronwy. *A Chapter of Accidents* (London: Chatto & Windus, 1972).

Reile, O. 'Wer taüschte die deutsche militärische Führung über die Stärke der in England für die Invasion bereitgestellten Streitkräfte?', *Wehrwissenschaftliche Rundschau*, no. 3 (1979).

Reilly, Sidney. *The Adventures of Sidney Reilly* (London: Elkin Mathews & Marrot, 1931).

Rings, Werner. *Life with the Enemy: Collaboration and Resistance in Hitler's Europe 1939–1945* (London: Weidenfeld & Nicolson, 1982).

Rohwer, J., and Jäckel, E. (eds). *Die Funkaufklärung und ihre Rolle im Zweiten Weltkrieg* (Stuttgart: Motorbuch, 1979).

Romanov, A. I. *Nights Are Longest There* (London: Hutchinson, 1972).

Ronge, Max (ed.). *Kriegs und Industrie Spionage* (Vienna: Amalthea, 1930).

Rositzke, Harry. 'America's Secret Operations: a Perspective'. *Foreign Affairs*, vol. 53 (January 1975).

Rositzke, Harry. *The CIA's Secret Operations* (New York: Reader's Digest Press, 1977).

Rositzke, Harry. *The K.G.B. The Eyes of Russia* (London: Sidgwick & Jackson, 1982).

Rowan, Richard Wilmer, and Deindorfer, Robert G. *Secret Service* (London: Kimber, 1969).

Rusbridger, James. 'The Sinking of the *Automedon*, the Capture of the *Nankin*'. *Encounter*, May 1985.

Sakharov, Vladimir, and Tosi, Umberto. *High Treason* (New York: Ballantine, 1981).

Salisbury, Harrison. *Vietnam Reconsidered* (New York: Harper & Row, 1984).

Schellenberg, W. *The Schellenberg Memoirs* (London: Deutsch, 1956).

Scoville, Herbert. 'Is Espionage Necessary for Our Security?' *Foreign Affairs*, vol. 54, no. 3 (April 1976).

Shirreff, F. D. 'Some Experience with Special Signals'. *Mercury. The Magazine of the Royal Signals Amateur Radio Society* (1981–2).

Smiley, David. *Albanian Assignment* (London: Chatto & Windus, 1984).

Smith, Bradley F. *The Shadow Warriors: O.S.S. and the Origins of the C.I.A.* (London and New York: Deutsch and Basic Books, 1983).

Smith, R. Harris. *OSS* (Los Angeles, Calif.: University of California Press, 1972).

Snepp, Frank. *Decent Interval* (Harmondsworth, Middx: Penguin, 1980).

Snepp, Frank. 'The Intelligence of the Central Intelligence Agency in Vietnam'. Part 1 in Harrison Salisbury (ed.), *Vietnam Reconsidered* (New York: Harper & Row, 1984).

Spiller, Roger J. 'Assessing Ultra'. *Military Review*, vol. 59, no. 8 (August 1979).

Stafford, David. 'The Detonator Concept: British Strategy, SOE and European Resistance after the Fall of France'. *Journal of Contemporary History*, vol. 10 (1975).

Stafford, David. *Britain and European Resistance, 1940–1945* (London: Macmillan, 1980).

Steven, Stewart. *The Spymasters of Israel* (New York: Macmillan, 1980).

Stevenson, William. *A Man Called Intrepid: the Secret War 1939–1945* (London: Macmillan, 1976).

Stockwell, John, *In Search of Enemies: A CIA Story* (New York: Norton, 1979; revised in paperback, 1984).

Straight, Michael. *After Long Silence* (London: Collins, 1983).

Sweet-Escott, Bickham. *Baker Street Irregular* (London: Methuen, 1965).

Swetschin, A. 'The Strategy'. In Max Ronge (ed.), *Kriegs und Industrie Spionage* (Vienna: Amalthea, 1930).

Taylor, Edmond. *Richer by Asia* (Boston, Mass.: Houghton Mifflin, 1947).

Taylor, Edmond. *Awakening from History* (Boston, Mass.: Gambit, 1969).

Toscano, M. *Designs in Diplomacy* (Baltimore, Md: Johns Hopkins Press, 1970).

Trefousse, Hans L. 'The Failure of German Intelligence in the United States, 1939–1945'. *Mississippi Valley Historial Review*, vol. 42, no. 1 (June 1955).

Trumpener, Ulrich. 'War Premeditated? German Intelligence Operations in July 1914'. *Central European History*, vol. 9, no. 1 (March 1976).

Van der Rhoer, Edward. *Master Spy* (New York: Scribner's, 1981).

Vassall, John. *Vassall: the Autobiography of a Spy* (London: Sidgwick & Jackson, 1975).

Verrier, Anthony. *Through the Looking Glass* (London: Cape, 1983).

Waagenaar, Sam. *The Murder of Mata Hari* (London: Barker, 1964).

Wark, Wesley K. 'British Intelligence on the German Air Force and Aircraft Industry, 1933–1939'. *Historical Journal*, vol. 25, no. 3 (1982).

Waters, W. H. H. *Secret and Confidential* (London: John Murray, 1926).

Watt, George. *China Spy* (London: Johnson, 1972).

Werner, Ruth (pseudonym for Kuczynski). *Sonjas Rapport* (East Berlin: Verlag Neues Leben, 1977).

West, Nigel. *MI5. British Security Service Operations 1909–1945* (London: The Bodley Head, 1981).

West, Nigel. *A Matter of Trust. MI5 1945–1972* (London: Weidenfeld & Nicolson, 1982).

West. Nigel. *MI6. British Secret Intelligence Service Operations 1909–1945* (London: Weidenfeld & Nicolson, 1983).

West, Nigel. *The Branch – a History of the Metropolitan Police Special Branch, 1883–1983* (London: Secker & Warburg, 1983).

West, Nigel. *Unreliable Witness. Espionage Myths of the Second World War* (London: Weidenfeld & Nicolson, 1984).

Whaley, Barton. 'Covert Rearmament in Germany 1919–1939: Deception and Misperception'. *Journal of Strategic Studies*, part 5 (March 1982).

Wheeler, Mark. 'The SOE Phenomenon'. In Walter Laqueur (ed.), *The Second World War* (London and Beverley Hills, Calif.: Sage, 1982).

Whitwell, John. *British Agent* (London: Kimber, 1966).

Winterbotham, F. W. *Secret and Personal* (London: Kimber, 1969).

Winterbotham, F. W. *The Ultra Secret* (London: Weidenfeld & Nicolson, 1974).

Wise, David, and Ross, Thomas B. *The Invisible Government* (London: Cape, 1965).

Wise, David, and Ross, Thomas B. *The Espionage Establishment* (New York: Random House, 1967).

Yardley, Herbert O. *The American Black Chamber* (New York: Ballantine, 1981).

Yergin, Daniel. *Shattered Peace* (London: Deutsch, 1978).

Young, Kenneth. *The Diaries of Sir Robert Bruce Lockhart: Vol. I 1915–1938* (London: Macmillan, 1973)

# Index

Abel, Colonel, 293
Abse, Leo, 292
Abwehr (Germany), 99, 194, 246;
  anti-Nazi elements, 137, 144, 146–7,
  151; Canaris, 96, 101, 146–7, 151;
  "double-cross", 144–53; Enigma code
  machine, 164; forbidden sabotage in
  US, 220; Himmler, 151; Hooper, 140;
  Kolbe, 138–9; other intelligence
  agencies, 96–7; Popov, 148; purge &
  merger with RHSA, 151; US
  technological secrets, 102–3; Venlo
  kidnapping, 130; view of SIS, 144
Abwehr, Section I, 147
Abwehr, Section V, 147, 198
Acheson, Dean, 267–8
Adams, Donald, 99
Afirenko, Joseph Ilitch: alias of Paul
  Dukes, q.v.
Agee, Philip, 298, 341–2, 367
Ahmed, Gulzar, 141
Alamos, Los, 263, 264, 265
Albania, 252, 254
Aldrich, Winthrop W., 211
Alexander, General Sir Harold, 161
Alexandra, Queen, 13
Allason, Rupert, 173 (as Nigel West),
  356–7, 359–60, 361
Amory, Robert (Jnr), 254, 288, 295, 318
American Protection League (APL), 36–7
Amtorg, 176, 211
Andrew, Dr Christopher, 110
"Andrey", 309
Andropov, Yuri, 367–8
Angleton, James Jesus, 311–2, 318, 342;
  Philby, 296; Golitsyn, 307–9
Angola, 365
Arbenz, Guzman Jacob, 255
Armas, Carlos Castillo, 255
Arnhem, 166
Ashleigh, Charles, 80
Ashworth, John, a.k.a. Charles Ashleigh,
  q.v.
Asquith, Herbert Henry, 10
Astor, David, 131

Astor, Hon. J. J., 135n
Astor, Vincent, 211, 212
Atom bomb, Russian, 258–67
Auchinleck, General Sir Claude, 162
Australian Secret Intelligence Service,
  84
Automeden codebooks incident, 170–1

Babu, Abdul Raman Mohammed, 330–1
Baldwin, Stanley, 85–6, 89
Ball, George, 207
Balfour, Harold, 135n
"Barbarossa", 189, 194–7, 208
Barbie, Klaus, 274
Barclay, Cecil, 173
Barrett, Michael J., 388
Baruch, Bernard, 258
Bateson, Gregory, 266
Bats as a terror weapon, 221
Baun, Hermann, 223–4
Bazna, Elyesa ("Cicero"), 143
B-Dienst (Beobachtungsdienst)
  (Germany), 168, 169
Beaumont-Nesbitt, Major-General
  Frederick ("Paddy"), 114–5, 215
Bedell-Smith, General Walter:
  becomes CIA director, 258, 267;
  Philby, 275, 278; mistrust after Philby
  affair, 286, 295
Belfrage, Cedric, 354n
Bell, Walter, 211
Benn, Tony, 289
Bentley, Nick, 199
Beobachtungsdienst (Germany), see
  B-Dienst
Bermann, Georg, alias of Sidney Reilly,
  q.v.
Beria, Lavrenti Pavlovich, 176
Berlin Tunnel, 291
Bernhardi, General F. von, 34
"Bernhardt", 186
Bernhardt, Sarah, 14
Berzin, General Antonovich, 70, 72, 192
Best, Captain Sigismund Payne:
  after WW1, 132; battle of Cambrai,

# The Second Oldest Profession

Hinsley, Professor F. H. – *cont.*
  of British intelligence, 111, 357–8
Hitler, Adolf: 92, 147, 208; Abwehr
  opposition elements, 144, 146–8, 153;
  Abwehr purge, 151; Ambassador
  Kennedy, 146; astrology, 153n;
  attitude towards intelligence, 142;
  compromise peace plans in 1939,
  133–4; forbids sabotage in USA, 220;
  Hess' visit to Britain, 135; Holland &
  Belgium invasion, 137; judgement of
  US political leadership, 104; Luftwaffe,
  92–3; opposition to him before WWII,
  131–2; remilitarisation evidence
  ignored, 88; "seize control of USA",
  218; SIS encourages dissent in
  Germany, 132; SIS reaction to his rise,
  82, 91; Stalin's views of his intentions
  towards Russia, 196; Stalin warned of
  his hostility, 177
Ho Chi Minh, 232, 239
Hoare, Sir Samuel, 116, 117, 135n
Hoetzendorf, General Conrad von, 50
Hohenlohe, Prince, 133
Holburn, James, 108
Hollis, Roger: affair assessed, 361–3;
  Blunt, 348–9; case evidence reviewed,
  347–9; Gouzenko, 344, 348;
  information leaks, 353; investigation
  clears him, 350–1; launches "mole
  hunt" (1964–), 345; Thatcher
  statement, 353; "Young Turks", 346–7,
  356, 361
Home, Lord; see Lord Dunglass
Hooper, William John, 140–1
Hoover, J. Edgar, 233, 286, 447, 366;
  character, 150; contact with SIS 1940,
  213; "Fedora", 309; opposes Donovan,
  222; Philby exposure attempt, 282–5;
  Popov, 149–50; "Red Menace", 37n;
  Russian atom bomb, 259
Horne, Alistair, 273
Hoxha, Enver, 252, 253
Hughes, John, 374
Humphrey, Hubert, 352

IB (Indian Intelligence Bureau), 79–81
IIC (Industrial Intelligence Centre) (UK),
  84–6, 93
Indian Intelligence Bureau, see IB
Indian Secret Intelligence Section, 32
Industrial Intelligence Centre (UK),
  see IIC
Infomationsstelle III (Germany), 97
International Brigades, 82
Inter-Services Research Bureau (i.e.
  SOE), 122

Inverlair Lodge, 123
Iran, 255, 365
Iraq, 138
Italy, 250, 251, 254
Ivanov, Yevgeny M., 325n, 343n

"James" (Kuczynski Ring), 205
"James" (in Penkovsky affair), 314
Jaruzelski, General, 270
Jebb, Gladwyn, 120
Jebsen, Johann, 148–9, 151
"Jeff", alias of Pepita Reilly, q.v.
JIC (Joint Intelligence Committee) (UK),
  114–5, 126, 219–20, 370, 379–80
John, Otto, 200
Johnson, Herschel, 145
Johnson, Lyndon B., 327, 333–4
Joint Intelligence Committee (UK), see
  JIC
Jones, Dr R. V., 136
Jong, Dr Louis de, 220
Jordan, Mrs Jessie, 99
Joynson-Hicks, William, 89
Judenitch, General, 71

Kane, Jock, 373
Kanovalov, Anton, alias of Jankel Lock,
  q.v.
Kaplan, Dora, 59, 71–2
Karume, President, 331
Kaye, Sir Cecil, 80
Kean, Gwynne, 85
Kell, Captain (later Colonel) Vernon, 50,
  55, 113
Kelly, Joseph, 99
Kennedy, John F.: Bay of Pigs, 317–8;
  Cuban missile crisis, 321–2, 326–7;
  fascination with espionage, 8;
  Khrushchev, 318–9, 325
Kennedy, Ambassador Joseph P., 317;
  anti-British views & reports, 146, 214;
  Donovan's visit to Britain, 214, 223;
  leaks of despatches, 145–6; Lindbergh
  on German air power, 94
Kennedy, Robert, 302, 308, 318
Kent, Tyler, 145–6
Kerby, Henry, 54, 231, 289
Kerensky, Alexander, 65
Kernochan, Frederick, 211
KGB (USSR):
  Blake, 290–5; Blunt, 183, 201; budget,
  4; Burgess, 183, 201; changed image in
  1980s, 367–9; changed priorities, 176,
  197 (1941), 206 (1944); covert activities,
  270; economic intelligence, 383–4;
  Golitsyn, 301–2, 306–9, 308–313;
  Gouzenko, 272; King, 180; Kuczynski